Edited by Aliyah Morgenstern and Susan Goldin-Meadow
Gesture in Language

Language and the Human Lifespan Series

Bilingualism Across the Lifespan
Factors Moderating Language Proficiency
Edited by Elena Nicoladis and Simona Montanari

Entrenchment and the Psychology of Language Learning
How We Reorganize and Adapt Linguistic Knowledge
Edited by Hans-Jörg Schmid

Gesture in Language
Development Across the Lifespan
Edited by Aliyah Morgenstern and Susan Goldin-Meadow

Innovative Investigations of Language in Autism Spectrum Disorder
Edited by Letitia R. Naigles

María Blume and Barbara C. Lust
Research Methods in Language Acquisition
Principles, Procedures, and Practices

Gesture in Language

Development Across the Lifespan

Edited by
Aliyah Morgenstern and Susan Goldin-Meadow

 AMERICAN PSYCHOLOGICAL ASSOCIATION

Copyright © 2023 by the American Psychological Association and Walter de Gruyter GmbH. All rights reserved. Ex-cept as permitted under the United States Copyright Act of 1976, no part of this publication may be reproduced or distributed in any form or by any means, including, but not limited to, the process of scanning and digitization, or stored in a database or retrieval system, without the prior written permission of the publishers. The opinions and statements published are the responsibility of the authors, and such opinions and statements do not necessarily represent the policies of the American Psychological Association or Walter de Gruyter GmbH. This volume is text- and page-identical with the hardback published in 2022.

Published by
American Psychological Association
750 First Street, NE
Washington, DC 20002
https://www.apa.org
To order in the United States and Canada:
APA Order Department
https://www.apa.org/pubs/books
order@apa.org

Walter de Gruyter GmbH
Genthiner Strasse 13
10785 Berlin / Germany
http://www.degruyter.com
To order in Europe:
HGV Hanseatische Gesellschaft für Verlagsservice mbH
Holzwiesenstr. 2
72127 Kusterdingen / Germany
Tel.: +49 (0)7071 9353 – 55
orders@degruyter.com

Other customers, including those in the United Kingdom, may order from either publisher.

Typeset in DG Meta Serif Science by Circle Graphics, Inc., Reisterstown, MD
Printer (U.S. & Canada): Sheridan Books, Chelsea, MI
Printer (Europe): CPI books GmbH, Leck, Germany
Cover Designer: Mercury Publishing Services, Inc., Glenwood, MD

Library of Congress Cataloging-in-Publication Data
Names: Morgenstern, Aliyah, editor. | Goldin-Meadow, Susan, editor. |
  American Psychological Association.
Title: Gesture in language : development across the lifespan / edited by
  Aliyah Morgenstern and Susan Goldin-Meadow.
Description: Washington : American Psychological Association, [2022] |
Series: Language and the human lifespan | Includes bibliographical
references and index.
Identifiers: LCCN 2021021511 (print) | LCCN 2021021512 (ebook) |
  ISBN 9781433836299 (hardcover) | ISBN 9781433838422 (ebook)
Subjects: LCSH: Body language. | Gesture. | Cognition.
Classification: LCC BF637.N66 G48 2022 (print) | LCC BF637.N66 (ebook) |
  DDC 153.6/9—dc23
LC record available at https://lccn.loc.gov/2021021511
LC ebook record available at https://lccn.loc.gov/2021021512

Gesture in Language: Development Across the Lifespan has been published by De Gruyter Mouton under the following ISBNs: ISBN 978-3-11-125523-1 | e-ISBN (PDF) 978-3-11-056752-6 | e-ISBN (EPUB) 978-3-11-056505-8

Bibliographic information published by the Deutsche Nationalbibliothek
The Deutsche Nationalbibliothek lists this publication in the Deutsche Nationalbibliografie; detailed bibliographic data are available in the internet at http://dnb.dnb.de.

https://doi.org/10.1037/0000269-000
Printed in the United States of America and Germany

Contents

Contributors —— vii

        Aliyah Morgenstern and Susan Goldin-Meadow
1   Introduction to Gesture in Language —— 3

I An Emblematic Gesture: Pointing

        Kensy Cooperrider and Kate Mesh
2   Pointing in Gesture and Sign —— 21

        Aliyah Morgenstern
3   Early Pointing Gestures —— 47

II Gesture Before Speech

        Meredith L. Rowe, Ran Wei, and Virginia C. Salo
4   Early Gesture Predicts Later Language Development —— 93

        Olga Capirci, Maria Cristina Caselli, and Virginia Volterra
5   Interaction Among Modalities and Within Development —— 113

III Gesture With Speech During Language Learning

        Eve V. Clark and Barbara F. Kelly
6   Constructing a System of Communication With Gestures and Words —— 137

        Pauline Beaupoil-Hourdel
7   Embodying Language Complexity: Co-Speech Gestures Between Age 3 and 4 —— 157

        Casey Hall, Elizabeth Wakefield, and Susan Goldin-Meadow
8   Gesture Can Facilitate Children's Learning and Generalization of Verbs —— 185

IV Gesture After Speech Is Mastered

Jean-Marc Colletta
9   On the Codevelopment of Gesture and Monologic Discourse in Children —— 205

Susan Wagner Cook
10   Understanding How Gestures Are Produced and Perceived —— 243

Tilbe Göksun, Demet Özer, and Seda Akbıyık
11   Gesture in the Aging Brain —— 269

V Gesture With More Than One Language

Elena Nicoladis and Lisa Smithson
12   Gesture in Bilingual Language Acquisition —— 297

Marianne Gullberg
13   Bimodal Convergence: How Languages Interact in Multicompetent Language Users' Speech and Gestures —— 317

Gale Stam and Marion Tellier
14   Gesture Helps Second and Foreign Language Learning and Teaching —— 335

Aliyah Morgenstern and Susan Goldin-Meadow
Afterword: Gesture as *Part of Language* or *Partner to Language* Across the Lifespan —— 365

Index —— 371

About the Editors —— 383

Contributors

Seda Akbıyık, MA
Harvard University
Cambridge, MA, United States

Pauline Beaupoil-Hourdel, PhD
Sorbonne University
Institut National Supérieur du Professorat et de l'Education
UR 7332
Center for Linguistics at the Sorbonne
Paris, France

Olga Capirci, PhD
Institute of Cognitive Sciences and Technologies
Consiglio Nazionale delle Ricerche
Rome, Italy

Maria Cristina Caselli, PhD
Institute of Cognitive Sciences and Technologies
Consiglio Nazionale delle Ricerche
Rome, Italy

Eve V. Clark, PhD
Stanford University
Stanford, CA, United States

Jean-Marc Colletta, PhD
Grenoble Alpes University
Grenoble, France

Susan Wagner Cook, PhD
University of Iowa
Iowa City, IA, United States

Kensy Cooperrider, PhD
University of Chicago
Chicago, IL, United States

Tilbe Göksun, PhD
Koç University
Istanbul, Turkey

Susan Goldin-Meadow, PhD
University of Chicago
Chicago, IL, United States

Marianne Gullberg, PhD
Lund University
Lund, Sweden

Casey Hall, PhD
University of Chicago
Chicago, IL, United States

Barbara F. Kelly, PhD
University of Melbourne
Melbourne, Australia

Kate Mesh, PhD
Lund University
Lund, Sweden

Aliyah Morgenstern, PhD
Sorbonne Nouvelle University
Paris, France

Elena Nicoladis, PhD
University of Alberta
Edmonton, AB, Canada

Demet Özer, PhD
Koç University
Istanbul, Turkey

Meredith L. Rowe, EdD
Harvard University
Cambridge, MA, United States

Virginia C. Salo, PhD
Vanderbilt University
Nashville, TN, United States

Lisa Smithson, PhD
University of Alberta
Edmonton, AB, Canada

Gale Stam, PhD
National Louis University
Chicago, IL, United States

Marion Tellier, PhD
Aix-Marseille University
The French National Centre for Scientific Research
Laboratoire Parole et Langage
Aix-en-Provence, France

Virginia Volterra, PhD
Institute of Cognitive Sciences and Technologies
Consiglio Nazionale delle Ricerche
Rome, Italy

Elizabeth Wakefield, PhD
Loyola University, Chicago
Chicago, IL, United States

Ran Wei, PhD
Harvard University
Cambridge, MA, United States

Edited by Aliyah Morgenstern and Susan Goldin-Meadow
Gesture in Language

Aliyah Morgenstern and Susan Goldin-Meadow
1 Introduction to Gesture in Language

From childhood to old age, our bodies move as they go about the mundane activities of our daily lives, resonating with our environment as we interact with others through actions, speech, sign, and gestures. The body is the existential basis of culture and perception (Bourdieu, 1977), and it is through the kinetic and multimodal coordination of our productions and our perceptions that we become fully cooperative participants within our own cultural community (Merleau-Ponty, 1972). In order to capture the full complexity of language, new approaches are needed to analyze all our semiotic resources as they are deployed in their natural habitat. This habitat involves the orchestration of bodies engaged in communicating through speech or sign and gestures.

The purpose of this edited volume is to focus on the forms, functions, and roles of gesture in language across the lifespan, as it is deployed in a multitude of skillful variations in the collective coordination of communicative bodies.

We examine the role of gesture over the lifespan in its complex interaction with language. We explore the forms and uses of gesture before, during, and after language development over the lifespan, and when there is more than one language in bilingual people and second-language learners. We thus investigate how gesture, language, and multimodal communication can be studied in relation to developmental time. Rather than view gesture in language as a stable phenomenon, as is usually done in large corpus studies relying on big data, our aim is to examine the relation between gesture and language both in time and over time. Most chapters target communicative development over multiple data collection points, either in naturalistic environments or in experiments conducted longitudinally with the same participants or cross-sectionally with participants of different ages. Some chapters also include the moment-to-moment unfurling of semiotic resources in a sequence, as in conversation analysis, which details the mutual adjustment of communication partners to each other's gestures, facial expressions, gaze, speech, or sign.

One of the aims of this book is to provide a forum for different perspectives on how gesture is related to language—should it be considered part of language or a distinct representational form produced along with language?

1.1 Approaches to Gesture in Language

Interest in gestures dates back at least to Cicero and Quintilian, who analyzed gesture as rhetorical vehicles of influence. They viewed gesture as a universal language, a view shared by Bonifacio, Montanus, and Bulwer in the 16th and 17th centuries, as reported by Kendon (2004). De Jorio, one of the scholars who studied gestures in the 19th century, focused on continuities over time between gestures used in antique Greece and those used by his Neapolitan contemporaries. By contrast, in the 20th century, Efron (1941) rekindled scholars' interest in gesture by studying differences across cultures. Authors representing a wide range of fields, including biology (Darwin, 1877), philosophy (Wittgenstein, 1953), psychology (Goldin-Meadow, 2003; Kendon, 2004; McNeill, 1992; Wundt, 1912), anthropology (Haviland, 1998; Jousse, 1974), and linguistics (Calbris, 1990; Cienki, 2012; Müller, 2009), have contributed to creating a new and exciting scientific domain.

The debates about the links between gesture and language were stirred by the challenging title of McNeill's paper "So You Think Gestures Are Non-verbal" (1985). The dominant view at the time clearly dissociated gesture and language (Ekman & Friesen, 1969), as opposed to the seamless integration suggested in the late 19th century and early 20th century by authors such as Darwin (1877) and Wundt (1912). Gesture studies were given new life and propelled forward by McNeill's 1992 monograph. Thanks to McNeill, gesture was reappraised as a necessary and valuable object of study for psychologists and linguists. He presented speech and gesture as an integrated system that expresses two different types of thought (imagistic vs. propositional).

Despite his focus on the importance of gesture, McNeill still viewed gesture as having a different representational form from language. He described gestures as holistic and imagistic on-the-spot creations by speakers and language as conventionalized and categorical forms that must be learned. As Müller (2018) explained (supported by Goldin-Meadow & Brentari, 2017), this difference could be a consequence of their focus on spontaneously used gestures that are neither lexicalized nor conventionalized.

Kendon (1980), whose work had not yet been widely read but had influenced McNeill, described gesture and speech as "two aspects of the process of utterance" (p. 207). Kendon demonstrated the integration of gesture and speech by studying the temporal alignment of gesticulation and spoken units. Kendon also studied sign languages in Central Australian Aboriginal speech communities (Kendon, 1989), which inspired McNeill's (1992) formulation of "Kendon's continuum" (McNeill, 1992, p. 37). Gestural phenomena are ordered according to their degree of conventionality (among other parameters):

Gesticulation > Language-like gestures > Pantomime > Emblem > Sign language

Gesture for Kendon included the entire range of kinesic forms and functions, from gesticulation (i.e., spontaneously created forms encoding meaning in a holistic fashion) to emblems and signs. This continuum, in which emblems and signs are the most lexicalized/linguistic/symbolic, takes into account the presence or absence of coarticulated speech with gestures. However, as shown by Müller (2018),

"Kendon's continuum" does not do justice to Kendon's strong views about the historical continuity between spontaneously created singular gestures and standardized manual forms that function like words (signs). These views are in line with Wilcox (2005, 2007), who documented grammaticalization of gestures into sign in American, Catalan, French, and Italian Sign Languages. Note, however, that here we are talking about change over historical time. McNeill focused on processing change over momentary time.

Kendon (2004) also examined processing and, in these analyses, showed how gestures are integrated in the vocal utterance and used like words by making detailed analyses of conversational data and its "mixed syntax" (see Slama-Cazacu, 1976, who coined the term). These multimodal structures have been referred to as "multimodal grammatical integration" (Fricke, 2013), "composite signals" (Clark, 1996), "composite utterance" (Enfield, 2009), or, when referring to child language, "multimodal constructions" (Andrén, 2010; Morgenstern, 2014).

Gesture studies are now a dynamic emerging field in which scholars take different theoretical approaches and apply a variety of methods to the study of what Kendon (2004) called "visible action as utterance." Utterances may be constructed from speech, from gesture, or from combinations of both. Nevertheless, McNeill's (1992) original point still stands—gesture and language form an integrated system, but make use of different representational formats to do so.

This book deals with all types of gestures. *Emblems* are the most lexicalized and conventional, and can be used with or without speech. *Gesticulation* co-occurs with speech and is typically categorized into several types: *iconic* or *representational gestures*, which are the least conventional and the most imagistic, expressive, and individualized gestures; *deictic gestures* (including pointing), which index the objects, people, and places to which they refer; *beat gestures*, which play a prosodic role as they structure and punctuate the flow of speech; and *pragmatic gestures* (also called *recurrent gestures*, Ladewig, 2014), which have a high degree of conventionality and are used to regulate conversation.

Gesture theories vary with respect to their view of the relation between language and gesture, and this variability may go hand-in-hand with the type of gesture that is the focus of the theory. Kendon (2004) has studied gestures that accompany speech, as well as sign languages used in place of speech, and considers both types of behaviors to be visible action. In contrast, Singleton et al. (1995; see also Goldin-Meadow et al., 1996) made a clear distinction between co-speech gesture and language, both sign language and spoken language. They focused on representational and deictic gestures, which display either concrete or abstract properties of their referents. One reason to make a distinction between these types of gestures and the language (speech or sign) they accompany is that a mismatch between the information conveyed in gesture and the information conveyed in the accompanying language has cognitive implications—speakers who produce gesture–speech mismatches when explaining a task are ready to learn that task, and are more likely to profit from instruction on the task, than speakers who produce only gesture–speech matches (Alibali & Goldin-Meadow, 1993; Breckinridge Church & Goldin-Meadow, 1986; Goldin-Meadow, 2003; Perry et al., 1988). The same holds true for signers who produce gesture–sign mismatches (Goldin-Meadow et al., 2012). Under this view, it is essential to make a distinction between gesture and language in order to detect mismatch between information conveyed categorically (i.e., in language—speech or sign), and information conveyed imagistically (i.e., gesture; see Goldin-Meadow & Brentari, 2017).

Other scholars insist on the tight links between action, gesture, and language, and how the gestural modality can take on linguistic properties (Capirci et al., 2005; Capirci & Volterra, 2008; Goodwin, 2017; Morgenstern et al., 2018). Following this perspective, in some studies, gestures are considered part of language, especially when the focus is on recurrent, pragmatic gestures or emblems (Ladewig, 2014; Morgenstern, 2014). Pragmatic gestures are culturally shared and grounded in conventionalized and embodied experiential frames. They are the product of experiences that have resulted in recurrent multimodal scripts over different time frames: over the history of a community of users who share a culture and a language (historical time), over each individual's development (ontogenetic time), and over time spent with interactional partners from one moment to the next in the course of one conversation or repeated conversations with many interactional partners (conversational time). These gestures may indeed have become fully conventionalized and, thus, part of language (see also Boutet, 2010, who made the same argument about beats and iconic gestures, which he argued are sketches of emblems).

Cienki (2012) proposed a widely integrated view of language. For hearing adults, speech is the default medium for expressing and sharing ideas. But other behaviors, including actions, object manipulations, nonlexical sounds, prosodic patterns, facial expressions, and gestures, may acquire symbolic or communicative value according to the affordances of the context. In Cienki's theory, language has flexible boundaries—the body segment used to communicate meaning is determined by the context, interlocutor, availability of the body parts in the situation, and activity. A meaning can migrate from one body part to another: if hands are not available, shoulders can be used, or head or both or speech, and if the rest of the body is engaged in another activity (e.g., cooking), a mouth shrug or a frown will suffice. A family of meanings is thus dynamically paired with a family of forms. An important question to explore is when and how meaning migrates from speech or sign to other body parts, and whether we can find regularities in this process.

In order not to prejudge the issues of how gesture and language relate to one another, we have chosen the title *Gesture in Language*, and we hope that this book leads to informed and informative discussions of the question.

1.2 Methods

Different methods have been used to study gesture in language across the lifespan, using either naturalistic or experimental data. Both types of methods are essential in moving forward our understanding of how gesture and language work together to create meaning.

1.2.1 The Naturalistic Approach

Adam Kendon (2004), inspired by David Efron (1941) and Wilhelm Wundt (1912), made a plea for studies of gesture in context. In grounded situations where bodies in movement interact, using multimodal approaches to language (Morgenstern, 2014) has the potential to transform not only gesture studies but also linguistic theories. Linguistic theory has long been focused on *langue* [language] and on written texts rather than *parole* [speech] (de Saussure, 1959), which in Cienki's (2012) view can include gesture as a "relevant behavior."

Video-recording tools have advanced the detailed analysis of the organization of human action and interaction (Mondada, 2019). Although the recorded sessions represent only a small portion of the participants' lives, those snippets can help us capture sediments of their past experiences, as they are reactivated in their daily activities and exchanges—what we could call their "habitus," as defined by Husserl (1931). The recorded sessions index multiple dimensions of broader interactional-linguistic practices that can be replayed, transcribed, coded, and thoroughly analyzed over and over, from a variety of perspectives.

Not only can gesture be coarticulated with speech (and sign [Lu & Goldin-Meadow, 2018], even though sign languages are themselves compositional) and coarticulated with gaze, facial expressions, and posture, but each gesture produced with one of the upper limbs is potentially composed of movements of the shoulder, arms, forearms, hands, and fingers, and is often coordinated with the movements of the other upper limb. By studying gesture in its ecological environment in interactive situations, we put a lens on the fine and complex orchestration of all our body segments and our multilinear way of expressing meaning. But each speaker's body is also coordinated with other interacting bodies, as well as with manipulable objects, during daily activities. The materiality of the body has always had the potential to shape our environment, our tools, our objects, and the spaces we inhabit (Leroi-Gourhan, 1993). By adopting a naturalistic approach, researchers can capture language in its environment and articulate its actional roots and symbolic functions. Multimodal analyses of language (Cienki, 2012; Morgenstern, 2014) informed by moving bodies might, in turn, transform our linguistic theories.

Child language research is one of the first fields in which spontaneous interaction data have been systematically collected, initially through diary studies (Ingram, 1989;

Morgenstern, 2009), and later through audio and video recordings shared worldwide, thanks to the CHILDES project (MacWhinney, 2000). Research in language acquisition has developed tools, methods, and theoretical approaches to analyze children's situated multimodal productions, as they provide evidence for links between motor and psychological development, cognition, affectivity, and language (see Morgenstern, Chapter 3, this volume, for a more detailed presentation). Longitudinal interactive data collected in home environments require the researchers' involvement in data collection and analysis over a long period of time. This process creates a useful familiarity with the participants and the situations. It allows observers to annotate various kinesic features of the gestures and identify their meanings based not only on form but also on context and speech.

However, the analysis of naturalistic data can be tedious and costly, and it provides only a small sample of communication around and with children or among adults in everyday life. Nor can naturalistic data provide compelling insight into cause. Other methods are therefore necessary to capture gesture in language throughout the lifespan.

1.2.2 The Experimental Approach

Experimental methods are essential to convincingly address certain questions. For example, naturalistic data are particularly difficult to work with if we are interested in children's language comprehension. A child who brings two sneakers back in response to mother's request to "Go upstairs and get your sneakers" may understand the plural "s" form. But it's just as likely that the child understood the word "sneakers," and sneakers typically come in pairs. Finding just the right naturalistic situation in which the child is relying on linguistic form to respond appropriately is difficult. But it is relatively easy to set up experimental situations to test particular linguistic constructions (see, e.g., Fraser et al., 1963; Johnson et al., 2005; Goldin-Meadow et al., 1976). These situations are essential to determine which linguistic forms a child understands and whether adding gesture makes it more likely that the child will respond appropriately to those forms.

Experimental methods can also be used to complement naturalistic methods. For example, Motamedi et al. (2020) asked how children learn associations between words and meanings in their early language development. They hypothesized that because onomatopoeia (e.g., *knock, meow*) evokes imagery of the referent, it has the potential to bootstrap vocabulary acquisition when referents are present, and when they are absent. Using naturalistic observations of caregiver–child interactions, the authors explored whether onomatopoeia is, in fact, used in caregivers' speech to children and under what conditions. Using experimental data, they tested whether children can learn from onomatopoeia. The authors found that onomatopoeia is present in child-directed language, most often at the early stages and when the referent of the intended word is absent. They also found that children learn onomatopoeic word forms more easily than nononomatopoeic word forms. Together, the data from naturalistic and experimental situations combine to give us a more complete picture of early word-learning. Using both naturalistic and experimental studies of caregivers' use of gesture to young children will help us determine whether gesture plays a role in word learning.

Experimental evidence is best when used in conjunction with naturalistic data. We can generate hypotheses on the basis of naturalistic data and then test those hypotheses on experimental data. For example, English-speaking children ages 2½ to 3 years tend to put agents in the first position of their sentences and patients in the second position. On the basis of these naturalistic data, we hypothesize that children use animacy categories as the basis for their early ordering patterns. However, in the real world, agents tend to be animate and patients tend to be inanimate. As a result, the young child's ordering bias could be based on animacy categories (animate/inanimate), rather than semantic role categories (agent/patient). To distinguish between these two hypotheses, we need situations in which an inanimate object is playing an agent role and animate agent is playing a patient role. But these situations rarely arise in the child's world. To solve this problem, we turn to experimental data—we present children with these relatively artificial situations and ask them to talk about what happened. When we follow this plan, we find that children put inanimate objects in first position of their sentences when they play agent roles and animate objects in second position when they play patient roles (Angiolillo & Goldin-Meadow, 1982), confirming the hypothesis that children base their early ordering patterns on semantic role categories. We thus need experimental evidence to be convinced that children talk about the role an entity plays independent of its animateness and that they use role-defined categories like *agent* and *patient* to communicate these relational intentions.

As a second example from the field of gesture studies, researchers have found in longitudinal naturalistic studies that children's early gestures predict the size of their vocabularies several years later (e.g., Rowe & Goldin-Meadow, 2009). But the naturalistic data cannot tell us whether the act of gesturing plays a causal role in increasing the size of a child's vocabulary or merely reflects skills that are themselves responsible for the increase. To test this hypothesis, we need to experimentally manipulate a young child's gestures early in development and examine the child's spoken vocabulary at some later time. LeBarton et al. (2015) did just that, instructing only some children to point at objects in a picture book. Two months later, after 7 weeks of at-home experimental sessions, children who were instructed to point not only produced more pointing gestures when interacting with their parents than children who were not told to point, but they also produced more different spoken words. It is impossible to test a causal theory about gesture's role in language learning without experimental data. As an aside, it is worth noting that LeBarton et al. conducted their study in the children's homes—experimental studies need not be conducted in the lab.

1.3 Analyzing Gesture Across the Lifespan

This volume examines gesture over the lifespan by considering three developmental periods because there is evidence that gesture plays a different role during each period. Early in development, most children go through a time when they are able to communicate with others using gesture, but do not yet use speech (Goldin-Meadow, 2015)—gesture is their primary means of communication. During this period, children produce a variety of gestures that engage others in interaction. For example, they hold up or point at an object in order to bring attention to it; they extend an object in order to get their communication partners to take it and perhaps act on it; they extend an open palm to request an object. Children also produce conventional emblem gestures, which enter their repertoire either through everyday playful scripts or songs and nursery rhymes, such as "bye-bye" (waving hands), "peek-a-boo" (playfully hiding face with hands), "bravo" (clapping hands), "*ainsi font font font les petites marionnettes*" (a French song that is accompanied by hand gestures representing puppets). Emblems derive from the culture in which children are being raised and have very strong social and symbolic values.

Early gesture sets the stage for the language that is to come. Indeed, De Laguna (1927) noted that "in order to understand what the baby is saying you must see what the baby is doing" (p. 91). More recently, Zlatev (1997) suggested that sensorimotor schemas provide the "grounding" of language in experience and will then lead to children's access to the symbolic function. Infants' imitation and general production of gestures has been studied as a precursor to constructing prelinguistic concepts, as a pathway into the symbolic function of language, and as a bridge between language and embodiment. Gestures are viewed as representational structures, often constructed through imitation, which are enacted overtly and can be shared with others.

During the next period, children begin to produce single words, initially on their own and then eventually combined with gesture. Gesture-plus-word combinations mark the child's transition to a system in which gesture and speech are integrated both temporally and semantically. Prior to this point, children do produce gestures along with sounds, but those sounds are not coordinated with the stroke of the gesture, that is, they are not temporally integrated with gesture. But when children begin to combine points with meaningful words, the word *is* produced on the stroke of the gesture, heralding the onset of a semantically and temporally integrated gesture–speech system (Butcher & Goldin-Meadow, 2000). Gesture has begun to share the stage with speech/sign and must be described in relation to language. During this period, gestures (particularly pointing gestures) may be functioning like words, as they often take the place of words (e.g., the child points at his mother's hat and says "mama" to indicate who owns the hat; the point substitutes for the word "hat"). Indeed, using two modalities for two different semantic elements systematically precedes the onset of two-word speech by about 3 months (Goldin-Meadow & Butcher, 2003; Iverson & Goldin-Meadow, 2005; Özçalışkan & Goldin-Meadow, 2005). Although adults do, at times, produce gestures (particularly emblems) that stand in for a word, for the most part, adult gesture conveys information in a mimetic form that complements the categorical information conveyed in speech/sign (McNeill, 1992). Children thus have several steps to take before they achieve the gesture–speech system used by adults.

The third period is after language is mastered and gesture has the potential to be integrated with language, as it is in adults. Gesture is a lifelong behavior, used in combination with vocal productions by all adults (H. Marcos, 1998). Pointing not only remains functional but also diversifies in form and function as children become skilled multimodal conversationalists, and continues to be used by both adult speakers and signers (Fenlon et al., 2019). Once speech has been mastered, children can use their gestures not to acquire speech, but along with speech, as adults do. Gesture and speech (or sign) work together throughout childhood and old age. Age-related decline in motor control is due to modifications in the central nervous system (Ketcham & Stelmach, 2001). The decline in motor control has an effect on everyday life and might also have an effect on the production of co-speech gestures. Older adults might also benefit from seeing others produce gesture as their hearing declines. Analysis of the use of gesture at the end of the lifespan can thus inform theories of language production and comprehension across the lifespan.

If gesture is learned in relation to the language that the child is acquiring, what happens if two languages are learned? Studying second-language acquisition allows us to explore how gestures can change in connection to language development. There is evidence that the lower the proficiency in a second language, the greater the number of gestures (Nicoladis, 2007). Bilingual people also use more gestures when they speak in their weaker language (Benazzo & Morgenstern, 2014; L. R. Marcos, 1979). In addition, languages with different language conceptualization might be complemented by different co-speech gestures (Kita & Özyürek, 2003). Studies on the use of gestures in language teaching can also be useful to understand the role of gesture in learning a second language.

We use this developmental framework to organize the chapters in this volume.

1.4 Overview of the Volume

The volume is organized in five parts. Part I focuses on the most studied gesture in the literature and a foundational communicative tool: pointing (following Kita's seminal overview, 2003), which brings together issues on the (dis)continuities between gesture and sign. We chose to begin with an exploration across space and cultures in adults before turning to the beginning of the lifespan. In Chapter 2, Cooperrider and Mesh take us on a fascinating voyage around the world, as they synthesize the many uses of pointing in gesture and sign with specific details on forms and functions across cultures. Their chapter nourishes the larger debate on similarities and differences between gesture and sign. In Chapter 3, Morgenstern takes us back to the roots of multimodal language through an overview of the literature on early pointing, its integration in speech and sign, and the role of the adult. She then illustrates the range of uses drawing on detailed analyses of a collection of interactive sequences from longitudinal data. She analyzes pointing gestures from their various functions when used in isolation in interactive contexts to the use of multimodal constructions combining gesture, gaze, and speech. This section illustrates how one type of gesture, pointing, is a central tool across cultures and throughout the lifespan, and how it can be used productively to "refer to and conjure up visible and invisible, present and absent, actual and imaginary entities and events" (Chapter 3, this volume, p. 82).

Part II is centered on early gestures before children have fully entered language. Chapter 4 authors Rowe, Wei, and Salo clearly distinguish gesture and language, and explain how early gesture predicts later language development. They first present the various types of relations between gesture and language skills across children's early communicative development, and then show how gesture has the potential to reveal children's social cognitive skills. They carefully unravel the links between specific types of gestures and specific language skills, and show how analyzing early gestures may provide a better understanding of how children learn language. In Chapter 5, derived from their team's extensive research devoted to gesture, sign, and language development, Capirci, Caselli, and Volterra present a different view of the relation between gesture and language, focusing on the period between the end of the 1st year and the end of the 2nd year. They trace continuities between actions, gestures, and words, and emphasize the role of caregivers as they scaffold children's entry into symbolic meaning. They focus particularly on different categories of gestures derived from children's handling of objects. Their aim is to illustrate how language is grounded in an array of cognitive skills that are manifest in the analysis of early gestures within children's intentional and meaningful communication with their caretakers.

In Part III, the authors illustrate how gesture can be used in coordination with speech to form a system or facilitate language use. In Chapter 6, Clark and Kelly pursue the double aim of laying the foundations of the field and describing children's early multimodal communicative system. Through a historical overview of the field of language development and relevant illustrations, they highlight the role of adults and show how children's early gestures and words form an integrative communicative system that continues to be used, even once they have started producing multiword utterances with more complex multimodal constructions. In Chapter 7, Beaupoil-Hourdel's study is centered on co-speech gestures between the ages of 3 and 4 years. The combination of quantitative and detailed qualitative analyses of longitudinal data video (recorded at home) illustrates how children progressively learn to deploy all the semiotic resources at their disposal to convey negation and opposing stance through complex multimodal constructions. She focuses on co-speech gestures and how children can rely on the moment-to-moment interactive process with others and within a sequence to unfurl complex meanings. Chapter 8 authors Hall, Wakefield, and Goldin-Meadow emphasize the power of gesture in language-learning, with a focus on verb learning. Using an experimental paradigm, they demonstrate how gesture—either the gestures children see others produce or the gestures they themselves produce—can help children overcome the challenges of verb learning. Gestures' unique representational properties lay the groundwork for children not only to learn verbs, but also to generalize those newly learned verbs to appropriate contexts.

Part IV is dedicated to the use of gesture after language has been mastered, from older children to adults. In Chapter 9, Coletta analyzes the codevelopment of gesture and monologic discourse. He asserts that "gesture contributes to the full meaning of the bimodal utterance, thanks to its pragmatic, indexical, imagistic, and structuring properties" (p. 205). The chapter reviews his unique scientific contribution to describing older children's multimodal and narrative skills in studies conducted over the past 20 years. On the basis of a large range of findings, he discusses the relation between gesture and speech over time and how gesture scaffolds children's social, discursive, and narrative skills. In Chapter 10, Wagner Cook presents candidate processes underlying gesture production and perception, and explores how these processes are used over the lifespan. She argues that uncovering the mechanisms of gesture production will require studying gestures in complex communicative situations, as they are flexible behaviors that serve a variety of functions. She proposes the use of a range of methods and approaches to capture gesture's specific features according to its use and combinations with speech/sign. Chapter 11, by Göksun, Özer, and Akbıyık, is about gesture and the aging brain. They address how the decline in cognitive skills can affect gesture, whether gesture use can help improve speech problems, and how aging adults with neurodegenerative disorders use and comprehend gesture. They discuss the implications of these studies for understanding the interaction between speech and gesture. They demonstrate that additional studies on elderly adults' language and communicative skills are needed to have a better grasp of the mechanisms underlying gesture in language.

Part V includes three chapters on the use of gesture with more than one language. In Chapter 12, Nicoladis and Smithson present an extensive overview of gesture in bilingual language acquisition and highlight the impact of both cognitive and cultural factors. As bilingual people tend to have lower verbal abilities in their weaker language, some authors have predicted that they would use more gestures than monolingual people, particularly when speaking their weaker language. However, some studies have not confirmed this hypothesis. At the cultural level, bilingual people might be expected to differentiate their gestures according to the language they are using. The authors show that the same gestures (convergence) are often used by bilingual people in both of their languages. They support their argument by describing gesture use in bilingual children and adults. They propose that there might not be significant age-related changes in bilingual speakers' use of gesture. In Chapter 13, Gullberg grounds the concept of convergence by showing how languages interact in multicompetent language users' speech and gesture. The chapter illustrates how languages do not exist in isolation. When languages come into contact, cross-linguistic influence impacts gesture. The chapter promotes "a bimodal view of language in which speech and gesture are partners" (p. 317). The volume closes with Chapter 14, in which Stam and Tellier highlight the role of gesture in second-language learning and teaching. They posit that the study of verbal language only provides a partial picture of second language acquisition. Gesture is a powerful medium of communication in contexts of asymmetrical language proficiency, as between a native and nonnative speaker or between a learner and a teacher. As in first-language acquisition, gesture is used by experts to facilitate comprehension and to scaffold communication with novices, who themselves deploy their multimodal semiotic resources to express their communicative intent. The chapter highlights the importance of using pedagogical gestures in second-language teaching and demonstrates the value of analyzing kinesic activity in the classroom with both experimental methods and naturalistic data.

The detailed overviews and studies presented in this volume are a tribute to the role of gesture in language across the lifespan. We have, of course, given only a partial picture of the variety and complexity of the issues at stake, but we hope we have demonstrated that gesture studies form a vibrant, rich, and complex field of research that demands attention.

References

Alibali, M. W., & Goldin-Meadow, S. (1993). Gesture–speech mismatch and mechanisms of learning: What the hands reveal about a child's state of mind. *Cognitive Psychology*, *25*(4), 468–523. https://doi.org/10.1006/cogp.1993.1012

Andrén, M. (2010). *Children's gestures from 18 to 30 months* [Doctoral dissertation, Center for Cognitive Semiotics, Lund University]. https://portal.research.lu.se/portal/en/publications/childrens-gestures-from-18-to-30-months(f3e27d0e-a023-475a-af6d-c23c3e9c19f1).html

Angiolillo, C. J., & Goldin-Meadow, S. (1982). Experimental evidence for agent–patient categories in child language. *Journal of Child Language*, *9*(3), 627–643. https://doi.org/10.1017/S0305000900004943

Benazzo, S., & Morgenstern, A. (2014). A bilingual child's multimodal path into negation. *Gesture*, *14*(2), 171–202. https://doi.org/10.1075/gest.14.2.03ben

Bourdieu, P. (1977). *Outline of a theory of practice*. Cambridge University Press. https://doi.org/10.1017/CBO9780511812507

Boutet, D. (2010). Structuration physiologique de la gestuelle: Modèle et tests [Physiological structuring of body language: Model and tests]. *Lidil. Revue de Linguistique et de Didactique des Langues*, *42*, 77–96. https://doi.org/10.4000/lidil.3070

Breckinridge Church, R., & Goldin-Meadow, S. (1986). The mismatch between gesture and speech as an index of transitional knowledge. *Cognition*, *23*(1), 43–71. https://doi.org/10.1016/0010-0277(86)90053-3

Butcher, C., & Goldin-Meadow, S. (2000). Gesture and the transition from one- to two-word speech: When hand and mouth come together. In D. McNeill (Ed.), *Language and gesture* (pp. 235–258). Cambridge University Press. https://doi.org/10.1017/CBO9780511620850.015

Calbris, G. (1990). *The semiotics of French gestures*. Indiana University Press.

Capirci, O., Contaldo, A., Caselli, C., & Volterra, V. (2005). From action to language through gesture: A longitudinal perspective. *Gesture, 5*(1–2), 155–177. https://doi.org/10.1075/gest.5.1.12cap

Capirci, O., & Volterra, V. (2008). Gesture and speech. The emergence and development of a strong and changing partnership. *Gesture, 8*(1), 22–44. https://doi.org/10.1075/gest.8.1.04cap

Cienki, A. (2012). Usage events of spoken language and the symbolic units we (may) abstract from them. In J. Badio & K. Kosecki (Eds.), *Cognitive processes in language* (pp. 149–158). Peter Lang.

Clark, H. (1996). *Using language*. Cambridge University Press. https://doi.org/10.1017/CBO9780511620539

Darwin, C. (1877). A biographical sketch of an infant. *Mind, os-2*(7), 285–294. https://doi.org/10.1093/mind/os-2.7.285

De Laguna, G. A. (1927). *Speech: Its function and development*. Yale University Press.

de Saussure, F. (1959). *Course in general linguistics* (W. Baskin, Trans.), Philosophical Library.

Efron, D. (1941). *Gesture and environment*. King's Crown Press.

Ekman, P., & Friesen, W. V. (1969). The repertoire of nonverbal behavior: Categories, origins, usage and coding. *Semiotica, 1*(1), 49–98. https://doi.org/10.1515/semi.1969.1.1.49

Enfield, N. J. (2009). *The anatomy of meaning: Speech, gesture, and composite utterances*. Cambridge University Press. https://doi.org/10.1017/CBO9780511576737

Fenlon, J., Cooperrider, K., Keane, J., Brentari, D., & Goldin-Meadow, S. (2019). Comparing sign language and gesture: Insights from pointing. *Glossa: A Journal of General Linguistics, 4*(1), 2. https://doi.org/10.5334/gjgl.499

Fraser, C., Bellugi, U., & Brown, R. (1963). Control of grammar in imitation, comprehension, and production. *Journal of Verbal Learning and Verbal Behavior, 2*(2), 121–135. https://doi.org/10.1016/S0022-5371(63)80076-6

Fricke, E. (2013). Towards a unified grammar of gesture and speech: A multimodal approach. In C. Müller, A. Cienki, E. Fricke, S. Ladewig, D. McNeill, & S. Tessendorf (Eds.), *Body—language—communication: An international handbook on multimodality in human interaction* (38.1, pp. 733–754). De Gruyter Mouton. https://doi.org/10.1515/9783110261318.733

Goldin-Meadow, S. (2003). *Hearing gesture: How our hands help us think*. Belknap Press of Harvard University Press.

Goldin-Meadow, S. (2015). Gesture as a window onto communicative abilities: Implications for diagnosis and intervention. *Perspectives on Language Learning and Education, 22*(2), 50–60. https://doi.org/10.1044/lle22.2.50

Goldin-Meadow, S., & Brentari, D. (2017). Gesture, sign, and language: The coming of age of sign language and gesture studies. *Behavioral and Brain Sciences, 40*, e46. https://doi.org/10.1017/S0140525X15001247

Goldin-Meadow, S., & Butcher, C. (2003). Pointing toward two-word speech in young children. In S. Kita (Ed.), *Pointing: Where language, culture, and cognition meet* (pp. 85–107). Lawrence Erlbaum Associates.

Goldin-Meadow, S., McNeill, D., & Singleton, J. (1996). Silence is liberating: Removing the handcuffs on grammatical expression in the manual modality. *Psychological Review, 103*(1), 34–55. https://doi.org/10.1037/0033-295X.103.1.34

Goldin-Meadow, S., Seligman, M., & Gelman, R. (1976). Language in the two-year-old. *Cognition, 4*(2), 189–202. https://doi.org/10.1016/0010-0277(76)90004-4

Goldin-Meadow, S., Shield, A., Lenzen, D., Herzig, M., & Padden, C. (2012). The gestures ASL signers use tell us when they are ready to learn math. *Cognition*, *123*(3), 448–453. https://doi.org/10.1016/j.cognition.2012.02.006

Goodwin, C. (2017). *Co-operative action*. Cambridge University Press. https://doi.org/10.1017/9781139016735

Haviland, J. (1998). Early pointing gestures in Zincantán. *Journal of Linguistic Anthropology*, *8*(2), 162–196. https://doi.org/10.1525/jlin.1998.8.2.162

Husserl, E. (1931). *Ideas: General introduction to pure phenomenology* [W. R. B. Gibson, Trans.]. Macmillan.

Ingram, D. (1989). *First language acquisition: Method, description and explanation*. Cambridge University Press.

Iverson, J. M., & Goldin-Meadow, S. (2005). Gesture paves the way for language development. *Psychological Science*, *16*(5), 367–371. https://doi.org/10.1111/j.0956-7976.2005.01542.x

Johnson, V. E., de Villiers, J. G., & Seymour, H. N. (2005). Agreement without understanding: The case of third person singular /s/. *First Language*, *25*(3), 317–330. https://doi.org/10.1177/0142723705053120

Jousse, M. (1974). *L'anthropologie du geste* [The anthropology of gesture]. Gallimard.

Kendon, A. (1980). Gesture and speech: Two aspects of the process of utterance. In M. R. Key (Ed.), *The relationship of verbal and nonverbal communication* (pp. 207–228). De Gruyter Mouton.

Kendon, A. (1989). *Sign languages of Aboriginal Australia: Cultural, semiotic and communicative perspectives*. Cambridge University Press.

Kendon, A. (2004). *Gesture: Visible action as utterance*. Cambridge University Press. https://doi.org/10.1017/CBO9780511807572

Ketcham, C. J., & Stelmach, G. E. (2001). Age-related declines in motor control. In J. E. Birren & K. W. Schaie (Eds.), *The handbook of the psychology of aging* (5th ed., pp. 313–348). Academic Press.

Kita, S., & Özyürek, A. (2003). What does cross-linguistic variation in semantic coordination of speech and gesture reveal? Evidence for an interface representation of spatial thinking and speaking. *Journal of Memory and Language*, *48*(1), 16–32. https://doi.org/10.1016/S0749-596X(02)00505-3

Ladewig, S. H. (2014). Recurrent gestures. In C. Müller, A. Cienki, E. Fricke, S. H. Ladewig, D. McNeill, & J. Bressem (Eds.), *Body—language—communication: An international handbook on multimodality in human interaction* (pp. 1558–1574). De Gruyter Mouton.

LeBarton, E. S., Goldin-Meadow, S., & Raudenbush, S. (2015). Experimentally induced increases in early gesture lead to increases in spoken vocabulary. *Journal of Cognition and Development*, *16*(2), 199–220. https://doi.org/10.1080/15248372.2013.858041

Leroi-Gourhan, A. (1993). *L'homme et la matière: Evolution et techniques* [Man and matter: Evolution and techniques]. Albin Michel.

Lu, J. C., & Goldin-Meadow, S. (2018). Creating images with the stroke of a hand: Depiction of shape and size in sign language. *Frontiers in Psychology*, *9*, 1276. https://doi.org/10.3389/fpsyg.2018.01276

MacWhinney, B. (2000). *The CHILDES project: Tools for analyzing talk* (3rd ed.). Lawrence Erlbaum Associates.

Marcos, H. (1998). *De la communication prélinguistique au langage: Formes et fonctions* [From prelinguistic communication to language: Forms and functions]. L'Harmattan.

Marcos, L. R. (1979). Nonverbal behavior and thought processing. *Archives of General Psychiatry*, *36*(9), 940–943. https://doi.org/10.1001/archpsyc.1979.01780090026003

McNeill, D. (1985). So you think gestures are nonverbal? *Psychological Review*, *92*(3), 350–371. https://doi.org/10.1037/0033-295X.92.3.350

McNeill, D. (1992). *Hand and mind: What gestures reveal about thought*. University of Chicago Press.

Merleau-Ponty, M. (1972). *Phénoménologie de la perception* [Phenomenology of perception] (C. Smith, Trans.). Gallimard. (Original work published 1945)

Mondada, L. (2019). Contemporary issues in conversation analysis: Embodiment and materiality, multimodality and multisensoriality in social interaction. *Journal of Pragmatics*, *145*, 47–62. https://doi.org/10.1016/j.pragma.2019.01.016

Morgenstern, A. (2009). *L'enfant dans la langue* [The child in the language]. Presses Sorbonne Nouvelle.

Morgenstern, A. (2014). Children's multimodal language development. In C. Fäcke (Ed.), *Manual of language acquisition* (pp. 123–142). De Gruyter. https://doi.org/10.1515/9783110302257.123

Morgenstern, A., Blondel, M., Beaupoil-Hourdel, P., Benazzo, S., Boutet, D., Kochan, A., & Limousin, F. (2018). The blossoming of negation in gesture, sign and oral production. In M. Hickman, E. Veneziano, & H. Jisa (Eds.), *Sources of variation in first language acquisition: Languages, contexts, and learners* (pp. 339–364). Trends in Language Acquisition Research (TiLAR). https://doi.org/10.1075/tilar.22

Motamedi, Y. Murgiano, M., Perniss, P., Wonnacott, E., Marshall, C., Goldin-Meadow, S., & Vigliocco, G. (2020). Bootstrapping language from sensory experience: Onomatopoeia in early word learning. *Developmental Science*. Advance online publication. e13066. https://doi.org/10.1111/desc.13066

Müller, C. (2009). Gesture and language. In K. Malmkjaer (Ed.), *Routledge's linguistics encyclopedia* (pp. 214–217). Routledge.

Müller, C. (2018). Gesture and sign: Cataclysmic break or dynamic relations? *Frontiers in Psychology*, *9*, 1651. https://doi.org/10.3389/fpsyg.2018.01651

Nicoladis, E. (2007). The effect of bilingualism on the use of manual gestures. *Applied Psycholinguistics*, *28*(3), 441–454. https://doi.org/10.1017/S0142716407070245

Özçalışkan, S., & Goldin-Meadow, S. (2005). Gesture is at the cutting edge of early language development. *Cognition*, *96*(3), B101–B113. https://doi.org/10.1016/j.cognition.2005.01.001

Perry, M., Breckinridge Church, R., & Goldin-Meadow, S. (1988). Transitional knowledge in the acquisition of concepts. *Cognitive Development*, *3*(4), 359–400. https://doi.org/10.1016/0885-2014(88)90021-4

Rowe, M. L., & Goldin-Meadow, S. (2009). Differences in early gesture explain SES disparities in child vocabulary size at school entry. *Science*, *323*(5916), 951–953. https://doi.org/10.1126/science.1167025

Singleton, J. L., Goldin-Meadow, S., & McNeill, D. (1995). The cataclysmic break between gesticulation and sign: Evidence against an evolutionary continuum of manual communication. In K. Emmorey & J. Reilly (Eds.), *Language, gesture, and space* (pp. 287–312). Psychology Press.

Slama-Cazacu, T. (1976). Nonverbal components in message sequence: "Mixed syntax." In W. C. McCormack & S. A. Wurm (Eds.), *Language in man: Anthropological issues* (pp. 127–148). De Gruyter Mouton.

Wilcox, S. (2005). Routes from gesture to language. *Revista da Abralin*, *4*(1–2), 11–45. https://doi.org/10.5380/rabl.v4i1/2.52651

Wilcox, S. (2007). Routes from gesture to language. In E. Pizzuto, P. Pietrandrea, & R. Simone (Eds.), *Verbal and signed languages: Comparing structures, constructs and methodologies* (pp. 107–131). Mouton de Gruyter.

Wittgenstein, L. (1953). *Philosophical investigations*. Basil Blackwell.

Wundt, W. M. (1912). *Völkerpsychologie: Die sprache* [Ethnic psychology: The language]. Engelmann.

Zlatev, J. (1997). *Situated embodiment, Studies in the emergence of spatial meaning*. Gotab Press.

I An Emblematic Gesture: Pointing

Kensy Cooperrider and Kate Mesh
2 Pointing in Gesture and Sign

2.1 Introduction

Human communication is composite (e.g., H. H. Clark, 2016; Enfield, 2009; Ferrara & Hodge, 2018; Holler & Levinson, 2019). It involves the voice, face, hands, and the rest of the body. It integrates categorical elements and gradient ones, highly conventional and ad hoc forms, and both arbitrary symbols and motivated signals. This is true of spoken communication, and it is true—in equal measure—of signed communication. Both speakers and signers stitch these different types of components into a seamless whole. Some of these components are historically considered a core part of language, others marginal, and still others are thought to be something else entirely—gestural, expressive, paralinguistic (see, e.g., Dingemanse, 2018; Goldin-Meadow & Brentari, 2017; Müller, 2018). Regardless of whether one considers the language/nonlanguage divide fundamental, fuzzy, or fictitious, there is widespread agreement that certain communicative phenomena haunt the boundaries in ways that prove revealing. Chief among these are cases where both speakers and signers make use of the same bodily raw material, but in putatively very different ways: flashes and furrows of the brow; imitations of actions; depictions of size, shape, and arrangement. Here, we analyze one of these similar-looking forms in detail: *pointing*. The case of pointing shows, first, how a single semiotic tool can be put to many uses and, second, how speakers and signers use this tool in some ways that are similar and other ways that are different.

Pointing is an especially powerful and pervasive tool in the semiotic kit, used across the lifespan, across cultures, and across contexts. It's a major way that humans coordinate attention, anchor words to the world, and build common ground with each other. Following others, we here define *pointing* as a bodily movement toward a *target*—someone, something, somewhere—with the intention of reorienting attention to it (Eco, 1976; see also Cooperrider et al., 2018; Kendon, 2004). Often this gesture is done with the index finger—a preeminently "pointy" articulator that projects an imaginary vector, but it can also be done by tossing the head, pursing the lips, or extending a machete, among other ways. Pointing is a means of *indicating*—that is, of establishing attention to something by creating a spatiotemporal connection to it (Peirce, 1940; see also H. H. Clark, 2003). It is not the only way of indicating; one can also pat something or hold it up for inspection (H. H. Clark, 2003). Indicating, in turn, is one of the three major methods of meaning-making that humans have, along with *depicting* (i.e., using iconic representations) and what is sometimes called *describing* (i.e., using symbolic resources; H. H. Clark, 2003, 2016; Enfield,

2009; Ferrara & Hodge, 2018; Peirce, 1940). (The term *symbolic* is used in many ways in linguistics and cognitive science, but here refers to meaning conveyed by rule or convention, e.g., that a green traffic light means "go.") On purely theoretical grounds, then, pointing is a basic building block of communication (Kita, 2003b). And so it is on empirical grounds, too. Pointing is an early-emerging communicative act—among the earliest, in fact (see Morgenstern, Chapter 3, this volume)—and it is found universally in both spoken and signed communication (Kendon, 2010; Kita, 2003b; Morgenstern, 2014; Pfau, 2011).

Unsurprisingly, this elemental gesture has attracted the attention of both gesture researchers and sign language linguists. However, scholars in these two traditions have looked at pointing through different lenses and have gravitated toward different aspects of it. Gesture researchers, for example, have usually treated pointing as an adjunct to language but not really part of it; sign researchers, in contrast, have often treated pointing as a core part of sign language grammar rather than as a separate, gestural component (e.g., Meier & Lillo-Martin, 2010). These differing frameworks and foci contribute to an impression that—superficial similarities notwithstanding—pointing gestures and pointing signs are, deep down, fundamentally different. Recently, however, there has been a new push to compare pointing gestures and pointing signs directly, using similar data sets and similar analytical criteria. These direct comparisons underscore the fact that pointing gestures and pointing signs share many commonalities, and help sharpen our understanding of where exactly the differences lie.

Pointing may be a basic, foundational communicative tool, but—as we emphasize here—it is also a multifarious one. We thus examine pointing in all its formational, functional, contextual, and cultural variety. We begin by looking closely at the major foci of research on pointing in gesture studies (Section 2.2) and in sign language linguistics (2.3). We then review recent efforts to directly compare the two (2.4). A major refrain throughout is that, contrary to its assumed simplicity, pointing is multiform and multifunctional in both gesture and sign.

2.2 Pointing Gestures

Though there is a rich tradition of research on pointing in children (e.g., Bates, 1976; Cochet & Vauclair, 2010; Tomasello et al., 2007; see also Morgenstern, Chapter 3, this volume), research on adult pointing gestures has been more sporadic and diffuse. It has originated from diverse disciplinary quarters, including anthropology, psychology, linguistics, and conversation analysis. Despite this diversity of approaches, these efforts have had a few recurring foci, including (a) the variety of uses of pointing, with some uses considered primary and others secondary; (b) the relationship of pointing to spoken language; (c) how pointing varies in form from one use to the next; and (d) how pointing varies across cultures. We now consider these foci in turn.

2.2.1 Primary and Secondary Functions of Pointing

One focus of research in gesture studies has been the variety of functions pointing serves in communication. By definition, pointing always serves the function of drawing attention somewhere. But, under this broad umbrella, pointing has certain uses that are widely considered *primary* (Enfield et al., 2007), *prototypical* (Langacker, 2008), or *canonical* (Cooperrider, 2014), and others that are usually considered *secondary*.[1] The primary use of pointing, in these treatments, involves indicating something in the real world—such as a star in the sky, a mountain on the horizon, a fish in an aquarium—and, in doing so, inviting a listener to look at that something. Such points occur in many contexts, including ostension-based language learning (e.g., E. V. Clark & Estigarribia, 2011), direction giving (e.g., Kita, 2003a), sightseeing (e.g., Kendon, 2004), museum visits (Dimitra, 2012), and a variety of other joint activities (e.g., Bangerter, 2004). By definition, primary points not only invite listeners to reorient their gaze, they also convey crucial information about where something is or which of several is meant (Enfield et al., 2007). Without the information conveyed by such gestures, the communicative message would be incomplete.

But pointing is also used in a number of other ways that are often considered secondary, even within the category of real-world points to entities or places (see Figure 2.1). One example is when people point to something or somewhere, but without necessarily intending to redirect listener gaze and without relying on the point to communicate message-critical information. Enfield et al. (2007) described pointing in such cases as a kind of pragmatic safety net; it is used when the speaker thinks the listener knows the referent but is not entirely sure. Relatedly, speakers point in cases where the listener is already attending to the pointed-to target and where the referent is perfectly clear. A good example is seen in points to the self (Cooperrider, 2014). When speakers point to their own bodies along with pronouns like "I," "my," or "mine," they are drawing attention but not necessarily reorienting listener gaze—according to the norms of conversation, listeners should already be looking at the speaker, and the referent of "I" is rarely ambiguous. Similarly, when pointing to the listener with "you" or "yours," listeners know where they are and the referent is usually not ambiguous. In these cases, pointing serves to reorient discourse attention but not visual attention per se; it adds emphasis but does not contribute message-critical information.

Another type of secondary pointing occurs when people point to one thing to refer to another. In the above examples, what the speaker points to—the *target*—is recognizably

---

[1] "Primary" and "secondary" are, of course, theoretically loaded terms, inviting the question: Primary in what sense? One idea is that primary points are more frequent—as far as we know, there is no work suggesting this. Another idea is that they loom larger in folk theories of pointing—this has been claimed, but without any direct evidence. A third idea is they are learned first. This seems likely to be the case, but, again, we are not aware of direct evidence.

Fig. 2.1: Examples of points to real-world entities in gesture (top row) and sign (bottom row). (A) An English speaker points to an array of novel creatures while carrying out a referential communication task. (B) A Yupno (Papua New Guinea) man, far right, asks a "where" question, and his three interlocutors point as part of their answers: a nose point (far left), an index finger point (man behind, face occluded), and another nose point (middle). (C) A deaf signer of San Juan Quiahije Chatino Sign Language (Mexico) points to a plant while he explains its various uses. (D) A deaf signer of Israeli Sign Language points to a foam block on the table in front of him while carrying out a referential communication task. We thank Wendy Sandler and the Sign Language Research Lab at the University of Haifa for granting permission to use this image.

the same as what is referred to in speech—the *referent*. This is sometimes called *direct pointing* (Le Guen, 2011). But, at other times, the pointed-to target is associated with the referent but not identical to it (e.g., Borg, 2002; H. H. Clark, 2003; Le Guen, 2011). This phenomenon has gone by different labels, including *metonymic pointing*, *deferred ostension*, and *indexical chaining*. A classic example involves pointing to a speedometer to refer to a car's speed (Quine, 1960); other examples include pointing to the chest to refer to a "we" (Cooperrider, 2014) or pointing to a house to refer to one of its occupants (Levinson, 2006).

People also point to things that, strictly speaking, are not there. This phenomenon is commonly known as *deixis am phantasma* (Bühler, 1934/1990) or *abstract deixis* (Stukenbrock, 2014), and it takes a number of different forms. In some cases, people point metaphorically, such as to a temporal landmark like "tomorrow," which has no physical location in space (Cooperrider et al., 2014). In other cases, people point to empty locations to invest them with meaning (see Haviland, 2000, on *baptismal pointing*), a behavior that has been studied in storytelling situations (McNeill, 1992) and in joint activities (Bavelas et al., 2011). This general technique of assigning referents to empty locations in space has been the subject of direct comparisons between speakers and signers, as discussed later. Finally, people also point to apparently empty space when they are gesturing *under transposition*: During storytelling, people may point as if from some imagined there–then rather than from the actual location here–now of the speech event (Haviland, 1993, 2003).

All of the uses of pointing considered so far serve *referential* functions—they serve to draw attention to a person, place, object, or idea being overtly referred to in the discourse. But points sometimes also serve more narrowly *interactive* functions. This often involves pointing to present people. For instance, speakers taking over a turn may point to the last speaker as a way of showing agreement with what they just said, even though that speaker goes unmentioned in the discourse (Healy, 2012). Similarly, in multiparty conversations such as meetings, people point as a way of tacitly citing others present (Bavelas et al., 1992). Conversely, pointing to the addressee is also used to mock (Sherzer, 1973) or scold (Andrén, 2014). Generally, such social functions of pointing have not been as widely examined as the more prototypical referential uses. Note that these interactive functions still involve the same overarching function of orienting attention to a region of space—in the case of the person being agreed with, cited, mocked, or scolded—but take on a richer meaning in context. Moreover, even a point that is prototypically referential—such as a point to someone while addressing them—may do important social work, as when it conveys authority or reprimand.

2.2.2 Coproduction With Speech

Another focus for gesture researchers has been how pointing is organized in relation to spoken language. Importantly, pointing does sometimes occur on its own, without accompanying speech—early in development but also in adult communication. Generally, like depicting gestures, points can occur on their own, in sequence with speech, or overlapping with speech (H. H. Clark, 2016). When pointing does overlap with speech, it is most prototypically associated with a distinctive class of words known as *demonstratives*—including, in English, "this," "that," "these," "those," "here," and "there" (Diessel, 2006). Indeed, demonstratives have sometimes been dubbed "pointing words" (Diessel, 2012). This is partly because demonstratives commonly co-occur with pointing—some describe pointing as obligatory when demonstratives are used (e.g., Levelt et al., 1985)—and partly because both serve to indicate something in the world. Going further, Cooperrider (2016) emphasized that demonstratives and pointing are designed in relation to each other, or *co-organized*. In particular, the choice of whether to point to an entity is entwined with the choice of whether to use a demonstrative and, if so, whether to use "this" or "that," "here" or "there" (or their parallels in other languages; see Mesh, 2017, in press; Piwek et al., 2008).

Pointing also commonly co-occurs with spoken language beyond demonstratives, of course. Because points are often used for conveying "where" or "which" information, pointing is regularly used along with location or feature descriptions (Bangerter, 2004). In fact, the range of spoken referents that pointing can partner with is essentially unbounded. By making use of metonymy, metaphor, and imagination, speakers can talk about a wide world of possible referents—nonpresent, invisible, nonphysical—while simultaneously directing attention to regions of space in the here-and-now (Cooperrider, 2014).

2.2.3 Variation in Pointing Across Contexts

Gesture researchers have also examined how points vary in form from use to use and context to context. Such variation is usually not assumed to be arbitrary, but rather to reflect fine-grained differences in function. Some aspects of this variation stem from culture-specific conventions, as discussed later, but others may reflect general principles. For example, Kendon (2004) described how different pointing handshapes are tailored to different discourse purposes. He noted that when British and Italian speakers indicate something for the purposes of presenting it for "inspection" (p. 224) they tend to point with the palm open and facing up. In other cases, variation in pointing handshape reflects the incorporation of iconic features, thus fusing indicating and depicting elements (Cooperrider, 2014; Goodwin, 2007; Kendon, 2004). Recently, Talmy (2018) analyzed in detail such deviations from the prototypical case of index finger pointing, creating a typology of how different ways of pointing evoke targets that are static or moving, 2D or 3D, punctate or extended (see also Hassemer & McCleary, 2018).

Beyond incorporating iconic features, pointing gestures also vary from use to use in how much effort the speaker puts into them. Drawing on interviews with Lao speakers, Enfield et al. (2007) observed that points serving the primary function of conveying location information involved greater arm extension and were more likely to involve speaker gaze to the target; the secondary points they observed, in contrast, were smaller in form. Relatedly, Bangerter and Chevalley (2007) observed that *communicative points*—produced when speaker and listener were visible to each other—were more likely to involve arm extension than *noncommunicative points*—produced when a barrier separated the participants. These and other findings suggest that pointing gestures embody varying degrees of effort. They also suggest a candidate general principle that merits further investigation: The more central a pointing gesture is to the message at hand, the more effort the speaker will put into it.

2.2.4 Variation in Pointing Across Cultures

A final focus has been on how pointing varies from one culture to the next. Pointing, by all accounts, is a human universal (e.g., Cooperrider et al., 2018), but it varies in several ways across communities. Some of this variation is due to particular conventions of pointing form. Speakers of Arrernte, an Indigenous Australian language, have several pointing handshapes that are codified for particular purposes—for instance, an open hand with palm facing to the side is used when indicating the direction of an absolutely oriented path (Wilkins, 2003). Some communities have a conventional practice of raising the height of the pointing arm to reflect the distance of the target— the higher the arm, the farther away the target (e.g., Eco, 1976). People in Mesoamerica show an especially exaggerated version of this far-is-up strategy, sometimes using a near-vertical point to indicate distant referents (Le Guen, 2006; Levinson, 2003; Mesh, 2017, in press). Different communities also have different conventions for pointing nonmanually, with the head and face. Some form of pointing with the head—such as tossing, thrusting, tilting—appears to be universal (e.g., McClave, 2007). In certain cultures, however, there are also conventional facial pointing actions. These include *lip-pointing*, which consists of protruding, funneling, or pursing the lips (Enfield, 2001; Mihas, 2017; Sherzer, 1973), and *nose-pointing*, which consists of scrunching the nose (Cooperrider & Núñez, 2012). Both of these types of facial points are usually accompanied by a meaningful shift of gaze in the direction of the target (Adone & Maypilama, 2014; Enfield, 2001). Ethnographers have frequently claimed that such facial gestures are a major—or even preferred—form of pointing in the communities where they are used (e.g., Sherzer, 1983). In one case, this claim has been borne out quantitatively. Using a referential communication task, Cooperrider et al. (2018) found that people in the Yupno valley of Papua New Guinea, where nose-pointing is used, were just as likely to point nonmanually as manually.

Pointing also varies across cultures by virtue of being bound up with broader communicative practices and cognitive patterns. For example, Blythe et al. (2016) described how pointing becomes an especially critical communicative resource in Murrinhpatha conversation because of cultural taboos on naming certain people and the places associated with those people. Elsewhere, pointing is recruited into a conventional practice for referring to the time of day. The best-studied case is found in the Brazilian Amazon (Floyd, 2016). Nheenghatú speakers will point to an accurately oriented arc of the sun, running east to west, in order to refer to particular times (e.g., noon, by pointing directly overhead) or to more extended intervals (e.g., all afternoon, by sweeping a hand over the corresponding segment of the arc). Similar practices are found much more widely in speaking communities (see also Le Guen & Pool Balam, 2012), as well as in some village sign languages (de Vos, 2014). Finally, it is reported that people in some Indigenous communities remain absolutely oriented and maintain accurate cognitive maps as they move through the world (Levinson, 2003). There is thus a cultural expectation in such groups that people will point accurately, even to distant, unseen locations (Haviland, 1993; Le Guen, 2011). In Western cultural groups, there appears to be no such expectation; Americans, for instance, sometimes point with comic inaccuracy, even to familiar locations (e.g., Schegloff, 1984).

A final source of variation across cultures is taboos that regulate how you can point or what you can point to. In Ghana, for instance, pointing with the left hand is considered impolite, and this prohibition has consequences for direction-giving (Kita & Essegbey, 2001). Among Indigenous Australians, where avoidance registers are used during certain social interactions, speakers will often point in a more constrained fashion by using a fist or the elbow (Green, 2019; see also Adone & Maypilama, 2014). Elsewhere, taboos govern what you can point to. Famously, in some cultures, it is unacceptable to point to rainbows (Lee & Fraser, 2001); in many Western cultures, it is considered rude to point to people, though this norm is unevenly observed and commonly violated (e.g., Jarmołowicz-Nowikow, 2015).

2.3 Pointing Signs

Signers, like speakers, point prodigiously. Every sign language documented thus far—whether used by a deaf child without access to a sign language model (i.e., a *homesigner*), a group of deaf people in an urban or village setting, or even by hearing people as an alternative to speech—relies heavily on pointing to serve multiple functions. Despite this fact, research on sign languages has historically focused on only a small subset of the many functions of pointing signs. When sign linguistics arose as a field of study in the 1960s, its practitioners were intent on demonstrating that sign languages are not merely elaborate gestural systems, but instead exhibit the same structures found in spoken language (see, e.g., Klima & Bellugi, 1979). As a result, early research on pointing signs focused on those features that could be directly compared with speech and sidelined pointing features with analogues in gesture. Only relatively recently has a welcome sea change begun: more and more, sign linguists are attending to the full set of features of pointing signs, taking interest in the many features that are shared with pointing gestures. The major foci of research on pointing signs include (a) similarities between pointing signs and spoken pronouns, demonstratives, and locative expressions; (b) uses of pointing signs to establish and maintain reference; (c) other uses of pointing, some analogous to secondary pointing gestures; and finally, (d) cross-linguistic comparisons of pointing signs. We now discuss each in turn.

2.3.1 Pronouns, Demonstratives, and Locatives: Analogues to Pointing Signs?

Signers, of course, point toward the objects, spaces, and people around them; pointing is as fundamental to their communication as it is for speakers. However, the push to compare sign with speech led sign language linguists to largely focus on just one type of real-world pointing: points toward present people. These were compared systematically with pronouns, the most basic resource for referring to persons in speech. There was a rich set of comparisons to be made, first in terms of function: Both pointing signs and pronouns refer, that is, they identify speech act participants and track reference to those participants throughout the discourse (e.g., Engberg-Pedersen, 1993; Liddell, 1996; Lillo-Martin & Klima, 1990; Meier, 1990; Petitto, 1987; Senghas & Coppola, 2001; van Hoek, 1992). In addition, signed points to persons can take different forms based on whether the target is the signer, addressee, or another present person—and whether that target is singular or plural—a fact that many sign linguists take as evidence for the grammatical person- and number-marking that is found on pronouns (e.g., Meier & Lillo-Martin, 2013). Moreover, person-referring pointing signs are subject to the same principles that determine the placement of pronouns in spoken languages, including the so-called binding conditions on anaphora (for discussion, see Meier & Lillo-Martin, 2010). In accounting for this evidence, sign linguists have disagreed, sometimes quite contentiously, about whether person-referring pointing signs are true pronouns, or can even be called *linguistic*. At the heart of the argument is the question of whether a language's lexicon needs to contain a finite, listable set of forms. Some authors claim that because some features of pointing are gradient—in particular, the direction of the point, which may be modified in indefinitely many ways—signed points should be understood as *gestural* components of the language (i.e., formed at least partly from gradient features) rather than *linguistic* (i.e., organized around a finite set of categorical oppositions, e.g., Liddell, 2000, 2003; Liddell & Metzger, 1998). Other authors argue that pointing signs are organized in a way that makes them linguistic, but the types of distinctions they encode are limited and are thus closer to a simplified demonstrative system than to a pronominal one (Ahlgren, 1990; Koulidobrova & Lillo-Martin, 2016; McBurney, 2002). Still others argue that the person- and number-marking features seen in some sign languages' person-referring points justifies treating them not only as linguistic but also as clear pronouns (see Cormier et al., 2013). A growing trend in the discipline is to sidestep the debate altogether and not worry as much about categorizing pointing signs as linguistic or gestural. Such treatments focus instead on identifying similarities and differences between pointing signs and pronouns or demonstratives on the one hand, and pointing signs and pointing gestures on the other (see Cormier et al., 2013; Johnston, 2013a, 2013b); or they focus on the cognitive processes that account for how speakers and signers use points (see Wilcox & Occhino, 2016).

Of course, signers point toward not only people in the world around them but also objects and locations. Pointing signs targeting objects have been described as *demonstrative expressions* (Koulidobrova & Lillo-Martin, 2016; McBurney, 2004), while pointing signs targeting locations have been called *locatives* (e.g., de Vos, 2013; Padden, 1983; Shepard-Kegl, 1985). Notably, signers appear to distinguish points toward locations from points toward people by modifying two formational features of points: palm orientation and handshape. Points toward locations are typically formed with the palm facing downwards, whereas points toward people are more often formed with the palm facing to the side; this observation has been made for a number of the world's sign languages (for a review, see Pfau, 2011), including in a quantitative analysis of British Sign Language (BSL, Fenlon et al., 2013). Studies of American Sign Language (ASL) and of BSL have also shown that points toward locations are produced more often with an index finger (Bayley et al., 2002; Fenlon et al., 2013). Notably, in the ASL and BSL studies, signers were more consistent in how they formed points toward locations and showed more variation in their points toward people. Fenlon et al. (2013) suggested that this result is due to different patterns of coarticulation with the surrounding signs—a possibility that underscores how closely pointing signs are prosodically integrated with the signs surrounding them.

2.3.2 Pointing Signs to Establish and Maintain Reference

Some of the most interesting features of pointing in sign language arise when the point is directed toward nothing at all. Signers sometimes *anchor* a referent in space by first naming the referent and then pointing to a location in the empty space in front of them (Barberà & Zwets, 2013). An ASL signer recounting a story about her pet, for example, could introduce the animal with the lexical sign DOG, preceded or followed by a point. The noun-accompanying point appears to share the function of spoken language determiners, and its presence and ordering relative to the noun provides information about whether the reference is definite (*the* dog) or indefinite (*a* dog; MacLaughlin, 1997; Zimmer & Patschke, 1990). Crucially, this type of point toward empty space—with or without an accompanying noun—has a second function: It associates the referent with the selected empty space (often called a *referential locus*, or *R-locus*), making it possible to point toward this same space later to refer back to the same referent. The ASL signer from our example points alongside the sign DOG, and in so doing, associates the notion of the dog with a specific location in the space in front of her. It is thus possible for her to continue to point to this same location throughout her narrative, referring again and again to the dog as she narrates his adventures (see Cormier et al., 2013; Perniss & Özyürek, 2015). Once a signer has associated a referent to a given R-locus, they can use a variety of deictic mechanisms beyond the point to refer back to the referent. Many sign languages contain a specialized set of main verbs that are produced using movements to or from R-loci, conveying that the subject or object of the verb is the referent associated with that space (e.g., Padden, 1983; see also Hou & Meier, 2018; Schembri et al., 2018). In our ASL example, the signer might modulate the location and movement of the verb BITE, making the starting-place of the moving hand the dog's R-locus (and thus identifying the dog as the biter) or moving the hand toward the dog's R-locus (identifying the dog as the bitee). *Spatial agreement* or *spatial modulation* of the kind exemplified by the movement of the verb BITE in this example is dependent on the meaningful association of referents with empty space, and this association is most often established by an initial pointing act. In this way, a seemingly marginal function of points—to establish reference to nonpresent entities—becomes foundational for verb inflection processes in many sign languages.

2.3.3 Other Pointing Phenomena in Sign Languages

Across signing communities, points are also regularly used metonymically—that is, points toward real-world spaces are used for referents that are not in those spaces, but are conceptually related to them (see Table 2.1). This, of course, is analogous to the metonymic pointing gestures described earlier. In Yolngu Sign Language and Kata Kolok, languages used in small-scale communities where the location of everyone's home is common knowledge, a signed point toward a particular home refers to the

Tab. 2.1: Overview of Studies on Uses of Pointing in Gesture and Sign

	Gesture	Sign
Direct points to real-world entities		
Objects	Bangerter, 2004; Cooperrider, 2016	Koulidobrova & Lillo-Martin, 2016; McBurney, 2004
Locations	Enfield et al., 2007; Mesh, 2017, in press; Wilkins, 2003	de Vos, 2013; Padden, 1983; Shepard-Kegl, 1985
Persons	Cooperrider, 2014; Jarmołowicz-Nowikow, 2015	Cormier et al., 2013; Meier & Lillo-Martin, 2010, 2013
Metonymic points		
Locations for person reference	Levinson, 2006	Bauer, 2014; Butcher et al., 1991; de Vos, 2013
Locations for temporal reference	Floyd, 2016; Le Guen & Pool Balam, 2012	de Vos, 2013; Le Guen, 2012
Body parts for experiential concepts	Cooperrider, 2014	Evans & Wilkins, 2000; Kendon, 1980; Östling et al., 2018
Body parts for colors	not attested	de Vos, 2011; Woodward, 1989; Zeshan & Sagara, 2016
Points to empty space		
Referential loci	McNeill, 1992; Perniss & Özyürek, 2015	Cormier et al., 2013; Engberg-Pedersen, 1993; Liddell, 2003
Metaphorical	Cooperrider et al., 2014	Yano & Matsuoka, 2018
Transposed targets	Haviland, 1993	Liddell, 2003
Interactive functions of pointing	Bavelas et al., 1992; Healy, 2012	Ferrara, 2020

person who lives in it (Bauer, 2014; de Vos, 2013). Among not only speakers of Yucatec Maya but also signers of Yucatec Maya Sign Language, a point to the sky refers to the time of day when the sun is at that location (Le Guen & Pool Balam, 2012; see also de Vos, 2013). In young sign languages and more established ones alike, points to the hair, teeth, and lips are regularly used to refer to the colors black, white, and red (de Vos, 2011; Nonaka, 2004; Woodward, 1989; Zeshan & Sagara, 2016). The human propensity toward developing metonymic reference is so great that even when homesigners get little exposure to metonymic pointing in gesture, they nevertheless develop it. Using this strategy substantially expands the communicative potential of pointing (Butcher et al., 1991).

Sign languages also incorporate pointing into fully lexical signs. For example, in ASL and other sign languages, body parts terms are most often formed by a pointing movement toward the body part. Often these are not simply prototypical points with an index finger extended, but involve different handshapes (e.g., open hand) or motion (e.g., reduplication) (Pyers, 2006). Indeed, many lexical signs, while not obviously "pointy," are articulated in relation to parts of the body—such as the head, face, or abdomen—and thus motivated, in part, by metonymic indexicality (Cooperrider, 2014; Kendon, 1980). For instance, words related to cognition are often articulated near the head (Evans & Wilkins, 2000; Kendon, 1980); in contrast, words related to hunger may be articulated near the stomach, and words related to eating may be articulated near the mouth (Östling et al., 2018).

2.3.4 Pointing Signs in Crosslinguistic Comparison

When discussing the variety of functions for pointing signs, it can be easy to forget that the sign languages in which pointing is found are themselves remarkably diverse. There is no one context for "pointing in sign language"; rather, pointing signs are found in sign languages young and old, in urban and rural environments, with high or low numbers of users in a variety of different social configurations. What is common to the pointing signs found in all of these environments is that they are frequent and indispensable. For homesigners still in the process of conventionalizing vocabularies, pointing is a reliable tool for identifying not only present objects but also the properties that they embody (Coppola & So, 2006; Torigoe & Takei, 2002). For signers of more established sign languages, pointing takes on additional functions (Pfau & Steinbach, 2006) and in at least some contexts it is used even more frequently than in homesign (Coppola & Senghas, 2010). There are certainly aspects of variation in pointing across sign languages. For example, pointing signs draw attention to the physical environment in ways that reflect the different topographies and direction-giving traditions where sign languages emerge (de Vos, 2013; Mesh, 2017, in press; Nonaka, 2015), and they direct attention beyond the here-and-now in ways particular to the narrative practices of specific cultures (Green & Wilkins, 2014). Just how uniformly pointing is integrated into different sign languages, and how much diversity there may be in sign language pointing practices, are promising areas for further study.

2.4 Comparing Gesture and Sign

Much of the work on pointing gestures has been done without drawing any comparisons to pointing signs—and vice versa. Fortunately, this is starting to change. Increasingly, for instance, sign linguists are comparing phenomena in sign both to analogous phenomena in spoken language and to analogous phenomena in co-speech gesture (e.g., Cormier et al., 2013; Johnston, 2013a; Meier & Lillo-Martin, 2013; Pfau, 2011). A number of insightful observations have come out of such theoretical comparisons, and a range of similarities and differences between pointing gestures and pointing signs have been proposed. One limitation of such theoretical treatments, however, is that they often rely on an "armchair" understanding of pointing, rather than an empirically informed one. Moreover, because gesture researchers and sign researchers have so often gravitated to different aspects of pointing, it is tempting to conclude from the existing literature that gesturers don't really do *this*, or signers don't do much of *that*. But, in reality, we simply lack studies spanning the full range of pointing behaviors in gesture and sign. To overcome this limitation, direct comparisons are critical (as some have noted, e.g., Cormier et al., 2013). In this vein, several studies have, for instance, compared how signers and gesturers use pointing (and other forms of deictic anchoring) during reference tracking (Barberà & Zwets, 2013; Perniss & Özyürek, 2015). Here, we consider two recent lines of our own work; both are efforts to quantitatively compare pointing in gesture and sign using similar data sets and similar analytic criteria.

2.4.1 Comparing Pointing in Chatino Gesture and Sign

A first study to systematically compare pointing by signers and gesturers in the same community, taking a quantitative approach to a sizable data set, was performed by Mesh (2017) in a Chatino community of Mexico. This study compared points to landscape-scale referents—including schools, churches, and trade locations in the surrounding mountainous terrain—produced by gesturers and signers as they gave route directions.

The Chatino people traditionally inhabit a region at the base of the southern Sierra Madre mountain range in the state of Oaxaca, Mexico. While Chatinos are in no way socially isolated, there are social barriers to sending children to residential schools in mestizo (i.e., non-Indigenous) cities. As a result, deaf Chatinos have minimal exposure to the national sign language transmitted in residential schools for the deaf. In the Chatino community of San Juan Quiahije, 13 of the approximately 3,600 community members are deaf, and these 13 people, along with their hearing family members, are developing an interrelated set of family sign languages: San Juan Quiahije Chatino Sign Language (SJQCSL). Signers of SJQCSL draw on the rich gestural practices found in the surrounding community. An interesting question that arises in this context is thus how much signers alter these practices as they incorporate them into a fully visual–manual language (Mesh & Hou, 2018). Mesh (2017) approached this question by focusing on pointing practices in particular.

In a series of semistructured interviews, deaf and hearing citizens of San Juan Quiahije were asked how to reach local and regional landmarks on footpaths and via the roads that have more recently been built for travel by truck to distant locations. Thirty-one people were interviewed: 29 hearing speakers of San Juan Quiahije Chatino (providing more than 6 hours of footage) and two deaf signers of SJQCSL, representing two distinct family sign varieties (providing 31 minutes of footage). Since pointing in Mesoamerica has been described as obeying the far-is-up principle (see Section 2.4), and as using different handshapes to indicate nearby, visible objects versus distant directions (e.g., Haviland, 2003), all points were coded for the distance of the target (measured in meters) and for two formational features of the point: elbow height and handshape. A later extension of the study took a third formational feature into account: arm extension (Mesh, 2017, in press).

Chatino speakers showed a strong pattern of marking referent distance in their gestures, using all three coded features: they frequently indicated nearby targets using points with a low elbow, partial extension of the arm, and an extended index finger (Figure 2.2A). By contrast, they were significantly more likely to indicate distant targets using points with a high elbow, full extension of the arm, and an open handshape (Figure 2.2B). Remarkably, the two deaf SJQCSL signers mirrored the hearing speaker-gesturers' pointing system in only one respect: like gesturers, the signers used elbow height to mark distance, but unlike gesturers, the signers frequently used a fully extended arm and an extended index finger to indicate targets regardless of their distance (Figures 2.3A and 2.3B).

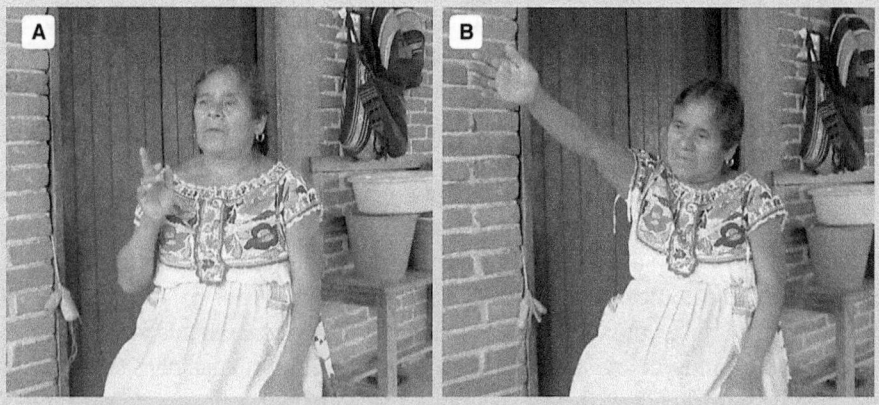

Fig. 2.2: A speaker of San Juan Quiahije Chatino follows the far-is-up pointing principle. She points to a nearby street with a low, unextended arm and an outstretched index finger (A) and to a distant city using a high, extended arm with an open hand (B).

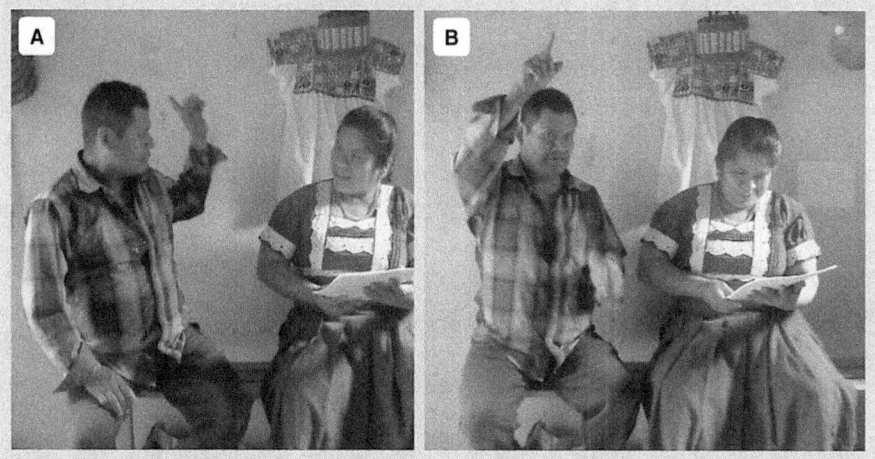

Fig. 2.3: Signers of San Juan Quiahije Chatino sign language also follow the far-is-up pointing principle. Unlike speakers, though, they point with the same handshape for nearby targets (A) and distant ones (B).

How can this result shed light on what is shared, and what is distinct, in pointing signs and pointing gestures? The area of similarity between gesturers and signers provides an important first clue: the use of elbow height to mark referent distance has been argued to be a universal feature of human pointing (see, e.g., Eco, 1976), and even to extend to pointing in other species (Gonseth et al., 2017), but the instantiation of the far-is-up strategy varies across human communities. In particular, the use of near-vertical pointing to mark distant referents has been described as especially prominent in the Mesoamerican context (e.g., Levinson, 2003). The pointing feature shared by signers and gesturers in San Juan Quiahije, then, is community-particular, and was evidently acquired in a process of cultural transmission involving both deaf and hearing recipients.

The differences between gesturers and signers in this study are equally important for our understanding of how pointing enters sign languages. Neither of the two family sign languages represented in this study had a pointing system identical to that of gesturers in the surrounding community. This gives us evidence that signers of emerging languages do not adopt the pointing practices around them wholesale. Rather, they differentially integrate features of pointing practices into their emerging linguistic systems, in ways that are likely sensitive to the contrasts already developing in their language's phonology and morphology. If differences are to be found between pointing gestures and pointing signs in communities with older, more established sign languages, these differences may well be due to language-specific constraints imposed on the adoption and adaptation of gestures during the early stages of the sign languages' emergence.

2.4.2 Pointing in BSL, ASL, and Spoken English

Fenlon, Cooperrider, and their colleagues recently compared pointing signs and pointing gestures using existing corpora in a first study (Fenlon et al., 2019), and controlled elicitation in a second (Cooperrider et al., 2021). The first study examined points to the self, addressee, and other entities (thus corresponding to first-, second-, and third-person pronouns, Fenlon et al., 2019). The data came from two existing corpora of dyadic conversation; they included 27 English speakers from the Tavis Smiley Corpus (Cooperrider, 2014), who contributed a total of 543 pointing gestures, and 24 signers from the conversational component of the British Sign Language Corpus (Fenlon et al., 2014), who contributed a total of 574 pointing signs. A number of prior researchers had suggested that pointing signs differ in their function from pointing gestures (e.g., Barberà & Zwets, 2013; Meier & Lillo-Martin, 2013). Fenlon and colleagues (2014) took a different tack, examining whether pointing signs might differ in their *form* from pointing gestures, by virtue of being more "linguistic" in nature. If so, the authors reasoned, the pointing signs should show a heightened degree of *conventionalization*, *reduction*, and *prosodic integration*, since these three characteristics are considered to be formational hallmarks of linguistic status.

By examining a range of features—such as handshape, hand use, duration, and others—the authors found that pointing signs did indeed differ from pointing gestures on these three dimensions. First, pointing signs appeared to be more conventionalized than pointing gestures. The signers were more consistent in their handshape preference, strongly favoring points with index finger extension; more consistent in using one hand instead of two; and more consistent in using their dominant hand. Second, pointing signs were much more reduced than pointing gestures, especially in terms of duration, lasting roughly a third as long as pointing gestures. Finally, the pointing signs were integrated into utterance-level prosody in a way that pointing gestures were not. Specifically, utterance-final pointing signs were longer in duration than nonfinal pointing signs—a pattern of lengthening widely observed for other types of signs (e.g., Wilbur, 1999). Pointing gestures, in contrast, did not show this pattern.

These findings about form are thus consistent with the proposal that pointing signs are more linguistic than pointing gestures. However, the authors also noted an alternative possibility. Several of the observed differences might be explained instead by another crucial difference between sign and gesture: pointing signs are produced within the same articulatory channel as the rest of the referential content (i.e., the hands), whereas pointing gestures are produced in a different articulatory channel from the rest of the referential content. This same-channel constraint offers an intuitive explanation for the shorter duration of pointing signs, as they have to be wedged into a stream of other signs. But the constraint could also have more subtle effects. For instance, it could add pressure to conserve effort when signing, leading signers to strongly favor one hand; it could also lead to pointing signs becoming more tightly integrated into broader prosodic structures because those structures are produced with the same articulators. In sum, it remains an open question whether the differences observed by Fenlon et al. (2019) are primarily driven by the linguistic status of pointing signs per se, or whether at least some might be driven by a same-channel constraint that exerts certain pressures on pointing signs.

A second study by the same researchers sought to further investigate commonalities and differences in pointing in gesture and sign, this time using controlled elicitation in the lab (Cooperrider et al., 2021). The participants were 12 English speakers and 12 ASL signers. Whereas the corpus study focused on pronoun-like points (to self, addressee, and other entities), the elicitation study focused on points to visible locations and objects. Of particular interest were two issues. A first was whether both pointing gestures and pointing signs would exhibit that pattern observed by Enfield et al. (2007) for Lao speakers, in which *location-focus* points—that is, points carrying message-critical information about "which" or "where"—were bigger in form. To examine this, Cooperrider and colleagues (2021) designed a paradigm to elicit location-focus utterances in response to "which" or "where" questions (e.g., "That chair"), as well as explanatory utterances involving more than "which" or "where" information (e.g., "She walked to the chair in the back"; Figure 2.4). The expected pattern was that points embedded in location-focus utterances would be bigger in form than points embedded in explanatory utterances. Indeed, this pattern was found, but with an important additional wrinkle. The researchers further distinguished two types of points occurring within location-focus utterances: (a) "load-bearing points" in which the point exclusively carried the locative information (e.g., "That chair") and (b) "load-sharing points" in which the point coexpressed the locative information alongside other locative words (e.g., "That chair on the right"). In both gesturers and signers, only the load-bearing points were larger in form; the load-sharing points were no bigger than those embedded in explanatory utterances.

A second issue was how the same-channel constraint described above might affect the integration of pointing signs with other signs (and, conversely, how the *absence* of this constraint might affect the integration of pointing gestures with spoken language). In line with the findings of Fenlon et al. (2019), pointing signs were markedly shorter in duration than pointing gestures. This was likely due to the contrasting ways in which pointing signs and pointing gestures were integrated into the surrounding linguistic materials. Pointing signs were far more likely to slot in between other signs (93%) than they were to overlap with those signs (7%; i.e., by pointing with one hand while signing with the other); pointing gestures showed the opposite pattern, occasionally slotting in between spoken words (7%) but far more often overlapping with them (93%). Both signers and speakers thus make some use of both structural possibilities—slotting in and overlapping—but each group strongly favors one or the other.

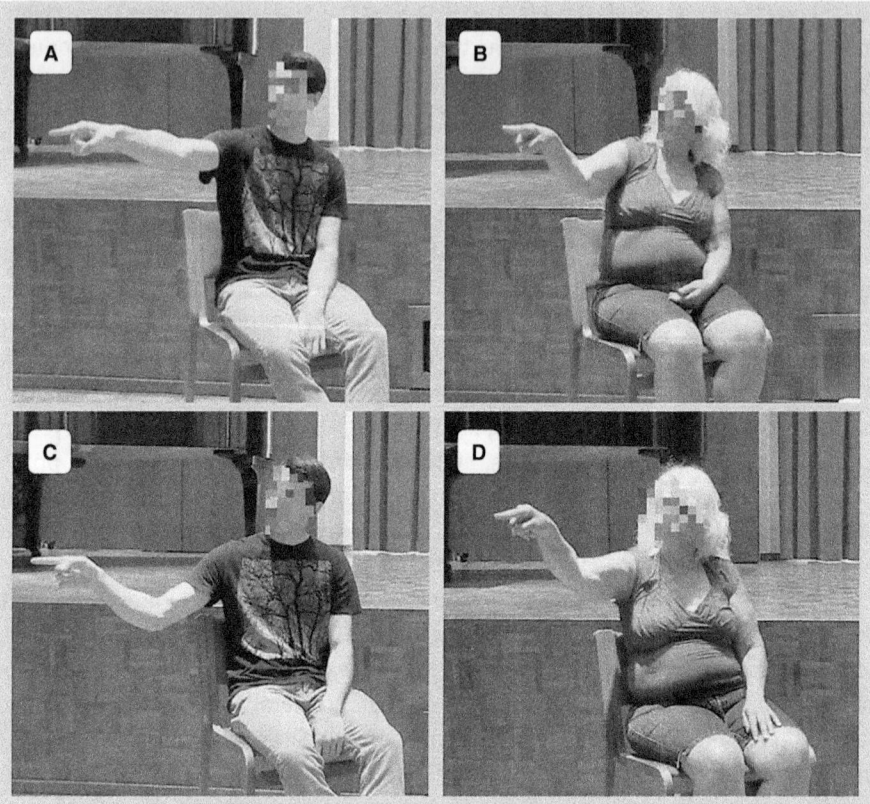

Fig. 2.4: Examples of points to objects and locations produced by an English speaker (A, C) and an American Sign Language signer (B, D). Points were produced as part of a referential communication task (Cooperrider et al., 2021), and were embedded in location-focus utterances (top row) or in explanatory utterances (bottom row).

Taking both studies together, several generalizations emerge. On the one hand, pointing gestures and pointing signs show a number of broad similarities. Both are used in similar ways, such as to point to present persons, nonpresent others, visible locations, and objects. Both are sometimes used along with other lexical material, and other times on their own. Both are responsive to similar functional pressures, such as the pressure to use more effort when the point carries central information. On the other hand, a number of broad differences were evident. Pointing signs are more consistent in form and tend to be more reduced, both in duration and in the bodily effort expended to produce them. This marked reduction may stem from a same-channel constraint that operates in sign but not in gesture. Of course, to corroborate these generalizations, more work is needed with different speaking and signing communities.

2.5 Conclusion

Everyone points—children and adults, signers and speakers, urbanites and rural farmers. By any criterion we might choose—frequency of use, cross-cultural universality, developmental priority, semiotic simplicity—pointing is a basic communicative act. As such, pointing is sometimes treated as a monolith. But, in fact, pointing takes different forms and does different things; it varies from moment to moment and community to community; it has an over-arching function of directing attention, and a host of more fine-grained functions, too. It is integrated into spoken and signed communication in different ways, and this fact is sometimes reflected in its form. But this does not imply that pointing gestures and pointing signs are fundamentally, irreconcilably different. Nor does it imply that they sit on opposite sides of a language/nonlanguage divide. As we have shown, many of the uses of pointing found in gesture—points to real-world people, objects, and places; metonymic points; points to empty space; points that serve interactive functions; and more—are also found in sign. Signers and speakers both point in a way that makes use of common conceptual mappings (e.g., the far-is-up mapping) and common pragmatic principles (e.g., the principle that more effort should be put into a point if it makes a critical contribution to the message).

Though we have sketched in broad strokes the similarities and differences between pointing gestures and pointing signs, it bears emphasis that there is much work left to do; in particular, there is much promise in further systematic, direct comparisons that will sharpen our understanding of these similarities and differences. As we continue to delve into other aspects of pointing—how it is formed, how it combines with gaze, how it is fitted into utterances, how it is deployed in particular interactive sequences—we will no doubt uncover more commonalities, as well as more points of divergence. Such direct, zoomed-in comparisons are not just critical for our understanding of pointing; they are critical for our understanding of human communication more broadly, of how speakers and signers make communicative wholes out of disparate parts.

References

Adone, M. C. D., & Maypilama, E. (2014). Bimodal bilingualism in Arnhem land. *Australian Aboriginal Studies*, *1*(2), 101–106.

Ahlgren, I. (1990). Deictic pronouns in Swedish and Swedish Sign Language. In S. D. Fischer & P. Siple (Eds.), *Theoretical issues in sign language research: Vol. 1. Linguistics* (pp. 167–174). University of Chicago Press.

Andrén, M. (2014). Multimodal constructions in children: Is the headshake part of language? *Gesture*, *14*(2), 141–170. https://doi.org/10.1075/gest.14.2.02and

Bangerter, A. (2004). Using pointing and describing to achieve joint focus of attention in dialogue. *Psychological Science*, *15*(6), 415–419. https://doi.org/10.1111/j.0956-7976.2004.00694.x

Bangerter, A., & Chevalley, E. (2007). Pointing and describing in referential communication: When are pointing gestures used to communicate? In I. van der Sluis, M. Theune, E. Reiter, & E. Krahmer (Eds.), *CTIT proceedings of the workshop on multimodal output generation (MOG)*. Aberdeen, Scotland.

Barberà, G., & Zwets, M. (2013). Pointing and reference in sign language and spoken language: Anchoring vs. identifying. *Sign Language Studies*, *13*(4), 491–515. https://doi.org/10.1353/sls.2013.0016

Bates, E. (1976). *Language and context: The acquisition of pragmatics*. Academic Press.

Bauer, A. (2014). *The use of signing space in a shared sign language of Australia*. De Gruyter Mouton. https://doi.org/10.1515/9781614515470

Bavelas, J., Gerwing, J., Allison, M., & Sutton, C. (2011). Dyadic evidence for grounding with abstract deictic gestures. In G. Stam & M. Ishino (Eds.), *Integrating gesture: The interdisciplinary nature of gesture* (pp. 49–60). John Benjamins. https://doi.org/10.1075/gs.4.05bav

Bavelas, J. B., Chovil, N., Lawrie, D. A., & Wade, A. (1992). Interactive gestures. *Discourse Processes*, *15*(4), 469–489. https://doi.org/10.1080/01638539209544823

Bayley, R., Lucas, C., & Rose, M. (2002). Phonological variation in American Sign Language: The case of 1 handshape. *Language Variation and Change*, *14*(1), 19–53. https://doi.org/10.1017/S0954394502141020

Blythe, J., Mardigan, K. C., Perdjert, M. E., & Stoakes, H. (2016). Pointing out directions in Murrinhpatha. *Open Linguistics*, *2*(1), 132–159. https://doi.org/10.1515/opli-2016-0007

Borg, E. (2002). Pointing at Jack, talking about Jill: Understanding deferred uses of demonstratives and pronouns. *Mind & Language*, *17*(5), 489–512. https://doi.org/10.1111/1468-0017.00209

Bühler, K. (1990). *Theory of language: The representational function of language* (D. F. Goodwin, Trans.). John Benjamins. (Original work published 1934) https://doi.org/10.1075/fos.25

Butcher, C., Mylander, C., & Goldin-Meadow, S. (1991). Displaced communication in a self-styled gesture system: Pointing at the nonpresent. *Cognitive Development*, *6*(3), 315–342. https://doi.org/10.1016/0885-2014(91)90042-C

Clark, E. V., & Estigarribia, B. (2011). Using speech and gesture to introduce new objects to young children. *Gesture*, *11*(1), 1–23. https://doi.org/10.1075/gest.11.1.01cla

Clark, H. H. (2003). Pointing and placing. In S. Kita (Ed.), *Pointing: Where language, culture, and cognition meet* (pp. 243–268). Lawrence Erlbaum.

Clark, H. H. (2016). Depicting as a method of communication. *Psychological Review*, *123*(3), 324–347. https://doi.org/10.1037/rev0000026

Cochet, H., & Vauclair, J. (2010). Features of spontaneous pointing gestures in toddlers. *Gesture*, *10*(1), 86–107. https://doi.org/10.1075/gest.10.1.05coc

Cooperrider, K. (2014). Body-directed gestures: Pointing to the self and beyond. *Journal of Pragmatics*, *71*, 1–16. https://doi.org/10.1016/j.pragma.2014.07.003

Cooperrider, K. (2016). The co-organization of demonstratives and pointing gestures. *Discourse Processes*, *53*(8), 632–656. https://doi.org/10.1080/0163853X.2015.1094280

Cooperrider, K., Fenlon, J., Keane, J., Brentari, D., & Goldin-Meadow, S. (2021). How pointing is integrated into language: Evidence from speakers and signers. *Frontiers in Communication*, *6*(567774). https://doi.org/10.3389/fcomm.2021.567774

Cooperrider, K., & Núñez, R. (2012). Nose-pointing: Notes on a facial gesture of Papua New Guinea. *Gesture*, *12*(2), 103–129. https://doi.org/10.1075/gest.12.2.01coo

Cooperrider, K., Núñez, R., & Sweetser, E. (2014). The conceptualization of time in gesture. In C. Müller, A. Cienki, E. Fricke, S. Ladewig, D. McNeill, & J. Bressem (Eds.), *Body—language—*

communication: An international handbook on multimodality in human interaction (Vol. 2, pp. 1781–1788). De Gruyter Mouton.

Cooperrider, K., Slotta, J., & Núñez, R. (2018). The preference for pointing with the hand is not universal. *Cognitive Science, 42*(4), 1375–1390. https://doi.org/10.1111/cogs.12585

Coppola, M., & Senghas, A. (2010). Deixis in an emerging sign language. In D. Brentari (Ed.), *Sign languages: A Cambridge language survey* (pp. 543–569). Cambridge University Press. https://doi.org/10.1017/CBO9780511712203.025

Coppola, M., & So, W. C. (2006). The seeds of spatial grammar: Spatial modulation and coreference in homesigning and hearing adults. In D. Bamman, T. Magnitskaia, & C. Zaller (Eds.), *BUCLD 30: Proceedings of the 30th Annual Boston University Conference on Language Development* (pp. 119–130). Cascadilla Press.

Cormier, K., Schembri, A., & Woll, B. (2013). Pronouns and pointing in sign languages. *Lingua, 137*, 230–247. https://doi.org/10.1016/j.lingua.2013.09.010

de Vos, C. (2011). Kata Kolok color terms and the emergence of lexical signs in rural signing communities. *The Senses and Society, 6*(1), 68–76. https://doi.org/10.2752/174589311X12893982233795

de Vos, C. (2013). *Sign-spatiality in Kata Kolok: How a village sign language of Bali inscribes its signing space* [Unpublished doctoral dissertation]. Radboud University Nijemgen.

de Vos, C. (2014). The Kata Kolok pointing system: Morphemization and syntactic integration. *Topics in Cognitive Science, 7*(1), 150–168. https://doi.org/10.1111/tops.12124

Diessel, H. (2006). Demonstratives, joint attention, and the emergence of grammar. *Cognitive Linguistics, 17*(4), 463–489. https://doi.org/10.1515/COG.2006.015

Diessel, H. (2012). Bühler's two-field theory of pointing and naming and the deictic origins of grammatical morphemes. In K. Davidse, T. Breban, L. Brems, & T. Mortelmans (Eds.), *New perspectives on grammaticalization: Theoretical understanding and empirical description* (pp. 37–50). John Benjamins. https://doi.org/10.1075/slcs.130.02die

Dimitra, C. (2012). *Does "pointing at" museum exhibits make a point? A study of visitors' performances in three museums for the use of reference as a means of initiating and prompting meaning-making* [Unpublished doctoral dissertation]. University College.

Dingemanse, M. (2018). Redrawing the margins of language: Lessons from research on ideophones. *Glossa: A Journal of General Linguistics, 3*(1), 4. https://doi.org/10.5334/gjgl.444

Eco, U. (1976). *A theory of semiotics*. Indiana University Press.

Enfield, N. J. (2001). 'Lip-pointing': A discussion of form and function with reference to data from Laos. *Gesture, 1*(2), 185–211. https://doi.org/10.1075/gest.1.2.06enf

Enfield, N. J. (2009). *The anatomy of meaning: Speech, gesture, and composite utterances*. Cambridge University Press. https://doi.org/10.1017/CBO9780511576737

Enfield, N. J., Kita, S., & de Ruiter, J. P. (2007). Primary and secondary pragmatic functions of pointing gestures. *Journal of Pragmatics, 39*(10), 1722–1741. https://doi.org/10.1016/j.pragma.2007.03.001

Engberg-Pedersen, E. (1993). *Space in Danish Sign Language: The semantics and morphosyntax of the use of space in a visual language*. SIGNUM-Press.

Evans, N., & Wilkins, D. (2000). In the mind's ear: The semantic extensions of perception verbs in Australian languages. *Language, 76*(3), 546–592. https://doi.org/10.2307/417135

Fenlon, J., Cooperrider, K., Keane, J., Brentari, D., & Goldin-Meadow, S. (2019). Comparing sign language and gesture: Insights from pointing. *Glossa: A Journal of General Linguistics, 4*(1), 2. https://doi.org/10.5334/gjgl.499

Fenlon, J., Schembri, A., Rentelis, R., & Cormier, K. (2013). Variation in handshape and orientation in British Sign Language: The case of the '1' hand configuration. *Language & Communication*, *33*(1), 69–91. https://doi.org/10.1016/j.langcom.2012.09.001

Fenlon, J., Schembri, A., Rentelis, R., Vinson, D., & Cormier, K. (2014). Using conversational data to determine lexical frequency in British Sign Language: The influence of text type. *Lingua*, *143*, 187–202. https://doi.org/10.1016/j.lingua.2014.02.003

Ferrara, L. (2020). Some interactional functions of finger pointing in signed language conversations. *Glossa: A Journal of General Linguistics*, *5*(1), 88. https://doi.org/10.5334/gjgl.993

Ferrara, L., & Hodge, G. (2018). Language as description, indication, and depiction. *Frontiers in Psychology*, *9*, 716. https://doi.org/10.3389/fpsyg.2018.00716

Floyd, S. (2016). Modally hybrid grammar? Celestial pointing for time-of-day reference in Nheengatú. *Language*, *92*(1), 31–64. https://doi.org/10.1353/lan.2016.0013

Goldin-Meadow, S., & Brentari, D. (2017). Gesture, sign, and language: The coming of age of sign language and gesture studies. *Behavioral and Brain Sciences*, *40*, e46. https://doi.org/10.1017/S0140525X15001247

Gonseth, C., Kawakami, F., Ichino, E., & Tomonaga, M. (2017). The higher the farther: Distance-specific referential gestures in chimpanzees (*Pan troglodytes*). *Biology Letters*, *13*(11), 20170398. https://doi.org/10.1098/rsbl.2017.0398

Goodwin, C. (2007). Environmentally coupled gestures. In S. D. Duncan, J. Cassell, & E. T. Levy (Eds.), *Gesture and the dynamic dimensions of language: Essays in honor of David McNeill* (pp. 195–212). John Benjamins. https://doi.org/10.1075/gs.1.18goo

Green, J. (2019). Embodiment and degrees of respect in speech and action. *Gesture*, *18*(2–3), 370–395.

Green, J., & Wilkins, D. P. (2014). With or without speech: Arandic sign language from central Australia. *Australian Journal of Linguistics*, *34*(2), 234–261. https://doi.org/10.1080/07268602.2014.887407

Hassemer, J., & McCleary, L. (2018). The multidimensionality of pointing. *Gesture*, *17*(3), 417–463. https://doi.org/10.1075/gest.17018.has

Haviland, J. B. (1993). Anchoring, iconicity, and orientation in Guugu Yimithirr pointing gestures. *Journal of Linguistic Anthropology*, *3*(1), 3–45. https://doi.org/10.1525/jlin.1993.3.1.3

Haviland, J. B. (2000). Pointing, gesture spaces, and mental maps. In D. McNeill (Ed.), *Language and gesture* (pp. 13–46). Cambridge University Press. https://doi.org/10.1017/CBO9780511620850.003

Haviland, J. B. (2003). How to point in Zinacantán. In S. Kita (Ed.), *Pointing: Where language, culture, and cognition meet* (pp. 139–170). Lawrence Erlbaum.

Healy, C. (2012). Pointing to show agreement. *Semiotica*, *2012*(192), 175–195. https://doi.org/10.1515/sem-2012-0073

Holler, J., & Levinson, S. C. (2019). Multimodal language processing in human communication. *Trends in Cognitive Sciences*, *23*(8), 639–652. https://doi.org/10.1016/j.tics.2019.05.006

Hou, L., & Meier, R. P. (2018). The morphology of first-person object forms of directional verbs in ASL. *Glossa: A Journal of General Linguistics*, *3*(1), 114. https://doi.org/10.5334/gjgl.469

Jarmołowicz-Nowikow, E. (2015). How Poles indicate people and objects, and what they think of certain forms of pointing gestures. *Lingua Posnaniensis*, *56*(1), 85–95. https://doi.org/10.2478/linpo-2014-0005

Johnston, T. (2013a). Towards a comparative semiotics of pointing actions in signed and spoken languages. *Gesture*, *13*(2), 109–142. https://doi.org/10.1075/gest.13.2.01joh

Johnston, T. (2013b). Formational and functional characteristics of pointing signs in a corpus of Auslan (Australian sign language): Are the data sufficient to posit a grammatical class of 'pronouns' in Auslan? *Corpus Linguistics and Linguistic Theory*, *9*(1), 109–159.

Kendon, A. (1980). A description of a deaf-mute sign language from the Enga Province of Papua New Guinea with some comparative discussion. Part III: Aspects of utterance construction. *Semiotica*, *32*(3–4), 245–313. https://doi.org/10.1515/semi.1980.32.3-4.245

Kendon, A. (2004). *Gesture: Visible action as utterance*. Cambridge University Press. https://doi.org/10.1017/CBO9780511807572

Kendon, A. (2010). Pointing and the problem of "gesture": Some reflections. *Rivisti Di Psicolinguistica Applicata*, *10*(3), 19–30. http://www.pitt.edu/~icl/publications/Parlade_Iverson_RIPLA_3_2010.pdf

Kita, S. (2003a). Interplay of gaze, hand, torso orientation, and language in pointing. In S. Kita (Ed.), *Pointing: Where language, culture, and cognition meet* (pp. 307–328). Lawrence Erlbaum. https://doi.org/10.4324/9781410607744-17

Kita, S. (2003b). Pointing: A foundational building block of human communication. In S. Kita (Ed.), *Pointing: Where language, culture, and cognition meet* (pp. 1–8). Lawrence Erlbaum. https://doi.org/10.4324/9781410607744-5

Kita, S., & Essegbey, J. (2001). Pointing left in Ghana: How a taboo on the use of the left hand influences gestural practice. *Gesture*, *1*(1), 73–95. https://doi.org/10.1075/gest.1.1.06kit

Klima, E. S., & Bellugi, U. (1979). *The signs of language*. Harvard University Press.

Koulidobrova, E., & Lillo-Martin, D. (2016). A 'point' of inquiry: The case of the (non-) pronominal IX in ASL. In P. Grosz & P. Patel-Grosz (Eds.), *The impact of pronominal form on interpretation* (pp. 221–250). De Gruyter Mouton. https://doi.org/10.1515/9781614517016-009

Langacker, R. W. (2008). *Cognitive grammar: A basic introduction*. Oxford University Press.

Lee, R. L., & Fraser, A. B. (2001). *The rainbow bridge: Rainbows in art, myth, and science*. Penn State University Press.

Le Guen, O. (2006). *L'organisation et l'apprentissage de l'espace chez les Mayas Yucatèques du Quintana Roo, Mexique* [Organization and learning of space among the Yucatecan Maya of Quintana Roo, Mexico] [Unpublished doctoral dissertation]. Université Paris X-Nanterre.

Le Guen, O. (2011). Modes of pointing to existing spaces and the use of frames of reference. *Gesture*, *11*(3), 271–307. https://doi.org/10.1075/gest.11.3.02leg

Le Guen, O. (2012). An exploration in the domain of time: From Yucatec Maya time gestures to Yucatec Maya Sign Language time signs. In U. Zeshan & C. de Vos (Eds.), *Endangered sign languages in village communities: Anthropological and linguistic insights* (pp. 209–250). De Gruyter Mouton. https://doi.org/10.1515/9781614511496.209

Le Guen, O., & Pool Balam, L. I. (2012). No metaphorical timeline in gesture and cognition among Yucatec Mayas. *Frontiers in Psychology*, *3*, 271. https://doi.org/10.3389/fpsyg.2012.00271

Levelt, W. J. M., Richardson, G., & La Heij, W. (1985). Pointing and voicing in deictic expressions. *Journal of Memory and Language*, *24*(2), 133–164. https://doi.org/10.1016/0749-596X(85)90021-X

Levinson, S. C. (2003). *Space in language and cognition: Explorations in cognitive diversity*. Cambridge University Press. https://doi.org/10.1017/CBO9780511613609

Levinson, S. C. (2006). On the human "interaction engine." In N. J. Enfield & S. C. Levinson (Eds.), *Roots of human sociality: Culture, cognition and interaction* (pp. 39–69). Berg.

Liddell, S. K. (1996). Spatial representations in discourse: Comparing spoken and signed language. *Lingua*, *98*(1–3), 145–167. https://doi.org/10.1016/0024-3841(95)00036-4

Liddell, S. K. (2000). Indicating verbs and pronouns: Pointing away from agreement. In K. Emmorey & H. Lane (Eds.), *The signs of language revisited: An anthology to honor Ursula Bellugi and Edward Klima* (pp. 303–320). Lawrence Erlbaum.

Liddell, S. K. (2003). *Grammar, gesture and meaning in American Sign Language.* Cambridge University Press. https://doi.org/10.1017/CBO9780511615054

Liddell, S. K., & Metzger, M. (1998). Gesture in sign language discourse. *Journal of Pragmatics, 30*(6), 657–697. https://doi.org/10.1016/S0378-2166(98)00061-7

Lillo-Martin, D., & Klima, E. S. (1990). Pointing out differences: ASL pronouns in syntactic theory. In S. D. Fischer & P. Siple (Eds.), *Theoretical issues in sign language research* (Vol. 1, pp. 191–210). University of Chicago Press.

MacLaughlin, D. (1997). *The structure of determiner phrases: Evidence from American Sign Language* [Unpublished doctoral dissertation]. Boston University.

McBurney, S. L. (2002). Pronominal reference in signed and spoken language: Are grammatical categories modality-dependent? In R. P. Meier, K. Cormier, & D. Quinto-Pozos (Eds.), *Modality and structure in signed and spoken languages* (pp. 329–369). Cambridge University Press. https://doi.org/10.1017/CBO9780511486777.017

McBurney, S. L. (2004). *Referential morphology in signed languages* [Unpublished doctoral dissertation]. University of Washington.

McClave, E. C. (2007). Potential cognitive universals: Evidence from head movements in Turkana. In S. D. Duncan, J. Cassell, & E. T. Levy (Eds.), *Gesture and the dynamic dimension of language: Essays in honor of David McNeill* (pp. 91–98). John Benjamins. https://doi.org/10.1075/gs.1.10mcc

McNeill, D. (1992). *Hand and mind: What gestures reveal about thought.* Chicago University Press.

Meier, R. P. (1990). Person deixis in American Sign Language. In S. D. Fischer & P. Siple (Eds.), *Theoretical issues in sign language research* (Vol. 1, pp. 175–190). University of Chicago Press.

Meier, R. P., & Lillo-Martin, D. (2010). Does spatial make it special? On the grammar of pointing signs in American Sign Language. In D. B. Gerdts, J. Moore, & M. Polinsky (Eds.), *Hypothesis A/ hypothesis B: Linguistic explorations in honor of David M. Perlmutter* (pp. 345–360). MIT Press.

Meier, R. P., & Lillo-Martin, D. (2013). The points of language. *Humana.Mente Journal of Philosophical Studies, 24*, 151–176. https://lillomartin.linguistics.uconn.edu/wp-content/uploads/sites/1112/2016/11/Meier_Lillo-Martin_2013_Humana_f.pdf

Mesh, K. (2017). *Points of comparison: What indicating gestures tell us about the origins of signs in San Juan Quiahije Chatino Sign Language* [Unpublished doctoral dissertation]. The University of Texas at Austin.

Mesh, K. (in press). It's as far as the arm can raise: Pointing height marks target distance among the San Juan Quiahije Chatino. *Lingua.*

Mesh, K., Cruz, E., van de Weijer, J., Burenhult, N., & Gullberg, M. (2021). Effects of scale on multimodal deixis: Evidence from Quiahije Chatino. *Frontiers in Psychology, 11*, 3183. https://doi.org/10.3389/fpsyg.2020.584231

Mesh, K., & Hou, L. (2018). Negation in San Juan Quiahije Chatino Sign Language: The integration and adaptation of conventional gestures. *Gesture, 17*(3), 330–374. https://doi.org/10.1075/gest.18017.mes

Mihas, E. (2017). Interactional functions of lip funneling gestures: A case study of Northern Kampa Arawaks of Peru. *Gesture, 16*(3), 432–479. https://doi.org/10.1075/gest.00004.mih

Morgenstern, A. (2014). Shared attention, gaze and pointing gestures in hearing and deaf children. In I. Arnon, M. Casillas, C. Kurumada, & B. Estigarribia (Eds.), *Language in interaction: Studies in honor of Eve V. Clark* (pp. 139–156). John Benjamins. https://doi.org/10.1075/tilar.12.12mor

Müller, C. (2018). Gesture and sign: Cataclysmic break or dynamic relations? *Frontiers in Psychology, 9*, 1651. https://doi.org/10.3389/fpsyg.2018.01651

Nonaka, A. M. (2004). The forgotten endangered languages: Lessons on the importance of remembering from Thailand's Ban Khor Sign Language. *Language in Society, 33*(5), 737–767. https://doi.org/10.1017/S004740450404504X

Nonaka, A. M. (2015). Toponyms in Ban Khor Sign Language. *Learning Communities: International Journal of Learning in Social Contexts* [Special Issue: Indigenous Sign Languages], *16*, 66–91. https://doi.org/10.18793/LCJ2015.16.06

Östling, R., Börstell, C., & Courtaux, S. (2018). Visual iconicity across sign languages: Large-scale automated video analysis of iconic articulators and locations. *Frontiers in Psychology, 9*, 725. https://doi.org/10.3389/fpsyg.2018.00725

Padden, C. A. (1983). *Interaction of morphology and syntax in American Sign Language* [Unpublished doctoral dissertation]. University of California, San Diego.

Peirce, C. S. (1940). *Philosophical writings of Peirce* (J. Buchler, Ed.). Dover.

Perniss, P., & Özyürek, A. (2015). Visible cohesion: A comparison of reference tracking in sign, speech, and co-speech gesture. *Topics in Cognitive Science, 7*(1), 36–60. https://doi.org/10.1111/tops.12122

Petitto, L. A. (1987). On the autonomy of language and gesture: Evidence from the acquisition of personal pronouns in American Sign Language. *Cognition, 27*(1), 1–52. https://doi.org/10.1016/0010-0277(87)90034-5

Pfau, R. (2011). Response: A point well taken: On the typology and diachrony of pointing. In G. Mathur & D. J. Napoli (Eds.), *Deaf around the world: The impact of language* (pp. 144–163). Oxford University Press.

Pfau, R., & Steinbach, M. (2006). Modality-independent and modality-specific aspects of grammaticalization in sign languages. *Linguistics in Potsdam, 24*, 5–98.

Piwek, P., Beun, R.-J., & Cremers, A. (2008). 'Proximal' and 'distal' in language and cognition: Evidence from deictic demonstratives in Dutch. *Journal of Pragmatics, 40*(4), 694–718. https://doi.org/10.1016/j.pragma.2007.05.001

Pyers, J. E. (2006). Indicating the body: Expression of body part terminology in American Sign Language. *Language Sciences, 28*(2–3), 280–303. https://doi.org/10.1016/j.langsci.2005.11.010

Quine, W. V. O. (1960). *Word and object*. MIT Press.

Schegloff, E. A. (1984). On some gestures' relation to talk. In J. M. Atkinson, J. Heritage, & K. Oatley (Eds.), *Structures of social action* (pp. 266–298). Cambridge University Press.

Schembri, A., Cormier, K., & Fenlon, J. (2018). Indicating verbs as typologically unique constructions: Reconsidering verb 'agreement' in sign languages. *Glossa: A Journal of General Linguistics, 3*(1), 89. https://doi.org/10.5334/gjgl.468

Senghas, A., & Coppola, M. (2001). Children creating language: How Nicaraguan sign language acquired a spatial grammar. *Psychological Science, 12*(4), 323–328. https://doi.org/10.1111/1467-9280.00359

Shepard-Kegl, J. A. (1985). *Locative relations in American Sign Language word formation, syntax and discourse* [Unpublished doctoral dissertation]. Massachusetts Institute of Technology.

Sherzer, J. (1973). Verbal and nonverbal deixis: The pointed lip gesture among the San Blas Cuna. *Language in Society, 2*(1), 117–131. https://doi.org/10.1017/S0047404500000087

Sherzer, J. (1983). *Kuna ways of speaking: An ethnographic perspective*. University of Texas Press.

Stukenbrock, A. (2014). Pointing to an 'empty' space: *Deixis am Phantasma* in face-to-face interaction. *Journal of Pragmatics, 74*, 70–93. https://doi.org/10.1016/j.pragma.2014.08.001

Talmy, L. (2018). *The targeting system of language*. MIT Press. https://doi.org/10.7551/mitpress/9780262036979.001.0001

Tomasello, M., Carpenter, M., & Liszkowski, U. (2007). A new look at infant pointing. *Child Development*, *78*(3), 705–722. https://doi.org/10.1111/j.1467-8624.2007.01025.x

Torigoe, T., & Takei, W. (2002). A descriptive analysis of pointing and oral movements in a home sign system. *Sign Language Studies*, *2*(3), 281–295. https://doi.org/10.1353/sls.2002.0013

van Hoek, K. (1992). Conceptual spaces and pronominal reference in American Sign Language. *Nordic Journal of Linguistics*, *15*(2), 183–199. https://doi.org/10.1017/S0332586500002596

Wilbur, R. B. (1999). Stress in ASL: Empirical evidence and linguistic issues. *Language and Speech*, *42*(2–3), 229–250. https://doi.org/10.1177/00238309990420020501

Wilcox, S., & Occhino, C. (2016). Constructing signs: *Place* as a symbolic structure in signed languages. *Cognitive Linguistics*, *27*(3), 371–404. https://doi.org/10.1515/cog-2016-0003

Wilkins, D. (2003). Why pointing with the index finger is not a universal (in sociocultural and semiotic terms). In S. Kita (Ed.), *Pointing: Where language, culture, and cognition meet* (pp. 171–216). Laurence Erlbaum.

Woodward, J. (1989). Basic color term lexicalization across sign languages. *Sign Language Studies*, *63*, 145–152. https://doi.org/10.1353/sls.1989.0021

Yano, U., & Matsuoka, K. (2018). Numerals and timelines of a shared sign language in Japan: Miyakubo Sign Language on Ehime-Oshima Island. *Sign Language Studies*, *18*(4), 640–665. https://doi.org/10.1353/sls.2018.0019

Zeshan, U., & Sagara, K. (Eds.). (2016). *Semantic fields in sign languages: Colour, kinship and quantification*. De Gruyter Mouton. https://doi.org/10.1515/9781501503429

Zimmer, J., & Patschke, C. G. (1990). A class of determiners in ASL. In C. Lucas (Ed.), *Sign language research: Theoretical issues* (pp. 201–210). Gallaudet University Press.

Aliyah Morgenstern
3 Early Pointing Gestures

Not only is pointing abundantly used with a variety of functions across the globe in different cultures by adults, but it is one of the first gestures that enters children's productive repertoire (see Figure 3.1), often preceding first recognizable spoken words (Carpenter et al., 1998). It is considered a developmental cognitive and social milestone, as well as one of the first forms of communication used as humankind developed and thus a basic tool for cooperation (see Figure 3.2; Tomasello, 2008).

Despite being regarded as the simplest, most primary form of communicative action (Wundt, 1912) because of its phylogenetic and ontogenetic role as a precursor to human language, pointing is a fascinating, rich semiotic process that is resourcefully used long after children have mastered the complexities of language.

In most parts of the world, pointing pervades all types of conversations (see Cooperrider & Mesh, Chapter 2, this volume) as an unmatched tool for orienting attention (Peirce, 1897/1932), as is well epitomized in several art forms.[1] As pointed out by Cooperrider (2020),

> Pointing may also be seen as a semiotic primitive, a philosophical puzzle, a communicative workhorse, a protean universal, a social tool, a widespread taboo, a partner of language, a part of language, a fixture of art, a graphical icon, a cognitive prop, a developmental milestone, a diagnostic window, a cross-species litmus test, and an evolutionary stepping-stone. (p. 1)

Pointing can be described as the first communicative gesture or a gesture used to complement speech, a symbolic resource of its own, or incorporated into sign languages in a grammaticalized form and used, for example, as the equivalent of demonstrative or personal pronouns.[2] There have been descriptions of its various functions in child development and ongoing debates about its being separate from (Petitto, 1992) or part of (Haviland, 1998) language, of its being a ritualized extension of natural reaching movements (Vygotsky, 1934/1985), or a highly conventionalized form of expression that needs to be learned (Wittgenstein, 1953/1958).

In this chapter, I do not reduce the abundant literature on this multifaceted process to a few pages (but see Cooperrider, 2020, for a beautiful panorama), nor do I give definite answers to all the ongoing debates. Rather, by adopting a usage-based, functional approach, I focus on the emergence and uses of pointing in child–adult

---
[1] As in the Bayeux tapestry, Leonardo Da Vinci's paintings or Alberto Giacometti's, *l'homme au doigt* [man pointing], 1947 (see Boutet, 2018; Cooperrider, 2020).
[2] But see the debate between Cormier et al., 2013; Fenlon et al., 2019; Johnston, 2013; Meier and Lillo-Martin, 2013; and Pizzuto and Capobianco, 2008.

Fig. 3.1: Ellie pointing at the heart of the flower.

Fig. 3.2: Théo and his father pointing at each other.

interactions and illustrate its semiotic potential through its integration in the multimodal discursive flow of children's *languaging* (Linell, 2009) with adult interlocutors. Our approach is supported by dialogic data and enriched by results from experimental studies. In a usage-based and constructivist approach to language acquisition (Tomasello, 2003), the study of pointing is situated within the more general framework of the child's interactive experience and competence, and takes into account the semantic and pragmatic dimensions of the child's language use, as well as adult input. Pointing is thus viewed in terms of its function in dialogue. Bruner's (1975) classical account is focused on the adult–child social interaction involved in pointing events grounded in meaningful social exchanges. Pointing is analyzed within the framework of joint attentional formats seen as a type of scaffolding that helps infants share information and affects with helpful adults, as observed by Werner and Kaplan (1963), who named them "primordial sharing situations" (p. 8).

The first part of the chapter addresses the status of early pointing in the development of language and communicative skills. My account of language development carefully considers children's social experience and, in particular, adult–child interactions, and highlights the role of adult caretakers. In the second part, I follow children's reception and production of pointing through qualitative detailed analyses of examples extracted from our longitudinal data (the *Paris Corpus*; Morgenstern & Parisse, 2012). Thanks to the ease of producing pointing gestures, they are often displayed before articulated speech. However, pointing gestures are not as simple in terms of pragmatic and symbolic qualities as they might appear. Children need to have developed complex cognitive and social skills to use them appropriately. Just like any other symbolic form, pointing can only be paired with a function when it is analyzed in association with the conversational content, the affordances of the situation, other multimodal cues (e.g., gaze, facial expression, vocal productions, words/signs), and the interlocutor's response.

3.1 The Pointing Gesture in Children's Development of Communicative Skills

Following Piaget (1962) and Vygotsky (1934/1985), functional scientists agree that language is usage-based and emerges from interaction and from nonverbal cognitive and social development in infancy. The subsequent research has striven to investigate how early perceptual–cognitive capacities pave the way for language and communication. Even though children have innate biological and cognitive capacities, they need to learn conventions and formal patterns from communication and language in their environment. Social interaction in infancy is dependent on the interplay between infants' affects, their neural learning processes, their perceptual and motor skills, and the structure of their social and affective environment (Cole & Cole, 1993). Social information helps infants decipher the meaning of others' language acts (Tomasello, 1999). Adults' drive to attend to the same objects facilitates infants' entrance into the language community. Infants gradually become fully developed interacting speakers, building on such cognitive and social skills as the ability to follow another's gaze, to draw and maintain their attention, to imitate, to read others' intentions, to make analogies, to categorize, and to symbolize.

A wealth of studies (Bruner, 1983; Clark, 2003; Ochs & Schieffelin, 1989; Trevarthen, 1977; among others) have shown that it is the interaction and complementarity between basic perceptual, cognitive, affective processes and a favorable environment involving caretakers or older siblings constantly adjusting their behavior to the infants' that seem to trigger and guide the emergence of shared attention and intentionality, which will then lead the child into symbolic communication epitomized in the pointing gesture.

3.1.1 The Grounding of Pointing in Shared Attention

Infants' capacity for attention sharing plays a critical role in their communication with older children and adults (Baldwin, 1993; Brazelton et al., 1974; Bruner, 1983; Tomasello, 1999). The notion of shared or joint attention[3] is used for a whole range of skills that include gaze following, request gestures and postures, and especially pointing. By 7 to 9 months, even though there are individual differences in their rhythm of development, most infants follow adults' gaze and pointing gestures, and learn to discriminate what is important for them in their environment based on the attention shown and the feedback given by more expert caregivers.

The onset of joint attentional skills is often viewed as occurring early in infancy and marked by deictic gaze. Infants' ability to follow the other's gaze develops gradually (Butterworth, 1995). At 6 months, infants follow the adult's gaze with some variability in their attention span. At 12 months, in an experimental design, they reliably followed gaze and deictic gestures, and identified a target. Some studies have found that children are sensitive to the dynamic motion of the pupils (Golinkoff & Hirsh-Pasek, 2006) and the pointing index finger (Rohlfing et al., 2004). Of course, pointing gestures are rare in comparison with gaze shifting, but they are more salient for infants because of the hand and arm movement they involve. They also imply more effort, and children may assume the target is even more interesting when pointing is used. The combination of gaze and pointing seems particularly effective in creating joint attention, especially when performed by an experimenter rather than the caregiver (Amano et al., 2004). Multimodality may thus compensate for the fact that an interlocutor is unfamiliar.

Multimodal cues produced by adults (gazing, pointing, touching, manipulating) have been found to facilitate word learning (Booth et al., 2008). By providing redun-

---

3 Some authors have different definitions of these two notions, but I use them interchangeably.

dant sensory information, pointing gestures can influence infants' selective attention. Symbolic gestures, especially pointing (Iverson et al., 1999), have been shown to facilitate children's comprehension by reinforcing the vocal information.

While hearing adults communicate with infants using speech, they also employ other semiotic resources, including communicative actions, gestures—such as pointing—gaze, and facial expressions. Those resources permeate children's engagements with their caregivers. Infants grow up in a social world infused with social motivation, in which daily mundane activities resonate with the accompanying forms of expression that shape children's entrance into language.

3.1.2 Extracting Meaning

Scholars have puzzled for centuries over how children construct the referential process and meaning, and have recognized the importance of children's pointing in this process. Saint Augustine stressed its crucial role in his account of his own acquisition of language (as quoted by Wittgenstein, 1953/1958, p. 2). He described how, when adults named and pointed at an object, he could grasp what the thing was called. Wittgenstein (1953/1958), when discussing this process, questioned whether language can really be captured so straightforwardly; he gives the example of shapes and colors, and how it would be difficult to learn them just by pointing at an object. This problem is echoed in Quine's (1960) *gavagai* example. If we are in a foreign land with a speaker of another language, and that person points at a rabbit running in front of both of us and says "gavagai," what meaning do we attribute to this vocal production? Does it refer to an object, an action, a quality, all of those? Is it even a word or a string of words? Does it mean "rabbit," "furry animal," the rabbit's "long ears," "running," "tonight's dinner," "let's catch tonight's dinner"? Is the meaning to be attributed to the combined production of the gesture, gaze, and vocal discourse? The pointing gesture does not in itself identify a referent; it orients attention to the object or event of interest. The reconstruction must be done by the interlocutor, who then connects the gesture to the vocal flow and the context according to their experience. Pointing is therefore not transparent, and children can only identify the referent in interaction by using context, other multimodal cues, shared knowledge with the person pointing, and experience (Morgenstern et al., 2016).

Caregivers all around the world point for their infants. Communicative pointing becomes the basis for referential behavior and reciprocity established in common activities between children and their parents (Bruner, 1975). As explained by Butterworth (2003),

> Pointing serves not only to individuate the object, but also to authorize the link between the object and speech from the baby's perspective. Pointing allows visual objects to take on auditory qualities, and this is the royal road (but not the only route) to language. (p. 29)

Children are described as able to extract meaning from pointing gestures at a young age (Thompson & Massaro, 1986). Recent studies showed that parents accompany their pointing with distinct prosody, and use distinct hand shapes to express different social intentions (Esteve-Gibert et al., 2016, 2017). These studies make clear how infants retrieve the social intentions of pointing from spatial information, social activity, and the form of the act (prosody and hand shape). They illustrate how infants understand pointing as an intentional communicative–referential act with distinct illocutionary forces. Children rely on pointing more than words when the two are in conflict (see Clark & Kelly, Chapter 6, this volume). Liszkowski (2018) argued there is a *prelinguistic* basis to language that is driven by social interactional experiences in the first year of life. This basis is apparent in the use of canonical pointing gestures modelled by adults and understood and taken up by infants.

3.1.3 Role of the Input

The extension of the arm, hand, and index finger toward an object is so widespread in different cultures that researchers sometimes forget its conventional nature. In most data sets scholars have analyzed around the world, finger pointing predominates. However, people can point with chin or lips (Sherzer, 1973), or with a different finger or fingers, or with distinct handshapes (Poyatos, 1983). Children take up the most widely spread pointing gestures around them, which underscores the role of the surrounding culture and input.

The comparison between the use of pointing in the input of signing families and families using vocal languages also illustrates the role of the input. For the child who is surrounded by sign language, pointing gestures are progressively incorporated into their formal linguistic system and used for personal reference, among other functions. According to Schick (2011),

> for the child who produces spoken English, the point is considered a gesture. But for the child learning [American Sign Language] because points are considered linguistic in the adult system, it is tempting to consider the child's points as linguistic. (p. 221)

How are observers to decide whether the nature of pointing is linguistic or nonlinguistic? Petitto (1986) found that the deaf signing child whom she studied longitudinally started pointing at 10 months. Up to 12 months, the child pointed freely at persons and objects. Between 12 and 18 months, points at individuals disappeared. Petitto interpreted this disappearance as indicating a discontinuity between nonlinguistic pointing and linguistic pronouns. Another child studied by Petitto even made reversal errors, pointing toward her interlocutor to refer to herself (similarly to speaking children who use "you" instead of "I" to designate themselves). By 27 months, all the deictic pronouns were used to refer to the relevant referent. Petitto's hypothesis is that the child interpreted the pronoun "you" as a lexical sign equivalent to the child's own name (see the "name hypothesis" in Clark, 1978). The reversal would therefore reveal that the child treated pointing as having linguistic properties and did not take advantage of the transparency of the form–referent relation (which would lead the child to point toward the interlocutor to refer to the interlocutor and not to herself; but for arguments on pronominal reversals, see Caët & Morgenstern, 2015; Morgenstern et al., 2016).

While discontinuity between pointing gestures and points used as personal pronouns has been found in children exposed to American Sign Language, the same phenomenon has not been observed in children exposed to Italian Sign Language (Pizzuto & Capobianco, 2008), Greek Sign Language (Hatzopoulou, 2008), or *Langue des Signes Française* [French Sign Language] (Morgenstern et al., 2016). There was no clear interruption of pointing toward persons and no pronoun reversal. For some scholars, pointing signs in sign language users do not look different on the surface from pointing in nonsigners (Kendon, 2004; Kita, 2003), but variations have been shown by Fenlon et al. (2019). In both cases, points belong to the deictic system; they index locations of objects, persons, and events in the deictic space.

Some studies have focused on specific features of pointing in deaf adults and children and on their ability to use different forms and types of pointing for different functions, such as combinatorial dimensions of finger, wrist, and arm configuration; movement; intensity; and speed (see Hoiting & Slobin, 2007). According to Hoiting (2009), not only do deaf children use an impressive number of pointing gestures from very early on, but the functions of these points are "integrated into the process of conventionalization of gesture and control of the signing space" (p. 84). Her observations and analyses support a very clear impact of child-directed language on children's use of pointing, but also show that the distinction between gestures and signs are not clear-cut. Speakers also use pointing gestures toward objects, persons, or activities, but signers' points seem to be more rigidly conventionalized and thus appear to be "more word-like" (Cooperrider, 2020; Fenlon et al., 2019). These debates indicate that detailed analyses of the different types of pointing used both by hearing and deaf children and their functions in context are still needed to capture whether there are continuities or discontinuities between pointing gestures and signs.

Far from Saint Augustine's opinion (354–430/1996), which sees gestures as "the natural language of all peoples," for Wittgenstein (1953/1958), children's reactions to pointing have to be learned along with words or signs. Several studies have found synchronic correlations between the amount of adult pointing and infant pointing at 14 months (Rowe & Goldin-Meadow, 2009), at 12 months (Liszkowski & Tomasello, 2011), and in a cross-culturally diverse sample of infants between 10 and 14 months (Liszkowski et al., 2012). A subsequent study (Salomo & Liszkowski, 2013) showed that age-matched 8- to 15-month-old infants from three cultural groups varied in the amount of pointing as a function of caregivers' amount of attention directing gestures.

Adults have been shown to interpret children's pointing and produce feedback for them (Morgenstern, 2014). This helps to render children's behaviors intentionally communicative. Adult feedback takes the form of spoken reformulations of children's multimodal productions (e.g., pointing in context + gaze + vocalizations) that are offered in dialogue and can be, in time, understood and productively taken up by the children themselves. When children are treated as interactive participants, and their pointing gestures are endowed with meaning, recognized, and taken up as part of language and discourse, they become aware of their own semiotic power and use it productively.

3.1.4 Early Pointing and Language Development

In most university course books published in the second half of the 20th century, children's language development was described as starting with children's first vocalizations without much attention to early gestures. The maturation of children's phonic capacities was analyzed but seldom their body movements. However, thanks to pioneering scholars such as Bates et al. (1975) and Bruner (1975, 1983), more and more studies have demonstrated how pointing gestures, combined with other cues in context, do play an important role in the language acquisition process (see Clark & Kelly, Chapter 6, this volume). Pointing gestures are grounded in joint attention, they trigger interaction, and they may also facilitate children's entry into word combination and syntax (Iverson & Goldin-Meadow, 2005; Kelly, 2011; see also Capirci et al., Chapter 5, this volume).

The pioneers of the study of child development and language in the 19th century had great intuitions about the importance of gestures and their relation to language. Romanes (1888/1891) and Sully (1896) had already considered pointing as a gestural precursor of grammatical tools used later on in speech. In his notes on his son's development, Darwin (1877) stressed the importance of observing the transition from uncontrolled body movements to intentional gestures. W. Stern (1914) viewed pointing, in particular, as a precursor of intentional marking.[4] For Werner and Kaplan (1963), pointing represented children's ability to discriminate between external objects and their own person. Wundt (1973) explained that "pointing appears to be the very earliest [gesture] among human beings, and whose spontaneous origin may be observed in infants" (p. 127).

Infants extend the isolated index finger even before birth, as ultrasound pictures attest. Various configurations of infants' hands with a pointed index finger have been observed as early as 3 months old (Fogel & Hannan, 1985). Around 8 months of age, infants develop the fine motor skills to manipulate objects with the extended index finger and the pincer grip, which could be one key element of pointing (Butterworth & Morissette, 1996). Intentional pointing seems to become productive at around 10 to 11 months, not long before children produce their first spoken words. In native signers

---

4 See Morgenstern (2009) for a detailed account of diary studies.

(i.e., children—deaf or hearing—who grow up using a sign language as their first language), pointing has been observed as emerging in parallel with other signs. Pointing is described as giving children the extraordinary power of localizing for themselves and their interlocutors an object of attention, without having to touch it or be very close to it. Pointing thus opens up vast possibilities for intersubjective interactions (Cabrejo-Parra, 1992). The use of their extended arm and pointed index finger at a distance from the object of their attention is a deictic act that is the foundation for verbal or signed designation of the object. It can also be seen as a transition toward *displacement*, which is one of the most important aspects of language. Children first use language about objects and events that they perceive in the here and now. But, over time, they refer to objects and events that they have perceived, manipulated, ingested, liked, disliked, in the past. They have memorized the scenarios with their strings of events and the temporal unfolding of language. Action and language are organized in scripts and performed interactively in daily situations. If, as proposed by Boas (1911/1965), Gumperz and Levinson (1991), Sapir (1927), and Whorf (1956), language shapes experience, language is also the vehicle for displaced reference, as it can create worlds of its own out of our remembrance of things past, our projects or dreams of things to come, and the figments of our imagination. Those worlds are inhabited and shared with others thanks to the linguistic forms people perform with all the semiotic resources at their disposal. Through the mediation of pointing, a designated object takes on a very special status, as it is distinguished and detached from the rest of its environment (Bruner, 1983). This process can be viewed as the foundation of the ability to refer to absent entities, inner thoughts, and past, future, or fictive events. Children thus accomplish their first symbolic operation in a "meeting of minds" (Tomasello, 1999) with their interlocutor.

Monitoring and checking are basic ingredients of communicative acts. Before they monitor, check, and repair their speech (Clark, 1982), children learn to monitor and check adults' attention. Pointing enables children to organize joint gaze and triangulation, which is a necessary step toward the recognition of psychic otherness (theory of mind), which may be a human characteristic.

Indeed, according to Butterworth (2003), pointing is specific to human beings. In most studies, it is considered a uniquely human mode of joint-attentional behavior (Povinelli et al., 2003; Tomasello, 2006). But, as summarized by Cooperrider (2020), this claim has been challenged. Field observations of bonobos in Zaire describes them as pointing (Veà & Sabater-Pi, 1998). Other very rare accounts have been made of chimpanzees pointing in the context of reaching for distant desired objects (Hobaiter et al., 2014). When given sufficient scaffolding in interaction, primates have been shown to point. Indeed, different groups of chimpanzees (in the wild vs. in captivity) sampled from the same gene pool differ in whether they point. This finding indicates that pointing can emerge in our nearest living relatives when the environment provides a function for it (Leavens et al., 2005). According to Tomasello (2008), what is distinctive in our species is a cooperative mode, which has led to declarative pointing in order to share an object of attention (as opposed to pointing to obtain the object, i.e., imperative pointing; see Section 3.1.5). Adult pointing and its uptake by children could thus be powerful evidence showing that people live in a shared social world permeated with communicative potential (but see Baron-Cohen, 1989, for pointing impairment in autistic children). Interestingly enough, at around age 12 to 14 months, children start pointing to places where there used to be an object, person, or event of interest that is no longer present in the context (Liszkowski et al., 2009). This finding indicates that children understand that pointing is a communicative tool outside the presence of a target. Through their bodies (arm, hand, and finger intentionally aligned toward a target), infants create a link between the immediate world of sensory experience and the world of discourse.

3.1.5 Origin and Functions of Pointing

For some authors, pointing is assumed to develop out of prehension (Wundt, 1912). According to this hypothesis, unsuccessful grasping movements are interpreted by the adult as a gesture of request addressed to others (Vygotsky 1934/1985). Alternatively, pointing may emerge from index finger extension used to touch, press, or feel objects and to explore the surrounding world. Before they point in communicative situations, infants extend their index fingers (Masataka, 2003) as they explore objects with their fingertips. In both cases, the extended finger and arm establish a link between the child and the object. These two scenarios result in two possible interpretations of children's uses of pointing (Marcos, 1998). In line with Vygotsky (1934/1985), the use of pointing emerges from social interaction between adults and infants. Children's gestures toward an object that is out of reach are interpreted by adults as expressing the child's desire to take the object. According to another explanation associated with Werner and Kaplan (1963), children first point for themselves to isolate an object from its environment, which is the foundation of a referential act; they then use the point interactively (see also Bates et al., 1975; Carpendale & Carpendale, 2010). Liszkowski et al. (2008) demonstrated that 12-month-old children can tailor their pointing toward a recipient and even increase their pointing behavior if the recipient does not react. Others consider that pointing is learned through imitation of adult interlocutors who use it abundantly to draw the child's attention (Kaye, 1982).

When infants' pointing is interpreted as intentional, it is interactively endowed with a function. A behavior is considered intentional if it is directed toward an interlocutor. Pointing gestures are often accompanied by visual-orienting gaze alternation between the interlocutor and the object or event. However, gaze alternation is not required. The interlocutor's general attention might already be engaged in a shared activity with the same visual perspective (as in book-reading or joint playful activities). Gaze alternation seems to be used more expertly by deaf signing children, who do not add vocalizations to pointing to attract a deaf parent's attention. When pointing does not succeed in attracting the other's attention, children are often found to repeat the gesture. Their persistence is interpreted as marking intentionality. In order to establish whether pointing is intentional and what its function in dialogue might be, authors thus must take into account the accompanying cues, such as vocalizations, gaze, posture, facial expressions, the context, the interlocutor's reaction, and the child's subsequent behavior (Morgenstern, 2014).

On the basis of these features, studies using *speech act theory* (Bates, 1976; Bates et al., 1979) classically distinguish between (a) *protoimperative* pointing, where children point to a desirable object or place that the adult can help them to obtain or to reach (and which may be replaced by reaching or grasping gestures); and (b) *protoassertive* (also called *protodeclarative*) pointing, where children point in order to share attention to some interesting or surprising object or event.

In Figure 3.3, Théophile is making a protodeclarative pointing gesture with gaze on his grandmother's hands, as she is peeling apples for a pie. He simultaneously produces a very brief vocalization with falling intonation ("uh").

In Figure 3.4, Madeleine requests that her mother go and open the drawer of a closet that is quite high. She is in her mother's arms and uses gesture, gaze, posture, and vocalization to make her request in several stages. In Figure 3.4a, she points and gazes at the location of the drawer. Her mother's reaction is not immediate, and,

Fig. 3.3: Théophile, 11 months, protodeclarative pointing. Pointing + gaze on activity + vocal production "uh."

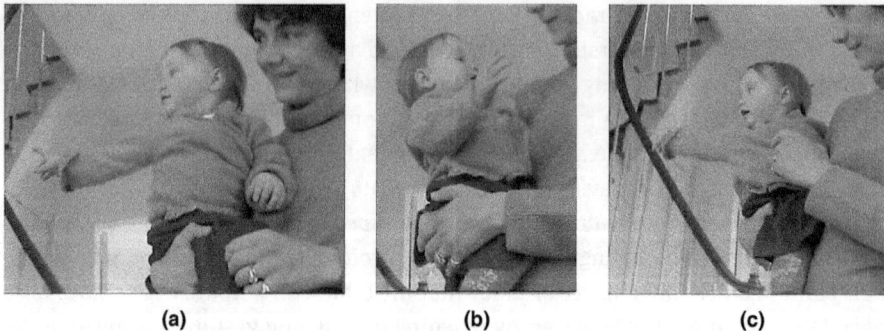

Fig. 3.4: Madeleine, 11 months. **Note.** (a) protoimperative pointing + [la] + gaze on target location; (b) turning to mother + gaze; (c) protodeclarative pointing + [la] + gaze on location.

as seen in Figure 3.4b, Madeleine then turns to her mother and makes a gesture to urge her to move. In Figure 3.4c, Madeleine turns back toward the drawer and points at it again.

A third category, called *informative pointing* has been documented experimentally. Babies as young as 12 months old were found to point to inform another person of the location of an object they were looking for (Liszkowski et al., 2006). This evidence suggested that infant pointing depends on human skills and motivations for cooperation and shared intentionality (e.g., joint intentions and attention with others), which both serve as a platform for prelinguistic communication. Southgate et al. (2007) proposed a fourth, alternative account. In this account, infant pointing is neither declarative, imperative, nor informative, but interrogative; rather than being motivated by the drive to share or help, pointing is assumed to serve a cultural learning mechanism by which infants can obtain information from adults.

Supporting a distinction between functions of pointing, Leroy et al. (2009) showed that the vocalizations associated with imperative and declarative pointing display different prosodic patterns. In a similar vein, Grünloh and Liszkowski (2015) established that infants' imperative points differ in prosody and hand shape from infants' declarative points in experimental studies. The child's gaze to the adult or the target object has also been considered a cue to distinguish requests (or protoimperative pointing) from comments (or protodeclarative pointing): "It seems unquestionable that gaze direction is an essential, defining component in the production and comprehension of different types of pointing" (Pizzuto & Capobianco, 2008, p. 8). However, Povinelli and O'Neill (2000) questioned the determination of the function and meaning of pointing gestures used by children. They noted that the function of pointing depends highly on the context in which it is performed and may not be inherent to the actual formal components of the pointing gesture itself. But the functional distinction is also supported by differences between human children and primates, as well as primates in captivity and primates in the wild. When captive primates do point, the gesture has a request function for daily food provisions. There are environmental differences between primates in captivity and primates in the wild because of the restraining pressure of captivity and of the interaction with humans (Leavens et al., 2005). The functional differences between declarative and imperative pointing are also supported by the literature on children with autism; for instance, Baron-Cohen (1989) noted that children with autism produced imperative pointing but not declarative pointing.

Declarative pointing is not only more cognitively complex than imperative pointing, but is also more linguistic, in the sense that it is comparable to exophoric uses like demonstrative determiners or pronouns. Exophora serves a language independent function. Pointing thus contributes to the acquisition of speech by highlighting and identifying entities in the outside world (see Rowe et al., Chapter 4, this volume). The pointing gesture can pinpoint the referent in conjunction with prior discourse or nonlinguistic factors such as context or salience of the referent. First uses of declarative pointing gestures require the spatiotemporal presence of the object, but children progressively acquire the capacity to use pointing when not supported by the discursive and extralinguistic context. Declarative pointing is therefore a fundamental act in language development because it is a means to integrate reference into the child's communication system.

Thus, children have different motives underlying their pointing gestures, and those gestures can be analyzed as having different functions. But mostly, their pointing involves an understanding of their addressees' behaviors and of their intentions based on the ongoing context and interactions.

3.1.6 Early Pointing and Speech

As demonstrated by Iverson and Goldin-Meadow (2005), pointing precedes and predicts speech: the words that are going to enter a child's vocabulary can be anticipated by taking into account what objects they point to.

Not only is pointing considered a key element in the communicative system of children, but developmental continuity between pointing and early linguistic productions such as demonstratives was being discussed as early as the 18th century by Condillac (1756/1997). For Clark (1978), the early vocal demonstratives used by children follow pointing gestures as children shift rather fluidly from prelinguistic to linguistic communication in a sequence of stages.

Pointing is argued to also facilitate the transition from gestures to nondeictic words. Adults often respond to children's pointing gestures by labeling the entity at stake, which may in turn trigger children's own labeling of the designated entity (Goldin-Meadow et al., 2007; Ninio & Bruner, 1978). Thus, in the development of spoken language in hearing children, pointing facilitates access to verbal naming and may predict lexical development (Bates et al., 1979; for a review, see Rowe et al., Chapter 4, this volume).

First pointing gestures are thus generally observed before children's first decipherable words; a few months later, they are associated with lexical elements and later on with longer and more complex verbalizations. "Assuming that gestures and speech are functioning as a unit" (Butcher & Goldin-Meadow, 2000, p. 86), pointing gestures may facilitate access to combinations and early syntax (Bates et al., 1977). For Goldin-Meadow and Butcher (2003), pointing has a crucial role in the transition from one- to two-word speech: Gesture–word combinations help trigger the onset of two-word speech. They facilitate children's entry into syntax as cross-modal gesture–word combinations precede and announce utterances made of two or more vocal elements (Butcher & Goldin-Meadow, 2000; Capirci et al., 1996; Goldin-Meadow & Butcher, 2003; Volterra et al., 2005). Using a gesture combined with a word might be less demanding than conveying the same meaning in the verbal modality and puts less strain on memory. Pointing gestures are physically easy to produce once motor control over the hand is fine enough, easy to remember (the cognitive load is therefore lighter), and easy to generate on the spot.

When children produce what in the literature is called a *holophrase* (one-word utterance; De Laguna, 1927), they are in fact often combining a word with gestures, gaze, or facial expressions. When a word is combined with pointing, the word could be a deictic or a localizer. French children abundantly use pointing + [sa] (interpreted as "that") or pointing + [la] (interpreted as "there"; see Mathiot et al., 2009). The word could be a label for the object that is pointed at, such as pointing toward a doll + [bebe] (baby). The age when children first point to an entity while offering a spoken label for it (pointing at a dog and saying "dog") predicts the age at which they will produce noun + determiner combinations in speech ("the dog"; see Cartmill et al., 2014; see also Cooperrider, 2020).

The word used can also designate an absent entity, such as pointing toward the mother's necklace + [mama] (Guidetti, 2003; Morford & Goldin-Meadow, 1992). This last category could serve as a transition toward two-word utterances combining two distinct semantic elements (Capirci et al., 1996; Goldin-Meadow & Butcher, 2003; Iverson & Goldin-Meadow, 2005; Özçalışkan & Goldin-Meadow, 2005; Volterra et al., 2005).

Pointing is thus part of the set of gestures that are considered to be "the cutting edge of early language development" (Özçalışkan & Goldin-Meadow, 2005, p. B101) as a result of gesture–speech combinations that precede by several months multiword constructions performed solely in the vocal modality. A child's ability to convey utterance-like meaning across modalities, and the types of gesture–speech combinations that children produce, changes over time. Those combinations predict the production of multiword combinations.

Pointing gestures therefore play a crucial role in children's cognitive, social, and linguistic development: they allow children to segment their environment, extract an element of the world that surrounds them, and direct the adults' attention and speech to it. Inserted in a protosyntactic structure formed of two elements combining gesture and word, they mark children's entry into syntax through multimodal constructions.

3.2 Pointing Gestures in Longitudinal Interactive Data

This section illustrates the use of pointing gestures in real-world adult–child interactive data. Before presenting detailed analyses of extracts of early pointing gestures produced in context, I present my theoretical approach and method.

3.2.1 Theoretical Approach

The theoretical framework used here combines language socialization, cognitive grammar, and interactive and multimodal approaches to languaging. I borrow the term *languaging* to refer to multimodal language use—"linguistic actions and activities in actual communication and thinking" (Linell, 2009, p. 274)—expanding the term to include speaking, signing, and gesturing. I consider how children's socialization to a variety of modes of expression in their daily experiencing (Ochs, 2012) shapes their language development. The framework of *cognitive grammar* provides a means of taking into account all semiotic resources as a consequence of the usage-based (Langacker, 1988) nature of the theory. The theory allows for linguistic signs (in the Saussurian sense, 1916/1995) to be multimodal to varying degrees, based on the extent of schematization and entrenchment, but including an interactive and multimodal component grounded in everyday experience. Thus far, humans cannot yet be imitated in their skill to coordinate the semiotic resources at their disposal, varying the use of "the scope of relevant behaviors" as needed (Cienki, 2012, p. 155), adjusting to the context of interaction, the activity, the age and identity of the interlocutor, the time of day, and so on. Each language provides a certain set of options for grammatically encoding characteristics of objects and events. Slobin (1987) suggested that children are "guided in how they choose to talk about experience by the most available grammatical means provided by their native language" (p. 443) as they are *thinking for speaking*. I apply this approach to *thinking for multimodal languaging*.

Human beings mobilize their representational skills and combine semiotic modalities in order to coconstruct meaning, to refer to present and absent entities and events, and to express intentions, desires, and feelings. As shown by Vygotsky (1934/1985), interaction is a crucial locus for children to develop such cognitive and linguistic skills, which are socially coconstructed between collaborating partners within a cultural context. The scaffolding role of adults (Wood et al., 1976) is paramount in the development of children's interactional competencies. Scaffolding involves cooperation between adults and children in order to facilitate the children's participation in interactional practices and help them learn to use available semiotic resources so as to coconstruct meaning within their cultural and linguistic community.

Children's first productions are permeated with echoes of the constructions heard in the adult input. To actually learn linguistic constructions (Tomasello, 2003), be they sound patterns, gestures, words, or multimodal constructions, children must repeat and manipulate the forms, play with them—with others and on their own—to test a wide range of sounds and prosodic patterns, gestural configurations, and movements. Children progressively internalize the adult's role and appropriate the linguistic tools, social codes, and behaviors used in their community in dialogue.

3.2.2 Data and Method

Thanks to combinations of experimental and ecological studies, video recordings, a variety of specialized software, international databases, theoretical approaches that include multimodality and multiple levels of analyses, and rich collaborations among experts of several scientific fields related to language development, researchers now have the tools to create new methods of studying the blossoming of gesture in everyday interactive language practices.

In order to capture language development with a true usage-based perspective (Tomasello, 2003), I focus on children's engagement in spontaneous interactional activities through situated practices. Video-recording tools have transformed the detailed analysis of interaction (Mondada, 2019). These tools have shaped new avenues of research on language in interaction, as it is deployed in multiple ecologies, both in time (the moment-to-moment unfurling of an interaction) and over time (multiple recordings over several years of the same children in their family environment). Child language research is one of the first fields in which spontaneous interaction data was systematically collected, initially through diary studies (Ingram, 1989; Morgenstern, 2009), and later by audio and video recordings shared worldwide thanks to the CHILDES project (MacWhinney, 2000). This data-centered method has allowed many researchers to confirm that, in the course of their development, children make their way through successive transitory multimodal systems with their own internal coherence (Cohen, 1924). This phenomenon can be observed at all levels of linguistic analysis. Children's productions are like evanescent sketches of adult language and can only be transcribed and analyzed in their interactional context by taking into account shared knowledge, actions, manual gestures, facial expressions, body posture, head movements, and all types of vocal productions, along with the recognizable words used by children (Morgenstern & Parisse, 2007; Parisse & Morgenstern, 2010). Research in language acquisition has developed tools, methods, and theoretical approaches to analyze children's situated multimodal productions, as they provide evidence for links between motor and psychological development, cognition, affectivity, and language.

The excerpts analyzed in this section are drawn from the *Forrester Corpus* (Forrester, 2008) and the *Paris Corpus* (Morgenstern & Parisse, 2012). The children have middle-class, college-educated parents, and were filmed at home about once a month for an hour in daily life situations (playing, taking a bath, having dinner). The transcriptions were done in CHAT format, thus enabling the use of CLAN software tools for analyzing and searching the data (mean length of utterance, word frequency, number of word types and word tokens, morphological categorization, word and expression search). The transcriptions were aligned with the video data and can be analyzed with a variety of computerized tools. For the purpose of this chapter, I use a more reader-friendly format, with the original French production, its English translation between brackets, and nonverbal information in italics.

3.2.3 Parents' Input and Pointing

There are multiple illustrations of the role of parental input in our data. Kaye (1982) suggested that in order to understand intentions, infants must themselves be treated by adults as intentional beings. Just as described by Haviland (1998) in the case of Zinacantec infants, adults in the data sets analyzed in this chapter belong to a culture in which they endow their children's behaviors with significance and celebrate their actions by reacting with interpretations. They decipher their children's every move and action as having some meaning or some goal and provide various types of feedback to this effect. They give meaning to the child's every gaze, gesture, facial expression, and vocal production, projecting some kind of agency onto the infant. This begins very early on and creates the mental context for the emergence of the infant's intentional action. In the first months of life, parent–infant synchrony has a formative role in brain maturation. It was found to be predictive of children's self-regulation, symbolic play, and more general cognitive skills (Feldman & Eidelman, 2004). Indeed, infants engage in *protoconversations* from as young as 2 months old (Trevarthen, 1974), which involve rhythmic attunement of adult and infant vocalizations. However, the caregiver's role is not symmetrical, as they produce amplified enhanced versions of their child's sounds (Papoušek, 1989). Those exchanges are accompanied with smiles, mutual gaze, gestures that D. Stern (1985) has called "supportive emotional colored attunements" (p. 142) and are therefore enriched with affect.

Parents might attribute intentionality to their infants but be deceiving themselves and contributing all the meaning in the exchange. When the child moves or vocalizes and seems to change her focus of attention, she might not be gazing at anything in particular, and the movement or vocal emission might not be intentional. However, the parent's illusion could be essential for the child's development, as it bootstraps the child into their shared social and cultural world. Through repetition of similar situations and interpretations, the child can grow into a full-blown intentional agent.

When children take up and imitate the forms produced by their parents, parents then seize and take up the sounds and movements produced by their children in order to endow those sounds and movements with as much meaning as possible, and shape them into a form that could be compatible with the adult communicative system. In the following example taken from the Forrester Corpus (Forrester, 2008; MacWhinney, 2000), the father takes up his daughter's gesture, which might not have been intentional or communicative when the child first produced it. As previously shown by Caët (2014), he transforms it into a game that serves as a transition toward meaning.

> Example 3.1 *Ella 1;02*[5]
> The link to the video of this example can be found with this book's supplementary materials online (https://www.apa.org/pubs/books/gesture-in-language).
> *The father and the daughter are having breakfast.*
> FATHER: Are you tired?
> *Ella whimpers and rubs her face.*
> FATHER: Oh, a little bit.
> *She then makes a very unexpected gesture. Her hand goes down along her hair. She hits her head and looks at her father as she produces a short vocalization.*
> ELLA: eh!
> *He repeats his daughter's gesture and points to her head.*
> FATHER: Baby's head.
> *He then points at his own head.*
> FATHER: Daddy's head.

In Figure 3.5, the father takes up what seems to be a nonintentional, noncommunicative gesture. In Figure 3.6, he shapes her movement into a conventional pointing gesture, through which he can designate, alternatively, his own head and his daughter's head by combining the gesture with spoken utterances.

---

[5] Age is indicated in [X years;Y months]: 1;02: 1 year and 2 months. This example was first presented by Stéphanie Caët and analyzed in the doctoral seminar I conducted in 2011. An analysis was published to illustrate the use of gestures (Caët, 2014). The original transcription followed the CHAT format (MacWhinney, 2000), which creates a hierarchy between speech and actions/gestures/gaze. We simplified the transcription conventions and used italics instead of secondary lines to transcribe all information outside speech, and did not change the priority artificially given to speech in our examples taken from the *Paris Corpus*.

Early Pointing Gestures —— 65

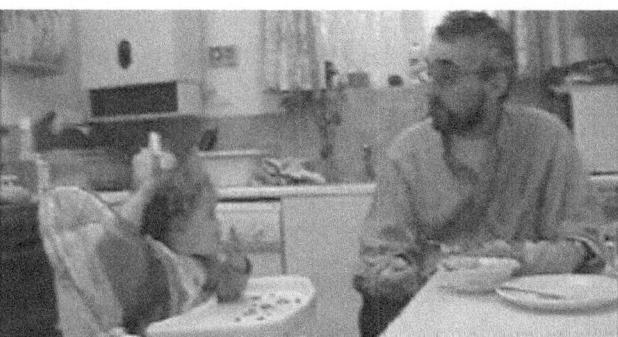

Fig. 3.5: Ella's movement.

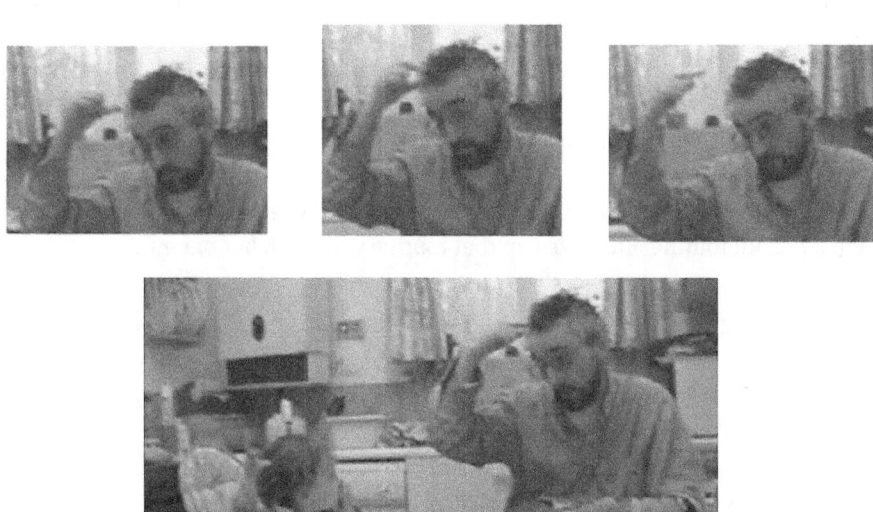

Fig. 3.6: Father's reenactment.

He has transformed the child's movement into a social gesture, which is part of the string of routinely used pointing gestures associated with speech of the various members of the family, and which Ella will take up and replay herself in the following sessions in the data. The child's movement, expressed in what the father interprets and performs himself as a gesture, has been converted into a multimodal performance.

In our analysis of Example 3.1, we illustrated the moment-to-moment unfurling of a father/daughter interaction and the adult's introduction of a playful routine involving pointing gestures. However, this performance was repeated daily in a variety of contexts by all the adults in the family, so that it became what Bruner (1983) calls a *format*, which the little girl took up herself as illustrated in the following example which was recorded 2 months later. We thus illustrated the importance of recording longitudinal data and being able to observe the unfurling of children's use of pointing over time.

3.2.4 Children's Interactive Pointing

The following example is continuous with Example 3.1 where Ella's father used pointing in a playful routine. Ella takes up that routine with both her parents.

> Example 3.2 *Ella 1;04*
> The link to the video of this example can be found with this book's supplementary materials online (https://www.apa.org/pubs/books/gesture-in-language).
> MOTHER: Have you got all your big toothies coming through?
> MOTHER: Oh the big [/] big toothies ! Oh, you got even more toothies coming through!
> MOTHER: She's got another one at the back coming through at the bottom.
> ELLA: Mummy.
> *She points at her mother's teeth (with contact on one of her teeth, mother has her mouth wide open).*
> MOTHER: Oh, big toothies. Oh, the big toothies. Oh, the big toothies.
> *ELLA points at her dad.*
> MOTHER: Oh, daddy's got toothies, too.
> *ELLA points at her own teeth.*
> MOTHER: Baby's got big toothies.
> *ELLA points at her mother's teeth.*
> MOTHER: And Mummy's got big toothies.
> *ELLA points at her father's teeth.*

MOTHER: And Daddy's got big toothies.
MOTHER: Yeah.
MOTHER: Here.
MOTHER: Don't have to get up!
FATHER: Show me!
Father comes close for Ella to be able to reach to him.
MOTHER: Where's the Daddy toothies?
Ella stops her pointing teeth tour and hands her food to her mother.

After her mother explains that Ella's teeth are growing, the child leans toward her mother, opens her own mouth, and points to her own teeth. She thus shares the topic and enters the dialogue through her actions and her gesture (Figure 3.7). Ella's mother then addresses the father, and continues her explanation, enacting the illustration of the teeth growing on herself (Figure 3.8 and Figure 3.9).

This triggers Ella's pointing tour. She touches her mother's teeth in response to her mother's own gesture and initiates a comparison/association between herself, her mother, and her father by successively pointing at their teeth. Ella is even simultaneously pointing at her mother's and father's teeth with her two arms (Figure 3.10).

Ella's mother is close enough for the pointing gesture to be associated with touching the teeth, whereas her father is standing farther away. The father then comes closer in order to be part of the tactile designation of teeth. This sequence could be viewed as an echo to all previous situations in which the parents have explicitly compared themselves to the child, initiated routines by pointing at several body parts, such as the one described in Example 3.1.

Fig. 3.7: Ella pointing at her teeth.

Fig. 3.8: Ella and her mother both pointing at their teeth.

Fig. 3.9: Ella pointing at mother's teeth.

Fig. 3.10: Ella Pointing at both mother's and father's teeth.

3.2.5 Monologic Pointing

In the literature, pointing has been analyzed as emerging for the child's own benefit before being addressed to interlocutors (Werner & Kaplan, 1963). We started filming Théo when he was 7 months old and did not use pointing yet. Because we filmed him at least once a month, we could observe the emergence of pointing in our data. In our recordings, monologic pointing was produced by Théo for the first time at 11 months old, in the same session as his very first dialogical pointing. Théo would go around the house pointing for himself outside his mother's presence (she could be in another room or have her back turned to him). The most frequent occurrences were counted at 1;02. They decreased until 1;06 and then became quite rare. However, at 1;09, as they arrived at his grandparents' house in the countryside, his parents observed him going around in the garden and then running from room to room excitedly pointing at different locations and objects and vocalizing for himself as he was discovering the premises (Figure 3.11).

Théo's pointing could be considered as a *reported gesture* (or as fictive gestural interaction, Pascual, 2014) with roots in actual gesture-in-interaction, and it could be analyzed as enabling the child to borrow the interactive role of the adult interlocutor. In these scenes, Théo is interacting with himself; he is both the one who points and the receiver of the pointing. Just like his parents, who from the very beginning of our data sessions continuously pointed to designate interesting objects or events, the child showed himself target phenomena. He was thus performing mini dialogic sequences for himself. Pointing created a triadic link between Théo as the perceiver of an object, the object itself, and the Théo who could then view the object as interesting.

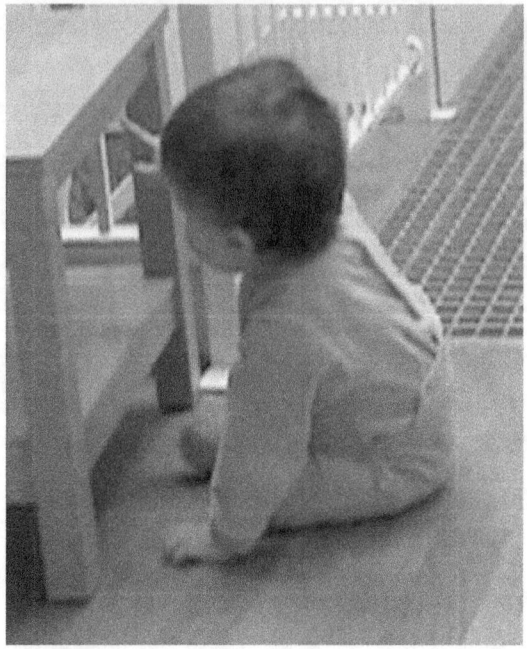

Fig. 3.11: Théo points at a plant leaf showing under the coffee table.

In a Vygotskyan framework (1934), Théo has internalized pointing as part of his repertoire to think in gesture.

3.2.6 Playful Imperative Pointing as Demonstration of Power

In the following example, Théo takes on the role of orchestra conductor.

> Example 3.3 *Théo 1;3*
> The link to the video of this example can be found with this book's supplementary materials online (https://www.apa.org/pubs/books/gesture-in-language).
> *MOTHER feeds Théo with a spoon.*
> *THEO opens his mouth and eats, but is not looking at his mother; he claps his hands, applauding, for no apparent reason.*
> MOTHER: Tu as envie d'applaudir ce soir? [You want to applaud tonight?]
> THEO: Mhm

He looks intently at FATHER, leaning forward, pointing at him with his index finger.
FATHER raises both arms, high up.
MOTHER: Tu le fais! [You do it!] *to Theo*
THEO raises both arms, high up; beaming with a proud smile.
MOTHER: Ouais [yeah!]
FATHER: Ouais! Oh là oh là! [Yeah! Oh là!]
THEO points at FATHER with his index finger.
FATHER points at THEO with his index finger.
THEO again points at FATHER with his index finger.
FATHER: Oh pourquoi—pourquoi toujours moi? [Oh why—why always me?]
THEO points at MOTHER with his index finger.
MOTHER: À moi? [My turn?]
Raising arms high and wide above her head.
MOTHER: *Ah oui à toi!* [Yes, now your turn!]
Points at THEO.
THEO lifts his arms high and wide; smiling beamingly.
THEO applauds.
FATHER: Bravo!
THEO claps his hands beamingly; shakes head in excitement.

When Théo claps his hands, his mother interprets his clapping as a wish for attention and joint activity at the dinner table. She treats him as the master of ceremonies. Théo then uses imperative pointing, singling out his father who immediately and eagerly raises his arms as if obeying his son's order (Figure 3.12).

The pointing thus regulates which participants perform this playful action, in some kind of improvised family performance at the dinner table. His mother then tells Théo himself to act ("you do it"), and he raises both arms and hands, with a proud facial expression. Both parents celebrate his action, through gleeful response cries (Goffman, 1978). When asked by his child through a new pointing gesture to perform again, his father makes a more elaborate play enactment by both raising his arms and waiving his hands (Figure 3.13).

The child points to him once more, thus making a request for a repetition but Father then protests and points at Mother. This becomes another act in the family game, as she performs and raises both hands and then points at Théo for him to perform his part in the hand raising game. The participants thus reverse roles but the meaning of each gesture remains the same: pointing is the act required by the participant imbued with *imperative power*. The recipient of the pointing gesture is then transformed into a performer who can raise both hands and be celebrated (Figure 3.14; Aronsson & Morgenstern, 2021).

Fig. 3.12: Théo points imperatively.

Fig. 3.13: Father raises both arms.

Fig. 3.14: Théo raises both arms.

This all takes place nonverbally on the young child's part. Théo does not use much speech at this stage in his development, but he is eager to take his part in this meaningful collective performance and takes on both roles: pointing to trigger his parents' hand raising, and being the target of pointing to be the hand-raiser himself. He demonstrates his power as both giving the cue/the order, and as receiving it and performing the playful hand raising gesture.

3.2.7 Protodeclarative Pointing

In the following example, Madeleine's bunny has been left in the next room while she is in her high chair ready for her meal. The bunny is visible from where the little girl is sitting.

> Example 3.4 *Madeleine 1;0*
> The link to the video of this example can be found with this book's supplementary materials online (https://www.apa.org/pubs/books/gesture-in-language).
> MADELEINE *is in her high chair, ready to eat. She points toward the room where her stuffed rabbit has been placed before her meal.*
> MOTHER *holds out a spoon full of soup.*

MADELEINE: /œga gagagaa/
She turns around toward the other room where they left the bunny.
MOTHER: Madeleine
She holds out a spoon full of soup and waits.
MADELEINE: /ka/
She gazes toward the bunny.
MOTHER: Oui, il est là. Madeleine tu veux de la soupe? [Yes, it's there. Madeleine, do you want some soup?]
MADELEINE: /œga/
She gazes toward the bunny.
MOTHER: Madeleine?
She is still holding out the spoon full of soup and waiting.
MOTHER: Et si t'as ton lapin il va être tout tâché. [If you have your bunny with you, it will be all stained.]
She gives her a spoonful.
MOTHER: Il va avoir plein de soupe. [It will be full of soup.]
MADELEINE: /gagaga/
She gazes at the bunny.
MOTHER: Oui, il est là. [Yes, it's there.]
MADELEINE: /keza/
MOTHER: Hum. Il t'attend, il attend que tu aies fini ta soupe. [Hum. It's waiting, it's waiting for you to finish your soup.]

In this example, although Madeleine only produces vocalizations that cannot be interpreted as words yet, her mother understands that the little girl is focused on her bunny, thanks to a pointing gesture associated with gaze. Every possible visible and audible cue is thus interpreted by the mother in order to create a fruitful conversation with her daughter, in which she will not only refer to the bunny and state its permanence, but also provide an explanation for why it has been left aside during the meal (it will be preserved from being stained with soup). After Madeleine's first pointing gesture, her mother understands that Madeleine is referring to her bunny, because she can see the direction of the pointing gesture, and she has shared the previous context. As Madeleine continues to point and gaze in the same direction repeatedly, her mother continues to refer to the bunny but maintains her goal, which is to feed Madeleine. The conversation about the bunny is densely scaffolded by Madeleine's mother who provides the name of the referent, reassures Madeleine (who does not abandon her pointing gestures and gaze) by telling her that it is still where they left it and provides the explanation. As long as Madeleine is only using vocal productions that are not semantically transparent, the mother relies on every semiotic resource at the child's disposal to interpret her meaning but transforms every cue into a spoken reformulation. Pointing and gaze are interpreted as referring to the bunny, making sure it is where it was left, and questioning the motivation for its having been left behind during the meal.

However, as soon as Madeleine, who is a precocious speaker, produces words, those words will become the primary source of semantic information.

3.2.8 Combining Modalities

Using two modalities for two different elements is described as preceding the onset of two-word speech (see Clark & Kelly, Chapter 6, this volume, for a thorough discussion). The skills to express more than one element or aspect of an event in the same turn (as opposed to what Scollon, 1976, called "vertical constructions," i.e., different elements expressed in two successive turns that are often united in parents' reformulations) are necessary for children to be able to combine two words. The multifaceted character of an event is first expressed through two complementary modalities, with a gesture and a word referring to two different elements. Those word–gesture combinations have been documented in the 2nd year and could be considered a transition toward two-word utterances (Goldin-Meadow & Butcher, 2003). In book-reading, for example, a caregiver will very often repeat the multimodal construction "look" (or "here") plus pointing. Example 3.5 shows that Madeleine takes up the exact same construction with the directive verbal element *"regarde"* (look) and the gestural deictic element toward the illustration on the book:

Example 3.5 *Madeleine 1;01*
>The link to the video of this example can be found with this book's supplementary materials online (https://www.apa.org/pubs/books/gesture-in-language).
>MOTHER: Oh, regarde le petit Popi! [Oh, look at little Popi!]
>*MOTHER points at a character (Popi) on the magazine with her index finger.*
>*Madeleine looks at the magazine.*
>MOTHER: Oh, il met les pieds dans l'eau. [Oh, he is dipping his feet in the water.]
>*Madeleine tries to turn the page but her mother is still showing her other elements in the same picture.*
>MOTHER: Regarde, c'est quoi ça? [Look, what's that?]
>*MOTHER points at an element on the picture.*
>MOTHER: C'est quoi ça? [What's that?] C'est un–? [It's a–?]
>MADELEINE: Ver
>*Madeleine turns the page.*
>MOTHER: Oh, petit ours! [Oh, little bear!]

> MADELEINE: Regarde. [Look] (phonetic transcription: /œga/)
> *She points at an element on the picture.*
> MOTHER: Oui. [Yes.]

In this extract, Madeleine uses the same prosodic pattern as her mother when she produces her incomplete string of phonemes "œga" for the word "*regarde*" (look). Children are quite skilled at using the right prosodic patterns at a very early age (Konopczynski, 1990) to transmit their intentions through a range of speech acts (request, directive, comment), and it compensates for their incomplete phonological system. Prosodic patterns associated with pointing therefore help them make the transition from prelinguistic vocalizations to first verbal predications. If we see in this moment-by-moment example how the little girl takes up the multimodal construction [pointing + *regarde*] from the mother's productions (the mother performs 12 occurrences of the construction in that sequence before Madeleine produces it herself for the first time in our data), thanks to our longitudinal recordings that began when she was 8 months old, we could observe the multimodal constructions being used over and over by the mother both in book-reading situations and during other activities. Madeleine internalized its form and function *over time*.

3.2.9 Complex Multimodal Productions

The transition from gesture–word combinations to word–word combinations is scaffolded by the adult communicative strategies, as when the adult replies to the child's gesture–word combination by translating it into a unimodal spoken utterance (Goldin-Meadow, 2009) as illustrated in the following example:

> Example 3.6 *Ellie 1;09*
> *Robert, Ellie's uncle, shows Ellie a black record sleeve and asks her what color it is.*
> ELLIE: Blue.
> *She looks at the object and takes it in her hands.*
> ROBERT: Oh (*he raises his eyebrows*). I think it might be black. Oh it's definitely black.
> ELLIE: No. Blue.
> *She points at the object.*

Ellie uses a pointing gesture to refer to the object; her uncle takes up the reference by using an anaphoric pronoun (it). The pointing gesture and the pronoun could be considered as having the same referential function in each participant's utterance. The child produces two multimodal utterances equivalent to "it's blue" and "no, it's blue." The pointing gesture is used to refer to the record sleeve, but it also combines with the adjective "blue" and has a predicative function similar to the presence of the auxiliary "be" or the modal "might" in the uncle's speech. Children's gestures are thus constantly taken up by adults and reformulated into words. Parents rely on children's pointing gestures in order to interpret their communicative intention.

Over time, Ellie's spoken syntax becomes richer and more complex. In the following example, even though her verbalization is now quite complete in itself (although with nonstandard syntax), she still uses pointing gestures to clarify the location she is referring to. Her pointing gestures create a link between her spoken words and the visible world that surrounds her and her father.

> Example 3.7 *Ellie 2;05*
> *Ellie's father has just dug a hole in the garden. Her mother has forbidden her to go near the hole or go in it.*
> ELLIE: You not go in.
> *She points toward the hole her father has dug in the garden.*
> FATHER: In here?
> ELLIE: No.
> FATHER: Oh, he's bitten my foot. Ah!
> *He place one foot in the hole and pretends the hole is eating the foot up.*
> MOTHER: Daddy!
> FATHER: Oh!
> [...]
> ELLIE: You not go in there, Daddy!
> *She points at the hole and shakes her head.*
> MOTHER: No!

Ellie is recycling a prohibition made to her by her mother. As she is not supposed to go too close, Ellie compensates for the distance between her body and the hole by using an extended pointing gesture to create a link between her words and the reality of the danger, the hole. The father playfully takes up the association of the preposition "in" and the pointing gesture by reformulating them in a deictic verbal expression "in here?" Ellie's pointing gesture in this sequence is thus equivalent to the deictic adverb "here." The referent, the hole in the ground, which she was pointing at, is then physically explored by the father with his foot as he goes against the prohibition. The playful atmosphere created by the father and mother is only possible because of their status as adults. The projection of the prohibition made to Ellie onto her adult father is put into question by her father, who replaces pointing, that symbolic gestural link between his body and the hole, by an enactment of the dangerous action itself. But Ellie has perfectly understood that, as a little girl, she cannot perform the action herself, and that she can only allow herself to represent the danger by a symbolic gesture, pointing.

Continuing on our longitudinal journey, we now illustrate Ellie's full integration of gesture and speech as she progressively masters language.

> Example 3.8 *Ellie 2;08*
> The link to the video of this example can be found with this book's supplementary materials online (https://www.apa.org/pubs/books/gesture-in-language).
> *Ellie and her mother are going to paint a cardboard box. The mother places newspaper on the kitchen floor in order to avoid stains.*
> ELLIE: Where's the big box?
> *Palm-up with both hands.*
> MOTHER: Where's the big box?
> ELLIE: There.
> *Pointing toward the box.*
> MOTHER: Can you get it?
> *The mother is still pointing at the paper on the floor.*
> ELLIE: Can I?
> *She points at the newspaper on the floor in front of her. Gazes at her mother.*
> MOTHER: Yeah, you can walk on that.
> *She nods several times, gazes at Ellie.*

In this last example, Ellie now has good speech skills, and she is still using coverbal gestures and especially pointing. Some of the recurrent gestures in this example (Ellie's palm up gesture and the mother's nods) are emphasizing equivalent vocal productions and could be considered redundant (Capirci et al., 1996; Goldin-Meadow & Morford, 1990; Özçalışkan & Goldin-Meadow, 2005). Ellie's palm up gesture is associated with "Where's the big box?" and enacts the absence of the box. However there is a clear articulation created by associating the WH pronoun "where" and the epistemic gesture relying a lack of information both addressed to the mother. This multimodal construction can be interpreted as having a meaning that is not expressed if only her words are taken into account: "The big box is not visible by me right now. I don't know where it is so I am asking Mummy."[6]

---

6 See Beaupoil-Hourdel (2015, p. 380).

Similarly, gesture, words, and gaze are used by the mother to grant permission to step on the newspaper on the floor. The mother's nods and gaze toward her daughter are associated with "Yeah, you can walk on that." Despite their semantic equivalence, gestures and words remain somewhat complementary in these multimodal productions. However, the pointing gestures used by Ellie in this sequence are supplying other types of information than her words. The first pointing gesture enables Ellie to give the precise location of the box in the space around her, which could not be accomplished by the simple emission of words. The second pointing gesture is even more complex as, by pointing at the newspaper on the floor, she is providing not only a referent missing in her words (the newspaper) but also, implicitly, the missing predicate "walk" or "step" referring to the action her body must accomplish in order for her to fulfil her mother's request. Her added gaze on her mother is asking for permission, her body is prepared for the motion, but she will not engage in it without that permission. Her mother has enough shared context to fully interpret her multimodal production and grant the permission to step on the newspaper.

As we have seen throughout these examples, not only are pointing gestures deployed in our moment-to-moment interactions, but their functions diversify greatly over the course of the longitudinal recordings (Morgenstern, 2014). At first, pointing gestures are produced in isolation with either a protodeclarative (comment) or a protoimperative (request) function. When the child is around age 1 year, these gestures begin to be complemented by vocal productions with the same overall functions. Around age 1;06, pointing gestures are produced with deictics or nouns and clearly localize the objects shown or requested. The verbal productions simultaneous with pointing then become more and more complex: first with predicates, then with whole utterances. Between 1;06 and 2;0, children start pointing to absent entities. At 2;06 they point to several locations during fictive narratives. They also start using more diversified coverbal gestures. After 3;0, their speech becomes more complex (even earlier for Ellie and Madeleine) with embedded clauses and diversification of their tense system, and in parallel they go through what McNeill (2005) called "the gesture explosion" (p. 183) with more and more coverbal gestures.

Around 3;06 to 4;0, the functions of children's pointing gestures become more and more diverse. For example, Madeleine uses her fingers to count the dolls she is talking about, but she also then points to those same fingers as they embody the dolls themselves (as if they were classifiers in sign language).

By the age of 4;0, the children's pointing gestures are integrated in fluid coverbal gesturing. Pointing can follow the rhythmic variation of their prosody: gestures and vocal productions are linked with great subtlety. They demonstrate excellent mastery of the location, the orientation, and the motion of pointing gestures, which enables children to differentiate among their functions. The children's gesturing illustrates, specifies, reinforces, or modalizes the meanings of their vocal productions. Gestures thus continue to enhance the blossoming of children's communication skills after their first words and the first gesture–word combinations. They are part of an intersubjective multimodal communicative system, in which it is more and more complex to tease apart gestures from speech. The performative, interactional, and sociocultural nature of language involves the cooperation of both modalities, with one constantly supporting, extending, or modifying the other.

3.3 Conclusion

Before children start using words or signs, they communicate through gaze, facial expressions, postures, and gestures. In Western culture, as well as many others (see Cooperrider & Mesh, Chapter 2, this volume), their most frequent conventional gesture is pointing. This behavior emerges quite early in infancy (sometimes as early as 7–8 months, most often around 10–11 months old) to locate, request, or comment upon an object that is present and in the child's eyesight.

Pointing is used as a sociopragmatic tool in dialogue and therefore should not only be studied in isolation but also in rich social contexts. It is accompanied by a number of communicative behaviors such as gaze, facial expressions, and vocalizations. Scaffolding adults can interpret the function of children's pointing by taking into account the situation, the communicative context, the target of the pointing, its position, and that of the participants in order to adjust their own reaction and behavior.

Pointing continues to enhance the blossoming of children's communication skills after the prelinguistic period and the first pointing–word combinations. The performative, interactional, and sociocultural nature of language involves the cooperation of visual-gestural and auditory-vocal modalities, with one constantly supporting, extending, or modifying the other.

Kendon (2004) presented an approach in which he invited us "to engage in a comparative semiotics of the utterance uses of visible actions" (p. 88), thanks to which we need not try to differentiate gesture and sign or call them linguistic, prelinguistic, or nonlinguistic. He suggested comparing the range of forms of visible actions, how systematically they are used, and the types of semiosis they display in order to approach the performances of pointing in terms of gradience and consider them as part of languaging if they are composed of certain features and are part of specific configurations.

As Goodwin (2003) suggested,

Pointing provides an opportunity to investigate within a single interactive practice the details of language use, the body as a socially organized field for temporally unfolding displays of meaning tied to relevant action, and material and semiotic phenomena in the surround. (p. 29)

Through the analysis of pointing in combination with gaze, vocalization, speech, and posture, we have the opportunity to investigate the range of semiotic resources deployed by children in interaction with scaffolding adult interlocutors to build meaning in a variety of situations within the social world they inhabit. Our posture as analysts could be modelled from caretakers who integrate their children's pointing gestures in the flow of their conversations and characterize them as linguistic communicative acts in their own glosses, in Zinacantec Tzotzil (Haviland, 1998) as well as in French, British, or American Sign Language. Pointing can thus be viewed not only as a precursor, but as an integral part of language. It is intricately linked to the development of speech in what could be seen as children's first multimodal communicative constructions. As Haviland (1998) also highlighted, pointing has the language-like properties of emblems, as it can be autonomous from speech or a full component of sign language, but it also appears together with verbalization as a necessary referential or pragmatic accompaniment. It is thus a central tool to refer to and conjure up visible and invisible, present and absent, actual and imaginary entities and events. It is used cross-culturally and throughout the lifespan. It is transmitted to and produced by children through multimodal languaging in their everyday collective and individual experience.

References

Amano, S., Kezuka, E., & Yamamoto, A. (2004). Infant shifting attention from an adult's face to an adult's hand: A precursor of joint attention. *Infant Behavior and Development, 27*(1), 64–80. https://doi.org/10.1016/j.infbeh.2003.06.005

Aronsson, K., & Morgenstern, A. (2021). "*Bravo!*": Co-constructing praise in French family life. *Journal of Pragmatics, 173*, 1–14. https://doi.org/10.1016/j.pragma.2020.12.002

Augustine of Hippo, Saint. (1996). *Confessions*. Harvard University Press. (Original work published AD 354–430)

Baldwin, D. A. (1993). Infants' ability to consult the speaker for clues to word reference. *Journal of Child Language, 20*(2), 395–418. https://doi.org/10.1017/S0305000900008345

Baron-Cohen, S. (1989). Perceptual role taking and protodeclarative pointing in autism. *British Journal of Developmental Psychology, 7*(2), 113–127. https://doi.org/10.1111/j.2044-835X.1989.tb00793.x

Bates, E. (1976). *Language and context: The acquisition of pragmatics (language, thought, and culture)*. Academic Press.

Bates, E., Benigni, L., Bretherton, I., Camaioni, L., & Volterra, V. (1977). From gesture to the first word: On cognitive and social prerequisites. In M. Lewis & L. Rosenblum (Eds.), *Interaction, conversation and the development of language* (pp. 247–307). Wiley.

Bates, E., Benigni, L., Bretherton, I., Camaioni, L., & Volterra, V. (1979). *The emergence of symbols: Cognition and communication in infancy*. Academic Press.

Bates, E., Camaioni, L., & Volterra, V. (1975). The acquisition of performatives prior to speech. *Merrill-Palmer Quarterly, 21*(3), 205–226.

Beaupoil-Hourdel, P. (2015). *Multimodal acquisition and expression of negation. Analysis of a videotaped and longitudinal corpus of a French and an English mother–child dyad* [Unpublished doctoral dissertation]. Sorbonne Nouvelle University, Paris.

Boas, F. (1965). *The mind of primitive man*. Free Press. (Original work published 1911)

Booth, A., McGregor, K., & Rohlfing, K. J. (2008). Socio-pragmatics and attention: Contributions to gesturally guided word learning in toddlers. *Language Learning and Development, 4*(3), 179–202. https://doi.org/10.1080/15475440802143091

Boutet, D. (2018). *Pour une approche kinésiologique de la gestualité* [For a kinesiological approach to body language]. [Habilitation à diriger des recherches, Université de Rouen-Normandie]. https://hal.archives-ouvertes.fr/tel-02357282

Brazelton, T. B., Koslowski, B., & Main, M. (1974). The origins of reciprocity: The early mother–infant interaction. In M. Lewis & L. Rosenblum (Eds.), *The effect of the infant on its care-giver* (pp. 49–76). Wiley-Interscience.

Bruner, J. (1975). The ontogenesis of speech acts. *Journal of Child Language, 2*(1), 1–19. https://doi.org/10.1017/S0305000900000866

Bruner, J. (1983). *Child's talk: Learning to use language*. W. W. Norton.

Butcher, C., & Goldin-Meadow, S. (2000). Gesture and the transition from one- to two-word speech: When hand and mouth come together. In D. McNeill (Ed.), *Language and gesture* (pp. 235–258). Cambridge University Press. https://doi.org/10.1017/CBO9780511620850.015

Butterworth, G. (1995). Origins of mind in perception and action. In C. Moore & P. Dunham (Eds.), *Joint attention: its origins and role in development* (pp. 29–40). Psychology Press.

Butterworth, G. (2003). Pointing is the royal road to language for babies. In S. Kita (Ed.), *Pointing: Where language, culture, and cognition meet* (pp. 9–33). Lawrence Erlbaum.

Butterworth, G., & Morissette, P. (1996). Onset of pointing and the acquisition of language in infancy. *Journal of Reproductive and Infant Psychology, 14*(3), 219–231. https://doi.org/10.1080/02646839608404519

Cabrejo-Parra, E. (1992). Deixis et opérations symboliques [Deixis and symbolic operations]. In L. Danon-Boileau & M.-A. Morel (Eds.), *La deixis* [The deixis] (pp. 409–414). P.U.F.

Caët, S. (2014). Quand un père emprunte les gestes de sa fille : Fonctions discursive et intersubjective de la reprise gestuelle [When a father borrows his daughter's gestures: Discursive and intersubjective functions of gestural recovery]. Travaux neuchâtelois de linguistique [Neuchâtel linguistics works]. *Revue Tranel, 60*, 47–56.

Caët, S., & Morgenstern, A. (2015). First and second person pronouns in two mother–child dyads. In L. Gardelle & S. Sorlin (Eds.), *The pragmatics of personal pronouns* (pp. 173–194). John Benjamins Publishing. https://doi.org/10.1075/slcs.171.09cae

Capirci, O., Iverson, J., Pizzuto, E., & Volterra, V. (1996). Gestures and words during the transition to two-word speech. *Journal of Child Language, 23*(3), 645–673. https://doi.org/10.1017/S0305000900008989

Carpendale, J., & Carpendale, A. (2010). The development of pointing: From personal directedness to interpersonal direction. *Human Development*, *53*(3), 110–126. https://doi.org/10.1159/000315168

Carpenter, M., Nagell, K., Tomasello, M., Butterworth, G., & Moore, C. (1998). Social cognition, joint attention, and communicative competence from 9 to 15 months of age. *Monographs of the Society for Research in Child Development*, *63*(4), i–vi, 1–143. https://doi.org/10.2307/1166214

Cartmill, E. A., Hunsicker, D., & Goldin-Meadow, S. (2014). Pointing and naming are not redundant: Children use gesture to modify nouns before they modify nouns in speech. *Developmental Psychology*, *50*(6), 1660–1666. https://doi.org/10.1037/a0036003

Cienki, A. (2012). Usage events of spoken language and the symbolic units we (may) abstract from them. In K. Kosecki & J. Badio (Eds.), *Cognitive processes in language* (pp. 149–158). Peter Lang.

Clark, E. V. (1978). From gesture to word: On the natural history of Deixis in language acquisition. In J. S. Bruner & A. Garton (Eds.), *Human growth and development* (pp. 340–408). C.U.P.

Clark, E. V. (1982). Language change during language acquisition. In M. E. Lamb & A. L. Brown (Eds.), *Advances in developmental psychology* (Vol. 2, pp. 173–197). Lawrence Erlbaum Associates.

Clark, E. V. (2003). *First language acquisition*. Cambridge University Press.

Cohen, M. (1924). *Sur les langages successifs de l'enfant* [On the successive languages of the child]. In *Mélanges linguistiques offerts à M. J. Vendryès par ses amis et ses élèves* [Linguistic mixtures offered to Mr. J. Vendryès by his friends and his pupils]. Paris, Champion, collection published by the Société de Linguistique, XVII (pp. 109–127).

Cole, M., & Cole, S. (1993). *The development of children* (2nd ed.). Scientific American Books.

Condillac, E. B. (1997). *Traité des sensations* [Treatise on sensations]. Fayard. (Original work published 1756)

Cooperrider, K. (2020). Fifteen ways of looking at a pointing gesture. *PsyArXiv*. https://doi.org/10.31234/osf.io/2vxft

Cormier, K., Schembri, A., & Woll, B. (2013). Pronouns and pointing in sign languages. *Lingua*, *137*, 230–247. https://doi.org/10.1016/j.lingua.2013.09.010

Darwin, C. (1877). A biographical sketch of an infant. *Mind*, *os-2*(7), 285–294. https://doi.org/10.1093/mind/os-2.7.285

De Laguna, G. M. A. (1927). *Speech: Its function and development*. Yale University Press.

de Saussure, F. (1995). *Cours de linguistique générale* [Course in general linguistics]. Payot. (Original work published 1916)

Esteve-Gibert, N., Liszkowski, U., & Prieto, P. (2016). Prosodic and gestural features distinguish the intention of pointing gestures in child-directed communication. In M. E. Armstrong, N. Henriksen, & M. D. M. Vanrell (Eds.), *Interdisciplinary approaches to intonational grammar in Ibero-Romance* (pp. 249–276). John Benjamins.

Esteve-Gibert, N., Prieto, P. P., & Liszkowski, U. (2017). Twelve-month-olds understand social intentions based on prosody and gesture shape. *Infancy*, *22*(1), 108–129. https://doi.org/10.1111/infa.12146

Feldman, R., & Eidelman, A. I. (2004). Parent–infant synchrony and the social–emotional development of triplets. *Developmental Psychology*, *40*(6), 1133–1147. https://doi.org/10.1037/0012-1649.40.6.1133

Fenlon, J., Cooperrider, K., Keane, J., Brentari, D., & Goldin-Meadow, S. (2019). Comparing sign language and gesture: Insights from pointing. *Glossa, 4*(1–2), 1–26. https://doi.org/10.5334/gjgl.499

Fogel, A., & Hannan, T. (1985). Manual acts of nine- to fifteen-week-old human infants during face-to-face interaction with their mothers. *Child Development, 56*, 1271–1279.

Forrester, M. (2008). The emergence of self-repair: A case study of one child during the early pre-school years. *Research on Language and Social Interaction, 41*(1), 99–128. https://doi.org/10.1080/08351810701691206

Goffman, E. (1978). *The presentation of self in everyday life.* Anchor/Doubleday.

Goldin-Meadow, S. (2009). How gesture promotes learning in development. *Child Development Perspectives, 3*(2), 106–111. https://doi.org/10.1111/j.1750-8606.2009.00088.x

Goldin-Meadow, S., & Butcher, C. (2003). Pointing toward two-word speech in young children. In S. Kita (Ed.), *Pointing: where language, culture, and cognition meet* (pp. 85–107). Erlbaum.

Goldin-Meadow, S., Goodrich, W., Sauer, E., & Iverson, J. (2007). Young children use their hands to tell their mothers what to say. *Developmental Science, 10*(6), 778–785. https://doi.org/10.1111/j.1467-7687.2007.00636.x

Goldin-Meadow, S., & Morford, M. (1990). Gesture in early child language. In V. Volterra & C. J. Erting (Eds.), *From gesture to language in hearing and deaf children* (pp. 249–262). Springer-Verlag. https://doi.org/10.1007/978-3-642-74859-2_20

Golinkoff, R., & Hirsh-Pasek, K. (2006). Baby wordsmith: From associationist to social sophisticate. *Current Directions in Psychological Science, 15*(1), 30–33. https://doi.org/10.1111/j.0963-7214.2006.00401.x

Goodwin, C. (2003). Pointing as situated practice. In S. Kita (Ed.), *Pointing: Where language, culture and cognition meet* (pp. 217–241). Lawrence Erlbaum.

Grace, D. L. (1927). *Speech, its function and development.* Yale University Press.

Grünloh, T., & Liszkowski, U. (2015). Prelinguistic vocalizations distinguish pointing acts. *Journal of Child Language, 42*(6), 1312–1336. https://doi.org/10.1017/S0305000914000816

Guidetti, M. (2003). *Pragmatique et psychologie du développement* [Pragmatics and developmental psychology]. Editions Belin.

Gumperz, J. J., & Levinson, S. C. (1991). Rethinking linguistic relativity. *Current Anthropology, 32*(5), 613–623. https://doi.org/10.1086/204009

Hatzopoulou, M. (2008). *Acquisition of reference to self and others in Greek Sign Language: From pointing gesture to pronominal pointing signs* [Unpublished doctoral dissertation]. Stockholm University.

Haviland, J. (1998). Early pointing gestures in Zincantán. *Linguistic Anthropology, 8*(2), 162–196. https://doi.org/10.1525/jlin.1998.8.2.162

Hobaiter, C., Leavens, D. A., & Byrne, R. W. (2014). Deictic gesturing in wild chimpanzees (*Pan troglodytes*)? Some possible cases. *Journal of Comparative Psychology, 128*(1), 82–87. https://doi.org/10.1037/a0033757

Hoiting, N. (2009). *The myth of simplicity: Sign language acquisition by Dutch deaf toddlers* [Unpublished doctoral dissertation]. University of Groningen.

Hoiting, N., & Slobin, D. (2007). From gestures to signs in the acquisition of sign language. In S. D. Duncan, J. Cassell, & E. T. Levy (Eds.), *Gesture and the dynamic dimension of* language: Essays in honor of David McNeill (pp. 51–65). John Benjamins. https://doi.org/10.1075/gs.1.06hoi

Ingram, D. (1989). *First language acquisition: Method, description and explanation*. Cambridge University Press.

Iverson, J., Capirci, O., Longobardi, E., & Caselli, C. (1999). Gesturing in mother–child interactions. *Cognitive Development, 14*(1), 57–75. https://doi.org/10.1016/S0885-2014(99)80018-5

Iverson, J. M., & Goldin-Meadow, S. (2005). Gesture paves the way for language development. *Psychological Science, 16*(5), 367–371. https://doi.org/10.1111/j.0956-7976.2005.01542.x

Johnston, T. (2013). Towards a comparative semiotics of pointing actions in signed and spoken languages. *Gesture, 13*(2), 109–142. https://doi.org/10.1075/gest.13.2.01joh

Kaye, K. (1982). *The mental and social life of babies: How parents create persons*. University of Chicago Press.

Kelly, B. F. (2011). A new look at redundancy in children's gesture and word combinations. In I. Arnon & E. V. Clark (Eds.), *Experience, variation, and generalization: Learning a first language* (pp. 73–90). John Benjamins. https://doi.org/10.1075/tilar.7.05kel

Kendon, A. (2004). *Gesture: Visible action as utterance*. Cambridge University Press. https://doi.org/10.1017/CBO9780511807572

Kita, S. (2003). Interplay of gaze, hand, torso orientation, and language in pointing. In S. Kita (Ed.), *Pointing: Where language, culture, and cognition meet* (pp. 307–328). Lawrence Erlbaum. https://doi.org/10.4324/9781410607744-17

Konopczynski, G. (1990). *Le langage emergent: Caractéristiques rythmiques* [The emerging language: Rhythmic characteristics]. Buske Verlag.

Langacker, R. W. (1988). A view of linguistic semantics. In B. Rudzka-Ostyn (Ed.), *Topics in cognitive linguistics* (pp. 49–90). John Benjamins. https://doi.org/10.1075/cilt.50.04lan

Leavens, D. A., Hopkins, W. D., & Bard, K. A. (2005). Understanding the point of chimpanzee pointing: Epigenesis and ecological validity. *Current Directions in Psychological Science, 14*(4), 185–189. https://doi.org/10.1111/j.0963-7214.2005.00361.x

Leroy, M., Mathiot, E., & Morgenstern, A. (2009). Pointing gestures, vocalizations and gaze: Two case studies. In J. Zlatev, M. Andrén, M. Johansson Falck, & C. Lundmark (Eds.), *Studies in language and cognition* (pp. 402–420). Cambridge Scholars Publishing.

Linell, P. (2009). *Rethinking language, mind and world dialogically: Interactional and contextual theories of human sense-making*. Information Age Publishing.

Liszkowski, U. (2018). Origins and complexities of infant communication and social cognition. In A. Newen, L. D. Bruin, & S. Gallagher (Eds.), *Oxford handbook of 4E cognition* (pp. 661–684). Oxford University Press.

Liszkowski, U., Brown, P., Callaghan, T., Takada, A., & de Vos, C. (2012). A prelinguistic gestural universal of human communication. *Cognitive Science, 36*(4), 698–713. https://doi.org/10.1111/j.1551-6709.2011.01228.x

Liszkowski, U., Carpenter, M., Striano, T., & Tomasello, M. (2006). 12- and 18-month-olds point to provide information for others. *Journal of Cognition and Development, 7*(2), 173–187. https://doi.org/10.1207/s15327647jcd0702_2

Liszkowski, U., Carpenter, M., & Tomasello, M. (2008). Twelve-month-olds communicate helpfully and appropriately for knowledgeable and ignorant partners. *Cognition, 108*(3), 732–739. https://doi.org/10.1016/j.cognition.2008.06.013

Liszkowski, U., Schäfer, M., Carpenter, M., & Tomasello, M. (2009). Prelinguistic infants, but not chimpanzees, communicate about absent entities. *Psychological Science, 20*(5), 654–660. https://doi.org/10.1111/j.1467-9280.2009.02346.x

Liszkowski, U., & Tomasello, M. (2011). Individual differences in social, cognitive, and morphological aspects of infant pointing. *Cognitive Development, 26*(1), 16–29. https://doi.org/10.1016/j.cogdev.2010.10.001

MacWhinney, B. (2000). *The CHILDES Project: Tools for analyzing talk: Vol. 2. The database* (3rd ed.). Lawrence Erlbaum Associates.

Marcos, H. (1998). *De la communication prélinguistique au langage: formes et fonctions* [From prelinguistic communication to language: forms and functions]. Harmattan.

Masataka, N. (2003). *The onset of language*. Cambridge University Press. https://doi.org/10.1017/CBO9780511489754

Mathiot, E., Limousin, F., Leroy, M., & Morgenstern, A. (2009). Premiers pointages chez l'enfant sourd signeur et l'enfant entendant: deux suivis longitudinaux entre 7 mois et 2 ans et 7 mois [First scores in the deaf signing child and the hearing child: two longitudinal follow-ups between 7 months and 2 years and 7 months]. *Acquisition et interaction en langue étrangère* [Acquisition and interaction in a foreign language], *Aile ... Lia, 1*, 141–168. https://doi.org/10.4000/aile.4515

McNeill, D. (2005). *Gesture and thought*. Chicago University Press. https://doi.org/10.7208/chicago/9780226514642.001.0001

Meier, P., & Lillo-Martin, D. (2013). The points of language. *Humana.Mente: Journal of Philosophical Studies, 6*(24), 151–176. http://www.humanamente.eu/index.php/HM/article/view/154

Mondada, L. (2019). Contemporary issues in conversation analysis: Embodiment and materiality, multimodality and multisensoriality in social interaction. *Journal of Pragmatics, 145*, 47–62. https://doi.org/10.1016/j.pragma.2019.01.016

Morford, M., & Goldin-Meadow, S. (1992). Comprehension and production of gesture in combination with speech in one-word speakers. *Journal of Child Language, 19*(3), 559–580. https://doi.org/10.1017/S0305000900011569

Morgenstern, A. (2009). *L'enfant dans la langue* [The child in the language]. Presses de la Sorbonne Nouvelle.

Morgenstern, A. (2014). Shared attention, gaze and pointing gestures in hearing and deaf children. In B. E. Inbal, M. Tice, & C. Kurumada (Eds.), *Language in interaction. Studies in honor of Eve V. Clark* (pp. 139–156). John Benjamins Publishing. https://doi.org/10.1075/tilar.12.12mor

Morgenstern, A., Caët, S., & Limousin, F. (2016). Pointing and self-designation in deaf and hearing children. *Open Linguistics, 2*(1), 768–787.

Morgenstern, A., & Parisse, C. (2007). Codage et interprétation du langage spontané d'enfants de 1 à 3 ans [Spontaneous language coding and interpretation of children aged 1 to 3]. *Corpus No. 6 Interprétation, Contextes, Codage* [Corpus 6: Interpretation, Contexts, Coding], 55–78. https://doi.org/10.4000/corpus.922

Morgenstern, A., & Parisse, C. (2012). The Paris corpus. *French Language Studies, 22*(1), 7–12. https://doi.org/10.1017/S095926951100055X

Ninio, A., & Bruner, J. (1978). The achievement and antecedents of labelling. *Journal of Child Language, 5*(1), 1–15. https://doi.org/10.1017/S0305000900001896

Ochs, E. (2012). Experiencing language. *Anthropological Theory*, *12*(2), 142–160. https://doi.org/10.1177/1463499612454088

Ochs, E., & Schieffelin, B. (1989). Language has a heart. *Text: Interdisciplinary Journal for the Study of Discourse*, *9*(1), 1989, 7–26. https://doi.org/10.1515/text.1.1989.9.1.7

Özçalışkan, S., & Goldin-Meadow, S. (2005). Gesture is at the cutting edge of early language development. *Cognition*, *96*(3), B101–B113. https://doi.org/10.1016/j.cognition.2005.01.001

Papoušek, M. (1989). Determinants of responsiveness to infant vocal expression of emotional state. *Infant Behavior and Development*, *12*(4), 507–524. https://doi.org/10.1016/0163-6383(89)90030-1

Parisse, C., & Morgenstern, A. (2010). A multi-software integration platform and support for multimedia transcripts of language. *LREC 2010, Proceedings of the workshop on multimodal corpora: Advances in capturing, coding and analyzing multimodality*, May 2010, La Valette, Malta (pp. 106–110).

Pascual, E. (2014). *Fictive interaction: The conversation frame in thought, language and discourse*. John Benjamins. https://doi.org/10.1075/hcp.47

Peirce, C. (1932). *Sanders. 1897. Division of signs in*. Collected Papers. (Original work published 1897)

Petitto, L. A. (1986). From gesture to symbol: the relationship between form and meaning in the acquisition of personal pronouns in American Sign Language. *Dissertation Abstracts International*, *45*(4-B), 1304.

Petitto, L. A. (1992). Modularity and constraints in early lexical acquisition: Evidence from children's early language and gesture. In M. R. Gunnar & M. Maratsos (Eds.), *The Minnesota symposia on child psychology: Vol. 25. Modularity and constraints in language and cognition* (pp. 25–58). Lawrence Erlbaum Associates.

Piaget, J. (1962). *Play, dreams and imitation in childhood*. W. W. Norton.

Pizzuto, E. A., & Capobianco, M. (2008). Is pointing "just" pointing? Unraveling the complexity of indexes in spoken and signed discourse. *Gesture*, *8*(1), 82–103. https://doi.org/10.1075/gest.8.1.07piz

Povinelli, D., Bering, J., & Giambrone, S. (2003). Chimpanzees' "pointing": Another error of the argument by analogy? In S. Kita (Ed.), *Pointing: Where language, culture, and cognition meet* (pp. 35–68). Laurence Erlbaum.

Povinelli, D., & O'Neill, D. (2000). Do chimpanzees use their gestures to instruct each other? In S. Baron-Cohen, H. Tager-Flusberg, & D. J. Cohen (Eds.), *Understanding other minds: Perspectives from developmental cognitive neuroscience* (2nd ed., pp. 459–488). Oxford University Press.

Poyatos, F. (1983). *New perspectives on nonverbal communication*. Pergamon Press.

Quine, W. V. O. (1960). *Word and object*. MIT Press.

Rohlfing, K., Longo, M. R., & Bretenthal, B. (2004). *Following pointing: Does gesture trigger shifts of visual attention in human infants?* [Poster presentation.] 14th Biennial International Conference on Infant Studies, Chicago, IL, United States.

Romanes, G. J. (1891). *L'évolution mentale chez l'homme: Origine des facultés humaines* [Mental evolution in man: Origin of human faculty]. Alcan. (Original work published 1888)

Rowe, M. L., & Goldin-Meadow, S. (2009). Differences in early gesture explain SES disparities in child vocabulary size at school entry. *Science*, *323*(5916), 951–953. https://doi.org/10.1126/science.1167025

Salomo, D., & Liszkowski, U. (2013). Sociocultural settings influence the emergence of prelinguistic deictic gestures. *Child Development, 83*(6), 1296–1307. https://doi.org/10.1111/cdev.12026

Sapir, E. (1927). The unconscious patterning of behavior in society. In C. M. Child, K. Koffka, J. E. Anderson, J. B. Watson, E. Sapir, W. I. Thomas, M. E. Kenworthy, F. L. Wells, & W. A. White (Eds.), *The unconscious: A symposium* (pp. 114–142). Alfred A. Knopf. https://doi.org/10.1037/13401-006

Schick, B. (2011). The development of American Sign Language and manually-coded English systems. In M. Marschark & P. E. Spencer (Eds.), *Oxford handbook of deaf studies, language, and education* (Vol. 1, 2nd ed., pp. 229–240). Oxford University Press.

Scollon, R. (1976). *Conversations with a one-year-old: A case study of the developmental foundations of syntax*. University of Hawaii Press.

Sherzer, J. (1973). Verbal and nonverbal deixis: The pointed lip gesture among the San Blas Cuna. *Language in Society, 2*(1), 117–131. https://doi.org/10.1017/S0047404500000087

Slobin, D. I. (1987). Thinking for speaking. *Proceedings of the Thirteenth Annual Meeting of the Berkeley Linguistics Society* (pp. 435–445). https://doi.org/10.3765/bls.v13i0.1826

Southgate, V., van Maanen, C., & Csibra, G. (2007). Infant pointing: Communication to cooperate or communication to learn? *Child Development, 78*(3), 735–740. https://doi.org/10.1111/j.1467-8624.2007.01028.x

Stern, D. (1985). *The interpersonal world of the infant: A view from psychoanalysis and developmental psychology*. Basic Books.

Stern, W. (1914). *Psychologie der frühen Kindheit bis zum sechsten Lebensjahr* [Psychology of early childhood: Up to the sixth year of age]. Quelle & Meyer.

Sully, J. (1896). *Studies of childhood*. D. Appleton & Co.

Thompson, L. A., & Massaro, D. W. (1986). Evaluation and integration of speech and pointing gestures during referential understanding. *Journal of Experimental Child Psychology, 42*(1), 144–168. https://doi.org/10.1016/0022-0965(86)90020-2

Tomasello, M. (1999). *The cultural origins of human cognition*. Harvard University Press.

Tomasello, M. (2003). *Constructing a language: a usage-based theory of language acquisition*. Harvard University Press.

Tomasello, M. (2006). Why don't apes point? In N. J. Enfield & S. C. Levinson (Eds.), *Roots of human sociality: Culture, cognition and interaction* (pp. 506–524). Berg.

Tomasello, M. (2008). *Origins of communication*. MIT Press. https://doi.org/10.7551/mitpress/7551.001.0001

Trevarthen, C. (1974). Conversations with a two-month-old. *New Scientist, 62*, 230–235.

Trevarthen, C. (1977). Descriptive analyses of infant communication behaviour. In H. R. Schaffer (Ed.), *Studies in mother–infant interaction* (pp. 227–270). Academic Press.

Veà, J., & Sabater-Pi, J. (1998). Spontaneous pointing behaviour in the wild pygmy chimpanzee (*Pan paniscus*). *Folia Primatologica, 69*, 289–290. https://doi.org/10.1159/000021640

Volterra, V., Caselli, C., Capirci, O., & Pizzuto, E. (2005). Gesture and the emergence and development of language. In M. Tomasello & D. Slobin (Eds.), *Beyond nature–nurture: Essays in honor of Elizabeth Bates* (pp. 3–40). Lawrence Erlbaum.

Vygotsky, L. (1985). *Thought and language* (Rev. ed.; E. Hanfmann & G. Vakar, Trans.). MIT Press. (Original work published 1934)

Werner, H., & Kaplan, B. (1963). *Symbol formation: An organismic-developmental approach to language and the expression of thought.* Wiley.

Whorf, B. (1956). *Language, thought, and reality: selected writings.* The MIT Press.

Wittgenstein, L. (1958). *Philosophical investigations* (2nd ed., G. E. M. Anscombe, Trans.) Blackwell. (Original work published 1953)

Wood, D., Bruner, J. S., & Ross, G. (1976). The role of tutoring in problem solving. *Journal of Child Psychology and Psychiatry, and Allied Disciplines, 17*(2), 89–100. https://doi.org/10.1111/j.1469-7610.1976.tb00381.x

Wundt, W. (1912). *Völkerpsychologie: Die sprache* [Ethnic psychology: The language]. Engelmann.

Wundt, W. (1973). *The language of gestures.* De Gruyter Mouton. https://doi.org/10.1515/9783110808285

II Gesture Before Speech

Meredith L. Rowe, Ran Wei, and Virginia C. Salo
4 Early Gesture Predicts Later Language Development

Young children communicate via gesture before they communicate through speech; research has documented strong associations between early gesture use and later language development (e.g., Iverson et al., 2008; Rowe & Goldin-Meadow, 2009a). The goal of this chapter is to summarize the literature on relations between early gesture production and comprehension and language development in typically developing children with a focus on describing the nature of these relations and considering the mechanisms involved. In the first half of this chapter, we review relations between gesture and language skills at different points across early development. In the second half, we offer some potential non–mutually exclusive reasons, and corresponding evidence, for why early gesture might predict later language skills. We see gesture, in addition to being an important means of communication, as a useful indicator of concurrent social–cognitive abilities, a key predictor of later skills, and a potential area for early-intervention research.

In this chapter, we define *gestures* as nonverbal communicative actions that are symbolic, or representational, in nature (Iverson & Goldin-Meadow, 2005), and we use the term *language* to refer to children's oral language skills, including their vocabulary knowledge and ability to produce multiword utterances (spoken or signed). Early in development, most gestures tend to be deictic, such as pointing and showing, and conventional (e.g., waving, nodding or shaking the head [Bates et al., 1975], giving a thumbs-up [Bates et al., 1975]). Later in toddlerhood, however, children also produce representational or iconic gestures (e.g., holding arms out wide to indicate "big"; Acredolo & Goodwyn, 1988; Özçalışkan et al., 2014). Actions that are noncommunicative are not considered gestures. For instance, many actions performed on objects (e.g., grabbing a block, turning pages) are not gestures, because they do not request a response from the interlocutor and hence are not communicative. However, holding up an object for the interlocutor to see is a deictic gesture because it serves the same deictic function (i.e., showing) as many pointing gestures. Because pointing is the most common gesture used by young children, our review highlights the role of pointing in language development while also examining other early gestures.

4.1 Relations Between Gesture and Language Development

In the following sections, we review the research on the links between gesture and language development. We begin by discussing the association between gesture production and vocabulary and then address the association between gesture production and syntactic development. Then we discuss the association between gesture comprehension and vocabulary development. Later in this chapter, we discuss several potential reasons why gesture predicts (or is an indicator of) language development, but first we review the literature on the relations themselves.

4.1.1 Gesture Production and Vocabulary

A growing number of studies have shown associations between children's early use of gesture and their vocabulary acquisition. "Show" and "give" gestures are typically the first to emerge, around 10 months of age and before pointing gestures. In fact, use of show and give gestures at 10 months predicts later use of points at 12 months (Cameron-Faulkner et al., 2015). Furthermore, use of show and give gestures at 10 months predicts expressive vocabulary at 18 months, whereas at 14 months it is pointing gestures (but not show and give gestures) that predict vocabulary at 18 months (Choi et al., in press). In a more nuanced analysis of specific lexical items, Iverson and Goldin-Meadow (2005) found that the objects that infants (10+ months) pointed to or held up to show parents during interactions with their caregivers were likely to be the words that entered their verbal lexicon several months later, indicating that these gestures precede and predict lexical acquisition during the early stages of language learning. *Gesture types* are the different meanings represented by gesture. For example, a pointing gesture to a ball would be given the gloss or meaning BALL, a waving-hello gesture would be given the gloss HELLO, and the total number of different gesture meanings or glosses assigned for each child is the gesture types total. Rowe and Goldin-Meadow (2009a) found that 14-month-olds who produced more unique gesture types (e.g., pointing to objects, waving "bye-bye") during interactions with their caregivers had larger receptive vocabularies as measured by the Peabody Picture Vocabulary Test when they were 54 months-old than the 14-month-olds who produced fewer meanings in gesture, even with early spoken vocabulary controlled. A study that compared typically developing children with children with language delay found that using more pointing gestures in interactions with caregivers at age 12 to 14 months was associated with typical development, whereas using more pointing gestures later—around 21 months—was associated with language delay (Lüke et al., 2017). Early gesture use also predicts vocabulary growth. For example, Brooks and Meltzoff (2008) found that infants who were pointing at 10 to 11 months showed faster growth over time in receptive vocabulary on the MacArthur–Bates Communicative Developmental Inventory. Similarly, children who produced more gesture types at 14 months showed faster growth in productive vocabulary use (word types) between 14 and 46 months, controlling for socioeconomic status (SES) and parent verbal input (Rowe et al., 2012). Furthermore, a 2010 meta-analysis on the topic found a large effect size for the concurrent relation between infant pointing and language and a medium to large effect size for longitudinal relations between pointing and later vocabulary size or vocabulary growth (Colonnesi et al., 2010). Thus, a growing body of evidence indicates that, during the period between 10 and 15 months, the specific objects children gesture about predict the words that will later enter their verbal lexicon, and the amount and diversity of infant gestures during this time predict vocabulary size and growth.

The intention or motivation behind the pointing gesture, specifically, is also differentially associated with vocabulary development. Studies have consistently found that declarative pointing (e.g., when the child uses pointing to share information or to influence the adults' attention), which tends to be more advanced, is positively associated with language skill, whereas imperative pointing (e.g., when the child points at an object because they want the adult to retrieve it for them) does not predict language in any systematic way (e.g., Carpenter et al., 1998; Colonnesi et al., 2010; Desrochers et al., 1995). Declarative pointing has also been found to relate to children's understanding of others' intentions (e.g., Camaioni et al., 2004). It is of interest to note that nonhuman primates do not naturally produce pointing gestures (Tomasello, 2007). Admittedly, in experimental settings, apes raised by humans can be trained to point for human beings (e.g., to indicate the location of a tool so that humans can get them food; Call & Tomasello, 1994), but there is no evidence that apes ever point for each other without previous human intervention (Tomasello, 2007). The hand shape used while producing the gesture also moderates the relation between infant pointing and language. A study conducted with fifty-nine 12-month-olds found that whether or not an infant produced index finger points, rather than full hand or palm points, was actually a better predictor of later language skills than was the intention of the point (e.g., declarative vs. imperative). It is interesting to note that a similar percentage of index finger points versus full hand points were used across the declarative and imperative experimental conditions (Lüke et al., 2017). Thus, hand shape seems to give a unique insight into the sophistication of an infant's pointing ability and their communicative skill.

As children transition from infancy to toddlerhood, their gesture repertoires expand and continue to predict language. For example, by 19 months the number of symbolic gestures children produce positively predicts productive vocabulary at 24 months (Acredolo & Goodwyn, 1988), and children begin to combine gesture and speech together in important ways that predict other features of language development besides vocabulary.

4.1.2 Gesture Production and Syntactic Development

As children become more advanced in their gesture use, but before they can combine two words together in speech, they begin to combine gestures with speech to convey two ideas. For example, a child might point at a cookie while saying the word "mine"—in essence, using a gesture + speech combination to convey the idea "my cookie" (Butcher & Goldin-Meadow, 2000; Capirci et al., 1996; Greenfield & Smith, 1976). It turns out that the age at which children first produce these combinations in gesture + speech reliably predicts the age at which they will begin to produce two-word utterances in speech alone (Goldin-Meadow & Butcher, 2003; Iverson et al., 2008; Iverson & Goldin-Meadow, 2005). Furthermore, research suggests that early gesture use selectively predicts language development in that different uses of gesture are uniquely associated with different language skills. To be specific, Rowe and Goldin-Meadow (2009b) found that, at age 18 months, children's gesture types predicted their receptive vocabulary at 42 months, yet the number of gesture + speech combinations at 18 months did not predict later vocabulary. However, the number of gesture + speech combinations at 18-months did predict the children's productive sentence complexity at 42 months, whereas their 18-month gesture types did not. This specificity of relations between gesture and speech skills continues even into the school-age years; for example, 5-year-olds who use gesture to convey a character's viewpoint when telling a story have greater oral narrative discourse skills later on than 5-year-olds who don't use gesture in this particular way (Demir et al., 2015). Thus, gesture production predicts later language skills in a finely tuned fashion (e.g., Rowe & Goldin-Meadow, 2009b).

In sum, these studies on early gesture production in relation to language suggest that by watching how children communicate through their use of gesture early in development we can gain some insight into their future language abilities as well as their ability to represent and understand others' intentions (as we discuss further in the next section). These are, of course, correlational studies that present average effects, and there are always exceptions, for example, linguistically precocious children who don't gesture much. However, the consistency of the effects across studies lends support to the argument that specific features of gesture production, as noted earlier, can be a good indicator of language ability and a lack thereof a potential sign of language delay. We now turn to the research on gesture comprehension as a predictor of language.

4.1.3 Gesture Comprehension and Vocabulary

The literature on the link between gesture *comprehension* and language development is relatively sparse. In large part this is likely due to the difficulty in measuring preverbal infants' understanding of gestures. However, infants are able to follow others' points by around age 9 months (Carpenter et al. 1998), and there is evidence that infants do indeed understand the communicative intentions behind others' deictic gestures by around the end of their first year. For example, Woodward and Guajardo (2002) found that, after habituating to a scene in which an experimenter pointed to one of two objects, 12-month-old infants looked longer during a test phase in which the experimenter pointed to a new object as compared to when the experimenter pointed to the habituated object in a new location. Nine-month-old infants, however, did not show this discriminating pattern during the test phase, suggesting that the older infants understand the relation between gesture and referent, whereas the younger infants did not. Similarly, Behne and colleagues (2012) found that 12-month-old infants understand that pointing gestures can be used to convey information about a hidden object. Moreover, Aureli et al. (2009) found that older infants (16- to 20-month-olds) respond differentially and appropriately depending on whether an experimenter pointed with an informative intention (to identify the location of a hidden object) or an attention-sharing motive. Thus, infants do seem to understand that gestures—specifically, deictic gestures—can be used to direct attention and to share information. However, studies that have used these measures of gesture understanding have yet to examine whether individual differences in understanding are linked to developing language ability.

Findings in the closely related area of joint attention research can provide insight into how infants' understanding of others' nonverbal communicative behavior, including gestures, may be related to their own language development. Engaging in joint attention involves sharing attention with a partner to a third entity, such as when an infant is attending simultaneously to both a parent and a toy (Seibert et al., 1982; Tomasello & Farrar, 1986). Correctly responding to a parent's or experimenter's bids for joint attention is often interpreted as indicating that a child understands the communicative intention behind said bid. A common measure of an infant's ability to respond to joint attention typically includes correctly following a pointing gesture to a target referent, often in addition to correctly following a gaze shift (Mundy et al., 2003). Research has found links between responding to joint attention (RJA) and developing language skills. A study conducted with 14- to 17-month-olds (Mundy & Gomes, 1998) found that, above and beyond the effects of initial receptive language and general cognitive ability, RJA was a significant predictor of receptive language skill measured 16 months later. Markus et al. (2000) found evidence that RJA at 12 months predicted expressive vocabulary at both 18 and 21 months, again above and beyond the effect of concurrent language skills and general cognitive development. Morales, Mundy, and colleagues have even found evidence that RJA measured at 6 months predicted both receptive and expressive language skills as far out as 30 months (Morales et al., 2000, 1998).

It is important to note that infants' production of gestures is related to their understanding of gestures (e.g., Salo et al., 2018; Woodward & Guajardo, 2002); therefore, more research is needed to tease apart whether infants' understanding of gestures might contribute to their developing language skills above and beyond their own production of gestures. We, along with others, have argued that this link between early gesture understanding and later language ability may reflect a common shared underlying mechanism, namely, the ability to understand the goals and intentions behind others' actions (Capirci et al., 2005; Charman et al., 2000; Salo et al., 2018; Woodward, 2004), be they instrumental or communicative goals.

4.2 Why Do Children Vary So Much in Their Early Gesture Use?

The above-mentioned relations between gesture and speech are grounded in the fact that there is considerable variation across children in gesture use and language abilities at any given age. For instance, in a sample of forty-eight 10-month-olds from families of diverse SES backgrounds, we found notable individual differences in their production of gesture tokens (sheer number of gestures) and types (number of different gestures) as well as vocabulary knowledge. In a 15-minute interaction during which parent–child dyads read books and played with toys, children produced, on average, 3 gestures, but there was a range from 0 to 24, and they produced 2.13 gesture types, on average, with a range from 0 to 12. Given that early variability in gesture use predicts later language, this might lead one to wonder where the early variability in gesture use comes from. One answer is their caregivers. Evidence suggests that children are socialized to gesture more or less on the basis of how often their parents gesture with them. For example, Rowe and Goldin-Meadow (2009a) found socioeconomic differences in children's use of gesture at 14 months, with children from higher SES backgrounds gesturing more, and about more objects, than children from lower SES backgrounds. Rowe and Goldin-Meadow also showed, however, that the children from higher SES homes were gesturing more not because they were born to gesture more but because their parents were gesturing more with them. In other words, the relation between SES and child gesture use was mediated, or explained, by parent gesture use. Thus, children who are exposed to more gestures during interactions tend to use more gestures themselves. Furthermore, cross-cultural studies have found average differences in how much parents gesture across cultures, but they also have found consistent associations between parent and child gesture use within cultures (e.g., Salomo & Liszkowski, 2013). Therefore, one primary reason why children might vary so much in their gesture production early in development is because of variation in their exposure to gesture. This conclusion echoes findings that children who are exposed to a greater amount of, and more diverse, child-directed speech tend to also have stronger oral language skills (e.g., Hoff, 2003; Huttenlocher et al., 2010).

4.3 Are Relations Between Gesture and Language Causal?

Although the studies mentioned above found associations between gesture and language, they do not show that gesturing *causes* language learning. Thus, we turn to the few training or intervention studies that attempted to examine causal effects. In one study, 17-month-old infants were visited in the home by an experimenter weekly for 6 weeks. Half of the infants received instructions to point to objects that the experimenter was labeling during play, whereas the other half heard the same labels for the objects but were not instructed to point. The results showed that the children who were told to point increased more over the 8-week period in the number of different objects they gestured to, and expressed larger vocabularies at follow-up, than the children who were not told to point in the training phase (LeBarton et al., 2015). Thus, telling children to point when they are interacting may lead them to point more in general, which may lead to vocabulary growth. Next, we address the mechanisms further to try and understand why this increase in pointing might promote vocabulary development.

Because of the literature showing that parents who gesture more tend to have children who gesture more, several studies have attempted to increase child gesture and language development by intervening with parents around their own gesture use with children. These studies have had mixed findings. For example, Matthews et al. (2012) trained parents of 9- to 11-month-olds to expose their children to 15 minutes a day of activities when the parent pointed a lot and compared them with a group of parents who received a music training. They found that the parents in the pointing training did point more with their children at the follow-up visits than the parents who received the music training, so the training affected parents' pointing behaviors. The training did not influence children's ability to point declaratively in a task with an experimenter, yet child pointing frequency was associated with parent pointing frequency. In a separate study, Rowe and Leech (2019) implemented a pointing intervention with parents of 10-month-olds. The intervention incorporated a growth mindset component by encouraging parents to point with their children because it will make a big difference in their children's pointing and vocabulary development. The families were given toys and told to play for 15 minutes a day and point a lot during the interaction. Compared with parents in the control group, parents in the training group in this study pointed more at follow-up 2 months later (child age 12 months), yet the results faded after child age 14 months. It is important to note that there was also a main effect of the intervention on children's pointing at 12 months during the follow-up interaction with their parents. Furthermore, the effect of the intervention was stronger for parents who endorsed fixed mindsets at baseline and had an added benefit of increased vocabulary growth from 10 to 18 months for children of parents who endorsed fixed mindsets. Thus, there is some evidence that training parents to point more may result in increases in child pointing and vocabulary development, at least in some families.

There is also evidence that training parents to gesture more may enhance how children perceive gestures they see other people produce (Salo et al., 2021). In a study with 10- to 12-month-olds that used the same pointing gesture intervention as that in Rowe and Leech's (2019) study, Salo et al. (2021) found that increases in parents' pointing production were related to infants' perception of pointing gestures produced by experimenters in the laboratory. Using electroencephalography, infants' perception of pointing was measured in terms of changes in μ rhythm activity. The electroencephalography μ rhythm reflects fluctuation of the sensorimotor cortex during both observation and execution of actions. It has been shown to effectively measure sensorimotor activity across the lifespan (Cuevas et al., 2014; Fox et al., 2016), and has been found to reflect neural processes related to understanding the goal structure of observed actions (Filippi et al., 2016; Southgate et al., 2010, 2009).

In finding a relation between increased parent pointing with their child and increased μ rhythm activity during observation of pointing after the training, Salo et al.'s (2021) results suggest that exposure to pointing gestures influences an infant's ability to understand the communicative goal behind those pointing gestures. This may support infants' subsequent ability to learn from the communicative context in which a gesture is produced. In line with this, Salo et al.'s results also show that increases in μ rhythm activity after training were, in turn, related to increases in infants' receptive vocabulary.

Taken together, these training studies provide evidence that increasing infants' exposure to and experience with gestures may be causally linked with their vocabulary development. Furthermore, one specific mechanism for this link, suggested by Salo et al.'s (2021) findings, may be an increased ability to represent the communicative goal of the pointing gesture. However, more experimental work is needed to determine whether these relations are stable and replicable.

4.4 Potential Mechanisms for Why Gesture Predicts Language

We have thus far discussed the literature on the extent and nature of relations between children's early gesture use—in particular, pointing—and later language development, but the question of *why* children's production of and exposure to gestures predict their later language skills still remains. There are several different, but non–mutually exclusive, explanations to this important question. First, children's use of gestures may merely reflect their existing language and cognitive skills that pave the way for future language acquisition. Second, children's gestures often elicit contingent input from caregivers that supports language development (e.g., Goldin-Meadow, 2007; Goldin-Meadow & Alibali, 2013). Third, children are particularly effective at encoding information that they proactively seek through gesturing (e.g., Harris, 2019). Finally, children's exposure to caregiver gestures may not only promote their own gesture production but also directly contribute to their language acquisition by facilitating their comprehension of adult input (e.g., Goldin-Meadow & Alibali, 2013; Özçalışkan & Dimitrova, 2013). In the remainder of the chapter we provide some evidence for each of these potential mechanisms.

4.4.1 Gesture Reflects Existing Skills

To begin, children's early use of gestures may simply reflect their existing language and cognitive abilities, which lay the foundation for language acquisition. Cartmill et al. (2014), for example, found that the age at which children started combining a point and a noun (e.g., point at bottle + "bottle" = that bottle) predicted the age at which they started producing determiner + noun phrases (e.g., a wagon). The authors suggested that young children's ability to produce point + noun combinations reflects their emerging understanding that nouns are modifiable speech units and that one could refer to a particular member of a conceptual category (*that* bottle out of all bottles). This nascent understanding precedes, and may contribute to, children's ability to produce determiner phrases in speech. In addition, children's use of gestures may also reflect advances in their social cognition. Demir et al. (2015) found that, in narrative production tasks, 5-year-olds who produced more iconic gestures to express a character's first-person viewpoints tended to produce better structured narratives at later ages. Demir and colleagues argued that children's use of character-viewpoint gestures demonstrates their ability to take the character's perspective, a skill crucial to narrative processing and production. Children who have stronger perspective-taking skills were therefore better at producing narratives at later ages. Furthermore, as we mentioned earlier, infants' gesturing and their developing language ability, in addition to other higher order social cognitive skills (e.g., theory of mind), may build from a shared underlying ability to recognize the goals and intentions behind others' actions (Capirci et al., 2005; Charman et al., 2000; Salo et al., 2018; Woodward, 2004). Children's understanding of shared goals and intentions may then pave the way for their language development (Tomasello et al., 2005, 2007).

4.4.2 Gesture Elicits Helpful Input From Caregivers

Many studies have shown that children can use gestures to indicate their communicative intentions and attentional foci to interlocutors (e.g., Golinkoff, 1986; Liszkowski et al., 2004; Tomasello et al., 2007). Parents habitually use multiple cues to infer infants' and toddlers' interests and intents, including but not limited to children's gestures, vocalizations, and eye gaze. However, gestures, especially points, clearly target specific referents and are thus easier to interpret (Goldin-Meadow et al., 2007). Caregivers are sensitive to children's gestures and often respond with contingent information, including labels that describe objects and events children are attending to (Bruner, 1983; Ger et al., 2018; Kishimoto et al., 2007; Marcos, 1991; Olson & Masur, 2011). Goldin-Meadow and colleagues (2007), for example, found that parents routinely translated infants' pointing gestures into corresponding object labels. If a child pointed to a dog, the parent would respond, "Yes, that's a dog." Similarly, Olson and Masur (2011) found that parents spontaneously labeled objects and actions that 1-year-olds gesture toward (e.g., bear, bubbles, dance, spin). Parents also respond with internal state labels such as "like," "want," and "think" (e.g., "You like bubbles"; Olson & Masur, 2011). Moreover, Wu and Gros-Louis (2015) found that parents were more likely to provide labels in response to 1-year-olds' points than to their vocalizations, suggesting that children's early gestures are particularly effective in signaling children's attentional foci and eliciting contingent responses from parents. Parents' labeling of objects and events following children's attention foci then helps children reduce mapping errors and supports their acquisition of novel words (Olson & Masur, 2015; Tomasello & Farrar, 1986; Tomasello & Todd, 1983).

In addition to indicating their communicative intents and attentional foci, children use gestures to convey meanings that they are not yet able to express with spoken language, for example, pointing to a llama when the lexical item "llama" is not in the child's vocabulary (Goodwyn et al., 2000). Objects children refer to usually appear in their deictic gestures, including pointing and showing (e.g., holding up a LEGO® to show parents), before the corresponding labels enter children's spoken lexicon (Goldin-Meadow et al., 2007; Iverson & Goldin-Meadow, 2005). For many phrasal and syntactic constructions, gesture + speech combinations tend to precede the corresponding spoken structures (Goldin-Meadow & Butcher, 2003; Goldin-Meadow & Morford, 1985; Iverson et al., 2008; Iverson & Goldin-Meadow, 2005; Özçalışkan & Goldin-Meadow, 2009). For example, a child might say "eat" and point to a cracker before they are able to produce the two-word structure "eat cracker." On average, children combine gestures and speech to produce argument + argument(s), predicate + argument(s), and predicate + predicate structures several months before they produce such structures in speech alone (Özçalışkan & Goldin-Meadow, 2005). Caregivers, on the other hand, routinely translate messages children convey with gestures or gesture + speech combinations into phrases or sentences and thus model for young children how ideas and structures can be expressed in spoken language. For example, upon seeing a dog chewing on a bone, a child may say "doggy" and gesture "eat" at the same time. In this case, the predicate "eat" is gestured, and the argument (agent) "doggy" is expressed linguistically. The mother may respond "Yeah, the doggy is eating," thus modeling the complete spoken form for the child. Goldin-Meadow and colleagues (2007) found that parents often translated children's gesture + word combinations into utterances. Such translation has been shown to promote children's syntactic development (Dimitrova et al., 2016; Goldin-Meadow et al., 2007); specifically, when parents labeled objects that infants referred to with gestures, those labels were more likely to enter children's spoken lexicon than objects that parents did not translate.

Similarly, parents who more frequently translated children's gesture + speech combinations into utterances had children who started producing two-word utterances earlier. Together, these findings suggest that, in response to children's gestures, parents spontaneously model labels and syntactic structures that children are not yet able to verbalize, which facilitates children's vocabulary and syntactic development.

In sum, children's use of communicative gestures provides a mechanism by which they can elicit contingent and informative responses from caretakers, and such input may then promote children's language development. Although studies substantiating causal mechanisms among children's gestures, caregiver responses, and child language development are lacking, correlational studies have provided indirect evidence that caregivers' responses to children's gestures may at least partially explain the relations between children's early gestures and language development (Masur, 1982; Olson & Masur, 2015). Olson and Masur (2015) found that mothers' use of object labels in response to children's deictic, declarative gestures that indicate objects mediated the association between 1-year-olds' gestures and their concurrent noun vocabulary. Mothers' object labeling responses to infants' declarative gestures predicted children's noun vocabulary at 1;5 (years;months). Mothers' action-labeling responses to infants' requestive gestures (e.g., pointing gestures toward a wind-up toy that the infant cannot operate independently) were predictive of infants' action verb lexicon at 1;5. Moreover, it is noteworthy that maternal responses to children's nongestural communicative acts (e.g., vocalizations and a searching gaze) were not concurrently or predictively related to children's size of vocabulary, indicating that children's communicative gestures play a unique role in eliciting maternal input and facilitating language learning.

4.4.3 Gesture Helps Children Solicit Information That They Prioritize

Some researchers argue that, in addition to optimizing caregiver input, children's use of gestures may promote their language acquisition by directly affecting their cognition. In other words, young children can intentionally seek information through gesturing, and they more readily and effectively process and memorize the solicited information than information they passively receive. Young children produce gestures, especially pointing gestures, not only to share interests and attention but also to proactively elicit information from interlocutors (Begus & Southgate, 2012; Kovács et al., 2014; for reviews, see Harris, 2019, and Ronfard et al., 2018). For example, Begus and Southgate (2012) found that 12-month-olds were more likely to point to objects when interacting with a knowledgeable interlocutor than with a poorly informed interlocutor who had incorrectly named familiar objects before, suggesting they were pointing to seek information from the knowledgeable informant. Kovács and colleagues (2014) found that when infants' points elicited informative, rather than mere sharing, responses from adults, infants were more motivated to point. Taken together, these findings suggest that infants point to seek information they are genuinely interested in and that they expect to gain contingent and informative responses from communicative partners. Because people better memorize information that they are interested in (Kang et al., 2009; Loewenstein, 1994), infants can better encode information they proactively seek with gestures in memory (Begus et al., 2014; Lucca & Wilbourn, 2018). With regard to language learning, gestures, especially points, indicate children's interest in obtaining, and readiness to learn, information related to the referent. Hence, children are better at learning labels provided in the wake of their gestures. Lucca and Wilbourn (2018) found that 18-month-olds better remembered object labels provided immediately in response to their points than those they referred to via other communicative acts, such as vocalization.

4.4.4 Exposure to Gesture Aids Language Comprehension and Promotes Gesture Production

Researchers have also found associations between caregiver gestures and children's vocabulary skills (Acredolo & Goodwyn, 1988; Iverson et al., 1999; Pan et al., 2005). Why does young children's exposure to caregivers' gestures contribute to their language skills? There are three general reasons. First, parent gestures may indirectly affect children's language development through influencing children's own production of gestures (Özçalışkan & Dimitrova, 2013; Rowe & Goldin-Meadow, 2009a). As we discussed, parents who gesture more when interacting with their children have children who produce more gestures and more diverse gestures (Iverson et al., 1999; Namy et al., 2000; Salomo & Liszkowski, 2013). Children's production of gestures then facilitates their language development. Rowe and Goldin-Meadow (2009a) found that parents' use of gestures at 14 months was not directly related to children's vocabulary size, yet parents who produced more gestures had children who used more gestures at 14 months, and children's production of gestures at 14 months predicted their size of vocabulary at 54 months.

Second, parents' use of gestures aids children's comprehension of caregiver input (Goldin-Meadow & Alibali, 2013; Özçalışkan & Dimitrova, 2013). Children can follow adults' pointing gestures and gesture–word combinations early in life (Carpenter et al., 1998; Stanfield et al., 2014). Twelve-month-olds can successfully retrieve hidden objects guided by adults' pointing gestures (Behne et al., 2012). One-word speakers between 14 and 28 months of age can understand adults' gestures that reinforce speech (e.g., an experimenter points at a big stuffed dog and says "dog") as well as those supplementing speech (e.g., an experimenter points at a big stuffed dog and says "big"; Morford & Goldin-Meadow, 1992). Furthermore, parents' object-directed gestures may help children comprehend messages that parents intend to convey, reduce children's mapping errors, and help children more efficiently acquire words (e.g., Cartmill et al., 2014). Similarly, children may be able to better comprehend phrases and sentences accompanied by caregiver gestures and thus more efficiently acquire phrasal and syntactic constructions.

Third and last, parents' use of gestures helps establish parent–child joint attention. Yu and Smith (2013) showed that 1-year-olds paid close attention to their caregivers' hands when playing with novel toys. Moment-to-moment tracking of infants' eye movements demonstrated that parents' holding behaviors, including holding gestures, had an immediate and direct effect on infants' looking. Hence, parents' use of gestures likely leads to joint visual attention and, as discussed, parents' attempts to label objects and events during joint-attention episodes facilitate children's word learning (e.g., Tomasello & Farrar, 1986; Tomasello & Todd, 1983).

It is noteworthy that the mechanisms we have discussed in this section are not mutually exclusive. They are all potentially at work concurrently and may jointly explain the predictive relations between children's production of and exposure to gestures and their language development. For instance, infants who are more adept at using gestures to indicate their intentions and attention foci may elicit more contingent, and a larger variety of, object labels from caregivers. Infants may then effectively acquire these labels provided in the wake of their gestures. Furthermore, infants of parents who gesture frequently may be socialized to gesture more themselves, driving toward language development in one way while simultaneously growing their vocabulary by acquiring information about their world from the gestures their parents are using with them.

4.5 Conclusion

Young children's gesture comprehension and production precede and predict their language development. In this chapter, we summarized the growing body of empirical work that is uncovering more and more details about the specific types of gestures that relate to specific language skills at different points in early development, and we highlighted recent intervention work that shows some evidence of causal effects. Furthermore, we described multiple, non–mutually exclusive explanations for why gesture might be such a good predictor of later language ability, including the theoretical perspective that both gesture comprehension and language rely on a shared understanding of the intentions behind others' actions, as well as more practical explanations, such as the fact that gesture elicits informative responses from adults that may promote learning. There very well may be more reasons why early gesture predicts language development. We encourage more research in this area because continued attention to the gestures infants use and the mechanisms linking gesture with language development can provide critical insights into how children learn language.

References

Acredolo, L., & Goodwyn, S. (1988). Symbolic gesturing in normal infants. *Child Development*, *59*(2), 450–466. https://doi.org/10.2307/1130324

Aureli, T., Perucchini, P., & Genco, M. (2009). Children's understanding of communicative intentions in the middle of the second year of life. *Cognitive Development*, *24*(1), 1–12. https://doi.org/10.1016/j.cogdev.2008.07.003

Bates, E., Camaioni, L., & Volterra, V. (1975). The acquisition of performatives prior to speech. *Merrill-Palmer Quarterly of Behavior and Development*, *21*(3), 205–226.

Begus, K., Gliga, T., & Southgate, V. (2014). Infants learn what they want to learn: Responding to infant pointing leads to superior learning. *PLOS ONE*, *9*(10), e108817. https://doi.org/10.1371/journal.pone.0108817

Begus, K., & Southgate, V. (2012). Infant pointing serves an interrogative function. *Developmental Science*, *15*(5), 611–617. https://doi.org/10.1111/j.1467-7687.2012.01160.x

Behne, T., Liszkowski, U., Carpenter, M., & Tomasello, M. (2012). Twelve-month-olds' comprehension and production of pointing. *British Journal of Developmental Psychology*, *30*(3), 359–375. https://doi.org/10.1111/j.2044-835X.2011.02043.x

Brooks, R., & Meltzoff, A. N. (2008). Infant gaze following and pointing predict accelerated vocabulary growth through two years of age: A longitudinal, growth curve modeling study. *Journal of Child Language*, *35*(1), 207–220. https://doi.org/10.1017/S030500090700829X

Bruner, J. S. (1983). *Child's talk: Learning to use language*. W. W. Norton.

Butcher, C., & Goldin-Meadow, S. (2000). Gesture and the transition from one- to two-word speech: When hand and mouth come together. In D. McNeill (Ed.), *Language and gesture* (pp. 235–258). Cambridge University Press. https://doi.org/10.1017/CBO9780511620850.015

Call, J., & Tomasello, M. (1994). Production and comprehension of referential pointing by orangutans (*Pongo pygmaeus*). *Journal of Comparative Psychology*, *108*(4), 307–317. https://doi.org/10.1037/0735-7036.108.4.307

Camaioni, L., Perucchini, P., Bellagamba, F., & Colonnesi, C. (2004). The role of declarative pointing in developing a theory of mind. *Infancy*, *5*(3), 291–308. https://doi.org/10.1207/s15327078in0503_3

Cameron-Faulkner, T., Theakston, A., Lieven, E., & Tomasello, M. (2015). The relationship between infant holdout and gives, and pointing. *Infancy*, *20*(5), 576–586. https://doi.org/10.1111/infa.12085

Capirci, O., Contaldo, A., Caselli, M. C., & Volterra, V. (2005). From action to language through gesture: A longitudinal perspective. *Gesture*, *5*(1–2), 155–177. https://doi.org/10.1075/gest.5.1.12cap

Capirci, O., Iverson, J. M., Pizzuto, E., & Volterra, V. (1996). Gestures and words during the transition to two-word speech. *Journal of Child Language*, *23*(3), 645–673. https://doi.org/10.1017/S0305000900008989

Carpenter, M., Nagell, K., & Tomasello, M. (1998). Social cognition, joint attention, and communicative competence from 9 to 15 months of age. *Monographs of the Society for Research in Child Development*, *63*(4), i–vi, 1–143. https://doi.org/10.2307/1166214

Cartmill, E. A., Hunsicker, D., & Goldin-Meadow, S. (2014). Pointing and naming are not redundant: Children use gesture to modify nouns before they modify nouns in speech. *Developmental Psychology*, *50*(6), 1660–1666. https://doi.org/10.1037/a0036003

Charman, T., Baron-Cohen, S., Swettenham, J., Baird, G., Cox, A., & Drew, A. (2000). Testing joint attention, imitation, and play as infancy precursors to language and theory of mind. *Cognitive Development*, 15(4), 481–498. https://doi.org/10.1016/S0885-2014(01)00037-5

Choi, B., Wei, R., & Rowe, M. L. (in press). Show, give and point gestures across infancy differentially predict language development. *Developmental Psychology*.

Colonnesi, C., Stams, G. J. J. M., Koster, I., & Noom, M. J. (2010). The relation between pointing and language development: A meta-analysis. *Developmental Review*, 30(4), 352–366. https://doi.org/10.1016/j.dr.2010.10.001

Cuevas, K., Cannon, E. N., Yoo, K., & Fox, N. A. (2014). The infant EEG mu rhythm: Methodological considerations and best practices. *Developmental Review*, 34(1), 26–43. https://doi.org/10.1016/j.dr.2013.12.001

Demir, Ö. E., Levine, S. C., & Goldin-Meadow, S. (2015). A tale of two hands: Children's early gesture use in narrative production predicts later narrative structure in speech. *Journal of Child Language*, 42(3), 662–681. https://doi.org/10.1017/S0305000914000415

Desrochers, S., Morissette, P., & Ricard, M. (1995). Two perspectives on pointing in infancy. In C. Moore & P. J. Dunham (Eds.), *Joint attention: Its origins and role in development* (pp. 85–101). Erlbaum.

Dimitrova, N., Özçalışkan, Ş., & Adamson, L. B. (2016). Parents' translations of child gesture facilitate word learning in children with autism, Down syndrome and typical development. *Journal of Autism and Developmental Disorders*, 46(1), 221–231. https://doi.org/10.1007/s10803-015-2566-7

Filippi, C. A., Cannon, E. N., Fox, N. A., Thorpe, S. G., Ferrari, P. F., & Woodward, A. L. (2016). Motor system activation predicts goal imitation in 7-month-old infants. *Psychological Science*, 27(5), 675–684. https://doi.org/10.1177/0956797616632231

Fox, N. A., Bakermans-Kranenburg, M. J., Yoo, K. H., Bowman, L. C., Cannon, E. N., Vanderwert, R. E., Ferrari, P. F., & van IJzendoorn, M. H. (2016). Assessing human mirror activity with EEG mu rhythm: A meta-analysis. *Psychological Bulletin*, 142(3), 291–313. https://doi.org/10.1037/bul0000031

Ger, E., Altınok, N., Liszkowski, U., & Küntay, A. C. (2018). Development of infant pointing from 10 to 12 months: The role of relevant caregiver responsiveness. *Infancy*, 23(5), 708–729. https://doi.org/10.1111/infa.12239

Goldin-Meadow, S. (2007). Pointing sets the stage for learning language—And creating language. *Child Development*, 78(3), 741–745. https://doi.org/10.1111/j.1467-8624.2007.01029.x

Goldin-Meadow, S., & Alibali, M. W. (2013). Gesture's role in speaking, learning, and creating language. *Annual Review of Psychology*, 64(1), 257–283. https://doi.org/10.1146/annurev-psych-113011-143802

Goldin-Meadow, S., & Butcher, C. (2003). Pointing toward two-word speech in young children. In S. Kita (Ed.), *Pointing: Where language, culture, and cognition meet* (pp. 85–107). Erlbaum.

Goldin-Meadow, S., Goodrich, W., Sauer, E., & Iverson, J. (2007). Young children use their hands to tell their mothers what to say. *Developmental Science*, 10(6), 778–785. https://doi.org/10.1111/j.1467-7687.2007.00636.x

Goldin-Meadow, S., & Morford, M. (1985). Gesture in early child language: Studies of deaf and hearing children. *Merrill–Palmer Quarterly*, 31(2), 145–176.

Golinkoff, R. M. (1986). "I beg your pardon?": The preverbal negotiation of failed messages. *Journal of Child Language*, 13(3), 455–476. https://doi.org/10.1017/S0305000900006826

Goodwyn, S. W., Acredolo, L. P., & Brown, C. A. (2000). Impact of symbolic gesturing on early language development. *Journal of Nonverbal Behavior*, *24*(2), 81–103. https://doi.org/10.1023/A:1006653828895

Greenfield, P., & Smith, J. (1976). *The structure of communication in early language development*. Academic Press.

Harris, P. L. (2019). Infants want input. In V. Grover, P. Uccelli, M. L. Rowe, & E. Lieven (Eds.), *Learning through language: Towards an educationally informed theory of language learning* (pp. 31–39). Cambridge University Press. https://doi.org/10.1017/9781316718537.004

Hoff, E. (2003). The specificity of environmental influence: Socioeconomic status affects early vocabulary development via maternal speech. *Child Development*, *74*(5), 1368–1378. https://doi.org/10.1111/1467-8624.00612

Huttenlocher, J., Waterfall, H., Vasilyeva, M., Vevea, J., & Hedges, L. V. (2010). Sources of variability in children's language growth. *Cognitive Psychology*, *61*, 343–365. https://doi.org/10.1016/j.cogpsych.2010.08.002

Iverson, J. M., Capirci, O., Longobardi, E., & Caselli, M. C. (1999). Gesturing in mother–child interactions. *Cognitive Development*, *14*(1), 57–75. https://doi.org/10.1016/S0885-2014(99)80018-5

Iverson, J. M., Capirci, O., Volterra, V., & Goldin-Meadow, S. (2008). Learning to talk in a gesture-rich world: Early communication in Italian vs. American children. *First Language*, *28*(2), 164–181. https://doi.org/10.1177/0142723707087736

Iverson, J. M., & Goldin-Meadow, S. (2005). Gesture paves the way for language development. *Psychological Science*, *16*(5), 367–371. https://doi.org/10.1111/j.0956-7976.2005.01542.x

Kang, M. J., Hsu, M., Krajbich, I. M., Loewenstein, G., McClure, S. M., Wang, J. T., & Camerer, C. F. (2009). The wick in the candle of learning: Epistemic curiosity activates reward circuitry and enhances memory. *Psychological Science*, *20*(8), 963–973. https://doi.org/10.1111/j.1467-9280.2009.02402.x

Kishimoto, T., Shizawa, Y., Yasuda, J., Hinobayashi, T., & Minami, T. (2007). Do pointing gestures by infants provoke comments from adults? *Infant Behavior and Development*, *30*(4), 562–567. https://doi.org/10.1016/j.infbeh.2007.04.001

Kovács, Á. M., Tauzin, T., Téglás, E., Gergely, G., & Csibra, G. (2014). Pointing as epistemic request: 12-month-olds point to receive new information. *Infancy*, *19*(6), 543–557. https://doi.org/10.1111/infa.12060

LeBarton, E. S., Goldin-Meadow, S., & Raudenbush, S. (2015). Experimentally-induced increases in early gesture lead to increases in spoken vocabulary. *Journal of Cognition and Development*, *16*(2), 199–220. https://doi.org/10.1080/15248372.2013.858041

Liszkowski, U., Carpenter, M., Henning, A., Striano, T., & Tomasello, M. (2004). Twelve-month-olds point to share attention and interest. *Developmental Science*, *7*(3), 297–307. https://doi.org/10.1111/j.1467-7687.2004.00349.x

Loewenstein, G. (1994). The psychology of curiosity: A review and reinterpretation. *Psychological Bulletin*, *116*(1), 75–98. https://doi.org/10.1037/0033-2909.116.1.75

Lucca, K., & Wilbourn, M. P. (2018). Communicating to learn: Infants' pointing gestures result in optimal learning. *Child Development*, *89*(3), 941–960. https://doi.org/10.1111/cdev.12707

Lüke, C., Grimminger, A., Rohlfing, K. J., Liszkowski, U., & Ritterfeld, U. (2017). In infants' hands: Identification of preverbal infants at risk for primary language delay. *Child Development*, *88*(2), 484–492. https://doi.org/10.1111/cdev.12610

Marcos, H. (1991). How adults contribute to the development of early referential communication? *European Journal of Psychology of Education*, *6*(3), 271–282. https://doi.org/10.1007/BF03173150

Markus, J., Mundy, P., Morales, M., Delgado, C. E. F., & Yale, M. (2000). Individual differences in infant skills as predictors of child–caregiver joint attention and language. *Social Development*, *9*(3), 302–315. https://doi.org/10.1111/1467-9507.00127

Masur, E. F. (1982). Mothers' responses to infants' object-related gestures: Influences on lexical development. *Journal of Child Language*, *9*(1), 23–30. https://doi.org/10.1017/S0305000900003585

Matthews, D., Behne, T., Lieven, E., & Tomasello, M. (2012). Origins of the human pointing gesture: A training study. *Developmental Science*, *15*(6), 817–829. https://doi.org/10.1111/j.1467-7687.2012.01181.x

Morales, M., Mundy, P., Delgado, C. E., Yale, M., Neal, A. R., & Schwartz, H. K. (2000). Gaze following, temperament, and language development in 6-month-olds: A replication and extension. *Infant Behavior and Development*, *23*(2), 231–236. https://doi.org/10.1016/S0163-6383(01)00038-8

Morales, M., Mundy, P., & Rojas, J. (1998). Following the direction of gaze and language development in 6-month-olds. *Infant Behavior and Development*, *21*(2), 373–377. https://doi.org/10.1016/S0163-6383(98)90014-5

Morford, M., & Goldin-Meadow, S. (1992). Comprehension and production of gesture in combination with speech in one-word speakers. *Journal of Child Language*, *19*(3), 559–580. https://doi.org/10.1017/S0305000900011569

Mundy, P., Delgado, C., Block, J., Venezia, M., Hogan, A., & Seibert, J. M. (2003). *A manual for the abridged Early Social Communication Scales [ESCS]*. University of Miami, Coral Gables.

Mundy, P., & Gomes, A. (1998). Individual differences in joint attention skill development in the second year. *Infant Behavior and Development*, *21*(3), 469–482. https://doi.org/10.1016/S0163-6383(98)90020-0

Namy, L., Acredolo, L., & Goodwyn, S. (2000). Verbal labels and gestural routines in parental communication with young children. *Journal of Nonverbal Behavior*, *24*(2), 63–79. https://doi.org/10.1023/A:1006601812056

Olson, J., & Masur, E. F. (2011). Infants' gestures influence mothers' provision of object, action and internal state labels. *Journal of Child Language*, *38*(5), 1028–1054. https://doi.org/10.1017/S0305000910000565

Olson, J., & Masur, E. F. (2015). Mothers' labeling responses to infants' gestures predict vocabulary outcomes. *Journal of Child Language*, *42*(6), 1289–1311. https://doi.org/10.1017/S0305000914000828

Özçalışkan, Ş., & Dimitrova, N. (2013). How gesture input provides a helping hand to language development. *Seminars in Speech and Language*, *34*(4), 227–236. https://doi.org/10.1055/s-0033-1353447

Özçalışkan, Ş., Gentner, D., & Goldin-Meadow, S. (2014). Do iconic gestures pave the way for children's early verbs? *Applied Psycholinguistics*, *35*(6), 1143–1162. https://doi.org/10.1017/S0142716412000720

Özçalışkan, S., & Goldin-Meadow, S. (2005). Gesture is at the cutting edge of early language development. *Cognition*, *96*(3), B101–B113. https://doi.org/10.1016/j.cognition.2005.01.001

Özçalışkan, S., & Goldin-Meadow, S. (2009). When gesture–speech combinations do and do not index linguistic change. *Language and Cognitive Processes*, *24*(2), 190–217. https://doi.org/10.1080/01690960801956911

Pan, B. A., Rowe, M. L., Singer, J. D., & Snow, C. E. (2005). Maternal correlates of growth in toddler vocabulary production in low-income families. *Child Development*, *76*(4), 763–782. https://doi.org/10.1111/j.1467-8624.2005.00876.x

Ronfard, S., Bartz, D. T., Cheng, L., Chen, X., & Harris, P. L. (2018). Children's developing ideas about knowledge and its acquisition. *Advances in Child Development and Behavior*, *54*, 123–151. https://doi.org/10.1016/bs.acdb.2017.10.005

Rowe, M. L., & Goldin-Meadow, S. (2009a, February 13). Differences in early gesture explain SES disparities in child vocabulary size at school entry. *Science*, *323*(5916), 951–953. https://doi.org/10.1126/science.1167025

Rowe, M. L., & Goldin-Meadow, S. (2009b). Early gesture *selectively* predicts later language learning. *Developmental Science*, *12*(1), 182–187. https://doi.org/10.1111/j.1467-7687.2008.00764.x

Rowe, M. L., & Leech, K. A. (2019). A parent intervention with a growth mindset approach improves children's early gesture and vocabulary development. *Developmental Science*, *22*(4), e12792. https://doi.org/10.1111/desc.12792

Rowe, M. L., Raudenbush, S. W., & Goldin-Meadow, S. (2012). The pace of vocabulary growth helps predict later vocabulary skill. *Child Development*, *83*(2), 508–525. https://doi.org/10.1111/j.1467-8624.2011.01710.x

Salo, V. C., Debnath, R., Rowe, M. L., & Fox, N. A. (2021). *Mirroring mediates the relation between gesture experience and language development in infancy*. Manuscript submitted for publication.

Salo, V. C., Rowe, M. L., & Reeb-Sutherland, B. (2018). Exploring infant gesture and joint attention as related constructs and as predictors of later language. *Infancy*, *23*(3), 432–452. https://doi.org/10.1111/infa.12229

Salomo, D., & Liszkowski, U. (2013). Sociocultural settings influence the emergence of prelinguistic deictic gestures. *Child Development*, *84*(4), 1296–1307. https://doi.org/10.1111/cdev.12026

Seibert, J. M., Hogan, A. E., & Mundy, P. C. (1982). Assessing interactional competencies: The Early Social-Communication Scales. *Infant Mental Health Journal*, *3*(4), 244–258. https://doi.org/10.1002/1097-0355(198224)3:4<244::AID-IMHJ2280030406>3.0.CO;2-R

Southgate, V., Johnson, M. H., El Karoui, I., & Csibra, G. (2010). Motor system activation reveals infants' on-line prediction of others' goals. *Psychological Science*, *21*(3), 355–359. https://doi.org/10.1177/0956797610362058

Southgate, V., Johnson, M. H., Osborne, T., & Csibra, G. (2009). Predictive motor activation during action observation in human infants. *Biology Letters*, *5*(6), 769–772. https://doi.org/10.1098/rsbl.2009.0474

Stanfield, C., Williamson, R., & Özçalışkan, S. (2014). How early do children understand gesture–speech combinations with iconic gestures? *Journal of Child Language*, *41*(2), 462–471. https://doi.org/10.1017/S0305000913000019

Tomasello, M. (2007). If they're so good at grammar, then why don't they talk? Hints from apes' and humans' use of gestures. *Language Learning and Development*, *3*(2), 133–156. https://doi.org/10.1080/15475440701225451

Tomasello, M., Carpenter, M., Call, J., Behne, T., & Moll, H. (2005). Understanding and sharing intentions: The origins of cultural cognition. *Behavioral and Brain Sciences*, *28*(5), 675–691. https://doi.org/10.1017/S0140525X05000129

Tomasello, M., Carpenter, M., & Liszkowski, U. (2007). A new look at infant pointing. *Child Development*, *78*(3), 705–722. https://doi.org/10.1111/j.1467-8624.2007.01025.x

Tomasello, M., & Farrar, M. J. (1986). Joint attention and early language. *Child Development*, *57*(6), 1454–1463. https://doi.org/10.2307/1130423

Tomasello, M., & Todd, J. (1983). Joint attention and lexical acquisition style. *First Language*, *4*(12), 197–211. https://doi.org/10.1177/014272378300401202

Woodward, A. L. (2004). Infants' use of action knowledge to get a grasp on words. In D. G. Hall & S. R. Waxman (Eds.), *Weaving a lexicon* (pp. 149–172). MIT Press.

Woodward, A. L., & Guajardo, J. J. (2002). Infants' understanding of the point gesture as an object-directed action. *Cognitive Development*, *17*(1), 1061–1084. https://doi.org/10.1016/S0885-2014(02)00074-6

Wu, Z., & Gros-Louis, J. (2015). Caregivers provide more labeling responses to infants' pointing than to infants' object-directed vocalizations. *Journal of Child Language*, *42*(3), 538–561. https://doi.org/10.1017/S0305000914000221

Yu, C., & Smith, L. B. (2013). Joint attention without gaze following: Human infants and their parents coordinate visual attention to objects through eye–hand coordination. *PLOS ONE*, *8*(11), e79659. https://doi.org/10.1371/journal.pone.0079659

Olga Capirci, Maria Cristina Caselli, and Virginia Volterra
5 Interaction Among Modalities and Within Development

In this chapter, we describe the relations among different modalities of expression during the very critical phases of early child development, between 6 and 36 months of age. During these first phases of development, infants engage in several different forms of expression. Along with vocalizations, babbling, and first tentative words, infants produce functional actions in relation to toys and tools that show their understanding of the nature of these objects and how they are used. They also produce other types of motor behaviors that do not involve object manipulation, which acquire a meaning through dyadic child–caregiver interaction.

Meanings (both vocal and gestural) are built on general abilities shared with other cognitive domains and are mediated by common domain-general neural systems (Bates & Dick, 2002; Capirci & Volterra, 2008; Iverson, 2010; Karmiloff-Smith, 2013). The period between the end of the first year and the end of the second year is characterized by a transition from a contextualized to a symbolic, decontextualized use of these communicative behaviors.

We present herein developmental evidence for the continuity from actions to gestures to words in child language acquisition and for the key role of adult scaffolding in interaction. Our main aim is to provide stronger grounding for an embodied, multimodal approach to language that considers not only gesture and speech but also their common origin in motor actions. Much of these developmental data derive from research conducted in our laboratory over the past 40 years (the Language and Communication Across Modalities Laboratory at the Institute of Cognitive Sciences and Technologies of the Italian National Research Council, Rome, Italy).

In the sections that follow, we describe not only complex interrelations between modalities (e.g., between spoken words and gestures) but also their relationship within development. The different modalities that are frequently used together in adulthood follow a specific developmental progression in infancy; specifically, it is possible to trace a continuity between actions, gestures, and words.

In analyzing the path from actions to words it is essential to consider the role of caregivers and social interactions because these people play an essential and active role in modulating the way in which we may choose to convey information and to build a bridge for children into symbolic meaning. Given that human communication is essentially an act in which one connects with others by building a space of shared meanings, to fully capture the complex development of human communication it is essential to turn from considering only the person being studied to also considering the interactions in which they engage.

The chapter is organized in three sections, according to three main topics: (a) the continuity between actions, gestures, and words, taking into consideration the key role of motor development; (b) the interrelation among actions, gestures, and words and its predictability in both comprehension and production; and (c) the role of mother–child interaction—in particular, the mother's use of actions and gestures—in supporting the child's construction of meanings.

It is important to mention that, in the studies we review here, the terminology used for different types of gestures observed in children's development has constantly changed over the years, even within the work of the same author(s), often reflecting parallel changes in methodology and/or theoretical perspectives. We have chosen not to alter the terminology used in the original studies, but we will attempt to use both older and more recent terminology.

5.1 Developmental Continuity Between Actions, Gestures, and Words in Infants and Toddlers

Many studies have provided consistent, convincing evidence showing continuity from actions to gestures and words and supporting the relationship between the emergence of symbols in cognitive and communicative development. Early in development, gestures provide a means for infants and young toddlers to communicate before the development of spoken language. Showing off is one of the first indications the infant gives of intentional communication (Bates et al., 1979, 1975). Young infants repeat behaviors that previously have been successful in gaining adult attention, often provoking laughter in the caregiver. These showing-off behaviors precede the use of objects as a means to obtain adult attention, as evident in the following example, provided by Bates and colleagues (1975) in their first pioneering study description:

> [Carlotta] is in her mother's arms, drinking milk from a glass. When she has finished drinking, she looks around at the adults watching her, and makes a comical noise with her mouth . . . adults laugh and [Carlotta] repeats the activity several times. (p. 216)

The use of objects to gain adult attention marks the entry into use of deictic gestures for requesting, showing, giving, and pointing (Capone & McGregor, 2004; Crais et al., 2004). These behaviors have also been referred to as "performatives" because they are first constructed on the plane of action, using objects rather than propositions.

The following are examples of deictic gestures:

- *Ritualized requests:* Acts inducing specific responses in caregivers or agents to effect a change in the ongoing situation (e.g., children often raise their arms to be picked up).

- *Showing:* Acts that display the presence of an object or event or specific characteristics of an object or event to caregivers (e.g., the child is able to extend their arm toward the adult, holding a toy, and to open the hand to show the toy).
- *Giving:* Acts that imply the transfer of an object from child to caregiver (e.g., a child picks up an object on the other side of the room, crosses the room, and drops it into the caregiver's lap).
- *Pointing:* Acts to direct the caregiver's attention toward a desired object or an interesting event (e.g., a child may point to a cat while looking at the adult).

Deictic gestures constitute cases in which familiar actions—those already present in the child's motor repertoires (e.g., holding a small ball in the palm of the hand and opening the hand)—performed in specific contexts (e.g., in the presence of the caregiver and of a toy box with a round hole), attract the other's attention and induce specific reactions (e.g., the adult may say "Do you want to put the ball into the box?" and/or perform the action for the child). These actions, through repetition (e.g., the child might show again the ball in presence of the box), lead to ontogenetic ritualization (e.g., the entire sequence of actions becomes a shared game with the adult).

Deictic gestures and showing off are often accompanied by vocalizations, which enhance their main scope as attention-grabbers, providing a means of directing caregivers' attention toward things and events present in the environment while also building relevant shared experiences.

Given their origin on the plane of action and the fact that they soon lead to more ritualized gestural behaviors, deictic gestures form a link between motor acts and communication. To understand the origin of this link, however, we need to look at the development of basic motor skills in infants, which precede the emergence of deictic gestures and their frequency. We now discuss some examples.

Acts of showing and giving may be linked to infants' early exploration of objects through different types of grasping, whereas ritualized requests may be traced back to actions performed with the whole body. For example, at approximately age 3 to 4 months, infants begin to repeatedly produce basic forms of voluntary grasping that then undergo major transformations between ages 4 and 13 months. The development of this ability is itself linked to achieving postural control (i.e., independent sitting) and in reaching skills (Oztop et al., 2006). It is interesting to note that infants begin exploring different types of palmar grips and initial changes in voluntary grasping mostly by shifting the object within the palm. The first year of life is thus characterized by significant shifts in the areas of the hand involved in voluntary grasping, involving an ulnar–radial shift and a proximal–distal shift (Connolly & Elliott, 1972). These shifts in palm use are precursors to the emergence of opposable-thumb use in precision grips between ages 9 and 13 months. Around the same time that these palmar shifts are performed (10 months), the palm of the hand also becomes the locus for performative acts of showing and giving, in which the infant opens the hand and shows or gives an object that previously was firmly held in the palm. Palmar grasps are characterized by being stable, but allow only a partial view of the object, which is mainly hidden by the grasping fingers. The infant's motor exploration at this stage is thus characterized by movements such as opening the hand in order to better explore the object's appearance. These acts of opening the hand, performed in presence of a caregiver and often repeated, may become ontogenetically ritualized communicative acts, in which the other is induced to join in an observation of a common object, thereby establishing forms of shared experience (Sparaci & Volterra, 2017).

Acts of pointing are preceded by early index finger extensions without an outstretched arm movement and can be observed during mother–infant interactions at age 2 months (Fogel & Hannan, 1985; Masataka, 2003). Pointing to explore proximal objects by poking is present at 9 months, and pointing with the extended index figure emerges around 11 to 12 months, often accompanied by vocalizations (Bates et al., 1979; Kita, 2003).

Development of deictic gestures may be traced back not only to fine motor hand actions but also to the development of gross motor skills, as in the case of ritualized requests or of showing off. Whole-body actions (e.g., lifting the arms to be picked up), initially induced by specific constants in the surrounding environment (i.e., the adult is usually in a physically higher position with respect to the child), may be constantly repeated up to the point that they become ritualized requests produced to elicit an adult's response. As infants progressively explore the full potential of their moving bodies, these behaviors capture caregivers' attention and are often interpreted as meaningful or as linked to specific contexts (e.g., bringing the palms of the hands together may be interpreted as a form of clapping). These interpretations are manifest in adults' reaction to specific motor acts, which in turn lead infants to repeat behaviors that appear successful or elicit positive reactions (e.g., after receiving reactions such as "Bravo!") by caregivers (see the video clip with this book's supplementary materials online, https://www.apa.org/pubs/books/gesture-in-language). In this way, gross motor acts that do not involve objects may become early representational gestures.

Sequences of acts involving objects lead to other types of representational gestures. Various studies have reported that, at the same age that infants start mastering precision grips (around 12 months), short action sequences with objects begin to emerge. These action sequences are usually related to the object's function, for example, using a spoon to eat (Bates et al., 1979; Caselli, 1990). Soon afterward, these same action sequences may be performed in the absence of objects while maintaining their meaning (e.g., the child places an empty spoon in their mouth as if eating).

To summarize these studies, one can say that motor repertoires and handshapes exploited by infants in grasping precede and prepare for the emergence of representational gestures that are performed with the same handshape, but without the object in hand, and denote a specific referent while remaining relatively stable across different contexts (Sparaci & Volterra, 2017).

These actions, through repetition, lead to *ontogenetic ritualization*, a process of mutual anticipation in which particular social behaviors come to function as intentional communicative signals (Myowa-Yamakoshi, 2018; Tomasello, 2008). Caregivers' attention is attracted to a specific action performed by the child. Caregivers, in turn, provide comments on and attribute meanings to infants' actions scaffolded by objects and/or contexts (which we discuss more extensively in section 5.3). For example, caregivers often readily identify an action produced by the child as a representational gesture, incorporating it into the gesture repertoires they use with their child (e.g., if the child brings an empty hand to the mouth, they may say "Is Baby hungry? Does Baby want cookie?"). These identifications are supported also by the fact that handshapes produced during actions and gestures involving object manipulation often suggest physical characteristics of objects that can be grasped and manipulated (e.g., a hand shaped how it would be if grasping a spoon and brought to the mouth may suggest a spoon's affordance).

The conceptual meaning is suggested by the goal-like structure of the action or gesture (e.g., the gesture is built as a sequence of motor acts that involve shaping the hand and bringing it to the mouth, reminiscent of sequences of actions that characterize the functional act of eating). It is important to stress that, at approximately age 12 months, children are learning to organize simple action schemes, which are differentiated according to specific objects and are within structured functional acts that allow them to reach practical goals (e.g., bringing a comb to the hair for combing). The process we describe here, built largely out of initial explorations of objects, supports the development of object categorization and recognition. Furthermore, the linking of objects to their functions also leads to a more structured understanding of the world that surrounds the infant.

Content-loaded gestures have been classified in some studies as "symbolic play schemes." Other studies have referred to them as "recognitory" (later defined as "representational"), "referential," or "conventional" gestures and included not only those performed while holding objects but also empty-handed gestures (Acredolo & Goodwyn, 1990; Caselli, 1990). Subsequent observational studies have considered actions with objects and empty-handed gestures as separate categories (Capirci et al., 2005). These studies are particularly relevant in that they provide evidence of continuity from what has been considered prelinguistic to linguistic development and they document interesting correspondences between linguistic milestones and nonlinguistic abilities (see Iverson & Goldin-Meadow, 2005, among others). These studies demonstrate that language is not solely a product of domain-specific, dedicated processes but instead a skill that is heavily built on neighboring cognitive domains. Symbolic abilities are manifested not only in language comprehension and production. Bates et al. (1979) found striking parallels between early vocal productions and gestural schemes of symbolic play produced by infants between ages 9 and 13 months from two different cultures and languages. Play-related actions have been traditionally considered beyond the realm of linguistic communication. Bates et al.'s study, as well a subsequent longitudinal single-case study (Caselli, 1990), found that infants initially acquired representational gestures and first words while acting on prototypical objects in the context of highly stereotyped routines. These gestures and words gradually became decontextualized and extended to a wider and more flexible range of objects and events, providing children with the opportunity to practice *naming*, extending meaning initially assigned to an individual referent across a variety of different referents.

Another study conducted by colleagues at our laboratory at the Consiglio Nazionale delle Richerce in Rome explored the interplay between gestures and words in the early vocabulary of 12 Italian children at ages 16 and 20 months (Iverson et al., 1994). The representational gestures produced by children were classified according to their semantic meaning into a set of categories. The study distinguished between predicate and nominal gestures. *Predicate gestures* describe qualities or characteristics of an object or situation (e.g., raising the arms high for TALL or waving the hands for TOO HOT). *Nominal gestures* are those that seem to provide a label for a specific object in one of two ways: (a) by replicating the action performed by an agent with the object referent (e.g., drinking from a cup, combing with a comb) or (b) by copying the movement performed by the object referent itself (e.g., opening and closing the mouth for FISH or flapping the hands for BIRD). Within these nominal and predicate gesture categories, Iverson et al. (1994) included both gestures made with the object referent in the hand as well as those that were empty handed.

Iverson et al.'s (1994) data showed gradual processes of decontextualization that occurred in symbolic development. For example, they observed a decline between ages 16 and 20 months in the use of action-by-agent nominal gestures (now called "action with object") produced while holding the object and a co-occurring increase in the production of form of the referent or "movement-of-object nominal and predicate gestures" (now called "representational gestures"), all of which were empty handed. In a subsequent longitudinal study of three Italian children ages 10 to 23 months, Capirci et al. (2005) confirmed a close link among early action schemes, gestures, and the appearance of first words. Their aim was to determine whether meaningful manual actions precede and pave the way for the development of language and whether they share a semantic link with gestures and words. Capirci et al. considered all the actions and gestures produced in a communicative context, that is, if they were accompanied by eye contact with another person and/or vocalization or other clear evidence of an effort to direct the attention of another person present in the room (Thal & Tobias, 1992).[1] The "gesture" category included the following types:

- gestures iconically related to actions performed by or with the referent (e.g., bringing the empty hand to the lips for SPOON, holding an empty fist to the ear for TELEPHONE);

---

[1] The distinction between actions and gestures was sometimes difficult to determine. Actions and gestures produced in a communicative context are not clearly separate categories; instead, they should be considered a continuum. Even adults can produce gestures with an object in hand for communicative purposes.

- gestures describing qualities or characteristics of an object or situation (e.g., extending the arms for BIG or waving the hands for TOO HOT);
- gestures representing intransitive actions (e.g., moving the body rhythmically without music for DANCING, covering the eyes with one hand for PEEK-A-BOO);
- conventional gestures (e.g., shaking the head for NO) as well as gestures culturally specific to the Italian repertoire (e.g., bringing the index finger to the cheek and rotating it for GOOD).

The "action" category included all communicative and intelligible manual actions associated with specific objects (e.g., bringing a phone or handset to the ear, pushing a little car) and intransitive actions (e.g., dancing with the music, hiding oneself under the table).

Capirci et al. (2005) found that all three children produced meaningful communicative actions from the first session (at age 10 months), which was even before they produced their first representational gestures or words. Almost all the actions produced by the three children had a "meaning correspondence" with representational gestures or words that were produced later, indicating that the emergence of a particular action preceded the production of the gesture or word with the corresponding meaning.

Examples Capirci et al. (2005) found in their sample of the semantic overlap among actions, gestures, and words in which the items in the repertoire conveyed the same meaning were the following:

- action: holding a toy phone to the ear; gesture: holding an empty fist to the ear for TELEPHONE/TO PHONE; word: "Pronto" ("Hello"; see Figures 5.1 and 5.2), and

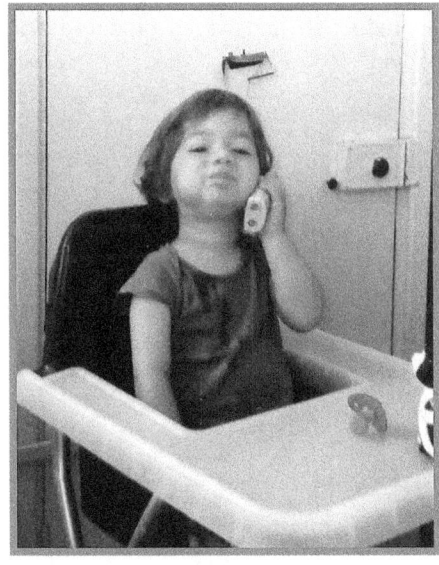

Fig. 5.1: PHONING action.   **Fig. 5.2:** PHONING gesture.

- action: holding a toy bottle to the mouth (see Panel A, Figure 5.3); gesture: holding an empty hand with fingers closed to the mouth; word: "Glu-glu" (see Panel B, Figure 5.3).

The meanings shared through the goal-directed action were almost all later expressed in a symbolic way with gestures and/or words. It is, however, important to note that the meaning expressed by a gesture did not necessarily precede the corresponding meaning expressed by the word, and both forms of expressions could appear at the same or different times.

It is also important here to highlight the fact that almost all actions were produced by the three children in a situation in which the caregiver was present and was making comments and attributing meaning to the action performed by the child. We now review in more detail studies that have considered the ways in which imitation, especially assisted imitation, contributes to communicative development, and how caregiver support can speed up learning and communicative abilities.

To summarize, the consideration of deictic gestures allows us to trace back the origins of gestural forms to early motor actions and both fine and gross motor skills exercised by infant–caregiver dyads in specific contexts. This, in turn, supports the emergence of ontogenetic ritualization and participatory sense-making. Early deictic gestures constitute the basis for the emergence of more complex gestural forms. We have described how they lay the groundwork for the emergence of representational gestures. These gestures allow us to make another step forward in the development of human communication: the emergence of both gestural and vocal symbols.

In this first section of the chapter our focus has been mainly on the continuity from action to gestures and first-spoken productions. Now we look more carefully at the relationship between action/gesture production and words produced and comprehended.

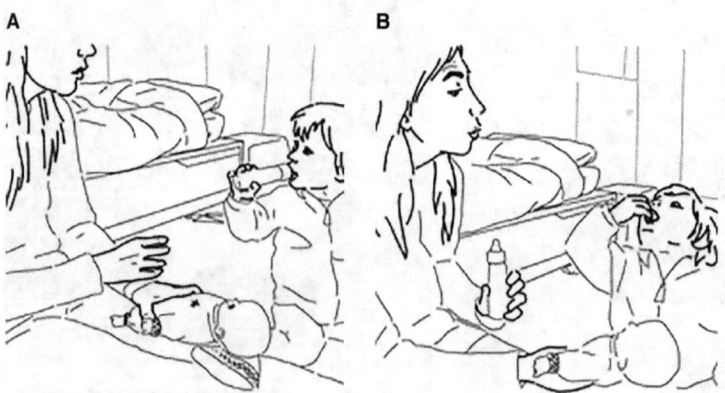

Fig. 5.3: (a) BOTTLE action; (b) BOTTLE gesture.

5.2 Actions, Gestures, and Early Vocabulary: Interrelation and Mutual Predictability

Several of the studies we have described also analyzed the relationships between gestural and spoken modalities, not only in terms of developmental continuity but also in terms of semantic content expressed and the predictive value of nonverbal communicative signals on lexical comprehension and production.

Iverson et al. (1994) observed 12 children at ages 16 and 20 months interacting with their mothers and reported that almost half of the children, at the first observation, produced a larger number of different gestures than different words and that lexical overlap was minimal. Gestural vocabularies tapped the same semantic domains in a complementary way but rarely duplicated their verbal lexicons. At approximately age 20 months, a higher production of words than gestures indicated a shift from gestural to spoken modality.

Capirci et al. (2005) reported similar findings in their longitudinal study of three children observed monthly from ages 10 to 23 months. They found that at around 15 to 17 months there was a basic "equipotentiality" between gestures and words. This could be defined as what Abrahamsen (2000) called a *bimodal period*, in which words are not as distinct from gestures and gestures are not as distinct from words. Both modalities were used productively to communicate something about a specific referent in a decontextualized, symbolic manner. At around age 2 years, a shift was noted from symbolic/representational communication in the gestural modality to symbolic/representational communication in the vocal modality. The authors argued that this transition could not be attributed to a contraction of the infants' gestural repertoire but instead is due to a parallel and comparatively greater expansion of the spoken vocabulary. Despite a larger repertoire of words, however, gestures are still used very frequently at the end of the second year together with or in substitution of words.

In two subsequent studies, Caselli et al. (2012, 2015) used the Italian version of the MacArthur–Bates Communicative Development Inventory (MB-CDI), Words and Gestures (WG) form, to analyze the relationships among action, gesture, and word comprehension and production. Longer and shorter forms of the Italian WG questionnaire were developed and standardized for Italian-speaking children between ages 8 and 24 months (Caselli et al., 2015). The longer complete form of the WG includes 408 words and 63 actions and gestures organized into five sections: (a) First Communicative Gestures, (b) Games and Routines, (c) Actions Performed on and With Objects, (d) Pretending to Be a Parent, and (e) Imitating Other Adult Actions. The WG short form includes 100 words and 18 actions and gestures belonging to these same five categories.

In a cross-sectional study of 495 infants ages 8 to 16 months, Caselli et al. (2012) collected data with the Italian MB-CDI WG complete form. The results showed that, in the period considered, the relationship between actions/gestures and word comprehension was stronger than the relationship between actions/gestures and word production, confirming the results of previous studies of children acquiring languages other than Italian (e.g., Eriksson & Berglund, 1999; Fenson et al., 1994, 2007; Kern, 2007). The production of what Caselli et al. called "actions/gestures" was strongly correlated with word comprehension, probably because the meanings of these gestures are shared with caregivers who often produce the related word before or after the child's gesture production, reinforcing the link between action/gesture and word. The order of appearance of early actions/gestures was also analyzed with consideration of the motor execution of the gestures. The results outlined a developmental pattern for different gesture types and introduced the distinction between actions/gestures with and without object manipulation. This distinction was necessary in order to underline different origins, times of emergence, and further outcomes of these gestures. As we described in the preceding section, gestures not involving objects derive from showing-off behaviors performed very early in dyadic child–caregiver interactions (Reddy, 2003), whereas gestures involving objects derive from object manipulation behaviors. Caselli et al. also analyzed the relationship between age of production of actions/gestures and the comprehension/production of words with related meaning. Although they found no significant difference in the age of appearance between actions/gestures with and without object manipulation, the actions/gestures production and the comprehension of words related to actions/gestures not involving object manipulation appeared approximately 1 month earlier than the actions/gestures production and the comprehension of words related to actions/gestures involving object manipulation. By contrast, the production of words related to actions/gestures with object manipulation (which were primarily nouns for objects) preceded by approximately 2 months the production of words related to actions/gestures without object manipulation, although again, the differences were not significant.

The relationships among actions, gestures, word comprehension, and production were also investigated in a collaborative longitudinal study in which monthly data were collected from infants ages 10 to 17 months, using the Italian MB-CDI WG short form (Sansavini et al., 2010). The authors reported that gestures (e.g., deictics, conventional gestures) significantly correlated with word comprehension at ages 10 and 11 months and with word production at ages 14 and 15 months. This relationship is no longer evident in subsequent months, when these gestures have been completely mastered and verbal abilities increase. Other studies have found that the combinations of gestural and vocal elements become not only strictly related to verbal abilities at the same age but also appear as early predictive indexes of later word production (Capirci et al., 1996; Capobianco et al., 2017; Özçalışkan & Goldin-Meadow, 2009; Pizzuto & Capobianco, 2005; Rowe et al., 2008). Sansavini and colleagues (2010) also reported that, in contrast, actions related to objects (i.e., brief actions associated with specific objects, which they defined in that article as "object-actions") showed tight relationships with word comprehension, but not with word production, during the entire period of observation. The authors suggested that at a later stage, when the expressive vocabulary is larger, the relationship of these object-actions with word production should be more evident. Infants first produce object-actions directed toward a goal linked to daily routines (e.g., eat with a spoon or fork). Later, these actions become coordinated into more complex sequences, involving greater cognitive as well as motor complexity (e.g., put a puppet to bed), and word comprehension increases. Object-actions produced within an interactional context contribute to the coconstruction of meanings. Infants become progressively able to understand words beyond the original contexts in which they first encountered them and to construct symbolic (more decontextualized) lexical meanings.

Caselli et al.'s (2012) and Sansavini et al.'s (2010) results on Italian children are consistent with the findings from previous longitudinal studies of children acquiring languages different from Italian. Among others, Bavin and colleagues (2008), using the complete form of the MB-CDI, showed a positive and strong relationship between production of actions and gestures and comprehension (i.e., contextualized phrases and vocabulary). Until age 16 months, however, only a weak relationship was documented between actions and gestures with word production (Bavin et al., 2008).

A recent article reported data collected by means of both indirect assessment instruments and direct observation (Sparaci et al., 2018). The aim of this study was to provide a longitudinal assessment of the emergence of functional actions in infants at high risk for autism spectrum disorder (high-risk siblings of older children with autism spectrum disorder) and to evaluate whether functional action production may predict later language development in these infants. Children were observed during a semistructured assessment involving spontaneous spoon use in a standardized play-like task. Videos of 41 high-risk infants at 10, 12, 18, and 24 months of age were coded. In line with data from previous studies of typically developing children, the authors reported that actions with objects at age 10 months significantly predicted word comprehension at age 12 months. They also found that actions with objects at age 10 months significantly predicted words produced at ages 24 and 36 months (but not at 12 months). The data indicate that for children of younger ages, words comprehended may be a more appropriate measure, whereas at older ages words produced are also affected. This is understandable given that word comprehension often precedes word production, so effects on production may be captured only later in development, when children produce more words (as was also suggested by Sansavini et al., 2010). These results also seem to support the theory that difficulties in relating to objects may have significant cascading effects in communication and social interaction in high-risk infants at later ages (Bhat et al., 2012; Iverson, 2010). Volterra et al. (2017, 2018) have discussed new data on the transition from actions to language through gestures, providing new strength to and support for the view highlighted by research on the mirror neuron system (Arbib et al., 2018; Rizzolatti & Arbib, 1998). Moreover, we suggest that, through observation and execution of object-actions directed toward a goal within an interactional context with the caregiver, infants start to recognize the functions of objects in their social and physical environment and build a vocabulary of actions and gestures for representing meanings, as we now discuss.

5.3 Actions, Gestures, and Words in Caregiver–Child Interactions

According to Zukow-Goldring (2006; see also Zukow-Goldring & Arbib, 2007) caregivers guide infants through *assisted imitation* to direct their attention to relevant affordances and functionalities that are detectable in aspects of ongoing events. This type of interaction may contribute to a common understanding of events and constitutes a prerequisite for subsequent steps of language development. In a variety of cultures, caregivers, when infants pay attention to objects, "say and do," synchronizing words and gesture in order to demonstrate actions or properties of these objects (Zukow-Goldring, 1997). This type of practice helps infants 8 to 15 months old understand early word–object associations (Gogate et al., 2001; de Villiers Rader & Zukow-Goldring, 2010).

Sansavini et al. (2010) and Caselli et al. (2012), underscoring the importance of word comprehension in establishing shared meanings between infants and caregivers, have supported this perspective and suggested that the model of assisted imitation could be applied also to deictic and conventional gestures that do not involve action manipulation. The form of the actions-without-object, the meaning of conventional gestures, originates mainly through adult tutoring because, through interaction, caregivers invite infants to imitate games and routines (e.g., SLEEPING with a lullaby) whose goal is intrinsically communicative. In contrast, the form of the gesture may derive from schemas already present in the infant's motor repertoire: As these behaviors are associated with words produced by caregivers, new schemas emerge and acquire meaning (see Figure 5.4). (A fuller discussion of this can be found in Capirci et al., 2005.)

Fig. 5.4: SLEEP gesture.

In the case of actions-without-object, the main goal is the interaction with caregivers. (see also Iverson et al. 1999, which we discuss shortly). In the case of actions-with-objects, an external object is incorporated and the partner's attention is attracted to that object (Arbib et al., 2008). Furthermore, the word produced by caregivers interacting with infants helps them create a conceptual meaning for their motor actions (e.g., CLAP HANDS = "Bravo"; the link to the video clip can be found with this book's supplementary materials at https://www.apa.org/pubs/books/gesture-in-language). The results of Caselli et al.'s (2012) study, based on questionnaires for parents (i.e., the Italian MB–CDI; Caselli et al., 2015) support this perspective. The link between action and gesture production and the comprehension of words with related meaning emerges about a month earlier for actions-without-object, with respect to actions-with-object manipulation, as we reported earlier. These hypotheses have also been confirmed in other studies based on direct observations conducted in our laboratory, as well as by other research teams.

Several studies, beginning with Snow and Ferguson (1977), have identified characteristics of maternal communicative behaviors that appear to support infants' communication development. For example, when adults interact with very young children they modify their speech in a consistent fashion, and the types and frequencies of these modifications predict later child language development. More recently, a growing number of studies have considered the presence and the role of actions and gestures produced by the caregiver interacting with infants and toddlers, as well as the relationship between the multimodal input and the language and communication development in children (see Özçalışkan & Dimitrova, 2013, for a review).

Iverson et al. (1999) examined the nature and content of gestures produced by 12 Italian mothers interacting with their children at 16 and 20 months. In that study, Iverson et al. considered only empty-handed gestures, regardless of their origins and typology, that is, deictic, conventional (e.g., BYE-BYE), or representational (e.g., COMB, BLOWING). The results showed that only about 15% of sentences were accompanied by gesture. This is particularly striking in light of the fact that, for children at both ages, the proportion of maternal utterances containing gesture was much lower than that of the utterances of the child itself. The relatively low rate of maternal gesture was not, in other words, a simple reflection of low gesture rates in the children. Most maternal gestures were either deictic or conventional, and most functioned to reinforce the message conveyed in speech. In other words, the mothers' gestures rarely provided information that was not already present in the spoken utterance. In adult–adult interactions a different pattern has been reported: Gesture complements or supplements information conveyed in speech (McNeill, 1992).

One possible explanation for the difference between mother–child communication and adult–adult communication is that the enhanced use of gestures to reinforce or disambiguate, rather than supplement, portions of the verbal utterance reflects an effort on the part of the mother to accommodate the needs of a young listener. Given that young children may have difficulty processing information conveyed uniquely in gesture, mothers may shift the burden of information communication to speech and use gestures primarily to highlight and reinforce aspects of their verbal message.

Overall, Iverson et al.'s (1999) results on maternal gesture production suggest that mothers modify their gestures in consistent and unique ways when talking to their children. Mothers appear to be using a kind of "gestural motherese" that is characterized by fewer and more concrete gestures redundant to and reinforcing of their speech. Mothers' gestures appear to have the function of attracting attention to particular words or objects tightly linked with the immediate context. Iverson et al. reported large individual differences in the amount of gestures and words that mothers produce during interaction with their children but a relative stability over time in respect to the tremendous changes occurring in children's relative use of gesture and speech between ages 16 and 20 months. This has been seen before in the transition to two-word speech (e.g., Iverson et al., 1994) when the spoken language progressively becomes the primary mode of communication, and gesture shifts from a position of relative communicative equivalence with respect to speech to one of a secondary support system integrated with speech, but the changes in children's developing communicative systems are not simply a direct reflection of changes in maternal gestural input.

Mothers who offer plenty of communication (using multimodal expressions) may elicit a richer communication from their children—and vice versa. A similar pattern of gestural motherese was observed for children learning English in the United States. Özçalışkan and Goldin-Meadow (2005), who analyzed maternal gestures at three child age points (14, 18, and 22 months) in spontaneous mother–child interactions, showed that American mothers predominantly used deictic and conventional gestures in their nonverbal communications addressed to their children and very rarely produced more representational gestures. Similarly, British mothers interacting with their 20-month-old children were reported to produce largely deictic gestures, which accounted for 90% of their overall gesture production (O'Neill et al., 2005).

Taken together, these findings point to a gestural motherese somewhat akin to motherese in speech, characterized by higher rates of simpler gesture forms (points and conventional gestures) indicating objects or conveying culturally shared conventionalized meanings as well as the use of simpler gesture–speech combinations, typically conveying the same information across the two modalities. One interesting difference, however, was that, unlike their parents, who mostly used reinforcing combinations, the children used predominantly supplementary combinations, and they increased their use of such combinations with increasing age (Özçalışkan & Dimitrova, 2013).

Another line of studies has considered the importance of sensitive maternal responses, such as those that rely on the infant's requests and interests, for the development of infants' communication skills. These maternal responses have been termed "contingent" when promptly provided and "relevant" when focused on infants' behaviors and attributing meaning to them. Results have shown that both these types of maternal responses are predictive of later language abilities in young children (Baumwell et al., 1997; Goldstein & Schwade, 2008; Gros-Louis et al., 2014; Rollins, 2003; Tamis-LeMonda et al., 2001). In particular, contingent communicative behaviors, such as comments, descriptive expressions, vocal imitations, verbal expansions, and reformulations of infants' vocal utterances, have positive effects on lexical comprehension and production as well as on grammatical development (Rollins, 2003; Tamis-LeMonda et al., 2001). Moreover, when a caregiver produces a word with a meaning that corresponds to the meaning expressed by the infant's vocal and/or gestural production, they offer a highly relevant input for language development. Goldin-Meadow and colleagues (2007) showed that when a mother reformulates the infant's gesture meaning into words, those referents were more likely to get in the infant's spoken vocabulary than nontranslated referents.

In a recent study, Benassi and colleagues (2018) examined maternal responses to infants' spontaneous communicative behaviors in a sample of 20 extremely low-gestational-age (ELGA) infants and 20 full-term (FT) infants during 30 minutes of play interaction, when infants were age 12 months. Among other things, they examined the relationships between maternal relevant responses involving a repeated label and infants' communication skills (verbal and gestural) at 12 and 24 months. The results indicated that these kinds of maternal responses were positively and significantly related to infants' gestures; however, the nature of this relation varied by group: In FT dyads, the relation was observed for conventional and representational gestures, produced frequently and clearly by these infants in daily contexts. Pointing and giving gestures in ELGA dyads, though, were more frequently produced by these infants than the conventional and representational gestures.

Taken as a whole, the literature shows that the use of gestural motherese may be a consistent feature of maternal communication with young children. Moreover, the sensitivity of mothers in adapting their response behaviors to their infants' current developmental level plays a crucial role in promoting language and communication in children. This is in line with a developmental approach that acknowledges the bidirectional nature of parent–infant interaction (Leezenbaum et al., 2014) and the role of the input that infants receive (Sameroff, 2009).

5.4 Conclusion

The developmental research on the relation among actions, gestures, and speech we have described in this chapter appears to be in accordance with the growing interest in the links between motor actions and communication in general. Today, many scholars, from various disciplines, consider human communication to be a multimodal system in which embodied actions play a crucial role (see Arbib et al., 2018, for a recent review).

This view of communication relies heavily on the coordination of infants' object manipulation and caregiver labeling. Moments of joint attention that occur when the labeled object is simultaneously being held by the infant (i.e., the right label at the right time) may provide the optimal sensorimotor input for infants to understand and produce novel labels.

The research results we have discussed in this chapter are consistent with this embodied perspective of early lexical acquisition, suggesting that infants' actions influence their language environment. According to West and Iverson (2017),

> It may be overly simplistic to consider infants' language acquisition as the output of the verbal input they receive; rather, it may be better described as emerging and developing within a feedback loop in which the infant and caregiver are both contributing. (p. 199)

The evidence reported and discussed in Section 5.2 of this chapter also show correlation and predictability, not only between actions and words but also between gestures and early receptive and expressive vocabulary.

Özçalışkan and colleagues (2017) recently tried to answer the question "How does gesture help with vocabulary development?" by proposing two possible, not mutually exclusive, explanations. One explanation is that the infant's gestures signal to the caregiver that the child is ready for taking up the relevant input. As shown in other work, and as we have shown in this chapter, caregivers are highly responsive to and frequently provide words for the majority of referents children convey only through their gestures. A second explanation is that the act of gesturing itself might help children take the next step in language learning, largely by reducing the cognitive load (see also Goldin-Meadow, 2014).

Finally, the research reported herein supports very clearly the theoretical perspective of a continuity between gesture and language. In particular, we have offered empirical developmental data about a gradual transition from action to gesture to words, showing how the process of language acquisition critically depends on engagement in dyadic encounters between infant and caregiver. The relation between the two expressive modalities is considered a dynamic one and is based on the concept of language as inherently multimodal (Müller, 2018). This theoretical perspective stands in contrast to the static and monadic view of language as being either present or not. Language did not come out of nowhere; neither did it arise as some bizarre genetic mutation unrelated to other aspects of human cognition and social life (Tomasello, 1999). Natural language is a symbolically embodied social institution that arose historically from previously existing social–communicative activities. Long before children learn to speak, they are able to communicate meaningfully and intentionally with their caretakers (Volterra et al., 2005).

The semiotic perspective used throughout this chapter reflects a continuing influence of Elizabeth Bates's pioneering conceptualization of language in its biological, developmental, and evolutionary frameworks. We would like to conclude with a quote from her cited in the book published in her honor:

> The emergence of symbols in human children may reflect the resulting interaction of old parts in the creation of a new system. . . . Language can be viewed as a new machine created out of various cognitive and social components that evolved initially in the service of completely different functions. (Bates et al., 1979, cited in Tomasello & Slobin, 2005, p. xxvii)

References

Abrahamsen, A. (2000). Explorations of enhanced gestural input to children in the bimodal period. In K. Emmorey & H. L. Lane (Eds.), *The signs of language revisited: An anthology to honor Ursula Bellugi and Edward Klima* (pp. 357–399). Erlbaum.

Acredolo, L. P., & Goodwyn, S. W. (1990). Sign language among hearing infants: The spontaneous development of symbolic gestures. In V. Volterra & J. Erting (Eds.), *From gesture to language in hearing and deaf children* (pp. 68–78). Springer-Verlag.

Arbib, M. A., Aboitiz, F., Burkart, J. M., Corballis, M., Coudé, G., Hecht, E., Liebal, K., Myowa-Yamakoshi, M., Pustejovsky, J., Putt, S., Rossano, F., Russon, A. E., Schoenemann, P. T., Seifert, U., Semendeferi, K., Sinha, C., Stout, D., Volterra, V., Wacewicz, S., & Wilson, B. (2018). The Comparative Neuroprimatology 2018 (CNP-2018) road map for research on how the brain got language. *Interaction Studies: Social Behaviour and Communication in Biological and Artificial Systems, 19*(1–2), 370–387. https://doi.org/10.1075/is.18013.arb

Arbib, M. A., Liebal, K., & Pika, S. (2008). Primate vocalization, gesture, and the evolution of human language. *Current Anthropology, 49*(6), 1063–1076. https://doi.org/10.1086/593015

Bates, E., Benigni, L., Bretherton, I., Camaioni, L., & Volterra, V. (1979). *The emergence of symbols: Cognition and communication in infancy*. Academic Press.

Bates, E., Camaioni, L., & Volterra, V. (1975). The acquisition of performatives prior to speech. *Merrill–Palmer Quarterly of Behavior and Development, 21*(3), 205–226.

Bates, E., & Dick, F. (2002). Language, gesture, and the developing brain. *Developmental Psychobiology, 40*(3), 293–310. https://doi.org/10.1002/dev.10034

Baumwell, L., Tamis-LeMonda, C. S., & Bornstein, M. H. (1997). Maternal verbal sensitivity and child language comprehension. *Infant Behavior and Development, 20*(2), 247–258. https://doi.org/10.1016/S0163-6383(97)90026-6

Bavin, E. L., Prior, M., Reilly, S., Bretherton, L., Williams, J., Eadie, P., Barrett, Y., & Ukoumunne, O. C. (2008). The Early Language in Victoria Study: Predicting vocabulary at age one and two years from gesture and object use. *Journal of Child Language, 35*(3), 687–701. https://doi.org/10.1017/S0305000908008726

Benassi, E., Guarini, A., Savini, S., Iverson, J. M., Caselli, M. C., Alessandroni, R., Faldella, G., & Sansavini, A. (2018). Maternal responses and development of communication skills in extremely preterm infants. *First Language, 38*(2), 175–197. https://doi.org/10.1177/0142723717736449

Bhat, A. N., Galloway, J. C., & Landa, R. J. (2012). Relation between early motor delay and later communication delay in infants at risk for autism. *Infant Behavior and Development, 35*(4), 838–846. https://doi.org/10.1016/j.infbeh.2012.07.019

Capirci, O., Contaldo, A., Caselli, M. C., & Volterra, V. (2005). From action to language through gesture: A longitudinal perspective. *Gesture, 5*(1–2), 155–177. https://doi.org/10.1075/gest.5.1-2.12cap

Capirci, O., Iverson, J. M., Pizzuto, E., & Volterra, V. (1996). Gestures and words during the transition to two-word speech. *Journal of Child Language*, *23*(3), 645–673. https://doi.org/10.1017/S0305000900008989

Capirci, O., & Volterra, V. (2008). Gesture and speech. The emergence and development of a strong and changing partnership. *Gesture*, *8*(1), 22–44. https://doi.org/10.1075/gest.8.1.04cap

Capobianco, M., Pizzuto, E. A., & Devescovi, A. (2017). Gesture–speech combinations and early verbal abilities: New longitudinal data during the second year of age. *Interaction Studies*, *18*(1), 55–76. https://doi.org/10.1075/is.18.1.03cap

Capone, N. C., & McGregor, K. K. (2004). Gesture development: A review for clinical and research practices. *Journal of Speech, Language, and Hearing Research*, *47*(1), 173–186. https://doi.org/10.1044/1092-4388(2004/015)

Caselli, M. C. (1990). Communicative gestures and first words. In V. Volterra & C. J. Erting (Eds.), *From gesture to language in hearing and deaf children* (pp. 56–67). Springer-Verlag. https://doi.org/10.1007/978-3-642-74859-2_6

Caselli, M. C., Bello, A., Rinaldi, P., Stefanini, S., & Pasqualetti, P. (2015). *Il Primo Vocabolario del Bambino: Gesti, parole e frasi. Valori di riferimento fra 8 e 36 mesi delle forme complete e delle forme brevi del questionario MacArthur–Bates CDI* [The first child's vocabulary: Gestures, words and phrases. Normative data between 8 and 36 months of the complete and short forms of the MacArthur–Bates CDI questionnaire]. FrancoAngeli.

Caselli, M. C., Rinaldi, P., Stefanini, S., & Volterra, V. (2012). Early action and gesture "vocabulary" and its relation with word comprehension and production. *Child Development*, *83*(2), 526–542. https://doi.org/10.1111/j.1467-8624.2011.01727.x

Connolly, K., & Elliott, J. (1972). The evolution and ontogeny of hand function. In N. Blurton-Jones (Ed.), *Ethological studies of child behavior* (pp. 329–381). Cambridge University Press.

Crais, E., Douglas, D. D., & Campbell, C. C. (2004). The intersection of the development of gestures and intentionality. *Journal of Speech, Language, and Hearing Research*, *47*(3), 678–694. https://doi.org/10.1044/1092-4388(2004/052)

de Villiers Rader, N., & Zukow-Goldring, P. (2010). How the hands control attention during early word learning. *Gesture*, *10*(2–3), 202–221. https://doi.org/10.1075/gest.10.2-3.05rad

Eriksson, M., & Berglund, E. (1999). Swedish early communicative development inventories: Words and gestures. *First Language*, *19*(55), 55–90. https://doi.org/10.1177/014272379901905503

Fenson, L., Dale, P. S., Reznick, J. S., Bates, E., Thal, D. J., Pethick, S. J., Tomasello, M., Mervis, C. B., & Stiles, J. (1994). Variability in early communicative development. *Monographs of the Society for Research in Child Development*. Serial No. 242, Vol. 59, No. 5.

Fenson, L., Marchman, V. A., Thal, D. J., Dale, P. S., Reznick, J. S., & Bates, E. (2007). *The MacArthur Communicative Development Inventories: User's guide and technical manual* (2nd ed.). Brookes.

Fogel, A., & Hannan, T. E. (1985). Manual actions of nine- to fifteen-week-old human infants during face-to-face interaction with their mothers. *Child Development*, *56*(5), 1271–1279.

Gogate, L. J., Walker-Andrews, A. S., & Bahrick, L. E. (2001). The intersensory origins of word comprehension: An ecological-dynamic system view. *Developmental Science*, *4*(1), 1–18. https://doi.org/10.1111/1467-7687.00143

Goldin-Meadow, S. (2014). Widening the lens: What the manual modality reveals about language, learning and cognition. *Philosophical Transactions of the Royal Society of London: Series B, Biological Sciences*, *369*(1651), 20130295. https://doi.org/10.1098/rstb.2013.0295

Goldin-Meadow, S., Goodrich, W., Sauer, E., & Iverson, J. (2007). Young children use their hands to tell their mothers what to say. *Developmental Science*, *10*(6), 778–785. https://doi.org/10.1111/j.1467-7687.2007.00636.x

Goldstein, M. H., & Schwade, J. A. (2008). Social feedback to infants' babbling facilitates rapid phonological learning. *Psychological Science*, *19*(5), 515–523. https://doi.org/10.1111/j.1467-9280.2008.02117.x

Gros-Louis, J., West, M. J., & King, A. P. (2014). Maternal responsiveness and the development of directed vocalizing in social interactions. *Infancy*, *19*(4), 385–408. https://doi.org/10.1111/infa.12054

Iverson, J. M. (2010). Developing language in a developing body: The relationship between motor development and language development. *Journal of Child Language*, *37*(2), 229–261. https://doi.org/10.1017/S0305000909990432

Iverson, J. M., Capirci, O., & Caselli, M. C. (1994). From communication to language in two modalities. *Cognitive Development*, *9*(1), 23–43. https://doi.org/10.1016/0885-2014(94)90018-3

Iverson, J. M., Capirci, O., Longobardi, E., & Caselli, M. C. (1999). Gesturing in mother–child interactions. *Cognitive Development*, *14*(1), 57–75. https://doi.org/10.1016/S0885-2014(99)80018-5

Iverson, J. M., & Goldin-Meadow, S. (2005). Gesture paves the way for language development. *Psychological Science*, *16*(5), 367–371. https://doi.org/10.1111/j.0956-7976.2005.01542.x

Karmiloff-Smith, A. (2013). Challenging the use of adult neuropsychological models for explaining neurodevelopmental disorders: Develop*ed* versus develop*ing* brains. *Quarterly Journal of Experimental Psychology: Human Experimental Psychology*, *66*(1), 1–14. https://doi.org/10.1080/17470218.2012.744424

Kern, S. (2007). Lexicon development in French-speaking infants. *First Language*, *27*(3), 227–250. https://doi.org/10.1177/0142723706075789

Kita, S. (Ed.). (2003). *Pointing: Where language, culture, and cognition meet*. Erlbaum. https://doi.org/10.4324/9781410607744

Leezenbaum, N. B., Campbell, S. B., Butler, D., & Iverson, J. M. (2014). Maternal verbal responses to communication of infants at low and heightened risk of autism. *Autism*, *18*(6), 694–703. https://doi.org/10.1177/1362361313491327

Masataka, N. (2003). From index-finger extension to index-finger pointing: Ontogenesis of pointing in preverbal infants. In S. Kita (Ed.), *Pointing: Where language, culture, and cognition meet* (pp. 69–109). Erlbaum.

McNeill, D. (1992). *Hand and mind: What the hands reveal about thought*. University of Chicago Press.

Müller, C. (2018). Gesture and sign: Cataclysmic break or dynamic relations? *Frontiers in Psychology*, *9*, 1651. https://doi.org/10.3389/fpsyg.2018.01651

Myowa-Yamakoshi, M. (2018). The evolutionary roots of human imitation, action understanding and symbols. *Interaction Studies*, *19*(1–2), 183–199. https://doi.org/10.1075/is.17034.myo

O'Neill, M., Bard, K. A., Linnell, M., & Fluck, M. (2005). Maternal gestures with 20-month-old infants in two contexts. *Developmental Science*, *8*(4), 352–359. https://doi.org/10.1111/j.1467-7687.2005.00423.x

Özçalışkan, Ş., Adamson, L. B., Dimitrova, N., & Baumann, S. (2017). Early gesture provides a helping hand to spoken vocabulary development for children with autism, Down syndrome and typical development. *Journal of Cognition and Development*, *18*(3), 325–337. https://doi.org/10.1080/15248372.2017.1329735

Özçalışkan, Ş., & Dimitrova, N. (2013). How gesture input provides a helping hand to language development. *Seminars in Speech and Language*, *34*(4), 227–236. https://doi.org/10.1055/s-0033-1353447

Özçalışkan, S., & Goldin-Meadow, S. (2005). Gesture is at the cutting edge of early language development. *Cognition*, *96*(3), B101–B113. https://doi.org/10.1016/j.cognition.2005.01.001

Özçalışkan, S., & Goldin-Meadow, S. (2009). When gesture–speech combinations do and do not index linguistic change. *Language and Cognitive Processes*, *24*(2), 190–217. https://doi.org/10.1080/01690960801956911

Oztop, E., Arbib, M. A., & Bradley, N. (2006). The development of grasping and the mirror system. In A. M. Arbib (Ed.), *Action to language via the mirror neuron system* (pp. 397–423). Cambridge University Press. https://doi.org/10.1017/CBO9780511541599.013

Pizzuto, E. A., & Capobianco, M. (2005). The link and differences between deixis and symbols in children's early gestural–vocal system. *Gesture*, *5*(1–2), 179–199. https://doi.org/10.1075/gest.5.1.13piz

Reddy, V. (2003). On being the object of attention: Implications for self-other consciousness. *Trends in Cognitive Sciences*, *7*(9), 397–402. https://doi.org/10.1016/S1364-6613(03)00191-8

Rizzolatti, G., & Arbib, M. A. (1998). Language within our grasp. *Trends in Neurosciences*, *21*(5), 188–194. https://doi.org/10.1016/S0166-2236(98)01260-0

Rollins, P. R. (2003). Caregivers' contingent comments to 9-month-old infants: Relationships with later language. *Applied Psycholinguistics*, *24*(2), 221–234. https://doi.org/10.1017/S0142716403000110

Rowe, M. L., Özçalışkan, S., & Goldin-Meadow, S. (2008). Learning words by hand: Gesture's role in predicting vocabulary development. *First Language*, *28*(2), 182–199. https://doi.org/10.1177/0142723707088310

Sameroff, A. (Ed.). (2009). *The transactional model of development: How children and contexts shape each other*. American Psychological Association. https://doi.org/10.1037/11877-000

Sansavini, A., Bello, A., Guarini, A., Savini, S., Stefanini, S., & Caselli, M. C. (2010). Early development of gestures, actions, word comprehension and word production and their relationships in Italian infants: A longitudinal study. *Gesture*, *10*(1), 52–85. https://doi.org/10.1075/gest.10.1.04san

Snow, C. E., & Ferguson, C. A. (1977). *Talking to children*. Cambridge University press.

Sparaci, L., Northrup, J. B., Capirci, O., & Iverson, J. M. (2018). From using tools to using language in infant siblings of children with autism. *Journal of Autism and Developmental Disorders*, *48*(7), 2319–2334. https://doi.org/10.1007/s10803-018-3477-1

Sparaci, L., & Volterra, V. (2017). Hands shaping communication: From gestures to signs. In M. Bertolaso & N. Di Stefano (Eds.), *Studies in applied philosophy, epistemology, and rational ethics: Vol. 38. The hand: Perception, cognition, action* (pp. 29–54). Springer International.

Tamis-LeMonda, C. S., Bornstein, M. H., & Baumwell, L. (2001). Maternal responsiveness and children's achievement of language milestones. *Child Development*, *72*(3), 748–767. https://doi.org/10.1111/1467-8624.00313

Thal, D. J., & Tobias, S. (1992). Communicative gestures in children with delayed onset of oral expressive vocabulary. *Journal of Speech, Language, and Hearing Research*, *35*(6), 1281–1289. https://doi.org/10.1044/jshr.3506.1289

Tomasello, M. (1999). The human adaptation for culture. *Annual Review of Anthropology*, *28*(1), 509–529. https://doi.org/10.1146/annurev.anthro.28.1.509

Tomasello, M. (2008). *The origin of human communication*. MIT Press. https://doi.org/10.7551/mitpress/7551.001.0001

Tomasello, M., & Slobin, D. I. (Eds.). (2005). *Beyond nature–nurture: Essays in honor of Elizabeth Bates*. Erlbaum.

Volterra, V., Capirci, O., Caselli, M. C., Rinaldi, P., & Sparaci, L. (2017). Developmental evidence for continuity from action to gesture to sign/word. *Language, Interaction and Acquisition*, *8*(1), 13–41. https://doi.org/10.1075/lia.8.1.02vol

Volterra, V., Capirci, O., Rinaldi, P., & Sparaci, L. (2018). From action to spoken and signed language through gesture. *Interaction Studies*, *19*(1–2), 216–238. https://doi.org/10.1075/is.17027.vol

Volterra, V., Caselli, M. C., Capirci, O., & Pizzuto, E. (2005). Gesture and the emergence and development of language. In M. Tomasello & D. I. Slobin (Eds.), *Beyond nature–nurture: Essays in honor of Elizabeth Bates* (pp. 3–40). Erlbaum.

West, K. L., & Iverson, J. M. (2017). Language learning is hands-on: Exploring links between infants' object manipulation and verbal input. *Cognitive Development*, *43*, 190–200. https://doi.org/10.1016/j.cogdev.2017.05.004

Zukow-Goldring, P. (1997). A social ecological realist approach to the emergence of the lexicon: Educating attention to amodal invariants in gesture and speech. In C. Dent-Read & P. Zukow-Goldring (Eds.), *Evolving explanations of development: Ecological approaches to organism–environment systems* (pp. 199–250). American Psychological Association. https://doi.org/10.1037/10265-006

Zukow-Goldring, P. (2006). Assisted imitation: Affordances, effectivities, and the mirror system in early language development. In M. A. Arbib (Ed.), *Action to language via the mirror neuron system* (pp. 469–500). Cambridge University Press. https://doi.org/10.1017/CBO9780511541599.015

Zukow-Goldring, P., & Arbib, M. A. (2007). Affordances, effectivities, and assisted imitation: Caregivers and the directing of attention. *Neurocomputing*, *70*(13–15), 2181–2193. https://doi.org/10.1016/j.neucom.2006.02.029

III Gesture With Speech During Language Learning

Eve V. Clark and Barbara F. Kelly
6 Constructing a System of Communication With Gestures and Words

Gestures, along with early words, are critical in children's construction of an early system of communication. From as young as 10 months old, children use locating gestures (usually points), iconic or depicting gestures (with or without props), and conventional gestures like waving or nodding, found in a specific cultural group. In this chapter, we trace the burgeoning field of developmental gesture studies and examine the emergence of gestures as visible utterances, adult responses to children's gestures, and the early use of gesture + word combinations that underpin children's early constructions and ongoing communication. We argue that children use gestures to communicate as a crucial part of language development, for example, pointing to focus attention and to inform and reaching to make requests. Children sometimes accompany early gestures with vocalizations to attract attention and elicit a response. Adults also use gestures to communicate: they gesture to enlist and maintain joint attention in their interactions with infants and young children, and they use gesture and speech together to identify objects as members of categories, to indicate their parts and properties, and to demonstrate motion and function.

In early studies of child language, gestures were not taken into account. Researchers were concerned with how children advanced from single-word utterances to their first two-word combinations, and the order in which they added inflections and other grammatical morphemes (e.g., Brown, 1973). Later studies began to look at lexical semantics and at how this affected the acquisition of increasingly complex syntactic constructions (e.g., E. V. Clark, 1973, 1993; Lieven et al., 1997, 2003). Only a handful of studies looked at children's early uses of gestures and words (e.g., Bates, 1976; Carter, 1979; Caselli, 1983). In the last 2 decades, though, researchers have shifted from an emphasis on the forms of children's grammars and now pay increasing attention to how very young children communicate with the people around them (e.g., E. V. Clark, 2017; Cochet & Vauclair, 2010; Wu & Gros-Louis, 2014). In this chapter, our focus is on how children employ multiple modalities to construct ways of communicating by combining gestures and language.

In Section 6.1, we review the general evidence that adults, as well as young children, use gestures in communicating with language. In Section 6.2, we look at when gestures and words emerge in children, their timing relative to each other, and the content conveyed by gesture and word combinations. In Section 6.3, we look at where children's gestures come from: the patterns of adult gestures used with young children. Then in Section 6.4, we consider how early child gesture and word production contribute to the construction of a system of communication.

6.1 Gestures as Visible Utterances

Gestures play an integral part in how people communicate with one another. Indeed, they have been characterized as *visible utterances* in adult–adult communication (Kendon, 2004). Here we consider gestures as they broadly divide into three major types: (a) *locating* or *deictic gestures* that locate an object or event of interest using hand and gaze, as when someone points and simultaneously looks at a specific eucalyptus tree; (b) *iconic* or *depictive gestures* that may designate objects or actions, as well as demonstrate movements and functions of objects, with or without props, as when someone shows how to tie a bow, say, or flicks the wheel of a toy car to show how it turns; and (c) *conventional gestures*, or emblems, specific to a particular cultural community, such as waving the hand for "goodbye," shaking the head to refuse, touching a finger to the forehead for "crazy," and so on (Calbris, 1990; Efron, 1941). These gestures can be used on their own, where they carry their own meanings in context, or together with speech. Gestures, then, can complement, augment, or sometimes emphasize, the meanings of spoken words. When combined, gesture and speech together function as *composite utterances*.

In communicative development, gestures play a role in both comprehension and production from very early on. Young infants are able to follow another person's gaze and pointing gestures from around 6 months, and begin to produce gestures themselves by 9 to 12 months of age, sometimes combining them with vocalizations. While caregivers and language-learning children use a variety of body parts as they gesture (e.g., hands, head, face, toes, shoulders), much of the research on gesture during early language development has focused on the hands. We, too, focus on the hands and how they are used with words as children construct the beginnings of a system of communication.

Drawing on our own and others' research, we address the following question: What range of meanings can children use their gesture + word combinations to convey? We argue that by combining gestures and words, children extend their communicative options. As a result, any adequate description of the process of language acquisition must consider communicative gestures as well as speech. Children rely on both modes from early on as they begin to construct a system of communication.

6.2 When do Gesture + Word Combinations Emerge in the Child?

Studies by Iverson et al. (1994), Kelly (2001), and Masur (1983) have shown that gestures appear first, before any recognizable words, toward the end of the first year, and typically fall into three main types: pointing, reaching, and showing. Early pointing and reaching, it has been proposed, are protoperformatives, with pointing used to mark early declarations or assertions of interest, and reaching used to mark early requests (e.g., Bates et al., 1975; Bruner, 1975; Werner & Kaplan, 1963).

One of the first researchers to focus on early communication, Elizabeth Bates (1976), showed that in spontaneous everyday interactions, young children *point* to call attention to objects and events, and to do this, they need to coordinate their points with looks to the parent or caregiver. For example, when they first point, they may then swing round with hand still extended for the point, looking toward the adult to check whether the adult is looking at the target of interest, then turning back so they are pointing again at the object they are interested in. Retaining their point on the object while looking round to check whether the adult is looking takes practice. Masur (1983) added to these findings by showing that children first learn how to point and coordinate their pointing and gaze as they monitor the other, before they start to produce any pointing combined with vocalizations or words. In pointing, children generally extend arm and hand with either the index finger or several fingers directed toward the object of interest. Golinkoff (1986) and Marcos (1991) extended this research by showing that young children *reach*, with an extended arm and hand, sometimes accompanied by opening and closing the hand, to make requests. They may also lean toward the object they want, and persist in the request until the adult gets right what it is the preverbal child wants. And children *show* objects to the adult by holding them out in the adult's field of vision (Masur, 1983). All three of these gesture-types emerge between 9 and 12 months, and all three may be produced initially with the occasional vocalization, and then, after a few months, combined with a word (see also Carter, 1979; Cochet & Vauclair, 2010; Iverson & Goldin-Meadow, 2005; Leung & Rheingold, 1981).

Carter (1979) showed in her case study of one child's early communicative schemas that early gestures may be accompanied by candidate protowords: together gesture + word combinations function to achieve specific goals. For example, between the ages of 1;1 and 1;4, David used a number of communicative schemas. To make a request, he would reach toward the object desired while producing an [m]-initial vocalization. To get someone to attend to something, he would point at the target or hold something out, along with a [d]- or [l]-initial vocalization. And to get an adult to attend to him, David would vocalize and say his own name or "Mommy."

David's uses of POINT and REACH were very frequent, and he also drew attention to objects by holding them out or SHOWING them to the other person. Besides these frequent schemas, he also made occasional use of shaking his head for "no" and smiling to mark surprise or recognition, both also accompanied by distinct vocalizations.

Masur's (1983) study noted a consistent shift from gesture + vocalization combinations to gesture + word combinations for all three gesture-types—POINT, REACH, and SHOW—with a gap of 3 to 7 months in each case between use of some vocalization followed by the subsequent production of a word in combination with the gesture. Masur also observed that 93% of pointing gestures were spontaneous, initiated by the child, while reaching and showing were often produced in response to something the adult did or said (38% of reaching and 59% of showing gestures). Children's early words accompanied pointing (29%) more often than they did showing (22%) or reaching (16%). She also observed that points, combined with vocatives like "mommy" or "daddy," appeared in their gesture + word combinations before children's use of any other nominals in such combinations (e.g., POINT + *book*).[1] Lastly, Masur noted that, on average, 36% of the words children produced appeared with more than one type of gesture. In short, children make use of the same word with different aims, marked by gestures that differentiate the meaning of each communication—making assertions about a specific referent or about its location, say, versus requesting that referent from someone else. They are already discovering the flexibility conferred by language on their emerging communication system.

6.2.1 Timing in Gesture + Word Combinations

While earlier studies focused on children's combinations of gesture and word, more recent studies have looked at the relative timing of the two modalities. Early gesture + word combinations may occur in the order of gesture first, then word, or the reverse. The two elements are not initially synchronized (Kelly, 2014; Murillo et al., 2018; see also Gogate et al., 2000). Butcher and Goldin-Meadow (2000), though, argued that although there is not synchronization for the first gesture + vocalization, there is for the first gesture + word combinations. More recently, Kelly (2014) and Murillo et al. (2018) have shown that when children begin to produce composite utterances, the stroke of their gesture is synchronous with the word they produce. Kelly (2014) followed five children in a small daycare center, and tracked their timing for production of three main gesture types—POINT, REACH (or GIMME), and SHOW (or ATTENTION FOCUS), from around 12 months of age on. She defined synchrony as coincidence of timing for gesture-stroke and word-production, and found that children seemed to go through two stages: at first, they displayed no synchrony between gesture and word, and their gesture sometimes preceded and sometimes followed the word; then they began to produce the gesture-stroke simultaneously with the word, as illustrated in Examples 6.1 and 6.2 (Kelly, 2014):

Example 6.1 a. Word, then gesture:
Brailey (12 months): [da]. Then B holds out toy to adult ([da] = that).
b. Word-&-gesture:[2]
Brailey (16 months): [də] as he holds up tissue to adult. ([də] = that). After adult looks at tissue, B drops his arm and moves away.

---

[1] Following Caselli (1990), we use CAPS for gestures and *italics* for words in children's gesture + word combinations.
[2] We use the convention of linking gesture and word with '&' when they are synchronous; when either the gesture or the word comes first, followed by the other element, the word + gesture combination is used.

Example 6.2 a. Gesture, then word:
Caitlin (13 months), points to banana in adult's hand, then she says [aːna].
ADULT: You want some banana?
Caitlin turns to look, then waits for a piece to be cut off for her.
b. Word-&-gesture:
Caitlin (14 months) says *beep* as she holds up broom to adult.
ADULT: aha.
Caitlin pulls the broom back toward herself.

Murillo and her coauthors (2018) also looked at the timing of gestures and words for 10 children, video-recorded every 3 months from the age of 9 to 18 months, as they moved from babbling to producing two-word combinations. They tracked POINT, REACH, SHOW, and any gestures that were iconic, with or without a prop (e.g., fingers raised to the mouth as though eating or empty spoon raised to mouth) or conventional (e.g., wave goodbye, nod head). At 9 months, gestures produced on their own outnumbered gestures combined with a vocalization, babble, or word (72 vs. 33). This dominance of gestures produced on their own continued to hold at 12 months (145 vs. 118) and at 15 months (189 vs. 80), but, by 18 months, the children produced more gestures accompanied by some kind of word or protoword than gestures alone (194 vs. 159). Murillo and her colleagues argued that this integration of gesture and speech at around 18 months is the precursor to synchrony in the production of gestures combined with single words, a synchrony that is well-established before children then move on to produce two-word combinations. Such combinations mark children's reliance on words for more precision in what they are trying to communicate.

6.2.2 Content of Gesture & Word Combinations

Researchers have shown that in constructing a system for communicating, children draw on whatever resources they control. Initially, this includes some gestures (see Capirci et al., Chapter 5, this volume), but not any recognizable words. But once children begin to produce protowords or approximations to some adult words, they supplement their gestures with these words, and the proportion of infant communications that involve some vocalization increases with age (Messinger & Fogel, 1998). This allows them to communicate more information with their still-limited resources. It is also possible that gestures at this stage lighten any cognitive load involved in retrieving and then producing the right word(s) by initially limiting children's planning to just one word per utterance, while doing the rest with gesture—pointing to attract attention, showing in order to focus adult attention, or reaching to make a request. For example, Kelly (2006) observed in one instance,

Lette (age 1;0) near a table where another child was being fed: Lette looks at the caregiver several times and then does a POINT gesture toward a plate of food. While her arm is still in a poststroke holding position, she says [da], possibly to clarify or attract attention to the object she is pointing at. On another occasion 6 months later (at 1;6), Lette produced the word "my" to refer to herself while using a GIMME gesture toward a bib.

Researchers have been interested in both the form and content of children's composite gesture-&-word combinations. What kinds of gestures and words do young children use? And what content do children manage to communicate? Capirci et al. (1996) looked at the spontaneous production of gestures and words from 12 Italian children videotaped at age 1;4 and again at age 1;8, and found a significant increase in the number of gesture-&-word and word + word combinations with age. They distinguished POINT, REACH, and SHOW gestures (all coded as deictic, DG), distinguishing them from referential gestures (RG), gestures that represented some property of a referent object or event (e.g., WAVE = "goodbye," "hi"; FLAP HANDS = "bird," OPEN AND CLOSE MOUTH = "fish"). They also included conventional gestures here, e.g., FINGER TO LIPS = "be quiet," WAVE = "hi, bye," PALMS UP = "all gone," FINGER WAGGED FROM SIDE TO SIDE = "no, don't." And they counted as gestures those where the child had a prop in hand. (Many researchers have excluded gestures with props from their analyses, but such omissions, as Capirci et al. (1996) noted, would lead to a considerable undercount of child gestures at this age, when the child is actually gesturing, albeit with a prop in the hand.) Deictic words (dw) could be locative, demonstrative, or pronominal (E. V. Clark, 1978), but children used very few of these at this stage. Referential words (rw) included any word forms based on adult nouns, verbs, or adjectives, as well as terms like "yes," "no," and "all gone." Unlike much of the research on gesture + word combinations that followed (e.g., Butcher & Goldin-Meadow, 2000; Kelly, 2014; Özçalışkan & Goldin-Meadow, 2009), Capirci et al. (1996) did not record the timing of gesture + word combinations but coded all combinations where the two elements produced by the children were simultaneous, overlapped, or followed each other in immediate succession, as composite utterances, as illustrated in Exhibit 6.1.

Exhibit 6.1: Some Examples of Gesture + Word Combinations

DG–rw	POINT (to flower) + *fiori* "flowers"; SHOW (cup) + *acqua* "water"
	POINT (drawing of pigeon) + *nanna* 'sleep'
DG–dw	POINT (to toy) + *eccoli* "there it is"; POINT (to game) + *te* "you"
RG–rw	BYEBYE (wave) + *ciao* "bye"; BIG (hands apart) + *grande* "big"
RG–dw	YES (nod) + *questo* "this one"

Note. Data from Capirci et al. (1996).

Capirci et al. (1996) also observed that children occasionally combined two gestures, e.g., POINT (drawing of fish) + FISH (open, close mouth), but they found that this was comparatively rare. And they noted that at 1;8 the children they observed had begun to produce some two-word combinations. These children expressed the same kinds of semantic relations in both gesture + word and in word + word combinations, as shown in Table 6.1 (see also Goldin-Meadow & Butcher, 2003; Özçalışkan & Goldin-Meadow, 2005, 2009), but their gesture + word combinations typically preceded their production of word + word combinations for conveying the same information. The relations expressed are those found cross-linguistically in other compilations of children's two-word combinations (see also Bowerman, 1973; Slobin, 1970).

Notice the continuity here: children convey the same semantic relations with their gesture + word combinations that they later convey with two-word combinations. This continuity also strongly suggests that children are building on their gesture + word combinations as they begin to produce their first constructions in spoken language, namely their first two-word combinations. Some of these, of course, are initially formulaic, picked up as chunks or phrases from the adult language (e.g., Arnon, 2015; Lieven et al., 1997), but the fact that most early two-word constructions (a) lack inflections, (b) do not neatly map onto constituents like *noun phrase* or *verb phrase*, and (c) often fail to observe word order rules, is strong evidence that these utterances are in fact early constructions put together from whatever lexical elements children have already extracted, stored in memory, and then learned to produce.

Such early constructions consist of form–meaning pairs in which sequences of forms are paired with conventional meanings, but with open slots to allow for choices in the specific meaning to be conveyed as well as variable size in the construction unit (see Clark & Kelly, 2006; see also Goldberg, 1995, 2006). This view of children's utterances, of course, differs from accounts based on generative grammars. Moreover, when these types of child utterances are inspected more closely, we find that they are typically accompanied by a gesture (Kelly, 2014). In fact, long before children

Tab. 6.1: Semantic Relations Expressed in Gesture + Word and in Word + Word Combinations

Semantic relations	Gesture–word combinations	Word–word combinations
Agent+Action	POINT (to oven) + *scotta* "burns"	*mette mama* "puts mommy"
Action+Object	POINT (to toy) + *toglie* (takes away)	*lo toglie* "takes it away"
Action+Location	POINT (to toy) + *giù* "down"	*vai dentro* "go inside"
Possessor+Object	POINT (to Fa's cup) + *papa*	*mama penna* "mommy pen"
Attribute+Object	POINT (to balloon) + *grande*	*questo grande* "this [one] big"
Notice	HI (wave) + *mama*	*ciao mama* "hi mommy"
Recurrence	REQUEST + *altra* "other"	*ancora altro* "more other"
Absence	ALLGONE + *pappa* "food"	*no acqua* "allgone water"

Note. Data from Capirci et al. (1996).

can distinguish between the syntactic categories "noun" and "verb" (with inflections and co-occurring function words like "the"; see Mintz, 2003), they can distinguish among gestures used to elicit actions (e.g., COME-HERE [beckon], FLAP-ARMS [= fly], HERE-YOU-ARE [holding out]) and words that refer to specific objects. Evidence that they understand such distinctions comes, for example, from child responses to adult pointing gestures and labels when 1-year-olds are introduced to unfamiliar objects that adults then label (e.g., E. V. Clark & Estigarribia, 2011; Estigarribia & Clark, 2007).

In their earliest spoken multiword utterances, children's first constructions are often item-based and built up from particular words, employed in systematic patterns of use (e.g., Tomasello, 1992). Earlier, Braine (1976) identified similar early patterns or constructions in spoken language that he called "pivot schemas," constructed with a relational, often verb-like, term and an open slot typically filled with a nominal, as in utterances like "want book," "want milk," "want it" (see also Bannard & Lieven, 2012). Kelly (2006) showed that, much like in Braine's pivot schemas, young children's speech and gesture combinations form a *relational matrix*, a combination of relational information encoded through gesture and speech. The matrix behaves as an operator that combines information across modalities, for example, as shown in Table 6.2, the pointing gesture always indexes a target referent, regardless of the range of words used with it (e.g., "book," "ball," "that") and so schematizes the information that children convey in their early communications.

As children move from gesture + word combinations to spoken constructions, more evidence for continuity comes from their POINT + nominal (DG + rw) combinations, e.g., POINT + *dog*. These appear to be the direct antecedents to children's first Determiner + Nominal forms in spoken language (e.g., *the/that dog*), as children participate in more extensive conversational exchanges (see Cartmill et al., 2014). Other gestures in children's gesture + word combinations, in particular iconic or depictive gestures representing actions, appear to be antecedents for early verb uses (see Acredolo & Goodwyn, 1988; Goodrich & Hudson Kam, 2009; Özçalışkan et al., 2014; see also Özçalışkan & Goldin-Meadow, 2009, for discussion of when gesture + word combinations do and do not index linguistic change in development). As children construct more complex spoken utterances, we might expect there to be additional

Tab. 6.2: The Relational Matrix Structure Across a POINT Gesture

Gesture		Word	
Handshape	Target	Object label	Caregiver response
POINT	book	book	look, comment
	orange	that	look, offer
	ball	ball	look, pick up

Note. Data from Kelly (2006).

patterns of development from specific gesture-types to particular word-types, but identifying these will require further research.

In summary, in the last few decades, researchers have shown that in constructing an initial system for communication, children build first on making their gestures and words into composite utterances by synchronizing them. This synchronization links gesture and word by exploiting properties of the two modalities: gestural and vocal. They then go on to add to their vocal lexical repertoire and start combining spoken words. And as they begin to produce longer sequences of these spoken words, they steadily expand their communicative resources (see, e.g., Butcher & Goldin-Meadow, 2000; Özçalışkan & Goldin-Meadow, 2009; and, for a review, Goldin-Meadow, 2014).

6.3 Where Do Children's Gestures Come From?

Although there has been considerable research on children's communicative gestures over the last 40 to 50 years, there has been less emphasis on adult gestures in adult–child interaction. But adults gesture as they talk, and in particular, they often gesture when they talk with their children (e.g., Iverson et al., 1999, 2008; Zammit & Schafer, 2011; Zukow-Goldring, 1996). Adults show children how to wave goodbye at a very young age, and also use exaggerated head nods with "yes" and head shakes along with "no." Aside from such conventional gestures, other researchers have also shown that adults make use of a variety of iconic gestures, with and without props, in pretend play; for example, pretending to eat and drink with the appropriate utensils; offering pretend food on a plate or pretend drink in a cup or glass; pretending to telephone with some prop or just a hand held to the ear, and so on, as they help children enact all kinds of daily routines and activities (e.g., Crawley & Sherrod, 1984; Lillard et al., 2011). From very early on, adults track infant gaze and coordinate their own pointing gestures with that infant gaze, following in to whatever the child is already attending to (e.g., Brooks & Meltzoff, 2014). In a study of early adult–child interactions, Escalona (1973) showed that adults offered things with a showing gesture, holding out an object or displaying it on the hand, in reciprocal exchange games with infants from around 9 to 10 months; and they also requested things (back) from the infant or young child by holding out an empty hand, palm up toward the child, as well as reaching toward something and making a verbal request (see also Messinger & Fogel, 1998).

Gestures like pointing and showing make clear, for example, what adults are talking about on any one occasion. These gestures *refer* (see Lyons, 1975; Zukow-Goldring, 2001). One necessary accompaniment of referring, of course, is making sure that both speaker and addressee are attending to the same entity, location, or event. That is, the reference needs to be grounded as part of the ongoing exchange, with both participants in the exchange attending to the same object or event (E. V. Clark, 2015; E. V. Clark & Bernicot, 2008; H. H. Clark, 1996). Adults are careful to attract young children's attention when they interact with them, starting out by pointing to or showing the object of current interest (e.g., Estigarribia & Clark, 2007; Rader & Zukow-Goldring, 2012). And adults also rely on gestures to help maintain attention during an interaction.

As part of their scaffolding of interactions with young children, when adults refer to an unfamiliar object, they make sure that they (adult and child) are both attending to that target object before they offer a new label along with whatever additional information they offer about the pertinent category (see E. V. Clark, 2007, 2010; E. V. Clark & Estigarribia, 2011). Adult offers of labels for new objects are typically accompanied by points or other gestures that demonstrate some property of the target object (E. V. Clark & Estigarribia, 2011; Zammit & Schafer, 2011). And when they introduce verbs for actions, they may accompany them with iconic gestures or demonstrations pertinent to the target action (Goodrich & Hudson Kam, 2009). Indeed, 2-year-old children give evidence of understanding iconic gestures for actions (e.g., an open palm flapping to indicate flying of a bird) before they understand gestures that depict properties (e.g., fingers spread to represent a bird's wing; see Hodges et al., 2018).

Adults also gesture to show the meaning of new prepositions, providing a demonstration of where something is if it is *under* something else, say (McGregor et al., 2009). And they make extensive use of gesture to locate the referents of third-person pronouns when there is more than one possibility visible in context (Goodrich Smith & Hudson Kam, 2012; see also Louwerse & Bangerter, 2005). Adults also tend to synchronize their gestures with the labels they are offering, thus making clear the referential link between label and object-type (see Gogate et al., 2000; Rader & Zukow-Goldring, 2012).

Finally, adults make stable uses of gestures in their interactions with young children. In a study of Italian mothers, Iverson et al. (1999) found a positive relation between adult gesture production and their children's verbal and gestural productions at ages 1;4 and 1;8. Adults used fewer gestures than in adult-to-adult exchanges, but their gestures were directly tied to the content of their spoken utterances (see also E. V. Clark & Estigarribia, 2011; Shatz, 1982). Iverson et al. (2008) found that mothers gestured less often than their children. At both ages 1;4 and 1;8, most mothers' gestures accompanied multiword utterances. Next most frequent were single words produced along with gestures. (Single words with multiple gestures, or multiple utterances with a single gesture, were both rare.) At both age points in Iverson's study, mothers' largest category of gestures, at or near 40%, was deictic (pointing, reaching, or showing), generally identifying the target referent in context; the next largest category was made up of conventional gestures, 30%–35%. Representational (iconic) gestures and emphatic gestures made up only around 5% each of maternal gestures. Finally, over 50% of maternal gestures served to reinforce the verbal content of the accompanying utterance. Gestures modelled *for* children are important for the production of gestures *by* children in their early communications, as are adult responses to children's gestures.

Adults are also more likely to respond to their very young children when the children themselves gesture. Kelly (2014) analyzed uses of gestures, words, and accompanying actions in young children attending a daycare center, and found that when the children produced gesture–word–action utterances (e.g., POINT + *de* + picking up food container), these elicited an adult response 96% of the time. When the children combined two of these options, they elicited responses from adults 79% of the time. But when they produced just one modality, they got an adult response only 38% of the time. Combinations of two options (these were generally synchronized) all elicited a high rate of response, with no significant differences among the various possible combinations of gesture, word, and action. For example, as shown in Table 6.3, (i) Lette's word + action communication, (ii) Caitlin's action + gesture communication, and (iii) Chera's word + gesture communication all elicited verbal responses from the caregiver.

In focusing on when adults respond here, as opposed to how they respond, Kelly (2014) showed that what's primary for the child is to receive a response, even if it is nonverbal. For example, in one instance a child aged 1;1 held a pointing gesture for 13 seconds without uttering a sound and without receiving an adult response. She then lowered her arm and raised it again while retracting her hand and extending her index finger to make a new pointing gesture. When she reiterated the gesture, she used a protoword [ba] after the point was fully established with retracted fingers and a hold. She moved her hand back to rest position only after the adult jointly attended by looking in the direction of the pointing gesture. So the child learns to use a range of modalities to elicit adult responses. Adults are also more likely to respond when 10- to 13-month-old children vocalize as they point, and young children typically vocalize when their caregivers are either not looking or when they don't respond to a pointing gesture alone. That is, even at 12 months or so, children produce vocalizations differentially, depending on whether the adult is attending or not, as they gesture and try to attract adult attention (Wu & Gros-Louis, 2014). This suggests that very young children monitor for attention in another person very early, and are already taking

Tab. 6.3: Two Element Combinations and Responses They Elicited

i. word + action	Lette (aged 1;5) sees a friend's mother and calls "yani" (Lani) in a loud voice while at the same time running toward her.
	ADULT RESPONSE: parent calls out "Hi Chera"
ii. action + gesture	Caitlin (aged 1;1) on hearing a plane, looks at the caregiver and points toward the plane while running in the direction in which the plane is moving.
	ADULT RESPONSE: caregiver says, "Do you see an airplane?"
iii. word + gesture	Chera (aged 1;3) says [baba] while pointing toward pasta in a container on a table and looking at the caregiver.
	ADULT RESPONSE: caregiver says "that's your pasta"

Note. Data from Kelly (2014).

this into account with their earliest uses of gestures (see also Bates, 1976; E. V. Clark, 2017). Children as young as 18 months display an ability to take their social partner's line of sight into account when engaging in joint attention (Franco & Gagliano, 2001). Finally, although Italian children grow up in a culture richer in gestures than American children, and tend to have a richer repertoire of gestures by age 2 or so, children in both cultures start to produce gesture + word combinations before they produce two-word utterances (Iverson et al., 2008). In both cultures, adults gesture to children, and children, in turn, gesture as they interact with adults.

In summary, parental gestures offer models for early child gestures. They also play an important role in attracting, maintaining, and directing young children's attention in adult–child interactions from very early on. Parental gestures also appear to play a role in helping children map words onto objects, actions, and relations during the earlier stages of language acquisition. And when young children use gestures to communicate, they combine them with vocalizations, and later with words, both to attract adult attention and to elicit responses to their calls for attention and to their requests.

6.4 Constructing a System of Communication

Having established that children combine speech and gesture, in this section we show how 1- and 2-year-old children combine these gestural and vocal modes from early on as they start constructing a multimodal system of communication. We propose that children start small in their construction of a system for communication. They begin with single gestures that they use to request (reaching), to assert (pointing), and to get another person to attend to something (showing; Goldin-Meadow et al., 2007). And on occasion, they may also produce some iconic gestures to communicate what they want, for example holding a cupped hand up toward a milk container. They can add vocalizations to their gestures as they draw attention to something or reach for something they want, sometimes with an accompanying whine (see Marcos, 1991; Masur, 1983). These vocalizations become babbles or even protowords that help further clarify and draw attention to their intentions in context. Their protowords are precursors to uses of recognizable words as their speech production improves (Carter, 1979; Murillo et al., 2018). Gestures here are not just manual but also encompass facial expressions and head movements, for example, to express early forms of negation (Beaupoil-Hourdel et al., 2015; Harrison, 2009).

Children also begin to make use of some conventional gestures, such as waving a hand to greet or say goodbye, hands held flat to the cheek with head tilted to indicate sleeping, a finger-wag for scolding. Some languages rely on a large range of conventional gestures or emblems (Calbris, 1990; Kendon, 1995), and children start to use some of them quite early if acquiring French and Italian (e.g., Iverson et al., 2008). Repertoires of conventional gestures are culture-specific in both form and meaning, and can differ considerably from one language to another. Iconic gestures, though, often stem from the actual actions or properties being depicted, and these remain a general communicative resource for adults as well (H. H. Clark, 2016).

After combining gestures with single words in their first composite utterances, children begin to expand their system. They start to combine words into two-word utterances, placing them under a single intonation contour (Fónagy, 1972). Some of these, depending on their intended meaning, continue to be combined with gestures like pointing, reaching, and showing. But as children add to the number of recognizable words they can produce, they become able to make increasing use of spoken lexical resources to convey their intentions. They also combine them in more and more complex constructions as they begin to observe the conventions on word order and inflection in their first language for expressing particular meanings.

Children also learn to differentiate, through caregiver responses, between the information encoded in gestures and the information encoded in words. Caregivers respond to children's gestures and words differently, as Wu and Gros-Louis (2015) showed: They measured parents' verbal responses to infants' object-directed pointing gestures and object-directed vocalizations at age 1;0, and found that when infants pointed, parents provided more verbal responses than when children simply vocalized. In light of different adult responses children begin to distinguish between gesture-based and word-based communication. The relations between them become paradigmatic, and lexical classes ultimately emerge from the multimodal relationship between gestures and words. For example, their differentiation between gestures interpreted as calls for action and spoken nominals or deictic *that* interpreted as object labels has important implications for children's later acquisition of constructions in the spoken language. Does this developmental sequence reflect a causal path from gesture to words? Not in general, it would seem, since gestures initially appear to supply protospeech acts (Bates et al., 1975; Bruner, 1975), with children making requests (with REACH) and declarations, as when they draw attention to something of interest (with POINT), as in their still-earlier protospeech acts. Gestures, then, supply the speech act, and words the content in composite utterances, as in REACH + *ball* as a request, or POINT + *dog* as a declarative.

At the same time, some early gesture + word combinations are replaced over time by small combinations of words, children's early constructions. For example, POINT + Nominal utterances evolve over time into Determiner + Noun phrases used for reference (Cartmill et al., 2014). But gestures intended to mark the location of an object are typically retained, and eventually supplemented with deictic terms like "here" and "that," as well as with pronouns like "I," "you," "he," and "she," rather than being replaced with words alone over time. And while adult speakers can point at things without producing a deictic term, when they do produce a deictic like "this," "that," or "there," it is virtually always accompanied by pointing (Louwerse & Bangerter, 2005). In short, deictic gestures and deictic words are closely linked in adult usage as well.

Gestures of showing or displaying objects are quite common in interaction but do not seem to be as closely associated with particular words or phrases (unlike pointing and deictic terms). While some deictic gestures combined with words do seem to develop into noun phrases, as in POINT + *dog* as a precursor to spoken combination "the dog" (Cartmill et al., 2014). Özçalışkan et al. (2014; Özçalışkan & Goldin-Meadow, 2009) have shown that REACH + word composites seem to be precursors of spoken requests. The early contrast between pointing alone, and reaching alone later becomes marked by use of such contrasting spoken phrases as "I think that—" for asserting, compared to "I'd like—" or "I want—" for requesting. But when young children refer, they rely on pointing along with a deictic term (POINT + *that?* for "what is that?") or with a category label (POINT + *dog*) to identify the object pointed at. As John Lyons (1975) observed, deixis is the source of reference in language. This is borne out in children's early construction of a system for communication.

Gestures can show that children already know the location of an object or event of interest. They can mark this right away with a pointing gesture either before or while they are retrieving a word for the object, actor, or action. Gesture then saves children some effort and time in retrieving one or more words to use in constructing their utterance, whether they are making an assertion, a request, or coming up with an answer to a question. They can readily convey information about location without needing to find a word for a specific location. In short, using gestures as well as words at this stage allows children to focus on retrieving a word for the action, agent, or object that is of interest in a particular location. In fact, children may know something they can indicate with a gesture faster than they can retrieve and execute the pertinent word. This is clear, for example, from the timing in 1- and 2-year-olds' responses to "where" and "which" questions. In answers to both question types, gestures are produced faster than words, and continue to be faster even when the child becomes able to respond with one or two words as well (e.g., E. V. Clark & Lindsey, 2015).

Research on multimodal interactions has shown that gesture offers a critical starting point as young children begin to construct a system for communicating, and then begin to produce different combinations of gestures and words to convey the events they are observing. For example, they see agents carrying out a range of actions (e.g., running, throwing, hopping, eating), with some of those actions being applied to objects (e.g., balls, toys, sticks, spoons), and some applied to people (Kelly, 2006). Combining gestures that attract attention or depict some action with a word for the agent or the object affected allows young children to represent for the adult interlocutor certain properties of the event they are interested in, and about which they are trying to communicate. At this stage of constructing a system for communicating, children rely on the meanings they have mapped both to the gestures they make use of and to the early words they have extracted from the adult speech stream. These gesture + word combinations form the basis of children's nascent multimodal constructions that gradually expand to reflect the kinds of communications common in adult multimodal interactions.

6.5 Conclusion

This view of early gesture and word at play in the first construction of a system for communication arose from our own research. E. V. Clark began with the relation between gesture and deixis (E. V. Clark, 1978), and then, over the years, took up the role of gesture and gaze in establishing joint attention (Estigarribia & Clark, 2007) and in providing supporting information with both indicating and demonstrating (or iconic) gestures about the properties of unfamiliar objects as adults offer young children new labels (e.g., E. V. Clark & Estigarribia, 2011; Zammit & Schafer, 2011; Zukow-Goldring, 2001)—and this in a setting where most studies of language acquisition in the 1970s and 1980s focused on children's discovery of grammar, in particular syntax and syntactic relations, with little or no attention devoted to communication. Kelly (2001, 2014) started out exploring communicative gestures and how children build on those as they start to produce their first linguistic constructions. Both our lines of research have focused on gestures and words, and the relation these bear to what children are trying to convey to their conversational partners.

In summary, it is evident in tracing children's gesture development that, from their earliest multimodal communications on, children draw on gesture + word combinations to convey a broad range of meanings. While gestures of pointing, showing, and reaching are general-purpose elements that can be used in a variety of contexts, iconic gestures are special-purpose gestures, sometimes used only once, with a specific meaning in context. Once children start to combine gestures with words, they add considerably more power to their emerging system of communication. The beginnings of this can be seen first in children's early gesture + word combinations, and then in their expanding combinations of words as they begin to master more complex constructions. What is important to keep in mind is that children continue to use gestures with a communicative function as they get older, and that their later gesture use is continuous with adult usage too.

References

Acredolo, L., & Goodwyn, S. (1988). Symbolic gesturing in normal infants. *Child Development*, *59*(2), 450–466. https://doi.org/10.2307/1130324

Arnon, I. (2015). What can frequency effects tell us about the building blocks and mechanisms of language learning? *Journal of Child Language*, *42*(2), 274–277. https://doi.org/10.1017/S0305000914000610

Bannard, C., & Lieven, E. (2012). Formulaic language in L1 acquisition. *Annual Review of Applied Linguistics*, *32*, 3–16. https://doi.org/10.1017/S0267190512000062

Bates, E. (1976). *Language and context: The acquisition of pragmatics*. Academic Press.

Bates, E., Camaioni, L., & Volterra, V. (1975). The acquisition of performatives prior to speech. *Merrill-Palmer Quarterly*, *21*(3), 205–226. http://www.jstor.org/stable/23084619

Beaupoil-Hourdel, P., Morgenstern, A., & Boutet, D. (2015). A child's multimodal negations from 1 to 4: The interplay between modalities. In P. Larrivée & C. Lee (Eds.), *Negation and polarity: Experimental perspectives* (pp. 95–123). Springer International. https://doi.org/10.1007/978-3-319-17464-8_5

Bowerman, M. (1973). Structural relationships in children's utterances: Syntactic or semantic? In T. E. Moore (Ed.), *Cognitive development and the acquisition of language* (pp. 197–213). Academic Press. https://doi.org/10.1016/B978-0-12-505850-6.50015-3

Braine, M. D. S. (1976). Children's first word combinations. [Serial No. 164]. *Monographs of the Society for Research in Child Development, 41*(1), 1–104. https://doi.org/10.2307/1165959

Brooks, R., & Meltzoff, A. N. (2014). Gaze following: A mechanism for building social connections between infants and adults. In M. E. Mikulincer & P. R. Shaver (Eds.), *Mechanisms of social connection: From brain to group* (pp. 167–183). American Psychological Association. https://doi.org/10.1037/14250-010

Brown, R. W. (1973). *A first language: The early stages*. Harvard University Press. https://doi.org/10.4159/harvard.9780674732469

Bruner, J. S. (1975). The ontogenesis of speech acts. *Journal of Child Language, 2*(1), 1–19. https://doi.org/10.1017/S0305000900000866

Butcher, C., & Goldin-Meadow, S. (2000). Gesture and the transition from one- to two-word speech: When hand and mouth come together. In D. McNeill (Ed.), *Language and gesture* (pp. 235–258). Cambridge University Press. https://doi.org/10.1017/CBO9780511620850.015

Calbris, G. (1990). *The semiotics of French gestures*. Indiana University Press.

Capirci, O., Iverson, J. M., Pizzuto, E., & Volterra, V. (1996). Gestures and words during the transition to two-word speech. *Journal of Child Language, 23*(3), 645–673. https://doi.org/10.1017/S0305000900008989

Capirci, O., & Volterra, V. (2008). Gesture and speech: The emergence and development of a strong and changing partnership. *Gesture, 8*(1), 22–44. https://doi.org/10.1075/gest.8.1.04cap

Carter, A. L. (1979). The disappearance schema: Case study of a second-year communicative behavior. In E. Ochs & B. B. Schieffelin (Eds.), *Developmental pragmatics* (pp. 131–156). Academic Press.

Cartmill, E. A., Hunsicker, D., & Goldin-Meadow, S. (2014). Pointing and naming are not redundant: Children use gesture to modify nouns before they modify nouns in speech. *Developmental Psychology, 50*(6), 1660–1666. https://doi.org/10.1037/a0036003

Caselli, M. C. (1983). Gesti communicativi e primi parole [Communicative gestures and first words]. *Età Evolutiva, 16*, 36–51.

Caselli, M. C. (1990). Communicative gestures and first words. In V. Volterra & C. L. Erting (Eds.), *From gesture to language in hearing and deaf children* (pp. 56–67). Springer. https://doi.org/10.1007/978-3-642-74859-2_6

Clark, E. V. (1973). What's in a word? On the child's acquisition of semantics in his first language. In T. E. Moore (Ed.), *Cognitive development and the acquisition of language* (pp. 65–110). Academic Press. https://doi.org/10.1016/B978-0-12-505850-6.50009-8

Clark, E. V. (1978). From gesture to word: On the natural history of deixis in language acquisition. In J. S. Bruner & A. Garton (Eds.), *Human growth and development: Wolfson College lectures 1976* (pp. 85–120). Oxford University Press.

Clark, E. V. (1993). *The lexicon in acquisition*. Cambridge University Press. https://doi.org/10.1017/CBO9780511554377

Clark, E. V. (2007). Young children's uptake of new words in conversation. *Language in Society, 36*(2), 157–182. https://doi.org/10.1017/S0047404507070091

Clark, E. V. (2010). Adult offer, word-class, and child uptake in early lexical acquisition. *First Language*, *30*(3–4), 250–269. https://doi.org/10.1177/0142723710370537

Clark, E. V. (2015). Common ground. In B. MacWhinney & W. O'Grady (Eds.), *Handbook of language emergence* (pp. 328–353). Wiley-Blackwell.

Clark, E. V. (2017). Becoming social and interactive with language. In F. N. Ketrez, A. C. Küntay, S. Özçalışkan, & A. Özyürek (Eds.), *Social environment and cognition in language development* (pp. 19–34). John Benjamins. https://doi.org/10.1075/tilar.21.02cla

Clark, E. V., & Bernicot, J. (2008). Repetition as ratification: How parents and children place information in common ground. *Journal of Child Language*, *35*(2), 349–371. https://doi.org/10.1017/S0305000907008537

Clark, E. V., & Estigarribia, B. (2011). Using speech and gesture to introduce new objects to young children. *Gesture*, *11*(1), 1–23. https://doi.org/10.1075/gest.11.1.01cla

Clark, E. V., & Kelly, B. F. (2006). Constructions and acquisition. In E. V. Clark & B. F. Kelly (Eds.), *Constructions in acquisition* (pp. 1–15). CSLI.

Clark, E. V., & Lindsey, K. L. (2015). Turn-taking: A case study of early gesture and word use in responses to WHERE and WHICH questions. *Frontiers in Psychology*, *6*, 890. https://doi.org/10.3389/fpsyg.2015.00890

Clark, H. H. (1996). *Using language*. Cambridge University Press. https://doi.org/10.1017/CBO9780511620539

Clark, H. H. (2016). Depicting as a method of communication. *Psychological Review*, *123*(3), 324–347. https://doi.org/10.1037/rev0000026

Cochet, H., & Vauclair, J. (2010). Pointing gestures produced by toddlers from 15 to 30 months: Different functions, hand shapes and laterality patterns. *Infant Behavior and Development*, *33*(4), 431–441. https://doi.org/10.1016/j.infbeh.2010.04.009

Crawley, S. B., & Sherrod, K. B. (1984). Parent–infant play during the first year of life. *Infant Behavior and Development*, *7*(1), 65–75. https://doi.org/10.1016/S0163-6383(84)80023-5

Efron, D. (1941). *Gesture and environment*. King's Crown Press.

Escalona, S. K. (1973). Basic modes of social interaction: Their emergence and patterning during the first two years of life. *Merrill-Palmer Quarterly*, *19*(3), 205–232. https://www.jstor.org/stable/23084035

Estigarribia, B., & Clark, E. V. (2007). Getting and maintaining attention in talk to young children. *Journal of Child Language*, *34*(4), 799–814. https://doi.org/10.1017/S0305000907008161

Fónagy, I. (1972). A propos de la génèse de la phrase enfantine [On the genesis of child utterances]. *Lingua*, *30*, 31–71. https://doi.org/10.1016/0024-3841(72)90042-3

Franco, F., & Gagliano, A. (2001). Toddlers' pointing when joint attention is obstructed. *First Language*, *21*(63), 289–321. https://doi.org/10.1177/014272370102106305

Gogate, L. J., Bahrick, L. E., & Watson, J. D. (2000). A study of multimodal motherese: The role of temporal synchrony between verbal labels and gestures. *Child Development*, *71*(4), 878–894. https://doi.org/10.1111/1467-8624.00197

Goldberg, A. E. (1995). *Constructions: A construction grammar approach to argument structure*. University of Chicago.

Goldberg, A. E. (2006). *Constructions at work: The nature of generalization in language*. Oxford University Press.

Goldin-Meadow, S. (2014). How gesture helps children learn language. In I. Arnon, M. Casillas, C. Kurumada, & B. Estigarribia (Eds.), *Language in interaction: Studies in honor of Eve V. Clark* (pp. 157–172). John Benjamins. https://doi.org/10.1075/tilar.12.13gol

Goldin-Meadow, S., & Butcher, C. (2003). Pointing toward two-word speech in young children. In S. Kita (Ed.), *Pointing: Where language, culture, and cognition meet* (pp. 93–116). Lawrence Erlbaum.

Goldin-Meadow, S., Goodrich, W., Sauer, E., & Iverson, J. (2007). Young children use their hands to tell their mothers what to say. *Developmental Science*, *10*(6), 778–785. https://doi.org/10.1111/j.1467-7687.2007.00636.x

Golinkoff, R. M. (1986). 'I beg your pardon?': The preverbal negotiation of failed messages. *Journal of Child Language*, *13*(3), 455–476. https://doi.org/10.1017/S0305000900006826

Goodrich, W., & Hudson Kam, C. L. (2009). Co-speech gesture as input in verb learning. *Developmental Science*, *12*(1), 81–87. https://doi.org/10.1111/j.1467-7687.2008.00735.x

Goodrich Smith, W., & Hudson Kam, C. L. (2012). Knowing 'who she is' based on 'where she is': The effect of co-speech gesture on pronoun comprehension. *Language and Cognition*, *4*(2), 75–98. https://doi.org/10.1515/langcog-2012-0005

Harrison, S. (2009). The expression of negation through grammar and gestures. In J. Zlatev, M. J. Andrén, M. J. Falck, & C. C. Lundmark (Eds.), *Studies in language and cognition* (pp. 421–435). Cambridge Scholars.

Hodges, L. E., Özçalışkan, Ş., & Williamson, R. (2018). Type of iconicity influences children's comprehension of gesture. *Journal of Experimental Child Psychology*, *166*, 327–339. https://doi.org/10.1016/j.jecp.2017.08.009

Iverson, J. M., Capirci, O., & Caselli, M. C. (1994). From communication to language in two modalities. *Cognitive Development*, *9*(1), 23–43. https://doi.org/10.1016/0885-2014(94)90018-3

Iverson, J. M., Capirci, O., Longobardi, E., & Caselli, M. C. (1999). Gesturing in mother–child interactions. *Cognitive Development*, *14*(1), 57–75. https://doi.org/10.1016/S0885-2014(99)80018-5

Iverson, J. M., Capirci, O., Volterra, V., & Goldin-Meadow, S. (2008). Learning to talk in a gesture-rich world: Early communication in Italian vs. American children. *First Language*, *28*(2), 164–181. https://doi.org/10.1177/0142723707087736

Iverson, J. M., & Goldin-Meadow, S. (2005). Gesture paves the way for language development. *Psychological Science*, *16*(5), 367–371. https://doi.org/10.1111/j.0956-7976.2005.01542.x

Kelly, B. F. (2001). The development of gesture, speech, and action as communicative strategies. In *Proceedings of the 27th annual meeting of the Berkeley Linguistics Society* (pp. 371–380). University of California, Berkeley, Department of Linguistics. https://doi.org/10.3765/bls.v27i1.1112

Kelly, B. F. (2006). The development of constructions through early gesture use. In E. Clark & B. F. Kelly (Eds.), *Constructions in acquisition* (pp. 15–30). CSLI. https://web.stanford.edu/group/cslipublications/cslipublications/CLRF/2004/06-Kelly.pdf

Kelly, B. F. (2014). Temporal synchrony in early multi-modal communication. In I. Arnon, M. Casillas, C. Kurumada, & B. Estigarribia (Eds.), *Language and interaction: Studies in honor of Eve V. Clark* (pp. 117–138). John Benjamins. https://doi.org/10.1075/tilar.12.11kel

Kendon, A. (1995). Gestures as illocutionary and discourse structure markers in Southern Italian conversation. *Journal of Pragmatics*, *23*(3), 247–279. https://doi.org/10.1016/0378-2166(94)00037-F

Kendon, A. (2004). *Gesture: Visible action as utterance*. Cambridge University Press. https://doi.org/10.1017/CBO9780511807572

Leung, E. L., & Rheingold, H. L. (1981). Development of pointing as a social gesture. *Developmental Psychology*, *17*(2), 215–220. https://doi.org/10.1037/0012-1649.17.2.215

Lieven, E., Behrens, H., Speares, J., & Tomasello, M. (2003). Early syntactic creativity: A usage-based approach. *Journal of Child Language, 30*(2), 333–370. https://doi.org/10.1017/S0305000903005592

Lieven, E., Pine, J., & Baldwin, G. (1997). Lexically-based learning and early grammatical development. *Journal of Child Language, 24*(1), 187–219. https://doi.org/10.1017/S0305000996002930

Lillard, A., Pinkham, A. M., & Smith, E. (2011). Pretend play and cognitive development. In U. Ghoswami (Ed.), *The Wiley-Blackwell handbook of childhood cognitive development* (2nd ed., pp. 285–311). Wiley-Blackwell. https://doi.org/10.1002/9780470996652.ch9

Louwerse, M. M., & Bangerter, A. (2005). Focusing attention with deictic gestures and linguistic expressions. In *Proceedings of the 27th annual meeting of the Cognitive Science Society* (pp. 1331–1336). http://csjarchive.cogsci.rpi.edu/proceedings/2005/docs/p1331.pdf

Lyons, J. (1975). Deixis as the source of reference. In E. L. Keenan (Ed.), *Formal semantics of natural language* (pp. 61–83). Cambridge University Press. https://doi.org/10.1017/CBO9780511897696.007

Marcos, H. (1991). Reformulating requests at 18 months: Gestures, vocalizations, and words. *First Language, 11*(33), 361–375. https://doi.org/10.1177/014272379101103304

Masur, E. F. (1983). Gestural development, dual-directional signaling, and the transition to words. *Journal of Psycholinguistic Research, 12*, 93–109. https://doi.org/10.1007/BF01067406

McGregor, K. K., Rohlfing, K. J., Bean, A., & Marschner, E. (2009). Gesture as a support for word learning: The case of under. *Journal of Child Language, 36*(4), 807–828. https://doi.org/10.1017/S0305000908009173

Messinger, D. S., & Fogel, A. (1998). Give and take: The development of conventional infant gestures. *Merrill-Palmer Quarterly, 44*(4), 566–590. https://www.jstor.org/stable/23093754

Mintz, T. H. (2003). Frequent frames as a cue for grammatical categories in child directed speech. *Cognition, 90*(1), 91–117. https://doi.org/10.1016/S0010-0277(03)00140-9

Murillo, E., Ortega, C., Otones, A., Rujas, I., & Casla, M. (2018). Changes in the synchrony of multimodal communication in early language development. *Journal of Speech, Language, and Hearing Research, 61*(9), 2235–2245. https://doi.org/10.1044/2018_JSLHR-L-17-0402

Özçalışkan, S., Gentner, D., & Goldin-Meadow, S. (2014). Do iconic gestures pave the way for children's early verbs? *Applied Psycholinguistics, 35*(6), 1143–1162. https://doi.org/10.1017/S0142716412000720

Özçalışkan, S., & Goldin-Meadow, S. (2005). Gesture is at the cutting edge of early language development. *Cognition, 96*(3), B101–B113. https://doi.org/10.1016/j.cognition.2005.01.001

Özçalışkan, S., & Goldin-Meadow, S. (2009). When gesture–speech combinations do and do not index linguistic change. *Language and Cognitive Processes, 24*(2), 190–217. https://doi.org/10.1080/01690960801956911

Rader, N. d. V., & Zukow-Goldring, P. (2012). Caregivers' gestures direct infant attention during early word learning: The importance of dynamic synchrony. *Language Sciences, 34*(5), 559–568. https://doi.org/10.1016/j.langsci.2012.03.011

Shatz, M. (1982). On mechanisms of language acquisition: Can features of the communicative environment account for development? In E. Wanner & L. R. Gleitman (Eds.), *Language acquisition: The state of the art* (pp. 102–127). Cambridge University Press.

Slobin, D. I. (1970). Universals of grammatical development in children. In G. B. Flores d'Arcais & W. J. M. Levelt (Eds.), *Advances in psycholinguistics* (pp. 174–186). North-Holland Publishing.

Tomasello, M. (1992). *First verbs: A case study of early grammatical development*. Cambridge University Press. https://doi.org/10.1017/CBO9780511527678

Werner, H., & Kaplan, B. (1963). *Symbol formation: An organismic-developmental approach to language and the expression of thought*. Wiley.

Wu, Z., & Gros-Louis, J. (2014). Infants' prelinguistic communicative acts and maternal responses: Relations to linguistic development. *First Language, 34*(1), 72–90. https://doi.org/10.1177/0142723714521925

Wu, Z., & Gros-Louis, J. (2015). Caregivers provide more labeling responses to infants' pointing than to infants' object-directed vocalizations. *Journal of Child Language, 42*(3), 538–561. https://doi.org/10.1017/S0305000914000221

Zammit, M., & Schafer, G. (2011). Maternal label and gesture use affects acquisition of specific object names. *Journal of Child Language, 38*(1), 201–221. https://doi.org/10.1017/S0305000909990328

Zukow-Goldring, P. (1996). Sensitive caregiving fosters the comprehension of speech: When gestures speak louder than words. *Early Development and Parenting, 5*(4), 195–211. https://doi.org/10.1002/(SICI)1099-0917(199612)5:4<195::AID-EDP133>3.0.CO;2-H

Zukow-Goldring, P. (2001). Perceiving referring actions: Latina and Euro-American infants and caregivers comprehending speech. In K. E. Nelson, A. Aksu-Koc, & C. E. Johnson (Eds.), *Children's language, Vol. 11: Interactional contributions to language development* (pp. 139–163). Lawrence Erlbaum.

Pauline Beaupoil-Hourdel
7 Embodying Language Complexity: Co-Speech Gestures Between Age 3 and 4

During their first 3 years of life, children rely on various semiotic resources to communicate. They learn to control their bodies to produce specific and meaningful movements and vocal productions in context. Gestures and speech are coordinated, but they do not necessarily play an equal part in the construction of meaning (Cartmill et al., 2014). The gesture–speech relationship develops following the children's age, motor, cognitive, and language development. Gestures are sometimes used alone and sometimes in combination with speech. Co-speech gestures are gestures that are used in combination with speech and that contribute to build meaning. The study of co-speech gestures consists of analyzing their use and function as well as assessing their status in the meaning-making process. This chapter proposes to analyze speech and co-speech gestures in children between ages 3 and 4 in order to show how children coordinate the two modalities to build complex meaning in interaction.

Complexity is often studied at the sentence level in linguistics, with work on the acquisition of complex sentences in children dealing with both syntax and semantics. Many papers also mention that children can perform cognitively complex actions, thus referring to mental processes (Antinucci & Volterra, 1979; Choi, 1988; Cuccio, 2012). The concept of complexity can also be applied to motor development studies, as learning to produce some gesture forms requires kinesthetic mastery over body movements. Complexity at the interaction level is another paradigm that should be analyzed. In this chapter, I investigate the notion of complex meaning in interaction by focusing on gestures that bear several functions simultaneously when a gesture is used to convey communicative stance and to add modality to a speech act or to index a mental state. I also scrutinize how the gestures coordinate with speech by focusing on the syntactic structures used and the semantic meaning of the spoken utterance.

This research aims at documenting the development of language and communication in early adult–child interactions. I adopt a holistic definition of language, as I consider that the semiotic resources each participant has at their disposal can contribute to make meaning in interaction. Therefore, I analyze all meaningful vocal

---

I thank Aliyah Morgenstern and Jean-Marc Colletta for their feedback on earlier drafts and analyses of this paper. I also thank the members of the NEGATION Group in Paris and of the Co-Operative Action Lab at UCLA for engaging in a vibrant academic discussion on some of the examples presented in this chapter.

This work was funded by the Labex EFL (ANR/CGI), a PhD grant from Sorbonne Nouvelle University and the ANR CoLaJE project (ANR-08-COM-021).

https://doi.org/10.1515/9783110675788-007
Gesture in Language: Development Across the Lifespan, A. Morgenstern and S. Goldin-Meadow (Editors)
Copyright © 2022 by the American Psychological Association and Walter de Gruyter GmbH. All rights reserved.

(speech and vocal productions) and visual productions (gestures, movements, postures, facial expressions) the child and her parents mobilize in conversation, taking into account the participants' spoken, cognitive, and motor development.

Negation is a central locus for the analysis of gesture acquisition, as children mobilize all the semiotic resources they have at their disposal when they need to refuse, reject, or deny something. The study of negation also enables researchers to simultaneously analyze children's psychological, cognitive, kinesthetic, and linguistic development. The first forms of negation are conveyed nonverbally (Beaupoil-Hourdel, 2015; Kochan, 2008; Morgenstern et al., 2018), but after 2;00, negations continue to develop along with speech productions. Their forms and functions diversify and specialize (Beaupoil-Hourdel et al., 2015) until after 3;00, when gesture fully complements speech to build meaning (Beaupoil-Hourdel, 2015; Beaupoil-Hourdel & Debras, 2017). After 3;00, gestures have been less studied because children enter complex sentences, and researchers have focused on their speech more than on their gestures. The goal of this chapter is therefore to analyze the role of gestures used to convey negation at the period when children's speech becomes more complex.

During the first 4 years, children's speech develops dramatically, but gestures also undergo major changes in their forms, the functions they help build in interaction, and in their relation to other modalities of expression, especially speech. In order to analyze the development of all semiotic resources that children mobilize to make meaning, I (along with a team of researchers specialized in interaction, prosody, and gesture and sign language studies) focused on the expression of negation in children.[1] Our previous work conducted on English, Italian, and French Sign Languages has shown that negation emerges early in children's communicative system, is often addressed to children by their caregivers, takes numerous visual and vocal forms, and serves a vast variety of pragmatic functions in interaction (Beaupoil-Hourdel et al., 2015; Benazzo & Morgenstern, 2014; Blondel et al., 2017; Morgenstern & Beaupoil, 2015; Morgenstern et al., 2016, 2018).

Negation is a complex communication act that consists of expressing counter-expectations in relation with the immediate environment (i.e., expression of absence, incapacity, powerlessness, or ignorance) or in displaying a negative stance toward others' actions or speech (i.e., refusal, rejection, prohibition, protest, denial). By saying "no," young children manage to express a vast range of pragmatic functions (Antinucci & Volterra, 1979; Beaupoil-Hourdel, 2015; Beaupoil-Hourdel et al., 2015; Bloom, 1970; Cameron-Faulkner et al., 2007; Choi, 1988; McNeill & McNeill, 1968; Pea, 1980; Vaidyanathan, 1991) that will eventually help them build their own self (Morgenstern, 2006). The development of negation in preschoolers has been studied extensively, but most studies have focused on speech. In contrast, multimodal analyses of the development of negation have recently documented the role of gestures prior to

---

1 *CoLaJE project* (http://colaje.scicog.fr) is funded by the Agence Nationale de la Recherche (Morgenstern & Parisse, 2012).

speech and as co-speech gestures in children before age 4 (Beaupoil-Hourdel, 2015; Beaupoil-Hourdel et al., 2015; Blondel et al., 2017; Morgenstern & Beaupoil, 2015; Morgenstern et al., 2016, 2018). Other researchers have focused on the development of specific gesture forms used by children to express negation, such as headshakes and head movements of avoidance (Andrén, 2010; Beaupoil-Hourdel, 2015), palm-ups and shrugs (Beaupoil-Hourdel & Debras, 2017; Morgenstern et al., 2016), as well as pushing-away actions (Beaupoil-Hourdel, 2015). The gestures that adults use in conversation to express negation have been thoroughly described (Calbris, 2011; C. Goodwin, 2017; Harrison, 2009a, 2009b, 2018; Kendon, 2002, 2004; Streeck, 2009), but there is no such similar scientific work on children's acquisition of gestures of negation.

This chapter presents an overview of the gesture forms that young children use to convey negation and opposite stance after they start using speech extensively. I adopt a developmental, constructivist, usage-based and interactionist approach to analyze the productions of two children between the ages of 3 and 4 years. My focus on two longitudinal follow-ups illustrates the complex use of multimodality in all its details. This chapter falls in the field of interactional linguistics (Beaupoil-Hourdel, 2015; Goffman, 1959, 1967; C. Goodwin, 2017; Morgenstern, 2014) and relies on the work produced by the CoLaJE research team in Paris (Morgenstern, 2009; Morgenstern & Parisse, 2012), whose members longitudinally analyzed language development in detail in seven children. The analyses presented in this chapter are thus grounded in a large body of research in first language acquisition.

After a short review of the literature on language acquisition and the gesture–speech relationship, I present the data and methodology and then the quantitative and detailed qualitative analyses and results. In the results section, I focus on the role of co-speech gestures during the process of building meaning multimodally in interaction.

7.1 State of the Art

The following section provides an overview of research relevant to the topic addressed in this chapter.

7.1.1 Language Emerging Through Context and Interaction With Others

Analyzing all semiotic dimensions of language can help capture children's language development in interaction in greater depth (Bakhtin, 1986; Duranti & C. Goodwin, 1992; C. Goodwin, 2017). Children learn to construct meaning in a rich context composed of words, gestures, actions, vocalizations, facial expressions, and the objects they manipulate or talk about in interaction with others. Language is often defined as a social phenomenon in which children learn to make meaning through context and input. Previous research has shown that some parents consider their infants' nonsymbolic movements as meaningful elements. Budwig (2003) explained that parents learn to decipher meaning by observing their children's movements and soon consider babies' actions, movements, and babbles as meaningful communication acts or attempts at communicating. Thus, parents almost systematically establish semantic continuity between movements, actions, gestures, and speech in the construction of meaning. They often verbalize the intended meaning they attribute to the child's production and assign either general meaning to actions or specific meaning to particular visual forms. In doing so, they position their children as inhabitants of the interaction (C. Goodwin, 2013) who can contribute by using the resources they have at their disposal, thereby conveying that both the parents and the child can cooperate to coconstruct meaning (Beaupoil-Hourdel et al., 2015). Language thus emerges through context and interaction with others. In order to understand how children manage to combine gestures and speech to linguistically and physically position themselves and display a negative stance in interaction, I also analyze parents' communicative input.

7.1.2 Gestures of Negation in Adults

The study of negation requires taking into account the overall linguistic and environmental context in which any form of negation, be it a headshake, a holophrastic "no," or a complex multimodal utterance is produced. Understanding why a young child says "no" supposes that the adult and the researcher can reconstruct the whole interactive sequence in which the utterance was produced as well as the possible unfolding action that it encapsulates. This is why C. Goodwin (2017) claimed that negation markers—verbal or nonverbal—indexically incorporate complex language structure as well as the talk of others, transforming them into new actions. To infer the function of the negations produced, researchers have proposed numerous functional typologies. However, most of these typologies do not rely on a full-fledged analysis of the interactional framework in which they are uttered. While many analyses of negation have dealt with its organization within speech, the emergence of negation in interaction has seldom been tackled. Researchers may also need to investigate other variables that contribute to building meaning in interaction, like who the addressee of the negation is, what the object or event that is being negated/rejected is, whether the child is displaying any negative stance toward the parent, the object, or the event, as well as how the parent reacts.

Research on adults points out that negation is a *transformative operation* (C. Goodwin, 2017) because it incorporates earlier talk and transforms the action by displaying a new stance toward the event when used in interaction. C. Goodwin (2017) showed that negation is an operation that requires a high degree of shared attention and semiosis among the speakers. He also explained that negation bears upon previous material in interaction and usually opens to a new unfolding of action within the interaction framework. In his work on an aphasic speaker (Chil) who was left with only three words of vocabulary ("yes," "no," and "and") after a stroke, Goodwin explained that the negation "no" was used by Chil to incorporate rich language structures created by others in previous turns. He also added that saying "no" while using gestures, body movements, and facial expressions helped Chil express meaning that he could not convey with words (C. Goodwin, 2010, 2017; C. Goodwin et al., 2002). Goodwin's work on interaction between proficient speakers and an aphasic man sheds light on the specificity of interactions between speakers who do not rely on the same semiotic resources to communicate together, which is the type of interactions researchers are dealing with when studying adult–child conversations. Indeed, there is an asymmetry between the child and the parents in the motoric mastery of semiotic resources, their coordination, and their function in interaction.

Previous studies have documented the gestures of negation used by adults (Calbris, 2011; Harrison, 2009b, 2018; Kendon, 2004; Streeck, 2009) and typically list the following forms as possible expressions of negation:

- Headshakes (Andrén, 2010, 2014; Calbris, 2011; M. H. Goodwin, 1980; Kendon, 2002, 2004) are used to express denial, refusal, or (sometimes) ignorance. They can also have discursive, expressive, or referential meaning (Colletta, 2004).
- Finger waggings (Calbris, 1990; Calbris & Montredon, 1986; Guidetti, 2005; Morgenstern et al., 2016) are often used to convey prohibition.
- Vertical palm (VP) gestures (Efron, 1941; Kendon, 2004) often convey refusal, prohibition, or denial.
- Open hand prone gestures (Calbris, 1990; Harrison, 2009a, 2009b, 2018; Kendon, 2004) consist of placing one or both hands palm-down and moving the arms apart from one another. They are often used with the markers "any," "at all," "never," or "nothing."
- Shoulder lifts (Debras, 2017; Givens, 1977; Jehoul et al., 2017; Streeck, 2009) are a form that is commonly used to express ignorance (Givens, 1977; Kendon, 2004; Morris, 1994; Streeck, 2009), but they can also mark disengagement, a lack of interest, incapacity, or powerlessness (Boutet, 2008, 2010; Debras, 2013, 2017; Streeck, 1994).
- Head tilts consist of moving the head laterally and often convey disengagement (Debras, 2013, 2017; Debras & Cienki, 2012; Streeck, 1994). They are often combined with adversative markers like "but" or "rather" (Beaupoil-Hourdel, 2015; Beaupoil-Hourdel & Debras, 2017).

- Open hand supine or palm-up gestures (Debras, 2013, 2017; Kendon, 2004; Müller, 1998; Streeck, 1994) are often used to express absence or ignorance.

All of these visual forms can contribute to convey negation and/or opposite stance in specific contexts. Therefore, they refer to the process of meaning making in interaction and to the management of interaction (see Bavelas et al., 1992, 1995, for a thorough description and distinction between topic gestures and interactive gestures).

7.1.3 Nonverbal Forms of Negation and Children's Multimodal Language

Acquisitionists adopting a multimodal approach to the development of language have shown that studying gesture productions is crucial to understanding how speech will develop as children start expressing themselves with nonverbal modalities like vocalizations, actions, and gestures (E. V. Clark, 2003; Guidetti & Colletta, 2010; Iverson, 2010; Iverson & Goldin-Meadow, 2005; Morgenstern, 2014). Adults interact with their children with speech and gestures, and they often interpret the children's visual productions as meaningful nonverbal utterances.

For the study of negation, Guidetti (2002, 2005) explained that gestures expressing refusal, along with pointing gestures, are the first gestures to emerge in children's productions, while H. H. Clark and E. V. Clark (1977) observed that the first negations children produce are conveyed through their body. Yet, even though visual modalities and negation are frequent and emerge early in young children's productions, little research has documented the acquisition and development of visual forms expressing negation in preschoolers. Some studies have shown that children start expressing negation with headshakes around 1;00 and 1;03 (Andrén, 2010, 2014; Spitz, 1957), and recent research on the production of gestures expressing negation in four French- and English-speaking children has shown that headshakes are quickly followed by the emergence of palm-ups and shoulder lifts used separately and in combination (Beaupoil-Hourdel & Debras, 2017; Morgenstern et al., 2016). Morgenstern et al. (2016) also mentioned that visual forms like finger wagging are rarely used by children in adult–child interaction, because in some families children are not easily entitled to forbid something to an adult. There is thus an asymmetry between the participants in the speech acts they produce. Yet, the authors added that children know the gesture and its meaning in context, as they sometimes use it in pretend play or when addressing their pet, other children, or their toys as in Example 7.1:

Example 7.1 *Finger wagging—Ellie 3;02*
The link to the video of this example can be found with this book's supplementary materials online (https://www.apa.org/pubs/books/gesture-in-language).

> Ellie is playing with her mother. The mother uses a toy and pretends
> that it is a thief. Ellie addresses the toy: [don't do it again!²
>   [Finger wagging

This body of literature highlights the fact that learning to say "no" to a cospeaker is a complex activity, as the speakers need to socially and morally adjust to the person they are interacting with and choose between a vast range of vocal and visual forms—the meaning of which will emerge in context (Bruner et al., 1956; Duranti & C. Goodwin, 1992). The development of negation should thus be addressed as a complex linguistic, cognitive, motor, and social process (Choi, 1988; Cuccio, 2012). In addition, communicating "no" also has an impact on the unfolding action within interaction, and forms of negation could therefore be analyzed as operating like discourse or interactional markers (C. Goodwin, 2000, 2017). Thus, learning to express negation is a complex process for children that involves choosing among the forms available to them in the input in order to express a specific function. It also implies taking and displaying a stance toward an event, an object, or the cospeaker and reorganizing the interaction by using visual and vocal cues that will have an impact on the unfolding action. This review illustrates the relevance of negation to study how children develop the expression of complex meaning in speech and gestures. It also sets the scene for a study on the coordination between modalities (speech and gestures) jointly mobilized by two children between the ages of 3 and 4 to convey negation.

7.2 Data and Method

This chapter is illustrated by a study on the emergence and the role of co-speech gestures expressing negation in two adult–child corpora from the Paris Corpus (Morgenstern & Parisse, 2012). The children (Ellie and Madeleine) were filmed monthly, at home, for 1 hour, in spontaneous and natural interactions with their mothers and sometimes with other family members. The video camera is set on the child and in some sequences, the mother is off screen. The children and their mothers are both monolinguals (French or English). They knew the films would be used to convey analyses on the children's language development, but they were unaware that a detailed study on visual forms of negation would be carried out. The corpus is composed of 66 hours of videos (30 hours for the French dyad and 36 hours for the English dyad). This chapter focuses on co-speech gestures expressing negation in the videos recorded between ages 3;00 and 4;02 (14 hours in total with 7 hours for each child) after the two little girls had achieved good mastery of speech.³ The French data

---

2 The bracket ([) is used to show that speech and gesture begin simultaneously.
3 See Beaupoil-Hourdel et al. (2015) and Morgenstern et al. (2018) for an analysis of their negations from 1 to 3.

were entirely transcribed using the CHAT format with CLAN (MacWhinney, 2000). Both data were tagged for negations, and I analyzed all the vocal (speech and vocal productions) and visual (actions, gestures, and facial expressions) forms of negation the children and the mothers produced in the videos using an Excel spreadsheet. Specific and detailed analyses of some gestural forms were done with ELAN (Wittenburg et al., 2006) to focus both on the forms of the visual productions and the coordination with other modalities of expression like speech or vocalizations. This methodology is based on the use of four analytical tools (CLAN, Excel, Praat and ELAN), and it makes it possible to list every single production of negation the children and the mothers produce and to convey detailed multilayered analyses. I used a mixed-method approach that relies on a quantitative and a qualitative treatment of the data. The term *mixed-method* refers to a methodology in applied linguistics that advocates for the integration of quantitative and qualitative approaches to provide a more comprehensive picture of the phenomenon under study (Hashemi, 2012; Reynolds, 2015). The work is time-consuming and resource-demanding, but in order to analyze interaction and the construction of meaning, combining complementary quantitative and qualitative analyses as well as macro- and microanalyses may help us highlight and illustrate the acquisition processes under study. Both data sets were also used by other researchers from the CoLaJE Project in Paris, and this chapter relies on the work that was previously done on Ellie and Madeleine, whose language development has been extensively described at various linguistic, morphosyntactic, prosodic, and pragmatic levels (Morgenstern, 2009, 2014).

Each occurrence of negation produced by the mother or the child in each dyad was coded according to its function in context (refusal, rejection, protest, nonexistence, absence, denial, negative assertion, ignorance, prohibition, and incapacity; Beaupoil-Hourdel, 2015; Beaupoil-Hourdel et al., 2015) as well as the modality or the combination of modalities used (speech, vocalization, facial expression, gesture, action). Our coding system was built in order to developmentally account for the evolution and transformation of visual and auditory forms in the children's productions. To do so, we divided the modalities of expression into two distinct categories that interact with each other, taking into account the channel of perception—either visual or auditory—on the one hand and the semiotic status of the modalities—symbolic or nonsymbolic—on the other hand (Figure 7.1).

The functions were coded based on the pragmatic and semantic functions of negative communication acts in young children proposed by Cameron-Faulkner et al. (2007). Using observation and a corpus-driven method, I tested all the functions proposed by the quoted authors in the data. I ended up with almost the same categories and added two more categories (refusal and protest), as Dodane and Massini-Cagliari (2010) found that prosody helped differentiate between a refusal, a rejection, and a protest. The typology was tested by four researchers partaking in the CoLaJE project who blind-coded a small portion of the data to assess the robustness of the coding system. All diverging results were discussed and solved collectively.

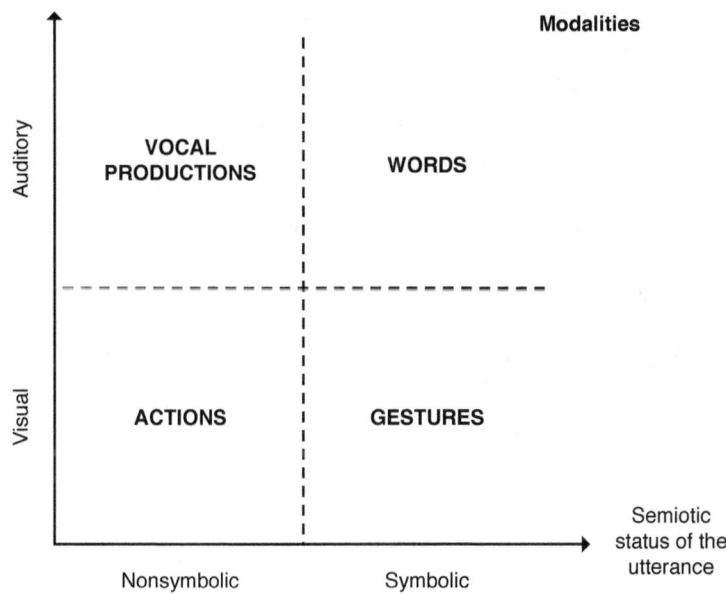

Fig. 7.1: Interaction between channel and semiotic status of the modalities of expression. From *Multimodal Acquisition and Expression of Negation: Analysis of a Videotaped and Longitudinal Corpus of a French and an English Mother–Child Dyad* [Unpublished doctoral dissertation] (p. 135), by P. Beaupoil-Hourdel, 2015, Sorbonne Nouvelle University, Paris. Copyright 2015 by P. Beaupoil-Hourdel; and from "A Child's Multimodal Negations From 1 to 4: The Interplay Between Modalities," by P. Beaupoil-Hourdel, A. Morgenstern, and D. Boutet, in P. Larrivée & C. Lee (Eds.), *Negation and Polarity: Experimental Perspectives* (p. 102), 2015, Springer International Publishing. Copyright 2015 by Springer Nature. Adapted with permission.

7.3 The Children's Gesture–Speech Productions Before and After 3;00

Results on negation in the data extending from 0;10 to 4;02 showed that a shift in the children's communicative system happens after 3;00. In the data, Ellie produces an overall 1,298 negations and Madeleine produces 1,518 negations. The children's pathways into negation are not the same in the data (Beaupoil-Hourdel, 2015; Morgenstern et al., 2016, 2018). Madeleine starts uttering her first words very early, and she delves into the spoken modality before using the visual modalities, whereas Ellie starts with the visual modalities and her speech develops only after 2;06. The two children enter language through different modalities. Madeleine's number of negations follows the development of her speech, whereas Ellie's number of negations remains almost the same throughout the data depending on the modalities she uses to communicate with others. Their individual preferences for the visual or vocal modalities led me to think that their use of gestures during the emergence of co-speech gestures around 3;00 and 3;06 would differ in forms and functions.

The graphs in Figures 7.2 and 7.3 show the interplay between the visual (gestures and actions) and the vocal (speech and vocal productions) modalities in Ellie and Madeleine's productions of negation before and after 3;00. Figure 7.2 shows that Ellie's system changes after 3;00 as the vocal channel becomes predominant with 67% of her productions being conveyed with the vocal modalities as compared with 35% before

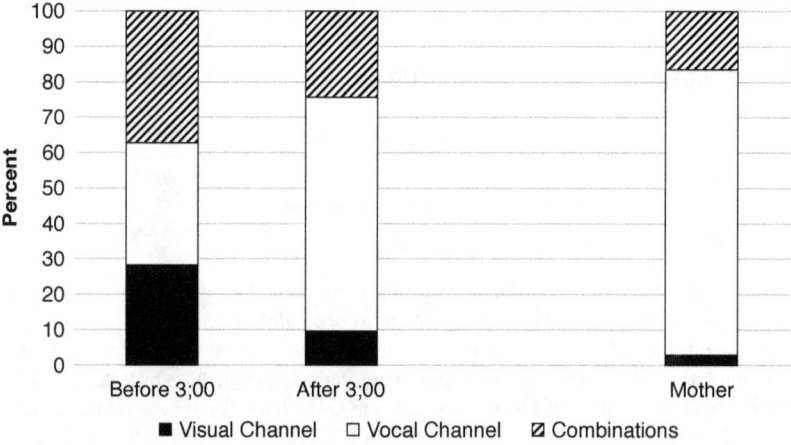

Fig. 7.2: Ellie's use of the channels of communication to convey her negations before and after 3;00 (*n* = 1,298) and her mother's communication systems (*n* = 711).

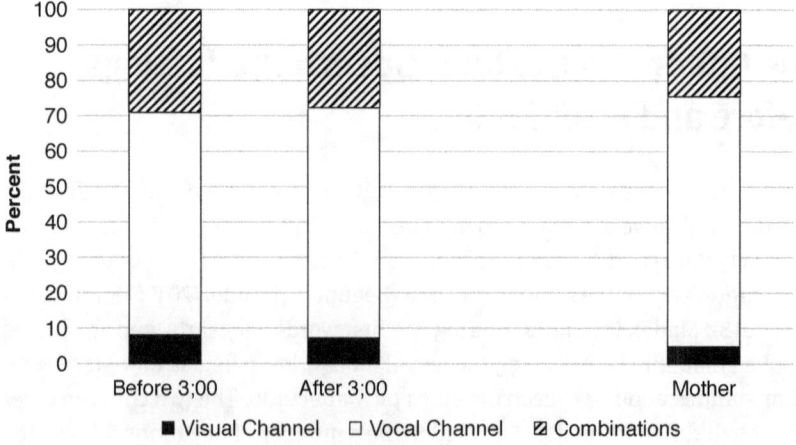

Fig. 7.3: Madeleine's use of the channels of communication to convey her negations before and after 3;00 (*n* = 1,518) and her mother's communication systems (*n* = 809).

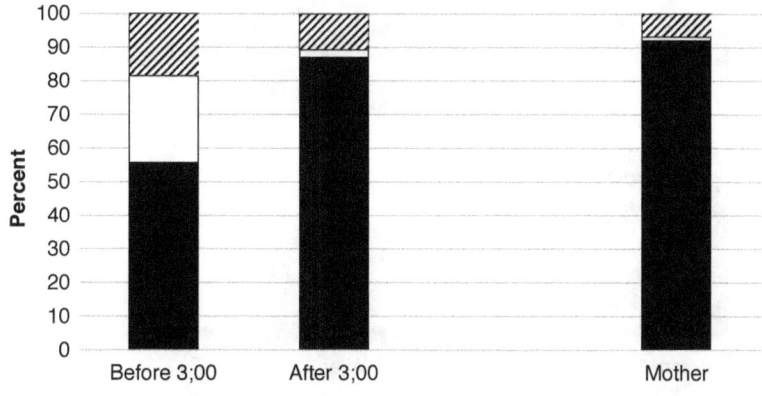

Fig. 7.4: Status of Ellie's productions of negation as being nonsymbolic (actions and vocal productions) or symbolic (gestures and speech) before and after 3;00 ($n = 1{,}298$). Mother ($n = 711$).

3;00 ($p < .001$). Madeleine's system (Figure 7.3) does not show any significant change ($p = .83$) yet, and it is worth pointing out that both the vocal and the spoken productions were coded in the vocal channel. Figures 7.2 and 7.3 show that the children's systems are becoming similar with the input but these graphs fail to represent the shift from nonsymbolic to symbolic modalities after 3;00 (see the graphs in Figure 7.4 and Figure 7.5). Indeed, Figures 7.4 and 7.5 show that as of age 3;00, both children rely

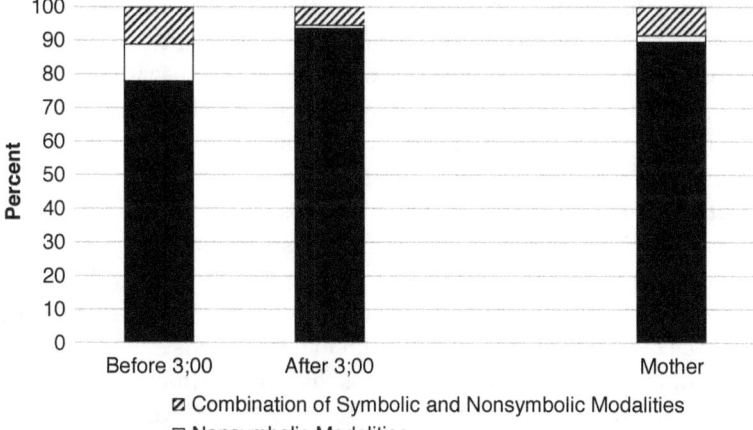

Fig. 7.5: Status of Madeleine's productions of negation as being nonsymbolic (actions and vocal productions) or symbolic (gestures and speech) before and after 3;00 ($n = 1{,}518$). Mother ($n = 809$).

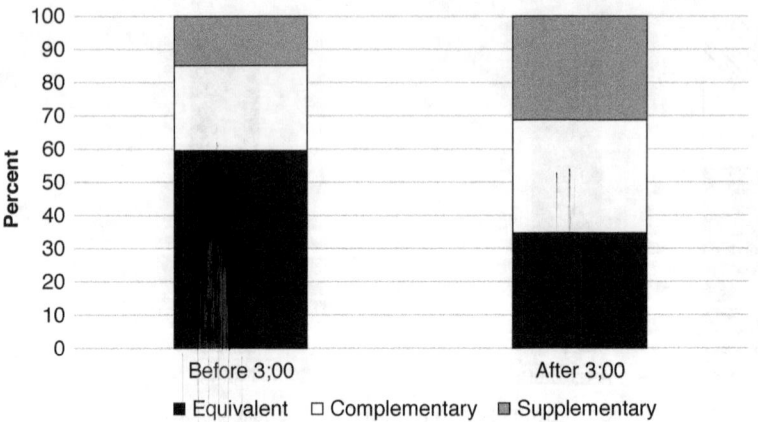

Fig. 7.6: Gesture–speech relationships in Ellie's data ($n = 658$).

predominantly on symbolic modalities (speech and gestures) to convey their negations ($p < .001$ for both children).

At 3;00, Ellie has a mean length of utterance (MLU) of 2.7 and Madeleine of 4.5. Madeleine's speech is already quite complex with a large set of vocabulary (309 types and 1,517 tokens). At the same age, Ellie produces 226 types and 833 tokens. In Ellie's data, the age of 3;00 marks both the emergence of co-speech gestures and the development of her speech. At 3;00, Ellie utters 4 times more tokens than at 2;00 and her number of types more than doubles. Between 3;00 and 4;02 her MLU continues to increase while the number of utterances she produces per session stabilizes. Her speech becomes lexically richer, even though she is not as talkative as Madeleine. The mothers' profiles are quite similar, and the children's modes of communication also become similar after 3;00, as they predominantly use the vocal channel (Figures 7.2 and 7.3)—more specifically speech (Figures 7.4 and 7.5)—to communicate. After 3;00, Ellie and Madeleine combine words with gestures to express their negations 20% to 30% of the time (Figures 7.2 and 7.3). However, a pure quantitative analysis of the data would not show any significant difference in the number of gestures produced before and after 3;00 in the children. The graphs in Figures 7.2 and 7.3 also fail to account for the status of the gesture–speech relationships. The graphs in Figures 7.6 and 7.7 are representations of the gesture–speech relationships. For each gesture produced in combination with speech, I coded whether it was equivalent with speech (*no* + a headshake to refuse), complementary (*no* + palm-up to express absence) or supplementary (*I don't want to tidy up* + shoulder lift to refuse to obey).[4]

The graphs show that the proportion of gestures that are equivalent with speech decreases a little after 3;00. They still represent about 30% of the gesture–speech

---

[4] I would like to thank Erica Cartmill for our rich discussions and her helpful suggestions on this topic during my stay at UCLA as a visiting scholar in 2014.

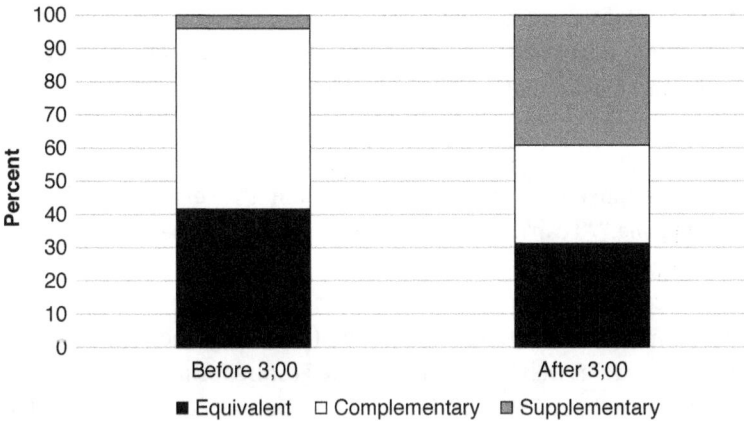

Fig. 7.7: Gesture–speech relationships in Madeleine's data ($n = 697$).

combinations because the children, just like the mothers, do not stop using the headshake in combination with holophrastic "no"s to express refusal. Yet, in proportion the number of supplementary gestures increases after 3;00 in both children, thus showing that the gesture–speech relationship after 3;00 undergoes some significant changes ($p < .001$ for both data). Qualitative interactional analyses also showed that after 3;00, the number of gesture productions may not increase but the function of the gestures changes. Indeed gestures take up the role of co-speech gestures as of age 3;00 and they contribute to build meaning differently in interaction, as they not only bear the negative scope of the utterance but, combined with speech, they help the children display physical negative stance toward an event. They are no longer mostly equivalent with speech, instead they complement and at times supplement speech.

7.4 Focus on Co-Speech Gestures and Their Contribution to the Process of Meaning Making

This section provides analyses of the data with a focus on the synchronization of the children's speech and gestures, and the contribution of both modalities to the expression of negation and negative stance display in interaction.

7.4.1 Gestures of Negation as Equivalent or Complementary Gestures

Before 3;00, gestures of negation are almost systematically used in isolation as monomodal utterances or combined with a one-word utterance like "no" or "gone."

Ellie produces 136 negations expressed with gestures alone or in combination with one word and only five gestures expressing negation are combined with a two-word utterance. Madeleine produces only 17 utterances with a gesture before 2;00, and 15 of them are expressed with only one word. Gestures are mostly equivalent to speech or complementary. There are numerous examples in the data based on the combination of a headshake with the spoken utterance "no, I don't want it" to express refusal or a palm-up gesture and "gone," "I can't," or "I don't know" to convey absence, incapacity, or ignorance.

Yet, some gestures are polysemic and help build a variety of functions as is the case for the gesture components of the shrug posture (palm-ups, shoulder lifts, and head tilts; Beaupoil-Hourdel & Debras, 2017). If all the gesture forms of negation are used in interaction in the data, Beaupoil-Hourdel and Debras (2017) showed that the shrug components are different, as they can be self-oriented or other-oriented. The question of (inter)subjectivity is indeed a parameter that changes the use of some gestural forms after 3;00 when the children start using gestures as co-speech gestures. The data show that gestures primarily used to construct negative meaning only, like a refusal or an absence, slowly take on a rather intersubjective meaning and function less on the level of meaning making than on that of displaying a stance (Goffman, 1959, 1963).

7.4.2 After 3;00, Gestures of Negation Help Build Complex Meaning

In this section, I use qualitative analyses of chosen sequences from Ellie's and Madeleine's corpus to analyze in detail the gesture–speech relationships that emerge after 3;00. In Example 7.2, Madeleine is age 3;03 and she uses speech and gestures in a complex manner to construct an adversative relation of two states of affairs (p and q) existing in a certain opposition to each other.

Example 7.2 *head tilt in a p but q sentence, Madeleine—3;03*
The link to the video of this example can be found with this book's supplementary materials online (https://www.apa.org/pubs/books/gesture-in-language).
MADELEINE: Peut-être que je peux te faire   [comme ça.
un collier
maybe I can make a necklace for you   [like this
[holds out two beads in front of her
RESEARCHER: Comment?
How?

MADELEINE: [comme ça.
　　　　　　like this.
　　　　　　[holds out two beads in front of her
RESEARCHER: hum hum.
　　　　　　uh uh
MADELEINE: (.) mais i(l) faudra　　[l'accrocher
　　　　　　(.) but I will have　　[to tie it
　　　　　　　　　　　　　　　　　[looks at the researcher
　　　　　　　　　　　　　　　　　[head tilt (Figure 7.8) and
　　　　　　　　　　　　　　　　　headshake [mouth shrug
　　　　　　　　　　　　　　　　　(Figure 7.9)
RESEARCHER: Faudrait trouver une ficelle.
　　　　　　We need to find a string.

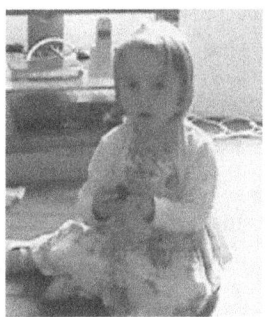  

Fig. 7.8: Madeleine 3;03, *head tilt.*　　　　**Fig. 7.9:** Madeleine 3;03, *mouth shrug.*

　　In Example 7.2, Madeleine tells the researcher who is filming her that she wants to make a necklace for her but she does not have a string on which to string the beads. Madeleine holds two beads in front of her, puts them next to each other and says "like this!" The researcher answers *"hum hum"* ["uh uh"] and indicates to the child that the beads will not stick together without a string. Madeleine then adds "but I will have to tie it [the necklace]" and produces a head tilt and a mouth shrug combined with falling prosodic contour. The gesture stroke is synchronized with the verb *accrocher* (to tie), which is produced at the end of the sentence in French because the pronoun is a clitic.

　　The adverb *mais* (but) in French is commonly used in *p but q* clauses and is generally analyzed as a marker expressing concession (Ducrot, 1984, 1989, 2001; Fontanier, 1968; Marconi & Bertinetto, 1984; Morel, 1996; Rossari, 2014). As such, it is employed to articulate two anti-oriented viewpoints. In this configuration the first clause *p* re-establishes the cospeaker's viewpoint and the coordinating conjunction "but" introduces the *q* clause, which is anti-oriented and which usually bears the speaker's viewpoint. In this sequence, Madeleine synchronizes several clauses in only one multimodal utterance: (a) she visually displays alignment with the interlocutor as she probably understands that she will not be able to make a necklace without a string; (b) she uses words to explain her intention to make a necklace and tie it; and (c) her posture, gestures, and prosodic contour also indicate that she is disappointed or powerless in this situation. A closer look at the gestures she produces reveals that the visual modality is articulated to the spoken utterance thanks to the adverb "but." In this excerpt, it appears that the *p* clause is expressed with speech and the anti-oriented clause is expressed simultaneously on the visual channel with a combination of the head tilt and the mouth shrug. Her full utterance could be glossed and described as presented in the alternate version of Example 7.2.

Example 7.2 *(alternate): head tilt in a p but q sentence, Madeleine—3;03*

"I will have to tie the necklace   but"   *head tilt* (Figure 7.10) and *mouth shrug* (Figure 7.11)

Gloss of the gesture: I need a string and I don't have it so I can't make a necklace.

Syntactic construction of the utterance:
p   *but*   *q*
(Speech)   (Gestures)

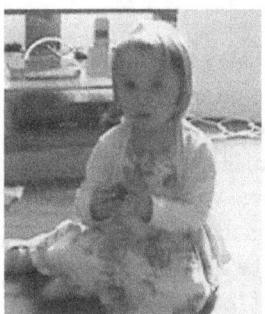
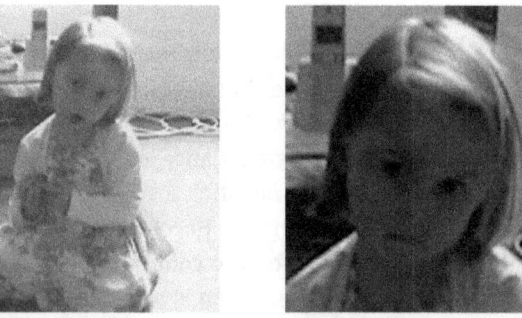

Fig. 7.10: Madeleine 3;03, *head tilt*.

Fig. 7.11: Madeleine 3;03, *mouth shrug*.

In this context, the head tilt not only contributes to the construction of the anti-oriented clause, it also displays a negative stance toward the action. In Example 7.2, the gesture supplements speech because it casts a new light on Madeleine's spoken utterance. Focusing solely on speech would lead to the conclusion that Madeleine does not consider the researcher's previous utterance "*hum hum*" ["uh uh"] that indexes doubts toward the projected event. In contrast, a multimodal analysis shows that the gestures and posture express a subjective discourse stance on the content of Madeleine's speech and on her intention. The visual modalities in this sequence incorporate previous talk (C. Goodwin, 2017) and illustrate that Madeleine knows that she will not be able to make a necklace without a string. Taken in isolation, her speech cannot lead to this understanding of the situation. At only 3;03, it is still difficult for Madeleine to construct complex meaning with words only, and it seems that the gestures help her in the language acquisition and meaning-making processes, as they help her create logical links between clauses and express a more nuanced meaning than the meaning she can build with words only. In fact, co-speech gestures emerge in her communicative system when she starts expressing complex meaning. Her vocabulary and syntax are quite rich already, but they are not complex enough from a linguistic and syntactic perspective for her to form complex sentences with words only. Co-speech gestures may therefore work as facilitators for the emergence of complex sentences and the expression of complex meaning, helping the child draw logical links between clauses and make meaning in a very condensed and multimodal manner before being able to express it with words only.

In this sequence, Madeleine is indeed able to synchronize visual and vocal modalities in a complex manner to express negation but the gestures do not only contribute to the construction of the complex *p but q* construction; they simultaneously help the child position herself toward the unfolding event. Her use of the visual modality is grammaticizing into logical and subjective markers, which are *publicly visible* (C. Goodwin, 2002; Leeuwen & Jewitt, 2000) and therefore contribute to the interaction in displaying her stance toward the event. Later on, Madeleine will probably become more fully aware of the impact of the visual resources she mobilizes on the unfolding action and on her coparticipants.

Ellie also uses head tilts in combination with *p but q* clauses. In a previous study on the use of shrugs in Ellie's data (Beaupoil-Hourdel & Debras, 2017), we showed that after 3;05 Ellie is able to express complex linguistic meaning thanks to the combination of both speech and gestures. To that extent, gestures and speech complement each other in a very complex manner as the use of multimodality and the possibility to combine speech and gestures simultaneously enables the child to construct the *p* and *q* clauses concurrently.

> Example 7.3 *Head tilt in a* p but q *sentence, Ellie—3;05 (Beaupoil-Hourdel & Debras, 2017)*
> The link to the video of this example can be found with this book's supplementary materials online (https://www.apa.org/pubs/books/gesture-in-language).

GRANDMOTHER: Have you been in that car?
ELLIE: *looks at a toy-car*
ELLIE: Been in mummy's   [car though
                                         [head tilt and right shoulder lift (Figure 7.12)

Syntactic construction of the utterance:
                q clause   but   p clause
GRANDMOTHER: What color is mummy's car?

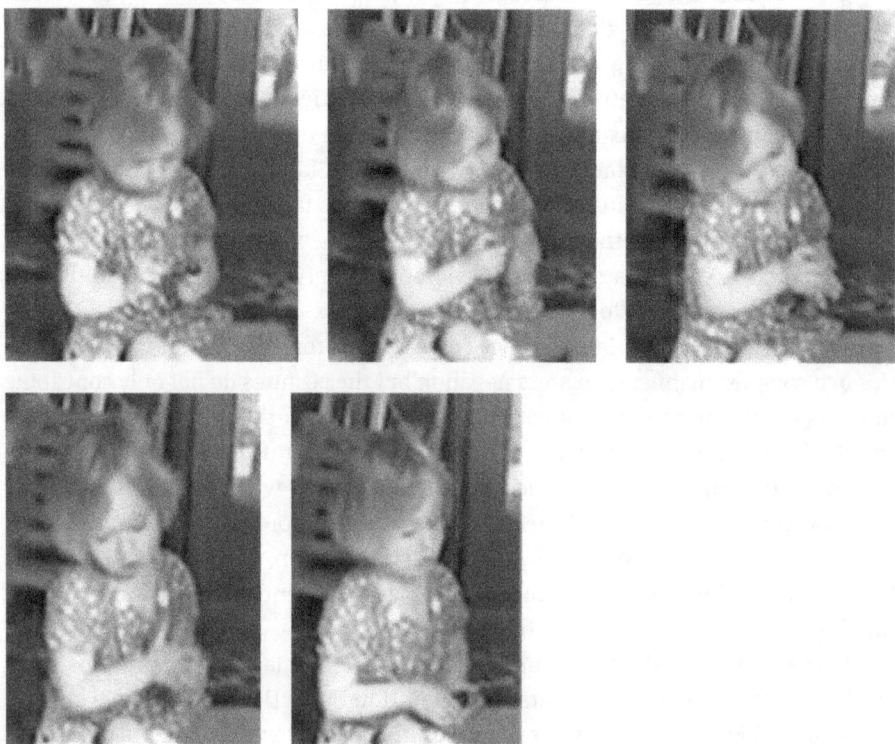

Fig. 7.12: Ellie's head tilt and one right shoulder lift.

The analysis of Example 7.3 shows that the synchronization of speech and gestures is dense and vertical, and it reveals underlying complex cognitive processes at work in the child's utterance. The gestures may not be intentionally addressed to the grandmother, but as they are visible and are produced in interaction, they constitute *publicly reusable* (C. Goodwin, 2017) and interpretable material the grandmother can rely on to understand the child's utterance and to build meaning subsequently.

In Example 7.4, Ellie continues to use gestures in a similar manner. Her palm-up and head tilt seem to be self-oriented, but because they are visible in interaction they take on a discursive function.

Example 7.4 *Palm-up and head tilt exhibiting Ellie's thinking process at work—3;06*
The link to the video of this example can be found with this book's supplementary materials online (https://www.apa.org/pubs/books/gesture-in-language).
GRANDMOTHER: Will you make me some toast and marmalade, please?
ELLIE: I can't because I haven't   [got any.
     [head tilt

[...]
GRANDMOTHER: But what can you make me? Can you make me something toasted please?
ELLIE: yeah.   [We::::::'ve got [(.) [jam!
     [head tilt [palm-up (Figure 7.13C)   [raises her fist
     (Figure 7.13A and Figure 7.13B)   (Figure 7.13F)
             [touches her face with her index finger
             (Figure 7.13D)
             [looks at the grandmother (Figure 7.13E)

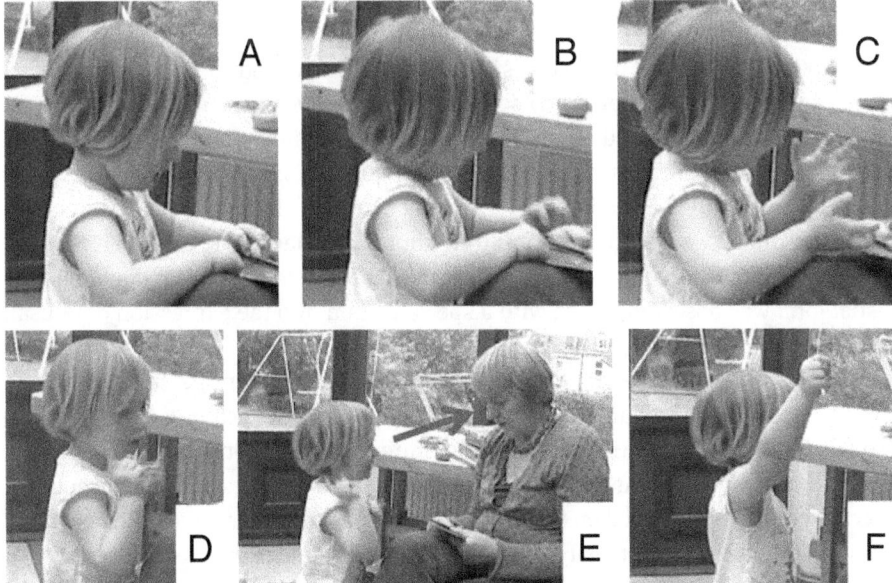

Fig. 7.13: Ellie's gesture sequence combined with "we've got marmalade."

In this sequence, Ellie needs some time to find ideas to answer her grandmother's question in a context of pretend play. The gestures she produces do not seem to be used primarily to sustain meaning making in interaction or to manage turn-taking but rather to help the child while she is engaged in a thinking process. Yet, the production of these gestures makes them visible and as soon as they are performed, they contribute to the *public substrate* (C. Goodwin, 2017). They are therefore available for the grandmother to analyze the situation and understand that the child is taking some time to think. This is probably why the grandmother keeps looking at the child and does not add anything. These gestures are thinking gestures and are not primarily communicative (C. Goodwin, 2017) because they are not directly addressed to the coparticipant in the interaction. Yet, because they are used in interaction, they highlight the thinking process Ellie is engaged in and, as such, they illustrate what McNeill described when he wrote that gestures are "a window onto mind and brain" (McNeill, 2013, p. 1). In this context, these gestures also take on a discursive function as Ellie manages to delay the moment when her grandmother is going to speak. Her gestures are meaningful for the grandmother, and they could be analyzed as early embodied practices for turn-taking management. Moreover, the palm-up and head tilt in Figure 7.13D are still used to express a function akin to ignorance or absence, but they also take on a more subjective function as they become markers of stance in interaction.

7.5 Discussion

After 3;00, it appears that the gestures Ellie and Madeleine produce to convey negation often express more than negation itself. Before 3;00, Ellie's occurrences of palm-ups, shoulder lifts, and head tilts mostly convey negation only. 48 out of the 57 coded productions of the shrug components between 1;00 and 3;00 contributed to express negation only. After 3;00, among Ellie's 36 occurrences of palm-ups, shoulder lifts, and head tilts, 25 were coded as multifunctional. In Madeleine's data, 108 out of 138 occurrences were coded as multifunctional. As for headshakes, a reduction of the visual form was observed, along with a specialization into the expression of refusal, denial, or ignorance.

These three sequences are examples among many others in the data. I use them to show that once the children start expressing complex meaning in the spoken modality, the status and the function of gestures seem to change and diversify. Yet the analyses illustrate that the emergence of co-speech gestures and their functional specialization are not based on the children's ability to fully convey complex meaning with words. Before using mostly speech and complex sentences, the children rely on multimodality and the synchrony between modalities. Research on early language acquisition has shown that gestures usually emerge during the prelinguistic period and are often described as facilitators for language development (Goldin-Meadow, 2015; Iverson & Goldin-Meadow, 2005). During the prelinguistic period, children use gestures instead of words to communicate their needs and desires to adults (Gentilucci et al., 2012; Iverson, 2010; Iverson & Goldin-Meadow, 2005; Morgenstern et al., 2010; Tomasello et al., 2007). These findings and this chapter highlight the specific role of gestures in combination with speech in language acquisition: if gestures facilitate the emergence of first words during what is called the *prelinguistic period* (before speech), they may also facilitate the emergence of complex sentences once children are more expert speakers. From that perspective, co-speech gestures between 3;00 and 4;00 may facilitate children's capacity to express complex meaning with words only later in their language development. Between 3;00 and 4;00, a functional complexification, as well as a grammaticization of the forms performed, occurs. Indeed, most gestures take on logical, discursive, intersubjective, and interactional values.

This chapter investigates the notion of complex meaning in interaction and tries to provide a definition for it. Our analyses of multimodal complex meaning making suggest that after 3;00, gestures add a variety of subtle meanings to speech. In this respect, the role of gesture is radically distinct between gestures that express communicative stance (refusal or absence), gestures that add subjectivity to a speech act (Examples 7.2, 7.3, and 7.4), and gestures that merely index a mental state (Example 7.4), but one gesture may bear several functions simultaneously or be deployed from one function to another as the interaction takes place.

Overall, Madeleine and Ellie enter language through different pathways, but the age of 3;00 marks a shift in their system: In Ellie's productions, the number of gestures decreases in favor of speech, but their functions and their contribution to meaning making complexify. Indeed, her gestures acquire more nuanced semantic values than before 3;00, and start supplementing speech. In Madeleine's productions, gestures are added to her already quite complex speech, and she starts developing symbolic combinations. Yet, co-speech gestures seem to emerge when both Madeleine and Ellie are cognitively capable of building complex meaning. At this stage, they express complex meaning in a dense and multimodal manner, mobilizing speech and gestures simultaneously. Eventually, their multimodal constructions will expand and diversify with the development of speech. In this perspective, multimodality enables children to embody and convey complex meaning at a stage when they would not be able to do so with words only. Co-speech gestures thus play a role in the acquisition of complex sentences in children, and the whole process of acquiring complex meaning may be in line with the *concertina effect* identified by Sekali (2012) for the development of spoken complex sentences in Madeleine. Sekali explained that the acquisition of complex sentences in Madeleine's speech relies on dynamic patterns of syntactic expansion, integration, and diversification of constructions in speech. In line with this research, I suggest that the acquisition of complex meaning relies on the densification of resources, their expansion, and their diversification. After a rich multimodal period leading to the emergence of complex sentences and syntax in the children's speech, the children adjust to the language addressed to them. In Madeleine's and Ellie's families, speech is the modality used the most, and the children, without leaving gestures aside, will primarily use speech.

7.6 Conclusion

In this chapter, I presented a study on the role of co-speech gestures when they emerge in the language of two monolingual children. Thanks to the use of quantitative and qualitative detailed interactive analyses, I was able to show that co-speech gestures contribute to the construction of complex meaning in the children's language and that they may even pave the way for the emergence of complex sentences in children's speech.

All the gestures the children produced after 3;00 were present in their input and used in child-directed speech. After 3;00, both children were proficient speakers of their native language and started expressing complex meaning with words. It appears from the data that the proficiency level in speech triggers a change in the functions of the gestures. The gestures that emerged before 2;06 were maintained to convey negation, but their meaning in context diversified. Gestures used before 2;06 to express negation took on discursive and interactional functions after 3;00. The gestures slowly developed from rather objective grammatical markers working as fixed semantic items to more subjective markers enabling the children to position themselves and manage interaction. In this respect, after 3;00, gestures can be considered as more grammaticized (Wilcox, 2004): Both children used them not only as markers of negation but also as stance, (inter)subjective markers, and as ways to manage turn-taking.

Neither qualitative nor quantitative analyses indicated any critical difference between the two children in the use of co-speech gestures after 3;00. This may indicate that whatever the semiotic path children follow to enter communication and language, when they are engaged in interaction, they develop language and a symbolic mode of communication similar to the one used by the other members of their community. In the end, both Madeleine and Ellie produced meaningful and complex sentences relying on gestures and speech. Between 3;00 and 4;00, their use of speech and gestures was still more condensed and vertical than the way their mothers combined these two modalities, but results show that the children's communication system was progressively becoming similar to their input.

This chapter raises new questions on the acquisition and development of complex speaking and thinking processes in young children. If previous studies have claimed that gestures facilitate the emergence of speech in the one- and two-word utterance period, the analyses presented here shed new light on the role of co-speech gestures. When Madeleine and Ellie start producing complex syntactic and semantic constructions but are not yet able to fully master the articulation of the clauses in the spoken modality, gestures play a role in the construction of meaning in interaction. In the production of a complex sentence like a *p but q* construction, co-speech gestures help children convey meaning rapidly, and linguistic complexity is supported by several modalities used simultaneously. Co-speech gestures create linguistic condensation, which will later on unfold and be taken over by linear speech. In this respect, this study showed that the acquisition of complex sentences is grounded in cognitive, linguistic, and motor development, and coordination.

From a developmental and ontogenetic perspective, this chapter demonstrated that analyzing the emergence and development of co-speech gestures in children's early complex productions may help clarify how language and meaning making in interaction coordinate and develop. This chapter also advocates for the systematic combination of quantitative and qualitative methods. A methodology combining several tools and approaches may be the best way to encapsulate the multimodal richness and the complexity of meaning making in children under 4;00.

References

Andrén, M. (2010). *Children's gestures from 18 to 30 months* [Unpublished doctoral dissertation]. Lund University: Centre for Languages and Literature.

Andrén, M. (2014). Multimodal constructions in children: Is the headshake part of language? *Gesture, 14*(2), 141–170. https://doi.org/10.1075/gest.14.2.02and

Antinucci, F., & Volterra, V. (1979). Negation in child language: A pragmatic study. In E. Ochs & B. Schieffelin (Eds.), *Developmental pragmatics* (pp. 281–304). Academic Press.

Bakhtin, M. M. (1986). *Speech genres and other late essays*. University of Texas Press.

Bavelas, J. B., Chovil, N., Coates, L., & Roe, L. (1995). Gestures specialized for dialogue. *Personality and Social Psychology Bulletin, 21*(4), 394–405. https://doi.org/10.1177/0146167295214010

Bavelas, J. B., Chovil, N., Lawrie, D. A., & Wade, A. (1992). Interactive gestures. *Discourse Processes, 15*(4), 469–489. https://doi.org/10.1080/01638539209544823

Beaupoil-Hourdel, P. (2015). *Multimodal acquisition and expression of negation. Analysis of a videotaped and longitudinal corpus of a French and an English mother–child dyad* [Unpublished doctoral dissertation]. Sorbonne Nouvelle University, Paris.

Beaupoil-Hourdel, P., & Debras, C. (2017). Developing communicative postures: The emergence of shrugging in child communication. *Language Interaction Acquisition, 1*(8), 91–118. https://doi.org/10.1075/lia.8.1.05bea

Beaupoil-Hourdel, P., Morgenstern, A., & Boutet, D. (2015). A child's multimodal negations from 1 to 4: The interplay between modalities. In P. Larrivée & C. Lee (Eds.), *Negation and polarity: Experimental perspectives* (pp. 95–123). Springer International Publishing.

Benazzo, S., & Morgenstern, A. (2014). A bilingual child's multimodal path into negation. *Gesture, 14*(2), 171–202. https://doi.org/10.1075/gest.14.2.03ben

Blondel, M., Boutet, D., Beaupoil-Hourdel, P., & Morgenstern, A. (2017). *La négation chez les enfants signeurs et non signeurs: Des patrons gestuels communs* [Negation in signing and non-signing children: Common gestural patterns]. *Language Interaction Acquisition*, *1*(8), 141–171.

Bloom, L. (1970). *Language development: Form and function emerging grammars*. MIT Press.

Boutet, D. (2008). Une morphologie de la gestualité: Structuration articulaire [A morphology of gestures: Joint structuring]. *Cahiers de Linguistique Analogique*, *5*, 81–115.

Boutet, D. (2010). Structuration physiologique de la gestuelle: Modèle et tests [Physiological structuring of gesture: Model and tests]. *Lidil: Revue de linguistique et de didactique des langues*, *42*, 77–96. https://doi.org/10.4000/lidil.3070

Bruner, J. S., Goodnow, J. J., & Austin, G. A. (1956). *A study of thinking*. Wiley.

Budwig, N. (2003). Context and the dynamic construal of meaning in early childhood. In C. Raeff & J. B. Benson (Eds.), *Social and cognitive development in the context of individual, social, and cultural processes* (pp. 103–130). Routledge.

Calbris, G. (1990). *The semiotics of French gestures*. Indiana University Press.

Calbris, G. (2011). *Elements of meaning in gesture*. John Benjamins. https://doi.org/10.1075/gs.5

Calbris, G., & Montredon, J. (1986). *Des gestes et des mots pour le dire* [Gestures and words to communicate]. Clé International.

Cameron-Faulkner, T., Lieven, E., & Theakston, A. (2007). What part of no do children not understand? A usage-based account of multiword negation. *Journal of Child Language*, *34*(2), 251–282. https://doi.org/10.1017/S0305000906007884

Cartmill, E. A., Hunsicker, D., & Goldin-Meadow, S. (2014). Pointing and naming are not redundant: Children use gesture to modify nouns before they modify nouns in speech. *Developmental Psychology*, *50*(6), 1660–1666. https://doi.org/10.1037/a0036003

Choi, S. (1988). The semantic development of negation: A cross-linguistic longitudinal study. *Journal of Child Language*, *15*(3), 517–531. https://doi.org/10.1017/S030500090001254X

Clark, E. V. (2003). *First language acquisition*. Cambridge University Press.

Clark, H. H., & Clark, E. V. (1977). *Psychology and language: An introduction to psycholinguistics*. Harcourt Brace Jovanovich.

Colletta, J.-M. (2004). *Le développement de la parole chez l'enfant âgé de 6 à 11 ans: Corps, langage et cognition* [Speech development in children age 6 to 11: Body, language and cognition]. Editions Mardaga.

Cuccio, V. (2012). Is embodiment all that we need? Insights from the acquisition of negation. *Biolinguistics*, *6*(3–4), 259–275.

Debras, C. (2013). *L'expression multimodale du positionnement interactionnel (multimodal stance-taking): Étude d'un corpus oral vidéo de discussions sur l'environnement en anglais britannique* [Unpublished doctoral dissertation]. Sorbonne Nouvelle University.

Debras, C. (2017). The shrug: Forms and meanings of a compound enactment. *Gesture*, *16*(1), 1–34. https://doi.org/10.1075/gest.16.1.01deb

Debras, C., & Cienki, A. (2012). Some uses of head tilts and shoulder shrugs during human interaction, and their relation to stancetaking. In *2012 International Conference on Privacy, Security, Risk and Trust and 2012 International Conference on Social Computing* (pp. 932–937). IEEE. https://doi.org/10.1109/SocialCom-PASSAT.2012.136

Dodane, C., & Massini-Cagliari, G. (2010). La prosodie dans l'acquisition de la négation: Étude de cas d'une enfant monolingue française [Prosody in the acquisition of negation: A case study of a French monolingual child]. *ALFA: Revista de Linguística*, *54*(2).

Ducrot, O. (1984). *Le dire et le dit* [Speaking and speech]. Editions de Minuit.
Ducrot, O. (1989). *Logique, structure, énonciation: Lectures sur le langage* [Logic, structure, enunciation: Readings on language]. Éditions de Minuit.
Ducrot, O. (2001). Quelques raisons de distinguer "locuteurs" et "énonciateurs" [Some reasons to distinguish "speakers" and "enunciators"]. *Polyphonie—Linguistique et Littéraire, 3*, 1–17.
Duranti, A., & Goodwin, C. (1992). *Rethinking context: Language as an interactive phenomenon*. Cambridge University Press.
Efron, D. (1941). *Gesture and environment*. King's Crown Press.
Fontanier, P. (1968). *Les figures du discours* [Figures of speech]. Editions Flammarion.
Gentilucci, M., De Stefani, E., & Innocenti, A. (2012). From gesture to speech. *Biolinguistics, 6*(3–4), 338–353.
Givens, D. B. (1977). Shoulder shrugging: A densely communicative expressive behaviour. *Semiotica, 19*(1–2), 13–28. https://doi.org/10.1515/semi.1977.19.1-2.13
Goffman, E. (1959). *The presentation of self in everyday life*. Anchor.
Goffman, E. (1963). *Behavior in public places: Notes on the social organization of gatherings* (Reissue edition). The Free Press.
Goffman, E. (1967). *Interaction ritual: Essays on face-to-face behavior*. Transaction Publishers.
Goldin-Meadow, S. (2015). Gesture as a window onto communicative abilities: Implications for diagnosis and intervention. *Perspectives on Language Learning and Education, 22*(2), 50–60. https://doi.org/10.1044/lle22.2.50
Goodwin, C. (2000). Action and embodiment within situated human interaction. *Journal of Pragmatics, 32*(10), 1489–1522. https://doi.org/10.1016/S0378-2166(99)00096-X
Goodwin, C. (2002). Time in action. *Current Anthropology, 43*(S4), S19–S35. https://doi.org/10.1086/339566
Goodwin, C. (2010). Constructing meaning through prosody in aphasia. In D. Barth-Weingarten, E. Reber, & M. Selting (Eds.), *Prosody in interaction* (pp. 373–394). https://doi.org/10.1075/sidag.23.29goo
Goodwin, C. (2013). The co-operative, transformative organization of human action and knowledge. *Journal of Pragmatics, 46*(1), 8–23. https://doi.org/10.1016/j.pragma.2012.09.003
Goodwin, C. (2017). *Co-operative action*. Cambridge University Press. https://doi.org/10.1017/9781139016735
Goodwin, C., Goodwin, M. H., & Olsher, D. (2002). Producing sense with nonsense syllables. In C. E. Ford, B. A. Fox, & S. A. Thompson (Eds.), *The language of turn and sequence* (pp. 56–80). Oxford University Press.
Goodwin, M. H. (1980). Processes of mutual monitoring implicated in the production of description sequences. *Sociological Inquiry, 50*(3–4), 303–317. https://doi.org/10.1111/j.1475-682X.1980.tb00024.x
Guidetti, M. (2002). The emergence of pragmatics: Forms and functions of conventional gestures in young French children. *First Language, 22*(3), 265–285. https://doi.org/10.1177/014272370202206603
Guidetti, M. (2005). Yes or no? How young French children combine gestures and speech to agree and refuse. *Journal of Child Language, 32*(4), 911–924. https://doi.org/10.1017/S0305000905007038
Guidetti, M., & Colletta, J.-M. (2010). Gesture and multimodal development. *Gesture, 10*(2–3), 123–128. https://doi.org/10.1075/gest.10.2-3.01gui

Harrison, S. (2009a). The expression of negation through grammar and gestures. In J. Zlatev, M. Andrén, M. Johansson Falck, & C. Lundmark (Eds.), *Studies in language and cognition* (pp. 421–435). Cambridge Scholars Publishing.

Harrison, S. (2009b). *Grammar, gesture, and cognition: The case of negation in English* [Unpublished doctoral dissertation]. Université de Bordeaux.

Harrison, S. (2018). *The impulse to gesture: Where language, minds, and bodies intersect*. Cambridge University Press. https://doi.org/10.1017/9781108265065

Hashemi, M. R. (2012). Reflections on mixing methods in applied linguistics research. *Applied Linguistics*, *33*(2), 206–212. https://doi.org/10.1093/applin/ams008

Iverson, J. M. (2010). Developing language in a developing body: The relationship between motor development and language development. *Journal of Child Language*, *37*(2), 229–261. https://doi.org/10.1017/S0305000909990432

Iverson, J. M., & Goldin-Meadow, S. (2005). Gesture paves the way for language development. *Psychological Science*, *16*(5), 367–371. https://doi.org/10.1111/j.0956-7976.2005.01542.x

Jehoul, A., Brône, G., & Feyaerts, K. (2017). The shrug as marker of obviousness: Corpus evidence from Dutch face-to-face conversations. *Linguistics Vanguard*, *3*(s1). https://doi.org/10.1515/lingvan-2016-0082

Kendon, A. (2002). Some uses of the headshake. *Gesture*, *2*(2), 147–182. https://doi.org/10.1075/gest.2.2.03ken

Kendon, A. (2004). *Gesture: Visible action as utterance*. Cambridge University Press. https://doi.org/10.1017/CBO9780511807572

Kochan, A. (2008). *The acquisition of negation: A socio-pragmatic study of a bilingual child* [Unpublished master's thesis]. Ecole Normale Supérieure Lettres et Sciences Humaines, Lyon.

Leeuwen, T. V., & Jewitt, C. (2000). *The handbook of visual analysis*. SAGE.

MacWhinney, B. (2000). *The CHILDES project: Tools for analyzing talk*. Lawrence Erlbaum.

Marconi, D., & Bertinetto, P. M. (1984). Analisi di "ma." Parte prima: Semantica e pragmatica [Analysis of "but." Part one: Semantics and pragmatics]. *Lingua e Stile*, *19*(2), 223–258.

McNeill, D. (2013). Gesture as a window onto mind and brain, and the relationship to linguistic relativity and ontogenesis. In C. Müller, E. Fricke, & A. Cienki (Eds.), *Body—language—communication* (Vol. 1, pp. 28–54). Mouton de Gruyter. https://doi.org/10.1515/9783110261318.28

McNeill, D., & McNeill, N. B. (1968). What does a child mean when he says no? In E. Zale (Ed.), *Proceedings of the Conference on Language and Language Behaviour* (pp. 51–62). Appleton-Century-Crofts.

Morel, M.-A. (1996). *La concession en français* [Concession in French]. Editions OPHRYS.

Morgenstern, A. (2006). *Un Je en construction: Genèse de l'auto-désignation chez le jeune enfant* [An I in construction: The genesis of self-designation in young children]. Ophrys.

Morgenstern, A. (2009). *L'enfant dans la langue* [The child in language]. Presses de la Sorbonne Nouvelle.

Morgenstern, A. (2014). Children's multimodal language development. In C. Fäcke (Ed.), *Manual of language acquisition* (pp. 123–142). De Gruyter. https://doi.org/10.1515/9783110302257.123

Morgenstern, A., & Beaupoil, P. (2015). Multimodal approaches to language acquisition through the lens of negation. *Vestnik of Moscow State University: Discourse as social practice: Priorities and prospects*, *6*(717), 435–451.

Morgenstern, A., Beaupoil-Hourdel, P., Blondel, M., & Boutet, D. (2016). A multimodal approach to the development of negation in signed and spoken languages: Four case studies. In L. Ortega,

A. E. Tyler, H. I. Park, & M. Uno (Eds.), *The usage-based study of language learning and multilingualism* (pp. 15–36). Georgetown University Press.

Morgenstern, A., Blondel, M., Beaupoil-Hourdel, P., Benazzo, S., Boutet, D., Kochan, A., & Limousin, F. (2018). The blossoming of negation in gesture, sign and oral productions. In M. Hickman, E. Veneziano, & H. Jisa (Eds.), *Sources of variation in first language acquisition: Languages, contexts, and learners* (pp. 339–364). John Benjamins. https://doi.org/10.1075/tilar.22.17mor

Morgenstern, A., Caët, S., Collombel-Leroy, M., Limousin, F., & Blondel, M. (2010). From gesture to sign and from gesture to word: Pointing in deaf and hearing children. *Gesture, 10*(2–3), 172–202. https://doi.org/10.1075/gest.10.2-3.04mor

Morgenstern, A., & Parisse, C. (2012). The Paris Corpus. *Journal of French Language Studies, 22*(1), 7–12. https://doi.org/10.1017/S095926951100055X

Morris, D. (1994). *Bodytalk: A world guide to gestures*. Random House.

Müller, C. (1998). Forms and uses of the palm up open hand: A case of a gesture family? In C. Müller & R. Posner (Eds.), *The semantics and pragmatics of everyday gestures: Proceedings of the Berlin conference April 1998* (pp. 233–256). Weidler Buchverlag.

Pea, R. D. (1980). The development of negation in early child language. In D. R. Olson (Ed.), *The social foundations of language and thought: Essays in honor of Jerome Bruner* (pp. 156–186). W. W. Norton.

Reynolds, B. L. (2015). A mixed-methods approach to investigating first- and second-language incidental vocabulary acquisition through the reading of fiction. *Reading Research Quarterly, 50*(1), 111–127. https://doi.org/10.1002/rrq.88

Rossari, C. (2014). How does a concessive value emerge? In C. Ghezzi & P. Molinelli (Eds.), *Discourse and pragmatic markers from Latin to the Romance languages* (pp. 237–260). Oxford University Press. https://doi.org/10.1093/acprof:oso/9780199681600.003.0013

Sekali, M. (2012). The emergence of complex sentences in a French child's language from 0;10 to 4;01: Causal adverbial clauses and the concertina effect. *Journal of French Language Studies, 22*(1), 115–141. https://doi.org/10.1017/S0959269511000615

Spitz, R. A. (1957). *No and yes: On the genesis of human communication*. International Universities Press.

Streeck, J. (1994). Gesture as communication II: The audience as co-author. *Research on Language and Social Interaction, 27*(3), 239–267. https://doi.org/10.1207/s15327973rlsi2703_5

Streeck, J. (2009). *Gesturecraft: The manu-facture of meaning*. John Benjamins. https://doi.org/10.1075/gs.2

Tomasello, M., Carpenter, M., & Liszkowski, U. (2007). A new look at infant pointing. *Child Development, 78*(3), 705–722. https://doi.org/10.1111/j.1467-8624.2007.01025.x

Vaidyanathan, R. (1991). Development of forms and functions of negation in the early stages of language acquisition: A study in Tamil. *Journal of Child Language, 18*(1), 51–66. https://doi.org/10.1017/S0305000900013295

Wilcox, S. (2004). Gesture and language: Cross-linguistic and historical data from signed languages. *Gesture, 4*(1), 43–73. https://doi.org/10.1075/gest.4.1.04wil

Wittenburg, P., Brugman, H., Russel, A., Klassmann, A., & Sloetjes, H. (2006). ELAN: A professional framework for multimodality research. In *Proceedings of the Fifth International Conference of Language Resources and Evaluation (LREC2006)* (pp. 1556–1559). Genoa, Italy.

Casey Hall, Elizabeth Wakefield, and Susan Goldin-Meadow
8 Gesture Can Facilitate Children's Learning and Generalization of Verbs

Imagine you are watching a game of catch with a young child and you comment, "The girl is throwing the ball." Although this sentence describes a relatively simple event in relatively simple language, some parts of the sentence may be more difficult for the child to map onto the event than others—"girl" and "ball" are concrete, stable objects, but throwing is a transient event. The referent of "throwing" is thus potentially more ambiguous than the referent of either "girl" or "ball." Now imagine explaining the event with the same words, but also producing an iconic gesture, representing the action of throwing, at the same time. Would the gesture help clarify the meaning of this transient event for the child?

As other chapters in this volume have established, gestures—movements of the hands that accompany speech—are an integral part of how humans communicate and serve important functions for language development. Even when interacting with young children, caregivers use co-speech gestures, which have the potential to provide information (Iverson et al., 1999; Özçalışkan & Goldin-Meadow, 2005a; Shatz, 1982). After having gesture modeled for them, children adopt these hand movements as a means of communication, first on their own and then in combination with spoken language (Bates et al., 1979; Goldin-Meadow & Morford, 1985; Greenfield & Smith, 1976; Masur, 1983; Morford & Goldin-Meadow, 1992; Zinober & Martlew, 1985). In this chapter, we focus on how gesture is developmentally tied to children's production and understanding of one particular class of words: verbs. We begin by reviewing the close relation between spoken language development and gesture (Section 8.1). Next, we review why verb learning might be particularly challenging for children (Section 8.2), and research showing that gesture may be a good tool for building verb knowledge (Section 8.3). Finally, we address some of the mechanisms by which gesture might have a positive effect on verb learning (Section 8.4) and end with a general discussion and thoughts about future directions (Section 8.5).

8.1 The Relation Between Gesture and Spoken Language Development

Typically developing infants enter a world in which they not only hear their parents speak but also see them gesture. Although gesture and other aspects of nonverbal communication are sometimes ignored in discussions of language acquisition, they

https://doi.org/10.1515/9783110675788-008
Gesture in Language: Development Across the Lifespan, A. Morgenstern and S. Goldin-Meadow (Editors)
Copyright © 2022 by the American Psychological Association and Walter de Gruyter GmbH. All rights reserved.

are nevertheless a routine part of the input early language-learners receive. Indeed, researchers have shown that the amount of gesture input children receive from their parents has an impact on language development. For example, across cultures, parents can promote children's gesture use by using gesture themselves (for review, see Özçalışkan & Dimitrova, 2013), which in turn predicts children's subsequent vocabulary development (Iverson et al., 1999; Pan et al., 2005; Rowe & Goldin-Meadow, 2009; Rowe et al., 2008). We return to the importance of gesture input later in this chapter when we discuss the role of gesture instruction in children's understanding of verbs.

Although gesture input is important, self-produced gesture also serves an important function in language development. The gestures children produce as they acquire spoken language reflect their developing understanding of linguistic structure, and children may even use gestures to compensate for challenges in developing articulatory and phonological systems (Acredolo & Goodwyn, 1988). Children produce their first gestures prior to their first words, usually around 9 to 12 months (see Morgenstern, Chapter 3, this volume), and these early gestures predict linguistic milestones (Bates, 1976; Bates et al., 1979; Iverson et al., 2008). Children's first gestures are *deictic* gestures: pointing gestures that refer to objects in the environment. These gestures predict when lexical items for objects first enter the child's verbal lexicon; for example, a child points at a teddy bear and then produces the word "bear" 3 months later (Iverson & Goldin-Meadow, 2005). Deictic gestures thus precede–and predict– the onset of nouns in speech (and have even been found to play a causal role in word learning; LeBarton et al., 2015). Children also use their early deictic gestures to supplement their speech, turning single words into utterances that convey sentence-like meanings (e.g., "eat" + point at cookie; Goldin-Meadow & Butcher, 2003). The onset of these gesture–word combinations predicts the onset of different types of word–word combinations. For example, a child points at a sleeping dog and says "nap" several months before producing an actor–act combination in speech (e.g., "dog nap"); or a child says "bottle" while extending his hand in a GIVE gesture several months before producing an act–object combination in speech (e.g., "give bottle"; Capirci et al., 1996; Capobianco et al., 2017; Iverson & Goldin-Meadow, 2005; Özçalışkan & Goldin-Meadow, 2005b).

Children's early deictic gestures thus reference objects and predict noun learning (see also Rowe et al., Chapter 4, this volume). In contrast, iconic gestures reference attributes and actions and thus have the potential to play a role in adjective and verb learning (i.e., in learning relational terms). Iconic gestures can convey physical attributes (e.g., placing the hand high above the head to convey the height of a tall person) or actions (e.g., quickly moving an empty fist forward to depict throwing) of a referent. It is because action iconic gestures represent aspects of movement that they have the potential to play a role in verb learning. Children produce their first iconic gestures as early as age 14 to 18 months, but they demonstrate a sharp increase in iconic gesture use around 2 years old (Özçalışkan et al., 2014). These early iconic gestures predominantly convey action information rather than information about physical attributes (Özçalışkan & Goldin-Meadow, 2005b, 2011). Children comprehend iconic gestures at the same time that they produce them (Namy, 2008; Namy et al., 2004), and display the same order of acquisition in comprehension as in production—they understand iconic gestures conveying action information earlier than iconic gestures conveying attribute information (Hodges et al., 2018).

Iconic gestures appear later in development than deictic gestures, and unlike deictic gesture's relation to nouns, the onset of iconic gestures conveying action information follows (rather than precedes) children's production of their first verbs in speech (Özçalışkan et al., 2014). Iconic gestures increase in frequency as spoken verbs do, and begin to reflect meanings not yet expressed in speech. For example, a child who does not know the word "stir" says, "go like this," while moving an empty fist in circles as though stirring with a spoon. Children thus use iconic gestures to represent information not yet expressed in speech, thereby filling in lexical gaps in their action vocabularies. This phenomenon hints at the possibility that gesture itself could be useful in acquiring new verbs.

As they get older, children continue to use gesture with speech to convey a variety of mental representations. For example, Stites and Özçalışkan (2017) found that when asked to retell a narrative story from a video, children ages 4 to 6 tracked story referents with gesture + speech combinations. Children use gesture to track transient information in a narrative; for example, they use gestures paired with transitive and intransitive verbs to help associate characters with the actions they perform. This process may require some of the same cognitive processes needed to learn verbs. As in the example with which we began this chapter, mapping the word "throw" to the girl's throwing action also requires an understanding of relationships between actions and entities. Evidence that children can use gesture to both articulate and comprehend action information suggests that gesture may be particularly useful for helping children understand how this type of abstract information maps onto spoken language. We turn now to work exploring how specific properties of verbs may make them difficult for children to learn. We then suggest how gesture may address these challenges.

8.2 Why Verb Learning Is Difficult for Children: Theories and Evidence

Although children come to understand language without targeted instruction, some aspects of language learning are more difficult than others. Children find verb learning, in contrast to noun learning, particularly challenging. On average, nouns are acquired before verbs, based on measures of both production (Bornstein et al., 2004; Caselli et al., 1995; Fenson et al., 1994; Goldfield, 2000; Greenfield & Smith, 1976;

Nelson, 1973; Ogura et al., 2006) and comprehension (Benedict, 1979; Goldin-Meadow et al., 1976; Golinkoff et al., 1987; Imai et al., 2008). This early noun-learning advantage is robust, observed in children across different languages and cultures (Au et al., 1994; Bornstein et al., 2004; Gentner, 1982; Kauschke et al., 2007; Kim et al., 2000; Tardif et al., 1999).

Many factors likely influence children's differential acquisition and understanding of nouns and verbs. For example, infants pay attention to the grammatical form of novel words and use them to distinguish nouns from verbs (Chemla et al., 2009; Mintz, 2003; Waxman et al., 2009). The difference between children's success in learning nouns compared to verbs may also lie in differences in the conceptual properties of the referents of nouns and verbs; namely, that nouns generally refer to stable objects (particularly in talk to young children) and verbs refer to transient events. This idea that children's difficulty with verb learning stems from conceptual differences between nouns and verbs grows out of the *natural partitions hypothesis*, proposed by Gentner (1982), and supported in more recent work (Gentner, 2006; Gentner & Boroditsky, 2001; Golinkoff & Hirsh-Pasek, 2008; Ma et al., 2009; McDonough et al., 2011). This hypothesis posits that the concepts nouns encode (persons and things) are more concrete and less variable than the concepts verbs encode (activities, changes of state, causal relations), which makes verb learning more conceptually challenging than noun learning (Gentner, 1982). In other words, verbs are less imageable, and therefore more difficult to learn, than nouns. As illustrated earlier in the example of the game of catch, nouns are often constrained or stabilized by their physical properties, whereas verbs can be more abstract, impacted by the direction, manner, and location in which they are performed (Gentner, 1982).

Children also differ in their ability to generalize nouns and verbs. In language learning, children have successfully generalized a word when they can recognize it in a different context from the one in which the word was originally learned. Children successfully generalize nouns, but struggle to generalize verbs (e.g., Gentner, 1982; Gleitman et al., 2005). Children's facility with learning and generalizing nouns may stem partially from their natural tendency to focus on the physical, concrete properties of objects during language learning; for example, starting around the age of 2 years, children tend to generalize labels for objects based on their shape (Gershkoff-Stowe & Smith, 2004; Landau et al., 1998; Smith, 2000; Smith et al., 2002). Children's focus on the shape of objects during early language-learning may help them learn and generalize noun labels for those objects, but this same focus could interfere with their ability to learn and generalize verb labels for actions (e.g., Kersten & Smith, 2002). Because the actions that verbs label are typically not tied to specific objects, generalization may be particularly difficult for verbs (Gentner, 1982, 2006; Golinkoff & Hirsh-Pasek, 2008; Ma et al., 2009; McDonough et al., 2011). An object that is the referent of a noun maintains its general physical properties from one context to another, but an event that is the referent of a verb may look different when it is performed in different contexts, depending on who is performing the action or the object on which it is being performed. If children are object-focused when first learning a verb, they may pay less attention to the transient action properties of the action referent of the verb, and thus struggle to recognize these properties when the action is performed in a different context, particularly if the action is performed by a different actor (Kersten & Smith, 2002; Maguire et al., 2002), or is performed by or on a different object (Behrend, 1995; Forbes & Farrar, 1993). Even when children do encode and remember the action labeled by a verb, they may still have difficulty mapping the verb onto the action when it appears in a new context (Imai et al., 2005).

It is important to note that evidence for a noun-learning advantage is not without controversy. Some studies of children acquiring verb-friendly languages—where verbs appear in a more salient position than nouns in input to children (e.g., Korean and Mandarin)—do not find evidence for a noun-learning advantage and, in some cases, find evidence for a verb-learning advantage (Choi, 2000; Choi & Gopnik, 1995; Gopnik et al., 1996; Stoll et al., 2012; Tardif, 1996; Tardif et al., 1997). For example, Choi and Gopnik (1995) analyzed spontaneous speech samples of Korean children and Korean parents' self-report measures of their children's vocabularies. They found that Korean-speaking children produced nouns and verbs with similar frequencies in their early vocabularies. Tardif (1996) used a similar methodology with Mandarin-speaking children and found a preponderance of verbs over nouns in children's early speech.

Although these results seem to challenge evidence for a noun-learning advantage, more recent work suggests that the methodologies used in these studies may underestimate children's acquisition of nouns (for a review, see Gentner & Boroditsky, 2009). For example, Tardif et al. (1999) examined naturalistic interactions between Mandarin- and English-speaking children in three different contexts: noun-favorable (reading a picture book together), verb-favorable (playing with a mechanical toy that could perform different actions), and neutral (playing with a variety of toys). They found that children's noun and verb use was highly context-dependent no matter what language was being learned, suggesting that small samples of transcribed speech may not be an effective method to estimate a child's total vocabulary. The researchers then pooled children's speech from the transcripts of all three contexts and compared the average numbers of nouns and verbs to those of the MacArthur Communicative Development Inventory, a vocabulary checklist completed by caregivers. They found that the transcripts severely underestimated children's vocabularies relative to the checklists, and that the checklist results revealed a clear noun advantage for both Mandarin- and English-speaking children.

These findings speak to the importance of considering the context in which a child's language production occurs, and the implications of this context-dependence for the child's overall understanding of language structure. Interestingly, however, in experiments where children are asked to explicitly use their knowledge of language, children acquiring both noun- and verb-friendly languages have been found to be better at mapping novel nouns to object categories than novel verbs to event categories (Arunachalam et al., 2013; Arunachalam & Waxman, 2011; Leddon et al., 2011). These studies illustrate children's more conservative, narrow understanding of the meaning of verbs, compared to their understanding of the meaning of nouns (e.g., Forbes & Poulin-Dubois, 1997; Huttenlocher et al., 1983). Difficulties with verbs persist into the preschool years and sometimes beyond (Imai et al., 2005, 2008; Kersten & Smith, 2002; Seston et al., 2009; Waxman et al., 2009; for a more general theoretical discussion, see Gleitman et al., 2005).

In the following sections, we discuss evidence showing that including gesture in verb-learning instruction can facilitate children's understanding of verbs. We suggest that gesture has the potential to focus a child's attention on the transient properties of an action referent, and thus facilitate a child's ability to map a verb onto its action referent and help the child navigate the unique challenges of verb learning.

8.3 Gesture Can Facilitate Children's Verb Learning

Broadly, gestures produced and observed by children can facilitate learning across many domains, including mathematical equivalence (Novack et al., 2014; Singer & Goldin-Meadow, 2005), symmetry (Valenzeno et al., 2003), conservation of matter and number (Ping & Goldin-Meadow, 2008), and language—in particular, nouns (Capone & McGregor, 2005; Vogt & Kauschke, 2017) and, most relevant to this chapter, verbs (de Nooijer et al., 2013; Goodrich & Hudson Kam, 2009; Wakefield et al., 2017).

Including gesture in instruction when teaching a new verb improves children's ability to pair the verb with its referent, both for verbs representing actions performed on objects (de Nooijer et al., 2013; Wakefield et al., 2017) and for verbs representing actions performed without objects (Goodrich & Hudson Kam, 2009). For example, Goodrich and Hudson Kam (2009) used gesture to teach 3- and 4-year-old children novel intransitive verbs. Children were shown a toy moving down a ramp. Following this event, an experimenter produced a novel label in speech (e.g., "dack") and, at the same time, performed either a relevant iconic gesture (e.g., an index finger tracing circles while moving downward at an angle to illustrate the manner and path of the toy moving down the ramp) or an interactive gesture that did not disambiguate the meaning of the verb (e.g., pointing at the child); a condition in which no gesture was presented served as a control. After the learning phase, children observed the original toy performing the original action, along with a new toy performing a new action, and were asked, "Which toy is 'dacking'?" Only children who had seen the iconic gestures during learning selected the correct action above chance, indicating that they had correctly paired the novel verbs with their corresponding gestures, and suggesting that they had used those gestures to map the verb onto its action referent. Gesture has also been shown to help children learn novel verbs for actions on objects (i.e., transitive verbs). Wakefield et al. (2017) found that children could successfully learn novel verbs (e.g., "ratching") for actions on objects (e.g., twisting a knob on an object) by producing or observing gestures representing that action (e.g., twisting near, but not on, the object; see Figure 8.1).

In most studies using gesture to teach children verbs (including Goodrich & Hudson Kam, 2009, and Wakefield et al., 2017), the object–action pairing shown during testing is identical to the object–action pairing shown during instruction. Thus, it is possible that children show evidence of learning because they associate the novel verb with a specific object or object–action pairing, rather than with the intended action referent (cf. Kersten & Smith, 2002). More recent literature addresses this concern, and asks whether gesture helps children generalize a newly learned verb to a new action context. Mumford and Kita (2014) showed 3-year-old children videos of an actor performing an action, such as placing felt pieces into a cloud shape. The actor then said a novel word (e.g., "blick") while producing either (a) a gesture highlighting the manner in which the felt-placing action was performed (e.g., depicting the vertical hand movements used to make the cloud), or (b) a gesture highlighting the outcome of the felt-placing action (e.g., depicting the shape of the cloud in midair); in a control group, the actor said the novel word for the action without performing a gesture. Children were then presented with two novel videos at the same time and asked to point to the video that showed "blicking." In one of the videos, the manner the actor used to perform the action was the same as the original event, but the end-state of the felt pieces had changed (i.e., she created a different shape out of felt). In the other video, the actor created the same shape as before (i.e., a cloud), but used

Fig. 8.1: Examples of action and gesture training. From "Gesture for Generalization: Gesture Facilitates Flexible Learning of Words for Actions on Objects," by E. M. Wakefield, C. Hall, K. H. James, and S. Goldin-Meadow, 2018, *Developmental Science*, *21*(5), e12656 (https://doi.org/10.1111/desc.12656). Copyright 2018 by John Wiley and Sons. Reprinted with permission.

different movements to do so. Children who saw the actor perform a manner gesture were more likely to choose the video showing the original manner (with a different outcome), compared with children who saw an end-state gesture or no gesture. Children who saw a gesture conveying manner information thus interpreted this information as relevant to the novel word that they heard, and used the information to correctly pair a novel action context with the word, suggesting that they were treating the newly learned word as a verb. The type of information conveyed through gesture in a verb-learning context can thus influence how children interpret and generalize the verb.

Wakefield et al. (2018) built on Mumford and Kita's work by exploring whether gestures produced in a verb-learning context influence whether children interpret the newly learned word as a label for an action, an action–object pairing, or an object. Four- to 5-year-old children learned novel verbs through producing or observing one of two types of movement experience: (a) actions on objects or (b) gestures near objects. Children learned to pair the newly learned word with the original object–action pairing whether they learned through action or gesture. However, they were significantly better at generalizing what they had learned to a new context if they had learned through gesture rather than action. For example, children learned, either through gesture or action, that "ratching" was associated with twisting a knob on an orange object. They were then shown two new videos playing simultaneously and were asked to point to the one that showed ratching—one video showed the twisting action performed on a new object; the other video showed a different action performed on the orange object (the object shown during initial learning of the word). Children in the gesture condition were significantly more likely to choose as "ratching" the video where twisting was performed on a new object than were children in the action condition, and this difference persisted 24 hours later (replicating previous work showing that gesture's beneficial effects on learning persist over time; e.g., Congdon et al., 2017; Cook et al., 2008). These findings suggest that children who learn a word through gesture (as opposed to action) are more likely to interpret the verb as a label for an action, that is, as a verb. In contrast, children who learn the same word through action are more likely to pay attention to the object on which the action was performed, thus interpreting the newly learned word as a label for a particular action–object pairing (i.e., as a verb with a restricted meaning) or as a label for the object (i.e., as a noun).

Gesture can thus facilitate verb learning. We now ask whether the degree to which gesture helps a learner depends on who is doing the gesture. Although children can benefit from receiving input from teachers, several studies suggest that asking children to produce the gesture themselves may have some advantages. De Nooijer et al. (2013) asked children ages 9 to 11 years to learn a verb through either doing or seeing a relevant gesture. Children were shown a video of an experimenter defining a verb in speech, followed by a video in which the experimenter again defined the verb while simultaneously producing a relevant gesture (e.g., defining "dismiss" followed by a shoo gesture). Children were asked to imitate the gesture at one of two timepoints:

(a) as they were watching the video (imitation during encoding [IE]) or (b) after they had watched the video and were told to recall the definition of the verb (imitation during retrieval [IR]). In a control condition, children were told to watch the video but not imitate the gesture. Children were then asked to recall the definition of the novel verb on a posttest. Children in both the IE and IR imitation conditions performed better on the posttest than children who observed the gestures but didn't produce them themselves (there were no differences between the two imitation conditions).

Wakefield et al. (2017) also directly compared learning through doing versus seeing gesture within the same study and found a similar result: 4- and 5-year-old children learned novel verbs for actions on objects more quickly when they learned through doing gestures themselves than when they learned through seeing the experimenter's gestures. Interestingly, however, this difference in performance between learning through doing versus seeing disappeared when children were asked to generalize the verbs—children in the doing and seeing conditions were equally likely to extend the novel word they had learned to the action performed on a new object (Wakefield et al., 2018). Although this null result must be interpreted with caution, it does suggest that learning through gesture can facilitate children's ability to generalize a verb to an appropriate new context whether they observe the gesture or produce it themselves.

8.4 The Unique Properties of Gesture May Alleviate Specific Challenges That Children Face When Learning Verbs

Gesture can facilitate children's ability to learn and generalize novel verbs, but why does gesture help? We now return to our discussion of the unique challenges that verb learning presents, compared with noun learning. We examine how specific properties of gesture may help alleviate these challenges, and thus may make gesture a useful instructional tool for improving children's learning and understanding of verbs. We consider three possibilities:

- Gesture can depict aspects of an action, such as the manner and path of a movement, which may make these transient properties more imageable for children trying to grasp the meaning of a verb referring to this action.
- Gestures can convey the relation between a movement and an object or objects without directly interacting with the object, helping to draw attention to the movement properties of the action itself, and away from the object on which the action is performed.
- Gesture can be flexibly used across different contexts, which may be particularly useful for facilitating children's ability to generalize verbs.

8.4.1 Gesture May Make the Concepts Underlying Verbs More Imageable

The key to gesture's success as a learning tool may be that it can represent important aspects of concepts underlying verbs that, according to the natural partitions hypothesis (Gentner, 1982), are conceptually more difficult for children to understand than the more concrete concepts underlying nouns. Gesture can represent information imagistically, a property that may help it highlight components of an action that are most relevant to a verb's meaning. For example, picture an adult explaining to a child the previously described event of a girl throwing a ball. The adult may use gestures to depict imagistic aspects of the event, such as the direction and force of the girl's throwing, by producing a grasping handshape and moving the hand in a throwing motion, or tracing the trajectory of the ball's movement in space to emphasize the direction of the throw. Through gesture, the adult can thus use concrete, visual cues to convey to the child important information about the action to which the verb "throwing" refers—information that is transient when children watch an action event themselves. Teaching verbs through gesture may therefore highlight and help children encode information that is most relevant to the meaning of a verb.

8.4.2 Gestures Can Draw Attention to a Movement Itself, Rather Than a Referential Object

Gesture can represent the relation between an action and an object without actually touching the object. Because gestures do not involve physical manipulation of objects, they have the unique ability to refer to changes in the world without implementing change. Performing a rotating gesture near an object does not change the position of the object, unlike physically rotating the object, which does. This aspect of gesture may help draw attention to the action and away from the object on which the action is performed, thus helping children overcome their natural bias to focus on objects and their physical properties when learning new words. In addition, when a gesture representing an action is performed near an object that can afford the action, the gesture can convey the relationship between the action and the object, a relationship that might be important to the meaning of the verb representing that action. Gesture's ability to guide children's attention to the action components of a verb's meaning while at the same time highlighting the action's relationship to an object may help children generalize the verb to a new context, one that maintains not only the essential components of the action but also the action–object relationship.

8.4.3 Gesture Can Be Used Flexibly Across Contexts

Gesture can be performed by different actors across different contexts, which mirrors the variability in how an action can be performed across different contexts. Indeed, providing children with a range of contexts in which a verb can be applied has a beneficial effect on verb learning (Behrend, 1995; Childers, 2011; Childers et al., 2012; Forbes & Farrar, 1995). For example, Childers (2011) found that 2.5-year-old children generalized a novel verb for an action better when they saw an experimenter perform that action on several different objects rather than on the same object multiple times. Seeing the same action performed on different objects presumably helps children recognize the core features of the action—features that are central to the verb's meaning—which then facilitates generalization of the verb to appropriate contexts (Childers, 2011). However, multiple exemplars may, in some cases, be confusing to a child. For example, Maguire et al. (2008) found that 2.5- and 3-year-old children learned and generalized intransitive novel verbs better when they were shown only one actor performing an action labeled by a novel verb four times, as opposed to four different actors performing the action. Varying the person who performs an action labeled by a verb can, at least at times, be detrimental to learning to generalize the verb.

Gesture may offer another route to exploiting the learning mechanism underlying varying exemplars and reduce potentially negative effects of varying an exemplar too much. Like actions, gestures can be and often are performed in reference to objects. Unlike actions, however, gesture does not involve physical manipulation of an object and thus is not constrained by object properties (e.g., the size and shape of the object, which determine an action's grasp size, force, etc.). Gestures may vary in form, handshape, manner, and path even when they are performed multiple times by the same actor and in relation to one object. Thus, gesture may help children understand that actions labeled by verbs can be performed on or by multiple objects by conveying variability within a single learning context. Although no studies have directly compared learning verbs through multiple exemplars versus learning verbs through gesture, Wakefield et al. (2018) did consider the potential impact that children's unscripted exploration of multiple exemplars had on verb learning. Recall that, in this study, children were taught a novel verb in a single context, with one action performed relative to one object, either through action or gesture; they then completed a generalization assessment. Before the assessment, children were allowed to play with all of the objects used to teach the novel verbs, as well as new objects that were later used in the generalization assessment videos. The children thus had a chance to perform the actions they had seen, not only on the original objects, but also on a variety of objects (many of which supported the action). Performing an action on a variety of objects could promote generalization. Children's extension of the learned verbs to novel objects did not predict their performance on the generalization assessment on Day 1 of the study, but did predict generalization performance on Day 2. However, learning through gesture during training continued to predict generalization, above and beyond the effects of performing the act on multiple objects. This finding adds support to previous literature showing that multiple exemplars can be profitably used to teach verbs but also makes it clear that gesture can aid in this process in a unique, powerful way.

8.5 General Discussion and Future Directions

Verbs are particularly challenging to learn, but gesture offers a promising avenue through which verb learning can be improved in children. Previous work has documented the flexible manner in which children naturally use gesture. These gestures not only reflect and predict changes in children's linguistic knowledge (Bates, 1976; Bates et al., 1979; Hodges et al., 2018; Iverson & Goldin-Meadow, 2005; Iverson et al., 2008; Özçalışkan et al., 2014; Rowe & Goldin-Meadow, 2009; Stites & Özçalışkan, 2017), but they may also play a causal role in bringing those changes about (LeBarton et al., 2015; Wakefield et al., 2018). Researchers have exploited this flexibility and have successfully used gesture as an instructional tool in verb-learning contexts, both when children observe a teacher's gestures (Goodrich & Hudson Kam, 2009; Wakefield et al., 2017) and when they are encouraged to produce their own gestures (de Nooijer et al., 2013; Wakefield et al., 2017).

Gesture's positive effects on verb learning may lie in its unique ability to convey the action properties of a fleeting movement, thus making the transient properties of the action labeled by a verb more imageable for children. At the same time, gesture does not require the presence of an object to convey action information, and thus may draw children's attention to the relevant movement of an action labeled by a to-be-learned verb, rather than to an object associated with the action (Mumford & Kita, 2014; Wakefield et al., 2018). Because gesture is not constrained by objects, it may also introduce variability into a verb-learning context, even when performed by the same actor in reference to one object. Furthermore, subtle differences in the gestures used to represent an action (e.g., a grasping vs. a pointing handshape) can make it clear which features of the action are not central to the meaning of the verb used to label that action, thus signaling to the learner how the verb can be generalized across contexts (Wakefield et al., 2018).

There are still open questions as to exactly how gesture benefits children's learning and generalization of verbs. For example, it would be useful to know whether and how the gestures that children and adults produce in learning contexts vary compared with other movement types, such as actions on objects. Specifically, researchers could measure and compare the movement properties of gestures and other types of movements used in teaching environments to determine whether gestural movements are, in fact, significantly more variable than other movement types, and whether this variability predicts learning. It is also important to understand how gesture focuses children's visual attention in a verb-learning context. Research in which children's eye movements are measured using an eye tracking device could help determine the aspects of a learning situation to which gesture does and does not draw attention.

Despite remaining questions about the mechanisms underlying gesture's effects on verb learning, the evidence to date overwhelmingly suggests that gesture can support children's verb learning. Parents and teachers should thus be encouraged to gesture—and should encourage their children to gesture—as children acquire a comprehensive understanding of verbs. Children see adults produce gestures when they explain many types of concepts, ranging from the concrete properties of nouns to the abstract relationships between actors and the movements they perform in verbs. As their vocabularies grow, children produce gestures with multiple linguistic components that map onto different pieces of conceptual information. Because gesture is a naturally occurring and ubiquitous part of children's linguistic environment, it is crucial for researchers to understand how gesture both reflects and facilitates children's understanding of language concepts as they gain linguistic fluency.

References

Acredolo, L., & Goodwyn, S. (1988). Symbolic gesturing in normal infants. *Child Development*, *59*(2), 450–466. https://doi.org/10.2307/1130324

Arunachalam, S., Leddon, E. M., Song, H.-j., Lee, Y., & Waxman, S. R. (2013). Doing more with less: Verb learning in Korean-acquiring 24-month-olds. *Language Acquisition*, *20*(4), 292–304. https://doi.org/10.1080/10489223.2013.828059

Arunachalam, S., & Waxman, S. R. (2011). Grammatical form and semantic context in verb learning. *Language Learning and Development*, *7*(3), 169–184. https://doi.org/10.1080/15475441.2011.573760

Au, T. K.-f., Dapretto, M., & Song, Y. K. (1994). Input vs. constraints: Early word acquisition in Korean and English. *Journal of Memory and Language*, *33*(5), 567–582.

Bates, E. (1976). *Language and context: The acquisition of pragmatics*. Academic Press.

Bates, E., Benigni, L., Bretherton, I., Camaioni, L., & Volterra, V. (1979). *The emergence of symbols: Cognition and communication in infancy*. Academic Press.

Behrend, D. A. (1995). Processes involved in the initial mapping of verb meanings. In M. Tomasello & W. Merriman (Eds.), *Beyond names for things: Young children's acquisition of verbs* (pp. 251–273). Lawrence Erlbaum.

Benedict, H. (1979). Early lexical development: Comprehension and production. *Journal of Child Language*, *6*(2), 183–200. https://doi.org/10.1017/S0305000900002245

Bornstein, M. H., Cote, L. R., Maital, S., Painter, K., Park, S.-Y., Pascual, L., Pêcheux, M.-G., Ruel, J., Venuti, P., & Vyt, A. (2004). Cross-linguistic analysis of vocabulary in young children: Spanish, Dutch, French, Hebrew, Italian, Korean, and American English. *Child Development*, *75*(4), 1115–1139. https://doi.org/10.1111/j.1467-8624.2004.00729.x

Capirci, O., Iverson, J. M., Pizzuto, E., & Volterra, V. (1996). Gestures and words during the transition to two-word speech. *Journal of Child Language*, *23*(3), 645–673. https://doi.org/10.1017/S0305000900008989

Capobianco, M., Pizzuto, E. A., & Devescovi, A. (2017). Gesture–speech combinations and early verbal abilities. *Interaction Studies*, *18*(1), 55–76. https://doi.org/10.1075/is.18.1.03cap

Capone, N. C., & McGregor, K. K. (2005). The effect of semantic representation on toddlers' word retrieval. *Journal of Speech, Language, and Hearing Research*, *48*(6), 1468–1480. https://doi.org/10.1044/1092-4388(2005/102)

Caselli, M. C., Bates, E., Casadio, P., Fenson, J., Fenson, L., Sanderl, L., & Weir, J. (1995). A cross-linguistic study of early lexical development. *Cognitive Development*, *10*(2), 159–199. https://doi.org/10.1016/0885-2014(95)90008-X

Chemla, E., Mintz, T. H., Bernal, S., & Christophe, A. (2009). Categorizing words using 'frequent frames': What cross-linguistic analyses reveal about distributional acquisition strategies. *Developmental Science, 12*(3), 396–406. https://doi.org/10.1111/j.1467-7687.2009.00825.x

Childers, J. B. (2011). Attention to multiple events helps two-and-a-half-year-olds extend new verbs. *First Language, 31*(1), 3–22. https://doi.org/10.1177/0142723710361825

Childers, J. B., Heard, M. E., Ring, K., Pai, A., & Sallquist, J. (2012). Children use different cues to guide noun and verb extensions. *Language Learning and Development, 8*(3), 233–254. https://doi.org/10.1080/15475441.2011.585285

Choi, S. (2000). Caregiver input in English and Korean: Use of nouns and verbs in book-reading and toy-play contexts. *Journal of Child Language, 27*(1), 69–96. https://doi.org/10.1017/S0305000999004018

Choi, S., & Gopnik, A. (1995). Early acquisition of verbs in Korean: A cross-linguistic study. *Journal of Child Language, 22*(3), 497–529. https://doi.org/10.1017/S0305000900009934

Congdon, E. L., Novack, M. A., Brooks, N., Hemani-Lopez, N., O'Keefe, L., & Goldin-Meadow, S. (2017). Better together: Simultaneous presentation of speech and gesture in math instruction supports generalization and retention. *Journal of Learning and Instruction, 50*, 65–74. https://doi.org/10.1016/j.learninstruc.2017.03.005

Cook, S. W., Mitchell, Z., & Goldin-Meadow, S. (2008). Gesturing makes learning last. *Cognition, 106*(2), 1047–1058. https://doi.org/10.1016/j.cognition.2007.04.010

de Nooijer, J. A., van Gog, T., Paas, F., & Zwaan, R. A. (2013). Effects of imitating gestures during encoding or during retrieval of novel verbs on children's test performance. *Acta Psychologica, 144*(1), 173–179. https://doi.org/10.1016/j.actpsy.2013.05.013

Fenson, L., Dale, P. S., Reznick, J. S., Bates, E., Thal, D. J., Pethick, S. J., Tomasello, M., Mervis, C. B., & Stiles, J. (1994). Variability in early communicative development. *Monographs of the Society for Research in Child Development, 59*(5), i–185. https://doi.org/10.2307/1166093

Forbes, J. N., & Farrar, M. J. (1993). Children's initial assumptions about the meaning of novel motion verbs: Biased and conservative? *Cognitive Development, 8*(3), 273–290. https://doi.org/10.1016/S0885-2014(93)80002-B

Forbes, J. N., & Farrar, M. J. (1995). Learning to represent word meaning: What initial training events reveal about children's developing action verb concepts. *Cognitive Development, 10*(1), 1–20. https://doi.org/10.1016/0885-2014(95)90016-0

Forbes, J. N., & Poulin-Dubois, D. (1997). Representational change in young children's understanding of familiar verb meaning. *Journal of Child Language, 24*(2), 389–406. https://doi.org/10.1017/S0305000997003127

Gentner, D. (1982). Why nouns are learned before verbs: Linguistic relativity versus natural partitioning. In Stan A. Kuczaj (Ed.), *Language development Vol. 2: Language, thought and culture*, 301–334. Lawrence Erlbaum.

Gentner, D. (2006). Why verbs are hard to learn. In K. Hirsh-Pasek & R. M. Golinkoff (Eds.), *Action meets word: How children learn verbs* (pp. 544–564). Oxford University Press. https://doi.org/10.1093/acprof:oso/9780195170009.003.0022

Gentner, D., & Boroditsky, L. (2001). Individuation, relativity, and early word learning. In M. Bowerman & S. C. Levinson (Eds.), *Language acquisition and conceptual development* (pp. 215–256). Cambridge University Press. https://doi.org/10.1017/CBO9780511620669.010

Gentner, D., & Boroditsky, L. (2009). Early acquisition of nouns and verbs: Evidence from Navajo. In V. C. Mueller Gathercole (Ed.), *Routes to language: Studies in honor of Melissa Bowerman* (pp. 5–36). Psychology Press.

Gershkoff-Stowe, L., & Smith, L. B. (2004). Shape and the first hundred nouns. *Child Development*, 75(4), 1098–1114. https://doi.org/10.1111/j.1467-8624.2004.00728.x

Gleitman, L. R., Cassidy, K., Nappa, R., Papafragou, A., & Trueswell, J. C. (2005). Hard words. *Language Learning and Development*, 1(1), 23–64. https://doi.org/10.1207/s15473341lld0101_4

Goldfield, B. A. (2000). Nouns before verbs in comprehension vs. production: The view from pragmatics. *Journal of Child Language*, 27(3), 501–520. https://doi.org/10.1017/S0305000900004244

Goldin-Meadow, S., & Alibali, M. W. (2013). Gesture's role in speaking, learning, and creating language. *Annual Review of Psychology*, 64, 257–283. https://doi.org/10.1146/annurev-psych-113011-143802

Goldin-Meadow, S., & Butcher, C. (2003). Pointing toward two-word speech in young children. In S. Kita (Ed.), *Pointing: Where language, culture, and cognition meet* (pp. 85–107). Lawrence Erlbaum.

Goldin-Meadow, S., & Morford, M. (1985). Gesture in early child language: Studies of deaf and hearing children. *Merrill-Palmer Quarterly*, 31(2), 145–176.

Goldin-Meadow, S., Seligman, M. E. P., & Gelman, R. (1976). Language in the two-year-old. *Cognition*, 4(2), 189–202. https://doi.org/10.1016/0010-0277(76)90004-4

Golinkoff, R. M., & Hirsh-Pasek, K. (2008). How toddlers begin to learn verbs. *Trends in Cognitive Sciences*, 12(10), 397–403. https://doi.org/10.1016/j.tics.2008.07.003

Golinkoff, R. M., Hirsh-Pasek, K., Cauley, K. M., & Gordon, L. (1987). The eyes have it: Lexical and syntactic comprehension in a new paradigm. *Journal of Child Language*, 14(1), 23–45. https://doi.org/10.1017/S030500090001271X

Goodrich, W., & Hudson Kam, C. L. (2009). Co-speech gesture as input in verb learning. *Developmental Science*, 12(1), 81–87. https://doi.org/10.1111/j.1467-7687.2008.00735.x

Gopnik, A., Choi, S., & Baumberger, T. (1996). Cross-linguistic differences in early semantic and cognitive development. *Cognitive Development*, 11(2), 197–225. https://doi.org/10.1016/S0885-2014(96)90003-9

Greenfield, P. M., & Smith, J. H. (1976). *The structure of communication in early language development*. Academic Press.

Hodges, L. E., Özçalışkan, Ş., & Williamson, R. (2018). Type of iconicity influences children's comprehension of gesture. *Journal of Experimental Child Psychology*, 166, 327–339. https://doi.org/10.1016/j.jecp.2017.08.009

Huttenlocher, J., Smiley, P., & Charney, R. (1983). Emergence of action categories in the child: Evidence from verb meanings. *Psychological Review*, 90(1), 72–93. https://doi.org/10.1037/0033-295X.90.1.72

Imai, M., Haryu, E., & Okada, H. (2005). Mapping novel nouns and verbs onto dynamic action events: Are verb meanings easier to learn than noun meanings for Japanese children? *Child Development*, 76(2), 340–355. https://doi.org/10.1111/j.1467-8624.2005.00849_a.x

Imai, M., Li, L., Haryu, E., Okada, H., Hirsh-Pasek, K., Golinkoff, R. M., & Shigematsu, J. (2008). Novel noun and verb learning in Chinese-, English-, and Japanese-speaking children. *Child Development*, 79(4), 979–1000. https://doi.org/10.1111/j.1467-8624.2008.01171.x

Iverson, J. M., Capirci, O., Longobardi, E., & Caselli, M. C. (1999). Gesturing in mother–child interactions. *Cognitive Development*, 14(1), 57–75. https://doi.org/10.1016/S0885-2014(99)80018-5

Iverson, J. M., Capirci, O., Volterra, V., & Goldin-Meadow, S. (2008). Learning to talk in a gesture-rich world: Early communication in Italian vs. American children. *First Language*, 28(2), 164–181. https://doi.org/10.1177/0142723707087736

Iverson, J. M., & Goldin-Meadow, S. (2005). Gesture paves the way for language development. *Psychological Science, 16*(5), 367–371. https://doi.org/10.1111/j.0956-7976.2005.01542.x

Kauschke, C., Lee, H.-W., & Pae, S. (2007). Similarities and variation in noun and verb acquisition: A crosslinguistic study of children learning German, Korean, and Turkish. *Language and Cognitive Processes, 22*(7), 1045–1072. https://doi.org/10.1080/01690960701307348

Kersten, A. W., & Smith, L. B. (2002). Attention to novel objects during verb learning. *Child Development, 73*(1), 93–109. https://doi.org/10.1111/1467-8624.00394

Kim, M., McGregor, K. K., & Thompson, C. K. (2000). Early lexical development in English- and Korean-speaking children: Language-general and language-specific patterns. *Journal of Child Language, 27*(2), 225–254. https://doi.org/10.1017/S0305000900004104

Landau, B., Smith, L., & Jones, S. (1998). Object shape, object function, and object name. *Journal of Memory and Language, 38*(1), 1–27. https://doi.org/10.1006/jmla.1997.2533

LeBarton, E. S., Goldin-Meadow, S., & Raudenbush, S. (2015). Experimentally-induced increases in early gesture lead to increases in spoken vocabulary. *Journal of Cognition and Development, 16*(2), 199–220. https://doi.org/10.1080/15248372.2013.858041

Leddon, E. M., Arunachalam, S., Waxman, S. R., Fu, X., Gong, H., & Wang, L. (2011). Noun and verb learning in Mandarin-acquiring 24-month-olds. In N. Danis, K. Mesh, & H. Sung (Eds.), *Online Proceedings Supplement, 35th Annual Boston University Conference on Language Development.* http://www.bu.edu/bucld/proceedings/supplement/vol35/

Ma, W., Golinkoff, R. M., Hirsh-Pasek, K., McDonough, C., & Tardif, T. (2009). Imageability predicts the age of acquisition of verbs in Chinese children. *Journal of Child Language, 36*(2), 405–423. https://doi.org/10.1017/S0305000908009008

Maguire, M. J., Hennon, E. A., Hirsh-Pasek, K., Golinkoff, R. M., Slutzky, C. B., & Sootsman, J. (2002). Mapping words to actions and events: How do 18-month-olds learn a verb? In B. Skarabela, S. Fish, & A. H. J. Do (Eds.), *Proceedings of the 26th Annual Boston University Conference on Language Development* (Vol. 2, pp. 371–382). Cascadilla Press.

Maguire, M. J., Hirsh-Pasek, K., Golinkoff, R. M., & Brandone, A. C. (2008). Focusing on the relation: Fewer exemplars facilitate children's initial verb learning and extension. *Developmental Science, 11*(4), 628–634. https://doi.org/10.1111/j.1467-7687.2008.00707.x

Masur, E. F. (1983). Gestural development, dual-directional signaling, and the transition to words. *Journal of Psycholinguistic Research, 12*, 93–109. https://doi.org/10.1007/BF01067406

McDonough, C., Song, L., Hirsh-Pasek, K., Golinkoff, R. M., & Lannon, R. (2011). An image is worth a thousand words: Why nouns tend to dominate verbs in early word learning. *Developmental Science, 14*(2), 181–189. https://doi.org/10.1111/j.1467-7687.2010.00968.x

Mintz, T. H. (2003). Frequent frames as a cue for grammatical categories in child directed speech. *Cognition, 90*(1), 91–117. https://doi.org/10.1016/S0010-0277(03)00140-9

Morford, M., & Goldin-Meadow, S. (1992). Comprehension and production of gesture in combination with speech in one-word speakers. *Journal of Child Language, 19*(3), 559–580. https://doi.org/10.1017/S0305000900011569

Mumford, K. H., & Kita, S. (2014). Children use gesture to interpret novel verb meanings. *Child Development, 85*(3), 1181–1189. https://doi.org/10.1111/cdev.12188

Namy, L. L. (2008). Recognition of iconicity doesn't come for free. *Developmental Science, 11*(6), 841–846. https://doi.org/10.1111/j.1467-7687.2008.00732.x

Namy, L. L., Campbell, A. L., & Tomasello, M. (2004). The changing role of iconicity in non-verbal symbol learning: A U-shaped trajectory in the acquisition of arbitrary gestures. *Journal of Cognition and Development, 5*(1), 37–57. https://doi.org/10.1207/s15327647jcd0501_3

Nelson, K. (1973). Structure and strategy in learning to talk. *Monographs of the Society for Research in Child Development, 38*(1/2), 1–136. https://doi.org/10.2307/1165788

Novack, M. A., Congdon, E. L., Hemani-Lopez, N., & Goldin-Meadow, S. (2014). From action to abstraction: Using the hands to learn math. *Psychological Science, 25*(4), 903–910. https://doi.org/10.1177/0956797613518351

Ogura, T., Dale, P. S., Yamashita, Y., Murase, T., & Mahieu, A. (2006). The use of nouns and verbs by Japanese children and their caregivers in book-reading and toy-playing contexts. *Journal of Child Language, 33*(1), 1–29. https://doi.org/10.1017/S0305000905007270

Özçalışkan, Ş., & Dimitrova, N. (2013). How gesture input provides a helping hand to language development. *Seminars in Speech and Language, 34*(04), 227–236. https://doi.org/10.1055/s-0033-1353447

Özçalışkan, Ş., Gentner, D., & Goldin-Meadow, S. (2014). Do iconic gestures pave the way for children's early verbs? *Applied Psycholinguistics, 35*(6), 1143–1162. https://doi.org/10.1017/S0142716412000720

Özçalışkan, Ş., & Goldin-Meadow, S. (2005a). Do parents lead their children by the hand? *Journal of Child Language, 32*(3), 481–505. https://doi.org/10.1017/S0305000905007002

Özçalışkan, Ş., & Goldin-Meadow, S. (2005b). Gesture is at the cutting edge of early language development. *Cognition, 96*(3), B101–B113. https://doi.org/10.1016/j.cognition.2005.01.001

Özçalışkan, Ş., & Goldin-Meadow, S. (2011). Is there an iconic gesture spurt at 26 months? In G. Stam & M. Ishino (Eds.), *Integrating gestures: The interdisciplinary nature of gesture* (pp. 163–174). John Benjamins. https://doi.org/10.1075/gs.4.14ozc

Pan, B. A., Rowe, M. L., Singer, J. D., & Snow, C. E. (2005). Maternal correlates of growth in toddler vocabulary production in low-income families. *Child Development, 76*(4), 763–782. https://doi.org/10.1111/1467-8624.00498-i1

Ping, R. M., & Goldin-Meadow, S. (2008). Hands in the air: Using ungrounded iconic gestures to teach children conservation of quantity. *Developmental Psychology, 44*(5), 1277–1287. https://doi.org/10.1037/0012-1649.44.5.1277

Rowe, M. L., & Goldin-Meadow, S. (2009). Early gesture selectively predicts later language learning. *Developmental Science, 12*(1), 182–187. https://doi.org/10.1111/j.1467-7687.2008.00764.x

Rowe, M. L., Özçalışkan, Ş., & Goldin-Meadow, S. (2008). Learning words by hand: Gesture's role in predicting vocabulary development. *First Language, 28*(2), 182–199. https://doi.org/10.1177/0142723707088310

Seston, R., Golinkoff, R. M., Ma, W., & Hirsh-Pasek, K. (2009). Vacuuming with my mouth?: Children's ability to comprehend novel extensions of familiar verbs. *Cognitive Development, 24*(2), 113–124. https://doi.org/10.1016/j.cogdev.2008.12.001

Shatz, M. (1982). On mechanisms of language acquisition: Can features of the communicative environment account for development? In E. Wanner & L. R. Gleitman (Eds.), *Language acquisition: The state of the art* (pp. 102–127). Cambridge University Press.

Singer, M. A., & Goldin-Meadow, S. (2005). Children learn when their teacher's gestures and speech differ. *Psychological Science, 16*(2), 85–89. https://doi.org/10.1111/j.0956-7976.2005.00786.x

Smith, L. B. (2000). Learning how to learn words: An associative crane. In R. M. Golinkoff & K. Hirsh-Pasek (Eds.), *Becoming a word learner: A debate on lexical acquisition* (pp. 51–80). Oxford University Press. https://doi.org/10.1093/acprof:oso/9780195130324.003.003

Smith, L. B., Jones, S. S., Landau, B., Gershkoff-Stowe, L., & Samuelson, L. (2002). Object name learning provides on-the-job training for attention. *Psychological Science, 13*(1), 13–19. https://doi.org/10.1111/1467-9280.00403

Stites, L. J., & Özçalışkan, Ş. (2017). Who did what to whom? Children track story referents first in gesture. *Journal of Psycholinguistic Research, 46*, 1019–1032. https://doi.org/10.1007/s10936-017-9476-0

Stoll, S., Bickel, B., Lieven, E., Paudyal, N. P., Banjade, G., Bhatta, T. N., Gaenszle, M., Pettigrew, J., Rai, I. P., Rai, M., & Rai, N. K. (2012). Nouns and verbs in Chintang: Children's usage and surrounding adult speech. *Journal of Child Language, 39*(2), 284–321. https://doi.org/10.1017/S0305000911000080

Tardif, T. (1996). Nouns are not always learned before verbs: Evidence from Mandarin speakers' early vocabularies. *Developmental Psychology, 32*(3), 492–504. https://doi.org/10.1037/0012-1649.32.3.492

Tardif, T., Gelman, S. A., & Xu, F. (1999). Putting the "noun bias" in context: A comparison of English and Mandarin. *Child Development, 70*(3), 620–635. https://doi.org/10.1111/1467-8624.00045

Tardif, T., Shatz, M., & Naigles, L. (1997). Caregiver speech and children's use of nouns versus verbs: A comparison of English, Italian, and Mandarin. *Journal of Child Language, 24*(3), 535–565. https://doi.org/10.1017/S030500099700319X

Valenzeno, L., Alibali, M. W., & Klatzky, R. (2003). Teachers' gestures facilitate students' learning: A lesson in symmetry. *Contemporary Educational Psychology, 28*(2), 187–204. https://doi.org/10.1016/S0361-476X(02)00007-3

Vogt, S., & Kauschke, C. (2017). Observing iconic gestures enhances word learning in typically developing children and children with specific language impairment. *Journal of Child Language, 44*(6), 1458–1484. https://doi.org/10.1017/S0305000916000647

Wakefield, E. M., Hall, C., James, K. H., & Goldin-Meadow, S. (2017). Representational gesture as a tool for promoting word learning in young children. In M. LaMendola & J. Scott (Eds.), *Proceedings of the 41st Annual Boston University Conference on Language Development* (pp. 718–729). Cascadilla Press.

Wakefield, E. M., Hall, C., James, K. H., & Goldin-Meadow, S. (2018). Gesture for generalization: Gesture facilitates flexible learning of words for actions on objects. *Developmental Science, 21*(5), e12656. https://doi.org/10.1111/desc.12656

Waxman, S. R., Lidz, J. L., Braun, I. E., & Lavin, T. (2009). Twenty four-month-old infants' interpretations of novel verbs and nouns in dynamic scenes. *Cognitive Psychology, 59*(1), 67–95. https://doi.org/10.1016/j.cogpsych.2009.02.001

Zinober, B., & Martlew, M. (1985). Developmental changes in four types of gesture in relation to acts and vocalizations from 10 to 21 months. *British Journal of Developmental Psychology, 3*(3), 293–306. https://doi.org/10.1111/j.2044-835X.1985.tb00981.x

IV Gesture After Speech Is Mastered

Jean-Marc Colletta
9 On the Codevelopment of Gesture and Monologic Discourse in Children

Since Kendon and McNeill's initial claim that gesture and speech are two aspects of a single process (Kendon, 1986, 1997, 2004; McNeill, 1992, 2005, 2014), extensive work has demonstrated that co-speech gesture does not solely add a touch of exoticism to the verbal utterance; instead, gesture contributes to the full meaning of the bimodal utterance, thanks to its pragmatic, indexical, imagistic, and structuring properties. Linguists consider gesture as one of the three aspects of language, along with the verbal content of speech and its prosody. They thus expect developmental changes in language skills to show both in the gestural and the verbal aspects of the child's communication behavior. This has been clearly demonstrated in the scientific investigation of infants' and young children's gestural means for communication (see the reviews in this volume by Morgenstern, Chapter 3; Rowe et al., Chapter 4; Capirci et al., Chapter 5; Clark and Kelly, Chapter 6; and Beaupoil-Hourdel, Chapter 7). Before the turn of the 21st century, significant data and results were already available on early gesture production and its relation to language acquisition; however, the study of older children's gestural behavior and its relation to later language development was far less advanced.

Preschool children make extensive use of nonverbal behavior when interacting with their peers (Montagner, 1978) and use conventional gestures to express basic speech acts (Guidetti, 1998). In regard to children who attend primary and secondary school, three studies conducted in the 1980s and 1990s yielded contrasting results on older children's gesture repertoire and the appearance of certain types of gestures. For instance, in a study conducted in a semi-experimental setting, Cosnier (1982) found a decrease in co-speech gesture production as children entered primary school

---

This chapter is dedicated to Chief Research Officer Maya Hickmann from the Centre National de la Recherche Scientifique, Paris, for her decisive work on child discourse development.
  I acknowledge the University of Grenoble Alpes (Lidilem Laboratory, Stendhal University, and the Institut Universitaire de Formation des Maîtres) for funding the JMacé data collection, the data collection regarding preschool explanations, and the P4C data on philosophical discussions (including the Philosophèmes data collection, which was funded by Maisons des Sciences de l'Homme, Auvergne, France, and Maisons des Sciences de l'Homme, Lorraine, France), as well as the French National Research Agency (ANR-05-BLANC-0178-01 and -02) for funding the Multimodality data collection.
  I am indebted to collaborators on studies that involved the above-mentioned data collections, who include Emmanuelle Auriac-Slusarczyk (University of Clermont-Ferrand, Clermont-Ferrand, France), Olga Capirci (Consiglio Nazionale Delle Ricerche, Rome, Italy), Susan Goldin-Meadow (University of Chicago, Chicago, IL, USA), Michèle Guidetti (University of Toulouse, Toulouse, France), Ramona Kunene Nicolas (University of the Witwatersrand, Johannesburg, South Africa), Catherine Pellenq (University of Grenoble Alpes, Grenoble, France), Asela Reig Alamillo (Stendhal University, Grenoble, France), and Jean-Pascal Simon (University of Grenoble Alpes, Grenoble, France).

https://doi.org/10.1515/9783110675788-009
Gesture in Language: Development Across the Lifespan, A. Morgenstern and S. Goldin-Meadow (Editors)
Copyright © 2022 by the American Psychological Association and Walter de Gruyter GmbH. All rights reserved.

(Grade 1), followed by an increase in gesture in older children (Grades 4 and 5) with the emergence of new types of gestures: beats and gestures that represent concepts and abstract entities. De Garitte et al. (1998) observed children in the same age range having lunch together at school and found that they used all kinds of gestures, including beats, from age 6 years on. In an investigation of children's gesture production during narratives, McNeill (1992) pointed out that iconic gestures appear as early as age 2½ years, whereas beats appear much later in children capable of metanarrative statements—around 8 years of age, in line with Cassell (1991)—and metaphoric gestures even later, no earlier than 11 years.

Such inconclusive results on the course of late gesture development and on the timing of emergent gesture types in children's repertoire could be explained by different objectives and methods, but in those days it was also the consequence of the lack of a developmental framework linking later language with cognitive and social abilities. Given that later language development involves the building of literacy abilities and the mastering of monologic discourse (i.e., monologue speech production of a speaker resulting in a complete text-type contribution such as an event report or an explanation; see section 9.2 for details), how do gesture use and the gestural repertoire evolve in older children? How do these relate to new language skills? Also, given the course of children's cognitive and social development, as modeled in developmental psychology, how do new language and gesture skills relate to emergent social and cognitive skills such as managing social interaction, monitoring one addressee's comprehension, taking the perspective of the other, using abstract concepts, reasoning, and arguing?

In this chapter, I offer an overview of the main results about children's gesture production in the context of monologic discourse in a series of studies conducted over the past 20 years. First, I present data that demonstrate that children as early as 6 years old start to use the whole range of gestures known to be used by adults (Section 9.1) and that they adapt their gestural resources to the type of discourse they engage in (Section 9.2). Second, data gathered from observational and semi-experimental studies on children's oral narratives provide evidence that children as early as 9 years old start to use gestures to mark narrative complexity and to introduce metanarrative comments (Section 9.3), that such changes in narrative abilities show both in gesture and in speech (Sections 9.4–9.5), and that they are robust enough to appear in cross-linguistic studies (section 9.6). Third, turning to oral expository discourse, I present evidence that children over age 6 years spontaneously express abstract concepts in gestures when giving an explanation (Section 9.7), that their gesturing indexes the emergence of abstract thinking and reasoning (Section 9.8), and that metaphoric gestures, which represent abstract concepts, are a great support for philosophical discussions in the classroom. Building on this set of findings, in the final section, 9.9, I discuss theoretical issues as regards gesture development, the relation between gesture and speech over time, and the role gesture plays in language and cognitive development.

9.1 From Age 6 Years Onward, Children's Functional Gesture Repertoire Is Adultlike

At the turn of the 21st century, and to better document children's gestures, I started an empirical study on gesture production in French children attending primary school (all details on the study are provided in Colletta, 2004). I hypothesized that the use of co-speech gestures, bodily postures, and facial expressions develops as a child acquires new discourse and social–cognitive abilities. To ensure comparability in bimodal language production across ages within a naturalistic framework, I opted for an interview paradigm in which children were asked causal why-questions on family and social topics such as rights and duties for adults and children at home and at school. Interviews were originally designed to investigate an understudied discourse genre in the literature on language development: causal explanation. The interviews were conducted in a semiformal manner by an experimenter with whom the participants were familiar. Most children thus freely expanded on their responses, enriched their explanations with narrations and depictions, and eventually discussed their personal views with a classmate. This empirical research (hereafter referred to as the "JMacé" study) involved 60 children ages 6 to 11 years, enrolled in the same primary school and video recorded in 19 interview sessions. Each session involved three or four classmates in the same grade. Some participants were more engaged in the interview than their classmates, but the experimenter made sure every child contributed somehow to the discussion.

Out of 7 hours of video recordings, using linguistic criteria, I was able to identify and extract an hour-long corpus of 334 monologue productions corresponding to a causal explanation, a narrative, a depiction, or an argument. Each production was transcribed and coded for hand, head, facial, and bodily gestures. Every gesture was categorized according to functional classifications authored by Cosnier (1993), Calbris (1997), Ekman and Friesen (1969), Kendon (2004, pp. 158–161), and McNeill (1992, pp. 12–16), which share most of their basic features despite different labeling. Reliability of the results was established by having two independent coders annotate 20% of the entire gestural data and a third coder selecting the most appropriate function(s) in case of disagreement while ensuring homogeneity across the whole data set. More than 1,500 coverbal gestures were identified (see Appendix 9.1 for details and examples):

- *performative gestures*, which are equivalent to a speech act
- *interactive gestures*, which help maintain joint action between interlocutors
- *framing gestures*, by which the speaker expresses feelings and communicates the utterance mood to frame the speech content
- *referential gestures of the concrete* (McNeill, 1992), which include indexical pointing (i.e., pointing to a referent that is physically accessible within the

Tab. 9.1: Mean Number and Percentage of Co-Speech Gestures in Children Ages 6–11 Years

Gestures of the abstract		Framing gestures		Gestures of the concrete		Pragmatic gestures	
n	%	n	%	n	%	n	%
562	37	472	31	398	26	77	5

Note. From *Le Développement de la Parole Chez L'enfant Âgé de 6 et 11 Ans: Corps, Langage et Cognition* [Speech development in children ages 6 and 11: Body, language and cognition] (pp. 243–244), by J.-M. Colletta, 2004, Mardaga. Copyright 2004 by Mardaga. Reprinted with permission.

setting) and iconic gestures (i.e., gestures that represent objects, characters, actions, and places)
- *referential gestures of the abstract* (McNeill, 1992), which include abstract pointing (i.e., pointing to a spot in a frontal space that holds for an absent referent) and metaphoric gestures (i.e., gestures that represent abstract entities)
- *speech and discourse parsing gestures*, which segment speech and mark discourse structure

Table 9.1 shows the proportion of gestures in each of the main categories that were identified in the JMacé data. In accordance with Kendon (2004), performative and interactive gestures were categorized as "pragmatic" gestures. As in Cosnier (1993), gestures that represent abstract entities and parsing gestures were categorized as "gestures of the abstract." Such grouping makes sense given that both dimensions are linked to advanced discourse abilities (McNeill, 1992). As shown in Table 9.1, from age 6 years onward a child's gestural repertoire includes all major dimensions that were identified in the above-mentioned literature. The surprisingly low proportion of pragmatic gestures (5%) in this pioneering study results from the fact that the data consisted of assertive speech acts (i.e., children's explanatory responses to the experimenter's questions) that promoted the use of framing gestures rather than pragmatic gestures (i.e., performative head nods and head shakes, interactive feedback, and synchronization signals). In contrast, the high proportion of gestures of the abstract (37%) relates to the focus on causal explanation. The results suggest that letting children talk about a large variety of topics will lead to their use of the whole range of gestural dimensions.

9.2 Like Adults, Children Adapt Their Gestures to the Discourse Genre

As stated, the data collected during interviews in the study (Colletta, 2004) did not consist only of elicited causal explanations. Thirty-two narrations (in the form of event reports), 25 depictions, and 23 debating sequences, all spontaneously produced by participants, together with 239 explanations, were extracted from the JMacé data. Such data enabled a comparison of gesture production across four types of oral discourse in order to investigate whether children age 6 and over adapt their gesture production to the discourse task.

Let us consider how discourse genres differ according to three major aspects: (a) their pragmatic purpose, (b) their texture, and (c) the type of content they refer to. First, depicting an object or a scene, narrating an event, giving an explanation, and exposing one's stance in a discussion serve different purposes, such as, in the context of the Colletta (2004) interviews, being serious and genuine when answering why-questions, being responsible for one's words when arguing with a peer, and being more entertaining when willing to report on an event or depicting something. Second, as European textual linguistics have demonstrated, each monologic discourse genre sets up a specific format or structure that can be highly constraining, as in narration and arguing (Adam, 1999; Brémond, 1973; Bronckart, 1996; Golder, 1996), and the use of specific cohesion devices—among which are connectives and verb mood and tenses (Halliday & Ruqaiya, 1976; Lundquist, 1980; Weinrich, 1989). Third, each discourse genre activates specific linguistic and cognitive resources, with expository discourse (i.e., causal explanation, reasoning, arguing) favoring logical and discourse relations (Grize, 1990; Roulet, 1999; Werlich, 1975), whereas narration prominently links together chronology and causality (Berman & Slobin, 1994; Peterson & McCabe, 1991) and depiction prominently activates objectal and spatial representations (Johnson-Laird, 1999; Talmy, 2000).

As illustrated in Table 9.2, gestures produced by children during interviews strongly varied across discourse tasks: Children mainly used abstract and discourse cohesion gestures (first row, first column of Table 9.2) when they answered why-questions, iconic gestures when they depicted objects and recounted events (second and third rows, second column), and framing gestures when they debated (fourth row, third column). The high proportion of gestures of the concrete in depictions and narrations is not surprising because these help represent objects' size and shape, their location and trajectories in space, and the behavior of animated objects and

Tab. 9.2: Proportion of Co-Speech Gestures in Four Discourse Tasks

	Gestures of the abstract	Gestures of the concrete	Framing gestures	Pragmatic gestures
Explaining	52.50	17.50	28.50	01.50
Depicting	22.00	57.50	17.50	03.00
Narrating	29.50	42.00	23.50	05.00
Debating	19.00	10.00	56.00	15.00

Note. From *Le Développement de la Parole Chez L'enfant Âgé de 6 et 11 Ans: Corps, Langage et Cognition* [Speech development in children ages 6 and 11: Body, language and cognition] (p. 244), by J.-M. Colletta, 2004, Mardaga. Copyright 2004 by Mardaga. Reprinted with permission.

characters (see Kendon, 2004 and Streeck, 2009, as well as the journal *Gesture* [https://benjamins.com/catalog/gest] because almost every issue has at least one article that focuses on iconic gestures). An adult speaker telling a story also tends to produce discourse parsing gestures to mark its structure and organize the speech content and framing gestures to express feelings and mood (Bouvet, 2001; McNeill, 1992), and so did some of the children involved in the JMacé study (in Table 9.2, third row, first and third columns), as I demonstrate in the next section. In regard to expository discourse (explaining and debating), adult speakers use representational gestures that help convey abstract thought, thanks to the metaphorical properties of gestures as evidenced in the literature (Calbris, 2003, 2011; Cienki & Müller, 2008; Johnson, 1987; McNeill, 1992) together with discourse cohesion gestures and framing gestures that either reinforce or connote speech content. In the data I discuss here, children behaved similarly, except they made scarce use of gestures of the abstract while they debated with each other (fourth row, first column of Table 9.2), but such discussions included little, if any, arguing.

In other words, from 6 years of age on, children adapt their gestures to the type of monologic discourse they engage in by selecting the gestural resources that are most appropriate to their communicative intention. Two more recent studies added evidence for such an early matching of speech and gesture resources in advanced language abilities. The first one contrasted a narrative task with an explanatory task, both of which are performed by the same children (Alamillo et al., 2013). It confirmed a strong effect of the task both on speech and gesture. The second one contrasted two types of oral explanations: an instructional explanation versus a noninstructional one (Mazur-Palandre et al., 2014). The results suggest that the managing of social interaction (as in instructional explanation) adds pragmatic constraints that are reflected both in linguistic and gestural resources.

9.3 Children Over Age 9 Use Gesture to Mark Narrative Complexity

Let us now look more carefully at the part gesture plays in children's narratives. Narration is highly constrained by textual properties attached to the goal of (re)telling an event from start to end, in a relevant if not complete account (Halliday & Ruqaiya, 1976), while marking the given versus new status of each piece of information (Firbas, 1992; Givón, 1995). Studies of children's narratives across languages and cultures have pointed out underlying abilities that are not yet fully mastered at the end of primary school. These include cognitive decentering (i.e., the ability to take the addressee's perspective) and abilities in theory of mind (i.e., the skilled narrator of an original report knows the addressee has no prior knowledge of the events they are recounting), knowledge of the storytelling text format, and the ability to plan text production both at the macrolevel of the narrative structure and the microlevel of linguistic content distributed into clauses chained together through the use of anaphora and connectives (Berman & Slobin, 1994; de Weck, 1991; Fayol, 2000; Hickmann, 2003; Jisa & Kern, 1998; Karmiloff-Smith, 1979; Peterson & McCabe, 1991; Tolchinsky, 2004). Two major milestones are identified in the literature. The first one occurs when the child is at the doorstep of primary school, which corresponds to the building of the concept of text, and the second one occurs when they are about to leave primary school, which corresponds to the emergence of new textual skills, including the building of a complete representation of a storyline, the ability to extract relevant information from a set of facts, and the ability to summarize linguistic information (Fayol, 2000; Hickmann, 2003; see also Colletta, Kunene-Nicolas, & Guidetti, 2018).

The first investigation of the role gesture plays in the child's narrative performance dates back to the late 1990s. Multimodal narrative performance was then scarcely documented except for isolated studies, such as work on oral storytelling in the tradition of African folklore (Klassen, 1999), on adults in France (Bouvet, 2001; Léonard & Pinheiro, 1993), and on English-speaking American adults (Lévy & McNeill, 1992; McNeill, 1992). In regard to children, only McNeill's (1992) pioneering observations were available. The starting questions in the Colletta (2004) study were the following: What is the typical multimodal narrative performance of a child at a certain age? Do gesture resources in narrative performance evolve with age? What does gesture production tell us about narrative development?

For the sake of this investigation, we used the JMacé data from which we extracted more than 30 event reports spontaneously produced by the participants. Analysis of the children's verbal performance was grounded both on the Labovian approach to oral narration (Labov & Waletzky, 1967) and on the European approach to the narrative structure (see Adam, 1999, for a presentation). In regard to the nonverbal aspects of performance, a glimpse at the video data was enough to realize that not only hand, head, face, and bodily gestures, but also gaze patterns and vocal–prosodic features, actively contributed to the narration, together with speech, hence our decision to follow Bouvet's (2001) holistic method to analyze narration in French.

A two-step analysis was conducted on the data. In this section, I discuss the first step, for which we focused on the narratives produced by three girls, ages 9, 10, and 11 years, whose verbal performances were selected because they were close to that of adults reporting on events during spontaneous talk (Colletta, 2004, 2009). All three narratives were analyzed according to four dimensions: (a) wording, (b) vocal and prosodic features, (c) gesture, and (d) gaze. (The transcription and annotation method are illustrated in Appendix 9.2.)

Detailed analyses of the speech content confirmed five broad findings: (a) that children this age are able to produce fairly long reports, including a background (i.e., "orientation" in the Labovian approach to narration) and a foreground (i.e., "complication" and "resolution"), and a detailed and dramatized account of the most striking events; (b) that they interrupt the telling of the narrative plot and move back to previous events or add side explanations when necessary; (c) that they use linguistic anaphora and connectives for cohesion purpose; (d) that they comment on the reported events or the narration itself at both the meta- and paranarrative levels (as defined in McNeill, 1992, pp. 185–189); and (e) that they frame their report within a socio-communicative strategy (i.e., "evaluation" in Labovian theory, such as "I'm telling you this because it is so funny, or because I want to share my indignation with you"), as adults commonly do (Laforest & Vincent, 1996; Traverso, 1996). The most exciting findings, however, emerged out of an analysis of the nonverbal dimension of the three narratives, with the speakers' vocal–prosodic features, gestures, and gaze patterns all contributing to the performance and therefore being inextricably linked to its speech content. I now present a synthesis of the main observations about the children (narrators) analyzed in our research.

Narrators use vocal and prosodic features (pitch, tone, intensity, voicing) to mimic the voice of a character whose speech is being reported, thanks to their iconic properties, and to help mark the structure of the ongoing narration, alternating vocal patterns (slow vs. fast speech, loud vs. low voice, emotional prosody) to highlight microdiscourse acts (e.g., reported speech, side explanation) and transitions between narrating and commenting, background and foreground, major versus minor information.

Narrators accompany their wording with gestures to enliven the story by representing characters, actions, places, and trajectories. They use facial expressions to mime the characters' behavior and emotions, to express their own emotion, and to frame their report as being humoristic or dramatic in its content.

Narrators gaze at their addressee(s) when closing their report and selecting the next speaker, but they avoid gaze contact when they start a new utterance, as adults tend to do (Goodwin, 1981; Kendon, 1967; Mondada, 2007; Streeck, 1993). Gaze patterns also help mark transitions between discourse acts, with the child avoiding gazing at the addressee when recounting an event versus searching for eye contact when making a meta- or paranarrative comment.

In other words, the results from Colletta's (2004) pioneering and qualitative study of three spontaneous oral narratives suggest that children age 9 years and over are able to share their experience with others in a narrative performance that does not fall short of French adults' multimodal narration as evidenced in work by Bouvet (2001) and Léonard and Pinheiro (1993). To summarize this point, children enrolled in the latest grades of primary school recount events they have lived or witnessed in an adultlike manner, making use of all communicative resources (i.e., words, voice, gesture, and gaze) to build the reference, structure its delivery in a coherent contribution, and adapt their performance to an addressee. Assuming that younger children are unable to achieve such performance, does this mean that narrative abilities develop both in speech and in gesture?

9.4 Changes in Narrative Abilities Are Present Both in Gesture and in Speech

For the second investigation, I considered the complete set of spontaneous event reports extracted from the data, including the three narratives mentioned in the preceding section (Colletta, 2009). Some children did not narrate anything during the interview, whereas others performed more than one narration. All in all, 32 monologue narratives produced by 23 children ages 6 to 11 were identified as genuine narratives (i.e., narratives including, at a minimum, a background, a foreground, and a closing or coda in Labovian theory) in which one single speaker narrates a past experience.

All reports were analyzed on the four above-mentioned dimensions (wording, vocal–prosodic features, gesture, and gaze), each one being scored on a 3-point scale, rating the obvious presence versus scarce presence versus absence of a complex pattern as shown in the older children's narratives (as illustrated in the performance of one of the three narrators; see the annotated example provided in Appendix 9.2). Example 9.1 is a very short account in which facts are briefly recounted in a linear way on the basis of a briefly described background (rated 1). Example 9.2 illustrates a longer and more detailed account, yet one that lacks a meta- or paranarrative comment (rated 2). An analysis of all reports showed a strong covariation between the verbal and the nonverbal dimensions, with short verbal accounts delivered with a monotone and flat prosody, sparse use of facial expressions and gestures, and basically no change in gaze and posture. Generally speaking, the more there was to be expressed in speech, the more our narrators made use of nonlinguistic resources. Appendix 9.3 includes a synthetic table that sums up typical features across modalities proper to each of the three levels.

> Example 9.1 **(7 years old)** moi - quand - moi un jour j'étais à la piscine - après - j'ai trainé par terre mon pied -
> j' me suis - cassé un p'tit peu l'ongle
> [me when, me I went to the swimming pool one day, after, I scraped my foot on the ground, I split off a bit of nail]
>
> Example 9.2 **(8 years old)** moi heu - avec mon papa et ma soeur - on s'est am' - on s'est amusé à - à jouer au ballon
> (xxx) - et pis ÷ chus tombée - contre un mur et j' me su's - j' me su's heu - ouvert le menton
> [. . .] et pis i' m'ont recoud avec un ciseau [. . .] i' voulaient me - i' - i' voulaient m'endormir
> et moi j'arrêtais pas d' pleurer pa'c'que ça faisait mal avec le ciseau - pour m'enlever les points

[me um, with my dad and my sister, we played, played ball (xxx), and then, I fell down, against a wall and I, um, I cut my chin [. . .] and then they sewed it up with scissors [. . .] they wanted, they wanted to put me to sleep and I couldn't stop crying because the scissors hurt so much, to take out the stitches]

To compare the children's performance across ages, each report was attributed a score representing the global score out of the four aspects taken into account (Colletta, 2004, 2009). Such computing led four narratives to be rated with intermediary values (Level 1–2, Level 2–3), as shown in Figure 9.1. In relation to the participants' school grades, the scores revealed a strong effect of age, with the sophisticated multimodal performance of older children age 9 years and over (Grades 4–5) greatly contrasting with that of their younger pairs (the light gray arrow in Figure 9.1 indexes the decreasing part of the Level 1 type of performance according to school grade, and the dark gray arrow indexes the increasing part of the Level 3 type of performance). This result confirms the existence of a crucial milestone corresponding to the emergence of new textual skills in children in Grades 4 to 5 (between 9 and 11 years old). To summarize, oral narration still constitutes a cognitively costly task in children age 6 years (Grade 1), who give short and hesitant accounts and makes little use of gesture and nonverbal resources. With age, spontaneous reports become more substantial on the verbal dimension and children start to comment on events, but not until age 9 do children

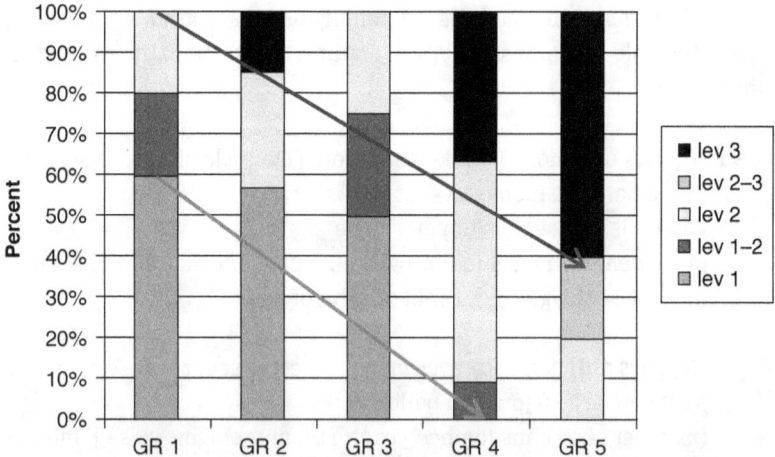

Fig. 9.1: Development of narrative behavior as a function of age (percentages in levels of performance according to school grade). GR = grade, lev = level. From "Comparative Analysis of Children's Narratives at Different Ages: A Multimodal Approach," by J.-M. Colletta, 2009, *Gesture, 9*(1), p. 88 (https://doi.org/10.1075/gest.9.1.03col). Copyright 2009 by John Benjamins. Reprinted with permission.

start to make detailed and lively reports that they easily comment on while taking into account the reactions of their addressees, thus acting as genuine narrators.

The most important finding from this study, however, is the evidence that gesture accompanies changes in performance at all levels (e.g., narrative content, metanarrative comments, and comments on the narration process) and that the better the linguistic performance, the more children rely on nonverbal and gestural resources to help the addressee understand the story and entertain them. Additional evidence for the codevelopment of gesture and speech was found by Graziano (2009) in a study of Italian children ages 4 to 9 years asked to narrate a story to an adult.

9.5 Learning to Narrate Is Learning to Comment, Both in Gesture and in Speech

The findings discussed in the two previous sections were observed within an empirical framework that lacked an accurate control of age, gender, and participants' productions, because these resulted from each child's free will. To check the robustness of the findings, Colletta et al. (2010) conducted a study of narrative performance across age using an elicitation method. Following McNeill's (1992) methodological paradigm, 120 French-speaking participants including 43 children age 10 years, 41 children age 6 years, and 38 adults (for reference data), were shown a wordless *Tom & Jerry* cartoon extract and were asked to tell the story it depicted to an addressee. The cartoon paradigm is widely used in psycholinguistic studies to investigate representational gesture production and its relation to mental imagery and the bimodal coding of space and movement (Fibigerová, 2012; Hickmann et al., 2011; Özyürek et al., 2005). Nonetheless, embedding the cartoon narration task in an interactional context leads participants to produce all kinds of gestures, just like in spontaneous event reports apart from a slightly higher rate of representational gestures. Participants in this study (hereafter referred to as the "Multimodality" study) were filmed and the data were transcribed and annotated with ELAN, using a coding system that included clauses and words, the pragmatics of the narrative (basically, narrating vs. commenting), discourse cohesion means (anaphora and connectives), and gestures (hand, head, and bodily enactments; see http://tla.mpi.nl/tools/tla-tools/elan/).

As expected, the 10-year-old children produced longer and more detailed verbal narratives (mean length as measured in number of clauses: 44) than the 6-year-olds (27 clauses). Surprisingly, adults produced shorter narratives than the 10-year-olds (37 clauses). The explanation lies, I believe, in the late development of summarizing abilities as evidenced in psycholinguistic studies (Fayol, 2000): Contrary to a 10-year-old child, who aims at being exhaustive in his retelling of the story, an adult tends to give a summarized account, to tell the main foreground events, and to ignore minor events or details. The 10-year-old children produced more gestures (mean number of gestures per clause: 0.50) than the 6-year-olds ($M = 0.27$). Given that adults' narratives are shorter than older children's narratives, one would expect the former to produce fewer gestures; however, adult participants produced more gestures ($M = 0.77$) than children in both age groups. This unexpected result suggests that co-speech gesture production does not depend solely on the amount of verbal information (i.e., the more one speaks or narrates, the more one gestures) and that it also varies with age (i.e., the older the speaker, the more they rely on gestural resources for communication purposes within a given language or discourse task). Indeed, when the length of the narrative was controlled, adults produced more gestures than children, as evidenced with a linear regression analysis conducted on the number of gestures as a dependent variable and age and narrative length as independent variables (see Figure 9.2 for the regression among age, number of gestures, and number of words as an index of narrative length).

Considering they deliver shorter accounts than children, why do adults gesture when narrating a story? From the results of the JMacé study we know that the type of verbal performance of the children is reflected in their gestures, as if speech and gesture were in a coexpressive relation as regards the pragmatics of narration. Consistent with this finding, the most striking difference between children and adults is in the amount of linguistic information allocated to narrating the story versus adding a side explanation, putting up an interpretation, or making a meta- or paranarrative comment (see Alamillo & Colletta, 2013, for details on coding the pragmatics of narration). The part devoted to the telling of the story dropped dramatically in adult participants ($M = 24$ clauses vs. $M = 38$ in older children) as a plausible effect of their superior summarizing abilities, whereas the part devoted to the three other discourse acts (explaining, interpreting, and commenting) increased by a factor of

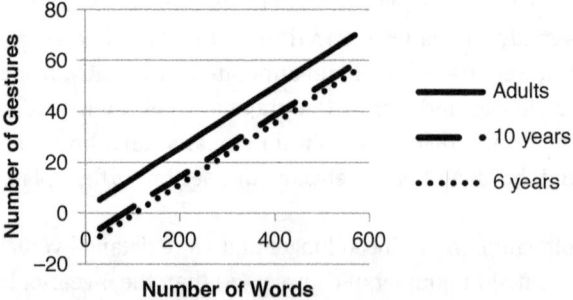

Fig. 9.2: Effect of age on gesture production when controlling the length of the narrative. From "Gestures and Multimodal Development: Some Key Issues for Language Acquisition," by M. Guidetti, K. Fibigerova, and J.-M. Colletta, in M. Seyfeddinipur and M. Gullberg (Eds.), *From Gesture in Conversation to Visible Action in Utterance* (p. 362), 2014, John Benjamins. Copyright 2014 by John Benjamins. Reprinted with permission.

four, as shown in the left-hand panel of Figure 9.3. In regard to gesture production, almost all gestures found in the Multimodality data were either *representational* (i.e., representing places, events, and newly introduced and reintroduced characters), *discursive* (i.e., marking discourse structure and the relation between clauses), or *framing* (i.e., expressing the speakers' feelings and mood and framing the utterance) gestures. Colletta et al. (2010) found that, contrary to children who mainly produced representational gestures, one gesture out of two in adult participants was a discourse parsing or a framing gesture (see Figure 9.3, right-hand panel). In other words, the way adult narrators allocate their gestures to these three basic functions is perfectly in line with the way they allocate their linguistic resources to the narrative, metanarrative, and paranarrative levels, spending much more time on structuring and framing their narrative than children.

To summarize the findings on gesture and narrative development, the picture that stands out from these two series of results is that children become gradually able to narrate the "adult way" by learning to distance themselves from the reported facts; to select the most relevant information; to insert a relevant comment that is in line with the dominant mood; and to plan and structure the interplay of the narrative, metanarrative, and paranarrative text in a performance where gesture and speech go hand in hand. Here again, it seems that the relation between speech and gesture is clearly a coexpressive one, regardless of age. Does this picture hold across different languages and cultures?

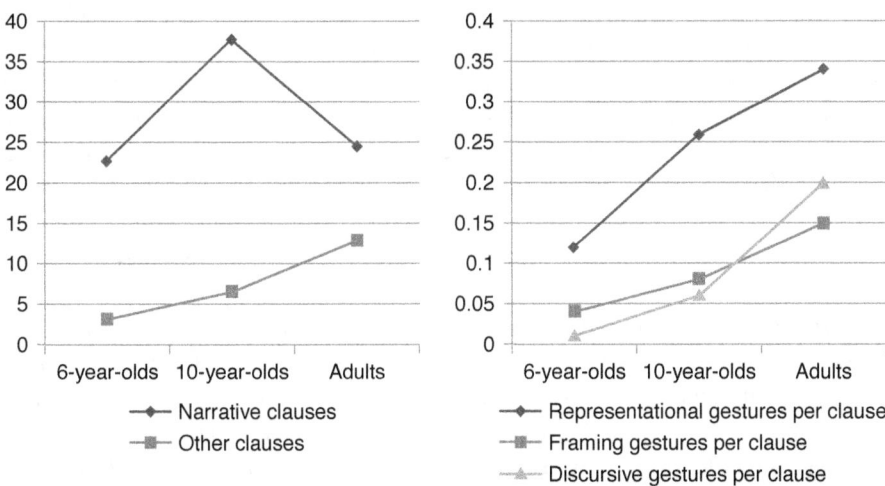

Fig. 9.3: Effect of age on the pragmatics of the narrative (left panel, numbers) and on main gesture types (right panel, rates/clause). From "Age-Related Changes in Co-Speech Gesture and Narrative: Evidence From French Children and Adults," by J.-M. Colletta, C. Pellenq, and M. Guidetti, 2010, *Speech Communication*, *52*(6), pp. 572 and 574 (https://doi.org/10.1016/j.specom.2010.02.009). Copyright 2010 by Elsevier. Reprinted with permission.

9.6 Gesture and Speech Go Hand in Hand Across Language and Culture

The Multimodality study included a cross-linguistic comparison between Italian-speaking and American English-speaking 6- and 10-year-old children who were age matched with French children. All participants were shown the *Tom & Jerry* cartoon extract used for the Multimodality study and were asked to tell, under similar conditions, the story it depicted (Colletta et al., 2015). The results yielded additional evidence for an increasing use of gesture resources for referential, discursive, and pragmatic purposes in the context of the narrative based on a cartoon and led the researchers to propose a model of multimodal narrative development that could be generalized to other languages despite linguistic specificities or cultural differences.

A study of narrative performance across ages in isiZulu, a Bantu language spoken in South Africa, brought to light a distinct picture of narrative development. Kunene (2010) compared adults and children ages 6, 10, and 12 years, speaking isiZulu as their mother tongue and narrating from the *Tom & Jerry* cartoon extract. Similar to French narrators, Zulu adults and older children produced longer and more detailed narratives and gestured more than younger children. Interestingly enough, male Zulu adults and older boys gestured more than their female counterparts, and they made more ample gestures, using the extreme periphery of the gestural space. This gender difference seems linked to gender socialization and to the common social practice of talk among young men in the urban context of townships in South Africa (Brookes, 2005), where the Zulu culture is among the dominant ones. Unlike French adults and older children, however, Zulu narrators favored a long and detailed, event-by-event account; produced comparatively fewer metanarrative and paranarrative comments; and accompanied their verbal narration with twice as many representational gestures and fewer discourse parsing and framing gestures than their French counterparts (Kunene Nicolas, 2010; Kunene Nicolas et al., 2017). The difference in the pragmatics of multimodal narration across the two languages likely reveals partly distinct cultural norms and expectations regarding oral literacy practice (Groenewald, 2003; Suzman, 1991).

Why, though, is the representational gesture rate in the Zulu adult narrator (0.85 gestures/clause) so high in the two above-mentioned studies compared with the French adult narrators (0.34 gestures/clause)? Studies of narratives produced by Italian children (Cristilli, 2014; Graziano, 2009) have linked a high rate of representational gestures to the need to disambiguate reference and compensate for the absence of explicit anaphora, as Italian is a pro-drop language in which the nominal or pronominalized subject is not used in the sentence unless required by the context. IsiZulu is a pro-drop language in which the verb agrees with both subject and object, thanks to a noun class system that groups nouns into 15 different classes, each one marked by a prefix. In the absence of a head noun or a pronoun it is the connective that marks a chronological relationship between clauses and takes the agreement prefix, hence acting as an anaphoric marker. To test the compensation hypothesis in the isiZulu data, Colletta, Kunene-Nicolas, and Guidetti (2018) looked for gesture + speech contexts in which an iconic gesture would disambiguate a connective incorporating a subject marker but found none except for a few occurrences in the younger children's narratives. It seems that Zulu narrators, whatever the age, do not use gestural means to disambiguate potential ambiguity in absence of explicit anaphora. Reasons for their high use of iconic gestures, I believe, are likely to be found in the Zulu culture, both in the tradition of oral storytelling and in social norms regarding the practice of everyday talk (Brookes, 2014).

In other words, despite the fact that changes in narrative abilities share a common timing, affect all dimensions of narration, and show up both in gesture and speech across language and culture, the tentative model of multimodal narrative development Colletta, Kunene-Nicolas, and Guidetti (2018) proposed on the basis of results pertaining to French, Italian, and American English cannot be extended, per se, to isiZulu. Only one aspect remains constant in these cross-linguistic investigations of narrative performance, that is, the tendency of all narrators to use gesture resources that are appropriate to the content and the pragmatics of the ongoing utterance. This finding supports McNeill's (1992, 2014) coexpressivity framework, according to which gesture and speech comprise one system, and it is consistent with results from experimental studies of the depiction of motion events that demonstrate that iconic gesture production in the clause tends to align with the clause content (Kita & Özyürek, 2003; Özyürek et al., 2005). Interestingly, studies that have investigated age differences in the depiction of motion events across languages (Fibigerová, 2012; Gullberg, Hendriks, & Hickmann, 2008; Hickmann et al., 2011; Özyürek et al., 2008) all pointed out changes in bimodal depiction patterns that become more adultlike with age, just like research found that bimodal narrative strategies become more adultlike with age, regardless of the language. Disregarding task, language, and culture specificities, speakers' gestures match the content of their speech, which in turn indicates an effect of underlying cognitive abilities.

9.7 Children Who Verbally Explain and Reason Express Abstract Concepts in Gesture

From the above-mentioned studies on bimodal narration within a developmental perspective, we know that both gesture and speech index growing language and cognitive abilities in the recounting of events, discourse abilities in the mastery of monologic discourse, and social–cognitive abilities in the framing of one's contribution, hence the common use of iconic gestures to refer to characters, events, and places and the emergence and use of discourse parsing and framing gestures as children grow older.

Generally speaking, however, children's gestural repertoire also includes gestures of the abstract, as reported in Section 9.1. What are these gestures, what emerging abilities do they index, and how do they contribute to child development?

In the JMacé study, gestures of the abstract were produced by children in Grades 1 to 5 who were asked to give causal explanations on family and social topics during interviews (see Section 9.1). Textually speaking, a causal explanation is complete when expressing the dual < P because Q > structure corresponding to expression of both an *explanandum* (i.e., a phenomenon or a behavior to be explained) and an *explanans* (i.e., a cause, reason, or motivation for this phenomenon or behavior; Adam, 1999; Grize, 1990). In young children, however, (Veneziano & Hudelot, 2002; Veneziano & Sinclair, 1995), as in the oral mode more generally, the two components are verbalized by two distinct speakers:

- Speaker 1: < why P >
- Speaker 2: < because Q >

In Colletta and Pellenq's (2009) data, all explanations were verbalized by children in response to a question from the experimenter and included some 680 gestures. Half of these were labeled as gestures of the abstract and were grouped into four subcategories after a more accurate analysis of their function: (a) gestures that introduce a referent, (b) gestures that represent an abstract concept, (c) gestures that represent an abstract process, and (d) gestures that express a modality.

9.7.1 Introduction of a Referent

By means of a hand flick or a hand or head abstract pointing, the speaker marks introduction of a referent (Example 9.3: an ancestor) or locates two related referents in distinctive spots in the frontal space (Example 9.4: grandmother and mother). Another gesture is the open-hand palm-up gesture known as the "conduit metaphor" (Kendon, 2004; McNeill, 1992), whereby a speaker introduces a new topic or referent (problems, in Example 9.5) while representing it as a content being offered to the addressee.

Example 9.3 Gestural introduction of a referent (boy, Grade 1)

moi j'ai plus d'arrière-grand-père ni d'arrière-gra'-mère - pas'que mon arrière-<u>grand-pè:re</u> heu: - il a fait la guerre
[I've no longer got a great grand-dad or a great-grandma - because my great <u>grand-dad</u>, eh -he fought in the war]
(head > Right)

Example 9.4 Gestural introduction of two related referents (boy, Grade 2)

pas'que [. . .] - et ma am' - ma - mo<u>n aut' mamie</u> - elle a <u>fait maman</u>
[because [. . .] - and my gra - nny - my <u>other granny</u> - she <u>had mum</u>]
(head > Right) (head > Left)

Example 9.5 Gestural introduction of a referent using the "content" gesture (girl, Grade 4)

ben - quand i' t'arrive des pro<u>blèmes tu</u> peux leur en parler: tu heu [. . .]
[well - if you have pro<u>blems you</u> can talk to them about it: you uh [. . .]]
(R hand > R in votive gesture)

9.7.2 Gestures Representing an Abstract Concept

Children use the metaphoric properties of hand gestures to represent concepts whose referent is not directly accessible or does not exist in the physical world, such as time (Example 9.6: the speaker gazes and points to upper left, fingers extended upwards, while referring to the past), quantity (Example 9.7: the speaker combines a slow shaking-head gesture and a lateral hand movement to express totality), or a logical relation (Example 9.8: the speaker's gestures compute two depictions while opposing two distinct entities to explain the fact that father and mother cannot originate from the same family).

Example 9.6 Gestural expression of time (boy, Grade 4)

pas'que - avant - <u>avant dans l' temps</u> - on pouvait faire c' qu'on veut y avait pas de truc de drogue [. . .]
[because - before – <u>long ago</u> - one was free to do all one wanted and there were no drugs and stuff [. . .]]
(gaze + L hand > L)

Example 9.7 Gestural expression of quantity (boy, Grade 5)

et là quand heu quand il aura fini <u>toutes ses études</u> il aura quarante-cinq ans - enfin- [. . .]
[and when he's finished <u>all his studies</u> he'll be forty-five years old - well - [. . .]]
(*head and R hand sweep through space from L to R*)

Example 9.8 Gestural expression of opposition (boy, Grade 4)

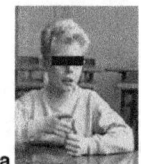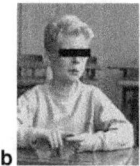

y a une CM1 - ses pa' - <u>un parent - son papa il est - heu: noir</u> - <u>et sa maman - elle est blanche</u> [. . .]
[there's a kid at school - his pa' - <u>one parent - his dad is - um: black</u> - <u>and his mum - she's white</u> [. . .]]
(*points to Left thumb with Right index finger*) (*points to Left index finger with Right index finger*)

9.7.3 Gestures Representing an Abstract Process

Children use the metaphoric properties of hand gestures to represent abstract processes, such as keeping an abstract attribute (Example 9.9: the family name that is transmitted over generations, with right hand in a fist as if holding something tightly) or learning (Example 9.10: the gesture represents learning as grasping something, presumably knowledge to be acquired).

Example 9.9 Gestural metaphor for "keeping an attribute" (boy, Grade 5)

Puisque le <u>père - i' garde - c'est lui qui:</u> - qui garde le nom d' famille [. . .]

[Because the <u>father keeps it – he is the one who</u> - who keeps the family name [. . .]]
(*R hand closes to form a fist*)

Example 9.10 Gestural metaphor for "learning" (boy, Grade 5)

a   b

Pas'que les jeunes (xxx) - i' <u>viennent heu d'apprendre</u> - alors [. . .]
[Because the young ones (xxx) - <u>have just learnt</u> - well [. . .]]
(*L hand makes a grasping gesture, illustrated in two sequential photos here*)

9.7.4 Gesturing a Modality

The head shake as the emblematic sign for negation, together with the shoulder shrug, are used to metaphorically express a subcategory of abstract concepts, such as lack of knowledge, inability, impossibility, or obligation (see Beaupoil-Hourdel, Chapter 7, this volume; Boutet, 2018; Calbris, 2011; Harrison, 2018), that speakers often use to express the utterance mood and modality. Such gestures that combine two dimensions (abstract reference plus framing the utterance) were the most common type of gestures expressing the abstract found in the data (Colletta & Pellenq, 2009).

More recently, Auriac-Slusarczyk and Colletta (2015) found children attending Philosophy for Children (P4C) workshops spontaneously using these four types of gestures. P4C gathers children from a certain grade into a discussion on an abstract concept or issue they have previously selected (see also Lipman, 1991). A leader supervises the discussion and elicits conceptualization, reasoning, and arguing from the children (Simon & Tozzi, 2017). Promoted by UNESCO (the United Nations Educational, Scientific and Cultural Organization), the regular setting of such practice is known to help children to develop reflexivity and critical thinking, among other language and social abilities (Daniel & Auriac-Slusarczyk, 2009). An analysis of four filmed discussions, two involving Grade 1 students and two involving Grade 5 students, revealed that one gesture out of three produced by Grade 5 students who actively participated was a gesture of the abstract (Colletta, 2015). In other words, given the opportunity to think abstractedly while reasoning or explaining something, children who have the ability for it show they do so in their gestures.

9.8 Gestures Index the Emergence of Abstract Thinking and Reasoning

The last finding from Colletta (2015) raises the following question: When do children start to think and reason abstractedly so as to show it in their gestures as well as in their speech? The first contextualized explanatory behavior appears as early as age 2 years in a child who provides a reason for a request or a refusal, using both speech and gesture (e.g., points to a glass out of reach while saying to the adult they are thirsty; Veneziano & Hudelot, 2002), and children attending preschool are known to provide explanans when asked why-questions (Kail & Weissenborn, 1984; Simon et al., 2009). When, though, do young children start to produce gestures of the abstract? To answer this question, Colletta and Pellenq (2009) assembled two sets of video data. The first set corresponds to the JMacé data collection (children ages 6–11 years) mentioned in the preceding section. The second set of data were collected in a collaborative study of early explanation in children ages 36 months to 6 years, attending preschool (Simon et al., 2009). For Colletta and Pellenq's study, 24 class sessions were identified, programmed, and filmed by participants (i.e., experimenters and teachers) as typical preschool activities that elicit causal explanations from the students. These included experiments relating to the topics of air and water, language and storytelling sessions, art workshops, and play sessions involving logical reasoning. The two sets of filmed data yielded a corpus of 500 oral explanations, 268 of which were collected in preschools.

In all contexts, explanations were verbalized in response to a why-question from an adult or a peer. This common pragmatic property allowed comparison of their formal aspects. Each explanation was therefore transcribed; measured for duration and syllabic content; and annotated for syntax, connectives, and co-speech gestures. The results showed a gradual and steady increase on all measures, as shown in Figure 9.4, for duration (left panel), syllabic content (middle panel), and gestures (right panel), as well as substantial changes in syntax and discourse structure, with explanations produced by children from the younger group limited to one clause and the single "because" connective greatly contrasting with explanations produced by children from the older group that often included several clauses and connectives.

To get a more accurate picture of changes in verbal performance across age, Colletta and Pellenq (2009) made a distinction between two types of causal explanations: (a) the "simple" explanation, composed of one single clause or including two clauses not linked by a logical or chronological connective (as in Example 9.11), and (b) the "complex" explanation, built out of two or more clauses linked by logical or chronological relations (as in Example 9.12). As expected, the proportion of simple explanations was extremely high (97%) in the younger age group and gradually decreased to 17% of all explanations in the older group. Conversely, the proportion of complex explanations, which were almost nonexistent in the first age group, increased to reach 83% of all explanations in Grades 4 and 5 children, given that the latter tended to produce text-like multi-clause explanations built on logical and chronological relations. On more

On the Codevelopment of Gesture and Monologic Discourse in Children — 225

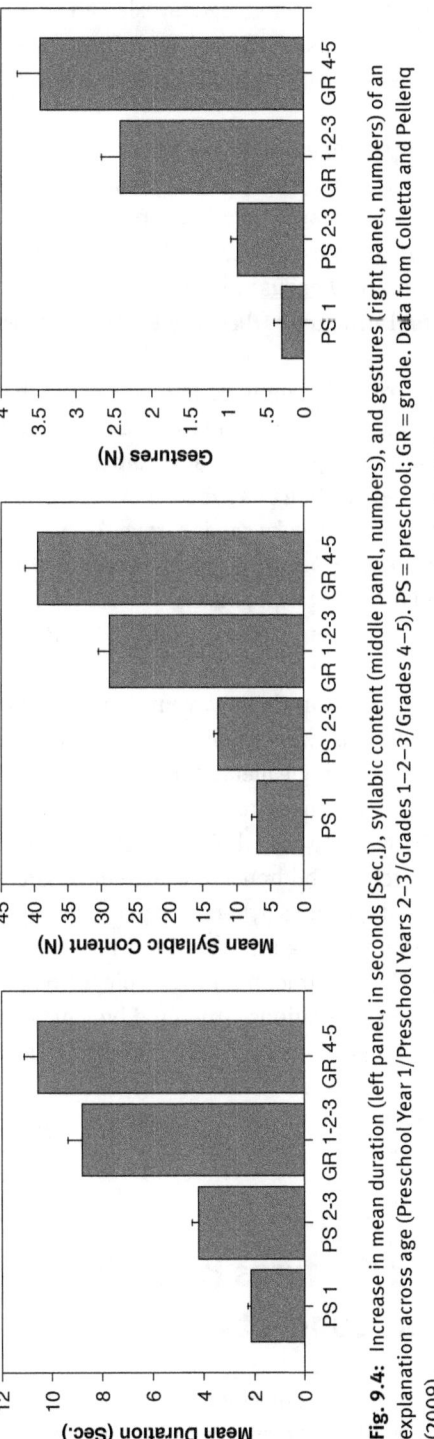

Fig. 9.4: Increase in mean duration (left panel, in seconds [Sec.]), syllabic content (middle panel, numbers), and gestures (right panel, numbers) of an explanation across age (Preschool Year 1/Preschool Years 2–3/Grades 1–2–3/Grades 4–5). PS = preschool; GR = grade. Data from Colletta and Pellenq (2009).

qualitative grounds, comparisons across age revealed an age-related expansion of the connectives paradigm, which is consistent with findings from other studies that investigated oral as well as written language (Alamillo et al., 2013; de Weck, 1991).

> Example 9.11 Simple explanation, verbatim example (girl, 4 years old):
> Explanandum: pourquoi elle pleure la p'tite fille ?
> **Explanans: <u>parce qu'elle est punie</u>**
> Explanandum: *why is the little girl crying?*
> **Explanans: <u>*because* she was punished</u>**
> Textual structure : < because P1 > (P1 = clause 1; P2 = clause 2, etc.)

> Example 9.12 Complex explanation, verbatim example (boy, 6 years old):
> Explanandum : pourquoi est-ce que ça peut faire mal ?
> **Explanans : <u>parce que si</u> tu lances en arrière ça tombe sur la tête <u>et après</u> ben t'es mort**
> Explanandum : *why can it hurt you?*
> **Explanans : <u>*because* if you throw it in the air it falls on your head *and then* well you die</u>**
> Textual structure: <because if P1, P2 and then P3>

In regard to gestures, not surprisingly, young preschool children, whose explanations, with a few exceptions, were rarely complex, produced little if no (8%) gestures of the abstract and not a single metaphoric gesture, in contrast to older children (Colletta & Pellenq, 2009). One must take into account the fact that the two sets of observations differed in regard to both their context and their content and that explanations produced by preschool children, embedded in classroom activities, promoted the use of deictic and iconic gestures, whereas explanations on social topics produced by primary school children during interviews did not. It is worth noting, however, that discourse gestures (i.e., abstract pointing, topic introduction, parsing gestures) appeared only in textlike explanations structured by logical and chronological relations and that metaphoric gestures appeared only in older children's explanations that involved abstract concepts and ideas. Linking verbal explanation performance to age, gesture production clearly indexes the emergence of new discourse and abstract thought abilities in children.

9.9 Metaphoric Gestures Help Children Reason and Discuss Concepts

Let us now consider the following question: Are co-speech gestures a mere index of language and cognitive abilities, or can they play an active role in the emergence of new abilities? Several studies of young children's language behavior have stressed the active part played by pointing and iconic gestures in the building of the first lexicon and the lengthening of the utterance at the end of the one-word utterance stage (for reviews, see Capirci & Volterra, 2008; Özçalışkan & Goldin-Meadow, 2005; Rowe & Goldin-Meadow, 2009; and Volterra et al., 2017). As for metaphoric gestures, thanks to their spatial and analogic properties, they prove highly relevant semiotic tools for speakers engaged in abstract thinking and reasoning (Calbris, 2011; Cienki & Müller, 2008; Stevens & Harrison, 2019). Could they play an active role in the emergence of such abilities in the child? A colleague and I tackled this issue in a recent investigation of metaphoric gestures participants spontaneously produce during P4C discussions (Lagrange-Lanaspre & Colletta, in press). Following an argument put forth by Müller (2008), we hypothesized that bimodal analogy (i.e., a verbal clause accompanied by a metaphoric gesture or a gestured verbal metaphor), because of its strong saliency in discourse, attracts attention from participants who repeat, reword, re-gesture, and extend the analogy. Our first results out of qualitative analysis do speak in favor of such a hypothesis: Metaphoric gestures do not merely show conceptualization and reasoning in the speaker; they also help generate and elaborate on new abstract concepts during collective reasoning (a similar effect has been found for gestures produced in a math lesson; teachers respond differently as a function of their pupils' gestures, thus providing the students with input targeted to their needs [Goldin-Meadow & Singer, 2003; see also Goldin-Meadow et al., 2007, who described the same phenomenon with respect to word learning]). Further work on extended P4C data is yet needed to fully support our claim.

A different methodological entry to tackle this issue is to turn to gesture and speech processing and to examine at what age and how children react to metaphoric gestures. Work by Boutet (2010, 2018) has shown that adults spontaneously attribute abstract meaning and values to hand gestures. In a series of experiments addressed to children in primary school, teenagers in middle school, and adults, Hadian-Cefidekhanie and Colletta (2015) showed participants short video clips of hand gestures bearing metaphoric properties (e.g., the palm-up, open-hand supine gesture; the palm-down pronation gesture; gestures that trace chasing, assembling, trenching, and separating actions; and the cyclic gesture). We first asked each participant to produce verbs and sentences one could say while making such gestures (Task 1); second, asked them to decide whether certain verbs and sentences whose meaning was either concrete or abstract matched with one of the gestures used as stimuli (Task 2); and, third, proposed Task 1 to them again. The first results showed a correlation among age, ability to understand verbal metaphor, and score: The older the participant, the better their understanding of idiomatic sentences and the better their score on detecting and using the metaphoric properties of gestures. In addition, we found a priming effect of the match/mismatch experiment: Detection of metaphoric properties in gestures improved after participants completed Task 2. On the basis of these first insights into iconic–metaphoric gesture processing, it seems that gestures, as semiotic tools, are good candidates to investigate the emergence of later and higher cognitive abilities involved in abstract thinking.

9.10 New Perspectives on Gesture and Discourse Development

Thanks to several funded research projects, data gathered and analyzed over the past 2 decades have enabled me and my colleagues to demonstrate that both gesture and speech codevelop as related means young speakers use in oral monologue speech, whether it be narration, explanation, or argumentation discourse. However, our findings raise three issues I now briefly discuss as unanswered questions and areas for further development: (a) gesture development per se, (b) the relation(s) between speech and gesture, and (c) the exact role gesture plays in language and cognitive development.

I first summarize what develops in gesture and what aspect(s) should be further investigated. As Guidetti et al. (2014, pp. 366–367) put it, there are at least three aspects that one should consider when studying gestures: (a) their function as regards the communication process, (b) their relation to the co-occurring speech, and (c) their morphology. The findings I discussed in Sections 9.1 and 9.2 supply evidence that children age 6 years and over use the complete range of functions described in the literature, contrary to early conclusions made by Cosnier (1982) and McNeill (1992; see Section 9.1). Whether children make use of them or not depends on the type of discourse behavior they engage in as well as on underlying language and social cognitive abilities. It is true, however, that co-speech gestures are "multifaceted" (McNeill, 2005, p. 38) and that one single gesture can simultaneously function at several levels, as in the example of the abstract pointing that conflates indexicality and iconicity (Colletta, 2017), or representational gestures that simultaneously bear pragmatic functions (Brookes, 2005). Moreover, one single iconic or metaphoric gesture often represents more than one single referent, as in the "dual viewpoint" gesture described by Parrill (2009), or in the concept of the "polysign" gesture proposed by Calbris (2011) in which each morphological feature (e.g., hand shape, movement, direction) holds for one aspect of the reference, or in the chaining of gestures, which increases the information load of each stroke (Ovendale et al., 2018).

How does morphology in children's gesture evolve with age? A few studies have focused on representational gestures in the context of narratives and detected changes in formal parameters (e.g., hand shape, location, orientation) and accuracy of execution (Capirci et al., 2011), as well as a move toward fewer body enactments, more hand gestures, and more standardized gestural forms with age (Graziano, 2009; McNeill, 1992). Nonetheless, such changes have been understudied so far. Apart from the standardization hypothesis, which should be limited to social emblems as well as to metaphoric and iconic gestures whose morphology is partly conventionalized, other changes could be tracked in the information load of gestures, in the proportion of polysign gestures in children's repertoire, and in the ability to chain iconic gestures in narration and the gestural backtracking of reference (Agyepong et al., 2018;

Alamillo et al., 2010). Boutet's (2018) kinesiological framework and the proximal–distal opposition could also help detect and explain morphological differences between gestures.

Let us now turn to the relation between speech and gesture. Studies of narratives whose results I discussed in Sections 9.3 to 9.6 all show the same tendency in narrators, whatever the age, to use gesture resources that are relevant to the content and the pragmatics of the utterance. Such co-expressivity remains constant across various types of monologic discourse, as exemplified in the abundant use of gestures of the abstract in expository discourse that involves explaining and reasoning (Sections 9.7–9.9). Yet coexpressivity at the pragmatic level of discourse is but one piece of the cake: There are other types of relations linked to distinct hypotheses that have been investigated. For instance, Italian and American studies have pointed out two types of relations between the linguistic and the gestural content of utterances young children produce at the prelinguistic stage, the first named "redundancy" and/or "complementation" when gesture and speech express the same content, the second named "supplementation" when they do not, the utterance therefore bearing two distinct meanings (see Capirci & Volterra, 2008, Özçalışkan & Goldin-Meadow, 2005, for reviews, and Rowe et al., Chapter 4, this volume). Contrary to the former, the supplementary relation was found to be a key predictor of the lengthening of the utterance and of expression of new semantic relations in children's verbal repertoire (Rowe & Goldin-Meadow, 2009).

The redundancy-versus-nonredundancy paradigm originally applied to bimodal point + word utterance was later adapted to the study of children's narratives by Alibali et al. (2009), who found children to be less redundant than adults in their use of representational gestures. Notwithstanding the methodological effort, one should note that, contrary to the pointing gesture, whose meaning can be considered as redundant with the corresponding naming—although one could discuss this claim from a pragmatic perspective (see, e.g., Cartmill et al., 2014)—the representational gesture, thanks to its visual–imagistic properties, always bears more meaning than, and never can be considered as strictly redundant with, the verbal expression it comes with (see the Kendon continuum and its discussion in McNeill, 2005), hence the coding of representational gestures as integrating with the related string of speech in our own coding system (see Colletta et al., 2009, for an example)—as if the bimodal compound integrated visual aspects of the reference thanks to the gesture's imagistic properties. Moreover, the complexity and multifunctionality of adults' iconic gestures as exemplified in the literature (Brookes, 2014; Calbris, 2011; Kendon, 2004) does not speak in favor of Alibali et al.'s claim.

The redundancy-versus-nonredundancy paradigm also relates to the *compensation hypothesis* by virtue of which a gesture can compensate for the lack of a word or verbal expression in the speaker. The compensation hypothesis is supported by evidence from psycholinguistic research on verbal production in adults who encounter speech disfluencies and, more generally, in populations who experience a language deficit (Feyereisen, 1994; Hadar & Butterworth, 1997; Krauss et al., 2000; McNeill, 2005), as well as in learners of a second language (Gullberg, de Bot, & Volterra, 2008; McCafferty & Stam, 2008; Yoshioka, 2008). In developmental studies, such a hypothesis was raised to account for the high rate of representational gestures in typically developing Italian children who supposedly use them to disambiguate referents in the absence of explicit anaphora (see Section 9.6). Nonetheless, no such disambiguating effect was found in Zulu children's narratives despite its also being a pro-drop language, and evidence for a compensatory use of gestures in narration and depiction has been challenged in studies of several languages (Alamillo et al., 2010; Hickmann et al., 2011; So et al., 2009). In other words, the gesture compensation hypothesis fits well with young children's attempts to express a whole utterance despite a limited vocabulary together with the adult missing a word, but it does not seem sufficiently appropriate to explain aspects of discourse development, unless it is called upon to explain speech disfluencies.

The last issue is that of the exact role played by gesture in language and social-cognitive development. From studies of early language acquisition we know that gesture production and comprehension play a critical role in the emergence of the early lexicon and the emergence of syntactic abilities (in this volume, see Rowe et al., Chapter 4; Capirci et al., Chapter 5; and Clark and Kelly, Chapter 6). Do gesture production and comprehension also enhance discourse development as well as the social-cognitive abilities that are linked to it? The best way to tackle this question is to identify contexts and discourse tasks that challenge children's linguistic abilities at a certain developmental step and lead them to rely on gesture as a supplementary semiotic resource. For instance, young children's attempts to link clauses in a story suggest that gesture enhances pre-narrative production (Batista, 2012; Batista et al., 2019), and gesture production in children's first narratives seems to predict some aspects of later narrative abilities (Demir et al., 2015). In regard to narration in older children, data and results (discussed in Sections 9.3–9.5) brought to light the subtle coevolution of speech and gesture over age in the pragmatic and textual dimensions of narratives, and I have illustrated how gesture plays a key role in expressing comments and marking discourse structure. Nonetheless, we still lack evidence from longitudinal studies that children use gestures rather than speech on their very first attempts at framing, structuring, and commenting on their own verbal production.

The study of complex language tasks brings additional results that support the claim that gesture production scaffolds new discourse and communication abilities, as evidenced by analyses of how children in the last years of primary school try to manage social interaction and monitor mutual understanding while building reference to addressees during instructions (Mazur-Palandre et al., 2014). In addition, the first insights regarding gesture production in the context of explanation and reasoning together with results from our pioneering investigation on gesture processing (discussed in Sections 9.7–9.9) also plead for an active role of gesture in cognitive development and support McNeill's (2005) claim that gesture, because of its specific properties, "fuels speech and thought" (p. 3). Clearly, there is more to investigate along this line. One should, however, bear in mind that, just like verbal language and prosody (Ferré, 2019), gesture production is highly sensitive to interactional context and the discourse genre in which speakers engage. Putting aside every other consideration (i.e., age, gender, language, or culture), studies of gestures and bimodality in human communication, whether observational or experimental, cannot be blind to the contextual, pragmatic, and textual constraints of everyday language (in its broad meaning) use.

Appendix 9.1
Main Functional Types of Coverbal Gestures Identified in the JMacé Data

Performative gestures: express an intentional communication act, such as a "yes" or a "no" answer (head nod or head shake), or that are equivalent to a verbal act, such as "I don't know" (shoulder shrug with head shake), or "Come close" (rapid flicks of index finger toward oneself).

Interactive gestures: help synchronize and maintain joint action between interlocutors (e.g., the head nod that serves as a feedback signal from the interlocutor, the touching gesture the speaker does to raise attention on their interlocutor, the open-hand supine gesture to elicit a response).

Framing gestures: facial expressions of emotion and bodily gestures emblematic of a mental state, such as a head shake for ignorance, a pout for irritation, or a shoulder shrug for fate, that the speaker performs to express their feelings, communicate the utterance mood, and frame the speech content by adding some cognitive distance or connotation.

Referential gestures of the concrete: include the "direct pointing" gesture that indexes a referent accessible within or from the physical setting (pointing to self or interlocutor, pointing to a nearby object), and the "iconic gesture" that represents a concrete referent, such as tracing the size and shape of an object that is not physically present, tracing the trajectory of an object or a character while narrating something, miming the character or his actions, and so on.

Referential gestures of the abstract: include indirect or "substitution" pointing that indexes an object physically present while referring to a similar object that is not accessible within the physical setting, "abstract" pointing (the index finger or hand gesture points to an empty spot in the speaker's frontal space, with the spot marking a discourse entity, such as a character in a story, a certain concept, or an abstract idea, whether the speaker relates to another entity marked by another spot or whether they will reactivate later while performing a gestural anaphora), and metaphoric gestures that represent abstract entities, thanks to the analogical properties of representational gestures.

Speech and discourse parsing gestures: short simple binary gestures (hand or head beats) that accompany the speech flow, help accentuate speech (syllable, word, clause), mark discourse transitions (e.g., alternation of narrative vs. metanarrative statements during storytelling), and segment the speech flow to mark discourse structure and components.

Note. From *Le Développement de la Parole Chez L'enfant Âgé de 6 et 11 Ans: Corps, Langage et Cognition* [Speech development in children ages 6 and 11: Body, language and cognition] (pp. 161–174), by J.-M. Colletta, 2004, Mardaga. Copyright 2004 by Mardaga. Reprinted with permission.

Appendix 9.2
Example of Narrative Performance From an 11-Year-Old French Girl: Multimodal Annotation and Translation

The annotation reads like a musical partition, one part after the other from left to right and from top to bottom. Within each block, each line is dedicated to one aspect of the narrator's performance:

<... gaze ...> optional (< marks its start ; > marks it stop)
<... facial expression and voice quality ...> optional (< marks its start ; > marks its stop)
↗↗ .... ↘ prosody (rising/falling tone)
Et aussi son frère il est mort heu - verbal transcription (French) *
(a) gesture representing headphones hand gestures **
And also his brother he is dead um, verbal translation

*Each underlining marks the presence of a co-occurring hand gesture.
**Each hand gesture labeled (a), (b), (c), and so on, is illustrated below the box representing the multimodal performance fully annotated.

Note. From "Comparative Analysis of Children's Narratives at Different Ages: A Multimodal Approach," by J.-M. Colletta, 2009, *Gesture*, 9(1), pp. 74–75 (https://doi.org/10.1075/gest.9.1.03col). Copyright 2009 by John Benjamins. Adapted with permission.

```
                      < gazes at the adult ............. >              < gazes at the adult ........................ >
                       ↗      ↗       ↗                                    ↗          ↗
Ama :  Et aussi son frère il est mort heu - pa'c'qu'il avait - il avait un casque sur la tête -  'fin c'est -
                                                        (a)     gesture representing headphones
       and also his brother he is dead um, because he had, he was wearing headphones,   but,
```

```
                               <  gazes at the adult  > < gazes at the camcorder ......................... >
       < wears an embarrassed smile ..................  .................   followed by an amused smile ..................... >
                       ↗       ↗ ↗                                                                     ↗ ↗
c'est une heu - famille un peu barjot quoi - (peut) dire ça -  'fin si vous lui montrez pas la cassette
(b)  metaphoric emblem for "mad" (repeated)            (c)     right hand points to camera filming her
     hum,  it's a bit of a loony family,     you could say,    well if you don't show them the tape
```

```
                             ↗↗ ........ ↘        ↗          ↗
       {interr.2s}   et ben il avait mis un casque sur la tête et il est mort à cause de -  parce qu'il
         [...]       well he put headphones on his head and he got killed because,        because he
```

```
                ↗↗ ........ ↘           ↗                      ↗↗ ........ ↘          ↗
                                          < face expresses bewilderment ............................ >
était allé chercher l' pain - et c'était pas un  le jour c'était la nuit chais pas pourquoi il était allé -
went out to get some bread, and it wasn't daylight it was very dark, I don't know why he went out,
```

```
                   < gazes at the adult ...................... >
               < low voice ............................................. >
                        ↗             ↗              ↗                 ↗↗ ...... ↘
'm'a raconté ça pa'c'que mon père il était présent -  et i' voulait traverser il écoutait d' la musique
I got told because my dad was there,        and he wanted to cross and he was listening to music
```

```
       ↗           ↗             ↗              ↗            ↗            ↗
et tout et au moment où i' ferme les yeux pour traverser y a un train qui passe -
                                                   (d)    R hand traces a straight line on the table
and just when he closed his eyes to cross there was a train going past,
```

```
       < gazes at the adult ........................... >
               ↗↗ .................... ↘        ↗↗ .. ↘
et il avait deux trous dans la tête - aaahhh
       (e) R hand points to own temple
and he had two holes in his head,  aaahhh
```

Pictures of the narrator's gestures:

(a) (b) (c) (d) (e)

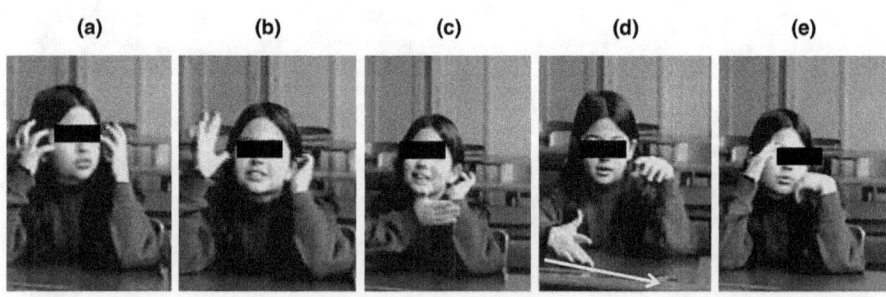

Appendix 9.3
Levels of Narrative Performance in Children's Behavior

Level	Verbal information	Voice and prosody	Gesture	Gaze
1	Short and uncomplete narrative reduced to a basic storyline (telling main events as they occurred)	Undifferentiated prosodic contours	Fixed posture and facial expression, no representational gestures	Either avoidance or continuous eye contact with addressee
2	Level 1 type of narrative including at least one distinctive feature of a Level 3 narrative	Sparsely differentiated prosodic contours	Sparse change in posture, facial expression and gestures	Synchronization glances to addressee
3	Detailed narrative with insertion of micro-discourse acts (e.g., description of background, side explanation, move back in the storyline to tell about an untold event, reported speech), meta- or paranarrative comment, evaluation, and coda	Prosodic contours differentiated as a function of narrative value of utterance (event level, parenthetical digression, comment), voice mimicking individuals involved in reported speech	Interactive and representational gestures, various facial expressions, dramatization of narrative through localization of objects and characters in available space, acting out of roles	Synchronization glances; gaze patterns differentiated according to the wordings' narrative function

Note. From "Comparative Analysis of Children's Narratives at Different Ages: A Multimodal Approach," by J.-M. Colletta, 2009, *Gesture*, *9*(1), p. 87 (https://doi.org/10.1075/gest.9.1.03col). Copyright 2009 by John Benjamins. Reprinted with permission.

References

Adam, J.-M. (1999). *Linguistique textuelle: Des genres de discours aux textes* [Textual linguistics: From genres of discourse to texts]. Nathan.

Agyepong, D., Mahura, O., Nteso, T., & Brookes, H. (2018, July 4–8). *Development of representational gestures in Sesotho speaking children's narratives* [Oral presentation]. Eighth International Society for Gesture Studies Conference, Cape Town, South Africa.

Alamillo, A. R., & Colletta, J-M. (2013). Apprendre à raconter, apprendre à commenter [Learning to make narratives and comments]. In M. Barbazan (Ed.), *Enonciation, texte, grammaire: De la linguistique à la didactique* (pp. 167–183). Presses Universitaires de Rennes.

Alamillo, A. R., Colletta, J.-M., & Guidetti, M. (2013). Gesture and language in narratives and explanations: The effects of age and communicative activity on late multimodal discourse development. *Journal of Child Language*, *40*(3), 511–538. https://doi.org/10.1017/S0305000912000062

Alamillo, A. R., Colletta, J-M., & Kunene, R. N. (2010). Reference tracking in gesture and speech: A developmental study on French narratives. *Rivista di Psicholinguistica Applicata*, *10*(3), 75–95.

Alibali, M. W., Evans, J. L., Hostetter, A. B., Ryan, K., & Mainela-Arnold, E. (2009). Gesture–speech integration in narrative: Are children less redundant than adults? *Gesture*, *9*(3), 290–311. https://doi.org/10.1075/gest.9.3.02ali

Auriac-Slusarczyk, E., & Colletta, J-M. (2015). *Les ateliers de philosophie: Une pensée collective en acte* [Philosophy workshops: Collective thinking in action]. Presses Universitaires Blaise Pascal.

Batista, A. (2012). *Etude du développement pragmatique multimodal au cours de la petite enfance* [A study of multimodal pragmatic development in early childhood] [Unpublished doctoral dissertation]. Université Stendhal, Grenoble, France.

Batista, A., Le Normand, M.-T., & Colletta, J.-M. (2019). Rôle et évolution des combinaisons bimodales au cours de l'acquisition du langage: Données chez l'enfant francophone âgé de 18 à 42 mois [Role and evolution of bimodal combinations during language acquisition: Data in French-speaking children aged 18 to 42 months]. In A. Mazur-Palandre & I. Colón de Carvajal (Eds.), *Multimodalité du langage dans les interactions et l'acquisition* (pp. 53–82). UGA Editions. https://doi.org/10.4000/books.ugaeditions.10947

Berman, R. A., & Slobin, D. I. (1994). *Relating events in narrative: A cross-linguistic developmental study*. Erlbaum.

Boutet, D. (2010). Structuration physiologique de la gestuelle: Modèle et tests [Physiological structuring of gesture: Model and tests]. *Lidil*, *42*, 77–96. https://doi.org/10.4000/lidil.3070

Boutet, D. (2018). *Pour une approche kinésiologique de la gestualité* [For a kinesiological approach to body gesture] [Note de synthèse pour l'habilitation à diriger des recherches] [Habilitation dissertation]. Université de Rouen.

Bouvet, D. (2001). *La dimension corporelle de la parole* [The bodily dimension of speech]. Peeters.

Brémond, C. (1973). *Logique du récit* [The logic of narratives]. Seuil.

Bronckart, J.-P. (1996). *Activité langagière, textes et discours: Pour un interactionnisme socio-discursif* [Language activities, texts, and discourse: For a socio-discursive interactionism]. Delachaux et Niestlé.

Brookes, H. (2005). What gestures do: Some communicative functions of quotable gestures in conversations among black urban South Africans. *Journal of Pragmatics*, *37*(12), 2044–2085. https://doi.org/10.1016/j.pragma.2005.03.006

Brookes, H. J. (2014). Gesture in the communicative ecology of a South African township. In M. Seyfeddinipur & M. Gullberg (Eds.), *Visible utterance in action: Festschrift for Adam Kendon* (pp. 59–74). John Benjamins.

Calbris, G. (1997). Multicanalité de la communication et multifonctionnalité du geste [Communication as multichannel and gesture as multifunctional]. In J. Perrot (Ed.), *Polyphonie pour Ivan Fonagy* (pp. 1–10). L'Harmattan.

Calbris, G. (2003). *L'expression gestuelle de la pensée d'un homme politique* [The gestural expression of a politician's thinking]. CNRS Editions.

Calbris, G. (2011). *Elements of meaning in gesture*. John Benjamins. https://doi.org/10.1075/gs.5

Capirci, O., Cristilli, C., De Angelis, V., & Graziano, M. (2011). Learning to use gesture in narratives: Developmental trends in formal and semantic gesture competence. In G. Stam & M. Ishino (Eds.), *Integrating gestures: The interdisciplinary nature of gesture* (pp. 187–200). John Benjamins. https://doi.org/10.1075/gs.4.16cap

Capirci, O., & Volterra, V. (2008). Gesture and speech: The emergence and development of a strong and changing partnership. *Gesture, 8*(1), 22–44. https://doi.org/10.1075/gest.8.1.04cap

Cartmill, E. A., Hunsicker, D., & Goldin-Meadow, S. (2014). Pointing and naming are not redundant: Children use gesture to modify nouns before they modify nouns in speech. *Developmental Psychology, 50*(6), 1660–1666. https://doi.org/10.1037/a0036003

Cassell, J. (1991). *The development of time and event in narrative: Evidence from speech and gesture* [Unpublished doctoral dissertation]. University of Chicago.

Cienki, A., & Müller, C. (Eds.). (2008). *Metaphor and gesture*. John Benjamins. https://doi.org/10.1075/gs.3

Colletta, J.-M. (2004). *Le développement de la parole chez l'enfant âgé de 6 et 11 ans: Corps, langage et cognition* [Speech development in children ages 6 and 11: Body, language and cognition]. Mardaga.

Colletta, J.-M. (2009). Comparative analysis of children's narratives at different ages: A multimodal approach. *Gesture, 9*(1), 61–96. https://doi.org/10.1075/gest.9.1.03col

Colletta, J.-M. (2015). Philosopher avec les mains [Philosophizing with your hands]. In E. Auriac-Slusarczyk & J.-M. Colletta (Eds.), *Les ateliers de philosophie: Une pensée collective en acte* (pp. 289–310). Presses Universitaires Blaise Pascal.

Colletta, J.-M. (2017). La deixis spatiale: Entre indexicalité et représentation [Spatial deixis: Between indexicality and representation]. *Langue Française, 193*(1), 127–142. https://doi.org/10.3917/lf.193.0127

Colletta, J.-M., Guidetti, M., Capirci, O., Cristilli, C., Demir, O. E., Kunene-Nicolas, R. N., & Levine, S. (2015). Effects of age and language on co-speech gesture production: An investigation of French, American, and Italian children's narratives. *Journal of Child Language, 42*(1), 122–145. https://doi.org/10.1017/S0305000913000585

Colletta, J.-M., Kunene, R. N., Venouil, A., Kauffman, V., & Simon, J.-P. (2009). Multitrack annotation of child language and gestures. In M. Kipp, J.-C. Martin, P. Paggio, & D. Heylen (Eds.), *Multimodal corpora: from models of natural interactions to systems and applications* (pp. 54–72). Springer.

Colletta, J.-M., Kunene-Nicolas, R., & Guidetti, M. (2018). Gesture and speech in adults' and children's narratives: A cross-linguistic investigation of Zulu and French. In M. Hickmann, E. Veneziano, & H. Jisa (Eds.), *Sources of variation in first language acquisition: Languages, contexts, and learners* (pp. 139–160). John Benjamins. https://doi.org/10.1075/tilar.22.08col

Colletta, J.-M., & Pellenq, C. (2009). Multimodal explanations in French children aged from 3 to 11 years. In M. A. Nippold & C. M. Scott (Eds.), *Expository discourse in children, adolescents, and adults: Development and disorders* (pp. 63–97). Erlbaum and Taylor & Francis.

Colletta, J.-M., Pellenq, C., & Guidetti, M. (2010). Age-related changes in co-speech gesture and narrative: Evidence from French children and adults. *Speech Communication*, *52*(6), 565–576. https://doi.org/10.1016/j.specom.2010.02.009

Cosnier, J. (1982). Communications et langages gestuels [Communication and gestural language]. In J. Cosnier, J. Coulon, A. Berrendonner, & C. Orecchioni (Eds.), *Les voies du langage: Communications verbales, gestuelles et animales* (pp. 255–304). Dunod-Bordas.

Cosnier, J. (1993). Etude de la mimogestualité [Study of mimogestuality]. In R. Pléty (Ed.), *Ethologie des communications humaines: Aide-mémoire méthodologique* (pp. 103–115). ARCI and Presses Universitaires de Lyon.

Cristilli, C. (2014). How gestures help children to track reference in narrative. In M. Seyfeddinipur & M. Gullberg (Eds.), *From gesture in conversation to visible action in utterance* (pp. 331–350). John Benjamins. https://doi.org/10.1075/z.188.15cri

Daniel, M.-F., & Auriac-Slusarczyk, E. (2009). Philosophy, critical thinking and philosophy for children. *Educational Philosophy and Theory*, *43*(5), 415–435. https://doi.org/10.1111/j.1469-5812.2008.00483.x

de Garitte, C., Le Maner, G., & Le Roch, E. (1998). La communication gestuelle dans une situation conversationnelle entre pairs du même âge de 6 à 10 ans [Gestural communication in a conversation between peers from 6 to 10 years old]. *Cahiers d'Acquisition et de Pathologie du Langage*, *18*, 71–89.

Demir, Ö. E., Levine, S. C., & Goldin-Meadow, S. (2015). A tale of two hands: Children's early gesture use in narrative production predicts later narrative structure in speech. *Journal of Child Language*, *42*(3), 662–681. https://doi.org/10.1017/S0305000914000415

de Weck, G. (1991). *La cohésion dans les textes d'enfants: Etude du développement des processus anaphoriques* [Cohesion in children's texts: A study of the development of anaphoric processes]. Delachaux et Niestlé.

Ekman, P., & Friesen, W. (1969). The repertoire of nonverbal behavior: Categories, origins, usage and coding. *Semiotica*, *1*(1), 49–98. https://doi.org/10.1515/semi.1969.1.1.49

Fayol, M. (2000). Comprendre et produire des textes écrits: L'exemple du récit [Understanding and producing written texts: Using narratives as an example]. In M. Kail & M. Fayol (Eds.), *L'acquisition du langage T2* (pp. 183–213). Presses Universitaires de France. https://doi.org/10.3917/puf.fayol.2000.02.0183

Ferré, G. (2019). *Analyse de discours multimodal: Gestualité et prosodie en discours* [Multimodal speech analysis: Gesture and prosody in discourse]. UGA Editions.

Feyereisen, P. (1994). *Le cerveau et la communication* [The brain and communication]. Presses Universitaires de France. https://doi.org/10.3917/puf.feyer.1994.01

Fibigerová, K. (2012). *L'effet de la langue sur le développement de l'expression verbale et gestuelle du "mouvement": Une comparaison entre Tchèques et Français d'âges différents* [The effect of language on the development of verbal and gestural expressions of "movement": A comparison between Czech and French people of different ages] [Unpublished doctoral dissertation]. Université de Toulouse, France.

Firbas, J. (1992). *Functional sentence perspective in written and spoken communication*. Cambridge University Press. https://doi.org/10.1017/CBO9780511597817

Givón, T. (1995). Coherence in text vs. coherence in mind. In M. A. Gernsbacher & T. Givón (Eds.), *Coherence in spontaneous text* (pp. 59–116). John Benjamins. https://doi.org/10.1075/tsl.31.04giv

Golder, C. (1996). *Le développement des discours argumentatifs* [The development of argumentative discourse]. Delachaux et Niestlé.

Goldin-Meadow, S., Goodrich, W., Sauer, E., & Iverson, J. (2007). Young children use their hands to tell their mothers what to say. *Developmental Science*, *10*(6), 778–785. https://doi.org/10.1111/j.1467-7687.2007.00636.x

Goldin-Meadow, S., & Singer, M. A. (2003). From children's hands to adults' ears: Gesture's role in the learning process. *Developmental Psychology*, *39*(3), 509–520. https://doi.org/10.1037/0012-1649.39.3.509

Goodwin, C. (1981). *Conversational organization: Interactions between speakers and hearers*. Academic Press.

Graziano, M. (2009). *Le développement de la relation entre les compétences verbale et gestuelle dans la construction d'un texte narratif chez l'enfant âgé de 4 à 10 ans* [The development of the relationship between verbal and gestural skills in the construction of a narrative text in children aged 4 to 10 years] [Unpublished doctoral dissertation]. Université Stendhal, Grenoble, and Universita degli Studi Suor Orsola Benincasa, Napoli.

Grize, J.-B. (1990). *Logique et langage* [Logic and language]. Ophrys.

Groenewald, H. C. (2003). Zulu oral art. *Oral Tradition*, *18*(1), 87–90. https://doi.org/10.1353/ort.2004.0017

Guidetti, M. (1998). Les usages des gestes conventionnels chez l'enfant [The uses of conventional gestures in children]. In J. Bernicot, H. Marcos, C. Day, M. Guidetti, V. Laval, J. Rabain-Jamin, & G. Babelot (Eds.), *De l'usage des gestes et des mots chez l'enfant* (pp. 27–50). Armand Colin.

Guidetti, M., Fibigerova, K., & Colletta, J.-M. (2014). Gestures and multimodal development: Some key issues for language acquisition. In M. Seyfeddinipur & M. Gullberg (Eds.), *From gesture in conversation to visible action in utterance* (pp. 351–370). John Benjamins. https://doi.org/10.1075/z.188.16gui

Gullberg, M., de Bot, K., & Volterra, V. (2008). Gestures and some key issues in the study of language development. *Gesture*, *8*(2), 149–179. https://doi.org/10.1075/gest.8.2.03gul

Gullberg, M., Hendriks, H., & Hickmann, M. (2008). Learning to talk and gesture about motion in French. *First Language*, *28*(2), 200–236. https://doi.org/10.1177/0142723707088074

Hadar, U., & Butterworth, B. (1997). Iconic gestures, imagery and word retrieval in speech. *Semiotica*, *115*(1–2), 147–172. https://doi.org/10.1515/semi.1997.115.1-2.147

Hadian-Cefidekhanie, A., & Colletta, J.-M. (2015, September 24–26). *Age-related variability in the processing of gestural information* [Oral presentation]. Fourth Protolang International Conference, Rome, Italy.

Halliday, M., & Ruqaiya, H. (1976). *Cohesion in English*. Longman.

Harrison, S. (2018). *The impulse to gesture: Where language, minds, and bodies intersect*. Cambridge University Press. https://doi.org/10.1017/9781108265065

Hickmann, M. (2003). *Children's discourse: Person, space and time across languages*. Cambridge University Press.

Hickmann, M., Hendriks, H., & Gullberg, M. (2011). Developmental perspectives on the expression of motion in speech and gesture: A comparison of French and English. *Language, Interaction and Acquisition*, *2*(1), 129–156. https://doi.org/10.1075/lia.2.1.06hic

Jisa, H., & Kern, S. (1998). Relative clauses in French children's narrative texts. *Journal of Child Language*, *25*(3), 623–652. https://doi.org/10.1017/S0305000998003523

Johnson, M. (1987). *The body in the mind: The bodily basis of meaning, imagination and reasoning*. University of Chicago Press. https://doi.org/10.7208/chicago/9780226177847.001.0001

Johnson-Laird, P. N. (1999). Space to think. In P. Bloom, M. A. Peterson, L. Nadell, & M. F. Garrett (Eds.), *Language and space* (pp. 437–462). MIT Press.

Kail, M., & Weissenborn, J. (1984). L'acquisition des connecteurs: Critiques et perspectives [The acquisition of connectives: Critical comments and perspectives]. In M. Moscato & G. Piérault-Le-Bonniec (Eds.), *Le langage, construction et actualisation* (pp. 101–118). Presses Universitaires de Rouen.

Karmiloff-Smith, A. (1979). *A functional approach to child language*. Cambridge University Press.

Kendon, A. (1967). Some functions of gaze-direction in social interaction. *Acta Psychologica*, *26*(1), 22–63. https://doi.org/10.1016/0001-6918(67)90005-4

Kendon, A. (1986). Some reasons for studying gesture. *Semiotica*, *62*(1–2), 1–2, 3–28. https://doi.org/10.1515/semi.1986.62.1-2.3

Kendon, A. (1997). Gesture. *Annual Review of Anthropology*, *26*(1), 109–128. https://doi.org/10.1146/annurev.anthro.26.1.109

Kendon, A. (2004). *Gesture: Visible action as utterance*. Cambridge University Press. https://doi.org/10.1017/CBO9780511807572

Kita, S., & Özyürek, A. (2003). What does cross-linguistic variation in semantic coordination of speech and gesture reveal? Evidence for an interface representation of spatial thinking and speaking. *Journal of Memory and Language*, *48*(1), 16–32. https://doi.org/10.1016/S0749-596X(02)00505-3

Klassen, D. H. (1999). *"You can't have silence with your palms up": Ideophones, gesture, and iconicity in Zimbabwean Shona women's ngano (storysong) performance* [Unpublished doctoral dissertation]. Indiana University.

Krauss, R. M., Chen, Y., & Gottesman, R. F. (2000). Lexical gestures and lexical access: A process model. In D. McNeill (Ed.), *Language and gesture* (pp. 261–283). Cambridge University Press. https://doi.org/10.1017/CBO9780511620850.017

Kunene Nicolas, R. (2010). *A comparative study of the development of multimodal narratives in French and Zulu children and adults* [Unpublished doctoral dissertation]. Université Stendhal.

Kunene Nicolas, R., Guidetti, M., & Colletta, J.-M. (2017). A cross-linguistic study of the development of gesture and speech in Zulu and French oral narratives. *Journal of Child Language*, *44*(1), 36–62. https://doi.org/10.1017/S0305000915000628

Labov, W., & Waletzky, J. (1967). Narrative analysis. In J. Helm (Ed.), *Essays on the verbal and visual arts* (pp. 12–44). University of Washington Press.

Laforest, M., & Vincent, D. (1996). Du récit littéraire à la narration quotidienne [From literary narrative to everyday storytelling]. In M. Laforest (Ed.), *Autour de la narration* (pp. 13–28). Nuit Blanche Editeur.

Lagrange-Lanaspre, S., & Colletta, J.-M. (in press). *Figures d'analogies verbo-gestuelles et raisonnement collectif* [Verb-gestural analogies and collective reasoning]. Presses Universitaires Blaise Pascal and Clermont-Ferrand.

Léonard, J.-L., & Pinheiro, M. B. (1993). Enonciation et non verbal: Aspects de la cohésion linguistique dans un récit oral poitevin [Enunciation and nonverbal forms of communication: Aspects of linguistic cohesion in an oral narrative from the Poitou region]. *Langage & Société*, *65*(1), 39–68. https://doi.org/10.3406/lsoc.1993.2623

Lévy, E., & McNeill, D. (1992). Speech, gesture, and discourse. *Discourse Processes, 15*(3), 277–301. https://doi.org/10.1080/01638539209544813

Lipman, M. (1991). *Thinking in education*. Cambridge University Press.

Lundquist, L. (1980). *La cohérence textuelle: Syntaxe, sémantique, pragmatique* [Textual coherence: Syntax, semantics, pragmatics]. Nyt Nordisk Forlag Arnold Busk.

Mazur-Palandre, A., Colletta, J. M., & Lund, K. (2014). Context sensitive "how" explanation in children's multimodal behavior. *Journal of Multimodal Communication Studies, 2*, 1–17.

McCafferty, S., & Stam, G. (Eds.). (2008). *Gesture: Second language acquisition and classroom research*. Routledge.

McNeill, D. (1992). *Hand and mind: What gestures reveal about thought*. University of Chicago Press.

McNeill, D. (2005). *Gesture and thought*. University of Chicago Press. https://doi.org/10.7208/chicago/9780226514642.001.0001

McNeill, D. (2014). Gesture–speech unity: Phylogenesis, ontogenesis, and microgenesis. *Language, Interaction and Acquisition, 5*(2), 137–184. https://doi.org/10.1075/lia.5.2.01mcn

Mondada, L. (2007). Multimodal resources for turn-taking: Pointing and the emergence of possible next speakers. *Discourse Studies, 9*(2), 194–225. https://doi.org/10.1177/1461445607075346

Montagner, H. (1978). *L'enfant et la communication* [The child and communication]. Stock-Laurence Pernoud.

Müller, C. (2008). What gestures reveal about the nature of metaphor. In A. Cienki & C. Müller (Eds.), *Metaphor and gesture* (pp. 219–245). John Benjamins. https://doi.org/10.1075/gs.3.12mul

Ovendale, A., Brookes, H., Colletta, J.-M., & Davis, Z. (2018). The role of gestural polysigns and gestural sequences in teaching mathematical concepts: The case of halving. *Gesture, 17*(1), 128–157. https://doi.org/10.1075/gest.00013.ove

Özçalışkan, Ş., & Goldin-Meadow, S. (2005). Gesture is at the cutting edge of early language development. *Cognition, 96*(3), B101–B113. https://doi.org/10.1016/j.cognition.2005.01.001

Özyürek, A., Kita, S., Allen, S., Brown, A., Furman, R., & Ishizuka, T. (2008). Development of cross-linguistic variation in speech and gesture: Motion events in English and Turkish. *Developmental Psychology, 44*(4), 1040–1054. https://doi.org/10.1037/0012-1649.44.4.1040

Özyürek, A., Kita, S., Allen, S., Furman, R., & Brown, A. (2005). How does linguistic framing of events influence co-speech gestures? Insights from cross-linguistic variations and similarities. *Gesture, 5*(1/2), 219–240.

Parrill, F. (2009). Dual viewpoint gestures. *Gesture, 9*(3), 271–289. https://doi.org/10.1075/gest.9.3.01par

Peterson, C., & McCabe, A. (Eds.). (1991). *Developing narrative structure*. Erlbaum.

Roulet, E. (1999). *La description de l'organisation du discours* [Description of the organization of discourse]. Didier.

Rowe, M. L., & Goldin-Meadow, S. (2009). Early gesture selectively predicts later language learning. *Developmental Science, 12*(1), 182–187. https://doi.org/10.1111/j.1467-7687.2008.00764.x

Simon, J.-P., Colletta, J.-M., Lepoire, S., Prévost, C., Sautot, J.-P., & Vuillet, J. (2009). *Apprendre à expliquer en maternelle* [Learning to explain in kindergarten]. Centre Régional de Documentation Pédagogique de Grenoble.

Simon, J.-P., & Tozzi, M. (Eds.). (2017). *Paroles de philosophes en herbe: Regards croisés de chercheurs sur une discussion sur la justice en CM2* [Words of budding philosophers: Crossed perspectives of researchers on a discussion on justice in CM2]. UGA Editions.

So, W. C., Kita, S., & Goldin-Meadow, S. (2009). Using the hands to identify who does what to whom: Gesture and speech go hand-in-hand. *Cognitive Science, 33*(1), 115–125. https://doi.org/10.1111/j.1551-6709.2008.01006.x

Stevens, M. P., & Harrison, S. (2019). Spectrums of thought in gesture: Using gestures to analyze concepts in philosophy. *Pragmatics & Cognition*, *24*(3), 441–473. https://doi.org/10.1075/pc.17024.ste

Streeck, J. (1993). Gesture as communication: Its coordination with gaze and speech. *Communication Monographs*, *60*(4), 275–299. https://doi.org/10.1080/03637759309376314

Streeck, J. (2009). *Gesturecraft: The manufacture of meaning*. John Benjamins. https://doi.org/10.1075/gs.2

Suzman, S. (1991). *Language acquisition in Zulu* [Unpublished doctoral dissertation]. University of the Witwatersrand, Johannesburg, South Africa.

Talmy, L. (2000). *Towards a cognitive semantics*. MIT Press.

Tolchinsky, L. (2004). The nature and scope of later language development. In R. A. Berman (Ed.), *Language development across childhood and adolescence* (pp. 233–248). John Benjamins. https://doi.org/10.1075/tilar.3.15tol

Traverso, V. (1996). *La conversation familière: Analyse pragmatique des interactions* [The familiar conversations: Pragmatic analysis of interactions]. Presses Universitaires de Lyon.

Veneziano, E., & Hudelot, C. (2002). Développement des compétences pragmatiques et théories de l'esprit chez l'enfant: Le cas de l'explication [Development of pragmatic skills and theory of mind in children: Focus on explanations]. In J. Bernicot, A. Trognon, M. Guidetti, & M. Musiol (Eds.), *Pragmatique et psychologie* (pp. 215–236). Presses Universitaires de Nancy.

Veneziano, E., & Sinclair, H. (1995). Functional changes in early child language: The appearance of references to the past and of explanations. *Journal of Child Language*, *22*(3), 557–581. https://doi.org/10.1017/S0305000900009958

Volterra, V., Capirci, O., Caselli, M. C., Rinaldi, P., & Sparaci, L. (2017). Developmental evidence for continuity from action to gesture to sign/word. *Language, Interaction and Acquisition*, *8*(1), 13–41. https://doi.org/10.1075/lia.8.1.02vol

Weinrich, H. (1989). *Grammaire textuelle du Français* [French textual grammar]. Didier/Hatier.

Werlich, E. (1975). *Typologie der texte* [Text typology]. Quelle und Meyer.

Yoshioka, K. (2008). Gesture and information structure in first and second language. *Gesture*, *8*(2), 236–255. https://doi.org/10.1075/gest.8.2.07yos

Susan Wagner Cook
10 Understanding How Gestures Are Produced and Perceived

What are the processes that underlie speech and gesture in communication? Does this link develop in the language system, or is it the result of more general cognitive processes? How can researchers design studies to understand a complex system like gesture? Current research provides evidence for a plethora of mechanisms by which gestures are produced and perceived; what is not known is how these putative processes work and interact with one another. In this chapter, I provide a selective overview of candidate processes underlying gesture production and perception and consider how these processes are used over the lifespan. I argue that uncovering the mechanisms of gesture production will require studying gestures in complex communicative situations. Given the multiplicity of candidate mechanisms along with the various functions served by gestures, understanding gesture production and perception will require moving beyond unidimensional accounts of production and perception to uncover how various processes interact with one another.

10.1 Gesture in Communication

When communicating, people encode information by means of rapid changes in a linguistic signal that is structured at multiple levels, including phonological, morphological, syntactic, and pragmatic. At the same time as they speak or sign, speakers and signers also modulate their hands in ways that coordinate with their linguistically structured signals. Although these hand gestures are not structured according to the rules of language, they are a robust feature of the linguistic system and are flexibly used for human communication across cultures, languages, and discourse contexts by speakers across the lifespan.

Gestures are produced by speakers of all known languages (Kita, 2009; McNeill, 1992). Children gesture from the very earliest stages of language production, and they integrate their gestures with their language over the course of development (Özçalışkan & Goldin-Meadow, 2005). Congenitally blind children and adults, who have never observed other person gesture, gesture along with their linguistic communication (Iverson & Goldin-Meadow, 1998, 2001). Signers also gesture (Emmorey, 1999; Marschark, 1994); however, because hand gestures and signs are produced with the same articulators the criteria for distinguishing gesture from sign are less agreed on than those used to identify gestures that accompany auditory language

(Goldin-Meadow & Brentari, 2017), and considerably less is known about the production and perception of gesture with sign language compared with the production and perception of gesture with spoken language.

Hand gestures are often categorized according to the form of the movement and the information that is contained within these movements (McNeill, 1992). For example, *deictic gestures* indicate locations or directions, often by means of pointing handshakes. *Iconic* and *metaphoric gestures* directly depict actions, movements, and shapes. Finally, *beat gestures* are movements that coordinate rhythmically with the accompanying linguistic signal but that do not appear to contain informationally structured features.

Two defining characteristics of gestures have been well documented: (a) gestures are *semantically* coordinated with linguistic signals and (b) gestures are *temporally* coordinated with linguistic signals. In children, both semantic and temporal coordination are evident from the onset of gesture use (Esteve-Gibert & Prieto, 2014). The precise coordination of gesture with language must be explained by any viable account of the processes supporting gesture production. These fundamental characteristics of gesture are likely also implicated in accounts of how observers perceive gestures, although of course observers need not be sensitive to all aspects of gesture as it is produced.

10.1.1 Semantic Coordination

Gestures and language coordinate to express semantic information at multiple linguistic levels, including the lexical level, the utterance level, and the pragmatic level. At times, the information in speech and gesture is highly redundant, with both expressing the same information. For example, when adult speakers are narrating stories, they are more likely to provide information about referents in gesture when this information is also available in the accompanying speech (So et al., 2009). Similarly, when adult speakers are describing entities in the immediate environment to listeners, they point more when they also use more locative descriptions in the accompanying speech, and speakers produce more iconic gestures when they use more feature descriptions in the accompanying speech (de Ruiter et al., 2012). Thus, gesture and speech often appear to emerge from the same information in mind.

At other times, it appears that information is distributed across speech and gesture, with some information being unique to gesture. For example, when adult speakers are referring to targets available in the immediate environment, they use more gestures and fewer words as targets get physically closer and thus could be more precisely indicated with a gesture (Bangerter, 2004). Along similar lines, adult speakers leave out more information from their linguistic descriptions of pictures when they gesture compared with when they do not (Melinger & Levelt, 2004). Children also distribute information across modalities.

Continuous, iconic representation of visual and spatial information in gesture can express information that would be cumbersome, and at times impossible, to communicate linguistically. For example, the trajectory of motion of a flying insect would be rather complicated to describe in words but can be readily depicted in a single gesture. Gestures offer a tool for continuous and iconic representation of visuospatial and motor information (Cook & Tanenhaus, 2009; Hilliard & Cook, 2017).

Even when gestures and speech appear to express the same information, however, they are not necessarily redundant with one another. Pointing at an object locates it in the immediate environment while naming that object classifies it. Language necessarily requires speakers to encode information using preestablished lexical and grammatical categories and following the rules of syntax. Gesture, in contrast, does not appear to be produced in a rule-governed way and, although gestures can be categorized, unlike words and sentences gestures are not necessarily produced according to preestablished categories. Instead, gesture is free to represent semantic information in a way that is flexibly adapted to the immediate environment and to the to-be-communicated information, whereas language represents the same information in a way that is necessarily adapted to the rules of the language used (Kita & Özyürek, 2003).

10.1.2 Simultaneous Production

Gestures and language also coordinate temporally. Gestures overlap in time with lexical items that express related semantic information (McNeill, 1992). In fact, gestures are more closely synchronized with language than comparable actions that co-occur with speech (Church et al., 2014).

The temporal coordination of gesture with lexical items is not perfectly simultaneous. The onset of speakers' gestures tends to anticipate the onset of related spoken words (Morrel-Samuels & Krauss, 1992). However, there is also often considerable variability in the temporal coordination of speech and lexical items. For example, in a corpus of German speakers describing routes, the modal asynchrony between gestures and related lexical items was 0 milliseconds, and the mean was 128 milliseconds, with gestures typically coming before the related words (Bergmann et al., 2011). Some of this variability is predictable from characteristics of the utterance and context. The degree of anticipation is related to the familiarity (Morrel-Samuels & Krauss, 1992) and predictability (Beattie & Shovelton, 2000) of the associated lexical item. The degree of anticipation is also related to the amount of semantic coordination, with greater semantic overlap being associated with closer temporal coordination (Bergmann et al., 2011).

Gesture is also coordinated with language beyond the lexical level. The points of maximum energy in speech are coordinated with points of maximum energy in gestures (Esteve-Gibert & Prieto, 2013). Gestures are also synchronized with intonation contours. The apex of pointing gestures (Loehr, 2012) and beat gestures

(Leonard & Cummins, 2011) is produced simultaneously with the pitch accent of the accompanying speech.

Thus, gestures are not epiphenomenal to the process of communication; instead, gestures have a variety of positive influences on producers and on observers. Much of my own work has investigated the effects of removing gesture from speakers and listeners in order to provide evidence for the function of gesture during communication and learning. I and others have found that removing gesture from an interaction influences speakers (Cook et al., 2012; Goldin-Meadow et al., 2001; Wagner et al., 2004) as well as listeners (Cook et al., 2013, 2017). For example, adult speakers who are restricted from gesturing are more disfluent (Morsella & Krauss, 2004; Rauscher et al., 1996), and they do not express as much information in their communicative signal (Driskell & Radtke, 2003), although this is not always the case (Hoetjes et al., 2014). Similarly, observers who do not have access to gesture expend more resources to access information (Morett et al., 2020), and they do not glean as much information as observers who view gestures (Goldin-Meadow & Sandhofer, 1999). Thus, gestures are functional behaviors that have positive consequences for producers and perceivers.

It is important to note that these positive effects are seen across ages. It is not the case that only developing producers and observers benefit from gesture, and it is also not the case that only developed producers and observers can use gesture to support communication (Goldin-Meadow et al., 2001; Wagner et al., 2004).

Although gestures are known to benefit producers and perceivers, this does not necessarily mean that producers and perceivers can always flexibly and optimally exploit gesture to achieve these benefits. Producers and perceivers must have a set of mechanisms supporting perception and production of gesture, but there is no reason to expect that these mechanisms are perfectly adapted to all communicative contexts or that these adaptations are the same across ages (McNamara & Houston, 2009).

Instead, given the diversity of human languages and communicative contexts and the inherent flexibility of human communication, it is highly likely that there are situations in which the mechanisms that underlie gesture production and perception lead to gestures being produced and perceived but in which the presence of gesture does not support improvements in function and perhaps even detracts from optimal outcomes.

10.2 How Is the Semantic and Temporal Coordination of Speech and Gesture Achieved by Producers?

Although the spatial and temporal coordination of gesture with speech is well documented, how this coordination is achieved is not known. One possibility is that speech and gesture are linked because of physiological processes in the body, whereby simultaneous motor plans are entrained to one another. According to this account, the tight links between speech and gesture may not reflect any underlying structure of the communicative system but instead may be a necessary feature of communication given that it is produced by embodied agents. Alternatively, speech and gesture may be linked via cognitive processes supporting thinking and communicating. According to this account, the tight links between speech and gesture may reflect an important characteristic of our communicative systems across development.

10.2.1 Physiological Processes Linking Hand and Mouth

The human body is a complex system, made up of multiple interacting subsystems serving a variety of simultaneous functions. One possibility is that speech and gesture emerge out of links between hand and mouth that are based in shared or overlapping processes.

10.2.1.1 Spontaneous Coordination

The spontaneous coordination of hand and mouth during communication may emerge out of fundamental links between instrumental hand actions and mouth actions. Single-cell recordings demonstrate that the same neurons that are involved in planning mouth movements are also involved in planning grasping actions (Rizzolatti et al., 1988). Newborns show coordination between hand movements and mouth movements (Rochat, 1993). In infancy, outside of communicative contexts, hand and mouth actions are frequently coordinated, and this coordination continues as infants develop communicative behaviors, providing a coordinated basis on which speech and gesture can develop (Iverson & Fagan, 2004; Iverson & Thelen, 1999).

There are structural and functional links between hand and mouth in adults as well. Hand and mouth share spatially proximal and synergistic neural representations (Desmurget et al., 2014). Thus, speech and gesture may not necessarily be linked in service of communication but instead at a more basic level in terms of how the brain is organized that may then shape communication (Vainio, 2019).

10.2.1.2 Entrainment

Even without higher order cognitive control, coupled oscillators self-organize into consistent patterns, and these patterns can be seen in simultaneous arm and mouth movements (Kelso, 1995) across the lifespan (Iverson & Fagan, 2004). When adult speakers move their hands along with their mouths, the movements produced can entrain to one another, resulting in close temporal coordination (Rusiewicz et al., 2013, 2014).

In adult speakers, it is clear that movements of the hand and mouth influence one another during communication. When speakers are asked to produce coordinated, meaningful movements along with their speech, there are reliable effects on both the speech and on the hand movements (Bernardis & Gentilucci, 2006). When speakers are asked to tap along with their speech, they are unable to desynchronize tapping and emphatic stress (Parrell et al., 2014). Deictic gestures are dynamically synchronized with prosody and stress in the accompanying words (Rusiewicz et al., 2013), and when auditory feedback is altered gesture trajectories change (Rusiewicz et al., 2014).

Synchronized motion does not seem to result in the same cognitive benefits that are associated with the production of meaningful hand gestures, however. Cook et al. (2012) compared the concurrent working memory performance of adult speakers who were asked to either use their hands while explaining, to make circular hand movements while explaining, or to hold their hand still, with individual speakers completing two of the possible three conditions. At the same time, speakers were asked to hold a list of letters in mind, and recall of the list was used to measure demand on working memory during the explanation task. Speakers performed better on the concurrent verbal working memory tasks when they were instructed to use their hands compared with when they were asked to make rhythmic movements or no movements at all. Simply moving one's hands is not enough to reduce speakers' demand on working memory; instead, the particular movements that are made are also important for some of the cognitive functions of gesture production.

10.2.2 Cognitive Processes Linking Hand and Mouth

Gesture and speech may be intentionally or automatically linked via specialized cognitive processes that support the development, expression, and communication of one's thoughts. Alternatively, gesture and speech may be linked by means of general-purpose cognitive processes such as attention, working memory, and memory that support cognition in a broad variety of tasks.

10.2.2.1 Gestures as Thinking

One possibility is that gestures emerge from the act of thinking, which underlies communication. One prominent example of this claim is *growth point theory*, developed by David McNeill (1992). For McNeill (1992), gesture and speech are two coordinated outputs of the act of thinking itself. Gesture emerges from the self-organizing dialectic process of communicating one's thoughts, and gestures are actively involved in the genesis of these thoughts. According to this account, it is not surprising that gestures are semantically and temporally coordinated with speech because both gesture and speech emerge from single acts of thinking, and the two modalities together both express and embody this thinking.

Experimental evidence suggests that gestures are associated with thinking from an early age. Alibali et al. (2000) studied 5-year-old children explaining their solutions to conservation problems and compared them with children simply describing the objects used in a conservation task. They found that children produced more representational gestures that conveyed substantial information in the explanation task compared with the description task, even though the children used essentially the same words and grammatical structures across the two tasks.

Other accounts suggest that gestures may reflect the underlying organization of our thoughts, especially as expressed in language. Embodied theories of language propose that our abstract thoughts and concepts are grounded in lower level perceptual and motor processes (Barsalou, 1999; Glenberg, 1997). Gestures may emerge as expressions of the lower level processes supporting higher cognition (Hostetter & Alibali, 2008, 2010, 2019).

10.2.2.2 Language Production Processes

An alternative is that gestures may emerge from processes specifically supporting language production (Butterworth & Hadar, 1989; de Ruiter, 1998; Morrel-Samuels & Krauss, 1992). In other words, gestures may emerge from the processes that are involved in translating a preverbal message into a linguistic form and then articulating this form. A variety of gesture production models have been put forth that postulate specialized processes within the language production system that are responsible for gesture.

Levelt (1993) proposed a three-level model of speech production that includes (a) a *conceptualizer* as the most abstract level, where a preverbal message is generated; (b) a *formulator*, where words and syntactic structures are activated; and (c) an *articulator*, where the necessary motor plans are generated and assembled. Models of adults' gesture production have been proposed that link gestures to Levelt's model via the conceptualizer and to the formulator (Butterworth & Hadar, 1989; de Ruiter, 1998; Melinger & Kita, 2007). These models typically propose that speakers' preverbal messages include both verbal and nonverbal aspects and that these aspects of the message are distributed across speech and gesture and are coordinated during articulation. Gestures have also been postulated to support lexical access in the formulator. Gestures reflect imagistic and motor aspects of one's thinking that may, by means of spreading activation, help activate lexical items (Krauss & Hadar, 1999; Rauscher et al., 1996) or phonological codes for lexical items (Butterworth & Hadar, 1989).

10.2.2.3 General Processes

During communication, speakers and listeners engage a variety of cognitive processes that are not specific to language or communication. Gesture may also emerge from more general cognitive processes, specifically, working memory and memory.

10.2.2.3.1 Working Memory

Language production makes use of available information in working memory. When speakers are asked to maintain irrelevant information in working memory, reducing the resources that are available for communication, they produce shorter, less elaborate sentences, and they pause more (Kemper et al., 2003; Power, 1985) and make more errors (Hartsuiker & Barkhuysen, 2006).

Gesturing helps both child and adult speakers reduce demand on their working memory processes. When speakers spontaneously gesture while explaining math problems, they perform better on current working memory tasks compared with explanations of problems during which they do not gesture. Similar patterns have been seen in children (Goldin-Meadow et al., 2001) and in adults (Wagner et al., 2004) for both verbal and spatial working memory (Cook et al., 2012; Goldin-Meadow et al., 2001; Wagner et al., 2004). Thus, speakers of all ages may be able to reduce their own demand on working memory by gesturing, by indexing referents, by spatializing ideas, and by reactivating relevant information.

10.2.2.3.2 Memory

Gesture has also been linked to memory processes. It is clear that information in memory can shape the form of a gesture given that gestures reflect characteristics of the to-be-communicated information that must arise from memory. Moreover, recalling information from memory seems to promote gesture production. When speakers describe a picture from memory, they gesture significantly more frequently than when they describe a picture that is in front of them (de Ruiter, 1998; Wesp et al., 2001), suggesting that the act of activating information in memory can support gesture production.

Cook and Tanenhaus (2009) investigated how adult speakers expressed information about a problem-solving task in speech and gesture. To do this, they varied the motor experience of speakers when they solved a well-studied problem-solving task, the Tower of Hanoi. One group of speakers solved the Tower of Hanoi using real objects on a physical board, and a second group of speakers solved the same task on a computer, using a mouse to click and drag virtual objects on a computer screen. After solving the task, speakers explained their solutions to an observer who was not present during the original task, in a room with none of the materials present. Speakers expressed information about *where* to move the disks in their speech and about *how* to move the disks in their gesture. Both speech and gesture reflected information from memory, but gesture additionally reflected motor information that was not available in the accompanying speech.

Gesture appears to help children access and communicate information from memory. When 6- and 7-year-old children are asked to gesture while they recall a previously experienced event, they report more information than children who are not instructed to gesture (Stevanoni & Salmon, 2005). Similar findings have been found with younger children who were asked to tell a story with either representational gesture or pointing gestures (Cameron & Xu, 2011).

Work taking a neuropsychological approach has revealed a multifaceted relation between gesture production and memory processes. Hilverman et al. (2016) studied patients with various profiles of memory impairment and found that particular memory systems are implicated in gesture production. Patients with hippocampal amnesia lacked a functioning declarative memory system. These patients gestured but did so significantly less frequently than comparison patients, especially when performing tasks that relied heavily on declarative memory. These findings suggest that some gestures are built on active representations in the declarative memory system. Klooster et al. (2015) studied patients with impairments in procedural memory and found that these patients did not express their prior motor experiences in their gesture, in contrast to comparison patients. These findings complement those seen in patients with amnesia and suggest that some gestures are built on activations in procedural memory systems. Thus, there is not a simple, unitary relation between memory systems and gestures. Instead, gesture production, like performance on many complex tasks, relies on diverse representations in memory (Knowlton et al., 1994).

10.2.3 Methodological Issues in Studying Gesture Production

Although gesture is a robust phenomenon, the processes implicated in gesture production are not clear. It is difficult to implicate specific processes in gesture production because gesture is a spontaneous behavior that is often produced without conscious awareness. It cannot be readily manipulated in experimental paradigms without also affecting other coordinated behaviors and without raising awareness of the behavior itself. This limits the sorts of experimental designs that can be used to study gesture and further restricts the nature of the causal inferences that can be drawn. As a result, much of the literature on gesture production has been developed with observational data, and many theories of gesture production lack strong causal evidence for the basic mechanisms postulated to underlie gesture production.

One solution to this is to examine more overt manipulations of gesture. Speakers can be instructed to gesture, to gesture in particular ways, or to refrain from gesturing, and listeners can be instructed to attend to or to ignore characteristics of the gestures they observe. The evidence to date reveals that overt manipulations of gesture may not change many of the fundamental properties of gestures. For example, gestures appear to facilitate working memory processes even when they are produced by instruction (Cook et al., 2012), and gestures iconically reflect stimulus characteristics even when these are not relevant to the task (Hilliard & Cook, 2017).

Gestures that are produced according to experimental instruction show additional similarities with spontaneously produced gestures. For example, gestures are known to reflect implicit knowledge that can catalyze the acquisition of new knowledge. Surprisingly, some children who are explicitly instructed to move their hands during an explanation also express knowledge in their gestures that is not expressed in the accompanying speech, and that can be coded and identified in the same way as spontaneously produced gestures. In addition, the knowledge that is expressed in gesture as a result of experimental instruction supports subsequent learning; Broaders et al. (2007) found that, as a group, children who were instructed to gesture learned more from subsequent instruction than children who were instructed not to gesture during the explanation task before the instruction. This difference was driven by the children who expressed new knowledge in their gestures in response to the instruction to gesture. These children subsequently learned more after instruction compared with children who were instructed to gesture but who did not express additional information in their gestures.

Finally, gestures appear to support learning even when they are produced as a result of explicit instruction. Cook et al. (2008) instructed children to repeat either spoken language, hand movements, or spoken language combined with hand movements and found that children who either repeated the hand movements or both the language and hand movements were more likely to maintain their learning compared with children who only repeated the spoken language.

These findings suggest that the experimentally produced gestures may engage mechanisms similar to those of spontaneously produced gestures. Although it is clear that speakers can modulate the rate of their gestures, other aspects of the speech–gesture system may be linked in ways that are less influenced by higher order cognitive processes. Thus, researchers may be able to successfully study gestures using more explicit instructions to vary the presence of gesture in experimental situations, increasing their ability to gather data that support causal inference. However, additional work will be necessary to elucidate whether similar functions are in fact arising from similar mechanism. It is also possible that the effects of experimentally produced gestures arise by means of different mechanisms than spontaneously produced gestures.

Experimental methods necessarily provide a limited perspective on processes supporting gesture production. By virtue of the fact that many variables are controlled, experiments strip away the fundamental richness of communication. Researchers may be more likely to uncover mechanisms of gesture production if they study the ways gesture production breaks down, which may require studying communication in complex situations. Studying gesture in situations where producers can readily produce the necessary speech and gesture may not stress the system enough to reveal its underlying organization.

Methods for testing causal models in observational data may allow gesture researchers to test causal models of gesture production using observational data gathered from rich contexts (Pearl, 2009). In particular, appropriate statistical techniques may allow them to investigate how multiple factors interact to shape one's propensity to gesture in a particular context, as well as the form that gesture takes. These approaches may offer a tool for researchers to better account for the complexity of gesture as it is produced, by better accounting for appropriate covariates in order to isolate variables of interest.

Gestures are complex, multifaceted behaviors, produced in conjunction with words and sentences that are also complex and multifaceted. An understanding of the processes that underlie gesture production over development will require integration of experimental and observational approaches as well as well-specified theoretical models.

10.3 How Is Gesture Perceived?

When observing another person communicate, listeners are faced with the task of deciphering the rapidly changing linguistic signal that is structured at multiple levels. Gestures are known to support the processing of this signal, facilitating understanding during communication. Sensitivity to information in gesture has been observed across ages (Morford & Goldin-Meadow, 1992), cultures (Graham & Argyle, 1975), and tasks (Dargue et al., 2019; Hostetter, 2011). For example, Cook et al. (2013) showed that children who are given instruction in math are more likely to learn and retain new knowledge when the instruction that they observe includes gesture compared with matched instruction that does not contain gesture, both for naturalistically produced gestures and for gestures produced by a computer generated avatar (Cook et al., 2017). Observers make use of both the semantic information in gesture as well as the simultaneity of speech and gesture during communication.

10.3.1 Integration of Semantic Information

Listeners integrate semantic information from language with semantic information from gesture. Influences of gesture on listeners' perception and recall of information have been demonstrated across ages in a variety of tasks and contexts (Beattie & Shovelton, 2001; Driskell & Radtke, 2003). For example, pointing gestures bias the perception of ambiguous speech signals for 5-year-old children as well as adults. When child and adult observers viewed a pointing hand indicating either a ball or a doll, they were more likely to perceive an ambiguous word that is between "ball" and "doll" as what is being indicated with the pointing hand (Thompson & Massaro, 1986). Gestures often express spatial and motoric information that is not available in the accompanying speech, and listeners detect this information (Beattie & Shovelton, 2001).

10.3.2 Perception of Coordinated Information

Even when there is not any additional semantic information evident in the available gestures, perception of coordinated information across speech and gesture seems to enhance processing. Infants can use coordinated visual and auditory information to extract higher order characteristics of stimuli (Bahrick & Lickliter, 2000), and coordination between visual and auditory information can help infants learn associations between syllables and words (Gogate, 2010). Even simple beat gestures, which do not seem to carry semantic information, have effects on memory for adults, although they do not seem to have similar effects for 4- to 5-year-old children (So et al., 2012). Thus, in addition to extracting information from the form of a gesture, observers of all ages are sensitive to the coordination of information across modalities and, in various contexts, observers can use coordination to facilitate processing.

10.3.3 What Are the Processes Listeners Use to Perceive Gestures?

How is the semantic and temporal coordination of speech and gesture perceived by observers? Although listeners are known to be influenced by gesture, how gestures are integrated with linguistically structured signals is not known. One possibility is that speech and gesture are linked via sensory processes that integrate information that co-occurs in time. On this account, listeners may be influenced by gesture not because it is a communicative signal that is produced by a speaker but because our perceptual systems integrate information that co-occurs in time. Alternatively, speech and gesture may be integrated via specialized cognitive processes that support understanding during communication. Gestures may modulate cognitive processes that function for comprehension, or they may recruit new processes during communication.

10.3.3.1 Perceptual and Motor Processes Integrating Sources of Information

The integrated perception of linguistic and gestural sources of information may arise because of how our perceptual systems combine sources of information across modalities and time scales. Simultaneous visual, auditory, and motor signals are automatically and obligatorily integrated by our perceptual systems. These effects are seen in infancy and become more precise over the course of development (Gori et al., 2012).

10.3.3.1.1 Entrainment

Much like gestures may emerge by means of the entrainment of articulators, integrated perception of speech or sign and gesture may also occur by means of entrainment. Neural entrainment to speech is important in determining the intelligibility of this speech in children and adults (Power et al., 2012; Riecke et al., 2018). Gestures may additionally promote entrainment, facilitating processing by shaping the perceptual system to expect useful information to occur at particular points in time. Gestures can provide a rhythmic undercurrent to speech that may adjust speakers' expectations in support of more efficient processing. Indeed, words that are presented in time with an expected rhythmic beat are processed more quickly than words that are not presented in time with the underlying beat (Cason & Schön, 2012; Quené & Port, 2005). Furthermore, beat gestures influence observers event-related potentials very early, suggesting that they modulate sensory aspects of perception (Biau & Soto-Faraco, 2013, 2015), and similar findings have been reported for representational gestures (Kelly, Creigh, & Bartolotti, 2010). Thus, gestures may influence perceivers by shaping neural oscillations and thereby enhancing perception.

10.3.3.1.2 Visual–Auditory Integration

Redundancy of information across modalities is known to have specific and robust effects on perception. For example, the timing of a sound stimulus influences the perception of an ambiguous motion stimulus (Sekuler et al., 1997). Moreover, the temporal coordination of visual and auditory information is important for determining whether information is integrated, with simultaneous signals more likely to be integrated than signals that are not temporally coordinated. In addition, when visual and auditory signals are not perfectly synchronous, integration is more likely when visual stimuli precede auditory stimuli, consistent with the faster speed of light relative to sound (Spence & Squire, 2003). Gesture provides a visual signal that coordinates with and anticipates speech. Thus, gesture has the potential to shape sensory processing in service of communication.

Ongoing work by me and my colleagues also suggests that observers integrate a variety of simultaneous visual signals with speech, so long as the temporal coordination between speech and these visual signals is appropriate (Cook, 2019). Moreover, integration of gesture with speech appears to be greater when gestures precede the accompanying speech rather than when speech precedes the accompanying gestures (Pruner & Cook, 2021).

10.3.3.1.3 Motor Simulation

Although gestures are not actions, in the sense that they do not change the state of the physical world, they share many features with actions (Novack & Goldin-Meadow, 2017). Observers may use the same mechanisms that they use to understand the actions produced by others to understand the gestures produced by others, specifically motor simulation. Child and adult observers appear to make sense of the actions produced by others by simulating these actions themselves (Blakemore & Decety, 2001; Filippi & Woodward, 2016; Sommerville et al., 2005). Similarly, speakers perceiving gestures may simulate the underlying action features, shaping processing.

Recall Cook and Tanenhaus's (2009) investigation, discussed earlier in this chapter, of how listeners perceived gesture information during a live interaction by observing listeners' responses to gestures depicting actions as produced in a Tower of Hanoi problem-solving and communication task. Recall that speakers' gestures were related to their experience solving the task. Speakers who solved the task with real objects produced more curved trajectories in their gestures, whereas speakers who solved it on the computer produced straighter trajectories in their gestures. In that study, listeners observed these explanations and subsequently solved the problem themselves, on a computer where their mouse movements were tracked. Listeners who observed explanations from speakers who had solved the problem with real objects produced more curved mouse trajectories compared with listeners who observed explanations from speakers who had solved the problem on the computer. Moreover, there was a positive correlation between the curvature of the gestures that were observed and the curvature of the mouse movements that an individual listener produced. Although these findings do not directly implicate motor simulation, they reveal that listeners can use gesture as a source of information to guide their future motor behaviors.

Behavioral research provides additional, more causal evidence that motor processes may be recruited in service of gesture perception; specifically, when adult observers are asked to perform motor tasks while observing stimuli, expected effects of gestures on comprehension are diminished (Ianì & Bucciarelli, 2018; Ping et al., 2014). Consistent patterns have also been observed using functional magnetic resonance imaging. Gestures are processed by means of a perceptual-motor network that is similar to that used to recognize actions (Ianì & Bucciarelli, 2018; Yang et al., 2015), and they activate motor brain networks (Özyürek, 2014). Studies using transcranial direct current stimulation also implicate motor processes in gesture perception. Disrupting the premotor cortex using transcranial magnetic stimulation decreases memory for action phrases accompanied by gesture (Ianì et al., 2018), and enhancing processing in motor cortex influences integration of gesture and speech (Hayek et al., 2018).

10.3.3.2 Cognitive Processes Linking Speech and Gesture

Gesture and speech may be linked by means of specialized cognitive processes that support language comprehension, either intentionally or automatically. Alternatively, gesture and speech may be linked via general purpose cognitive processes, such as attention, working memory, and memory, that support cognition in a broad variety of tasks.

10.3.3.2.1 Language Processing Models of Perception

Gesture perception might influence or modulate processes that are also engaged when processing language without accompanying gestures. Indeed, gestures influence language comprehension across levels of linguistic organization. At the lexical level, gestures support listeners' access to the meaning of words. Gestures can prime semantically related words (Wu & Coulson, 2007). Moreover, the effect of gestures on lexical processing appears to be at least partially driven by the semantic overlap between words and gestures. Words that are accompanied by weakly incongruent gestures are more likely to be processed accurately than words accompanied by strongly incongruent gestures, even when a person is given instructions to ignore the gestures, and both of these are less likely to be processed accurately than words that are not accompanied by gestures (Kelly, Özyürek, & Maris, 2010).

Gestures also influence syntactic processing. When observers viewed beat gestures that were timed with the grammatical subject of a sentence, these gestures appeared to reduce the processing costs associated with understanding sentences in a noncanonical order (Holle et al., 2012). Gestures can directly communicate prosodic information to listeners (Guellaï et al., 2014). Moreover, when gesture and prosody are put into conflict, observers tend to weigh the information from gesture more strongly than the information from prosody. Gestures also influence reference resolution even when they do not directly carry relevant semantic information. Points to locations in space that have previously been associated with one referent, but that are now produced with a different referent, can impair comprehension (Gunter et al., 2015).

Research reveals that gestures can shape language processing at a variety of levels. However, they do not directly implicate specific mechanisms in this influence. Evidence from functional magnetic imaging studies suggests that language with gestures may recruit neural processes similar to those of language without gestures. Symbolic gestures appear to be processed via the same functional neural network that processes spoken language (Dick et al., 2009; Holle et al., 2008; Hubbard et al., 2009; Straube et al., 2012; Xu et al., 2009), and the specific brain regions involved in the semantic processing of speech also appear to be involved in the semantic processing of gesture (Abrams & Christ, 2003; Özyürek, 2014).

10.3.3.3 General Cognitive Processes

Comprehension also involves a variety of general processes that are not specific to language or communication. Gesture may influence ongoing processing though its influence on general cognitive processes that are not specialized for language.

10.3.3.3.1 Attention

Moving stimuli are known to capture attention (Abrams & Christ, 2003). Gesture may function to both capture and modulate observers' attention. During language comprehension, observers quickly shift their attention to available referents in the immediate environment (Tanenhaus et al., 1995), and they do so in ways that are shaped both by characteristics of the environment as well as characteristics of the incoming linguistic information (Altmann & Kamide, 2007; Chambers et al., 2004). Ongoing work has been using eye tracking to investigate how observers' attention to the environment is modulated by gesture. Prior similar work reveals that gesture can shift children's attention; children observing gesture display different gaze patterns than children who do not observe gesture, even when the spoken language is identical (Wakefield et al., 2018). Gesture may also modulate attention to the accompanying linguistic information, enhancing attention at particularly informative moments (Cánovas et al., 2020). Finally, gesture may make a stimulus generally more engaging and appealing, enhancing overall attention and motivation (Zhang et al., 2014).

10.3.3.3.2 Working Memory

During language comprehension, observers rely on working memory to maintain relevant information in mind. Sensitivity to gesture may depend on a person's working memory profile, implicating working memory processes in gesture production. Aldugom et al. (2020) showed that adults with greater visuospatial working memory capacity are more likely to benefit from gesture in a learning task, whereas those with greater verbal working memory capacity are more likely to benefit from instructions that do not contain gesture. Similar findings have been demonstrated in a priming task, whereby individuals with higher spatial working memory capacity showed greater sensitivity to information in gesture and those with higher verbal working memory capacity showed greater sensitivity to information in speech (Özer & Göksun, 2020). Other research has suggested that kinesthetic working memory (Wu & Coulson, 2015) and verbal working memory (Schubotz et al., 2020) may support gesture perception.

10.3.3.3.3 Memory

Many studies have revealed that viewing language with gesture enhances later memory for the information that was communicated (Cook et al., 2012; Ianì et al., 2018; Klooster et al., 2015). Gestures may influence comprehenders by engaging memory processes during and after communication. For example, Cook et al. (2013) demonstrated that observing gesture during a mathematics lesson supported understanding during the lesson and was associated with improvements in performance over the next 24 hours, suggesting that gesture can engage consolidation processes.

Klooster et al.'s (2015) work with patients with disruptions in procedural memory suggests that procedural memory processing may support gesture perception. Patients with impairments in procedural memory did not show the effects of gesture on movement during Tower of Hanoi problem solving, whereas matched comparison patients without impairment showed the expected effects.

10.3.4 Methodological Limitations in the Study of Gesture Perception

Although video stimuli with and without gesture can be created, such research also has inherent limitations. Video presents gesture outside of the rich communicative context in which it is typically produced. Gestures are typically produced and processed in rich, shared communicative contexts, whereas participants in experimental studies often respond to decontextualized information presented in scripted, isolated, two-dimensional video clips. Speech and gestures used in experimental stimuli are specifically selected and may not represent the typical usage.

A number of nonverbal behaviors co-vary with gestures but are not considered gestures. Head and body motion beyond the hands and arms, speech prosody, and eye gaze and facial expressions are all coordinated with gesture and with language. Current approaches to investigating the perception of gesture rely on removing the face from the video or creating matching gesture and no-gesture videos that may not fully control these co-occurring characteristics of the stimuli. Moreover, perfectly controlling for the rich set of features that co-occur with gesture threatens naturalistic validity and carries the risk of artificially inflating attention to gestures by eliminating additional features that would typically influence processing. Studying behaviors that co-vary with one another by isolating them ignores the fact that co-occurring behaviors likely co-influence one another.

It is not clear how changing the communicative context and the reliability and informativity of the information that is available might shape the way that gesture is processed. Studies of gesture perception would be well served by considering whether and how one can disrupt listeners' perception of speech and gesture. It is well established that gestures can influence observers, but to understand how gestures influence observers researchers may need to study gesture in richer, more diverse paradigms.

10.4 Conclusion

There are a wide variety of candidate accounts underlying the processing of speech and gesture. It is unlikely that there is a single processing account that will explain how gestures are produced. Gestures are flexible behaviors, produced in a rich context, adapted to that context and to the accompanying language. Speakers express their intentions in language (Searle, 1980), and listeners use the information from speakers to understand those intentions and guide their own behavior. It seems most likely that gestures arise by means of a variety of interacting mechanisms (Cooperrider, 2017), and they serve a variety of functions in perception, likely mediated by multiple, interacting mechanisms (Kok et al., 2016). As the studies of various postulated mechanisms develop, so too will our ability to implicate these mechanisms in more complex behavior. If we are to truly understand how gestures are produced and processed, we will need to embrace gesture in all its complexity and to exploit a broad variety of approaches.

References

Abrams, R. A., & Christ, S. E. (2003). Motion onset captures attention. *Psychological Science*, *14*(5), 427–432. https://doi.org/10.1111/1467-9280.01458

Aldugom, M., Fenn, K., & Cook, S. W. (2020). Gesture during math instruction specifically benefits learners with high visuospatial working memory capacity. *Cognitive Research: Principles and Implications*, *5*(1), 27. https://doi.org/10.1186/s41235-020-00215-8

Alibali, M. W., Kita, S., & Young, A. J. (2000). Gesture and the process of speech production: We think, therefore we gesture. *Language and Cognitive Processes*, *15*(6), 593–613. https://doi.org/10.1080/016909600750040571

Altmann, G. T. M., & Kamide, Y. (2007). The real-time mediation of visual attention by language and world knowledge: Linking anticipatory (and other) eye movements to linguistic processing. *Journal of Memory and Language*, *57*(4), 502–518. https://doi.org/10.1016/j.jml.2006.12.004

Bahrick, L. E., & Lickliter, R. (2000). Intersensory redundancy guides attentional selectivity and perceptual learning in infancy. *Developmental Psychology*, *36*(2), 190–201. https://doi.org/10.1037/0012-1649.36.2.190

Bangerter, A. (2004). Using pointing and describing to achieve joint focus of attention in dialogue. *Psychological Science*, *15*(5), 415–419. https://doi.org/10.1111/j.0956-7976.2004.00694.x

Barsalou, L. W. (1999). Perceptual symbol systems. *Behavioral and Brain Sciences*, *22*(4), 577–660. https://doi.org/10.1017/S0140525X99002149

Beattie, G., & Shovelton, H. (2000). Iconic hand gestures and the predictability of words in context in spontaneous speech. *British Journal of Psychology*, *91*(4), 473–491. https://doi.org/10.1348/000712600161943

Beattie, G., & Shovelton, H. (2001). An experimental investigation of the role of different types of iconic gesture in communication: A semantic feature approach. *Gesture*, *1*(2), 129–149. https://doi.org/10.1075/gest.1.2.03bea

Bergmann, K., Aksu, V., & Kopp, S. (2011). The relation of speech and gestures: Temporal synchrony follows semantic synchrony. *Proceedings of the 2nd Workshop on Gesture and Speech in Interaction*, 1–6.

Bernardis, P., & Gentilucci, M. (2006). Speech and gesture share the same communication system. *Neuropsychologia*, *44*(2), 178–190. https://doi.org/10.1016/j.neuropsychologia.2005.05.007

Biau, E., & Soto-Faraco, S. (2013). Beat gestures modulate auditory integration in speech perception. *Brain and Language*, *124*(2), 143–152. https://doi.org/10.1016/j.bandl.2012.10.008

Biau, E., & Soto-Faraco, S. (2015). Synchronization by the hand: The sight of gestures modulates low-frequency activity in brain responses to continuous speech. *Frontiers in Human Neuroscience*, 9, 527.

Blakemore, S.-J., & Decety, J. (2001). From the perception of action to the understanding of intention. *Nature Reviews Neuroscience*, 2(8), 561–567. https://doi.org/10.1038/35086023

Broaders, S. C., Cook, S. W., Mitchell, Z., & Goldin-Meadow, S. (2007). Making children gesture brings out implicit knowledge and leads to learning. *Journal of Experimental Psychology: General*, 136(4), 539–550. https://doi.org/10.1037/0096-3445.136.4.539

Butterworth, B., & Hadar, U. (1989). Gesture, speech, and computational stages: A reply to McNeill. *Psychological Review*, 96(1), 168–174. https://doi.org/10.1037/0033-295X.96.1.168

Cameron, H., & Xu, X. (2011). Representational gesture, pointing gesture, and memory recall of preschool children. *Journal of Nonverbal Behavior*, 35(2), 155–171. https://doi.org/10.1007/s10919-010-0101-2

Cánovas, C. P., Valenzuela, J., Carrión, D. A., Olza, I., & Ramscar, M. (2020). Quantifying the speech–gesture relation with massive multimodal datasets: Informativity in time expressions. *PLOS ONE*, 15(6), e0233892. https://doi.org/10.1371/journal.pone.0233892

Cason, N., & Schön, D. (2012). Rhythmic priming enhances the phonological processing of speech. *Neuropsychologia*, 50(11), 2652–2658. https://doi.org/10.1016/j.neuropsychologia.2012.07.018

Chambers, C. G., Tanenhaus, M. K., & Magnuson, J. S. (2004). Actions and affordances in syntactic ambiguity resolution. *Journal of Experimental Psychology: Learning, Memory, and Cognition*, 30(3), 687–696. https://doi.org/10.1037/0278-7393.30.3.687

Church, R. B., Kelly, S., & Holcombe, D. (2014). Temporal synchrony between speech, action and gesture during language production. *Language, Cognition and Neuroscience*, 29(3), 345–354. https://doi.org/10.1080/01690965.2013.857783

Cook, S. W. (2019). *Audio–visual integration: Point light gestures influence listeners' behavior* [Abstract]. https://cogsci.mindmodeling.org/2019/papers/0744/0744.pdf

Cook, S. W., Duffy, R. G., & Fenn, K. M. (2013). Consolidation and transfer of learning after observing hand gesture. *Child Development*, 84(6), 1863–1871. https://doi.org/10.1111/cdev.12097

Cook, S. W., Friedman, H. S., Duggan, K. A., Cui, J., & Popescu, V. (2017). Hand gesture and mathematics learning: Lessons from an avatar. *Cognitive Science*, 41(2), 518–535. https://doi.org/10.1111/cogs.12344

Cook, S. W., Mitchell, Z., & Goldin-Meadow, S. (2008). Gesturing makes learning last. *Cognition*, 106(2), 1047–1058. https://doi.org/10.1016/j.cognition.2007.04.010

Cook, S. W., & Tanenhaus, M. K. (2009). Embodied communication: Speakers' gestures affect listeners' actions. *Cognition*, 113(1), 98–104. https://doi.org/10.1016/j.cognition.2009.06.006

Cook, S. W., Yip, T. K. Y., & Goldin-Meadow, S. (2012). Gestures, but not meaningless movements, lighten working memory load when explaining math. *Language and Cognitive Processes*, 27(4), 594–610. https://doi.org/10.1080/01690965.2011.567074

Cooperrider, K. (2017). Foreground gesture, background gesture. *Gesture*, 16(2), 176–202. https://doi.org/10.1075/gest.16.2.02coo

Dargue, N., Sweller, N., & Jones, M. P. (2019). When our hands help us understand: A meta-analysis into the effects of gesture on comprehension. *Psychological Bulletin*, 145(8), 765–784. https://doi.org/10.1037/bul0000202

de Ruiter, J. P. (1998). *Gesture and speech production* [Unpublished doctoral dissertation]. Radboud University Nijmegen.

de Ruiter, J. P., Bangerter, A., & Dings, P. (2012). The interplay between gesture and speech in the production of referring expressions: Investigating the tradeoff hypothesis. *Topics in Cognitive Science*, *4*(2), 232–248. https://doi.org/10.1111/j.1756-8765.2012.01183.x

Desmurget, M., Richard, N., Harquel, S., Baraduc, P., Szathmari, A., Mottolese, C., & Sirigu, A. (2014). Neural representations of ethologically relevant hand/mouth synergies in the human precentral gyrus. *Proceedings of the National Academy of Sciences of the United States of America*, *111*(15), 5718–5722. https://doi.org/10.1073/pnas.1321909111

Dick, A. S., Goldin-Meadow, S., Hasson, U., Skipper, J. I., & Small, S. L. (2009). Co-speech gestures influence neural activity in brain regions associated with processing semantic information. *Human Brain Mapping*, *30*(11), 3509–3526. https://doi.org/10.1002/hbm.20774

Driskell, J. E., & Radtke, P. H. (2003). The effect of gesture on speech production and comprehension. *Human Factors*, *45*(3), 445–454. https://doi.org/10.1518/hfes.45.3.445.27258

Emmorey, K. (1999). *Do signers gesture? Gesture, speech, and sign*. Oxford University Press.

Esteve-Gibert, N., & Prieto, P. (2013). Prosodic structure shapes the temporal realization of intonation and manual gesture movements. *Journal of Speech, Language, and Hearing Research*, *56*(3), 850–864. https://doi.org/10.1044/1092-4388(2012/12-0049)

Esteve-Gibert, N., & Prieto, P. (2014). Infants temporally coordinate gesture–speech combinations before they produce their first words. *Speech Communication*, *57*, 301–316. https://doi.org/10.1016/j.specom.2013.06.006

Filippi, C. A., & Woodward, A. L. (2016). Action experience changes attention to kinematic cues. *Frontiers in Psychology*, *7*, 19. https://doi.org/10.3389/fpsyg.2016.00019

Glenberg, A. M. (1997). What memory is for. *Behavioral and Brain Sciences*, *20*(1), 1–19. https://doi.org/10.1017/S0140525X97000010

Gogate, L. J. (2010). Learning of syllable–object relations by preverbal infants: The role of temporal synchrony and syllable distinctiveness. *Journal of Experimental Child Psychology*, *105*(3), 178–197. https://doi.org/10.1016/j.jecp.2009.10.007

Goldin-Meadow, S., & Brentari, D. (2017). Gesture, sign, and language: The coming of age of sign language and gesture studies. *Behavioral and Brain Sciences*, *40*, E46. https://doi.org/10.1017/S0140525X15001247

Goldin-Meadow, S., Nusbaum, H., Kelly, S. D., & Wagner, S. (2001). Explaining math: Gesturing lightens the load. *Psychological Science*, *12*(6), 516–522. https://doi.org/10.1111/1467-9280.00395

Goldin-Meadow, S., & Sandhofer, C. M. (1999). Gestures convey substantive information about a child's thoughts to ordinary listeners. *Developmental Science*, *2*(1), 67–74. https://doi.org/10.1111/1467-7687.00056

Gori, M., Sandini, G., & Burr, D. (2012). Development of visuo–auditory integration in space and time. *Frontiers in Integrative Neuroscience*, *6*, 77. https://doi.org/10.3389/fnint.2012.00077

Graham, J. A., & Argyle, M. (1975). A cross-cultural study of the communication of extra-verbal meaning by gestures. *International Journal of Psychology*, *10*(1), 57–67. https://doi.org/10.1080/00207597508247319

Guellaï, B., Langus, A., & Nespor, M. (2014). Prosody in the hands of the speaker. *Frontiers in Psychology*, *5*, 700. https://doi.org/10.3389/fpsyg.2014.00700

Gunter, T. C., Weinbrenner, J. E. D., & Holle, H. (2015). Inconsistent use of gesture space during abstract pointing impairs language comprehension. *Frontiers in Psychology*, *6*, 80. https://doi.org/10.3389/fpsyg.2015.00080

Hartsuiker, R. J., & Barkhuysen, P. N. (2006). Language production and working memory: The case of subject–verb agreement. *Language and Cognitive Processes*, *21*(1–3), 181–204. https://doi.org/10.1080/01690960400002117

Hayek, D., Flöel, A., & Antonenko, D. (2018). Role of sensorimotor cortex in gestural–verbal integration. *Frontiers in Human Neuroscience*, *12*, 482. https://doi.org/10.3389/fnhum.2018.00482

Hilliard, C., & Cook, S. W. (2017). A technique for continuous measurement of body movement from video. *Behavior Research Methods*, *49*(1), 1–12. https://doi.org/10.3758/s13428-015-0685-x

Hilverman, C., Cook, S. W., & Duff, M. C. (2016). Hippocampal declarative memory supports gesture production: Evidence from amnesia. *Cortex*, *85*, 25–36. https://doi.org/10.1016/j.cortex.2016.09.015

Hoetjes, M., Krahmer, E., & Swerts, M. (2014). Does our speech change when we cannot gesture? *Speech Communication*, *57*, 257–267. https://doi.org/10.1016/j.specom.2013.06.007

Holle, H., Gunter, T. C., Rüschemeyer, S. A., Hennenlotter, A., & Iacoboni, M. (2008). Neural correlates of the processing of co-speech gestures. *NeuroImage*, *39*(4), 2010–2024. https://doi.org/10.1016/j.neuroimage.2007.10.055

Holle, H., Obermeier, C., Schmidt-Kassow, M., Friederici, A. D., Ward, J., & Gunter, T. C. (2012). Gesture facilitates the syntactic analysis of speech. *Frontiers in Psychology*, *3*, 74. https://doi.org/10.3389/fpsyg.2012.00074

Hostetter, A. B. (2011). When do gestures communicate? A meta-analysis. *Psychological Bulletin*, *137*(2), 297–315. https://doi.org/10.1037/a0022128

Hostetter, A. B., & Alibali, M. W. (2008). Visible embodiment: Gestures as simulated action. *Psychonomic Bulletin & Review*, *15*(3), 495–514. https://doi.org/10.3758/PBR.15.3.495

Hostetter, A. B., & Alibali, M. W. (2010). Language, gesture, action! A test of the gesture as simulated action framework. *Journal of Memory and Language*, *63*(2), 245–257. https://doi.org/10.1016/j.jml.2010.04.003

Hostetter, A. B., & Alibali, M. W. (2019). Gesture as simulated action: Revisiting the framework. *Psychonomic Bulletin & Review*, *26*(3), 721–752. https://doi.org/10.3758/s13423-018-1548-0

Hubbard, A. L., Wilson, S. M., Callan, D. E., & Dapretto, M. (2009). Giving speech a hand: Gesture modulates activity in auditory cortex during speech perception. *Human Brain Mapping*, *30*(3), 1028–1037. https://doi.org/10.1002/hbm.20565

Ianì, F., & Bucciarelli, M. (2018). Relevance of the listener's motor system in recalling phrases enacted by the speaker. *Memory*, *26*(8), 1084–1092. https://doi.org/10.1080/09658211.2018.1433214

Ianì, F., Burin, D., Salatino, A., Pia, L., Ricci, R., & Bucciarelli, M. (2018). The beneficial effect of a speaker's gestures on the listener's memory for action phrases: The pivotal role of the listener's premotor cortex. *Brain and Language*, *180–182*, 8–13. https://doi.org/10.1016/j.bandl.2018.03.001

Iverson, J. M., & Fagan, M. K. (2004). Infant vocal–motor coordination: Precursor to the gesture–speech system? *Child Development*, *75*(4), 1053–1066. https://doi.org/10.1111/j.1467-8624.2004.00725.x

Iverson, J. M., & Goldin-Meadow, S. (1998, November 19). Why people gesture when they speak. *Nature*, *396*, 228. https://doi.org/10.1038/24300

Iverson, J. M., & Goldin-Meadow, S. (2001). The resilience of gesture in talk: Gesture in blind speakers and listeners. *Developmental Science*, *4*(4), 416–422. https://doi.org/10.1111/1467-7687.00183

Iverson, J. M., & Thelen, E. (1999). Hand, mouth and brain. The dynamic emergence of speech and gesture. *Journal of Consciousness Studies*, *6*(11–12), 19–40.

Kelly, S. D., Creigh, P., & Bartolotti, J. (2010). Integrating speech and iconic gestures in a Stroop-like task: Evidence for automatic processing. *Journal of Cognitive Neuroscience*, *22*(4), 683–694. https://doi.org/10.1162/jocn.2009.21254

Kelly, S. D., Özyürek, A., & Maris, E. (2010). Two sides of the same coin: Speech and gesture mutually interact to enhance comprehension. *Psychological Science*, *21*(2), 260–267. https://doi.org/10.1177/0956797609357327

Kelso, J. A. S. (1995). *Dynamic patterns: The self-organization of brain and behavior*. MIT Press.

Kemper, S., Herman, R. E., & Lian, C. H. T. (2003). The costs of doing two things at once for young and older adults: Talking while walking, finger tapping, and ignoring speech of noise. *Psychology and Aging*, *18*(2), 181–192. https://doi.org/10.1037/0882-7974.18.2.181

Kita, S. (2009). Cross-cultural variation of speech-accompanying gesture: A review. *Language and Cognitive Processes*, *24*(2), 145–167. https://doi.org/10.1080/01690960802586188

Kita, S., & Özyürek, A. (2003). What does cross-linguistic variation in semantic coordination of speech and gesture reveal? Evidence for an interface representation of spatial thinking and speaking. *Journal of Memory and Language*, *48*(1), 16–32. https://doi.org/10.1016/S0749-596X(02)00505-3

Klooster, N. B., Cook, S. W., Uc, E. Y., & Duff, M. C. (2015). Gestures make memories, but what kind? Patients with impaired procedural memory display disruptions in gesture production and comprehension. *Frontiers in Human Neuroscience*, *8*, 1054. https://doi.org/10.3389/fnhum.2014.01054

Knowlton, B. J., Squire, L. R., & Gluck, M. A. (1994). Probabilistic classification learning in amnesia. *Learning & Memory*, *1*(2), 106–120.

Kok, K., Bergmann, K., Cienki, A., & Kopp, S. (2016). Mapping out the multifunctionality of speakers' gestures. *Gesture*, *15*(1), 37–59. https://doi.org/10.1075/gest.15.1.02kok

Krauss, R. M., & Hadar, U. (1999). The role of speech-related arm/hand gestures in word retrieval. In L. Messing & R. Campbell (Eds.), *Gesture, speech, and sign* (pp. 93–116). Oxford University Press. https://doi.org/10.1093/acprof:oso/9780198524519.003.0006

Leonard, T., & Cummins, F. (2011). The temporal relation between beat gestures and speech. *Language and Cognitive Processes*, *26*(10), 1457–1471. https://doi.org/10.1080/01690965.2010.500218

Levelt, W. J. M. (1993). *Speaking: From intention to articulation*. MIT Press. https://doi.org/10.7551/mitpress/6393.001.0001

Loehr, D. P. (2012). Temporal, structural, and pragmatic synchrony between intonation and gesture. *Laboratory Phonology*, *3*(1), 71–89. https://doi.org/10.1515/lp-2012-0006

Marschark, M. (1994). Gesture and sign. *Applied Psycholinguistics*, *15*(2), 209–236. https://doi.org/10.1017/S0142716400005336

McNamara, J. M., & Houston, A. I. (2009). Integrating function and mechanism. *Trends in Ecology & Evolution*, *24*(12), 670–675. https://doi.org/10.1016/j.tree.2009.05.011

McNeill, D. (1992). *Hand and mind: What gestures reveal about thought*. University of Chicago Press.

Melinger, A., & Kita, S. (2007). Conceptualisation load triggers gesture production. *Language and Cognitive Processes*, *22*(4), 473–500. https://doi.org/10.1080/01690960600696916

Melinger, A., & Levelt, W. J. M. (2004). Gesture and the communicative intention of the speaker. *Gesture*, *4*(2), 119–141. https://doi.org/10.1075/gest.4.2.02mel

Morett, L. M., Roche, J. M., Fraundorf, S. H., & McPartland, J. C. (2020). Contrast is in the eye of the beholder: Infelicitous beat gesture increases cognitive load during online spoken discourse comprehension. *Cognitive Science*, *44*(10), e12912. https://doi.org/10.1111/cogs.12912

Morford, M., & Goldin-Meadow, S. (1992). Comprehension and production of gesture in combination with speech in one-word speakers. *Journal of Child Language*, *19*(3), 559–580. https://doi.org/10.1017/S0305000900011569

Morrel-Samuels, P., & Krauss, R. M. (1992). Word familiarity predicts temporal asynchrony of hand gestures and speech. *Journal of Experimental Psychology: Learning, Memory, and Cognition*, *18*(3), 615–622. https://doi.org/10.1037/0278-7393.18.3.615

Morsella, E., & Krauss, R. M. (2004). The role of gestures in spatial working memory and speech. *American Journal of Psychology*, *117*(3), 411–424. https://doi.org/10.2307/4149008

Novack, M. A., & Goldin-Meadow, S. (2017). Gesture as representational action: A paper about function. *Psychonomic Bulletin & Review*, *24*(3), 652–665. https://doi.org/10.3758/s13423-016-1145-z

Núria, E.-G., & Pilar, P. (2013). Prosodic structure shapes the temporal realization of intonation and manual gesture movements. *Journal of Speech, Language, and Hearing Research*, *56*(3), 850–864. https://doi.org/10.1044/1092-4388(2012/12-0049)

Özçalışkan, S., & Goldin-Meadow, S. (2005). Gesture is at the cutting edge of early language development. *Cognition*, *96*(3), B101–B113. https://doi.org/10.1016/j.cognition.2005.01.001

Özer, D., & Göksun, T. (2020). Visual–spatial and verbal abilities differentially affect processing of gestural vs. spoken expressions. *Language, Cognition and Neuroscience*, *35*(7), 896–914. https://doi.org/10.1080/23273798.2019.1703016

Özyürek, A. (2014). Hearing and seeing meaning in speech and gesture: Insights from brain and behaviour. *Philosophical Transactions of the Royal Society of London Series B: Biological Sciences*, *369*(1651), 20130296. https://doi.org/10.1098/rstb.2013.0296

Parrell, B., Goldstein, L., Lee, S., & Byrd, D. (2014). Spatiotemporal coupling between speech and manual motor actions. *Journal of Phonetics*, *42*, 1–11. https://doi.org/10.1016/j.wocn.2013.11.002

Pearl, J. (2009). Causal inference in statistics: An overview. *Statistics Surveys*, *3*, 96–146. https://doi.org/10.1214/09-SS057

Ping, R. M., Goldin-Meadow, S., & Beilock, S. L. (2014). Understanding gesture: Is the listener's motor system involved? *Journal of Experimental Psychology: General*, *143*(1), 195–204. https://doi.org/10.1037/a0032246

Power, A. J., Mead, N., Barnes, L., & Goswami, U. (2012). Neural entrainment to rhythmically presented auditory, visual, and audio-visual speech in children. *Frontiers in Psychology*, *3*, 216. https://doi.org/10.3389/fpsyg.2012.00216

Power, M. J. (1985). Sentence production and working memory. *The Quarterly Journal of Experimental Psychology Section A*, *37*(3), 367–385. https://doi.org/10.1080/14640748508400940

Pruner, T. J., & Cook, S. W. (2021). *Improved learning when hand gestures anticipate speech*. Unpublished manuscript.

Quené, H., & Port, R. F. (2005). Effects of timing regularity and metrical expectancy on spoken-word perception. *Phonetica*, *62*(1), 1–13. https://doi.org/10.1159/000087222

Rauscher, F. H., Krauss, R. M., & Chen, Y. (1996). Gesture, speech, and lexical access: The role of lexical movements in speech production. *Psychological Science*, *7*(4), 226–231. https://doi.org/10.1111/j.1467-9280.1996.tb00364.x

Riecke, L., Formisano, E., Sorger, B., Başkent, D., & Gaudrain, E. (2018). Neural entrainment to speech modulates speech intelligibility. *Current Biology, 28*(2), 161–169. https://doi.org/10.1016/j.cub.2017.11.033

Rizzolatti, G., Camarda, R., Fogassi, L., Gentilucci, M., Luppino, G., & Matelli, M. (1988). Functional organization of inferior area 6 in the macaque monkey: II. Area F5 and the control of distal movements. *Experimental Brain Research, 71*(3), 491–507. https://doi.org/10.1007/BF00248742

Rochat, P. (1993). Hand–mouth coordination in the newborn: morphology, determinants, and early development of a basic act. In G. J. P. Savelsbergh (Ed.), *Advances in psychology: Vol. 97. The development of coordination in infancy* (pp. 265–288). North-Holland. https://doi.org/10.1016/S0166-4115(08)60956-5

Rusiewicz, H. L., Shaiman, S., Iverson, J. M., & Szuminsky, N. (2013). Effects of prosody and position on the timing of deictic gestures. *Journal of Speech, Language, and Hearing Research, 56*(2), 458–470. https://doi.org/10.1044/1092-4388(2012/11-0283)

Rusiewicz, H. L., Shaiman, S., Iverson, J. M., & Szuminsky, N. (2014). Effects of perturbation and prosody on the coordination of speech and gesture. *Speech Communication, 57*, 283–300. https://doi.org/10.1016/j.specom.2013.06.004

Schubotz, L., Holler, J., Drijvers, L., & Özyürek, A. (2020). Aging and working memory modulate the ability to benefit from visible speech and iconic gestures during speech-in-noise comprehension. *Psychological Research*. Advance online publication. https://doi.org/10.1007/s00426-020-01363-8

Searle, J. R. (1980). Minds, brains, and programs. *Behavioral and Brain Sciences, 3*(3), 417–424. https://doi.org/10.1017/S0140525X00005756

Sekuler, R., Sekuler, A. B., & Lau, R. (1997, January 23). Sound alters visual motion perception. *Nature, 385*, 308. https://doi.org/10.1038/385308a0

So, W. C., Chen-Hui, C. S., & Wei-Shan, J. L. (2012). Mnemonic effect of iconic gesture and beat gesture in adults and children: Is meaning in gesture important for memory recall? *Language and Cognitive Processes, 27*(5), 665–681. https://doi.org/10.1080/01690965.2011.573220

So, W. C., Kita, S., & Goldin-Meadow, S. (2009). Using the hands to identify who does what to whom: Gesture and speech go hand-in-hand. *Cognitive Science, 33*(1), 115–125. https://doi.org/10.1111/j.1551-6709.2008.01006.x

Sommerville, J. A., Woodward, A. L., & Needham, A. (2005). Action experience alters 3-month-old infants' perception of others' actions. *Cognition, 96*(1), B1–B11. https://doi.org/10.1016/j.cognition.2004.07.004

Spence, C., & Squire, S. (2003). Multisensory integration: Maintaining the perception of synchrony. *Current Biology, 13*(13), R519–R521. https://doi.org/10.1016/S0960-9822(03)00445-7

Stevanoni, E., & Salmon, K. (2005). Giving memory a hand: Instructing children to gesture enhances their event recall. *Journal of Nonverbal Behavior, 29*(4), 217–233. https://doi.org/10.1007/s10919-005-7721-y

Straube, B., Green, A., Weis, S., & Kircher, T. (2012). A supramodal neural network for speech and gesture semantics: An fMRI study. *PloS ONE, 7*(11), e51207. https://doi.org/10.1371/journal.pone.0051207

Tanenhaus, M. K., Spivey-Knowlton, M. J., Eberhard, K. M., & Sedivy, J. C. (1995, June 16). Integration of visual and linguistic information in spoken language comprehension. *Science, 268*, 1632–1634. https://doi.org/10.1126/science.7777863

Thompson, L. A., & Massaro, D. W. (1986). Evaluation and integration of speech and pointing gestures during referential understanding. *Journal of Experimental Child Psychology, 42*(1), 144–168. https://doi.org/10.1016/0022-0965(86)90020-2

Vainio, L. (2019). Connection between movements of mouth and hand: Perspectives on development and evolution of speech. *Neuroscience and Biobehavioral Reviews, 100*, 211–223. https://doi.org/10.1016/j.neubiorev.2019.03.005

Wagner, S. M., Nusbaum, H., & Goldin-Meadow, S. (2004). Probing the mental representation of gesture: Is handwaving spatial? *Journal of Memory and Language, 50*(4), 395–407. https://doi.org/10.1016/j.jml.2004.01.002

Wakefield, E., Novack, M. A., Congdon, E. L., Franconeri, S., & Goldin-Meadow, S. (2018). Gesture helps learners learn, but not merely by guiding their visual attention. *Developmental Science, 21*(6), e12664. https://doi.org/10.1111/desc.12664

Wesp, R., Hesse, J., Keutmann, D., & Wheaton, K. (2001). Gestures maintain spatial imagery. *American Journal of Psychology, 114*(4), 591–600. https://doi.org/10.2307/1423612

Wu, Y. C., & Coulson, S. (2007). Iconic gestures prime related concepts: An ERP study. *Psychonomic Bulletin & Review, 14*(1), 57–63. https://doi.org/10.3758/BF03194028

Wu, Y. C., & Coulson, S. (2015). Iconic gestures facilitate discourse comprehension in individuals with superior immediate memory for body configurations. *Psychological Science, 26*(11), 1717–1727. https://doi.org/10.1177/0956797615597671

Xu, J., Gannon, P. J., Emmorey, K., Smith, J. F., & Braun, A. R. (2009). Symbolic gestures and spoken language are processed by a common neural system. *Proceedings of the National Academy of Sciences of the United States of America, 106*(49), 20664–20669. https://doi.org/10.1073/pnas.0909197106

Yang, J., Andric, M., & Mathew, M. M. (2015). The neural basis of hand gesture comprehension: A meta-analysis of functional magnetic resonance imaging studies. *Neuroscience and Biobehavioral Reviews, 57*, 88–104. https://doi.org/10.1016/j.neubiorev.2015.08.006

Zhang, J. R., Sherwin, J., Dmochowski, J., Sajda, P., & Kender, J. R. (2014). Correlating speaker gestures in political debates with audience engagement measured via EEG. In *MM '14: Proceedings of the 22nd ACM international conference on multimedia* (pp. 387–396). Association for Computing Machinery. https://doi.org/10.1145/2647868.2654909

Tilbe Göksun, Demet Özer, and Seda Akbıyık
11 Gesture in the Aging Brain

The effect of aging on communication has been extensively studied, but the effect of age-related changes on gesture comprehension and production has received less attention. A few studies have indicated that gesture comprehension (Cocks et al., 2011; Thompson, 1995; Thompson & Guzman, 1999), production (Arslan & Göksun, 2021; Cohen & Borsoi, 1996; Feyereisen & Havard, 1999), and imitation (Dimeck et al., 1998) could be impaired in older populations, yet these studies did not directly investigate the underlying mechanisms driving those age-related changes, nor did they offer detailed explanations of the impaired gesture use in older adults. People with certain cognitive, motor, or visuospatial deficits that are generally associated with aging can provide us with valuable information about gesture use in the aging brain (Özer & Göksun, 2020a). The examination of processing gestures and the function of gesture use in healthy and unhealthy older populations can also provide insights into the interaction between gesture and language.

Gesticulations are the most frequent type of gestures and are usually produced with speech. These co-speech gestures are different from emblems, pantomimes, or self-touch and grooming because they co-occur with speech. Co-speech gestures can be mainly divided into four categories: (a) *iconic* (representational gestures for entities, objects, and actions), (b) *metaphoric* (representational gestures for abstract entities), (c) *deictic* (pointing gestures), and (d) *beat* (rhythmic hand movements; McNeill, 1992). In this chapter, we focus on all four categories of co-speech gesture.

We first review the impact of aging on general language and cognitive abilities and how they might relate to gesture use and comprehension in older adults in light of different gesture theories. Then we address gesture use and comprehension in the aging brain and the effects on these processes of declines in cognitive skills such as verbal fluency, spatial and motor skills, and working memory (WM). Next, we focus on gesture use and comprehension in neurodegenerative disorders such as Alzheimer's disease (AD), semantic dementia (SD), and Parkinson's disease (PD) to provide further evidence about the mechanisms underlying gesture's role in cognition. We conclude the chapter by discussing the implications of these findings given that the functions of gestures can alter on the basis of the population being studied (Özer & Göksun, 2020a).

11.1 Aging and Gestures

Brain volume tends to decrease as we age, and this reduction is most salient in the frontal and parietal cortex, with the prefrontal cortex being the most affected (Peters, 2006). Because of this decline in brain volume, several cognitive functions, such as WM, inhibitory control, and executive function skills (Andrés & Van der Linden, 2000; Bélanger et al., 2010) as well as pragmatic communication skills, decay over time (for a review, see Zaidel et al., 2000). Compared with younger people, older people tend to exhibit more digression (i.e., moving away from the conversational theme), reducing their overall narrative coherence, and they produce more verbal repetitions than younger people (Gold & Arbuckle, 1995). The content and the grammatical complexity of utterances also change as people age (Kemper et al., 2001). In addition, older people often experience a decline in phonemic and semantic fluency (Troyer et al., 1997). Yet the morphological and syntactic abilities of older adults remain relatively preserved, unless WM load is high (Kemper, 1997). Different accounts have been proposed to explain the language problems older adults experience. General cognitive slowing, inhibitory deficits, WM, and executive function are generally linked to communicative deficiencies (Kemper, 2006). However, the studies suggest deficits in verbal communication in aging populations. How does aging affect nonverbal communication; more specifically, how does it affect the use and comprehension of gestures? Given that gesture is an integral part of language, investigating the gesture processing and production abilities of older adults is essential to delineate the effects of aging on communication.

Many theories argue for a close relationship between speech and gesture (e.g., de Ruiter, 2006; Kita, 2000; Kita & Özyürek, 2003; Krauss et al., 2000; McNeill, 2005), but theories of the proposed nature of this relationship vary. The first view suggests that speech and gesture stem from a single unified system and thus complement information presented in the other modality (McNeill, 1992, 2005). Other views argue that gesture and speech arise from different but interrelated representational systems (e.g., de Ruiter, 2006; Kita, 2000; Kita & Özyürek, 2003; Krauss et al., 2000). For instance, gestures can supplement spoken expressions (de Ruiter, 2006) and facilitate speech production, either by organizing spatial–motor information or facilitating word production (Kita, 2000; Kita et al., 2017; Krauss et al., 2000). Speech and gesture share neural substrates and are integrated at the neural level (Kelly et al., 2004). Furthermore, not only is gesture linked to speech, but it also serves psychological (Mol & Kita, 2012) and communicative (Evans et al., 2001) functions. Gesture is also tightly connected to a person's linguistic, spatial, motor, and cognitive functioning (Hostetter & Alibali, 2007, 2011; Özer & Göksun, 2020b; for a review, see Özer & Göksun, 2020a). These components of cognitive functioning are subject to age-related change.

If speech and co-speech gestures are derived from a common system of processing, then impairments in one system ought to be reflected in the other (Eling & Whitaker, 2009; McNeill, 1985, 1992; McNeill et al., 2008). In this case, older adults would use fewer co-speech gestures because of their decline in verbal communication abilities. If, however, gestures supplement verbal expressions and/or aid speech production by facilitating lexical retrieval or organizing spatial–motor information, one would expect an increase in the frequency of co-speech gestures in cases of decline in spoken communication (de Ruiter, 2006; Kita, 2000; Kita & Özyürek, 2003; Krauss et al., 2000). Hence, older adults would use more co-speech gestures to compensate for impairments and underspecifications in speech and to facilitate speech production.

It is important to note that gestures might serve multiple functions that vary across different populations (Özer & Göksun, 2020a). For example, older adults might use gestures mainly for communicative functions, supplementing spoken expressions, whereas people who have left frontal and/or temporal lesions and consequent speech impairments might use gestures for both communicative and restorative functions; that is, they use gestures to facilitate lexical retrieval and organize information into the linear format of speech (Özer et al., 2019). As a result, studying different populations in regard to gesture production and comprehension can shed light on both the mechanisms for speech–gesture relations and the functions of gestures. We next review gesture production and comprehension in aging populations.

11.1.1 Gesture Production

Earlier studies on aging and spontaneous gesture use suggest that older adults produce fewer representational gestures (i.e., iconic gestures) compared with young adults, whereas the use of nonrepresentational gestures (i.e., noniconic, such as conduit or beat gestures) in spontaneous discourse is comparable across young and older individuals (e.g., Cohen & Borsoi, 1996; Feyereisen & Havard, 1999; Glosser et al., 1998). One explanation for this finding could be that iconic and beat gestures are derived from different representational systems. Iconic gestures could originate from visual–spatial and motoric imagery, whereas the phonological encoding of sentences generates beats (Alibali et al., 2001; Rauscher et al., 1996). In this regard, the selective impairment in the use of spontaneous iconic gestures (but not beat gestures) might be due to the declining mental imagery that accompanies aging alongside preserved linguistic skills (Andersen & Ni, 2008; Copeland & Radvansky, 2007; Dror & Kosslyn, 1994; Mulder & Hulstijn, 2011).

In a recent study, Arslan and Göksun (2021) showed that older adults produced fewer representational gestures than younger ones, in particular in a spatial context, such as describing an address. The two groups had comparable overall gesture frequency. It is important to note that, regardless of the age, both groups' mental imagery scores, but not WM scores, were related to their representational gesture use in this spatial task. Feyereisen and Havard (1999), however, showed that older adults' speech paralleled young adults' in terms of the proportion of mental imagery words.

Even though young speakers used more iconic gestures than older adults when narrating a visual image (e.g., "Could you describe the room that you lived in?"), they used comparable number of iconic gestures when narrating a motor image (e.g., "Could you explain how to change the wheel of a car?").

What accounts for the differential use of gestures with aging? One candidate could be changes in speech characteristics: Older adults might rely more on speech as their main communication mode than young adults do (Adams et al., 2002; James et al., 1998; Schubotz et al., 2019). For example, a study that investigated the role of gestures in the resolution of the tip-of-the-tongue (TOT) situations showed that older adults had fewer TOT states and produced fewer iconic gestures than younger adults when asked to describe the function of objects that were computer generated (i.e., a pseudo-word paradigm; Theocharopoulou et al., 2015). However, this difference mainly comes from stylistic differences and strategies between young and older speakers. Whereas young adults generally tried to retrieve the word form, causing more TOT situations along with the higher use of iconic gestures, older adults produced circumlocutions. Instead of accessing the phonological form, they preferred to explain the function and identify the object using different words. However, when they were forced to retrieve the word form, older speakers faced higher TOT situations and used more iconic gestures to resolve lexical access difficulties. Thus, the diminished use of spontaneous iconic gestures among older adults might be due to declining mental imagery and visual–spatial skills, or to stylistic differences in speech.

Özer and colleagues (2017) asked young and older adults to describe routes on a map either in a condition where there was no mention of gesture (spontaneous speech) or in a condition in which gesture was restrained. The use of gestures in the spontaneous-speech condition was the same in the older and young adult groups, but when gestures were restrained the use of spatial information in speech increased only in the older adults. Older adults used gestures mainly for communicative purposes, supplementing and/or complementing spoken expressions. This suggests that not only the frequency of gesture use but also the functions gestures serve during communication might differ between young and older adults.

11.1.2 Gesture Comprehension

People integrate gestural information with speech information during comprehension (Kelly et al., 2010; for a review, see Özyürek, 2014). Studies conducted with aging populations have shown that older adults are impaired in multimodal integration in general, both in low-level sensory integration (e.g., the integration of lip movements with speech sounds; Huyse et al., 2014) as well as in high-level semantic integration of speech and gesture (Cocks et al., 2011; Thompson, 1995; Thompson & Guzman, 1999). Older adults rely more on visible speech and benefit less from gestures during comprehension compared with younger people in either clear speech or in difficult listening conditions (i.e., in noise; Schubotz et al., 2020; Thompson, 1995; Thompson & Guzman, 1999). Cocks and colleagues (2011) showed that although older adults could comprehend speech and gesture in isolation, they showed impairment in integrating two sources of information during comprehension. Put more specifically, they relied more on speech and disregarded gestural information. This impairment in semantic integration of speech and gesture mainly stems from the decline in WM resources that comes with normal aging. Reduced WM capacity in aging populations might make it more difficult to take information from two different modalities and lead to more reliance on one modality. In the case of older adults, WM resources might be consumed with speech processing, leaving fewer resources for processing gestural information. Declines in visual–spatial skills in aging populations might also affect how older adults process gestures given that individual differences in visual–spatial skills relate to how listeners attend to and process co-speech gestures (Özer & Göksun, 2020b).

In sum, studies conducted with older populations suggest that declines in the spontaneous use of co-speech iconic gestures and in the ability to integrate gestural information with speech might be due to reduced mental imagery, visual and spatial skills, WM resources, and stylistic or strategic differences in communication. These studies provide only indirect evidence about the possible mechanisms underlying these impairments in aging populations because they did not directly test these arguments.

11.2 Aging, Gestures, and Cognitive Correlates

WM, visual–spatial skills, and verbal skills are suggested to be correlated with gesture production and comprehension. In the next sections, we discuss each cognitive skill in relation to gestures and highlight how these cognitive functions change with aging. We also discuss how these changes in cognitive skills might play a role in the multimodal language use and processing of older people.

11.2.1 Working Memory

Many theories assert that gesture's primary role is to maintain spatial–motoric information in WM for speech production processes (Hadar & Butterworth, 1997; Morsella & Krauss, 1999, 2004; Wesp et al., 2001) or for problem solving, especially under conditions of high cognitive load (i.e., the lightening-the-load hypothesis; Chu & Kita, 2011; Goldin-Meadow et al., 2001; Ping & Goldin-Meadow, 2010; Wagner et al., 2004).

Chu et al. (2014) found that speakers with low visual and spatial WM capacities (as measured by the Corsi block span task and visual pattern task, respectively) used more spontaneous co-speech iconic gestures when describing abstract meanings of English phrases (e.g., to disclose something confidential) than speakers with high visual and spatial WM. Verbal WM resources also related to gesture use: Speakers with low verbal WM capacity (as measured by a listening span task) used more co-speech iconic gestures when narrating a cartoon story (Gillespie et al., 2014) than speakers with high verbal WM capacity. Verbal WM resources are a negative predictor of gesture use both in monolingual and bilingual speakers (Smithson & Nicoladis, 2013). Apart from speech production processes, gestures help lighten the cognitive load during problem solving. For example, Chu and Kita (2011) found that when participants were presented with complex information they used more gestures compared with when they were presented with simpler information. In addition, Pouw et al.'s (2016) participants who spontaneously used gestures, or were instructed to use gestures while mentally solving Tower of Hanoi (TOH) problems, performed better than participants not told to use gesture. However, gesture use was beneficial only under situations of high cognitive load, that is, for people with lower WM capacities. Children can also benefit from gestures' ability to reduce cognitive load. For instance, in a study conducted by Goldin-Meadow and colleagues (2001), children were presented with lists of words and then required to explain a mathematics task. Children who gestured during the explanation of the mathematics task performed better when asked to remember the items from the presented list. This can be a reduction in the burden of the explanation task, which in turn leaves more resources for the memory task.

In consideration of these findings with young adults, older adults are predicted to use more gestures than young adults during language production and problem solving because of their decreased WM capacity. The current literature, however, does not bear this out (e.g., Cohen & Borsoi, 1996). One reason could be that earlier studies investigated the spontaneous retellings and/or descriptions of mainly simple and nonspatial information (but see Arslan & Göksun, 2021; Feyereisen & Havard, 1999; Özer et al., 2017) with low cognitive load. Because of their decreased WM resources, older adults might especially use more iconic gestures during problem solving compared with young adults. To our knowledge, however, no study has yet investigated how older adults use gestures during problem solving and whether it benefits them. Future studies should investigate the effects of aging on the use of silent gestures (i.e., gestures executed without accompanying speech) or on tasks in which older adults are encouraged to gesture.

The role of WM resources in gesture comprehension and speech–gesture integration has also been established. Research shows that visual–spatial, but not verbal, WM capacity is positively related to gesture–speech integration. For example, people with higher visual WM capacity (as measured by Corsi block span task) make more errors and respond with longer latencies when speech and gesture expressed incongruent information than when it expressed congruent information (Wu & Coulson, 2014). Thus, the decline in spatial and visual WM resources in normal aging might be the reason older adults have difficulty in retaining two different sources of information and integrating them (Cocks et al., 2011; Thompson, 1995; Thompson & Guzman, 1999).

11.2.2 Spatial and Visual Skills

Gestures are visual and spatial phenomena and derive from the imagistic mental representations in WM (Hadar & Butterworth, 1997; Hostetter & Alibali, 2008; Krauss et al., 2000). Speakers use more gestures when talking about spatial and motoric content compared with neutral content (e.g., Alibali et al., 2001; Lavergne & Kimura, 1987; Rauscher et al., 1996; for a review, see Alibali, 2005). Some research suggests that speakers with higher spatial and visualization skills should have more perceptual and motoric simulations of events, compared with people who tend to encode information in a more propositional format, resulting in the higher use of gestures during imagistic speech (e.g., Hostetter & Alibali, 2008; Hostetter & Sullivan, 2011; Hostetter et al., 2011; Masson-Carro et al., 2016; Trafton et al., 2006). Speakers gesture more when speech is rated high on imageability (Beattie & Shovelton, 2002), and people with high visual–spatial skills (e.g., on a paper-folding task measuring the ability to mentally form, manipulate, and store spatial forms) used more iconic gestures while narrating a mouse cartoon and describing how to wrap a package compared with people with low visual–spatial skills (Hostetter & Alibali, 2007).

In contrast to these accounts, some studies have found that visual and spatial abilities are inversely related to gesture production (e.g., Chu et al., 2014; Göksun et al., 2013). For example, when asked to explain how people solve mental rotation problems, participants with low spatial skills (as measured by the Shephard–Metzler Mental Rotations Test) produced more gestures compared with participants with high spatial skills (Göksun, Goldin-Meadow, et al., 2013). It is worth noting, though, that these different patterns of results might have arisen from the nature of the gesture elicitation tasks. People with high spatial and visual abilities might use more iconic gestures in spontaneous speech of simple descriptions, whereas when the cognitive load is high (i.e., explaining a difficult problem), people with lower spatial and visual abilities might use more iconic gestures to lighten their cognitive load (for a review, see Özer & Göksun, 2020a). In other words, reduced visual and spatial abilities and mental imagery in aging (Copeland & Radvansky, 2007; Dror & Kosslyn, 1994) might be the mechanism driving the diminished use of spontaneous co-speech iconic gestures, especially in simple casual narratives or in a spatial context (Arslan & Göksun, 2021; Cohen & Borsoi, 1996; but see Feyereisen & Havard, 1999). However, older adults might use more iconic gestures compared with young adults while describing or explaining things that are spatially complex. A systematic understanding of the link between visual–spatial skills and gesture production in the older adult population is still lacking (but see Arslan & Göksun, 2021). Future studies should address how they use gestures when solving and describing spatially and visually complex phenomena.

11.2.3 Verbal Skills

Co-speech gestures help speakers formulate speech (Kita, 2000; Kita & Özyürek, 2003; Krauss et al., 2000), and they are likely to occur when speakers have difficulty producing speech. Individual differences in how skilled speakers are at expressing their thoughts in words can influence the production of representational gestures. More specifically, if gesture is likely to occur when speakers are having trouble producing speech, people with poor verbal skills should use more gestures.

The relation between different indicators of verbal skills and gesture use is somewhat mixed. For example, in an early study, Baxter et al. (1968) measured verbal skills with a verbal categorization task in which participants sorted different occupations into different semantic categories. They found that speakers with low verbal skills exhibited more nonverbal behavior (i.e., overall gestural behavior) than speakers with high verbal skills only when talking about unfamiliar topics (i.e., not necessarily spatial topics). When talking about familiar topics, speakers with higher verbal skills produced more gestures than speakers with low verbal skills. Yet it should be noted that this study measured gestural behavior as the subjective ratings of the amount of behavior expressed by the participants in their face, shoulders, arms, hands, and fingers. When gestural behavior was operationalized as representational hand gestures, no relation between these verbal scores and gesture was found. Verbal scores on the SAT and vocabulary knowledge are not related to the spontaneous use of iconic gestures (Frick-Horbury, 2002; Gillespie et al., 2014).

One measure of verbal ability is speech fluency; specifically, *semantic fluency* indexes a person's skill in accessing and retrieving words from existing semantic categories (e.g., "List as many unique animal names as possible in 60 seconds"), and *phonemic fluency* indexes skill in organizing and keeping track of the lexical space (e.g., "List as many words as possible starting with 'k' in 60 seconds"; Martin et al., 1994). Semantic fluency relies more on temporal lobe activity, whereas phonemic fluency relies on frontal lobe activities such as switching and strategic search (Troyer et al., 1997). Despite the fact that some studies have showed that verbal fluency does not predict spontaneous iconic gesture use (Chu et al., 2014; Gillespie et al., 2014), Hostetter and Alibali (2007) found that there was a relationship between the two, but it was a quadratic relationship: People with different verbal skill levels might use gestures for different purposes. Speakers with high phonemic fluency and speakers with low phonemic fluency produced more iconic gestures during motor (i.e., how to wrap a gift box) and spatial (i.e., a cartoon story) descriptions, compared with speakers with average phonemic fluency. The authors suggested that when speakers have high verbal skills, they might have more resources to devote to gesturing and, as a result, make their speech more engaging and entertaining for the benefit of listeners.

A more interesting pattern emerges when spatial and verbal skills are analyzed together. During a motor and spatial description task, people with poor verbal but high spatial skills gestured most frequently, and people with high verbal but poor spatial skills gestured least frequently (Hostetter & Alibali, 2007). This finding suggests that verbally dominant people, whose verbal abilities exceed their spatial abilities, tend to encode spatial information in a propositional format, and the production of gestures is especially increased when speakers have the spatial images in mind but are unable to efficiently convey them in speech.

How verbal abilities change with normal aging is controversial in the current literature. The contents as well as the grammatical complexity of spoken expressions decline with aging (Kemper et al., 2001), yet older adults do not exhibit deficits in rather low-level language processing. For example, there are no morphological or syntactic deficits unless there is high cognitive load (Kemper, 1997, 2006). Moreover, although older adults perform below younger adults in semantic fluency tasks, their performance on phonemic fluency tasks is comparable (Tomer & Levin, 1993). Older adults have larger vocabularies and use a more diverse set of lexical items than younger adults (Kemper & Sumner, 2001).

Earlier findings linking gesture use to verbal abilities in young adults suggest that older adults should use more gestures to compensate for their declining verbal abilities. It should be noted that low verbal abilities relate to higher gesture use only when coupled with intact visual–spatial imagery (Hostetter & Alibali, 2007, 2011; Özer & Göksun, 2020b). The impairment in spatial abilities and mental imagery in normal aging might account for the lower use of gestures in older people (Arslan & Göksun, 2021), despite a decline in verbal abilities.

Overall, both gesture production and gesture comprehension decline with aging. Compared with younger adults, older adults use co-speech gestures less frequently in spontaneous discourse and are relatively impaired in integrating gestural information with speech during comprehension. These impairments in gesture use and comprehension might be due to the declines in mental imagery, spatial abilities, and WM capacity that are a part of normal aging. Moreover, studies that focus on the cognitive correlates of gesture use and comprehension, and how these cognitive abilities change with aging, might provide insight into the mechanisms underlying gestural impairments in aging populations.

11.3 Gesture in Neurodegenerative Disorders of Aging

To date, research on the production and comprehension of gesture use with people who have neurodegenerative disorders is limited, with the exception of work on people with aphasia. In addition, there is accumulating evidence on gesture production with older patients who have speech impairments due to stroke (e.g., Akbyk et al., 2018; Akhavan et al., 2018; Göksun et al., 2013, 2015; Kemmerer et al., 2007; Özer et al., 2019). The findings suggest that spontaneous gesture production helps people communicate when they have difficulty retrieving words for spatial information (Akhavan et al., 2018; Göksun et al., 2015) or for creating narratives (Akbyk et al., 2018), in particular, when they have intact conceptual knowledge. People with speech problems can resolve lexical retrieval difficulties when they use iconic gestures (Akhavan et al., 2018). It is important to note that Özer et al. (2019) found that when patients were restrained from gesturing, the accurate use of verbs decreased, compared with the verbs used in a spontaneous-gesture condition.

Although this line of evidence is informative, different types of dementia, such as AD, primary progressive aphasia (PPA), and PD, are natural targets to study gesture in aging populations because the prevalence rates of these diseases increase with age (Brayne et al., 2006; Jorm et al., 1987). Findings from these lines of research not only provide information on the use of gestures in the aging brain but also present evidence with respect to theories in understanding the gesture–speech relationship.

11.3.1 Alzheimer's Disease

Dementia is an umbrella term that refers to a group of symptoms associated with different neurodegenerative disorders that result from progressive damage to neurons in the parts of brain that are related to cognitive functioning (Livingston et al., 2017). The symptoms comprise deficiencies in cognitive capacities, including, but not limited to, problem solving, attention, executive function, memory, and linguistic skills. Even though a general decline in these cognitive processes is expected during the course of normal aging, in dementia the symptoms are so severe that they interfere with daily functioning (World Health Organization, 2004).

The major cause of dementia in the elderly population, with 60% to 80% of cases, is AD (Fleming et al., 1995). Memory, attention, and executive function problems are among the initial cognitive declines in AD patients (Perry & Hodges, 1999). Limb apraxia has a low prevalence at the earlier stages of the disease but, as the severity increases, most people with severe AD suffer from an apraxia deficiency as well (Parakh et al., 2004). Evidence also suggests that approximately 75% of AD patients experience language-related disorders, even at the earlier stages of the disease (Becker et al., 1988; Carlomagno et al., 2005). AD is not a language-specific deficiency. With respect to the linguistic deficits, the grammatical aspects of language are generally preserved, but access to conceptual knowledge and semantic processes is distorted (Forbes-McKay & Venneri, 2005; Glosser et al., 1998). During the advanced stages of the disease, speech becomes unorganized and noninformative (Appell et al., 1982; Carlomagno et al., 2005), which can be attributed to attentional and executive function impairments (Perry & Hodges, 1999).

Multimodal assessments, or assessments that address different components of language and referential communication, can signal deficits even years before the emergence of memory deficits (Alberdi et al., 2016). Thus, assessing gestural abilities of people with AD would be helpful in aiding diagnosis. Identification of apraxia at the earlier stages can also be used as a proxy for the later trajectory of the disease. For instance, patients with AD who have limb apraxia decline more rapidly than those who do not (Yesavage et al., 1993). Another benefit of studying gesture is that gestures provide a more direct view of the organization of the conceptual meaning underlying communication, given that gestures require less conceptual transformation during the preparation of the concept for expression (Glosser et al., 1998). Furthermore, gesture use usually declines later than speech (McNamara & Durso, 2003), allowing researchers to study the cognitive system even at the late stages of the disorder.

Although apraxia has been more widely studied than gesture in the context of AD, the spontaneous gestures of these patients has been addressed. In fact, apraxia scores of AD patients need not associate with their gestural communication skills at all (Glosser et al., 1998). Thus, it is not appropriate to derive conclusions about co-speech gesture production from studies that assess apraxia skills. In an earlier study, people with AD did not differ from age-matched older participants in their overall rate of gesture production, yet patients with AD used gestures that were less complex in nature and with more nonidentifiable referents (Glosser et al., 1998). They also could not use gesture as a compensatory strategy, and the severity of the gestural impairment was positively associated with the information content in speech. Their numbers of meaningful gestures are also lower compared with age-matched neurotypical controls (Carlomagno et al., 2005).

As mentioned above, the most widely studied aspect of gesture processing in AD is apraxia. People with AD are deficient in the imitation of meaningless gestures and pantomimes, and the severity of apraxia is correlated with their linguistic abilities (Dumont et al., 2000; Rousseaux et al., 2012). AD patients' performance in iconic gesture production is slightly better than their performance in recognizing or producing pantomimes. This also reinforces the idea that their performances are tied to memory given that iconic gestures depict the meaning by means of similarity and are less memory bound (Foundas et al., 1999; Parakh et al., 2004).

11.3.2 Primary Progressive Aphasia

The most frequently studied aspect of the link between neuropsychological disorders and gesture is what happens to gesture production and comprehension when there is a deficiency in linguistic processes (e.g., Cicone et al., 1979; Cocks et al., 2013; Dipper et al., 2011; Wilkinson, 2013). A natural target for such an inquiry is PPA, a neurodegenerative disorder with an average onset of age 60, whereby the person experiences a progressive decline in linguistic abilities (Mesulam, 2001). This notion refers to a group of atrophy profiles that distort language processing without an additional structural abnormality in the brain (Grossman & Irwin, 2018). At least within the first 2 years of the disease, the only area of deficit is language (Mesulam et al., 2003).

The most prevalent deficit among different variants of PPA is word-finding difficulty (Mesulam et al., 2012). People with PPA have morphological, phonological, and syntactic deficits while suprasentential and macrolinguistic abilities are relatively preserved (Glosser & Deser, 1991; Pritchard et al., 2015). PPA provides valuable foundational information regarding the relationship between gesture and general linguistic abilities (e.g., Cocks et al., 2013; Sekine & Rose, 2013). There is also a strong clinical interest in the potential of gestures to enhance the communicative abilities of people with aphasia (Rose, 2006) because co-speech gestures can provide additional meaning to the semantic content of spoken language (Kendon, 2000) and compensate for linguistic problems by providing an alternative means of communication (Akbyk et al., 2018; Akhavan et al., 2018; Göksun et al., 2015; Hogrefe et al., 2012). Thus, people with PPA benefit from gesture production while they speak because they can compensate for their speech difficulty by conveying additional meaningful information by means of iconic gestures (Hadar et al., 1998; Kroenke et al., 2013).

People with nonfluent aphasia rely more on referential gestures than those with fluent aphasia (Duffy et al., 1984). The word retrieval difficulties of aphasic people also induce a higher rate of gesture production (Cicone et al., 1979). There is also evidence that people with aphasia use iconic gestures more frequently to provide additional meaning to the content of their speech (Kong et al., 2015). People with phonological or lexical difficulties produce more gestures than control participants or people with conceptual difficulties (Hadar et al., 1998). People with aphasia who have word finding difficulties tend to produce higher rates of iconic gestures (Cocks et al., 2011, 2013; Dipper et al., 2011; Kemmerer et al., 2007). People with nonfluent aphasia produce gestures for many reasons, including to increase the efficacy of communication. In a recent study, Akhavan and colleagues (2018) showed that people with aphasia (due to stroke) compensated for their speech impairment with gestures to resolve lexical retrieval difficulties and sometimes used gestures as social cues for the listener.

The semantic variant of PPA is characterized by disruptions in amodal conceptual processing (Hodges & Patterson, 2007), which results from bilateral atrophy in the ventral and lateral anterior temporal lobes (Gorno-Tempini et al., 2011). People with SD have difficulties in understanding word meanings (Hodges et al., 2000) while their episodic memory, syntactic abilities, and perceptual skills remain intact (Patterson et al., 2007). However, the morphological and syntactic complexity might be reduced (Patterson & MacDonald, 2006). A signature of this variant is a normal rate of speech with impairment at the comprehension and conceptual processing level (Grossman & Irwin, 2018). There is evidence for the importance of semantic processes for gesture production (see Göksun, Lehet, et al., 2013; Göksun et al., 2015; Özer et al., 2019). Studies conducted with people with SD therefore have the potential to shed further light on the importance of semantic processes for gesture (Buxbaum et al., 2007;

Hodges et al., 2000). SD is a selective impairment of semantic information in both the verbal and nonverbal domains, supporting the idea that the iconic gesture production patterns of people with SD would parallel their deficiencies in speech production.

People with SD have deficiencies in using familiar tools while their mechanical problem-solving skills remain intact, supporting the distinct but somewhat complementary role of semantic and mechanical knowledge in tool use (Baumard et al., 2016; Silveri & Ciccarelli, 2009). They perform better in situations where functional knowledge demands are low (Hodges et al., 2000). Gestures aid word retrieval and learning processes in neurotypical people, but those with semantic impairments tend to benefit less from the enhancements in learning provided by gesture compared with people with other patholinguistic profiles (Kroenke et al., 2013). SD patients are also deficient in the use of communicative gestures (Buxbaum et al., 2007), and they cannot use gesture as a compensatory or a complementary tool while speaking (Kroenke et al., 2013; see also Hogrefe et al., 2012). These findings reinforce the idea that the ability to convey semantic information through gestures depends on semantic abilities (Pritchard et al., 2015) and requires an intact inferior frontal network (Göksun et al., 2015).

11.3.3 Parkinson's Disease

Gesture also stands at the intersection point of motor movement and language. PD could provide a nice context for studying gesture because it is characterized by motor impairments (Jankovic, 2008) and a selective impairment for action-related language (Signorini & Volpato, 2006). PD is primarily an age-related disorder with the signature of motor dysfunction. The symptoms are caused by the progressive decrease in the brain's dopamine production in the basal ganglia as a result of the death of dopaminergic cells in the substantia pars compacta. Basal ganglia lesions are related to abnormalities in motor movement, which can reveal itself as increased or decreased movement (Grahn et al., 2008; Middleton & Strick, 1994). Other difficulties, such as problems in executive function and WM capacity, emerge as PD progresses (Lewis et al., 2003; Pell & Monetta, 2008). Investigating gesture in people with PD could yield valuable information regarding the importance of motor knowledge in relation to gesture production (Cleary et al., 2011; Humphries et al., 2016) and comprehension (Klooster et al., 2015) and help us understand how aging would affect these skills.

Language-related problems of patients with PD are usually related to the motor aspects of language, such as articulation, prosody, and intonation (Darkins et al., 1988; Goberman & Coelho, 2002). These directly affect the quality of the person's communication with the interlocutor (Pell et al., 2006). People with PD are also deficient in sentence comprehension (Grossman et al., 1991; Lieberman et al., 1990), syntactic integration (Friederici et al., 2003), understanding metaphors (Berg et al., 2003), and in inflecting and generating verbs (Crescentini et al., 2008; Ullman et al., 1997).

McNamara and Durso (2003) assessed verbal and nonverbal communicative skills of people with PD and showed that they had problems in pragmatic communication skills. There is further evidence that patients with PD with impaired procedural memory cannot benefit from the information content of the gestures of their interlocutors (Klooster et al., 2015). Moreover, PD patients have deficits in producing tool use pantomimes, both in imitation and verbal command conditions (Jaywant et al., 2016; Leiguarda et al., 1997, 2000), and they experience distortions in producing sequential movements with precision (Sharpe et al., 1983). Studies that have assessed gesture production patterns of people with PD have usually relied on pantomime, imitation, or tool use tasks that do not require speech, nor do they occur synchronously and in a natural flow with speech (e.g., Goldenberg et al., 1986). In regard to co-speech gestures, there is evidence for reduced gesture production in PD patients (Pitcairn et al., 1990). Their gestures are usually low in precision (Leiguarda et al., 2000) and informative content (Buck & Duffy, 1980). Cleary et al. (2011) examined a wide variety of gestures and showed that PD patients produced gestures at a rate similar to that of neurotypical control participants, but their gestures were semantically less precise in action-related gestures (which is consistent with previous literature, see Leiguarda et al., 2000). This deficiency was associated with their motor and speech symptoms. Humphries and colleagues (2021) confirmed these findings and indicated that people with PD produced fewer gestures for greater bodily motion and for specific manners of actions than neurotypical control participants. Overall, gestural deficiency in PD is suggested to derive from visual short-term memory and attentional deficiencies rather than a specific deficit in action-related processing per se (Bonivento et al., 2013).

Although research on the production and comprehension of gesture use with people who have neurodegenerative disorders is sparse (except for research on people with aphasia), there is evidence for impairments in gesture comprehension and production in AD, PPA, and PD. The differential patterns of gesture processing in these different diseases highlight the link between cognitive and gestural functioning and the benefits of studying this link from a neuropsychological perspective.

11.4 Conclusion

In this chapter, we have argued that the investigation of gestures in relation to language in both healthy and unhealthy aging adults could offer new insight into and evidence regarding gesture theories. Although gestures can serve several functions across different populations, the use of gestures for supplementing deteriorated spoken expressions would suggest a common mechanism for speech and co-speech gestures. In addition, the increase in co-speech gestures as a result of impaired speech can signal the role gestures play in facilitating lexical retrieval or underspecifications in spoken messages and organizing information for speech (Özer et al., 2019). For example, an older person who has trouble with spatial imagery who is asked to describe a geographical route would have difficulty organizing a mental image and therefore might produce only a beat gesture (rather than a representational gesture for the route) to reach the lexical item. On the other hand, if the person's spatial or mental imagery is intact, an iconic gesture showing the direction of the road would help the person reach the lexical item or facilitate the route description. For an older person who has a speech impairment but an intact frontotemporal network, the same representational gesture can supplement the intended message, which will not appear in speech. Thus, even though these two older persons, with and without speech problems, produce the same gestures, the function of these gestures would differ between the two.

Many studies also have found a decline in older populations in the spontaneous use of co-speech representational gestures and in the ability to integrate gestural information (e.g., Arslan & Göksun, 2021; Cocks et al., 2011; Cohen & Borsoi, 1996; Copeland & Radvansky, 2007; Feyereisen & Havard, 1999; Glosser et al., 1998; Schubotz et al., 2020). The reasons for these impairments in gesture production and comprehension might be due to a decline in cognitive abilities, such as mental imagery, spatial abilities, and WM capacity, that occurs in normal aging, yet there is not much research on the systematic analysis and function of different gesture types in older people (see Arslan & Göksun, 2021). There is a need for further studies to directly assess these hypotheses to uncover possible mechanisms of gesture use and comprehension in older adults, which will in turn benefit the current gesture theories.

Studying neurodegenerative disorders in older populations not only adds to the current debates on the mechanisms and functions of gestures but also has practical consequences. Because gesture use and functions can change according to the specific neurodegenerative problem (e.g., Carlomagno et al., 2005; Cocks et al., 2011; Hogrefe et al., 2012; Kroenke et al., 2013; Özer et al., 2019), the examination of gesture production during discourse in different patient groups can signal the speech impairment and diagnosis of the disease. Then, understanding gesture use might also aid the person's treatment. Understanding patients' communication abilities is also important for improving their living conditions given that patient–caregiver interactions also depend on such nonverbal communicative skills (Seidl et al., 2012).

Studies of people with aphasia present a good case for the positive outcomes of using gestures in speech therapies (Rose, 2006; Rose et al., 2013). For example, a combination of gesture and speech therapy can be helpful for people with aphasia. The gestures not only aid word retrieval but also enhance communication that may not appear in speech. It is important to note that gesture therapy alone does not yield the same beneficial effects as gesture and speech therapy combined (Rose et al., 2013). More research is needed to examine whether gestures can be useful to improve speech problems and communication difficulties for people with other neurodegenerative diseases.

The study of gesture use and comprehension in older adults with or without speech problems provides new angles for research addressing the interaction between speech and gesture to take. Gestures serve multiple functions that vary across populations. Examining the diverse functions of gestures, such as communicative, restorative, and cognitive, in older adults related to their language and other cognitive abilities will be fruitful in revealing the mechanisms underlying spoken and gestural language.

References

Adams, C., Smith, M. C., Pasupathi, M., & Vitolo, L. (2002). Social context effects on story recall in older and younger women: Does the listener make a difference? *The Journals of Gerontology: Series B: Psychological Sciences and Social Sciences*, *57B*(1), P28–P40. https://doi.org/10.1093/geronb/57.1.P28

Akbyk, S., Karaduman, A., Göksun, T., & Chatterjee, A. (2018). The relationship between co-speech gesture production and macrolinguistic discourse abilities in people with focal brain injury. *Neuropsychologia*, *117*, 440–453. https://doi.org/10.1016/j.neuropsychologia.2018.06.025

Akhavan, N., Göksun, T., & Nozari, N. (2018). Integrity and function of gestures in aphasia. *Aphasiology*, *32*(11), 1310–1335. https://doi.org/10.1080/02687038.2017.1396573

Alberdi, A., Aztiria, A., & Basarab, A. (2016). On the early diagnosis of Alzheimer's disease from multimodal signals: A survey. *Artificial Intelligence in Medicine*, *71*, 1–29. https://doi.org/10.1016/j.artmed.2016.06.003

Alibali, M. W. (2005). Gesture in spatial cognition: Expressing, communicating, and thinking about spatial information. *Spatial Cognition and Computation*, *5*(4), 307–331. https://doi.org/10.1207/s15427633scc0504_2

Alibali, M. W., Heath, D. C., & Myers, H. J. (2001). Effects of visibility between speaker and listener on gesture production: Some gestures are meant to be seen. *Journal of Memory and Language*, *44*(2), 169–188. https://doi.org/10.1006/jmla.2000.2752

Andersen, G. J., & Ni, R. (2008). Aging and visual processing: Declines in spatial not temporal integration. *Vision Research*, *48*(1), 109–118. https://doi.org/10.1016/j.visres.2007.10.026

Andrés, P., & Van der Linden, M. (2000). Age-related differences in supervisory attentional system functions. *The Journals of Gerontology Series B: Psychological Sciences and Social Sciences*, *55B*(6), P373–P380. https://doi.org/10.1093/geronb/55.6.P373

Appell, J., Kertesz, A., & Fisman, M. (1982). A study of language functioning in Alzheimer patients. *Brain and Language*, *17*(1), 73–91. https://doi.org/10.1016/0093-934X(82)90006-2

Arslan, B., & Göksun, T. (2021). Ageing, working memory, and mental imagery: Understanding gestural communication in younger and older adults. *Quarterly Journal of Experimental Psychology: Human Experimental Psychology*, *74*(1), 29–44. https://doi.org/10.1177/1747021820944696

Baumard, J., Lesourd, M., Jarry, C., Merck, C., Etcharry-Bouyx, F., Chauviré, V., Belliard, S., Moreaud, O., Croisile, B., Osiurak, F., & Le Gall, D. (2016). Tool use disorders in neurodegenerative diseases: Roles of semantic memory and technical reasoning. *Cortex*, *82*, 119–132. https://doi.org/10.1016/j.cortex.2016.06.007

Baxter, J. C., Winters, E. P., & Hammer, R. E. (1968). Gestural behavior during a brief interview as a function of cognitive variables. *Journal of Personality and Social Psychology*, *8*(3, Pt. 1), 303–307. https://doi.org/10.1037/h0025597

Beattie, G., & Shovelton, H. (2002). What properties of talk are associated with the generation of spontaneous iconic hand gestures? *British Journal of Social Psychology*, *41*(3), 403–417. https://doi.org/10.1348/014466602760344287

Becker, J. T., Huff, F. J., Nebes, R. D., Holland, A., & Boller, F. (1988). Neuropsychological function in Alzheimer's disease: Pattern of impairment and rates of progression. *Archives of Neurology*, *45*(3), 263–268. https://doi.org/10.1001/archneur.1988.00520270037018

Bélanger, S., Belleville, S., & Gauthier, S. (2010). Inhibition impairments in Alzheimer's disease, mild cognitive impairment and healthy aging: Effect of congruency proportion in a Stroop task. *Neuropsychologia*, *48*(2), 581–590. https://doi.org/10.1016/j.neuropsychologia.2009.10.021

Berg, E., Björnram, C., Hartelius, L., Laakso, K., & Johnels, B. (2003). High-level language difficulties in Parkinson's disease. *Clinical Linguistics & Phonetics*, *17*(1), 63–80. https://doi.org/10.1080/0269920021000055540

Bonivento, C., Rumiati, R. I., Biasutti, E., & Humphreys, G. W. (2013). The role of the basal ganglia in action imitation: Neuropsychological evidence from Parkinson's disease patients. *Experimental Brain Research*, *224*(2), 211–220. https://doi.org/10.1007/s00221-012-3300-8

Brayne, C., Gao, L., Dewey, M., Matthews, F. E., & The Medical Research Council Cognitive Function and Ageing Study Investigators. (2006). Dementia before death in ageing societies—The promise of prevention and the reality. *PLOS Medicine*, *3*(10), e397. https://doi.org/10.1371/journal.pmed.0030397

Buck, R., & Duffy, R. J. (1980). Nonverbal communication of affect in brain-damaged patients. *Cortex*, *16*(3), 351–362. https://doi.org/10.1016/S0010-9452(80)80037-2

Buxbaum, L. J., Kyle, K., Grossman, M., & Coslett, H. B. (2007). Left inferior parietal representations for skilled hand–object interactions: Evidence from stroke and corticobasal degeneration. *Cortex*, *43*(3), 411–423. https://doi.org/10.1016/S0010-9452(08)70466-0

Carlomagno, S., Santoro, A., Menditti, A., Pandolfi, M., & Marini, A. (2005). Referential communication in Alzheimer's type dementia. *Cortex*, *41*(4), 520–534. https://doi.org/10.1016/S0010-9452(08)70192-8

Chu, M., & Kita, S. (2011). The nature of gestures' beneficial role in spatial problem solving. *Journal of Experimental Psychology: General*, *140*(1), 102–116. https://doi.org/10.1037/a0021790

Chu, M., Meyer, A., Foulkes, L., & Kita, S. (2014). Individual differences in frequency and saliency of speech-accompanying gestures: The role of cognitive abilities and empathy. *Journal of Experimental Psychology: General*, *143*(2), 694–709. https://doi.org/10.1037/a0033861

Cicone, M., Wapner, W., Foldi, N., Zurif, E., & Gardner, H. (1979). The relation between gesture and language in aphasic communication. *Brain and Language*, *8*(3), 324–349. https://doi.org/10.1016/0093-934X(79)90060-9

Cleary, R. A., Poliakoff, E., Galpin, A., Dick, J. P. R., & Holler, J. (2011). An investigation of co-speech gesture production during action description in Parkinson's disease. *Parkinsonism & Related Disorders*, *17*(10), 753–756. https://doi.org/10.1016/j.parkreldis.2011.08.001

Cocks, N., Dipper, L., Pritchard, M., & Morgan, G. (2013). The impact of impaired semantic knowledge on spontaneous iconic gesture production. *Aphasiology*, *27*(9), 1050–1069. https://doi.org/10.1080/02687038.2013.770816

Cocks, N., Morgan, G., & Kita, S. (2011). Iconic gesture and speech integration in younger and older adults. *Gesture*, *11*(1), 24–39. https://doi.org/10.1075/gest.11.1.02coc

Cohen, R. L., & Borsoi, D. (1996). The role of gestures in description–communication: A cross-sectional study of aging. *Journal of Nonverbal Behavior*, *20*(1), 45–63. https://doi.org/10.1007/BF02248714

Copeland, D. E., & Radvansky, G. A. (2007). Aging and integrating spatial mental models. *Psychology and Aging*, *22*(3), 569–579. https://doi.org/10.1037/0882-7974.22.3.569

Crescentini, C., Mondolo, F., Biasutti, E., & Shallice, T. (2008). Supervisory and routine processes in noun and verb generation in nondemented patients with Parkinson's disease. *Neuropsychologia*, *46*(2), 434–447. https://doi.org/10.1016/j.neuropsychologia.2007.08.021

Darkins, A. W., Fromkin, V. A., & Benson, D. F. (1988). A characterization of the prosodic loss in Parkinson's disease. *Brain and Language*, *34*(2), 315–327. https://doi.org/10.1016/0093-934X(88)90142-3

de Ruiter, J. P. (2006). Can gesticulation help aphasic people speak, or rather, communicate? *Advances in Speech Language Pathology*, *8*(2), 124–127. https://doi.org/10.1080/14417040600667285

Dimeck, P. T., Roy, E. A., & Hall, C. R. (1998). Aging and working memory in gesture imitation. *Brain and Cognition*, *37*(1), 124–127.

Dipper, L., Cocks, N., Rowe, M., & Morgan, G. (2011). What can co-speech gestures in aphasia tell us about the relationship between language and gesture?: A single case study of a participant with conduction aphasia. *Gesture*, *11*(2), 123–147. https://doi.org/10.1075/gest.11.2.02dip

Dror, I. E., & Kosslyn, S. M. (1994). Mental imagery and aging. *Psychology and Aging*, *9*(1), 90–102. https://doi.org/10.1037/0882-7974.9.1.90

Duffy, R. J., Duffy, J. R., & Mercaitis, P. A. (1984). Comparison of the performances of a fluent and a nonfluent aphasic on a pantomimic referential task. *Brain and Language*, *21*(2), 260–273. https://doi.org/10.1016/0093-934X(84)90051-8

Dumont, C., Ska, B., & Joanette, Y. (2000). Conceptual apraxia and semantic memory deficit in Alzheimer's disease: Two sides of the same coin? *Journal of the International Neuropsychological Society*, *6*(6), 693–703. https://doi.org/10.1017/S1355617700666079

Eling, P., & Whitaker, H. (2009). History of aphasia: From brain to language In M. J. Aminoff, F. Boller, & D. F. Swaab (Eds.), *Handbook of clinical neurology: Vol. 95. History of neurology* (pp. 571–582). Elsevier. https://doi.org/10.1016/S0072-9752(08)02136-2

Evans, J. L., Alibali, M. W., & McNeil, N. M. (2001). Divergence of verbal expression and embodied knowledge: Evidence from speech and gesture in children with specific language impairment. *Language and Cognitive Processes*, *16*(2–3), 309–331. https://doi.org/10.1080/01690960042000049

Feyereisen, P., & Havard, I. (1999). Mental imagery and production of hand gestures while speaking in younger and older adults. *Journal of Nonverbal Behavior*, *23*(2), 153–171. https://doi.org/10.1023/A:1021487510204

Fleming, K. C., Adams, A. C., & Petersen, R. C. (1995). Dementia: Diagnosis and evaluation. *Mayo Clinic Proceedings*, *70*(11), 1093–1107. https://doi.org/10.4065/70.11.1093

Forbes-McKay, K. E., & Venneri, A. (2005). Detecting subtle spontaneous language decline in early Alzheimer's disease with a picture description task. *Neurological Sciences*, *26*(4), 243–254. https://doi.org/10.1007/s10072-005-0467-9

Foundas, A. L., Macauley, B. L., Raymer, A. M., Maher, L. M., Rothi, L. J., & Heilman, K. M. (1999). Ideomotor apraxia in Alzheimer disease and left hemisphere stroke: Limb transitive and intransitive movements. *Neuropsychiatry, Neuropsychology, and Behavioral Neurology*, *12*(3), 161–166.

Frick-Horbury, D. (2002). The effects of hand gestures on verbal recall as a function of high- and low-verbal-skill levels. *Journal of General Psychology*, *129*(2), 137–147. https://doi.org/10.1080/00221300209603134

Friederici, A. D., Kotz, S. A., Werheid, K., Hein, G., & von Cramon, D. Y. (2003). Syntactic comprehension in Parkinson's disease: Investigating early automatic and late integrational processes using event-related brain potentials. *Neuropsychology*, *17*(1), 133–142.

Gillespie, M., James, A. N., Federmeier, K. D., & Watson, D. G. (2014). Verbal working memory predicts co-speech gesture: Evidence from individual differences. *Cognition*, *132*(2), 174–180. https://doi.org/10.1016/j.cognition.2014.03.012

Glosser, G., & Deser, T. (1991). Patterns of discourse production among neurological patients with fluent language disorders. *Brain and Language*, *40*(1), 67–88. https://doi.org/10.1016/0093-934X(91)90117-J

Glosser, G., Wiley, M. J., & Barnoski, E. J. (1998). Gestural communication in Alzheimer's disease. *Journal of Clinical and Experimental Neuropsychology*, *20*(1), 1–13. https://doi.org/10.1076/jcen.20.1.1.1484

Goberman, A. M., & Coelho, C. (2002). Acoustic analysis of Parkinsonian speech: I. Speech characteristics and L-Dopa therapy. *NeuroRehabilitation*, *17*(3), 237–246. https://doi.org/10.3233/NRE-2002-17310

Göksun, T., Goldin-Meadow, S., Newcombe, N., & Shipley, T. (2013). Individual differences in mental rotation: What does gesture tell us? *Cognitive Processing*, *14*(2), 153–162. https://doi.org/10.1007/s10339-013-0549-1

Göksun, T., Lehet, M., Malykhina, K., & Chatterjee, A. (2013). Naming and gesturing spatial relations: Evidence from focal brain-injured individuals. *Neuropsychologia*, *51*(8), 1518–1527. https://doi.org/10.1016/j.neuropsychologia.2013.05.006

Göksun, T., Lehet, M., Malykhina, K., & Chatterjee, A. (2015). Spontaneous gesture and spatial language: Evidence from focal brain injury. *Brain and Language*, *150*, 1–13. https://doi.org/10.1016/j.bandl.2015.07.012

Gold, D. P., & Arbuckle, T. Y. (1995). A longitudinal study of off-target verbosity. *The Journals of Gerontology Series B: Psychological Sciences and Social Sciences*, *50B*(6), P307–P315. https://doi.org/10.1093/geronb/50B.6.P307

Goldenberg, G., Wimmer, A., Auff, E., & Schnaberth, G. (1986). Impairment of motor planning in patients with Parkinson's disease: Evidence from ideomotor apraxia testing. *Journal of Neurology, Neurosurgery, and Psychiatry*, *49*(11), 1266–1272. https://doi.org/10.1136/jnnp.49.11.1266

Goldin-Meadow, S., Nusbaum, H., Kelly, S. D., & Wagner, S. (2001). Explaining math: Gesturing lightens the load. *Psychological Science*, *12*(6), 516–522. https://doi.org/10.1111/1467-9280.00395

Gorno-Tempini, M. L., Hillis, A. E., Weintraub, S., Kertesz, A., Mendez, M., Cappa, S. F., Ogar, J. M., Rohrer, J. D., Black, S., Boeve, B. F., Manes, F., Dronkers, N. F., Vandenberghe, R., Rascovsky, K., Patterson, K., Miller, B. L., Knopman, D. S., Hodges, J. R., Mesulam, M. M., & Grossman, M. (2011). Classification of primary progressive aphasia and its variants. *Neurology*, *76*(11), 1006–1114. https://doi.org/10.1212/WNL.0b013e31821103e6

Grahn, J. A., Parkinson, J. A., & Owen, A. M. (2008). The cognitive functions of the caudate nucleus. *Progress in Neurobiology*, *86*(3), 141–155. https://doi.org/10.1016/j.pneurobio.2008.09.004

Grossman, M., Carvell, S., Gollomp, S., Stern, M. B., Vernon, G., & Hurtig, H. I. (1991). Sentence comprehension and praxis deficits in Parkinson's disease. *Neurology*, *41*(10), 1620–1626. https://doi.org/10.1212/WNL.41.10.1620

Grossman, M., & Irwin, D. J. (2018). Primary progressive aphasia and stroke aphasia. *Continuum*, *24*(3), 745–767. https://doi.org/10.1212/CON.0000000000000618

Hadar, U., Burstein, A., Krauss, R., & Soroker, N. (1998). Ideational gestures and speech in brain-damaged subjects. *Language and Cognitive Processes*, *13*(1), 59–76. https://doi.org/10.1080/016909698386591

Hadar, U., & Butterworth, B. (1997). Iconic gestures, imagery, and word retrieval in speech. *Semiotica*, *115*(1–2), 147–172. https://doi.org/10.1515/semi.1997.115.1-2.147

Hodges, J. R., Bozeat, S., Lambon Ralph, M. A., Patterson, K., & Spatt, J. (2000). The role of conceptual knowledge in object use evidence from semantic dementia. *Brain, 123*(9), 1913–1925. https://doi.org/10.1093/brain/123.9.1913

Hodges, J. R., & Patterson, K. (2007). Semantic dementia: A unique clinicopathological syndrome. *Lancet Neurology, 6*(11), 1004–1014. https://doi.org/10.1016/S1474-4422(07)70266-1

Hogrefe, K., Ziegler, W., Weidinger, N., & Goldenberg, G. (2012). Non-verbal communication in severe aphasia: Influence of aphasia, apraxia, or semantic processing? *Cortex, 48*(8), 952–962. https://doi.org/10.1016/j.cortex.2011.02.022

Hostetter, A., Alibali, M., & Bartholomew, A. (2011). Gesture during mental rotation. *Proceedings of the Annual Meeting of the Cognitive Science Society, 33*, 1448–1453. https://cogsci.mindmodeling.org/2011/papers/0331/paper0331.pdf

Hostetter, A., & Sullivan, E. (2011). Gesture production during spatial tasks: It's not all about difficulty. In L. Carlson, C. Hoelscher, & T. Shipley (Eds.), *Proceedings of the 33rd Annual Meeting of the Cognitive Science Society* (pp. 1965–1970). Cognitive Science Society.

Hostetter, A. B., & Alibali, M. W. (2007). Raise your hand if you're spatial: Relations between verbal and spatial skills and gesture production. *Gesture, 7*(1), 73–95. https://doi.org/10.1075/gest.7.1.05hos

Hostetter, A. B., & Alibali, M. W. (2008). Visible embodiment: Gestures as simulated action. *Psychonomic Bulletin & Review, 15*(3), 495–514. https://doi.org/10.3758/PBR.15.3.495

Hostetter, A. B., & Alibali, M. W. (2011). Cognitive skills and gesture–speech redundancy: Formulation difficulty or communicative strategy? *Gesture, 11*(1), 40–60. https://doi.org/10.1075/gest.11.1.03hos

Humphries, S., Holler, J., Crawford, T., & Poliakoff, E. (2021). Cospeech gestures are a window into the effects of Parkinson's disease on action representations. *Journal of Experimental Psychology: General*. Advance online publication. https://doi.org/10.1037/xge0001002

Humphries, S., Holler, J., Crawford, T. J., Herrera, E., & Poliakoff, E. (2016). A third-person perspective on co-speech action gestures in Parkinson's disease. *Cortex, 78*, 44–54. https://doi.org/10.1016/j.cortex.2016.02.009

Huyse, A., Leybaert, J., & Berthommier, F. (2014). Effects of aging on audio–visual speech integration. *The Journal of the Acoustical Society of America, 136*(4), 1918–1931. https://doi.org/10.1121/1.4894685

James, L. E., Burke, D. M., Austin, A., & Hulme, E. (1998). Production and perception of "verbosity" in younger and older adults. *Psychology and Aging, 13*(3), 355–367. https://doi.org/10.1037/0882-7974.13.3.355

Jankovic, J. (2008). Parkinson's disease: Clinical features and diagnosis. *Journal of Neurology, Neurosurgery, and Psychiatry, 79*(4), 368–376. https://doi.org/10.1136/jnnp.2007.131045

Jaywant, A., Wasserman, V., Kemppainen, M., Neargarder, S., & Cronin-Golomb, A. (2016). Perception of communicative and non-communicative motion-defined gestures in Parkinson's disease. *Journal of the International Neuropsychological Society, 22*(5), 540–550. https://doi.org/10.1017/S1355617716000114

Jorm, A. F., Korten, A. E., & Henderson, A. S. (1987). The prevalence of dementia: A quantitative integration of the literature. *Acta Psychiatrica Scandinavica, 76*(5), 465–479. https://doi.org/10.1111/j.1600-0447.1987.tb02906.x

Kelly, S. D., Kravitz, C., & Hopkins, M. (2004). Neural correlates of bimodal speech and gesture comprehension. *Brain and Language, 89*(1), 253–260. https://doi.org/10.1016/S0093-934X(03)00335-3

Kelly, S. D., Özyürek, A., & Maris, E. (2010). Two sides of the same coin: Speech and gesture mutually interact to enhance comprehension. *Psychological Science, 21*(2), 260–267. https://doi.org/10.1177/0956797609357327

Kemmerer, D., Chandrasekaran, B., & Tranel, D. (2007). A case of impaired verbalization but preserved gesticulation of motion events. *Cognitive Neuropsychology, 24*(1), 70–114. https://doi.org/10.1080/02643290600926667

Kemper, S. (1997). Metalinguistic judgments in normal aging and Alzheimer's disease. *The Journals of Gerontology Series B: Psychological Sciences and Social Sciences, 52B*(3), P147–P155. https://doi.org/10.1093/geronb/52B.3.P147

Kemper, S. (2006). Language in adulthood. In E. Bialystok & F. I. M. Craik (Eds.), *Lifespan cognition: Mechanisms of change* (pp. 223–237). Oxford University Press.

Kemper, S., Marquis, J., & Thompson, M. (2001). Longitudinal change in language production: Effects of aging and dementia on grammatical complexity and propositional content. *Psychology and Aging, 16*(4), 600–614. https://doi.org/10.1037/0882-7974.16.4.600

Kemper, S., & Sumner, A. (2001). The structure of verbal abilities in young and older adults. *Psychology and Aging, 16*(2), 312–322. https://doi.org/10.1037/0882-7974.16.2.312

Kendon, A. (2000). Language and gesture: Unity or duality? In D. McNeill (Ed.), *Language and gesture* (pp. 47–63). Cambridge University Press. https://doi.org/10.1017/CBO9780511620850.004

Kita, S. (2000). How representational gestures help speaking. In D. McNeill (Ed.), *Language and gesture* (pp. 162–185). Cambridge University Press. https://doi.org/10.1017/CBO9780511620850.011

Kita, S., Alibali, M. W., & Chu, M. (2017). How do gestures influence thinking and speaking? The gesture-for-conceptualization hypothesis. *Psychological Review, 124*(3), 245–266. https://doi.org/10.1037/rev0000059

Kita, S., & Özyürek, A. (2003). What does cross-linguistic variation in semantic coordination of speech and gesture reveal? Evidence for an interface representation of spatial thinking and speaking. *Journal of Memory and Language, 48*(1), 16–32. https://doi.org/10.1016/S0749-596X(02)00505-3

Klooster, N. B., Cook, S. W., Uc, E. Y., & Duff, M. C. (2015). Gestures make memories, but what kind? Patients with impaired procedural memory display disruptions in gesture production and comprehension. *Frontiers in Human Neuroscience, 8*, 1054. https://doi.org/10.3389/fnhum.2014.01054

Kong, A. P.-H., Law, S.-P., Wat, W. K.-C., & Lai, C. (2015). Co-verbal gestures among speakers with aphasia: Influence of aphasia severity, linguistic and semantic skills, and hemiplegia on gesture employment in oral discourse. *Journal of Communication Disorders, 56*, 88–102. https://doi.org/10.1016/j.jcomdis.2015.06.007

Krauss, R. M., Chen, Y., & Gottesman, R. F. (2000). Lexical gestures and lexical access: A process model. In D. McNeill (Ed.), *Language and gesture* (pp. 261–283). Cambridge University Press.

Kroenke, K.-M., Kraft, I., Regenbrecht, F., & Obrig, H. (2013). Lexical learning in mild aphasia: Gesture benefit depends on patholinguistic profile and lesion pattern. *Cortex, 49*(10), 2637–2649. https://doi.org/10.1016/j.cortex.2013.07.012

Lavergne, J., & Kimura, D. (1987). Hand movement asymmetry during speech: No effect of speaking topic. *Neuropsychologia, 25*(4), 689–693. https://doi.org/10.1016/0028-3932(87)90060-1

Leiguarda, R., Merello, M., Balej, J., Starkstein, S., Nogues, M., & Marsden, C. D. (2000). Disruption of spatial organization and interjoint coordination in Parkinson's disease, progressive supranuclear palsy, and multiple system atrophy. *Movement Disorders, 15*(4), 627–640. https://doi.org/10.1002/1531-8257(200007)15:4<627::AID-MDS1006>3.0.CO;2-5

Leiguarda, R. C., Pramstaller, P. P., Merello, M., Starkstein, S., Lees, A. J., & Marsden, C. D. (1997). Apraxia in Parkinson's disease, progressive supranuclear palsy, multiple system atrophy and neuroleptic-induced parkinsonism. *Brain*, *120*(1), 75–90. https://doi.org/10.1093/brain/120.1.75

Lewis, S. J. G., Cools, R., Robbins, T. W., Dove, A., Barker, R. A., & Owen, A. M. (2003). Using executive heterogeneity to explore the nature of working memory deficits in Parkinson's disease. *Neuropsychologia*, *41*(6), 645–654. https://doi.org/10.1016/s0028-3932(02)00257-9

Lieberman, P., Friedman, J., & Feldman, L. S. (1990). Syntax comprehension deficits in Parkinson's disease. *Journal of Nervous and Mental Disease*, *178*(6), 360–365. https://doi.org/10.1097/00005053-199006000-00003

Livingston, G., Sommerlad, A., Orgeta, V., Costafreda, S. G., Huntley, J., Ames, D., Ballard, C., Banerjee, S., Burns, A., Cohen-Mansfield, J., Cooper, C., Fox, N., Gitlin, L. N., Howard, R., Kales, H. C., Larson, E. B., Ritchie, K., Rockwood, K., Sampson, E. L., ... Mukadam, N. (2017). Dementia prevention, intervention, and care. *The Lancet*, *390*(10113), 2673–2734. https://doi.org/10.1016/S0140-6736(17)31363-6

Martin, A., Wiggs, C. L., Lalonde, F., & Mack, C. (1994). Word retrieval to letter and semantic cues: A double dissociation in normal subjects using interference tasks. *Neuropsychologia*, *32*(12), 1487–1494. https://doi.org/10.1016/0028-3932(94)90120-1

Masson-Carro, I., Goudbeek, M., & Krahmer, E. (2016). Can you handle this? The impact of object affordances on how co-speech gestures are produced. *Language, Cognition and Neuroscience*, *31*(3), 430–440. https://doi.org/10.1080/23273798.2015.1108448

McNamara, P., & Durso, R. (2003). Pragmatic communication skills in patients with Parkinson's disease. *Brain and Language*, *84*(3), 414–423. https://doi.org/10.1016/S0093-934X(02)00558-8

McNeill, D. (1985). So you think gestures are nonverbal? *Psychological Review*, *92*(3), 350–371. https://doi.org/10.1037/0033-295X.92.3.350

McNeill, D. (1992). *Hand and mind: What gestures reveal about thought.* University of Chicago Press.

McNeill, D. (2005). *Gesture and thought.* University of Chicago Press. https://doi.org/10.7208/chicago/9780226514642.001.0001

McNeill, D., Duncan, S. D., Cole, J., Gallagher, S., & Bertenthal, B. (2008). Growth points from the very beginning. *Interaction Studies*, *9*(1), 117–132. https://doi.org/10.1075/is.9.1.09mcn

Mesulam, M.-M. (2001). Primary progressive aphasia. *Annals of Neurology*, *49*(4), 425–432.

Mesulam, M.-M., Grossman, M., Hillis, A., Kertesz, A., & Weintraub, S. (2003). The core and halo of primary progressive aphasia and semantic dementia. *Annals of Neurology*, *54*(Suppl. 5), S11–S14. https://doi.org/10.1002/ana.10569

Mesulam, M.-M., Wieneke, C., Thompson, C., Rogalski, E., & Weintraub, S. (2012). Quantitative classification of primary progressive aphasia at early and mild impairment stages. *Brain*, *135*(5), 1537–1553. https://doi.org/10.1093/brain/aws080

Middleton, F. A., & Strick, P. L. (1994, October 21). Anatomical evidence for cerebellar and basal ganglia involvement in higher cognitive function. *Science*, *266*, 458–461. https://doi.org/10.1126/science.7939688

Mol, L., & Kita, S. (2012). Gesture structure affects syntactic structure in speech. *Proceedings of the Annual Meeting of the Cognitive Science Society*, *34*, 761–766. https://cogsci.mindmodeling.org/2012/papers/0141/paper0141.pdf

Morsella, E., & Krauss, R. M. (1999, October). *Electromyography of arm during the lexical retrieval of abstract and concrete words* [Poster]. Annual Convention of the Society for Psychophysiology, Grenada, Spain.

Morsella, E., & Krauss, R. M. (2004). The role of gestures in spatial working memory and speech. *The American Journal of Psychology*, *117*(3), 411–424. https://doi.org/10.2307/4149008

Mulder, K., & Hulstijn, J. H. (2011). Linguistic skills of adult native speakers, as a function of age and level of education. *Applied Linguistics*, *32*(5), 475–494. https://doi.org/10.1093/applin/amr016

Özer, D., & Göksun, T. (2020a). Gesture use and processing: A review on individual differences in cognitive resources. *Frontiers in Psychology*, *11*, 573555. https://doi.org/10.3389/fpsyg.2020.573555

Özer, D., & Göksun, T. (2020b). Visual–spatial and verbal abilities differentially affect processing of gestural vs. spoken expressions. *Language, Cognition and Neuroscience*, *35*(7), 896–914. https://doi.org/10.1080/23273798.2019.1703016

Özer, D., Göksun, T., & Chatterjee, A. (2019). Differential roles of gestures on spatial language in neurotypical elderly adults and individuals with focal brain injury. *Cognitive Neuropsychology*, *36*(5–6), 282–299. https://doi.org/10.1080/02643294.2019.1618255

Özer, D., Tansan, M., Özer, E. E., Malykhina, K., & Chatterjee, A. (2017). The effects of gesture restriction on spatial language in young and elderly adults. *Proceedings of the Annual Conference of the Cognitive Science Society*, *38*. http://www.tilbegoksunyoruk.com/documents/Ozer2_2017

Özyürek, A. (2014). Hearing and seeing meaning in speech and gesture: Insights from brain and behaviour. *Philosophical Transactions of the Royal Society of London Series B: Biological Sciences*, *369*(1651), 20130296. https://doi.org/10.1098/rstb.2013.0296

Parakh, R., Roy, E., Koo, E., & Black, S. (2004). Pantomime and imitation of limb gestures in relation to the severity of Alzheimer's disease. *Brain and Cognition*, *55*(2), 272–274. https://doi.org/10.1016/j.bandc.2004.02.049

Patterson, K., & MacDonald, M. (2006). Sweet nothings: Narrative speech in semantic dementia. In S. Andrews (Ed.), *From inkmarks to ideas: Current issues in lexical processing* (pp. 299–317). Psychology Press.

Patterson, K., Nestor, P. J., & Rogers, T. T. (2007). Where do you know what you know? The representation of semantic knowledge in the human brain. *Nature Reviews Neuroscience*, *8*(12), 976–987. https://doi.org/10.1038/nrn2277

Pell, M. D., Cheang, H. S., & Leonard, C. L. (2006). The impact of Parkinson's disease on vocal-prosodic communication from the perspective of listeners. *Brain and Language*, *97*(2), 123–134. https://doi.org/10.1016/j.bandl.2005.08.010

Pell, M. D., & Monetta, L. (2008). How Parkinson's disease affects non-verbal communication and language processing. *Language and Linguistics Compass*, *2*(5), 739–759. https://doi.org/10.1111/j.1749-818X.2008.00074.x

Perry, R. J., & Hodges, J. R. (1999). Attention and executive deficits in Alzheimer's disease: A critical review. *Brain*, *122*(3), 383–404. https://doi.org/10.1093/brain/122.3.383

Peters, R. (2006). Ageing and the brain. *Postgraduate Medical Journal*, *82*(964), 84–88. https://doi.org/10.1136/pgmj.2005.036665

Ping, R., & Goldin-Meadow, S. (2010). Gesturing saves cognitive resources when talking about nonpresent objects. *Cognitive Science*, *34*(4), 602–619. https://doi.org/10.1111/j.1551-6709.2010.01102.x

Pitcairn, T. K., Clemie, S., Gray, J. M., & Pentland, B. (1990). Impressions of Parkinsonian patients from their recorded voices. *International Journal of Language & Communication Disorders*, *25*(1), 85–92. https://doi.org/10.3109/13682829009011965

Pouw, W. T. J. L., Myrto-Foteini, M., van Gog, T., & Paas, F. (2016). Gesturing during mental problem solving reduces eye movements, especially for individuals with lower visual working memory capacity. *Cognitive Processing, 17*(3), 269–277. https://doi.org/10.1007/s10339-016-0757-6

Pritchard, M., Dipper, L., Morgan, G., & Cocks, N. (2015). Language and iconic gesture use in procedural discourse by speakers with aphasia. *Aphasiology, 29*(7), 826–844. https://doi.org/10.1080/02687038.2014.993912

Rauscher, F. H., Krauss, R. M., & Chen, Y. (1996). Gesture, speech, and lexical access: The role of lexical movements in speech production. *Psychological Science, 7*(4), 226–231. https://doi.org/10.1111/j.1467-9280.1996.tb00364.x

Rose, M. L. (2006). The utility of arm and hand gestures in the treatment of aphasia. *Advances in Speech Language Pathology, 8*(2), 92–109. https://doi.org/10.1080/14417040600657948

Rose, M. L., Raymer, A. M., Lanyon, L. E., & Attard, M. C. (2013). A systematic review of gesture treatments for post-stroke aphasia. *Aphasiology, 27*(9), 1090–1127. https://doi.org/10.1080/02687038.2013.805726

Rousseaux, M., Rénier, J., Anicet, L., Pasquier, F., & Mackowiak-Cordoliani, M. A. (2012). Gesture comprehension, knowledge and production in Alzheimer's disease. *European Journal of Neurology, 19*(7), 1037–1044. https://doi.org/10.1111/j.1468-1331.2012.03674.x

Schubotz, L. M. R., Holler, J., Drijvers, L., & Özyürek, A. (2020). Aging and working memory modulate the ability to benefit from visible speech and iconic gestures during speech-in-noise comprehension. *Psychological Research*. Advance online publication.

Schubotz, L. M. R., Holler, J., & Özyürek, A. (2019). Age-related differences in multimodal recipient design: Younger but not older adults adapt speech and co-speech gestures to common ground. *Language, Cognition, and Neuroscience, 34*(2), 254–271. https://doi.org/10.1080/23273798.2018.1527377

Seidl, U., Lueken, U., Thomann, P. A., Kruse, A., & Schröder, J. (2012). Facial expression in Alzheimer's disease: Impact of cognitive deficits and neuropsychiatric symptoms. *American Journal of Alzheimer's Disease & Other Dementias, 27*(2), 100–106. https://doi.org/10.1177/1533317512440495

Sekine, K., & Rose, M. L. (2013). The relationship of aphasia type and gesture production in people with aphasia. *American Journal of Speech-Language Pathology, 22*(4), 662–672. https://doi.org/10.1044/1058-0360(2013/12-0030)

Sharpe, M. H., Cermak, S. A., & Sax, D. S. (1983). Motor planning in Parkinson patients. *Neuropsychologia, 21*(5), 455–462. https://doi.org/10.1016/0028-3932(83)90002-7

Signorini, M., & Volpato, C. (2006). Action fluency in Parkinson's disease: A follow-up study. *Movement Disorders, 21*(4), 467–472. https://doi.org/10.1002/mds.20718

Silveri, M. C., & Ciccarelli, N. (2009). Semantic memory in object use. *Neuropsychologia, 47*(12), 2634–2641. https://doi.org/10.1016/j.neuropsychologia.2009.05.013

Smithson, L., & Nicoladis, E. (2013). Verbal memory resources predict iconic gesture use among monolinguals and bilinguals. *Bilingualism: Language and Cognition, 16*(4), 934–944. https://doi.org/10.1017/S1366728913000175

Theocharopoulou, F., Cocks, N., Pring, T., & Dipper, L. T. (2015). TOT phenomena: Gesture production in younger and older adults. *Psychology and Aging, 30*(2), 245–252. https://doi.org/10.1037/a0038913

Thompson, L. A. (1995). Encoding and memory for visible speech and gestures: A comparison between young and older adults. *Psychology and Aging, 10*(2), 215–228. https://doi.org/10.1037/0882-7974.10.2.215

Thompson, L. A., & Guzman, F. A. (1999). Some limits on encoding visible speech and gestures using a dichotic shadowing task. *Journals of Gerontology Series B: Psychological Sciences and Social Sciences*, *54B*(6), P347–P349. https://doi.org/10.1093/geronb/54B.6.P347

Tomer, R., & Levin, B. E. (1993). Differential effects of aging on two verbal fluency tasks. *Perceptual & Motor Skills*, *76*(2), 465–466. https://doi.org/10.2466/pms.1993.76.2.465

Trafton, J. G., Trickett, S. B., Stitzlein, C. A., Saner, L., Schunn, C. D., & Kirschenbaum, S. S. (2006). The relationship between spatial transformations and iconic gestures. *Spatial Cognition and Computation*, *6*(1), 1–29. https://doi.org/10.1207/s15427633scc0601_1

Troyer, A. K., Moscovitch, M., & Winocur, G. (1997). Clustering and switching as two components of verbal fluency: Evidence from younger and older healthy adults. *Neuropsychology*, *11*(1), 138–146. https://doi.org/10.1037/0894-4105.11.1.138

Ullman, M. T., Corkin, S., Coppola, M., Hickok, G., Growdon, J. H., Koroshetz, W. J., & Pinker, S. (1997). A neural dissociation within language: Evidence that the mental dictionary is part of declarative memory, and that grammatical rules are processed by the procedural system. *Journal of Cognitive Neuroscience*, *9*(2), 266–276. https://doi.org/10.1162/jocn.1997.9.2.266

Wagner, S. M., Nusbaum, H., & Goldin-Meadow, S. (2004). Probing the mental representation of gesture: Is handwaving spatial? *Journal of Memory and Language*, *50*(4), 395–407. https://doi.org/10.1016/j.jml.2004.01.002

Wesp, R., Hesse, J., Keutmann, D., & Wheaton, K. (2001). Gestures maintain spatial imagery. *The American Journal of Psychology*, *114*(4), 591–600. https://doi.org/10.2307/1423612

Wilkinson, R. (2013). Gestural depiction in acquired language disorders: On the form and use of iconic gestures in aphasic talk-in-interaction. *Augmentative and Alternative Communication*, *29*(1), 68–82. https://doi.org/10.3109/07434618.2013.767558

World Health Organization. (2004). *International statistical classification of diseases and related health problems* (Vol. 1).

Wu, Y. C., & Coulson, S. (2014). Co-speech iconic gestures and visuo-spatial working memory. *Acta Psychologica*, *153*, 39–50. https://doi.org/10.1016/j.actpsy.2014.09.002

Yesavage, J. A., Brooks, J. O., III, Taylor, J., & Tinklenberg, J. (1993). Development of aphasia, apraxia, and agnosia and decline in Alzheimer's disease. *The American Journal of Psychiatry*, *150*(5), 742–747. https://doi.org/10.1176/ajp.150.5.742

Zaidel, E., Kasher, A., Soroker, N., Batori, G., Giora, R., & Graves, D. (2000). Hemispheric contributions to pragmatics. *Brain and Cognition*, *43*(1–3), 438–443.

V Gesture With More Than One Language

Elena Nicoladis and Lisa Smithson
12 Gesture in Bilingual Language Acquisition

Co-speech gesture use can be influenced by both cognitive factors (e.g., proficiency in a language, cognitive resources) and cultural factors (e.g., as high–gesture-frequency cultures). Both of these sets of factors could affect gesture use among bilinguals. For the purposes of this chapter, we use "bilingual" to refer to any person who has fluency in two languages, even if they are not highly proficient in one of them. Bilinguals differ from monolinguals on both cognitive factors and cultural factors, in ways that could be related to gesture use.

Bilinguals differ from monolinguals (and from each other) on some cognitive factors, in particular, language proficiency and cognitive resources. Both of bilinguals' languages are continually active and accessible (Chee, 2006; Crinion et al., 2006; Kroll et al., 2006). Bilinguals must therefore inhibit the activation of one language in order to speak the other. The necessity of inhibition may be part of the reason that bilinguals have a harder time accessing words for speaking than monolinguals (Gollan & Acenas, 2004; Yan & Nicoladis, 2009). Gestures could play an important role in bilinguals' language access, in particular when their proficiency in the target language is weak.

One function of gestures is to lighten the load on working memory (Cook et al., 2012). Working memory is the dedicated system thought to underlie the processes responsible for thinking, speaking, and problem solving (Baddeley, 2003). Some components of working memory involve the ability to merely store and retrieve information as presented; other components are inextricably linked with executive functions (Baddeley, 2003). Krauss et al. (2000) laid out an explicit framework for the relationship between working memory and gesture production. They argued that information contained in long-term memory can be encoded in different representational formats. For example, for the word "house," a person may have numerous visual and verbal representations of this concept. According to Krauss et al., when one of these representational formats is activated in working memory, this can activate related concepts in other representational formats. When thinking about the visual layout of one's home, this could activate the verbal representations of "house" or "home." Relying on this framework, the activation of visuospatial working memory (e.g., the imagistic representations of house) tends to give rise to gesture production, and the activation of verbal working memory (e.g., the lexical representations of house) tends to give rise to speech articulation. According to this perspective, *representational gestures*—gestures that represent the referent through shape or movement—can facilitate speech production by cross-modally priming the lexical affiliate during the formulation of speech (Krauss et al., 2000). Difficulties in activating the relevant linguistic representations in verbal working memory would then be mitigated through the use of gesture production. In other words, gestures may serve a critical compensatory role in speech production (Chawla & Krauss, 1994; Frick-Horbury & Guttentag, 1998; Hostetter & Alibali, 2007; Iverson & Braddock, 2011; Melinger & Kita, 2007; Rauscher et al., 1996). In support of this claim, Hostetter and Alibali (2007) found that people with weaker verbal skills and stronger spatial skills tended to be the ones who use the most gestures. Further evidence comes from a study showing that the resolution of tip-of-the-tongue states is more likely when gesture is allowed in comparison to when it is restricted (Frick-Horbury & Guttentag, 1998).

Bilinguals can sometimes be characterized as having weaker verbal skills and stronger spatial skills than monolinguals. Bilinguals often have smaller receptive and expressive vocabularies than monolinguals in one or both of their languages (Gross et al., 2014; see the review in Bialystok, 2009) and a harder time accessing particular words than monolinguals (Gollan & Acenas, 2004; Yan & Nicoladis, 2009). For example, Gollan and Acenas (2004) showed that bilinguals experience more tip-of-the-tongue states than monolinguals. As for visuospatial skills, bilinguals are thought to rely heavily on imagistic encoding in order to speak about the same topics in both their languages (Paivio et al., 1988). Some studies have found that bilinguals outperform monolinguals on some measures of visuospatial working memory (Blom et al., 2014; McLeay, 2003). Given their weaker verbal skills and stronger visuospatial skills, bilinguals might use more gestures than monolinguals. The gestures might help with lexical access.

In addition to using gestures differently from monolinguals, bilinguals might also show differences across languages in gesture use. Bilinguals often speak one language better than the other (Silva-Corvalán & Treffers-Daller, 2016). They might therefore use gestures differently in their dominant and nondominant languages. Given the role of gestures in aiding lexical access (Krauss et al., 2000), bilinguals might gesture more in their nondominant language than in their dominant language (Nicoladis, 2007). A further rationale for this prediction comes from research on visuospatial skills. During the early stages of second-language acquisition, learners may be particularly highly dependent on visuospatial skills (Leonard et al., 2010). Because beginning second-language learners would necessarily be weak on verbal skills in that language, they might gesture more in their second (and weaker) language relative to their first language. Alternatively, given the role of gestures in constructing messages for speech (Kita, 2000), bilinguals might attempt to construct more complex messages in their dominant language and therefore gesture more in their dominant language than in their nondominant language (Gullberg, 1998).

Cultural factors might also affect bilinguals' use of gestures. Through each of their languages, bilinguals often have access to two different cultures. There are differences between cultures in the production of gestures (Efron, 1972; Kita, 2009; Sekine et al., 2015). For example, a single thumb held up by an American English speaker might mean "Okay" or "Good," while a single thumb held up in Germany might mean the number 1 (Pika et al., 2009). Furthermore, some studies have found cultural differences in the frequency of gesture production (So, 2010).

Bilinguals can differentiate their languages in terms of phonology, lexicon, morphology, syntax, and appropriate contexts for use from very early in development (Genesee & Nicoladis, 2007; Quay & Montanari, 2016), so it is possible that they might also differentiate their languages with regard to culturally specific gestures as well. However, bilinguals do not necessarily use their languages independently (Paradis & Genesee, 1996). In other words, bilinguals show differences from monolinguals in their language use in both languages. In fact, bilinguals often try to enhance the similarities between their two languages (Bullock & Toribio, 2004; Hartsuiker, 2013), such as by choosing linguistic constructions that are most similar in their two languages (Toribio, 2004). This phenomenon is called *convergence* (Bullock & Toribio, 2004). Bilinguals may have little motivation to differentiate their gesture use in their two languages, either in terms of the particular gestures used or in terms of frequency of gestures. Gestures most often accompany speech (McNeill, 1992), and so the speech alone can communicate the most important aspects of a message bilinguals wish to communicate. Furthermore, some kinds of gestures might also be understood in many cultures (Church et al., 2004). One could therefore predict that bilinguals will generally show convergence, rather than differentiation, in their gesture use.

In this chapter, we review the evidence for three questions: (a) Do bilinguals show differences from monolinguals in their gesture production? (b) Do bilinguals gesture differently in their nondominant language than their dominant language? and (c) Do bilinguals show differentiation or convergence in their gesture use?

12.1 Gesture Production: Bilinguals Versus Monolinguals

Some research has shown that people with weaker verbal skills and stronger spatial skills produce the most gestures (Hostetter & Alibali, 2007; cf. Chu & Kita, 2011). Bilinguals can often be described as having weaker verbal skills (Bialystok, 2009) and stronger spatial skills than monolinguals (e.g., Blom et al., 2014). Bilinguals might therefore gesture more than monolinguals in order to compensate for their weaker verbal skills.

Some studies have found that, indeed, bilinguals gesture more than monolinguals when telling a story. For example, Pika et al. (2006) found that English–Spanish and French–English bilinguals produced significantly more gestures than English monolinguals in a narrative task. Similarly, enhanced gesture use was found in comparisons of French–English bilingual children between 4 and 6 years of age with both English and French monolingual children (Nicoladis et al., 2009) and in comparisons of French–English bilingual children between 7 and 10 years of age with English monolinguals (Smithson, Nicoladis, & Marentette, 2011). These results are consistent with the argument that bilinguals may be more strongly reliant on gesture production than monolinguals in order to facilitate speech. It is important to note that these studies relied on purely quantitative analyses and did not explore the linguistic context in which the gestures were produced. Studies showing that bilinguals produce gestures more during word finding difficulties than monolinguals would help strengthen this argument.

Not all studies have shown that bilinguals gesture more than monolinguals. For example, Smithson et al. (2011) found that Chinese–English bilingual children did not differ from English monolinguals in their use of gestures. Furthermore, they found that the Chinese–English bilinguals gestured significantly less than French–English bilinguals. Similarly, one study showed that adult French–English bilinguals did not gesture more than English monolinguals (Smithson & Nicoladis, 2013). Yet another study with adults also showed no effect of bilingualism (Cavicchio & Kita, 2013). In this study, Italian–English bilinguals were asked to tell a story in both of their languages and their gesture use was compared with that of both Italian and English monolinguals. The Italian monolinguals gestured more than the English monolinguals, and the bilinguals gestured more in Italian than in English, corresponding to the monolinguals in each language. These results suggest that bilingualism alone may not lead to a high use of gestures.

Given the lack of consistency with regard to comparing monolinguals and bilinguals, some researchers have turned to an exploration of how cognitive resources might be related to gesture use in both monolinguals and bilinguals. With respect to verbal working memory, bilinguals may experience greater strain on these resources given that both of their languages are continually activated. Smithson and Nicoladis (2013) found that verbal memory was a significant predictor of representational gesture production both among monolinguals and bilinguals (with participants with lower verbal memory scores tending to produce higher rates of representational gestures). There were, however, no differences between the two groups on verbal working memory scores. So, one possible reason for the inconsistent results across bilinguals is that researchers have not controlled for the participants' verbal working memory capacity. Many studies have shown that bilinguals score lower than monolinguals on verbal memory measures (Barbosa et al., 2017; Gutiérrez-Clellen et al., 2004); however, some have shown no differences between bilinguals and monolinguals on verbal memory measures (Engel de Abreu, 2011). Thus, it is possible that there is variability in whether bilinguals gesture more than monolinguals because there is variability in whether bilinguals differ from monolinguals on measures of verbal working memory capacity.

In summary, because bilinguals have lower proficiency in each language relative to monolinguals and have a higher cognitive load due to their experience accessing and switching between languages, bilinguals might gesture more than monolinguals. Research has not, however, consistently supported that prediction. One possible reason for these inconsistent results is that individual differences in cognitive resources might outweigh differences between groups of language speakers. If so, then bilinguals' gesture use might be related to their proficiency in each of their languages. We now consider the evidence for that hypothesis.

12.2 Gesture Production and Language Proficiency

Because bilinguals often use their two languages with different people, in different contexts, for differing amounts of time, and for different purposes, they often speak one language better than the other (Silva-Corvalán & Treffers-Daller, 2016). Because gestures can play a compensatory role when verbal skills are weak (Hostetter & Alibali, 2007), one might predict that those who are less proficient in a language may gesture to a greater extent. This may be particularly the case when they are speaking in their weaker language (Krauss & Hadar, 1999). In favor of this argument, one study found that English–Mandarin bilingual children could express the distinction between new and old referents in discourse by using language alone in their dominant language (So et al., 2014). However, when speaking their nondominant language, the bilingual children used gestures to help make the distinction. The researchers argued that the children used gestures to communicate an important distinction that they did not yet know how to do with language in their nondominant language. Further evidence in favor of this argument comes from a case study of a French–Italian bilingual child followed longitudinally from 1;5 [years;months] to 3;5 (Benazzo & Morgenstern, 2014). When this child first started to speak, he produced a lot of code-mixed utterances and expressed negation nonverbally (e.g., shaking his head or shrugging his shoulders). As the child grew older, the nonverbal expressions of negation diminished, and he expressed negation primarily verbally. The authors concluded that nonverbal communication played a compensatory role for this child during a phase when his ability to express negation verbally was weak.

With regard to frequency of representational gesture use, do bilinguals gesture more in their weaker language than their stronger language? The answer has been inconsistent across studies. Some studies have found that, as predicted, bilinguals tend to gesture more when speaking in their weaker language than their stronger language (Nagpal et al., 2011; Nicoladis, 2007; Nicoladis et al., 2007). However, other studies have found greater gesture use when bilinguals are speaking their stronger language (Gullberg, 1998; Nicoladis et al., 1999), and still others have found no difference in gesture rate across both languages (Laurent & Nicoladis, 2015; Marcos, 1979; Sherman & Nicoladis, 2004). One study showed no correlation between measures of language proficiency and gesture frequency in bilingual adults (Nagpal et al., 2011).

Another possible way in which bilinguals might use gestures differently from one another is in terms of the kind of gestures. *Representational gestures* are those that have a physical resemblance to the referent (e.g., miming the action of throwing to mean throwing). Representational gestures have shown a particularly strong connection to visuospatial encoding for speaking (Hostetter & Alibali, 2008). *Nonrepresentational gestures* (e.g., pointing) are likely less connected to proficiency because children can start producing them even before they speak (Butterworth & Morissette, 1996). Nicoladis (2002) showed that French–English bilingual children used more representational gestures as their proficiency in a language increased (similar to Nicoladis et al., 1999), but nonrepresentational gestures showed no relationship whatsoever with proficiency. Most of the children's nonrepresentational gestures in that study were points. As for representational gestures, Nicoladis argued that they could have been associated with proficiency because they could fill in for word-finding difficulties. For example, one child said, "No, no I'll do that" (p. 262) while gesturing the action of attaching a pretend seatbelt. In this instance, the gesture could have specified the meaning of "that." However, not all studies have found similar results. For example, Nicoladis et al. (2007) found that Chinese–English bilinguals used both more representational and more nonrepresentational gestures in their second language than their first. Thus, it seems unlikely that the inconsistent results across studies relative to bilinguals and proficiency are due only to the kind of gesture under study. Other factors may be at play. For example, it may be that across proficiency levels of their languages, people may be investing differential degrees of motivation or may experience differential degrees of enjoyment and comfort with the task. In addition, content analyses of speech are required to examine differences in narrative quality produced in both languages to further understand how gestures relate to proficiency among bilinguals.

One study of narrative development in French–English bilingual children raised some further doubts about the relationship between proficiency and representational gesture use (Laurent et al., 2015). Storytelling is a challenging task and develops considerably between the ages of 4 and 10 years. If gestures are related to proficiency in bilingual children, they might gesture more when they are younger, to compensate for their weak ability to tell a story. In fact, Laurent et al. (2015) showed that bilingual children's storytelling developed between the ages of 4 and 10 in both of their languages, but the children's gesture production was related neither to their age nor to their storytelling ability. These results suggest that gesture use might be relatively independent of proficiency.

Even further evidence for doubting the link between proficiency and gesture use comes from a study on gesture restriction. Among monolinguals, gesture restriction has been found to result in an increase in speech disfluencies (Graham & Heywood, 1975; Rauscher et al., 1996), suggesting that gesture restriction interferes with verbal working memory. Laurent and Nicoladis (2015) restricted the gestures of French–English bilingual adults living in an English-majority-language part of Canada. The bilinguals were relatively balanced in the proficiency of their two languages. If gesture restriction interfered with verbal memory access, then the bilinguals should have shown language-access difficulties in both of their languages. Indeed, the bilinguals told shorter stories with fewer different types of words. However, these results were observed only in French.

One possible reason that gesture restriction affected only the bilinguals' French was that they were living in an English–majority-language part of Canada and did not necessarily have to use French on a day-to-day basis. Recall that gestures can sometimes be used to help access words (Krauss & Hadar, 1999). A follow-up study in the same region of Canada found some support for this interpretation (Aziz & Nicoladis, 2018). In this study, measures of proficiency in French and English showed no relationship with gesture production; however, English–French bilinguals, those who had learned French after learning English, showed significantly greater use of representational gestures in French than in English. The English–French bilinguals did not necessarily use French every day. These results are consistent with the argument that people use more gestures when lexical access is difficult (Krauss & Hadar, 1999).

In sum, although some studies have shown that bilinguals gesture more in their less proficient language, other studies have shown the reverse. Although the studies have not necessarily been consistent with what is meant by bilingualism, there is nonetheless growing evidence gathered by using different methods that proficiency and gesture use are not consistently related to each other. To date, there are more promising results with everyday usage of the two languages; that is, when speaking a language they do not use every day, bilinguals may use a lot of gestures in order to help access words or other linguistic constructions. The studies carried out thus far have relied only on quantitative analyses. Future studies could complement these studies by analyzing when bilinguals produce their gestures (e.g., perhaps in particular during word-finding difficulties).

12.3 Culture and the Gestures of Bilinguals

As we have noted, bilinguals can differentiate their languages from very early in development (Quay & Montanari, 2016), but they also often show convergence between their two languages (Bullock & Toribio, 2004). Do bilinguals differentiate gestures in their two languages, or do they show convergence? In order for bilinguals to be able to demonstrate gestural differentiation by language, there would have to be differences in gesture use among monolingual speakers, and indeed, there are differences among monolinguals in terms of conventional gestures, which aspects of motion events gestures encode, and gesture frequency (see Kita, 2009, for a review of cultural differences in gesture use).

The term "conventional gestures" refers to gestures used among members of a particular cultural group (Guidetti, 2002; Poortinga et al., 1993); for example, forming a "T" with two hands in North America indicates a desire for a time out or a break in the current line of discourse. Because they are known within a cultural group, conventional gestures can often be understood even without accompanying speech

(Guidetti, 2005). Number gestures are conventional gestures that indicate quantity. Monolinguals who speak different languages use different configurations of fingers to indicate quantities. Pika et al. (2009) found that German speakers in Germany used different finger configurations (e.g., a thumb and an index finger held up to indicate "2") than English- and French-speaking Canadians (who were likely to hold up an index finger and a middle finger to indicate "2"). Children use conventional number gestures appropriately early in development, from at least as young as 2 years of age (Nicoladis, Marentette, Pika, & Barbosa, 2018; Nicoladis et al., 2010).

Can bilinguals differentiate the use of conventional gestures between languages? Although we know of no study that has directly addressed that question with either children or adults, it is possible to elicit some hints from existing research as to the answer. One study elicited number gestures from three groups of preschool bilingual children living in Canada (French–English, German–English, and Mandarin–English bilinguals) and reported no difference by the language used to elicit number gestures (Nicoladis, Marentette, & Pika, 2018). This could mean that the children were showing convergence in their number gestures; however, the researchers did not systematically vary the language used to elicit number gestures. Another study showed that about half the conventional gestures produced by French–Romanian bilingual children corresponded to the appropriate language, and about one quarter corresponded to the inappropriate language (Garitte & Olteanu, 2013). These researchers did not, however, report how often the bilingual children produced both similar-meaning gestures appropriately for the target language. Nonetheless, these results suggest that bilingual children may be able to differentiate the conventional gestures associated with each language/culture while still exhibiting some degree of convergence. It would be interesting to know if older bilinguals also show this same pattern of mostly differentiating with some degree of convergence. At the moment, we do not know if this is a temporary phase in development or whether this pattern is characteristic of bilinguals of all ages.

Most studies on bilinguals' differentiation and/or convergence have focused on representational gestures rather than conventional gestures. Recall that representational gestures depict some aspect of the meaning of the referent in their form and/or their movement. One domain in which bilinguals might use representational gestures differentially in their two languages is in the encoding of motion events. Given that gestures can represent simulated action (Hostetter & Alibali, 2008), it is not surprising that speakers produce gestures when talking about how figures move against a ground (e.g., "She ran into the room"). These motion events are lexicalized differently by speakers of different languages (Talmy, 2000). For example, speakers of satellite-framed languages (e.g., English or German) tend to encode the manner of motion (e.g., "running," "hopping," "rolling") in the main verb and the path of motion in a satellite (e.g., "in," "out," "up"). In gesturing about motion events, speakers of satellite-framed languages often produce gestures that encode both the manner and path of motion (e.g., "rolling down") simultaneously (Kita & Özyürek, 2003). In contrast, speakers of verb-framed languages (e.g., French or Turkish or Japanese) tend to encode the path of motion as the main verb, and manner is optionally encoded as a dependent clause. The gestures of speakers of verb-framed languages tend to encode the path of motion; if manner of motion is encoded it is performed with a gesture separate from the path gesture (Kita & Özyürek, 2003). Monolingual children do not show the language-specific gesture patterns at 3 and 5 years of age, tending to gesture primarily about path (Özyürek et al., 2008). It is only at about age 9 years that the language-specific patterns in gestures begin to emerge (Özyürek et al., 2008).

Do bilinguals gesture differently in each of their languages when speaking about motion? Preschool French English bilingual children produce primarily gestures about path in both languages (Nicoladis & Brisard, 2002). For example, one child said, "You can fly like that" (Nicoladis & Brisard, 2002, p. 63) while moving his hand upward to show the path his LEGO® construction was going to take. Another child said, "Il vole!" [He flies] (Nicoladis & Brisard, 2002, p. 63) while moving his hand to indicate the path a toy superhero had taken. The children's high use of path gestures does not necessarily mean that bilinguals cannot differentiate between the gestures of motion events in their two languages, because even monolingual children of this age do not show signs of producing language-specific patterns in their gestures. Another study examined French–English bilingual children at ages 4 to 6 years on the one hand and 8 to 10 years on the other (Miller et al., 2018). The children showed evidence of using the language-specific motion event lexicalization in their speech, but not in their gestures. In English, the children used a lot of different manner verbs, whereas in French they used a lot of different path verbs. The children primarily encoded the path of movement in their gestures, regardless of the language they were speaking and even when they were speaking about the manner of motion alone. For example, one child said, "He ran" and gestured the path of motion off to one side (Miller et al., 2018, p. 82). Even adult bilinguals tend to produce the same pattern of gesture use in both of their languages (Brown, 2015; Özçalışkan, 2016). Taken together, these results suggest that bilinguals show convergence in their gesture use in their two languages when speaking about motion events.

What about gesture frequency? Some researchers have argued that Romance languages (e.g., Italian, French) are spoken with more gestures than Germanic languages (e.g., English, German), which are in turn spoken with more gestures than East Asian (e.g., Japanese, Korean) languages (Cavicchio & Kita, 2013; Sekine et al., 2015; So, 2010). Note that not all studies have supported this claim: Research has found no difference between monolingual speakers of Canadian English and Canadian French, either children (Nicoladis et al., 2009) or adults (Nicoladis & O'Carroll, 2012). Naturally, these studies do not cover all the possible cross-cultural comparisons that could be made, so future research needs to test this claim.

To the extent that there are differences between languages in gesture frequency among monolinguals, bilinguals might show differences in gesture frequency depending on which language they are speaking and, in fact, some research has supported that prediction. Cavicchio and Kita (2013) showed that both Italian monolinguals and Italian–English bilinguals gestured more when speaking Italian than English monolinguals or the bilinguals speaking in English. Another study conducted with children also showed results consistent with this prediction: Mandarin–English bilingual children were found to gesture at a rate equivalent to that of English monolinguals when telling a story in English, but less than French–English bilinguals (Smithson et al., 2011). However, other studies have not supported this prediction. Two studies have shown that French–English bilinguals gestured more than monolinguals in both languages, both for children (Nicoladis et al., 2009) and for adults (Nicoladis & O'Carroll, 2012). Yet another study showed that Mandarin–English bilingual adults gestured more than monolinguals in Mandarin but at a frequency equivalent to that of monolinguals in English (So, 2010). Thus, the results across studies do not consistently support the prediction that bilinguals will differentiate their languages in terms of gesture frequency. In contrast, one study showed that bilinguals' gesture frequency was highly correlated across languages (Nagpal et al., 2011). In other words, individual bilinguals who gesture a lot in one language tend to gesture a lot in another language.

One possible reason for the variable findings with regard to gesture frequency is that the effect of culture on gesture use may not be direct. Nicoladis, Nagpal, et al. (2018) found evidence for an indirect effect of language (or culture) on gesture use: There are cultural differences in the style of storytelling that people adopt and therefore how frequently they gesture. Culture differences in style of storytelling among Greek and American English monolinguals were observed by Tannen (1980). Tannen asked her participants to watch a movie and tell her the story of what happened. She found that English-speaking storytellers tended to tell the events factually, focusing on what had happened and how it happened. Their stories tended to be long. In contrast, Greek storytellers tended to focus not only on what happened but also why it happened. They provided commentary on their own feelings with regard to the story and inferred the feelings of characters. Their stories were relatively shorter.

Nicoladis, Nagpal, et al. (2018) argued that the chronicle style of storytelling (as used by the English speakers in Tannen's [1980] study) might lead to a high use of gestures. Because this style of storytelling focuses on what happened and how it happened, it is a highly imagistic style. An example from their study of a Canadian French speaker using a chronicle style is presented here; the specific, imagistic actions were formatted in boldface text by the authors:

> She is in the process of installing a clock. So <u>we see her</u> in the process of **hammering** on the wall to install it with um, in the process of setting it, we suppose. She **pulls** on the cord so we . . . yeah, I say, she to, um, we suppose that she is setting her clock. She **gets in** her bed. She **lies down**. So, <u>we see</u> [her], **turning and turning** some more, the hours passing. And then, just at the moment that the clock **begins to ring**, <u>we see</u> that there is a kind of of bird, that **comes out and sings**. The Pink Panther, the first thing she does is that she **turns around** and she uh **hits** the the table that is next (to her). She **breaks** it into a thousand pieces. (Nicoladis, Nagpal, et al., 2018, pp. 653–654)

Representational gestures may serve an important functional role of sustaining the activation of imagistic representations (Chu & Kita, 2011; Morsella & Krauss, 2004; Smithson & Nicoladis, 2014; Wesp et al., 2001). In contrast, the evaluative style (as used by the Greek speakers in Tannen's [1980] study) might lead to a low use of representational gestures because relatively more time is spent on evaluating feelings and motivations, concepts that are likely to have little imagistic content. An example from Nicoladis, Nagpal, et al. (2018) of an evaluative style is shown in the following excerpt. Again, the specific actions are in boldface type. The authors put in small caps the moral of the story.

> He was sleeping. It seemed that it was not morning. Probably, look, I don't know maybe it seemed that it was not morning [but] the alarm clock **was ringing**. He was very much *surprised*. So, later he **put** the bird on the bed to sleep together with him. I just think maybe THIS STORY EXPRESSES THE IDEA THAT LOST THINGS WOULD BE CONSIDERED TO BE BETTER. IF IT IS NOT LOST, MAYBE ONE WOULD FEEL IT WAS DISGUSTING BEFORE ONE WOULD TREASURE IT. (Nicoladis, Nagpal, et al., 2018, p. 655)

Nicoladis, Nagpal, et al. (2018) hypothesized that speakers adopting more of a chronicle style, as in the first block quote, would gesture more than those adopting more of an evaluative style, as in the second block quote, just presented. Some previous research supports this hypothesis. Kunene Nicolas et al. (2017) reported that Zulu speakers told longer stories (recall that the chronicle style is associated with longer stories) and produced more gestures while telling stories than French speakers. These researchers did not analyze their participants' storytelling style directly.

To examine whether storytelling style corresponds to representational gesture use, Nicoladis, Nagpal, et al. (2018) studied adult bilinguals who spoke English as a second language and one of the following four languages: Spanish, French, Mandarin Chinese, or Hindi. The bilinguals were asked to tell a story in both of their languages. Although the bilinguals did use significantly more gestures in their second language than in their first, the differences were small. There were much larger differences by language background: The Spanish and French speakers gestured more than the Mandarin and Hindi speakers. This difference corresponded to the storytelling style adopted by the participants. The Romance language speakers tended to use a chronicle style in telling their story, that is, longer stories with little evaluation. In contrast, the speakers of the Asian languages tended to use an evaluative style in their story, characterized by focusing on why the events had happened and what could be learned from the story. All of the participants adopted the same storytelling style in both of their languages.

These results are intriguing because they suggest that it may not so much be gesture frequency that differs by culture but rather discourse style that differs by culture, and gesture frequency depends on discourse style. The prediction follows that when bilinguals adopt the discourse style of two different cultures, they will show differences in gesture frequency. When they show convergence in their style, they will gesture at the same frequency in both of their languages. Future research can test that possibility.

The link between gesture frequency and discourse style was shown in bilingual adults. We do not know if these results will generalize to children who are still developing the ability to tell a story. Monolingual children as young as age 6 years show cultural differences in storytelling (Wang & Leichtman, 2000). We can therefore predict that it is by the age of 6 years that storytelling style mediates gesture use in bilinguals. We know of no study that has tested this prediction; however, one study showed that the gesture use of bilingual children between ages 7 and 10 years corresponded to this prediction: Mandarin–English bilingual children were found to gesture less often than French–English bilinguals (Smithson et al., 2011). This study did not, however, assess the children's storytelling style.

In sum, some preliminary evidence suggests that bilingual children can differentiate their conventional gestures by language (although they still show some signs of convergence, that is, using the same gesture in both languages; e.g., Garitte & Olteanu, 2013). In contrast, with regard to representational gestures conveying motion events and gesture frequency, bilinguals tend to show convergence, just as they do in many aspects of language use (Bullock & Toribio, 2004). These results are surprising because monolinguals can show differences between languages in gestures conveying motion events and gesture frequency (Cavicchio & Kita, 2013).

12.4 Summary and Discussion

In this chapter, we have considered how cognitive factors and cultural factors might affect bilinguals' gesture use. In terms of cognitive factors, we explored the possibility that bilinguals might use gestures to compensate for weak verbal skills by relying on visuospatial skills (and therefore gestures). Monolinguals gesture more when they have strong visuospatial skills and weak verbal skills (Hostetter & Alibali, 2007). Bilinguals are often characterized as having strong visuospatial skills and weak verbal skills in at least one language. It therefore follows that bilinguals should gesture more than monolinguals and gesture more in their weaker language than in the stronger language.

We did not see consistent support for either one of these predictions. Some studies found that, indeed, bilinguals gestured more than monolinguals, but other studies did not. Furthermore, research has not consistently found that the frequency of gesture use is related to bilinguals' proficiency. For example, some studies have found, as predicted, that bilinguals gesture more in their weaker language but other studies have not. Taken together, these results suggest that proficiency may simply not be the relevant variable to predict how frequently bilinguals gesture.

Proficiency—how well bilinguals know each language—is a multidimensional and complex construct (Silva-Corvalán & Treffers-Daller, 2016). One recent study showed that it may not be so much proficiency but day-to-day usage that predicts gesture frequency in bilinguals (Aziz & Nicoladis, 2018). In other words, gesture frequency will tend to increase if bilinguals do not have opportunities to use a language on an everyday basis. This interpretation is consistent with the argument that representational gestures can play an important role in accessing words and other linguistic constructions for speaking (Chawla & Krauss, 1994; Frick-Horbury & Guttentag, 1998; Rauscher et al., 1996).

In terms of cultural factors, we have observed that bilingual children may largely differentiate their conventional gestures by language (although they also show some signs of convergence). In contrast, with regard to representational gestures, bilinguals often show convergence. One possible interpretation of these results is that bilinguals tend to seek opportunities for convergence across languages that do not impede communication (Hartsuiker, 2013). Because conventional gestures can be produced without speech, it is important to get the right one to ensure comprehension. In contrast, representational gestures are most often produced with speech, and so the speech can carry the weight of communication. Furthermore, representational gestures often depict at least some part of co-occurring speech and so may not disrupt communication (Church et al., 2004). This point is illustrated nicely by a study that showed that bilinguals use the same storytelling style and a similar gesture frequency in both of their languages (Nicoladis, Nagpal, et al., 2018).

We have focused on gesture production in this chapter. There is a growing number of studies on the role of gestures in bilinguals' comprehension as well. Some studies have shown bilinguals may be able to benefit from gestures more than monolinguals in comprehension and learning (Church et al., 2004; Yow & Markman, 2011). For example, Church et al. (2004) showed that both monolingual and bilingual children can benefit from math instruction accompanied by gestures rather than instruction in speech alone, but the benefit of gestures is particularly noticeable among bilinguals. Church et al. argued that bilinguals can benefit from gestures even in their weak language because gesture meaning transfers across languages. Yow and Markman (2011) found that bilingual children attended more to gestures in interpreting speech than monolingual children did, perhaps to help their understanding.

We also have cited work in this chapter from both child and adult bilinguals in support of our arguments and only speculated about the possible role of developmental changes. At present, given the current state of the evidence, we believe that choice is justified because there is little reason to suspect age-related changes with regard to either the relationship between cognitive factors and gesture use or differential use of representational gestures by language. As further research is done, it will be important to review that stance and examine whether there are developmental changes in these domains.

In closing, we have shown that both cognitive and cultural factors affect bilinguals' gesture use, both in ways that are also observed in monolinguals (e.g., using gestures to help lexical access) as well as in ways that are unique to bilinguals (e.g., showing convergence in gesture use across languages, such as using the same nonverbal expressions of negation when speaking both languages; Benazzo & Morgenstern, 2014).

References

Aziz, J. R., & Nicoladis, E. (2018). "My French is rusty": Proficiency and bilingual gesture use in a majority English community. *Bilingualism: Language and Cognition*, 22(4), 826–835. https://doi.org/10.1017/S1366728918000639

Baddeley, A. (2003). Working memory: Looking back and looking forward. *Nature Reviews Neuroscience,* 4(10), 829–839. https://doi.org/10.1038/nrn1201

Barbosa, P., Jiang, Z., & Nicoladis, E. (2017). The role of working and short-term memory in predicting receptive vocabulary in monolingual and sequential bilingual children. *International Journal of Bilingual Education and Bilingualism*, 22(7), 801–817. https://doi.org/10.1080/13670050.2017.1314445

Benazzo, S., & Morgenstern, A. (2014). A bilingual child's multimodal path into negation. *Gesture*, 14(2), 171–202. https://doi.org/10.1075/gest.14.2.03ben

Bialystok, E. (2009). Bilingualism: The good, the bad, and the indifferent. *Bilingualism: Language and Cognition*, 12(1), 3–11. https://doi.org/10.1017/S1366728908003477

Blom, E., Küntay, A. C., Messer, M., Verhagen, J., & Leseman, P. (2014). The benefits of being bilingual: Working memory in bilingual Turkish–Dutch children. *Journal of Experimental Child Psychology, 128*, 105–119. https://doi.org/10.1016/j.jecp.2014.06.007

Brown, A. (2015). Universal development and L1–L2 convergence in bilingual construal of manner in speech and gesture in Mandarin, Japanese, and English. *Modern Language Journal*, 99(Suppl. 1), 66–82. https://doi.org/10.1111/j.1540-4781.2015.12179.x

Bullock, B. E., & Toribio, A. J. (2004). Introduction: Convergence as an emergent property in bilingual speech. *Bilingualism: Language and Cognition*, 7(2), 91–93. https://doi.org/10.1017/S1366728904001506

Butterworth, G., & Morissette, P. (1996). Onset of pointing and the acquisition of language in infancy. *Journal of Reproductive and Infant Psychology*, 14(3), 219–231. https://doi.org/10.1080/02646839608404519

Cavicchio, F., & Kita, S. (2013). Bilinguals switch gesture production parameters when they switch languages. In *Proceedings of the Tilburg Gesture Research Meeting (TiGeR) 2013* (pp. 305–309). https://www.semanticscholar.org/paper/Bilinguals-Switch-Gesture-Production-Parameters-Cavicchio/13e7e1b49819a6dabf9fd89e18ca83dc8028ed22

Chawla, P., & Krauss, R. (1994). Gesture and speech in spontaneous and rehearsed narratives. *Journal of Experimental Social Psychology*, 30(6), 580–601. https://doi.org/10.1006/jesp.1994.1027

Chee, M. W. L. (2006). Dissociating language and word meaning in the bilingual brain. *Trends in Cognitive Sciences*, 10(12), 527–529. https://doi.org/10.1016/j.tics.2006.09.009

Chu, M., & Kita, S. (2011). The nature of gestures' beneficial role in spatial problem solving. *Journal of Experimental Psychology: General*, 140(1), 102–116. https://doi.org/10.1037/a0021790

Church, R. B., Ayman-Nolley, S., & Mahootian, S. (2004). The role of gesture in bilingual education: Does gesture enhance learning? *International Journal of Bilingual Education and Bilingualism*, 7(4), 303–319. https://doi.org/10.1080/13670050408667815

Cook, S. W., Yip, T. K., & Goldin-Meadow, S. (2012). Gestures, but not meaningless movements, lighten working memory load when explaining math. *Language and Cognitive Processes, 27*(4), 594–610. https://doi.org/10.1080/01690965.2011.567074

Crinion, J., Turner, R., Grogan, A., Hanakawa, T., Noppeney, U., Devlin, J. T., Aso, T., Urayama, S., Fukuyama, H., Stockton, K., Usui, K., Green, D. W., & Price, C. J. (2006, June 9). Language control in the bilingual brain. *Science, 312*(5779), 1537–1540. https://doi.org/10.1126/science.1127761

Efron, D. (1972). *Gesture, race, and culture*. Mouton.

Engel de Abreu, P. M. (2011). Working memory in multilingual children: Is there a bilingual effect? *Memory, 19*(5), 529–537. https://doi.org/10.1080/09658211.2011.590504

Frick-Horbury, D., & Guttentag, R. E. (1998). The effects of restricting hand gesture production on lexical retrieval and free recall. *The American Journal of Psychology, 111*(1), 43–62. https://doi.org/10.2307/1423536

Garitte, C., & Olteanu, L. (2013). L'apprentissage des gestes conventionnels en Roumain et en Français chez les enfants bilingues de 7 et de 11 ans [Learning conventional gestures in Romanian and French in bilingual children aged 7 and 11]. *Langages, 4*(4), 45–55. https://doi.org/10.3917/lang.192.0045

Genesee, F., & Nicoladis, E. (2007). Bilingual first language acquisition. In E. Hoff & M. Shatz (Eds.), *Handbook of language development* (pp. 324–342). Blackwell.

Gollan, T. H., & Acenas, L.-A. R. (2004). What is a TOT? Cognate and translation effects on tip-of-the-tongue states in Spanish–English and Tagalog–English bilinguals. *Journal of Experimental Psychology: Learning, Memory, and Cognition, 30*(1), 246–269. https://doi.org/10.1037/0278-7393.30.1.246

Graham, J. A., & Heywood, S. (1975). The effects of elimination of hand gestures and of verbal codability on speech performance. *European Journal of Social Psychology, 5*(2), 189–195. https://doi.org/10.1002/ejsp.2420050204

Gross, M., Buac, M., & Kaushanskaya, M. (2014). Conceptual scoring of receptive and expressive vocabulary measures in simultaneous and sequential bilingual children. *American Journal of Speech-Language Pathology, 23*(4), 574–586. https://doi.org/10.1044/2014_AJSLP-13-0026

Guidetti, M. (2002). The emergence of pragmatics: Forms and functions of conventional gestures in young French children. *First Language, 22*(3), 265–285. https://doi.org/10.1177/014272370202206603

Guidetti, M. (2005). Yes or no? How young French children combine gestures and speech to agree and refuse. *Journal of Child Language, 32*(4), 911–924. https://doi.org/10.1017/S0305000905007038

Gullberg, M. (1998). *Gesture as a communication strategy in second language discourse*. Lund University Press.

Gutiérrez-Clellen, V. F., Calderón, J., & Ellis Weismer, S. (2004). Verbal working memory in bilingual children. *Journal of Speech, Language, and Hearing Research, 47*(4), 863–876. https://doi.org/10.1044/1092-4388(2004/064)

Hartsuiker, R. J. (2013). Bilingual strategies from the perspective of a processing model. *Bilingualism: Language and Cognition, 16*(4), 737–739. https://doi.org/10.1017/S1366728913000242

Hostetter, A. B., & Alibali, M. W. (2007). Raise your hand if you're spatial: Relations between verbal and spatial skills and gesture production. *Gesture, 7*(1), 73–95. https://doi.org/10.1075/gest.7.1.05hos

Hostetter, A. B., & Alibali, M. W. (2008). Visible embodiment: Gestures as simulated action. *Psychonomic Bulletin & Review, 15*(3), 495–514. https://doi.org/10.3758/PBR.15.3.495

Iverson, J. M., & Braddock, B. A. (2011). Gesture and motor skill in relation to language in children with language impairment. *Journal of Speech, Language, and Hearing Research*, *54*(1), 72–86. https://doi.org/10.1044/1092-4388(2010/08-0197)

Kita, S. (2000). How representational gestures help speaking. In D. McNeill (Ed.), *Language and gesture* (pp. 162–185). Cambridge University Press. https://doi.org/10.1017/CBO9780511620850.011

Kita, S. (2009). Cross-cultural variation of speech-accompanying gesture: A review. *Language and Cognitive Processes*, *24*(2), 145–167. https://doi.org/10.1080/01690960802586188

Kita, S., & Özyürek, A. (2003). What does cross-linguistic variation in semantic coordination of speech and gesture reveal? Evidence for an interface representation of spatial thinking and speaking. *Journal of Memory and Language*, *48*(1), 16–32. https://doi.org/10.1016/S0749-596X(02)00505-3

Krauss, R. M., Chen, Y., & Gottesman, R. F. (2000). Lexical gestures and lexical access: A process model. In D. McNeill (Ed.), *Language and gesture* (pp. 261–283). Cambridge University Press. https://doi.org/10.1017/CBO9780511620850.017

Krauss, R. M., & Hadar, U. (1999). The role of speech-related arm/hand gestures in word retrieval. In R. Campbell & L. Messing (Eds.), *Gesture, speech, and sign* (pp. 93–116). Oxford University Press. https://doi.org/10.1093/acprof:oso/9780198524519.003.0006

Kroll, J. F., Bobb, S. C., & Wodniecka, Z. (2006). Language selectivity is the exception, not the rule: Arguments against a fixed locus of language selection in bilingual speech. *Bilingualism: Language and Cognition*, *9*(2), 119–135. https://doi.org/10.1017/S1366728906002483

Kunene Nicolas, R., Guidetti, M., & Colletta, J. M. (2017). A cross-linguistic study of the development of gesture and speech in Zulu and French oral narratives. *Journal of Child Language*, *44*(1), 36–62. https://doi.org/10.1017/S0305000915000628

Laurent, A., & Nicoladis, E. (2015). Gesture restriction affects French–English bilinguals' speech only in French. *Bilingualism: Language and Cognition*, *18*(2), 340–349. https://doi.org/10.1017/S1366728914000042

Laurent, A., Nicoladis, E., & Marentette, P. (2015). The development of storytelling in two languages with words and gestures. *The International Journal of Bilingualism*, *19*(1), 56–74. https://doi.org/10.1177/1367006913495618

Leonard, M. K., Brown, T. T., Travis, K. E., Gharapetian, L., Hagler, D. J., Jr., Dale, A. M., Elman, J. L., & Halgren, E. (2010). Spatiotemporal dynamics of bilingual word processing. *NeuroImage*, *49*(4), 3286–3294. https://doi.org/10.1016/j.neuroimage.2009.12.009

Marcos, L. R. (1979). Nonverbal behavior and thought processing. *Archives of General Psychiatry*, *36*(9), 940–943. https://doi.org/10.1001/archpsyc.1979.01780090026003

McLeay, H. (2003). The relationship between bilingualism and the performance of spatial tasks. *International Journal of Bilingual Education and Bilingualism*, *6*(6), 423–438. https://doi.org/10.1080/13670050308667795

McNeill, D. (1992). *Hand and mind: What gestures reveal about thought*. University of Chicago Press.

Melinger, A., & Kita, S. (2007). Conceptualization load triggers gesture production. *Language and Cognitive Processes*, *22*(4), 473–500. https://doi.org/10.1080/01690960600696916

Miller, N., Furman, R., & Nicoladis, E. (2018). French–English bilingual children's motion event communication shows crosslinguistic influence in speech but not gesture. *Language, Interaction and Acquisition*, *9*(1), 69–100. https://doi.org/10.1075/lia.15006.mil

Morsella, E., & Krauss, R. M. (2004). The role of gestures in spatial working memory and speech. *The American Journal of Psychology*, *117*(3), 411–424. https://doi.org/10.2307/4149008

Nagpal, J., Nicoladis, E., & Marentette, P. (2011). Predicting individual differences in L2 speakers' gestures. *The International Journal of Bilingualism*, *15*(2), 205–214. https://doi.org/10.1177/1367006910381195

Nicoladis, E. (2002). Some gestures develop in conjunction with spoken language development and others don't: Evidence from bilingual preschoolers. *Journal of Nonverbal Behavior*, *26*(4), 241–266. https://doi.org/10.1023/A:1022112201348

Nicoladis, E. (2007). The effect of bilingualism on the use of manual gestures. *Applied Psycholinguistics*, *28*(3), 441–454. https://doi.org/10.1017/S0142716407070245

Nicoladis, E., & Brisard, F. (2002). Encoding motion in gestures and speech: Are there differences in bilingual children's French and English? http://web.stanford.edu/group/cslipublications/cslipublications/CLRF/2002/Pp_60 68,_Nicoladis.pdf

Nicoladis, E., Marentette, S., & Pika, S. (2018). How many fingers am I holding up? The answer depends on children's language background. *Developmental Science*, *22*(4), e12781. https://doi.org/10.1111/desc.12781

Nicoladis, E., Marentette, P., Pika, S., & Barbosa, P. G. (2018). Young children show little sensitivity to the representationality in number gestures. *Language Learning and Development*, *14*(4), 297–319. https://doi.org/10.1080/15475441.2018.1444486

Nicoladis, E., Mayberry, R. I., & Genesee, F. (1999). Gesture and early bilingual development. *Developmental Psychology*, *35*(2), 514–526. https://doi.org/10.1037/0012-1649.35.2.514

Nicoladis, E., Nagpal, J., Marentette, P., & Hauer, B. (2018). Gesture frequency is linked to storytelling style: Evidence from bilinguals. *Language and Cognition*, *10*(4), 641–664. https://doi.org/10.1017/langcog.2018.25

Nicoladis, E., & O'Carroll, S. (2012, July 24–27). *"I gesture a lot because I'm French": The myth of French as a high gesture frequency language* [Paper]. Fifth Conference of the International Society for Gesture Studies, Lund, Sweden.

Nicoladis, E., Pika, S., & Marentette, P. (2009). Do French–English bilingual children gesture more than monolingual children? *Journal of Psycholinguistic Research*, *38*(6), 573–585. https://doi.org/10.1007/s10936-009-9121-7

Nicoladis, E., Pika, S., & Marentette, P. (2010). Are number gestures easier than number words for preschoolers? *Cognitive Development*, *25*(3), 247–261. https://doi.org/10.1016/j.cogdev.2010.04.001

Nicoladis, E., Pika, S., Yin, H., & Marentette, P. (2007). Gesture use in story recall by Chinese–English bilinguals. *Applied Psycholinguistics*, *28*(4), 721–735. https://doi.org/10.1017/S0142716407070385

Özçalışkan, Ş. (2016). Do gestures follow speech in bilinguals' description of motion? *Bilingualism: Language and Cognition*, *19*(3), 644–653. https://doi.org/10.1017/S1366728915000796

Özyürek, A., Kita, S., Allen, S., Brown, A., Furman, R., & Ishizuka, T. (2008). Development of cross-linguistic variation in speech and gesture: Motion events in English and Turkish. *Developmental Psychology*, *44*(4), 1040–1054. https://doi.org/10.1037/0012-1649.44.4.1040

Paivio, A., Clark, J. M., & Lambert, W. E. (1988). Bilingual dual-coding theory and semantic repetition effects on recall. *Journal of Experimental Psychology: Learning, Memory, and Cognition*, *14*(1), 163–172. https://doi.org/10.1037/0278-7393.14.1.163

Paradis, J., & Genesee, F. (1996). Syntactic acquisition in bilingual children: Autonomous or interdependent? *Studies in Second Language Acquisition*, *18*(1), 1–25. https://doi.org/10.1017/S0272263100014662

Pika, S., Nicoladis, E., & Marentette, P. F. (2006). A cross-cultural study on the use of gestures: Evidence for cross-linguistic transfer? *Bilingualism: Language and Cognition, 9*(3), 319–327. https://doi.org/10.1017/S1366728906002665

Pika, S., Nicoladis, E., & Marentette, P. F. (2009). How to order a beer: Cultural differences in the use of conventional gestures for numbers. *Journal of Cross-Cultural Psychology, 40*(1), 70–80. https://doi.org/10.1177/0022022108326197

Poortinga, Y. H., Schoots, N. H., & van de Koppel, J. M. H. (1993). The understanding of Chinese and Kurdish emblematic gestures by Dutch subjects. *International Journal of Psychology, 28*(1), 31–44. https://doi.org/10.1080/00207599308246916

Quay, S., & Montanari, S. (2016). Early bilingualism: From differentiation to the impact of family language practices. In E. Nicoladis & S. Montanari (Eds.), *Bilingualism across the lifespan: Factors moderating language proficiency* (pp. 23–42). American Psychological Association and de Gruyter. https://doi.org/10.1037/14939-003

Rauscher, F. H., Krauss, R. M., & Chen, Y. (1996). Gesture, speech, and lexical access: The role of lexical movements in speech production. *Psychological Science, 7*(4), 226–231. https://doi.org/10.1111/j.1467-9280.1996.tb00364.x

Sekine, K., Stam, G., Yoshioka, K. Tellier, M., & Capirci, O. (2015). Cross-linguistic views of gesture usage. *Vigo International Journal of Applied Linguistics, 12*, 91–105.

Sherman, J., & Nicoladis, E. (2004). Gestures by advanced Spanish–English second-language learners. *Gesture, 4*(2), 143–156. https://doi.org/10.1075/gest.4.2.03she

Silva-Corvalán, C., & Treffers-Daller, J. (Eds.). (2016). *Language dominance in bilinguals: Issues of measurement and operationalization*. Cambridge University Press. https://doi.org/10.1017/CBO9781107375345

Smithson, L., & Nicoladis, E. (2013). Verbal memory resources predict representational gesture use among monolinguals and bilinguals. *Bilingualism: Language and Cognition, 16*(4), 934–944. https://doi.org/10.1017/S1366728913000175

Smithson, L., & Nicoladis, E. (2014). Lending a hand to imagery? The impact of visuospatial working memory interference upon representational gesture production in a narrative task. *Journal of Nonverbal Behavior, 38*(2), 247–258. https://doi.org/10.1007/s10919-014-0176-2

Smithson, L., Nicoladis, E., & Marentette, P. (2011). Bilingual children's gesture use. *Gesture, 11*(3), 330–347. https://doi.org/10.1075/gest.11.3.04smi

So, W.-C. (2010). Cross-cultural transfer in gesture frequency in Chinese–English bilinguals. *Language and Cognitive Processes, 25*(10), 1335–1353. https://doi.org/10.1080/01690961003694268

So, W.-C., Lim, J.-Y., & Tan, S.-H. (2014). Sensitivity to information status in discourse: Gesture precedes speech in unbalanced bilinguals. *Applied Psycholinguistics, 35*(1), 71–95. https://doi.org/10.1017/S0142716412000355

Talmy, L. (2000). *Toward a cognitive semantics*. MIT Press.

Tannen, D. (1980). A comparative analysis of oral narrative strategies: Athenian Greek and American English. In W. L. Chafe (Ed.), *The pear stories: Cognitive, cultural, and linguistic aspects of narrative production* (pp. 51–87). Ablex.

Toribio, A. J. (2004). Convergence as an optimization strategy in bilingual speech: Evidence from code-switching. *Bilingualism: Language and Cognition, 7*(2), 165–173. https://doi.org/10.1017/S1366728904001476

Wang, Q., & Leichtman, M. D. (2000). Same beginnings, different stories: A comparison of American and Chinese children's narratives. *Child Development*, *71*(5), 1329–1346. https://doi.org/10.1111/1467-8624.00231

Wesp, R., Hesse, J., Keutmann, D., & Wheaton, K. (2001). Gestures maintain spatial imagery. *The American Journal of Psychology*, *114*(4), 591–600. https://doi.org/10.2307/1423612

Yan, S., & Nicoladis, E. (2009). Finding *le mot juste*: Differences between bilingual and monolingual children's lexical access in comprehension and production. *Bilingualism: Language and Cognition*, *12*(03), 323–335. https://doi.org/10.1017/S1366728909990101

Yow, W. Q., & Markman, E. M. (2011). Young bilingual children's heightened sensitivity to referential cues. *Journal of Cognition and Development*, *12*(1), 12–31. https://doi.org/10.1080/15248372.2011.539524

Marianne Gullberg
13 Bimodal Convergence: How Languages Interact in Multicompetent Language Users' Speech and Gestures

Studies of speakers who learn, know, and use more than one language invariably show that languages do not exist in isolation but instead interact, affect, and change each other in various ways. A central issue in studies of second and foreign language acquisition and of bilingualism is to understand what happens when two or more languages come into contact within a person, a domain often referred to as *cross-linguistic influence* (CLI; Jarvis & Pavlenko, 2008; Kellerman & Sharwood Smith, 1986; Odlin, 1989, 2003). The classic example of CLI is foreign accent, whereby properties of one language "leak" into another one. But a particular case of CLI is when two languages in contact change to become more similar to each other than their monolingual versions. For example, when Belgian Flemish–French bilinguals talk about putting cups onto tables in French, they use the verb "mettre" [put], like monolingual French speakers. In Flemish, however, which has two placement verbs—"zetten" [set] and "leggen" [lay]—they often abandon one verb entirely and instead use only one verb in Flemish, "leggen," thus making the two languages more similar (Alferink & Gullberg, 2014). This phenomenon is known as *convergence*.

As with most aspects of (child and adult) language acquisition and bilingualism, convergence has thus far been studied in speech only (but see Stam and Tellier, Chapter 14, this volume, and Nicoladis and Smithson, Chapter 12, this volume, for overviews of bimodal acquisition studies). However, the evidence is rapidly mounting in support of a view in which speech and gestures form an integrated (McNeill, 1992, 2005) or co-orchestrated system (Kendon, 2004; for an overview, see Goldin-Meadow & Brentari, 2017). The evidence promotes a bimodal view of language in which speech and gesture are partners, in turn making it vital to consider both modalities when studying language development and bilingualism, including how emerging or stable languages interact. Bimodal convergence is especially challenging because a prevailing view (even within gesture studies) is that, because gestures can and do express slightly different information from that found in speech, gestures may compensate for expressive difficulties in learners or bilinguals and/or might reveal different meaning representations from those found in speech. In other words, convergence constitutes an interesting test bed for claims about the integrated nature of speech and gesture. Moreover, bimodal convergence also raises challenges for the traditional monomodal approach to convergence, especially if gestures reveal patterns that differ from speech alone. In this chapter I thus review what a bimodal analysis of speech and gesture can reveal about convergence in the language production of speakers who use more than one language.

A remark on terminology is in order. First, because this chapter deals with both what is traditionally known as *second language (L2) learners* and functional bilinguals, I adopt the term "multicompetent" user, drawing on the notion of multicompetence (Cook, 2012, 2016) to conveniently refer to the entire spectrum of users of more than one language, regardless of their acquisition history or formal proficiency levels. The term also partly circumvents the fact that the term "bimodal bilingual" (Emmorey et al., 2008) is now largely used to refer to users of a signed and a spoken language at the exclusion of users of two spoken languages who also gesture, even if their language use is arguably also bimodal.

I begin this chapter with an introduction to the notion of convergence and outline some key theoretical issues and empirical findings. In the following section, I introduce bimodal convergence, the semantic domain of motion used as a test case, and then offer some methodological remarks on the types of analyses performed to examine it. In the next two sections, I present examples of studies that have examined intermediate speakers of a second language, as well as fully functional bilinguals. In a brief section, I discuss potential convergence in multicompetent users of a signed and a spoken language (bimodal bilinguals). I conclude the chapter with a discussion of the implications for L2/bilingualism studies to consider bimodal data and a call for gesture studies to consider convergence.

13.1 Convergence in Multicompetent Spoken Language Production

The interactions among established, emerging, and multiple established languages is a big field of study in both adult second language acquisition (SLA) and bilingualism studies. The study of such CLI targets all levels of language (Jarvis & Pavlenko, 2008). Studies of SLA have tended to view CLI as unwanted, an uncontrolled intrusion of one language into another (categorized as transfer or interference) and to sometimes discuss the phenomenon in terms of incomplete acquisition. The ideal end state and ultimate sign of learning in SLA studies is a complete separation of languages to achieve a system like that of a monolingual native speaker (for discussions of the idealized native speaker, see chapters in Cook, 2003a). In contrast, in bilingualism studies it has long been recognized that a bilingual system is not typically the sum total of two neatly separated monolingual systems but a variety with unique properties of its own (Grosjean, 1982, 1989). Research in this domain has shown that full separation of systems may not be possible, providing evidence that the bilingual lexicon is organized and accessed as one rather than several stores (e.g., Costa, 2005;

Dijkstra, 2005), in which multiple languages can be active at the same time (e.g., van Hell & Dijkstra, 2002), as seen, for example, in code switching, whereby two languages are overtly used simultaneously in a single stretch of speech or a single clause (Muysken, 2000). CLI may therefore be a normal consequence of having more than one language at one's disposal.

One instantiation of CLI is convergence, in which a multicompetent speaker's languages show greater degrees of resemblance to each other than monolingual varieties of the same languages do (e.g., Ameel et al., 2005; Athanasopoulos, 2009; Brown, 2007; Bullock & Toribio, 2004; Clyne, 2003; Pavlenko, 2009; Thomason & Kaufman, 1988). These resemblances can be found in the sound system, such as when French–English bilinguals collapse two sounds, [ø] and [œ], into a single version [ə] in both languages (Bullock & Gerfen, 2004). Other resemblances are more covert, such as in semantic categorization. For example, Greek has two basic terms for blue ("ble" and "ghalazio" for "dark blue" and "light blue," respectively), whereas English has only one basic term (Athanasopoulos, 2009). Multicompetent Greek–English speakers who name colors in Greek shift their focal point for "ble" away from the point used by monolingual Greek speakers and closer to the focal point of monolingual English "blue." Interestingly, they also shift the focal point for the term "ghalazio" to still maintain a two-term system in Greek. Similar shifts are found for concrete nouns (e.g., Malt et al., 2015; Malt & Lebkuecher, 2017; Pavlenko & Malt, 2011; Zinszer et al., 2014). For instance, Belgian French–Flemish bilinguals name bottles and containers differently from monolingual speakers of those languages (Ameel et al., 2005, 2009). The objects named "fles" [bottle] in monolingual Flemish correspond to two categories in monolingual French: "bouteille" [bottle] and "flacon" [bottle]. Bilingual speakers retain the two labels in French but move some of the objects from the "flacon" category to the "bouteille" category, thus increasing the similarity between French "bouteille" and Flemish "fles." Convergence effects are also found in the categorization of nouns and verbs (Gathercole & Moawad, 2010), in adposition semantics (Indefrey et al., 2017; Yager & Gullberg, 2020), and in lexicalization patterns of motion (Brown & Gullberg, 2011; Hohenstein et al., 2006), to mention a few domains.

A prerequisite for convergence often mentioned is a preexisting similarity between two languages such that they can move closer together; that is, the structure undergoing change must be present in both monolingual varieties (e.g., Bullock & Gerfen, 2004). Another defining feature mentioned is that convergence is not a particular speaking style or jargon used intentionally under certain circumstances (such as code switching can be); instead, convergence is seen as an automatic phenomenon not normally under the speaker's volitional control. It is important to note that convergence does not imply that multicompetent speakers do not differentiate their languages (cf. Singleton, 2016). Multicompetent speakers know to speak Language X at one moment and Language Y at another (even if they may also code switch). Instead, convergence is typically a matter of subtle shifts. Convergence does not (necessarily) lead to ungrammatical or "deviant" structures. The changes can be subtle shifts of preferences in the frequency of use of available structures. A final observation is that convergence is not an all-or-nothing phenomenon across an entire language. Shifts may occur in some domains but not in others (e.g., Alferink, 2015; Pavlenko & Malt, 2011).

Studies of CLI typically examine the directionality of the influence. Traditionally, studies have focused only on influences from the first language (L1) to the second (L2). However, reverse influence (from L2 to L1) and bidirectional influence (from L1 to L2 and vice versa) have also been studied (see, e.g., Brown & Gullberg, 2008, 2010, 2011, 2012, 2013; and chapters in Cook, 2003a). For convergence, there is no agreement as to whether only one or both languages involved need to change and differ from the monolingual varieties (cf. Bassetti & Cook, 2011; Brown & Gullberg, 2012, 2013; Pavlenko, 2011; Treffers-Daller & Tidball, 2015) or whether bidirectional shifts are possible but not a defining feature (Bullock & Gerfen, 2004).

A further question is how systems become more similar—through reduction, redistribution, or accumulation of features (Alferink, 2015; Alferink & Gullberg, 2014). Several studies have found that convergence leads to reduced or simplified systems with fewer distinctions in one or both of a multicompetent user's languages. For example, Belgian French–Flemish bilinguals abandon a semi-obligatory semantic distinction in monolingual Flemish between the placement verbs "zetten" [set] and "leggen" [lay] (Alferink & Gullberg, 2014). The multicompetent Flemish system thus has a more general semantic system than monolingual Flemish, instead matching the French semantic system, which operates with one general placement verb (e.g., "mettre" [put]). The multicompetent Flemish system is reduced relative to the monolingual Flemish system, making it converge with and be more similar to French. In contrast, a redistributed system shows changes in distributional frequencies of available lexical elements; that is, when several options exist in one language and one of them also exists in the other language, then that option will become preferred even if it is not the most frequent in monolingual varieties. For example, French and Flemish speakers tend to express different semantic components of motion in verb roots, with the French favoring path (e.g., "traverser" [to cross]) and the Flemish favoring manner (e.g., "zwemmen" [swim]), expressing the path elsewhere. French–Flemish bilinguals decrease the frequency of path verbs in French, such as "traverser" [to cross], in favor of Flemish-like manner verbs such as "nager" [swim]. They also increase the use of French-like path verbs in Flemish, such as "oversteken" [to cross] (Alferink, 2015; cf. Hohenstein et al., 2006). The bilinguals thus show a shift in distributional preferences in both languages, reflecting frequency preferences from the other language. Finally, a cumulative system, in which semantic distinctions from both languages are maintained in both languages, is also logically possible but is less well supported in the literature (but see Berthele, 2004, and Daller et al., 2011). A mixture of these outcomes may also be possible depending on which part of the language system is under scrutiny (Pavlenko & Malt, 2011).

In sum, convergence is a phenomenon whereby all languages known influence each other. What remains largely unknown is how convergence manifests itself bimodally and whether multicompetent speakers' gestures reveal details about their language systems not visible in speech. Put more specifically, an analysis of gestures might reveal whether convergence is bimodally cumulative, that is, whether semantic distinctions from all languages are maintained, with some expressed in gesture and some in speech.

13.2 Bimodal Effects of Convergence

Studies of convergence have overwhelmingly focused on speech; however, if speech and gestures are seen as an integrated or co-orchestrated mode of expression, and language use as inherently bimodal, then convergence needs to be examined multimodally too. In addition to the descriptive value of understanding the interplay between speech and gesture in multicompetent language use, a bimodal analysis of convergence could shed important light on the nature of the multicompetent system. In particular, because gestures generally express somewhat different information than speech because of their format, gestures may reveal systems of richer underlying distinctions than are apparent in speech alone (cf. McNeill, 2000, 2005); that is, semantic distinctions not apparent in speech may instead appear in gestures. This view is particularly tempting for (adult) multicompetent language use (see Graziano & Gullberg, 2018, and Gullberg, 1998, 2011, for discussions of gestural compensation). To be specific, a bimodal analysis may reveal whether converged systems are mainly reduced, redistributed, or in fact cumulatively richer if gestures are used to express more distinctions and information than speech. To investigate convergence bimodally, analyses must focus on cross-modal information distribution, that is, on what information is expressed in which modality. Coexpressivity, or the extent to which speech and gesture express the same information, is a subtype of such analyses.

In the following sections, two lines of study are exemplified, one that focused on the L1 of L2 users with only intermediate proficiency skills in the L2 and the other on fully functional bilinguals. The studies operationalized coexpressivity differently, but both relied on an analysis of cross-modal information distribution. Both studies also used the domain of voluntary motion, whereby an entity moves on its own, as the sample domain. Voluntary motion is a popular domain for studying CLI. Talmy's (1985, 1991, 2000) typology of where languages express the path of motion sets up a useful typological contrast to be exploited in CLI studies. He distinguished verb-framed languages (e.g., Japanese, French), which express path in the verb root (e.g., "descend"), from satellite-framed languages (e.g., English, Dutch), which express path in so-called satellites (e.g., "down"). These typological groups also differ in regard to whether—and, if so, where—manner of motion is expressed (Slobin, 2004): in verb roots (typical of satellite-framed languages, e.g., English "roll") or in peripheral constructions (Hickmann & Hendriks, 2006) such as gerunds or full subordinate clauses, which are often omitted altogether (typical of verb-framed languages, e.g., Japanese, French). A slew of studies have examined the effects of such cross-linguistic differences for multicompetent speakers and their thinking-for-speaking patterns (Slobin, 1991, 1996) in speech (for an overview, see Cadierno, 2017) and in speech and gesture jointly (e.g., see Stam & Tellier, Chapter 14, this volume). Before I move on to the studies, a few methodological remarks are in order.

13.2.1 A Methodological Excursion

Analyses of cross-modal information distribution and of expressivity involve a number of challenges that are not always addressed overtly in the literature. First, for both speech and gesture, a decision must be made regarding what information is relevant (e.g., path, manner, direction, size) and how it is recognized. Although speech is obviously the easier domain, manner is notoriously tricky to handle and is often operationalized negatively as that which is not path (cf. Slobin, 2006). For instance, is "zig-zag" a manner verb, or does it instead define the trajectory of the motion? A further pitfall to avoid is translation equivalents. For example, the French word "grimper" is often translated only as "climb," but in fact it means "climb up" (cf. Gullberg et al., 2008). For gestures, deciding how to identify the gestural expression of a specific meaning is even harder. Even without discussing the problems of determining gestural functions (using terminology such as "representational" or "referential" gestures or, trickier still, "iconic" or "metaphorical" gestures, etc.), deciding how meaning such as path and manner of motion is recognized is not easy. Coding should really draw on very explicit criteria, preferably established pre hoc rather than post hoc once gestures have been identified (for a helpful definition of gestural manner of motion, see, e.g., Duncan, 2005, who suggested that it involves repeated or agitated movement).

Second, when coexpressivity is at stake, speech and gesture coding should really be done independently of each other to avoid circularity; specifically, gestures should be coded with sound turned off (and ideally by someone other than the speech coder) and rely only on form-based, structural criteria for determining which semantic elements are expressed in gesture (e.g., path, manner). Once gestural meaning is coded independently, a comparison can be made with meaning already identified in speech in order to establish (degrees of) coexpressivity (cf. Gullberg et al., 2008). If gestural meaning is influenced by knowledge of the meaning in speech, circularity cannot be avoided. Again, the literature does not always specify how coding is done in this regard.

Finally, coexpressivity can be examined at different levels of granularity. The literature often does not specify whether clause-level or narrow coexpressivity based on exact temporal alignment is considered, but there is a considerable difference between an analysis that identifies a semantic element in speech and a similar semantic element in gesture occurring somewhere in the same clause or utterance on the one hand and an analysis that identifies a semantic element in speech and in an exactly temporally aligned gesture on the other. It is important to clarify which is examined because outcomes can differ, as I discuss next.

13.2.2 Intermediate Second-Language Users

Convergence has traditionally not been studied in L2 users. It has been assumed that this is a phenomenon found only in functional bilingualism. However, psycholinguistic findings suggesting that all known languages affect each other raise the possibility that an emerging L2 might also affect an established L1 even at modest levels of proficiency and perhaps even lead to increased similarity between the L1 and the L2, to convergence. Furthermore, if it is assumed that gestures reveal more underlying meaning distinctions than speech alone, then speech and gestures may be less coexpressive in multicompetent speakers than in monolinguals. This should apply not only in the multicompetent speakers' L2, where they might be expressing in gesture what is inaccessible in speech, but also in their multicompetent L1.

McNeill (2000, 2005) himself has suggested that in verb-framed languages such as Spanish, manner might be expressed in gesture rather than in speech even in monolingual speakers; specifically, the *manner fog hypothesis* proposes that in verb-framed languages where there is no spoken manner with which a manner gesture can align, manner gestures may blanket an entire motion description in a "manner fog." Conversely, the *manner modulation hypothesis* suggests that in satellite-framed languages, where manner is almost obligatorily expressed in the main lexical verb (and path in a satellite), speakers might background or modulate manner by instead gesturing about path somewhere in the clause or utterance. McNeill thus proposed a manner foregrounding versus backgrounding function for gestures in verb- and satellite-framed languages, respectively. Notice that the hypotheses operate at the clause or utterance level, and no prediction is made about exact speech–gesture alignment.

To examine whether an emerging L2 affects an established L1 even at modest levels of proficiency, Brown and Gullberg (2008, 2010, 2011, 2012, 2013) probed in a series of studies how intermediate Japanese learners of English talked about voluntary motion in their L1 Japanese and in their L2 English. We thus explored the influence of an emerging satellite-framed language (English) on a verb-framed language (Japanese). We examined motion event descriptions from cartoon retellings in four groups of speakers: functionally monolingual English and monolingual Japanese speakers in the United States and in Japan, respectively, and Japanese intermediate L2 users of English, half of whom lived in Japan and the other half in the United States. We chose two groups of multicompetent speakers living in different language environments to control for possible effects of cultural exposure, including to gesture patterns in the target culture. Importantly, the multicompetent groups residing in the United States and in Japan were matched on formal L2 English proficiency (the Oxford Placement Test [Allan, 1992] and Cambridge University's First Certificate in English). The multicompetent Japanese–English speakers were tested in both L1 Japanese and L2 English, with order counterbalanced.

Speech analyses revealed that in L1 Japanese the multicompetent speakers differed significantly from the monolingual Japanese speakers in that they encoded more elements of path per clause than monolinguals, using not only verbs but also adverbials (Brown & Gullberg, 2010), especially adding goal expressions (Brown & Gullberg, 2011), and preferring to describe motion in several rather than single clauses (Brown & Gullberg, 2013). Remarkably, when their performance in multicompetent L1 Japanese and L2 English speech was compared, they did not differ from themselves on the measures taken, despite speaking two different languages. These findings suggest that an established L1 can change in the presence of an emerging language and shift toward the emerging L2, with the L1 displaying increased similarity to the emerging L2, that is, convergence. It is important to note that there were no differences between the groups in Japan and the United States on any of the measures, suggesting that cultural immersion was not the key factor. Also important is that multicompetent L1 production was completely grammatical. The convergence is therefore characterized by shifts in linguistic preference, not in grammaticality (cf. Bullock & Toribio, 2004). But what about the bimodal behavior?

The bimodal analyses focused on the expression of manner and traces of manner fog versus manner modulation in clause-level analyses (Brown & Gullberg, 2008). As expected, the monolingual English speakers mentioned significantly more manner in speech than any other group. The multicompetent speakers did not differ from their monolingual Japanese peers in L1 Japanese, but they mentioned significantly less manner in spoken L2 English than L1 English speakers, as expected. The gesture analyses showed that manner fog (i.e., manner in gesture with no manner in the spoken clause) was rare. It was entirely absent in monolingual English and rare in both monolingual and multicompetent Japanese. In contrast, manner modulation (i.e., manner in speech but path in the clause-accompanying gesture) did reveal differences. Monolingual English speakers mainly produced manner in speech and path in gesture (cf. Gullberg et al., 2008, for similar findings). In L1 Japanese the multicompetent speakers produced the same pattern—manner in speech and path in gesture—significantly more often than the monolingual Japanese. They thus resembled and did not differ from monolingual English speakers. In other words, although they were speaking their L1, they displayed a pattern more typical of English than Japanese: manner modulation or manner backgrounding. A striking finding is that when the multicompetent speakers were compared with themselves in L1 Japanese and L2 English, their bimodal performance in L1 and L2 was indistinguishable, again despite them speaking two different languages. In other words, in both languages they favored a manner modulation pattern, speaking about manner but gesturing about path. Overall, they looked more like themselves than like monolingual speakers of either language. Example 13.1 illustrates the pattern. Gestural strokes are in boldface, and expressions of manner are underlined.

Example 13.1
a. L1 Japanese   de   sonomama   **gorogoro**-to   korogatte
                  and   in.that.way   mimetic.COMP   roll.CON
                  "and in that way (it) rolls RUMBLE"
                  Path gesture: hand moving from speaker's left to right; no concurrent finger movement or wrist rotation. Manner in speech, not in gesture.
b. L2 English   and **rolled** up
                  Path gesture: hand moving from speaker's left to right; no concurrent finger movement or wrist rotation. Manner in speech, not in gesture. (Brown & Gullberg, 2008, p. 243)

These results do not support McNeill's manner fog hypothesis for verb-framed languages, but they do support the manner modulation hypothesis for satellite-framed languages. Moreover, there is little support for a view whereby gestures convey information left out from speech. Remember that the satellite-framed pattern has (path and) manner in speech but only path in gesture. In contrast, the findings do strongly suggest bimodal convergence between the multicompetent L1 and L2 varieties. Crucially, the shift leading to greater resemblance between multicompetent Japanese and English was seen not in speech (equal amounts of spoken manner was found) but in the cross-modal information distribution at the clause level, with an increase in manner backgrounding (i.e., manner in speech, path in gestures accompanying the clause). As before, there were no differences between the multicompetent groups in Japan and in the United States on any of the measures. Because the two groups were matched on formal proficiency, the results therefore suggest that the shift is due not to visual exposure to the English-speaking community's gestures but to an effect of having learned a language with a different rhetorical style, even at a modest level of proficiency. The results suggest convergence based on changes in distributional frequencies of available patterns to make two languages more similar, that is, on redistribution, not an accumulation of distinctions.

13.2.3 Functional Bilinguals

Functional bilinguals—speakers who use more than one language on a daily or regular basis for a range of functions and purposes (regardless of acquisition history and formal proficiency)—are a more common target group for the examination of convergence. However, bimodal convergence remains sorely understudied also in functional bilinguals.

In a series of studies of functional French–Flemish bilinguals in Belgium, Alferink and Gullberg (2014) examined motion event descriptions to probe whether these multicompetent speakers showed evidence of convergence, and specifically of cumulative convergence with additional distinctions made in gesture relative to speech (Alferink, 2015; Alferink & Gullberg, 2014). We exploited the typological contrast between French, a verb-framed language, and Flemish (i.e., Dutch) a satellite-framed language. We compared functional bilingual French–Flemish speakers (from bilingual Brussels) to functional monolingual speakers of French (from Namur in the French-speaking part of Belgium, Wallonia) and Flemish (from Leuven in the Flemish-speaking part of Belgium, Flanders). The bilinguals did not differ on self-rated formal proficiency in either language. They were tested in both languages with order counterbalanced. As before, we examined cross-modal information distribution, and specifically speech–gesture coexpressivity at the clause level (i.e., path or manner in the spoken clause and a gesture expressing the same information anywhere in that clause). We also investigated narrow coexpressivity (i.e., exactly temporally aligned information in speech and gesture).

The speech results showed that the monolingual French speakers expressed mainly path in speech, whereas monolingual Flemish speakers expressed both path and manner, in accordance with the typological expectations. The bilinguals expressed mainly path in French, and in Flemish both manner and path, in keeping with the preferences of each language. It is important to note, however, that in Flemish the bilinguals produced significantly less manner and path than the Flemish monolinguals; that is, in Flemish the bilinguals shifted the frequency distribution of path to be more similar to French in speech, showing convergence of Flemish toward French.

The bimodal analyses showed similar patterns. In the analysis of coexpressivity at the clause level, both monolingual and bilingual speakers of French expressed mainly path in speech and gesture. Conversely, the monolingual and bilingual Flemish speakers expressed manner and path in speech but only path in gesture, essentially displaying a manner modulation pattern (cf. Brown & Gullberg, 2008). The bilinguals did not differ from the monolinguals in either language in this clause-level analysis. In the narrow analysis of coexpressivity (exact temporal alignment), the French patterns remained the same, meaning that path gestures aligned exactly with spoken path elements; however, the Flemish results shifted. In clauses with spoken path and manner, path gestures aligned exactly with the spoken path elements. The manner modulation at the clause level now became exact coexpressivity at the narrow level. It is important to note that in this narrow analysis the bilinguals did not differ from themselves in French and Flemish, again despite speaking two different languages. This suggests bimodal convergence. Example 13.2 illustrates the bilingual pattern. Gestural strokes are in boldface, and expressions of manner are underlined.

Example 13.2
- a. Bilingual French et   ensuite elle **va**   **redes**cendre
                                     and   then   she will   redescend

  "and then she redescends"

  Path gesture: extended index moving vertically downwards. Path in speech, path in gesture.
- b. Bilingual Flemish en dan   kruipt   ie   **terug naar bene**den
                                     and then crawls   he   back   to   down

  "and then he crawls back down"

  Path gesture: extended index moving vertically downwards. Path and manner in speech, path only in gesture. (Alferink, 2015, p. 73)

As before, these results suggest multimodal convergence in functional bilinguals with a parallel pattern across speech and gesture in information distribution. There is no support for a view whereby gestures convey information left out from speech, nor is there any support for a view of gestures as revealing more semantic distinctions than speech. Instead, convergence is based on changes in distributional frequencies of available patterns to make two languages more similar, that is, on redistribution, not an accumulation of distinctions.

Despite the differences in multicompetent speakers types (intermediate L2 speakers vs. functional bilinguals), in the languages involved, and in the granularity of the analysis, both studies in Examples 13.1 and 13.2 thus show evidence of bimodal convergence. In both cases, multicompetent speakers produced speech–gesture ensembles that were similar across the two multicompetent varieties and showed evidence of shifts in distributional preferences, which in both cases means that speakers increased a pattern of manner modulation typical of satellite-framed languages also in their verb-framed language.

13.2.4 Is There Convergence in Bimodal Bilingualism With Sign and Spoken Language?

A particular group of multicompetent speakers are those who learn, know, and use a spoken and a signed language, referred to in the literature as "bimodal bilinguals"[1]

---

[1] This term largely refers to hearing bimodal bilinguals using a spoken and a signed language. Deaf bimodal bilinguals are sometimes referred to as "sign print" or "sign text" bilinguals; they use a sign language and written forms of the surrounding spoken language and may obviously also be able to lip read (cf. Emmorey et al., 2016).

(Emmorey et al., 2008, 2016), or L2M2 users (a second language in a second modality; Pichler, 2011). The term "bimodal bilingual" is somewhat unfortunate in that it implies that speakers using two spoken languages are "unimodal," thus disregarding the bimodal nature also of spoken language plus gesture. That said, the use of a signed and a spoken language raises particular challenges for the study of CLI in general and convergence in particular. Studies of functional bimodal bilinguals have revealed not only behaviors similar to other bilingual language use, such as code switching, but also modality-specific ones, such as the preference for so-called *code blends*, in which a sign and a corresponding spoken word co-occur (e.g., Emmorey et al., 2008). A small but growing literature has been examining what CLI between spoken and signed languages might look like, especially in L2 learning (for an overview, see Pichler & Koulidobrova, 2016), but no study has yet addressed convergence specifically. The production of spoken words following sign grammar, sometimes called "CODA talk" (CODA = child of deaf adult; Bishop & Hicks, 2005), does not qualify because its use is situationally governed. The same applies to the use of "simultaneous communication," or sign-supported speech, whereby sign and speech are deliberately produced in tandem (often to a mixed deaf–hearing audience) but in which the grammar and structure are mostly that of spoken language (e.g., Emmorey et al., 2016).

A promising avenue of study is to consider effects on gesture rather than speech or sign, much in the same way as gesture may show convergence effects even if speech does not (cf. manner modulation). There is already some evidence that knowledge of a sign language affects the co-speech gestures of bimodal multicompetent users, resulting in increased gesture rates, and greater handshape variation, for example (e.g., Casey et al., 2012). If this is convergence, it would predict effects also from gesture onto sign. As far as I know, this has not been examined to date.

Convergence in bimodal bilingualism thus remains largely unexplored empirically. But if one assumes that bimodal bilingualism is no different from other kinds of multicompetent language use, then one should expect it to show effects similar to those observed in unimodal bilingualism, including convergence.

13.3 Conclusion

Convergence, the phenomenon whereby two languages become more similar to each other in the production of multicompetent speakers, is as much a bimodal phenomenon as any other type of language use. As such, the study of convergence provides further evidence for the integrated nature of speech and gesture. The studies I have reviewed in this chapter provide evidence for bimodal convergence in a wide range of settings, in multicompetent speakers whose L2 is still emerging at an intermediate level of skill as well as in fully functional bilinguals. The observation that languages change even with relatively little knowledge and use of another language may be shocking to some, but it is in line with the psycholinguistic findings that all languages known interact in a multicompetent mind. Moreover, the studies provide evidence not only of changes in speech but also in how information is distributed across speech and gesture. It is important to note that there is no evidence that multicompetent speakers add information in gesture that is not available in speech or that gestures constitute a sneaky way to spy on richer underlying semantic representations. This is particularly evident when a finer lens is applied and the exact temporal alignment between speech and gesture is considered, as compared to clause-level analyses. The narrow analysis reveals that speech and gesture tend to express the same semantic information and therefore that convergence, on the whole, is parallel across the modalities. Gestures are thus not simply loci for compensation or facilitation in multicompetent language users but form part of a complex system that is internally consistent in the speaker. The benefit of looking at convergence and considering all of a multicompetent speaker's varieties is that it moves away from deficiency views of acquisition and bilingualism, promotes analyses of what multicompetent speakers do rather than what they do not do, and highlights the need to consider multimodal multicompetent varieties as a natural result of knowing and using more than one language.

Will these findings generalize to linguistic domains beyond motion, to other groups of multicompetent speakers, and to other ways of coding and analyzing speech and gesture? It is too early to tell, but it is an issue worth pursuing. Bimodal convergence has implications both for SLA/bilingualism studies and for gesture studies. The evidence that even moderate knowledge of an emerging language can influence and change the established L1 raises important challenges for the (idealized) monolingual native speaker as the benchmark for comparisons (cf. Cook, 2003b; Davies, 2003; Ortega, 2013). With a bimodal view of language the stakes are even higher (even if the empirical data are still largely missing). Multicompetent data and convergence also raise challenges for gesture studies. The evidence—including in the studies reviewed here—is strong for an integrated speech–gesture relationship and a bimodal view of language. However, the data also show that the speech–gesture relationship is complex and multifaceted. We do find parallelism across the modalities, but depending on how we analyze the data, different patterns may appear, as we have seen.

On the whole, bimodal convergence highlights the fact that models of language are overwhelmingly monolingual and monomodal. They should be neither. There is much work to do ahead to aim for multicompetent and multimodal models of language and learning instead.

References

Alferink, I. (2015). *Dimensions of convergence in bilingual speech and gesture* [Unpublished doctoral dissertation]. Radboud Universiteit.

Alferink, I., & Gullberg, M. (2014). French–Dutch bilinguals do not maintain obligatory semantic distinctions: Evidence from placement verbs. *Bilingualism: Language and Cognition*, *17*(1), 22–37. https://doi.org/10.1017/S136672891300028X

Allan, D. (1992). *Oxford Placement Test*. Oxford University Press.

Ameel, E., Malt, B. C., Storms, G., & Van Assche, F. (2009). Semantic convergence in the bilingual lexicon. *Journal of Memory and Language*, *60*(2), 270–290. https://doi.org/10.1016/j.jml.2008.10.001

Ameel, E., Storms, G., Malt, B. C., & Sloman, S. A. (2005). How bilinguals solve the naming problem. *Journal of Memory and Language*, *53*(1), 309–329. https://doi.org/10.1016/j.jml.2005.02.004

Athanasopoulos, P. (2009). Cognitive representation of colour in bilinguals: The case of Greek blues. *Bilingualism: Language and Cognition*, *12*(1), 83–95. https://doi.org/10.1017/S136672890800388X

Bassetti, B., & Cook, V. (2011). Relating language and cognition: The second language user. In V. Cook & B. Bassetti (Eds.), *Language and bilingual cognition* (pp. 143–190). Psychology Press.

Berthele, R. (2004). The typology of motion and posture verbs: A variationist account. Dialectology meets typology. In B. Kortmann (Ed.), *Dialect grammar from a cross-linguistic perspective* (pp. 93–126). Mouton de Gruyter.

Bishop, M., & Hicks, S. L. (2005). Orange eyes: Bimodal bilingualism in hearing adults from deaf families. *Sign Language Studies*, *5*(2), 188–230. https://doi.org/10.1353/sls.2005.0001

Brown, A. (2007). *Crosslinguistic influence in first and second languages: Convergence in speech and gesture* [Unpublished doctoral dissertation]. Boston University, and Max Planck Institute for Psycholinguistics.

Brown, A., & Gullberg, M. (2008). Bidirectional crosslinguistic influence in L1–L2 encoding of manner in speech and gesture: A study of Japanese speakers of English. *Studies in Second Language Acquisition*, *30*(2), 225–251. https://doi.org/10.1017/S0272263108080327

Brown, A., & Gullberg, M. (2010). Changes in encoding of path of motion after acquisition of a second language. *Cognitive Linguistics*, *21*(2), 263–286. https://doi.org/10.1515/COGL.2010.010

Brown, A., & Gullberg, M. (2011). Bidirectional crosslinguistic influence in event conceptualization? The expression of path among Japanese learners of English. *Bilingualism: Language and Cognition*, *14*(1), 79–94. https://doi.org/10.1017/S1366728910000064

Brown, A., & Gullberg, M. (2012). Multicompetence and native speaker variation in clausal packaging in Japanese. *Second Language Research*, *28*(4), 415–442. https://doi.org/10.1177/0267658312455822

Brown, A., & Gullberg, M. (2013). L1–L2 convergence in clausal packaging in Japanese and English. *Bilingualism: Language and Cognition*, *16*(3), 477–494. https://doi.org/10.1017/S1366728912000491

Bullock, B. E., & Gerfen, C. (2004). Phonological convergence in a contracting language variety. *Bilingualism: Language and Cognition*, *7*(2), 95–104. https://doi.org/10.1017/S1366728904001452

Bullock, B. E., & Toribio, A. J. (2004). Introduction: Convergence as an emergent property in bilingual speech. *Bilingualism: Language and Cognition*, *7*(2), 91–93. https://doi.org/10.1017/S1366728904001506

Cadierno, T. (2017). Thinking for speaking about motion in a second language. Looking back and forward. In I. Ibarretxe-Antuñano (Ed.), *Motion and space across languages: Theory and applications* (pp. 279–300). John Benjamins. https://doi.org/10.1075/hcp.59.12cad

Casey, S., Emmorey, K., & Larrabee, H. (2012). The effects of learning American Sign Language on co-speech gesture. *Bilingualism: Language and Cognition, 15*(4), 677–686. https://doi.org/10.1017/S1366728911000575

Clyne, M. G. (2003). *Dynamics of language contact: English and immigrant languages.* Cambridge University Press. https://doi.org/10.1017/CBO9780511606526

Cook, V. (Ed.). (2003a). *Effects of the second language on the first.* Multilingual Matters. https://doi.org/10.21832/9781853596346

Cook, V. (2003b). Introduction: The changing L1 in the L2 user's mind. In V. Cook & L. Wei (Eds.), *Effects of the second language on the first* (pp. 1–18). Multilingual Matters. https://doi.org/10.21832/9781853596346-003

Cook, V. (2012). Multi-competence. In C. Chapelle (Ed.), *The encyclopedia of applied linguistics.* Wiley-Blackwell. https://doi.org/10.1002/9781405198431.wbeal0778

Cook, V. (2016). Premises of multi-competence. In V. Cook & L. Wei (Eds.), *The Cambridge handbook of linguistic multi-competence* (pp. 1–25). Cambridge University Press. https://doi.org/10.1017/CBO9781107425965.001

Costa, A. (2005). Lexical access in bilingual production. In J. F. Kroll & A. M. de Groot (Eds.), *Handbook of bilingualism: Psycholinguistic approaches* (pp. 308–325). Oxford University Press.

Daller, M. H., Treffers-Daller, J., & Furman, R. (2011). Transfer of conceptualization patterns in bilinguals: The construal of motion events in Turkish and German. *Bilingualism: Language and Cognition, 14*(1), 95–119. https://doi.org/10.1017/S1366728910000106

Davies, A. (2003). *The native speaker: Myth and reality.* Multilingual Matters. https://doi.org/10.21832/9781853596247

Dijkstra, T. (2005). Bilingual visual word recognition and lexical access. In J. F. Kroll & A. M. de Groot (Eds.), *Handbook of bilingualism: Psycholinguistic approaches* (pp. 179–201). Oxford University Press.

Duncan, S. D. (2005). Co-expressivity of speech and gesture: Manner of motion in Spanish, English, and Chinese. In C. Chang, M. J. Houser, Y. Kim, D. Mortensen, M. Park-Doob, & M. Toosarvandani (Eds.), *Proceedings of the 27th Annual Meeting of the Berkeley Linguistic Society, Feb. 16–18, 2001* (pp. 353–370). Berkeley Linguistics Society.

Emmorey, K., Borinstein, H. B., Thompson, R., & Gollan, T. H. (2008). Bimodal bilingualism. *Bilingualism: Language and Cognition, 11*(1), 43–61. https://doi.org/10.1017/S1366728907003203

Emmorey, K., Giezen, M. R., & Gollan, T. H. (2016). Psycholinguistic, cognitive, and neural implications of bimodal bilingualism. *Bilingualism: Language and Cognition, 19*(2), 223–242. https://doi.org/10.1017/S1366728915000085

Gathercole, V. C., & Moawad, R. A. (2010). Semantic interaction in early and late bilinguals: All words are not created equally. *Bilingualism: Language and Cognition, 13*(4), 385–408. https://doi.org/10.1017/S1366728909990460

Goldin-Meadow, S., & Brentari, D. (2017). Gesture, sign, and language: The coming of age of sign language and gesture studies. *Behavioral and Brain Sciences, 40*, e46. https://doi.org/10.1017/S0140525X15001247

Graziano, M., & Gullberg, M. (2018). When speech stops, gesture stops: Evidence from developmental and crosslinguistic comparisons. *Frontiers in Psychology, 9*, 879. https://doi.org/10.3389/fpsyg.2018.00879

Grosjean, F. (1982). *Life with two languages.* Harvard University Press.

Grosjean, F. (1989). Neurolinguists, beware! The bilingual is not two monolinguals in one person. *Brain and Language, 36*(1), 3–15. https://doi.org/10.1016/0093-934X(89)90048-5

Gullberg, M. (1998). *Gesture as a communication strategy in second language discourse: A study of learners of French and Swedish*. Lund University Press.

Gullberg, M. (2011). Multilingual multimodality: Communicative difficulties and their solutions in second language use. In J. Streeck, C. Goodwin, & C. LeBaron (Eds.), *Embodied interaction: Language and body in the material world* (pp. 137–151). Cambridge University Press.

Gullberg, M., Hendriks, H., & Hickmann, M. (2008). Learning to talk and gesture about motion in French. *First Language, 28*(2), 200–236. https://doi.org/10.1177/0142723707088074

Hickmann, M., & Hendriks, H. (2006). Static and dynamic location in French and English. *First Language, 26*(1), 103–135. https://doi.org/10.1177/0142723706060743

Hohenstein, J., Eisenberg, A., & Naigles, L. (2006). Is he floating across or crossing afloat? Cross-influence of L1 and L2 in Spanish–English bilingual adults. *Bilingualism: Language and Cognition, 9*(3), 249–261. https://doi.org/10.1017/S1366728906002616

Indefrey, P., Şahin, H., & Gullberg, M. (2017). The expression of spatial relationships in Turkish/Dutch bilinguals. *Bilingualism: Language and Cognition, 20*(3), 473–493. https://doi.org/10.1017/S1366728915000875

Jarvis, S., & Pavlenko, A. (2008). *Crosslinguistic influence in language and cognition*. Routledge. https://doi.org/10.4324/9780203935927

Kellerman, E., & Sharwood Smith, M. (Eds.). (1986). *Crosslinguistic influence in second language acquisition*. Pergamon.

Kendon, A. (2004). *Gesture: Visible action as utterance*. Cambridge University Press. https://doi.org/10.1017/CBO9780511807572

Malt, B. C., & Lebkuecher, A. L. (2017). Representation and process in bilingual lexical interaction. *Bilingualism: Language and Cognition, 20*(5), 867–885. https://doi.org/10.1017/S1366728916000584

Malt, B. C., Li, P., Pavlenko, A., Zhu, H., & Ameel, E. (2015). Bidirectional lexical interaction in late immersed Mandarin–English bilinguals. *Journal of Memory and Language, 82*, 86–104. https://doi.org/10.1016/j.jml.2015.03.001

McNeill, D. (1992). *Hand and mind: What gestures reveal about thought*. University of Chicago Press.

McNeill, D. (2000). Imagery in motion event descriptions: Gestures as part of thinking-for-speaking in three languages. In M. L. Juge & J. L. Moxley (Eds.), *Proceedings of the 23rd Annual Meeting of the Berkeley Linguistics Society, Feb. 14–17, 1997* (pp. 255–267). Berkeley Linguistics Society.

McNeill, D. (2005). *Gesture and thought*. University of Chicago Press. https://doi.org/10.7208/chicago/9780226514642.001.0001

Muysken, P. (2000). *Bilingual speech: A typology of code-mixing*. Cambridge University Press.

Odlin, T. (1989). *Language transfer: Cross-linguistic influence in language learning*. Cambridge University Press. https://doi.org/10.1017/CBO9781139524537

Odlin, T. (2003). Cross-linguistic influence. In C. Doughty & M. H. Long (Eds.), *The handbook of second language acquisition* (pp. 436–486). Blackwell. https://doi.org/10.1002/9780470756492.ch15

Ortega, L. (2013). SLA for the 21st century: Disciplinary progress, transdisciplinary relevance, and the bi/multilingual turn. *Language Learning, 63*(S1), 1–24. https://doi.org/10.1111/j.1467-9922.2012.00735.x

Pavlenko, A. (2009). Conceptual representation in the bilingual lexicon and second language vocabulary learning. In A. Pavlenko (Ed.), *The bilingual mental lexicon: Interdisciplinary approaches* (pp. 125–160). Multilingual Matters. https://doi.org/10.21832/9781847691262-008

Pavlenko, A. (2011). Thinking and speaking in two languages: Overview of the field. In A. Pavlenko (Ed.), *Thinking and speaking in two languages* (pp. 237–257). Multilingual Matters. https://doi.org/10.21832/9781847693389-010

Pavlenko, A., & Malt, B. C. (2011). Kitchen Russian: Cross-linguistic differences and first-language object naming by Russian–English bilinguals. *Bilingualism: Language and Cognition, 14*(1), 19–45. https://doi.org/10.1017/S136672891000026X

Pichler, C. D. (2011). Sources of handshape error in first-time signers of ASL. In G. Mathur & D. J. Napoli (Eds.), *Deaf around the world: The impact of language* (pp. 96–121). Oxford University Press.

Pichler, C. D., & Koulidobrova, H. (2016). Acquisition of sign language as a second language (L2). In M. Marschark & P. E. Spencer (Eds.), *The Oxford handbook of deaf studies in language: Research, policy, and practice* (pp. 218–230). Oxford University Press.

Singleton, D. (2016). A critical reaction from second language acquisition research. In V. Cook & L. Wei (Eds.), *The Cambridge handbook of linguistic multi-competence* (pp. 502–520). Cambridge University Press. https://doi.org/10.1017/CBO9781107425965.024

Slobin, D. I. (1991). Learning to think for speaking. *Pragmatics, 1*(1), 7–25. https://doi.org/10.1075/prag.1.1.01slo

Slobin, D. I. (1996). From "thought and language" to "thinking for speaking." In J. J. Gumperz & S. C. Levinson (Eds.), *Rethinking linguistic relativity* (pp. 70–96). Cambridge University Press.

Slobin, D. I. (2004). How people move: Discourse effects of linguistic typology. In C. L. Moder & A. Martinovic-Zic (Eds.), *Discourse across languages and cultures* (pp. 195–210). John Benjamins. https://doi.org/10.1075/slcs.68.11slo

Slobin, D. I. (2006). What makes manner of motion salient? In M. Hickmann & S. Robert (Eds.), *Space in languages: Explorations in linguistic typology, discourse, and cognition* (pp. 59–81). John Benjamins. https://doi.org/10.1075/tsl.66.05slo

Talmy, L. (1985). Lexicalization patterns: Semantic structure in lexical forms. In T. Shopen (Ed.), *Language typology and syntactic description* (pp. 57–149). Cambridge University Press.

Talmy, L. (1991). Paths to realization: A typology of event conflation. In L. A. Sutton, C. Johnson, & R. Shields (Eds.), *Proceedings of the Berkeley Linguistics Society* (pp. 480–519). Berkeley Linguistics Society.

Talmy, L. (2000). *Toward a cognitive semantics*. MIT Press.

Thomason, S. G., & Kaufman, T. (1988). *Language contact, creolization, and genetic linguistics*. University of California Press. https://doi.org/10.1525/9780520912793

Treffers-Daller, J., & Tidball, F. (2015). Can L2 learners learn new ways to conceptualise events? Evidence from motion event construal among English-speaking learners of French. In P. Guijarro-Fuentes, K. Schmitz, & N. Müller (Eds.), *The acquisition of French in multi-lingual contexts* (pp. 145–184). Multilingual Matters. https://doi.org/10.21832/9781783094530-009

van Hell, J. G., & Dijkstra, T. (2002). Foreign language knowledge can influence native language performance in exclusively native contexts. *Psychonomic Bulletin & Review, 9*(4), 780–789. https://doi.org/10.3758/BF03196335

Yager, J., & Gullberg, M. (2020). Asymmetric semantic interaction in Jedek–Jahai bilinguals: Spatial language in a small-scale, non-standardized, egalitarian, long-term multilingual setting in Malaysia. *The International Journal of Bilingualism, 24*(3), 492–507. https://doi.org/10.1177/1367006918814378

Zinszer, B. D., Malt, B. C., Ameel, E., & Li, P. (2014). Native-likeness in second language lexical categorization reflects individual language history and linguistic community norms. *Frontiers in Psychology, 5*, 1203. https://doi.org/10.3389/fpsyg.2014.01203

Gale Stam and Marion Tellier

14 Gesture Helps Second and Foreign Language Learning and Teaching

From the perspective that language and language usage consist of both speech and gesture (McNeill, 1992, 2005, 2012), over the past 30 years, a number of studies have examined gesture's role in second language (L2) acquisition. These studies have demonstrated the important role that gesture plays in both second and foreign language learning and teaching[1] (for reviews, see Gullberg & McCafferty, 2008; Stam, 2013; Stam & Buescher, 2018; Stam & McCafferty, 2008; Tellier, 2014).

Despite the growing interest in gesture and second language (L2) learning and teaching among a number of researchers, the topic of gesture and its importance in understanding L2 acquisition is still not considered in most mainstream second language acquisition (SLA) studies. These studies on L2 learning and teaching have mainly focused on the analysis of speech production and have viewed gestures as peripheral to the process of learning and teaching. However, gestures play a very strong role in both learning and teaching because verbal language is only half of the picture: It provides a window only onto verbal thought, and not imagistic thought; therefore, it is not always the most efficient medium for communication, especially when there is an asymmetry in language proficiency between a learner and a teacher or a native speaker. L2 learning and teaching are interconnected and can be considered as two sides of the same coin: On the one hand, learners use gestures to facilitate their speech production and make it clearer, and on the other hand, teachers use gestures to scaffold their speech to make it more comprehensible for learners. In addition, learners' gestures indicate their language proficiency and comprehension of material, which are important aspects for teachers to take into consideration.

In this chapter, although it focuses on adult learners, we provide evidence for why it is important to consider gestures in both L2 learning and teaching for all age ranges. We begin by defining co-speech gestures and pedagogical gestures. Next, we discuss how learners' co-speech gestures show whether they are conceptualizing in their L1, their L2, or a combination of the two, and the extent to which different tasks affect the types of gestures learners produce. We then shift to pedagogical gestures and illustrate how teachers engage their bodies in different ways in the classroom, the various functions of the gestures teachers use, the manner in which teachers vary

---

[1] "Second language learning and teaching" refers to learning and teaching a language in a country where the language is spoken on a daily basis, whether it is the learner's second, third, or fourth language. "Foreign language learning and teaching" refers to learning and teaching another language in a person's home country, where it is not the language for communication. In this chapter, we use "L2" to refer to both.

their speech and gesture when engaging with nonnative speakers, and what this tells us about teaching and communication.

14.1 Speech and Gesture

When we communicate, we do not just move our mouths to make the sounds of a language; we also move our hands, our heads, and our bodies. These movements of the hands that accompany speech are referred to as "co-speech gestures" (Kendon, 2004; McNeill, 1992, 2005), and together with speech they form a unit that expresses both the speaker's verbal and imagistic thought (McNeill, 1992). Co-speech gestures, which are often produced without conscious awareness, are synchronous with speech, cannot be understood independently of speech, perform similar pragmatic functions as speech, and are multifunctional in that they perform both cognitive and communicative functions often at the same time (Stam, 2018a; Stam & McCafferty, 2008; Stam & Tellier, 2017). These gestures are often classified on the basis of their semiotic properties (McNeill, 2012; Stam, 2013), that is, what they represent, such as iconicity, metaphoricity, deixis, temporal highlighting, or social interactivity, or they are classified on the basis of their pragmatic function, that is, what their discourse function is, such as representational, discursive, deictic, interactive, or word searching (Kendon, 2004; Stam, 2018b).

In addition to co-speech gestures, there are a few other types of gestures and bodily movements that are relevant to L2 learning and teaching. These include speech-linked gestures, emblems, mimes, and pedagogical gestures. All of these are performed with some degree of conscious awareness (Stam, 2018a; Stam & Tellier, 2017). *Speech-linked gestures* are similar to co-speech gestures in that they also occur with speech, but they differ in terms of their synchrony (Stam, 2013). Speech-linked gestures are asynchronous with speech and occur during a pause in speech, thus filling a speech gap such as in the following utterance: "Sylvester went [gesture of an object flying out laterally]" (McNeill, 2005, p. 5). These gestures are used by learners when they lack vocabulary or by teachers as a teaching strategy when they leave a blank and perform a gesture so that learners can supply the missing word or words (Stam, 2018a).

Emblems are codified, culturally specific gestures such as the *thumbs down* gesture (fist with thumb down), that are known and learned by all members of a languacultural (Agar, 1994) group (Stam, 2013, 2018a). These gestures are performed with some degree of conscious awareness and occur both with and without speech. The form of an emblem is fixed, but its meaning can vary from culture to culture. Thus, emblems need special attention in the L2 classroom. They need to be taught (e.g., von Raffler-Engel, 1980; Wylie, 1985) so that L2 learners become competent in their usage (Stam, 2018a). It is also important for L2 teachers to be aware of their own usage of these gestures because they can be misunderstood if they are used without any explanation (see Hauge, 1998, 1999; Tellier & Cadet, 2013).

Mimes (or *pantomimes*) are gestures and body movements that are performed without speech and with conscious awareness (Stam, 2013). They depict actions, objects, or entire stories and are used by learners when they lack vocabulary or by teachers when they are attempting to get learners to guess.

Pedagogical gestures (Tellier, 2008a) are gestures that are used in the classroom. These gestures are often made with conscious awareness, and they perform several different functions. These include co-speech gestures (mainly deictics—[pointing gestures] and iconics—[gestures that represent concrete actions and objects]), speech-linked gestures, mimes, and emblems. We discuss pedagogical gestures further in the next section.

One interesting aspect of gestures and L2 learning and teaching is that the balance between gesture and speech may vary from that of a native speaker. Learners may use gestures to cope with weak language proficiency, or gesture frequency and timing may differ as learners work out their utterances in the L2 (Stam, 2006b). Similarly, when addressing a language learner, teachers (even preservice teachers) may use gestures in a way that helps the learner access meaning (Stam & Tellier, 2017; Tellier & Stam, 2012; Tellier et al., 2013, in press). Thus, studying gestures in L2 learning and teaching sheds new light on our comprehension of gestures and how they combine with speech and thought. We now turn to gesture and L2 learning.

14.2 Gesture and Second Language Learning

Empirical research on gesture and SLA over the past 30 years has examined gestures and L2 learning from a number of perspectives (for reviews, see Gullberg, 2010; Gullberg et al., 2008; Gullberg & McCafferty, 2008; Stam, 2013; Stam & Buescher, 2018; Stam & McCafferty, 2008). Among these are learners' rate of gesturing in their L2; the types and functions of the gestures learners produce; the impact of learners' gestures on oral proficiency assessments; the role of learners' gestures in lexical retrieval; what learners' gestures reveal about their thinking in their L2, in particular their thinking for speaking; and the role of gestures in enhancing L2 learning. In the sections that follow, we address the topics of oral proficiency assessment, lexical retrieval, learners' conceptualizations in their L2, task effects on gestures, and how gestures can enhance L2 learning.

14.2.1 Second Language Learners' Gestures Impact on Oral Proficiency Ratings

Several researchers (Gullberg, 1998; Jenkins & Parra, 2003; Nambiar & Goon, 1993; Neu, 1990; Stam, 2006a) have shown that learners' gestures have an effect on how their oral proficiency is rated. For example, Gullberg (1998) found that learners' oral proficiency was rated significantly higher in a video condition, in which the raters saw the learners' gestures, than in an audio-only condition, in which raters could only hear the learners' speech. Furthermore, in their comparison of ratings of oral proficiency interviews in a face-to-face and an audio-only condition, Nambiar and Goon (1993) found that learners' oral proficiency was rated significantly higher in the face-to-face condition. In both of these studies, hearing not only the speech of the learners' but also seeing their mouth movements and gestures benefited the raters (Drijvers & Özyürek, 2016). However, it is not just seeing learners' gestures that makes a difference in how their oral proficiency is rated. An important factor is the degree to which their gestures are close to those of the target language and culture. Neu (1990), Jenkins and Parra (2003), and Stam (2006a) all found that learners' oral proficiency was rated higher when their gestures were closer to the target language and culture than when they were not. When they were not, their oral proficiency was rated lower even if their speech was more fluent. Thus, as these studies indicate, the way learners gesture has an impact on how their oral proficiency is rated, regardless of whether the raters are aware that they are paying attention to the learners' gestures.

14.2.2 Second Language Learners' Gestures and Lexical Retrieval

According to the *lexical retrieval hypothesis*, iconic gestures (gestures that represent concrete actions and objects) are produced when speakers have difficulty finding words, and these gestures facilitate word finding (for a review, see Stam, 2012). However, G. Beattie and Coughlan (1998, 1999) have shown that lexical retrieval problems alone do not account for iconic gestures and that sometimes the gestures during lexical retrieval are iconic and sometimes they are not. This raises the question of what kinds of gestures L2 learners produce when they are having trouble finding a word. This is an interesting question because L2 learners may have gaps in their vocabulary based on their exposure to the L2 and proficiency level and may lack the vocabulary for different domains and tasks.

Only a few studies have examined this topic. For instance, Gullberg (1998) found that L2 learners sometimes used gestures as a communication strategy to deal with fluency, grammar, and lexical retrieval problems; these included metaphoric (gestures that represent abstract concepts) as well as iconic gestures. In addition, Stam (2001, 2012) investigated the types of gestures L2 learners produced during lexical searches (the word search phase), lexical retrievals (the word finding phase), and lexical failures (the inability to find a word). She found that the types of gestures learners produced depended on whether they knew the word and were trying to retrieve it or were asking the interlocutor for help. Searches that occurred with lexical retrieval often had iconic gestures with superimposed beats (small rhythmic movements of the hands or fingers produced on another gesture) and a larger superimposed beat occurring with the retrieved word, but these were not the only type of gesture that occurred during searches. There were also aborted (gestures that are started but not completed), word search, and deictic (pointing) gestures, to name a few. Gestures that occurred with failures were primarily iconic and aborted gestures that indicated what learners were thinking but did not express verbally. L2 gesture and lexical retrieval is an area that would benefit from further study.

14.2.3 What Second Language Learners' Gestures Reveal About Their Thinking in Their Second Language

L2 learners' gestures provide SLA researchers with a more complete picture of how they are thinking when they are speaking in their L2 than looking at speech alone (Stam, 2006b, 2008, 2016, 2018b). For example, Stam (2008) demonstrated that if we looked at only the speech of an L2 learner engaged in a cartoon narration task (Example 14.1), we see that the learner could produce the utterance "the Tweety has a / bowling ball /" and that the learner was having difficulty describing what she had seen before this. We do not know what she was thinking about.

> Example 14.1[2]
> and <uhm> the Tweety / / <uhm> /
> <mmm> / / / <mhff> #
> the Tweety has a / bowling ball / (Stam, 2008, p. 252)

In contrast, when the learner's gestures are also looked at (Example 14.2; Figures 14.1–14.4), it becomes clear that the learner was trying to describe part of the cartoon she had just watched, in which Tweety (one of the main characters) threw a bowling ball down a drainpipe. We can also see that even though she could produce the utterance "The Tweety has a / bowling ball /," her gestures reveal that her thinking is very segmented because she had a gesture for the subject and verb (the Tweety has), another one for the article (a), and a third gesture for the direct object (bowling ball).

The majority of studies that have examined L2 learners' gestures and what they tell us about learners' conceptualizations have focused on the domain of *motion events*. These studies (e.g., Aguiló Mora & Negueruela-Azarola, 2015; Brown, 2008, 2015; Brown & Gullberg, 2008; Choi & Lantolf, 2008; E. Kellerman & van Hoof, 2003; Negueruela et al., 2004; Stam, 2006b, 2008, 2010, 2014, 2015, 2017) have been conducted within the framework of Talmy's (2000) and Slobin's (2006) classification of languages into verb-framed (with path encoded on the verb), satellite-framed (with path encoded on a satellite, an adverb, or a preposition of movement), and equipollently framed (with both path and manner encoded on verbs) languages. They are also based on Slobin's (1991) *thinking-for-speaking hypothesis*, which proposes

---

[2] Transcription for Examples 14.1 to 14.10 use the following convention from McNeill (1992) < > = filled pauses and elongation, / = unfilled pauses, # = breath pauses, and * = repetitions or self-corrections.

Fig. 14.1: Example 14.2. and <uhm> t[he **Tweety** / / <uhm>]. Iconic: both hands at upper right and left, move away from body and down and repeat movement <Tweety throwing the bowling ball>

[/ <mmm>]

Note. All examples are coded according to McNeill's (1992) coding scheme, in which the gesture phrase (the movement of the hand from start to finish) is enclosed in square brackets, the stroke (the part of the gesture with meaning) is indicated in boldface, any holds—prestroke or poststroke (the maintaining of a hand shape in a particular position)—are indicated with underlining, and any gesture units (two or more gesture phrases that are related) are enclosed in another set of square brackets.

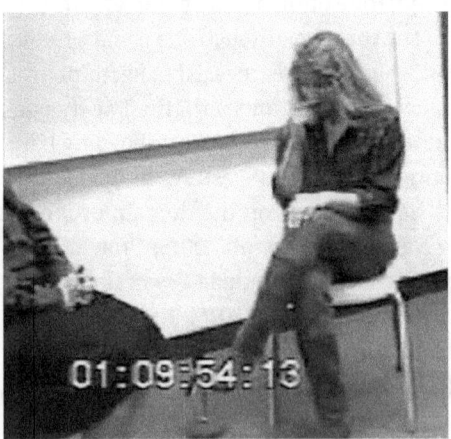

Fig. 14.2: Example 14.2. Word search: Left hand rises to nose, index finger touches nose, and retracts <trying to find the words>

[/ / /] <mhff> #

Note. Based on Stam (2008, p. 252).

Fig. 14.3: Example 14.2. Iconic (repetition to reduced repetition of previous iconic): Both hands at upper right and left, move away from body and down and repeat as a smaller movement <Tweety throwing the bowling ball>

[[the Tweety has] [a /] [bo<o>wling ball /]]

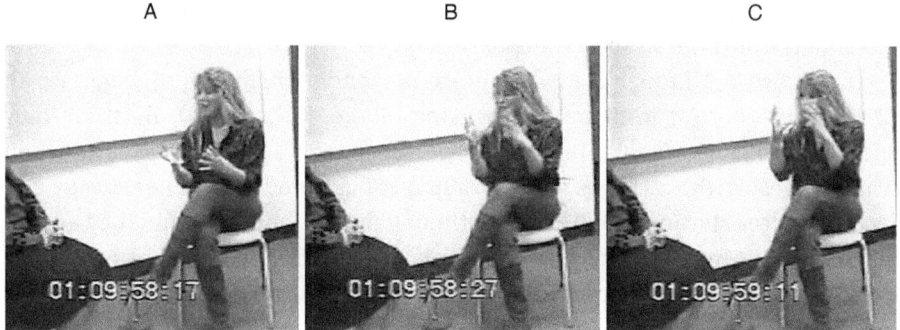

Fig. 14.4: Example 14.2. Panel A—Iconic: Both hands move to their respective sides and up to upper chest<Tweety holding bowling ball + shape of bowling ball>.
Panel B—Aborted iconic: Both hands continue from previous movement, move up to neck, out to respective sides, and back to neck<bowling ball>.
Panel C—Iconic: Both hands continue from previous movement, move up slightly open to their respective sides, then down to lower chest, and hold<showing shape of bowling ball>.

that "in acquiring a native language, a child learns a particular way of thinking for speaking" (p. 12). In other words, in first language (L1) acquisition, children learn the grammatical constructions and lexicon of the L1 that both provide them with a framework for the expression of thoughts, events, and feelings and guide their verbal expression as they engage in speaking (Stam, 2010). The typological differences that exist between languages are important in L2 acquisition, especially if different patterns of thinking for speaking exist between a learner's L1 and L2 because in order to become proficient in their L2 learners must learn another pattern of thinking for speaking (Cadierno & Lund, 2004; Stam, 1998). One way to have a more complete view of whether learners are thinking for speaking in their L2 is to examine not only their speech but also the timing of their gestures (Stam, 2006a, 2006b, 2008).

Studies that have explored learners' thinking for speaking have investigated how the motion events components of path, manner, and ground are expressed linguistically and gesturally in different languages and how L2 speakers express them in their L2. These studies have focused on what gestures are produced and what speech elements they accompany. They have found that the L2 learners were able to produce grammatically correct sentences in their L2 but that their gestures showed that the learners were not thinking for speaking in their L2: Their thinking for speaking was somewhere between their L1 and their L2. In other words, the learners' gestures indicated their interlanguage systems (Stam, 2008, 2010). This would not have been discernible by looking at speech alone.

Examples 14.3 through 14.5, which are from a longitudinal study of changes in an L2 learner's (Rosa's) thinking for speaking (Stam, 2017, p. 354), illustrate how speech alone is misleading. In describing a scene from a cartoon she had seen in which Sylvester (the cat) goes up the drainpipe, Rosa produces grammatically correct utterances starting in 1997 and continuing in 2006 and 2011, and they are not much different from that of a native English speaker (Example 14.6). All the utterances are complete sentences with subject–verb agreement and the inclusion of a satellite for path.

Example 14.3
Rosa—Speech 1997
he* the cat went through the* / / / the<e> pipe / and * but the*

Example 14.4
Rosa—Speech 2006
he goes inside the pipe the* /

Example 14.5
Rosa—Speech 2011
so h<e> // #breath goes through one of the pipes

Example 14.6
   Native English speaker—Speech
   a<a>nd // he goes<s> up / through the pipe this time #

From these data we could conclude that Rosa, whose L1 is Spanish, is thinking for speaking in her L2 English. However, when we look at her speech and gesture in Examples 14.7 through 14.9 compared with that of the native English speaker in Example 14.10, we see that is not the case, and we see how Rosa's thinking for speaking in English has changed from 1997 to 2011 (see Figure 14.5).

Rosa has five gestures in Example 14.7. This shows how segmented her thinking is in English in 1997. They indicate that, instead of thinking of the utterance as a whole, she is thinking of each constituent of the sentence individually. Also, besides having a path gesture with the satellite and article *through the* (Panel C of Figure 14.5), she also has a path gesture with the subject *the cat* (Panel A, Figure 14.5) and the verb *went* (see Panel B, Figure 14.6).

In 2006 (Example 14.8; see Figure 14.6), Rosa's gestures indicate that her thinking for speaking has changed in English. She is thinking of the utterance as a whole and produces one path and ground gesture with continual movement that co-occurs with the utterance as a whole, showing Sylvester going both inside and up the drainpipe.

The synchronization of Rosa's gestures in 2011 (Example 14.9; see Figure 14.7) shows that her thinking for speaking in English has continued to become more English-like. In 2011, she has one path and ground gesture that co-occurs with the satellite and ground elements of the sentence. This is similar to the native English speaker in Example 14.10, who produces two path and ground gestures with the satellite elements *up* and *through*.

Example 14.10
   Native English Speaker (Stam, 2008, p. 248)
   a<a>nd // he goe[[ss / **up** / **th| rough** the pipe]] *this time* #
                         a   b
   a: Iconic—Right hand at low right waist moves from right to left to next to left thigh <Sylvester goes into lower part of the pipe> PATH+GROUND
   b: Iconic—Right hand "O" shape pops open to loose curved hand and moves up vertically from next to left thigh to left lower chest level<Sylvester goes up inside pipe> PATH+GROUND

Thus, by looking at the speech and gesture examples above, it becomes clear that gesture more clearly indicates how learners are thinking in their L2 than speech alone does.

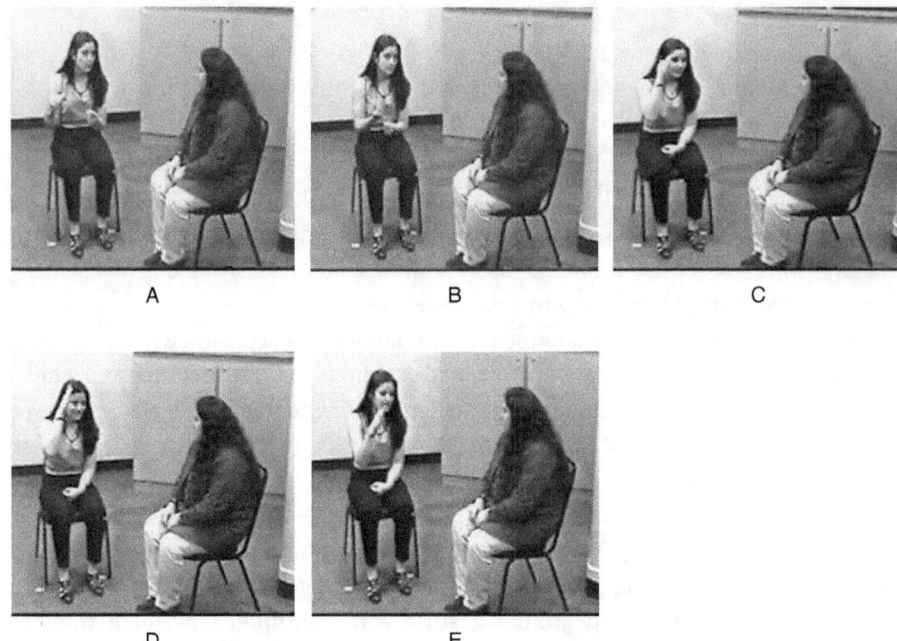

Fig. 14.5: Example 14.7. Rosa—Speech and gesture 1997

RH: [[he* **the ca**t] [**went** //] [**through the***] [///] [the<e> **pipe** / and * but the*]]

LH: [[he* **the ca**t] [**went** //] through the* /// the<e> pipe / and* but the*

Panel A—Iconic: Right hand at right, left hand, "O" shape at left waist<Sylvester entering the drainpipe>PATH.

Panel B—Iconic: Right hand at right chest moves up to right side of face, left hand,
"O" shape at waist lowers to lap as right hand rises<Sylvester going up inside drainpipe>PATH.

Panel C—Iconic: Right hand at right side of face moves in toward body and moves up to forehead changing hand orientation to palm toward down, fingers toward left <Sylvester going through the drainpipe>PATH.

Panel D—Iconic: Right hand at nose level and moves up to top of head then retracts to nose level<pipe>GROUND.

Panel E—Iconic (reduced repetition of previous gesture): right hand at upper chest moves up in toward body to chin level and down away from body to upper chest, small circular movement, and holds<pipe>GROUND.

Note. From "Verb Framed, Satellite Framed or in Between? A L2 Learner's Thinking for Speaking in Her L1 and L2 Over 14 Years," by G. Stam, in I. Ibarretxe-Antuñano (Ed.), *Motion and Space Across Languages: Theory and Applications* (p. 249), 2017, John Benjamins. Copyright 2017 by John Benjamins Publishing. Reprinted with permission.

 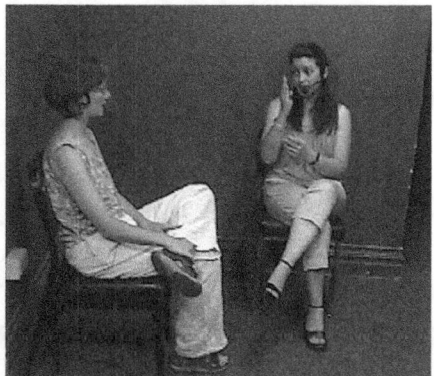

Fig. 14.6: Example 14.8. Rosa—Speech and gesture 2006

[he goes inside | the pipe the* /]

Iconic: Left hand C-shape at chest level <drainpipe>; right fingers extended thumb tucked in moves in toward left hand, up and around in a circular movement <entering> and then straight up to palm toward center, fingers toward up and retracts to just below right shoulder < left hand = pipe right hand = Sylvester, Sylvester entering and going up the drainpipe>PATH+GROUND.

Note. From "Verb Framed, Satellite Framed or in Between? A L2 Learner's Thinking for Speaking in Her L1 and L2 Over 14 Years," by G. Stam, in I. Ibarretxe-Antuñano (Ed.), *Motion and Space Across Languages: Theory and Applications* (p. 357), 2017, John Benjamins. Copyright 2017 by John Benjamins Publishing. Reprinted with permission.

14.2.4 Task Effects on Learners' Gestures

Most of the research on how learners' gestures reveal their conceptualizations has involved narrative tasks that use a cartoon stimulus. However, it is possible to examine learners' gestures in other tasks as well to see how task affects learners' use of gesture. So far only two studies (Stam, 2016; Tabensky, 2008) have looked at task effects on learners' gestures.

Tabensky (2008) investigated variation in learners' gestures during two tasks in an L2 classroom: (a) an expository task (a short presentation) and (b) a question-and-answer period that followed the presentation. She found that the gestures the learners produced were dependent on task: "The learners produced more presentational gestures, gestures that present information (e.g., metaphoric and interactive gestures), during the expository task and more representational gestures, gestures that present content (iconic, lexical, and topic gestures) answering questions" (Stam, 2016, p. 290).

Stam (2016) examined the speech and gesture of an L2 learner in two tasks (an oral proficiency interview and a narrative task) over a 14-year period (1997–2011). She found that the speech and gesture of the learner was greatly affected by the task.

Fig. 14.7: Example 14.9. Rosa—Speech and gesture 2011

[so h<e> // #breath goes **through one of the pipes**]

Iconic: Right hand facing down at right chest level moves down toward left hand at center chest, right hand palm facing left, and up to right chin level and holds <RH – Sylvester moving up through pipe; LH – pipe>PATH+GROUND.

Note. From "Verb Framed, Satellite Framed or in Between? A L2 Learner's Thinking for Speaking in Her L1 and L2 Over 14 Years," by G. Stam, in I. Ibarretxe-Antuñano (Ed.), *Motion and Space Across Languages: Theory and Applications* (pp. 357–358), 2017, John Benjamins. Copyright 2017 by John Benjamins Publishing. Reprinted with permission.

In the narrative task, the learner produced primarily iconic gestures and had more gestures per clause even though more clauses were produced in the oral proficiency task. In the oral proficiency task that more closely approximated a conversation on everyday topics such as work, school, and family, both the learner and the interviewer produced primarily metaphoric gestures. Stam also found that the interview task could be used to view the learner's conceptualizations and thinking for speaking as well as changes in the interaction between the learner and the interviewer. In Example 14.11, for example, the learner is talking about looking for a job and how she submitted her resume online (see Figure 14.8). She produces two iconic path gestures with the utterance: one on the word "through," a satellite element and one on the word "online," a ground element. This indicates that she is thinking for speaking about path according to the English pattern. Her speech alone would not have allowed us to see this.

In regard to the development of the interview interaction, Stam (2016) found that the last interview had become an actual conversation between peers with overlapping speech and gesture and use of each other's gestures. This would have all been missed had she looked at only the participant's speech.

A	B

Fig. 14.8: Example 14.11. Second language learner—2011 interview (Stam, 2016, pp. 303–304).

then I actually I send my resume twice [[/ **through the**][% swallow **online** /]]

Panel A—Iconic: Right hand curved with index finger extended at right shoulder arches down to right waist area changing to hand extended forward, palm flat <submitting resume>PATH.
Panel B—Iconic (reduced repetition of the previous gesture): Right hand curved at right shoulder moves down to waist area changing hand to hand extended forward, palm flat <submitting resume>PATH.

14.2.5 How Gestures Enhance Foreign Language Learning

As we have discussed, the gestures produced by learners shed light on their process of language learning, but gestures, especially gestures that are produced by teachers (pedagogical gestures) and taken into account by learners, can also scaffold and reinforce language learning.

Several studies have highlighted the positive effect of gestures and other kinesic (related to the body) cues on L2 listening comprehension (S. Kellerman, 1992; Sueyoshi & Hardison, 2005) including studies on young children (Tellier, 2008a, 2009). The question of how L2 learners perceive, use, and interpret teachers' gestures in the classroom has been addressed by several researchers, for example, Azaoui (2016), Hauge (1998, 1999), Sime (2001, 2006, 2008), and Tellier (2008a, 2009). They have shown that, even if gestures produced by a language teacher generally help learners' understanding, in some cases certain gestures can lead to misunderstanding because they are ambiguous, too symbolic, or culturally embedded.

14.2.6 Gestures and Second Language Memorization

A number of researchers have explored the question of whether gesture has an effect on L2 memorization. For example, Allen (1995) and Tellier (2008b) have explored the effect of gestures on L2 long-term memorization. Both found a significant effect of gestures on memorization of lexical items, and these results have been supported by more recent studies (de Nooijer et al., 2013; Krönke et al., 2013; Macedonia, 2013; Macedonia & Klimesch, 2014; Macedonia & Knösche, 2011; Macedonia et al., 2011; Rowe et al., 2013). On this topic, most research has taken place in artificial conditions (e.g., in a laboratory) except Nakatsukasa's (2016) study, which took place in a classroom context and evaluated the effect of a teacher's corrective reformulations on improving the learning of spatial prepositions (e.g., "in," "on," "under") in an English-as-a-second-language classroom.

The questions now to be addressed are how the ability to use gesture to scaffold language learning operates in the classroom and in what respects this ability can be developed by teachers as a professional skill.

14.3 Gestures Used by Language Teachers and Their Functions

Since the pioneering work of Grant and Grant Hennings in 1971 (*The Teacher Moves: An Analysis of Non-Verbal Activity*), teachers' bodies have been regarded as an important feature in the action of teaching. Among the studies of pedagogical gestures based on classroom observations or corpora are the works of S. Kellerman (1992), Allen (2000), Pavelin (2002), Lazaraton (2004), Tellier (2008a, 2016), Azaoui (2013, 2014), and Denizci and Azaoui (2015). With the evolution of audiovisual tools and technologies, and the recent development of multimodal annotation tools such as ELAN (Sloetjes & Wittenburg, 2008) research has become more precise and can be used on larger naturalistic corpuses. In addition to the various positive aspects of gestures for language learning that we have already discussed, teachers' gestures in the classroom (especially in language classes) adopt specific forms and perform particular functions. Some of teachers' pedagogical gestures are routinized and consciously used. They help learners focus their attention on the key words of sentences and thus enable an onomasiological approach (i.e., global) of the language. In previous work, Tellier (2008a) found three main pedagogical functions of gestures in the classroom. These are based on the three functions elaborated by Dabène (1984) for teacher talk: (a) informing, (b) managing, and (c) assessing.

14.3.1 Gestures to Inform About Language

Among information gestures, we find gestures of *grammatical information* that are used to transmit data related to morphosyntax and temporality (Matsumoto & Dobs, 2017); *gestures of lexical information* that illustrate a word or an idea of the oral speech of the teacher and *phonological and phonetic information gestures* that are created to help learners master pronunciation and prosody (e.g., Smotrova, 2017). The information function of the gesture especially during lexical explanation has been extensively studied in actual classrooms (e.g., Allen, 2000; Lazaraton, 2004; Seaver, 1992; Tellier, 2016) as well as in online teaching via videoconferencing (Holt et al., 2015).

Lexical explanation happens when a misunderstanding occurs in class and a teacher can explain the meaning of an item at the request of a learner or because the feedback (or absence of feedback) of the students indicates a misunderstanding. However, the gesture does not occur only when the learner has not understood and the teacher has to set up a repair sequence (Varonis & Gass, 1985). On the contrary, we have noticed in teachers' multimodal discourse an anticipation of the potential difficulties of comprehension. In short, a teacher anticipates the learner's knowledge, gaps, and needs. A gesture is produced by teachers to illustrate a word or idea from their oral speech. They may choose to illustrate one word over another for two main reasons (the two reasons can be combined): (a) because they consider this term particularly important for understanding the overall meaning of the sentence (this is the pivot) or (b) because they assume and anticipate that this word is unknown to the learner and will cause them a problem (Tellier, 2008a). Example 14.12 illustrates this; see Figure 14.9.

In Figure 14.9 the teacher wants some precision and asks whether the learner does not like to speak in front of one person in particular or in front of everybody. He produces two gestures, first an emblem to show the number 1 and then an iconic gesture with a flat hand, palm downward and moving sideways to represent a large amount. In his question, the two key words are connected to this contrast: one versus everybody. This is why he illustrates the two words with gestures synchronized with his key words. They are the pivots of the sentence, and he wants to make sure they are understood. It is interesting that the learner reproduces the second gesture when she answers, showing that she has paid attention to and assimilated the teacher's gesture.

Fig. 14.9: Example 14.12. In this French class, the student in black says that she does not like to speak in front of people. Teacher: "Juste une personne" [Just one person in particular] (Picture 1) "Ou tout le monde" [Or everybody?] (Picture 2)? [Just one person in particular or everybody?] Student: "Tout le monde" [Everybody] (Picture 3).

14.3.2 Gestures to Assess

The function of assessing (or evaluation) includes gestures to congratulate, approve, and report an error. Congratulatory and approving gestures appear more toward the end of a learner's intervention, allowing the teacher to seal the end of the answer with a positive assessment. When the statement contains errors, the teacher can either interrupt the learner or wait for the end of the statement to intervene. In Example 14.13, the teacher simply gives feedback on the learner's answer by repeating the correct form of the sentence and showing with a gesture that nothing else should be added (see Figure 14.10).

In general, if the teacher reports an error during the learner's production, they will tend to do so only nonverbally so as not to interrupt the learner's production. The teacher instead uses the gesture to indicate a problem in the student's response and not to give the correct answer. The learner, knowing where the wrong part is, simply has to correct it and can reflect on their mistakes. This evaluation function, especially in language classes, has been the subject of mainly descriptive research (Faraco, 2008; Mackey et al., 2007; Schachter, 1981).

In the context of the classroom, where several speakers contribute to the interaction, the teacher can use gestures to conduct the speech turns. A typical situation occurs when the teacher asks a question and several answers are produced at the same time by the students. In Example 14.14 (Figure 14.11), the learner in black has just provided an answer that was expected by the teacher (after asking a question to the whole class). He suddenly turns to her, looks at her with a smile, and points in her direction. Once again, the different kinesic cues coordinate to perform the function of assessing the learner's intervention.

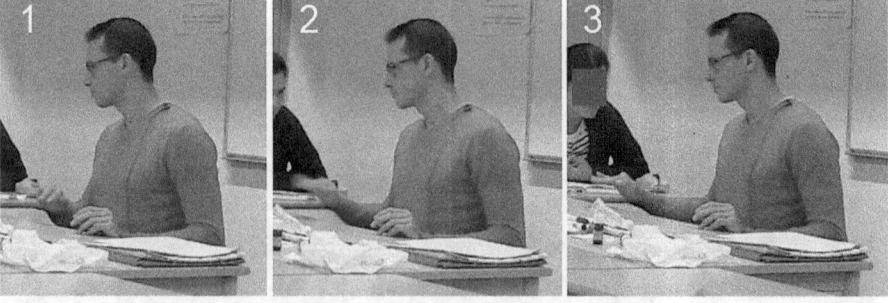

Fig. 14.10: Example 14.13. The students discuss what they enjoyed in the French class during the end of school term. They have to make sentences with "I enjoyed" [J'ai aimé] and "I less enjoyed" [J'ai moins aimé]. A student says "J'ai moins aimé beaucoup" [I less enjoyed a lot], which is grammatically incorrect. The teacher corrects by repeating "J'ai moins aimé" followed by a gesture that means "enough" to mean that the sentence is correct with nothing more.

Fig. 14.11: Example 14.14. Multimodal assessment of a student's answer.

14.3.3 Gestures to Manage the Class

The third major functional category of pedagogical gestures is the function of management that encompasses both class management gestures (change of activity, start and end of activity, placement of learners and material, give instructions) and the management of interactions and participation (regulate flow and volume, repeat, support, question, give voice, silence). This is a function that has received little attention in the analysis of teachers' gestures, and when it is mentioned, it is rarely the subject of careful analysis (Barnett, 1983; N. Beattie, 1977; Grant & Grant Hennings, 1971) with the exception of Azaoui's (2013, 2014, 2016) work. Is this due to the fact that the function of teacher as animator (i.e., making learning more animated), may seem less fundamental to some than informing or evaluating? This question remains. When instructions are being given, the key words typically can be accompanied by illustrative gestures like the one in Example 14.15 (Figure 14.12), when an emblem illustrates "three."

In Example 14.16 (Figure 14.13), a very interesting composition of kinesic movements accompanies the verbal instruction given by the teacher. He first points to the sheet of paper that the learners have received to show where they will have to write their answers; then he puts down the sheet to release his hands for the rest of the explanation. He starts to enumerate the kind of questions the students can create for their board game (only the first example is given here). Enumerating emblems are used to show different possibilities (the first here), and the emblem is pointed to in order to reinforce the enumeration. The example of "grammar questions" is nuanced by the head movement and the facial expression of the teacher, which imply that responding to grammar questions is a possibility, although it might not be the most exciting one. This interesting combination of kinesic cues added to verbal instruction is very typical of a teacher's multimodal discourse (see also Azaoui, 2014, 2016).

Fig. 14.12: Example 14.15. *Par groupes de trois* [in groups of three].

Finally, as we can see in Figure 14.13 (Example 14.16), the teacher's gaze sweeps the entire class to make sure everybody's attention is focused on him. It is a means of catching the learners' attention and including them as partners in the classroom conversation. It is also common to see teachers directing their gestures in order to make them visible to all. This phenomenon of orientation of the gesture toward the interlocutor was already highlighted by Özyürek (2000) in dyads or triads, in a semicontrolled context, and it is interesting to notice the same thing, in an ecological situation, in a class where the teacher is co-enunciator of several learners at the time to use Azaoui's (2014) phrasing. This capacity to gaze at the whole class to catch everybody's attention is not always acquired by young teachers (McIntyre et al., 2017;

Fig. 14.13: Example 14.16. The teacher gives instructions for an activity. The students have to write questions that will be used in the board game they are creating. Teacher: "Trouvez des questions pour chaque case" [Find questions for each box] (Picture 1), "Vous pouvez faire des questions de grammaire" [You can do grammar questions] (Picture 2), "Si vous voulez" [If you want] (Picture 3).

Tellier & Yerian, 2018). As we now discuss, the capacity to use and adapt kinesic cues to serve pedagogical functions is not completely innate but develops through training and experience.

14.4 Gestures of Future Teachers: A Developmental Approach

Using gestures as a pedagogical tool is not innate. It develops not only with time and experience but also through training. In this section, we discuss features of teachers' pedagogical gestures and how they can be improved with training.

14.4.1 Pedagogical Features of Co-Speech Gestures

As we have discussed, teachers can adapt their gestures to the language proficiency and the needs of their students to enhance learning. Strikingly, many language teachers are aware of the fact that they use gestures as a scaffold strategy in class: They can actually describe some of the gestures they use as a routine or postures that they tend to adopt for certain pedagogical functions (Tellier & Cadet, 2018). One can wonder how much of this adaptation is spontaneous and how much is developed through training and experience. Studies on foreigner talk (Ferguson, 1975, 1981) have shown that speakers adapt their speech to their foreign interlocutor (slow speech rate, simplification of lexical use, articulation, etc.), but little is known about the gestural adaptation that may occur. One study on gestures in foreigner talk (Adams, 1998) showed that little gestural adaptation is done when "regular" speakers address nonnative speakers although speakers did statistically produce more deictics when addressing nonnative speakers. Is this also true for future teachers (i.e., speakers who are sensitive to the difficulties that learners may encounter in oral comprehension)? In the *Gestures in Teacher Talk* project we launched in 2009, future teachers of French (enrolled in a training program in Aix en Provence, France) participated in a lexical explanation task with native and nonnative speakers of French. They had to explain 12 words to both partners to make them guess these words. Data enabled us to compare how future teachers use gesture and speech and adapt them to the proficiency level of their addressee (Tellier et al., in press).

To a certain extent, most future teachers use gestures as a "tool" to enrich their speech when talking to learners of French (Tellier et al., in press). For example, the degree of iconicity in their gestures is higher (more iconics and deictics are produced than metaphorics and emblems for instance) as well as the size of the gestures (larger gestures are produced with learners of French). Similar patterns are found when giving explanations in an L1 depending on the age of the addressee. For instance,

Campisi and Özyürek (2013) found that adult speakers produced gestures that were more informative and bigger for children than for adults.

In Example 14.17 from the *Gestures in Teacher Talk* corpus, the future teacher (on the left) explains the word "grimper" [to climb] first to a native partner, then a nonnative one (see Figure 14.14). In both conditions she says almost the same sentence and produces an iconic gesture (pretending to climb the rocks), but with the nonnative partner the gesture is larger and goes above her head.

Similarly, future teachers seem to adapt their gestures during their conversational exchange when their non-native partner does not understand them. In Example 14.18 (Figure 14.15), we can see a future teacher (on the left) explaining the phrase to "grate cheese" to a nonnative partner. He first produces an iconic gesture showing the size and the shape of a little piece of cheese. He explains the action of grating and says that the goal is to have little pieces of cheese in the end. The gesture is rather static and shows one referent (the small piece of cheese), which is a key word (i.e., a word whose comprehension is necessary to understand the meaning of the sentence). His nonnative interlocutor does not understand, so he explains again and focuses his gestures on the specific description of the action (the verbal explanation remains roughly the same: "little pieces [of cheese]"). This time, he shows the action of grating cheese and all the little pieces falling down from the grate. His gestures show the grate, the original piece of cheese, all the little grated pieces, and the action of the pieces falling from the grate. This sophisticated ensemble of gestures illustrates not only a single key word (like the other explanation) but the whole action. This happens because the first explanation with one gesture did not work. We can see that in case of misunderstanding, future teachers tend to add more meaning in their gestures and make them more complex.

A final feature specific to gestures produced in a pedagogical context is the use of gestures during speech pauses. In fact, future teachers (as well as experienced

Fig. 14.14: Example 14.17. To climb (from the Gestures in Teacher Talk corpus). A future teacher explains the word "grimper" [to climb] first to a native partner and then to a nonnative.
Left panel: Future teacher: "Quand tu montes à un arbre" [When you go up a tree].
Right panel: Future teacher: "*Quand on monte à un arbre*" [When one goes up a tree].

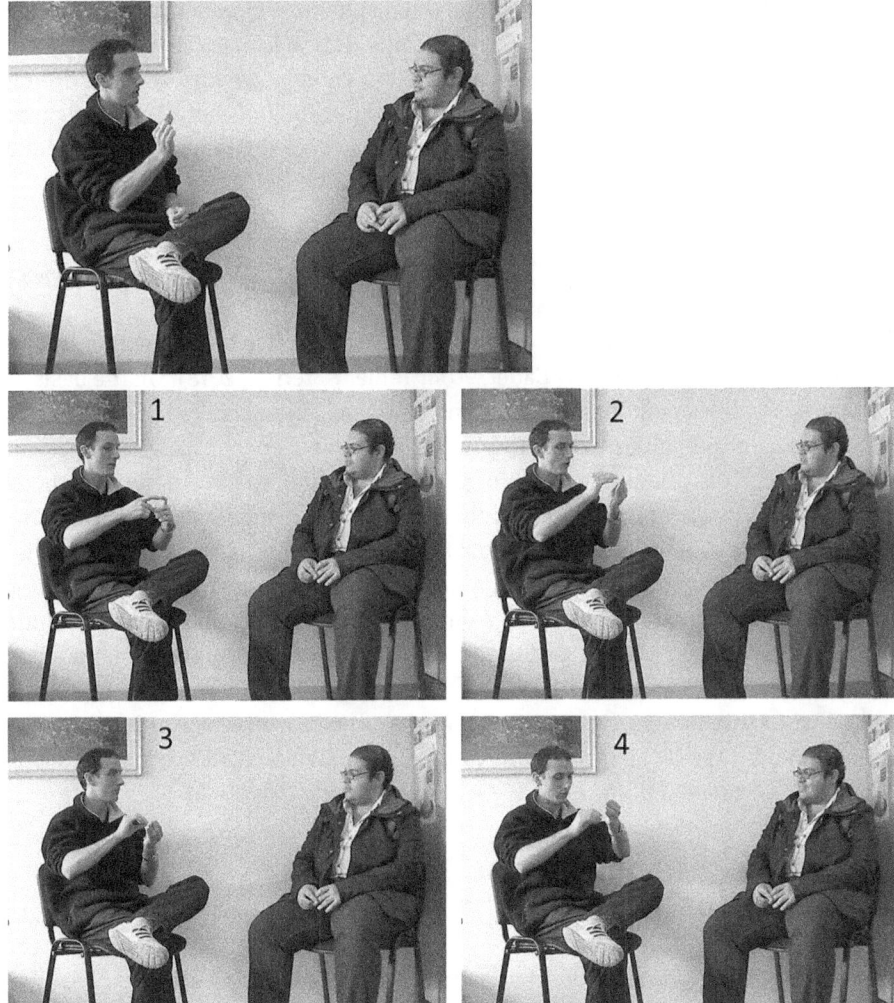

Fig. 14.15: Example 14.18. Top panel: "Pour avoir des petits euh des petits morceaux" [To get some small hum some small pieces].
Bottom panel: "Si j'ai un un morceau" [If I have a a piece] (Picture 1), "De fromage ouais" [Of cheese yeah] (390 ms) "Et je le frotte" [And I rub it] (Picture 2; 1,340 ms), "Ouais" [Yeah] (1,630 ms) "Et il y a des petits" [And there are little] (Picture 3), "Morceaux de fromage" [Pieces of cheese] (Picture 4). The numbers correspond to speech pauses.

teachers) use gestures during speech pauses to facilitate comprehension. They tend to produce speech pauses after and/or before key words to isolate them and facilitate the segmentation of the spoken chain, and they sometimes produce gestures during these pauses to help the learners understand the meaning of these key words (see Stam & Tellier, 2017; Tellier et al., 2013). Interestingly, they do not use this technique with native interlocutors in the *Gestures in Teacher Talk* corpus.

14.4.2 Pedagogical Gestures in Teacher Training

Pedagogical gestures and the use of the body in class receive little attention in language teacher training (Tellier & Cadet, 2014; Tellier & Yerian, 2018). On the basis of the analysis of classroom films and training sessions, Tellier and Yerian (2018) identified the major difficulties that future language teachers encounter with the use of their body in class: the relevant use of gaze, the posture and location of the body in class, and the use of the body (mainly the hands) to demonstrate meaning. This is why several researchers have advocated that effective use of the body as a pedagogical tool is an acquired skill and that teacher education programs should incorporate workshops or training modules on this topic. These modules could include (a) theoretical elements about gestures in communication and in teaching and how they can be culturally specific, (b) practice opportunities focused on exploiting embodied multimodality (integrating use of the body, voice, and other material support), and (c) sessions of self-observation in stimulated recall sessions (Tellier & Cadet, 2014; Tellier & Yerian, 2018).

14.5 Conclusion

Considering the importance of gestures in L2 learning and teaching that we have discussed in this chapter, we are convinced that studies in SLA and second language teaching should include more analyses of gestures to better understand how speech and gestures are linked in production and perception of a foreign language. As far as SLA is concerned, gestures tell us a lot about how L2 learners are thinking, and consequently they can be used as a means to assess both L2 development and L2 thinking. This can be done in both experimental tasks and in more naturalistic settings. Both kinds of data are necessary if we are to truly understand L2 acquisition. In addition, more studies are needed that look at learners' gestures in multiple tasks because this will give us a fuller picture of how they use the L2. Also needed are more longitudinal studies in multiple languages. Finally, more training is necessary for researchers who are interested in investigating L2 and gesture. This can be done as workshops at conferences or workshops sponsored by universities. Similarly, for second language teaching, the analysis of the kinesic activity (not only hand gestures but also gaze, facial expressions, postures) of teachers and learners would enable researchers in language education to gain a better understanding of what is going on in the classroom (in terms of interaction, activities, and learning). Future research should not only focus on assessing the effect of teacher training on the use of pedagogical gestures by young teachers but also look at professional development over a teacher's lifetime and the way experience can affect gesture production in class. Studies combining experimental methods and naturalistic data would lead to a better view on how pedagogical gestures are used in class and their effect on learning. Given what we know about gestures and what they can tell us about L2 learning and teaching, they can no longer be ignored in SLA and second language teaching research.

References

Adams, T. W. (1998). *Gesture in foreigner talk* [Unpublished doctoral dissertation]. University of Pennsylvania.

Agar, M. (1994). *Language shock: Understanding the culture of conversation*. William Morrow.

Aguiló Mora, F., & Negueruela-Azarola, E. (2015). Motion for the other through motion for the self: The conceptual complexities of giving-directions for advanced Spanish heritage learners. In K. Masuda, C. Arnett, & A. Labarca (Eds.), *Cognitive linguistics and sociocultural theory: Applications for second and foreign language teaching* (pp. 73–100). de Gruyter Mouton.

Allen, L. Q. (1995). The effects of emblematic gestures on the development and access of mental representations of French expressions. *Modern Language Journal*, 79(4), 521–529. https://doi.org/10.1111/j.1540-4781.1995.tb05454.x

Allen, L. Q. (2000). Nonverbal accommodations in foreign language teacher talk. *Applied Language Learning*, 11(1), 155–176.

Azaoui, B. (2013, June 19–21). *One teacher, two instructional contexts: Same teaching gestures?* [Paper]. Tilburg Gesture Research Meeting, Tilburg, the Netherlands. https://hal.archives-ouvertes.fr/file/index/docid/833026/filename/azaoui_tiger13_one_teacher_two_instructional_contexts_same_teaching_gestures.pdf

Azaoui, B. (2014). Multimodalité des signes et enjeux énonciatifs en classe de FL1/FLS [Multimodality of signs and enunciative issues in FL1/FLS class]. In M. Tellier & L. Cadet (Eds.), *Le corps et la voix de l'enseignant: Mise en contexte théorique et pratique* (pp. 115–126). Éditions Maison des Langues.

Azaoui, B. (2016). Mise en abyme des interactions didactiques [Putting didactic interactions in perspective]. *Recherches en Didactique des Langues et des Cultures*, 13(1). http://rdlc.revues.org/1472

Barnett, M. (1983). Replacing teacher talk with gestures: Nonverbal communication in the foreign language classroom. *Foreign Language Annals*, 16(3), 173–176. https://doi.org/10.1111/j.1944-9720.1983.tb01446.x

Beattie, G., & Coughlan, J. (1998). Do iconic gestures have a functional role in lexical access? An experimental study on the effects of repeating a verbal message on gesture production. *Semiotica*, 119(3/4), 221–249. https://doi.org/10.1515/semi.1998.119.3-4.221

Beattie, G., & Coughlan, J. (1999). An experimental investigation of the role of iconic gestures in lexical access using the tip-of-the-tongue phenomenon. *British Journal of Psychology*, *90*(1), 35–56. https://doi.org/10.1348/000712699161251

Beattie, N. (1977). Non-verbal aspects of the teaching and learning of foreign languages. *Audio-Visual Language Journal*, *15*(2), 175–181.

Brown, A. (2008). Gesture viewpoint in Japanese and English: Cross-linguistic interactions between two languages in one speaker. *Gesture*, *8*(2), 256–276. https://doi.org/10.1075/gest.8.2.08bro

Brown, A. (2015). Universal development and L1–L2 convergence in bilingual construal of manner in speech and gesture in Mandarin, Japanese, and English. *Modern Language Journal*, *99*(Suppl. 1), 66–82. https://doi.org/10.1111/j.1540-4781.2015.12179.x

Brown, A., & Gullberg, M. (2008). Bidirectional crosslinguistic influence in L1–L2 encoding of manner in speech and gesture: A study of Japanese speakers of English. *Studies in Second Language Acquisition*, *30*(2), 225–251. https://doi.org/10.1017/S0272263108080327

Cadierno, T., & Lund, K. (2004). Cognitive linguistics and second language acquisition: Motion events in a typological framework. In B. VanPatten, J. Williams, S. Rott, & M. Overstreet (Eds.), *Form–meaning connections in second language acquisition* (pp. 139–154). Erlbaum.

Campisi, E., & Özyürek, A. (2013). Iconicity as a communicative strategy: Recipient design in multimodal demonstrations for adults and children. *Journal of Pragmatics*, *47*(1), 14–27. https://doi.org/10.1016/j.pragma.2012.12.007

Choi, S., & Lantolf, J. P. (2008). Representation and embodiment of meaning in L2 communication: Motion events in the speech and gesture of advanced L2 Korean and L2 English speakers. *Studies in Second Language Acquisition*, *30*(2), 191–224. https://doi.org/10.1017/S0272263108080315

Dabène, L. (1984). Pour une taxinomie des opérations métacommunicatives en classe de langue étrangère [For a taxonomy of metacommunicative activities in the foreign language classroom]. *Études de Linguistique Appliquée*, *55*, 39–46.

Denizci, C., & Azaoui, B. (2015). Reconsidering gesture space for naturalistic teaching gesture research. *Istanbul Journal of Innovation in Education*, *1*(3), 97–109.

de Nooijer, J. A., van Gog, T., Paas, F., & Zwaan, R. A. (2013). Effects of imitating gestures during encoding or during retrieval of novel verbs on children's test performance. *Acta Psychologica*, *144*(1), 173–179. https://doi.org/10.1016/j.actpsy.2013.05.013

Drijvers, L., & Özyürek, A. (2016). Visual context enhanced: The joint contribution of iconic gestures and visible speech to degraded speech comprehension. *Journal of Speech, Language, and Hearing Research*, *60*(1), 212–222. https://doi.org/10.1044/2016_JSLHR-H-16-0101

Faraco, M. (2008, March 20–22). Gestes et prosodie didactiques dans l'enseignement des structures langagières en FLE [Didactic gestures and prosody in teaching language structures in FLE] [Paper]. *Actes du Colloque Enseigner les Structures Langagières en FLE*, Brussels, Belgium. http://gramm-fle.ulb.ac.be/95/enseigner-les-structures-langagieres-en-fle-bruxelles-20-22-mars-2008-actes/

Ferguson, C. (1975). Toward a characterization of English foreigner talk. *Anthropological Linguistics*, *17*, 1–14.

Ferguson, C. (1981). "Foreigner talk" as the name of a simplified register. *International Journal of the Sociology of Language*, *28*, 9–18. https://doi.org/10.1515/ijsl.1981.28.9

Grant, B. M., & Grant Hennings, D. (1971). *The teacher moves: An analysis of non-verbal activity*. Teachers College Press.

Gullberg, M. (1998). *Gesture as a communication strategy in second language discourse: A study of learners of French and Swedish*. Lund University Press.

Gullberg, M. (2010). Methodological reflections on gesture analysis in second language acquisition and bilingualism research. *Second Language Research, 26*(1), 75–102. https://doi.org/10.1177/0267658309337639

Gullberg, M., de Bot, K., & Volterra, V. (2008). Gestures and some key issues in the study of language development. *Gesture, 8*(2), 149–179. https://doi.org/10.1075/gest.8.2.03gul

Gullberg, M., & McCafferty, S. G. (2008). Introduction to gesture and SLA: Toward an integrated approach. *Studies in Second Language Acquisition, 30*(2), 133–146. https://doi.org/10.1017/S0272263108080285

Hauge, E. (1998). Gesture in the EFL class: An aid to communication or a source of confusion? In D. Killick & M. Parry (Eds.), *Cross-cultural capability—The why, the ways and the means—New theories and methodologies in language education—Proceedings of the Conference at Leeds Metropolitan University 15–16 December 1997* (pp. 271–280). Browns Books.

Hauge, E. (1999). Some common emblems used by British English teachers in EFL classes. In D. Killick & M. Parry (Eds.), *Cross-cultural capability: Promoting the discipline—Marking boundaries and crossing borders—Proceedings of the conference at Leeds Metropolitan University 12–14 December 1998* (pp. 405–420). Leeds Metropolitan University.

Holt, B., Tellier, M., & Guichon, N. (2015). The use of teaching gestures in an online multimodal environment: The case of incomprehension sequences. In G. Ferré & T. Mark (Eds.), *Gesture and speech in interaction* (4th ed., pp. 149–154). https://hal.archives-ouvertes.fr/hal-01195646/document

Jenkins, S., & Parra, I. (2003). Multiple layers of meaning in an oral proficiency test: The complementary roles of nonverbal, paralinguistic, and verbal behaviors in assessment decisions. *Modern Language Journal, 87*(1), 90–107. https://doi.org/10.1111/1540-4781.00180

Kellerman, E., & van Hoof, A.-M. (2003). Manual accents. *International Journal of Applied Linguistics, 41*, 251–269. https://doi.org/10.1515/iral.2003.011

Kellerman, S. (1992). "I see what you mean": The role of kinesic behaviour in listening and implications for foreign and second language learning. *Applied Linguistics, 13*(3), 239–258. https://doi.org/10.1093/applin/13.3.239

Kendon, A. (2004). *Gesture: Visible action as utterance*. Cambridge University Press. https://doi.org/10.1017/CBO9780511807572

Krönke, K. M., Mueller, K., Friederici, A. D., & Obrig, H. (2013). Learning by doing? The effect of gestures on implicit retrieval of newly acquired words. *Cortex, 49*(9), 2553–2568. https://doi.org/10.1016/j.cortex.2012.11.016

Lazaraton, A. (2004). Gestures and speech in the vocabulary explanations of one ESL teacher: A microanalytic inquiry. *Language Learning, 54*(1), 79–117. https://doi.org/10.1111/j.1467-9922.2004.00249.x

Macedonia, M. (2013). Learning a second language naturally: The voice movement icon approach. *Journal of Educational and Developmental Psychology, 3*(2), 102–116. https://doi.org/10.5539/jedp.v3n2p102

Macedonia, M., & Klimesch, W. (2014). Long-term effects of gestures on memory for foreign language words trained in the classroom. *Mind, Brain, and Education, 8*(2), 74–88. https://doi.org/10.1111/mbe.12047

Macedonia, M., & Knösche, T. R. (2011). Body in mind: How gestures empower foreign language learning. *Mind, Brain, and Education*, *5*(4), 196–211. https://doi.org/10.1111/j.1751-228X.2011.01129.x

Macedonia, M., Müller, K., & Friederici, A. D. (2011). The impact of iconic gestures on foreign language word learning and its neural substrate. *Human Brain Mapping*, *32*(6), 982–998. https://doi.org/10.1002/hbm.21084

Mackey, A., Maymona, A.-K., Gergana, A., Mika, H., Aubrey, L.-T., & Nakatsukasa, K. (2007). Teachers' intentions and learners' perceptions about corrective feedback in the L2 classroom. *Innovation in Language Learning and Teaching*, *1*(1), 129–152. https://doi.org/10.2167/illt047.0

Matsumoto, Y., & Dobs, A. M. (2017). Pedagogical gestures as interactional resources for teaching and learning tense and aspect in the ESL grammar classroom. *Language Learning*, *67*(1), 7–42. https://doi.org/10.1111/lang.12181

McIntyre, N., Mainhard, T., & Klassen, R. M. (2017). Are you looking to teach? Cultural, temporal and dynamic insights into expert teacher gaze. *Learning and Instruction*, *49*, 41–53. https://doi.org/10.1016/j.learninstruc.2016.12.005

McNeill, D. (1992). *Hand and mind: What gestures reveal about thought*. University of Chicago Press.

McNeill, D. (2005). *Gesture and thought*. University of Chicago Press. https://doi.org/10.7208/chicago/9780226514642.001.0001

McNeill, D. (2012). *How language began: Gesture and speech in human evolution*. Cambridge University Press. https://doi.org/10.1017/CBO9781139108669

Nakatsukasa, K. (2016). Efficacy of gestures and recasts on the acquisition of locative prepositions. *Studies in Second Language Acquisition*, *38*(4), 771–799. https://doi.org/10.1017/S0272263115000467

Nambiar, M. K., & Goon, C. (1993). Assessment of oral skills: A comparison of scores obtained through audio recordings to those obtained through face-to-face evaluation. *RELC Journal*, *24*(1), 15–31.

Negueruela, E., Lantolf, J. P., Jordan, S. R., & Gelabert, J. (2004). The "private function" of gesture in second language speaking activity: A study of motion verbs and gesturing in English and Spanish. *International Journal of Applied Linguistics*, *14*(1), 113–147. https://doi.org/10.1111/j.1473-4192.2004.00056.x

Neu, J. (1990). Assessing the role of nonverbal communication in the acquisition of communicative competence in L2. In R. C. Scarcella, E. S. Andersen, & S. D. Krashen (Eds.), *Developing communicative competence in a second language* (pp. 121–138). Newbury House.

Özyürek, A. (2000). The influence of addressee location on spatial language and representational gestures of direction. In D. McNeill (Ed.), *Language and gesture* (pp. 64–83). Cambridge University Press. https://doi.org/10.1017/CBO9780511620850.005

Pavelin, B. (2002). *Le geste à la parole* [Gesture to speech]. Presses Universitaires du Mirail.

Rowe, M. L., Silverman, R. D., & Mullan, B. E. (2013). The role of pictures and gestures as nonverbal aids in preschoolers' word learning in a novel language. *Contemporary Educational Psychology*, *38*(2), 109–117. https://doi.org/10.1016/j.cedpsych.2012.12.001

Schachter, J. (1981). The hand signal system. *TESOL Quarterly*, *15*(2), 125–138. https://doi.org/10.2307/3586404

Seaver, P. W., Jr. (1992). Pantomime as an L2 classroom strategy. *Foreign Language Annals*, *25*(1), 21–31. https://doi.org/10.1111/j.1944-9720.1992.tb00509.x

Sime, D. (2001). The use and perception of illustrators in the foreign language classroom. In C. Cavé, I. Guaïtella, & S. Santi (Eds.), *Oralité et gestualité: Interactions et comportements multimodaux dans la communication* (pp. 582–585). L'Harmattan.

Sime, D. (2006). What do learners make of teachers' gestures in the language classroom? *International Review of Applied Linguistics, 44*(2), 211–230. https://doi.org/10.1515/IRAL.2006.009

Sime, D. (2008). "Because of her gesture, it's very easy to understand": Learners' perceptions of teachers' gestures in the foreign language class. In S. G. McCafferty & G. Stam (Eds.), *Gesture: Second language acquisition and classroom research* (pp. 259–279). Routledge.

Slobin, D. I. (1991). Learning to think for speaking: Native language, cognition, and rhetorical style. *Pragmatics, 1*(1), 7–25. https://doi.org/10.1075/prag.1.1.01slo

Slobin, D. I. (2006). What makes manner of motion salient? Explorations in linguistic typology, discourse, and cognition. In M. Hickmann & S. Robert (Eds.), *Space in languages: Linguistic systems and cognitive categories* (pp. 59–81). John Benjamins. https://doi.org/10.1075/tsl.66.05slo

Sloetjes, H., & Wittenburg, P. (2008). Annotation by category—ELAN and ISO DCR. In *Proceedings of the 6th International Conference on Language Resources and Evaluation* (pp. 816–820). European Language Resources Association.

Smotrova, T. (2017). Making pronunciation visible: Gesture in teaching pronunciation. *TESOL Quarterly, 51*(1), 59–89. https://doi.org/10.1002/tesq.276

Stam, G. (1998). Changes in patterns of thinking about motion with L2 acquisition. In S. Santi, I. Guaïtella, C. Cavé, & G. Konopczynski (Eds.), *Oralité et gestualité: Communication multimodale, interaction* (pp. 615–619). L'Harmattan.

Stam, G. (2001). Lexical failure and gesture in second language development. In C. Cavé, I. Guaïtella, & S. Santi (Eds.), *Oralité et gestualité: Interactions et comportements multimodaux dans la communication* (pp. 271–275). L'Harmattan.

Stam, G. (2006a). *Changes in patterns of thinking with second language acquisition* [Unpublished doctoral dissertation]. University of Chicago.

Stam, G. (2006b). Thinking for speaking about motion: L1 and L2 speech and gesture. *International Review of Applied Linguistics, 44*, 145–171.

Stam, G. (2008). What gestures reveal about second language acquisition. In S. G. McCafferty & G. Stam (Eds.), *Gesture: Second language acquisition and classroom research* (pp. 231–255). Routledge.

Stam, G. (2010). Can a L2 speaker's patterns of thinking for speaking change? In Z. H. Han & T. Cadierno (Eds.), *Linguistic relativity in SLA: Thinking for speaking* (pp. 59–83). Multilingual Matters. https://doi.org/10.21832/9781847692788-005

Stam, G. (2012). Gestes et recherche de mots en langue seconde [Gestures and word search in a second language]. In R. Vion, A. Giacomi, & C. Vargas (Eds.), *La corporalité du langage: Multimodalité, discours et écriture* (pp. 55–71). Publications de l'Université de Provence.

Stam, G. (2013). Second language acquisition and gesture. In C. A. Chapelle (Ed.), *The encyclopedia of applied linguistics*. Blackwell. https://doi.org/10.1002/9781405198431.wbeal1049

Stam, G. (2014). Further changes in L2 thinking for speaking? In C. Müller, A. Cienki, E. Fricke, S. H. Ladewig, D. McNeill, & J. Bressem (Eds.), *Body language communication: An international handbook on multimodality in human interaction* (Vol. 2, pp. 1875–1886). Mouton de Gruyter. https://doi.org/10.1515/9783110302028.1875

Stam, G. (2015). Changes in thinking for speaking: A longitudinal case study. *Modern Language Journal, 99*(Suppl. 1), 83–99. https://doi.org/10.1111/j.1540-4781.2015.12180.x

Stam, G. (2016). Gesture as a window onto conceptualization in multiple tasks: Implications for second language teaching. *Yearbook of the German Cognitive Linguistics Association*, 4(1), 289–314. https://doi.org/10.1515/gcla-2016-0017

Stam, G. (2017). Verb framed, satellite framed or in between? A L2 learner's thinking for speaking in her L1 and L2 over 14 years. In I. Ibarretxe-Antuñano (Ed.), *Motion and space across languages: Theory and applications* (pp. 329–366). John Benjamins. https://doi.org/10.1075/hcp.59.14sta

Stam, G. (2018a). Gesture and speaking a second language. In R. Alonso (Ed.), *Speaking in a L2* (pp. 51–69). John Benjamins.

Stam, G. (2018b). Gesture as a window onto conceptualization in second language acquisition: A Vygotskian perspective. In J. P. Lantolf, M. E. Poehner, & M. Swain (Eds.), *Routledge handbook of sociocultural theory and second language development* (pp. 165–177). Routledge. https://doi.org/10.4324/9781315624747-11

Stam, G., & Buescher, K. (2018). Gesture research. In A. Phakiti, P. De Costa, L. Plonsky, & S. Starfield (Eds.), *Palgrave handbook of applied linguistics research methodology* (pp. 793–809). Palgrave Macmillan. https://doi.org/10.1057/978-1-137-59900-1_36

Stam, G., & McCafferty, S. G. (2008). Gesture studies and second language acquisition: A review. In S. G. McCafferty & G. Stam (Eds.), *Gesture: Second language acquisition and classroom research* (pp. 3–24). Routledge.

Stam, G., & Tellier, M. (2017). The sound of silence: The functions of gestures in pauses in native and non-native interaction. In R. B. Church, M. W. Alibali, & S. D. Kelly (Eds.), *Why gesture? How the hands function in speaking, thinking and communicating* (pp. 353–377). John Benjamins. https://doi.org/10.1075/gs.7.17sta

Sueyoshi, A., & Hardison, D. M. (2005). The role of gestures and facial cues in second language listening comprehension. *Language Learning*, 55(4), 661–699. https://doi.org/10.1111/j.0023-8333.2005.00320.x

Tabensky, A. (2008). Expository discourse in a second language classroom: How learners use gesture. In S. G. McCafferty & G. Stam (Eds.), *Gesture: Second language acquisition and classroom research* (pp. 298–320). Routledge.

Talmy, L. (2000). *Towards a cognitive semantics: Vol. II. Typology and process in concept structuring*. MIT Press.

Tellier, M. (2008a). Dire avec des gestes [Say it with gestures]. *Français Dans le Monde, Recherche et Application*, 44, 40–50.

Tellier, M. (2008b). The effect of gestures on second language memorisation by young children. *Gesture*, 8(2), 219–235. https://doi.org/10.1075/gest.8.2.06tel

Tellier, M. (2009). Usage pédagogique et perception de la multimodalité pour l'accès au sens en langue étrangère [Educational use and perception of multimodality for access to meaning in a foreign language]. In R. Bergeron, G. Plessis-Belaire, & L. Lafontaine (Eds.), *La place des savoirs oraux dans le contexte scolaire d'aujourd'hui* (pp. 223–245). Presses de l'Université du Québec.

Tellier, M. (2014). Donner du corps à son cours [Use your body in your course]. In M. Tellier & L. Cadet (Eds.), *Le corps et la voix de l'enseignant: Théorie et pratique* (pp. 101–114). Éditions Maison des Langues.

Tellier, M. (2016). Prendre son cours à bras le corps: De l'articulation des modalités kinésiques avec la parole [Embrace your course with your body: The articulation of kinesic modalities with speech]. *Recherches en Didactique des Langues et des Cultures*, 13(1). https://doi.org/10.4000/rdlc.474

Tellier, M., & Cadet, L. (2013). Dans la peau d'un natif: Etat des lieux sur l'enseignement des gestes culturels [In the skin of a native: State of play on the teaching of cultural gestures in French as a foreign language]. *La Revue Française d'Education Comparée, 9*, 111–140.

Tellier, M., & Cadet, L. (Eds.). (2014). *Le corps et la voix de l'enseignant: Théorie et pratique* [The teacher's body and voice: Theory and practice]. Éditions Maison des Langues.

Tellier, M., & Cadet, L. (2018). Si le corps vous en dit: Prendre conscience de son corps pédagogique en formation [As your body tells you: Become aware of your educational body in training]. In *Expertise au service des acteurs du français dans le monde: Mélanges pour les 50 ans du BELC* (pp. 57–65). CIEP Éditions.

Tellier, M., & Stam, G. (2012). Stratégies verbales et gestuelles dans l'explication lexicale d'un verbe d'action [Verbal and gestural strategies in the lexical explanation of an action verb]. In V. Rivière (Ed.), *Spécificités et diversité des interactions didactiques* (pp. 357–374). Riveneuve Éditions.

Tellier, M., Stam, G., & Bigi, B. (2013, June 19–21). Gesturing while pausing in conversation: Self-oriented or partner-oriented? [Paper]. Tilburg Gesture Research Meeting, Tilburg, the Netherlands.

Tellier, M., Stam, G., & Ghio, A. (in press). Handling language: How future language teachers adapt their gestures to their interlocutor. *Gesture*.

Tellier, M., & Yerian, K. (2018). Mettre du corps à l'ouvrage: Travailler sur la mise en scène du corps du jeune enseignant en formation universitaire [Put the body to work: Working on the staging of the body of pre-service teachers in university training]. *Recherche et Pratiques Pédagogiques en Langues de Spécialité—Cahiers de l'APLIUT, 37*(2). https://doi.org/10.4000/apliut.6079

Varonis, E. M., & Gass, S. (1985). Non-native/non-native conversations: A model for negotiation of meaning. *Applied Linguistics, 6*(1), 71–90. https://doi.org/10.1093/applin/6.1.71

von Raffler-Engel, W. (1980). Kinesics and paralinguistics: A neglected factor in second language research. *Canadian Modern Language Review, 36*(2), 225–237. https://doi.org/10.3138/cmlr.36.2.225

Wylie, L. (1985). Language learning and communication. *French Review, 58*(6), 777–785.

Aliyah Morgenstern and Susan Goldin-Meadow

Afterword: Gesture as *Part of Language* or *Partner to Language* Across the Lifespan

We have chosen to dedicate this volume to gestural expression used primarily by hearing speakers. The book illustrates how research—conducted with a range of different methods, on people of different ages, who use one or multiple languages, in a variety of situations, and within different theoretical frameworks—adds richness to the field of gesture studies. Within the limits of what can be done in a single volume, we have covered as many aspects of the dynamic relation between gesture and language across the lifespan as we could. But we did not cover them all. For example, we did not focus on sign languages or on the rich (dis)continuities between gesture and sign. Whether the relation between gesture and sign is presented as a "cataclysmic break" (Singleton et al., 1995; see also Brentari & Goldin-Meadow, 2017) or as naturally continuous (Müller, 2018) depends, in part, on the time span under consideration. Grammatical elements of sign languages can be traced to gestural origins over historical time (Blondel, 2020; Janzen, 1998, 2017; Wilcox, 2007, among others). But over ontogenetic time, sign and gesture have been found to be distinct vehicles (e.g., gesture–sign mismatches in signers learning math problems predict success on the problems, just as gesture–speech mismatches do; Goldin-Meadow et al., 2012).

As Cook explains in Chapter 10 of this volume, gesture and speech are generally placed in different categories because they are produced in different modalities. Gesture and sign are produced in the same modality, which often makes it difficult to separate the two. But gesture and speech also differ in the representational formats they use to convey information (McNeill, 1992), and so do gesture and sign (Goldin-Meadow & Brentari, 2017), which for certain categories of gesture could be considered as imagistic and continuous forms versus conventional and categorical forms in sign, other categories of gestures (e.g., emblems), and speech. There is consequently good reason to separate the two vehicles but also good reason to pay attention to how gesture and speech or sign work together; for example, to understand the role of the visual and kinesic modalities in language or to capture the conventionalization processes from idiosyncratic to socially transmitted grammaticalized forms.

The chapters in this book have taken different perspectives and used different methods and, as a result, have highlighted multiple issues. The relation between gesture and language depends on the definition of language a researcher uses (Morgenstern & Goldin-Meadow, Chapter 1). Whether gesture is considered *part of language* or *partner to language* also depends on the timespans, groups, and types of gestures studied. But all of the chapters consider gesture to be a crucial communicative and cognitive resource that serves multiple functions.

Some authors consider gesture to be a part of language. They integrate gesture into language or *languaging* (see Morgenstern, Chapter 3; Morgenstern, 2014), or promote a bimodal view of language (Gullberg, Chapter 13). Other authors consider gesture to be a partner to language, either a sign language (Goldin-Meadow et al., 2012) or a spoken language (Clark & Kelly, Chapter 6; Cooperrider & Mesh, Chapter 2; Rowe et al., Chapter 4). But this distinction may rest on semantics (and perhaps timespan)— if we define language as a system made entirely of discrete categories, mimetic and gradient, gesture can be viewed as not falling within this definition. But if we define language as including any device that has attained a degree of shared communicative value, gesture fits squarely within the definition. All researchers agree that gesture plays a role in communication. The argument may be over how seriously we take format— gesture can be considered as imagistic and continuous, language (as linguists typically define it) can be considered categorical and discrete. Along these lines, some authors highlight the imagistic power of gesture (Hall et al., Chapter 8) and how it can make words more learnable. Some underline the praxic roots of gesture and the affordances it provides to embody experience (Boutet & Morgenstern, 2020; Capirci et al., Chapter 5; Morgenstern, Chapter 3).

Although these distinctions may be a matter of definition and terminology, they underscore important differences in scientific domain (linguistics vs. psychology) and method (naturalistic interactive data vs. experimental data; qualitative vs. quantitative analyses). The type of gesture an author focuses on also affects whether gesture is treated as *part of* or *partner to* language. For example, spontaneous gestures are typically considered *partner to* language, whereas recurrent gestures or emblems are considered *part of* language (Müller, 2018). Gestures used without speech—for example "silent gestures" that speakers are asked to create on the spot (Goldin-Meadow et al., 1996), or homesign gestures that deaf children who are not exposed to sign language create over time (Goldin-Meadow, 2003)—are functioning as language (i.e., they are neither *partner to* nor *part of* language), and are evaluated in terms of the aspects of language that they display (Goldin-Meadow, 2006; Goldin-Meadow & Brentari, 2017).

Just as transcription systems may reveal an author's theory (Ochs, 1979), the choice of which type of gesture to study can reveal an author's views on what constitutes language. The distinctions are based on whether gestures are stable and conventionalized, rather than spontaneous; whether they are discrete, compositional, and linear, rather than global and synthetic; whether they are symbolic and have their own semiotic features, rather than being informed by co-occurrent speech or sign. One way of tackling these distinctions is to draw categories out of the heterogeneity of gestures and analyze their differences according to a continuum based on degree of communicative conventionality (Kendon, 1988; McNeill, 1992). Rather than give center stage to the entrenchment of form–function pairing, another approach is to create a multidimensional model based on a variety of parameters, including pragmatic transparency, social and cultural impact, recurrence, iconicity, indexicality, metaphoricity, salience, as well as arbitrariness or conventionality (see Irishkhanova & Cienki, 2018, for a multidimensional system with 12 parameters). It is only by creating dialogic spaces to discuss this array of perspectives that we can gain enough interdisciplinary expertise to capture the complexities of human polysemiotic interactive resources. Our volume represents a step along this path.

In the Age of Enlightenment and all the way to the end of the 19th century in Europe, gesture was viewed as the root of human language (Condillac, 1746/2014) or as a universal language that facilitated communication across cultures (Darwin, 1839). This interest in gesture was brought to an end when the Société de Linguistique de Paris (Paris Linguistic Society) was created in 1866 and forbade all study of the origin of language in France, which influenced research across Europe. In parallel, despite the inspiring role of L'Abbée de l'Epée in promoting the use of sign to educate deaf children, in 1880 at the Milan Congress, sign languages were banished from deaf children's education in favor of oral languages. Gesture and sign were thus "silenced" for a whole century.

In line with those historical circumstances, Clark and Kelly (Chapter 6) describe how gesture was not taken into account in early studies of child language development. Before the 1960s, linguists rarely integrated gesture or sign into their research. Models of language were overwhelmingly monolingual and monomodal (Gullberg, Chapter 13).

This collection of chapters clearly demonstrates that gesture is no longer invisible. All authors agree that gesture facilitates cognitive and linguistic development. Gesture plays a major role in language socialization (Morgenstern, Chapter 3). It has a variety of functions—communicative, restorative, cognitive—in perception and in production, across cultures and ages, particularly in aging adults as gesture often declines later than speech (Göksun et al., Chapter 11), in monolingual and multilingual populations (Nicoladis & Smithson, Chapter 12; Gullberg, Chapter 13), and in students and teachers (Stam & Tellier, Chapter 14). Gesture plays a role in constructing language skills and supporting the processing of linguistic signals (Cook, Chapter 10), transmitting language practices to children (Morgenstern, Chapter 3; Clark & Kelly, Chapter 6) and facilitating learning (Hall et al., Chapter 8).

The chapters in this volume also illustrate that gesture's role does not diminish over the lifespan but may change qualitatively. In his extensive overview of 2 decades of research, Colletta (Chapter 9) shows how co-speech gesture, bodily posture, and facial expression develop and are enriched as the child acquires new discourse and social–cognitive abilities. By the age of 9 years, children have begun to master and use gesture to mark narrative complexity.

The semiotic features of gestures are varied and variable, flexible, subject to a range of parameters and individual differences. But there may be gestural kinesic primitives stemming from the affordances of our bodies and others' bodies that unify gesture. The materiality of the body has the potential to shape our environment, our tools, our objects, the spaces we inhabit (Leroi-Gourhan, 1943/1993). Structuring these artifacts is closely linked to praxic gestures and is continuous with symbolic gestures (Boutet & Morgenstern, 2020).

Gesture, speech, and sign can therefore be considered semiotic systems that are integrated into language at large, at varying degrees according to the "dynamic scope of relevant behaviors" (Cienki, 2012, p. 155). Situation, population, culture, age, the affordances of the environment, and type of communicative context can all affect what counts as gesture, as exemplified through both quantitative and qualitative analyses in Beaupoil-Hourdel's study (Chapter 7), and in Capirci et al.'s comprehensive overview of 40 years of research (Chapter 5). All human communicative systems can dynamically and interactively evolve into symbolic units, as demonstrated by Edwards and Brentari (2021) in the illuminating case of tactile sign, in which the proprioceptive modality sustains language. When it is interactively deployed by participants who are both blind and deaf with each other using the four arms and hands of the conveyer and the receiver (rather than through the mediation of interpreters), it becomes a protactile language with its own phonology, privileging tactile space. It thus truly embodies Goodwin's powerful concepts of cooperative interaction and intertwined semiosis (2017). The signers' bodies are then what Boutet (2018) called the *support* (the instrument) and the *substrate* (the substance and structure) of language.

Across cultures, across situations, across populations, across human history, and across the lifespan, the construction of meaning is informed by the available and coordinated semiotic resources we use. Whether it is considered a *part of* or *partner to* language, gesture is shared with others during social interactions and thus is an important semiotic resource that can no longer be ignored.

References

Blondel, M. (2020). *Les langues des signes, des langues incarnées* [Sign languages, embodied languages] [Unpublished dissertation]. French Habilitation to Supervise Research, Université Paris 8.

Boutet, D. (2018). *Pour une approche kinésiologique de la gestualité* [For a kinesiological approach to gesture] [Unpublished *Habilitation* dissertation]. French Habilitation to Supervise Research, Université de Rouen-Normandie.

Boutet, D., & Morgenstern, A. (2020). Prelude et ode à l'approche kinésiologique de la gestualité [Prelude and ode to the kinesiological approach to gesture]. *TIPA, 36*. Advance online publication. https://doi.org/10.4000/tipa.3892

Brentari, D., & Goldin-Meadow, S. (2017). Language emergence. *Annual Review of Linguistics, 3*, 363–388. https://doi.org/10.1146/annurev-linguistics-011415-040743

Cienki, A. (2012). Usage events of spoken language and the symbolic units we (may) abstract from them. In J. Badio & K. Kosecki (Eds.), *Cognitive processes in language* (pp. 149–158). Peter Lang.

Condillac, E. (2014). *Essai sur l'origine des connaissances humaines* [Essay on the origin of human knowledge]. Vrin. (Original work published 1746)

Darwin, C. R. (1839). *Narrative of the surveying voyages of His Majesty's Ships Adventure and Beagle between the years 1826 and 1836, describing their examination of the southern shores of South America, and the Beagle's circumnavigation of the globe. Journal and remarks. 1832–1836*. Henry Colburn.

Edwards, T., & Brentari, D. (2021). The grammatical incorporation of demonstratives in an emerging tactile language. *Frontiers in Psychology, 11*, 579992. https://doi.org/10.3389/fpsyg.2020.579992

Goldin-Meadow, S. (2003). *The resilience of language: What gesture creation in deaf children can tell us about how all children learn language*. Psychology Press.

Goldin-Meadow, S. (2006). Talking and thinking with our hands. *Current Directions in Psychological Science, 15*(1), 34–39. https://doi.org/10.1111/j.0963-7214.2006.00402.x

Goldin-Meadow, S., & Brentari, D. (2017). Gesture, sign, and language: The coming of age of sign language and gesture studies. *Behavioral and Brain Sciences, 40*, e46. https://doi.org/10.1017/S0140525X15001247

Goldin-Meadow, S., McNeill, D., & Singleton, J. (1996). Silence is liberating: Removing the handcuffs on grammatical expression in the manual modality. *Psychological Review, 103*(1), 34–55. https://doi.org/10.1037/0033-295X.103.1.34

Goldin-Meadow, S., Shield, A., Lenzen, D., Herzig, M., & Padden, C. (2012). The gestures ASL signers use tell us when they are ready to learn math. *Cognition, 123*(3), 448–453. https://doi.org/10.1016/j.cognition.2012.02.006

Irishkhanova, O., & Cienki, A. (2018). The semiotics of gesture in cognitive linguistics: Contribution and challenges. *Voprosy Kognitivnoy Lingvistiki, 4*, 25–36. https://doi.org/10.20916/1812-3228-2018-4-25-36

Janzen, T. (2017). Composite utterances in a signed language: Topic constructions and perspective-taking in ASL. *Cognitive Linguistics, 28*(3), 511–538. https://doi.org/10.1515/cog-2016-0121

Janzen, T. D. (1998). *Topicality in ASL: Information ordering, constituent structure, and the function of topic marking* (Publication No. 9826632) [Doctoral dissertation, University of New Mexico]. ProQuest Dissertations Publishing.

Kendon, A. (1988). *Sign languages of Aboriginal Australia: Cultural, semiotic and communicative perspectives*. Cambridge University Press.

Leroi-Gourhan, A. (1993). *L'Homme et la matière: Evolution et techniques* [Man and matter: Evolution and techniques]. Albin Michel. (Original work published 1943)

McNeill, D. (1992). *Hand and mind: What gestures reveal about thought*. University of Chicago Press.

Morgenstern, A. (2014). Children's multimodal language development. In C. Fäcke (Ed.), *Manual of language acquisition* (pp. 123–142). De Gruyter. https://doi.org/10.1515/9783110302257.123

Müller, C. (2018). Gesture and sign: Cataclysmic break or dynamic relations? *Frontiers in Psychology, 9*, 1651. https://doi.org/10.3389/fpsyg.2018.01651

Ochs, E. (1979). Transcription as theory. In E. Ochs & B. Schieffelin (Eds.), *Developmental pragmatics* (pp. 43–72). Academic Press. http://www.sscnet.ucla.edu/anthro/faculty/ochs/articles/ochs1979.pdf

Singleton, J. L., Goldin-Meadow, S., & McNeill, D. (1995). The cataclysmic break between gesticulation and sign: Evidence against an evolutionary continuum of manual communication. In K. Emmorey & J. Reilly (Eds.), *Language, gesture, and space* (pp. 287–311). Erlbaum Associates.

Wilcox, S. (2007). Routes from gesture to language. In E. Pizzuto, P. Pietrandrea, & R. Simone (Eds.), *Verbal and signed languages: Comparing structures, constructs and methodologies* (pp. 107–131). Walter de Gruyter.

Index

Abrahamsen, A., 121
Abstract deixis, 24–25
Acenas, L.-A. R, 298
Actions, gestures vs., 118–120, 121–123
AD (Alzheimer's Disease), 278–279
African folklore, 211
Agency, 9
Age of Enlightenment, 367
Aging, 269–284
– and gesture comprehension, 272–273
– and gesture production, 271–272
– neurodegenerative disorders of, 277–282
– and spatial/visual skills, 275–276
– and verbal skills, 276–277
– and working memory, 273–275
Akhavan, N., 280
Alamillo, A. R., 210
Aldugom, M., 258
Alferink, I., 326
Alibali, M. W., 229, 249, 276–277, 298
Allen, L. Q., 347–348
Alzheimer's Disease (AD), 278–279
American Sign Language (ASL), 30, 53
Anaphora, 29, 77, 211, 212, 215, 218–219, 230, 232
Anchoring, 30
Animacy, 9
Animals, pointing in, 55, 58–59
Aphasia, 279–281
Apraxia, 279
Arm height, 27, 34–35
Arrernte speakers, 27
Arslan, B., 271
Articulators, 249
ASL (American Sign Language), 30, 53
Assisted imitation, 124
Attention, 50–51, 258, 278
Attunement, 63
Auditory–visual integration, 255
Augustine, Saint, 51, 53
Aureli, T., 97
Auriac-Slusarczyk, E., 223
Azaoui, B., 347, 348, 351–353

Babbling, 113, 141, 148, 160
Bangerter, A., 26
Baptismal pointing, 25
Baron-Cohen, S., 59
Basal ganglia, 281
Bates, E., 54, 57, 93, 114, 117, 128–129, 139
Bavin, E. L., 123
Baxter, J. C., 276
Beat gestures, 244, 269, 271
Beattie, G., 338
Beaupoil-Hourdel, P., 170
Begus, K., 103
Behne, T., 97
Benassi, E., 127
Bernardis, P., 248
Bilingualism studies, 318
Bilingual language acquisition, 297–310.
    See also Bimodal convergence
– and culture, 303–308
– and gesture production in monolinguals, 299–301
– and language proficiency, 301–303
Bimodal convergence, 317–329
– in functional bilinguals, 325–327
– in intermediate second-language users, 323–325
– methodology for analysis of, 322–323
– in multicompetent spoken language production, 318–321
– in sign language users, 327–328
Bimodal period, 121
Blindness, 243, 368
Blythe, J., 27
Boas, F., 55
Body, 3, 7, 23
Bonifacio, 3
Bonobos, 55
Bourdieu, P., 3
Boutet, D., 227, 229, 368
Bouvet, D., 211, 212
Braine, M. D. S., 144
Brain volume, aging and decreasing, 270
Brentari, D., 368
British Sign Language (BSL), 30, 36
British speakers, 26, 126
Brookes, H., 228
Brooks, R., 94–95
Brown, A., 323

Bruner, J., 49, 54, 55, 66
BSL (British Sign Language), 30, 36
Budwig, N., 160
Bulwer, J., 3
Butcher, C., 60, 140
Butterworth, G., 51, 55

Calbris, G., 207, 228
Cameron-Faulkner, T., 164
Canadian English, 305
Canadian French, 305
Canonical uses of pointing, 23
Capirci, O., 118–119, 121, 142–143
Caregivers
– actions/gestures/words in children's interactions with, 124–127
– developmental path from actions to words and role of, 113
– gestures to elicit helpful input from, 101–103
Carter, A. L., 139
Cartmill, E. A., 101
Caselli, M. C., 117–118, 121–123
Cassell, J., 206
Cavicchio, F., 306
Chaining, indexical, 24
CHAT format, 63
Chatino people, 24, 33–35
Chest, pointing to one's, 24
Chevalley, E., 26
Childers, J. B., 195
CHILDES project, 8, 62
Child language research, 7–8
Children. *See also* Infants; Toddlers
– communication system of. *See* Early communication system of gestures and words
– congenitally blind, 243
– co-speech gestures in. *See* Co-speech gestures in toddlers
– difficulty of verb learning for, 187–190
– gestures in. *See* Early gestures
– language development in. *See* Early language development
– modalities of expression in. *See* Early modalities of expression
– pointing gestures in. *See* Early pointing gestures
– reduction of cognitive load in, 274
– variation among, in gesture use, 98–100
Chimpanzees, 55

Chinese–English bilinguals, 300, 302
Chin-pointing, 52
Choi, S., 189
Chu, M., 273–274
Church, R. B., 309
Cicero, 3
Cienki, A., 6, 7, 61
CLAN software, 63, 164
Clapping, 116, 125
Clark, E., 162
Clark, E. V., 59, 151
Clark, H., 162
Cleary, R. A., 282
CLI (cross-linguistic influence), 317–321, 328
Code blends, 328
Code switching, 319
Coexpressivity, 321–323, 326
Cognition, indicating, 32
Cognitive descending, 210
Cognitive grammar, 61
Cognitive load, 60, 128, 141, 273–275, 277, 300
Cognitive processes
– attention, 258
– memory, 258–259
– speech and gesture linked via, 256–257
– working memory, 258
CoLaJE Project, 159, 164
Colletta, J.-M., 207, 209, 211–213, 215–220, 223, 224, 227–229
Comment, narrating and learning to comment, 215–217
Communication
– composite nature of, 21
– gesture in, 243–246
Communicative deficiencies, 270
Communicative points, 26
Communicative skills, early pointing gestures and development of, 49–60
Compensation hypothesis, 229–230
Complementary gestures, gestures of negation as, 169–170
Complexity, gesture for marking of narrative, 210–212
Complex meaning, gestures of negation for building, 170–176
Composite utterances, 138
Comprehension, 8, 11, 51, 93, 94, 96–98, 104–105, 121–125, 188, 257–259, 272–273
Conceptualizers, 249

Condillac, E. B., 59, 367
Conduit gestures, 271
Conduit metaphor, 220
Connectives, 209, 211, 212, 215, 224, 226
Context(s)
– variation in pointing across, 26
– verb learning and flexibility of, 194–195
Conventional gestures, 138, 303–304
Conventionalization, 36
Convergence, 299, 317. *See also* Bimodal convergence
Cook, S. W., 248, 250, 252, 253, 256, 258
Cooperrider, K., 25, 27, 36–38, 47, 53, 55
Corsi block span test, 273–274
Cosnier, J., 205–208, 228
Co-speech gestures, 205, 336
– categories of, 269
– in second and foreign language learning/teaching, 336, 353–356
Co-speech gestures in toddlers, 157–179
– data and methodology, 163–165
– and meaning making, 169–176
– negation, 169–176
– research overview, 159–163
– before vs. after 3;00, 165–169
Coughlan, J., 338
Cross-linguistic influence (CLI), 317–321, 328
Culture(s)
– and bilingual language acquisition, 298–299, 303–308
– connection of gesture and speech across, 218–219
– variation in pointing across, 27–28

Dabène, L., 348
Darwin, C., 4, 54, 367
Debras, C., 170
Declarative pointing, 59, 95
Deferred ostension, 24
De Garitte, C., 206
Deictic gaze, 50
Deictic gestures, 5, 97, 114–116, 118–120, 138, 149–151, 186, 244, 269
Deixis am phantasma, 24–25
De Jorio, 4
De Laguna, G. A., 10
Demir, Ö. E., 101
Demonstrative expressions, 29
Demonstratives, as analogues to pointing, 25–26, 28–30

Denizci, C., 348
De Nooijer, J. A., 192
De Saussure, F., 7, 61
Describing, 21–22
Diary studies, 7–8, 62
Digression, 270
Direction giving, pointing for, 23, 28
Direct pointing, 24
Dodane, C., 164
"Dual viewpoint" gesture, 228
Durso, R., 282

Early communication system of gestures and words, 137–151
– construction of, 148–150
– and content of gesture + word combinations, 141–145
– emergence of, in children, 138–145
– and modeling by parents, 145–148
– and timing in gesture + word combinations, 140–141
Early gestures, 93–105. *See also* Early pointing gestures
– and language development, 93–98
– variation in, 98–100
Early language development. *See also* Verb learning
– gestures and, 93–98, 103–105
– onomatopoeia in, 8–9
– and pointing gestures, 54–56
Early modalities of expression, 113–129
– in caregiver–child interactions, 124–127
– in pointing gestures, 75–80
– and vocabulary, 121–123
– and word development, 114–120
Early pointing gestures, 47–81
– adult feedback to, 53–54
– combined modalities in, 75–80
– complex multimodal productions in, 76–80
– data and methodology, 62–63
– and development of communicative skills, 49–60
– interactive pointing, 66–69
– and language development, 54–56
– monologic pointing, 69–70
– origins and functions of, 56–59
– and parents' input, 63–66
– playful imperative pointing, 70–73
– protodeclarative pointing, 73–75

- and speech development, 59–60, 95
- theoretical framework for analyzing, 61–62

East Asian languages, 305
Eating, 116
Edwards, T., 368
Efron, D., 4, 7
Ekman, P., 207
ELAN software, 164, 348
ELGA (extremely low-gestational-age) infants, 127
Emblems (emblem gestures), 5, 10, 336, 351
Emotional colored attunements, supportive, 63
Enfield, N. J., 23, 26, 37
English–Mandarin bilinguals, 301
English–Spanish bilinguals, 299
English speakers, 24, 36–38, 162, 189, 211, 218, 298, 306, 324, 325, 342–343
Entrainment, 255
Escalona, S. K., 145
Executive function, 270, 278
Exophora, 59
Experimental methodologies, 8–9
Explanandum/explanans, 220
Extremely low-gestational-age (ELGA) infants, 127
Eye contact, 118, 212, 235
Eye gazing, 212
Eye movements, 105, 196
Eye tracking, 196, 258

Facial pointing, 27
Fagan, M. K., 247
Fayol, M., 215
Feedback, to early pointing gestures, 53–54
Fenlon, J., 30, 36, 37, 53
Ferguson, C. A., 125
Feyereisen, P., 271
Fibigerova, K., 216
Fine motor skills, 116
Finger wagging, 142, 148, 161–163
Flanders, 326
Flemish–English bilinguals, 317
Foreign language learning and teaching, 335–337. *See also* Second language learning and teaching
- class management, gestures for, 351–353
- co-speech gestures, 336, 353–356
- and enhancement of learning via gestures, 347
- future teachers, gestures of, 353–356
- informing about language, gestures for, 348–349
- pedagogical gestures, 356
- performance assessment, gestures for, 350–351
Formats, 66
Formulators, 249
Forrester Corpus, 62–64
Framing gestures, 207, 232
French–English bilinguals, 299, 302–306
French–Flemish bilinguals, 319, 320, 326
French–Italian bilinguals, 301
French–Romanian bilinguals, 304
French Sign Language, 53
French speakers, 215, 307, 317, 326, 353–356
French-speaking Canadians, 304, 306
Friesen, W., 207
Frontal cortex, 270
Functional bilinguals, bimodal convergence in, 325–327

Gaze (gazing), 27, 356
- deictic, 50
- listener, 23
- speaker, 26
Gaze alternation, 56–57
Generalization, 188, 191, 195, 196
Gentilucci, M., 248
Gentner, D., 188
German–English bilinguals, 304
Germanic languages, 305
German speakers, 304
Gesticulation, 5
Gesticulations, 269
Gesture (journal), 210, 214
Gesture(s). *See also specific headings*
- actions vs., 118–120
- causality of relations between language and, 99–100
- in communication, 243–246
- as part of language, 366
- perception of, 253–259
- as predictor of language, 100–105
- as relevant behavior, 7
- semantic/temporal coordination of speech and, 246–253
- as visible utterances, 138
Gesture comprehension
- and aging, 272–273
- and vocabulary development, 96–98

Gesture–sign mismatches, 6
Gestures in Teacher Talk project, 353–356
Gestures of grammatical information, 348–349
Gestures of lexical information, 348–349
Gesture studies, 9
Gesture types, 94
Gesture + word combinations, 138–145
– content of, 141–145
– emergence of, in children, 139–140
– timing in, 140–141
Göksun, T., 271
Goldin-Meadow, S., 59, 60, 94, 96, 98, 102, 104, 126, 127, 140, 227, 274
Golinkoff, R. M., 139
Gollan, T. H., 298
Goodrich, W., 190
Goodwin, C., 80–81, 160, 161
Goon, C., 338
Gopnik, A., 189
Grammar, cognitive, 61
Grammatical information, gestures of, 348–349
Grant, B. M., 348
Grant Hennings, D., 348
Grasping, 115–116
Graziano, M., 215
Greek–English bilinguals, 319
Greek Sign Language, 53
Gros-Louis, J., 102, 149
Gross motor skills, 116
Growth point theory, 248–249
Grünloh, T., 58
Guajardo, J. J., 97
Guidetti, M., 162, 216, 217, 219, 228
Gullberg, M., 323, 326, 337–338
Gumperz, J. J., 55

Hadian-Cefidekhanie, A., 227
Hand–mouth linking, 246–251
– cognitive processes in, 248–251
– physiological processes in, 247–248
Handshakes, 161
Handshape, 26, 27, 36, 52, 95, 116
Hauge, E., 347
Havard, I., 271
Haviland, J., 63, 81
Headshakes, 71, 77, 145, 159–162, 168, 170, 171, 176, 208, 223, 232, 244
Head tilts, 148, 161, 170–176

Hilverman, C., 251
Hoiting, N., 53
Holophrases, 60
Homesigners, 28, 32
Hostetter, A. B., 276–277, 298
House, pointing to a, 24, 31, 32
Hudson Kam, C. L., 190
Humphries, S., 282
Husserl, E., 7

Iconic gestures, 5, 186–187, 269, 271
Imperative pointing, playful, 70–73
Imperative power, 71
Index finger, pointing with, 21, 24, 30, 34, 36, 50, 54–56, 95, 116, 139, 222, 232, 340, 347
Indexical chaining, 24
Indicating, via pointing, 21
Infants, 10, 247
– gestures and language development in, 94–95, 99–105
– gestures followed by, 63, 96–98, 138
– interaction among modalities in, 113–129
– noun–verb distinction in, 188
– pointing by, 49–56, 58, 95, 149
Information
– perception of gestures and coordinated, 254
– perception of gestures and integration of semantic, 253–254
– perceptual and motor processes integrating sources of, 254–256
– seeking of, through gesturing, 103–104
Informative pointing, 58
Informing about language, gestures for, 348–349
Inhibitory control, 270
Institute of Cognitive Sciences and Technologies (Italian National Research Council), 113
Interactional linguistics, 159
Interactive gestures, 207, 232
Interactive pointing, 66–69
Intermediate second-language users, bimodal convergence in, 323–325
Intonation contours, 245–246
isiZulu language, 218–219
Italian–English bilinguals, 300, 306
Italian National Research Council (Consiglio Nazionale delle Richerce), 113, 118
Italian Sign Language, 53

Italian speakers, 26
Iverson, J. M., 59, 118, 121, 125–126, 128, 138, 146, 247

Japanese speakers, 324
Jenkins, S., 338
JMacé study, 207–211, 216, 220, 224, 232
Joint attention, 97

Kaplan, B., 49, 54, 56
Kata Kolok, 31
Kaye, K., 63
Kellerman, S., 348
Kelly, B. F., 138, 140–142, 144, 147, 151
Kelso, J. A. S., 247
Kendon, A., 4–5, 7, 26, 81, 195, 207, 208
Kendon's continuum, 4–5
Kinesic cues, 351
Kita, S., 191–192, 274, 306
Klooster, N. B., 251, 259
Korean speakers, 189
Kovács, Á. M., 103–104
Krauss, R. M., 297–298
Kunene, R. N., 218
Kunene-Nicolas, R., 219, 307

L2 learners. *See* Second language learners
Labeling, 59, 102, 103, 128, 188
Labov, W., 211–212
Language. *See also* Early language development
– causality of relations between gesture and, 99–100
– connection of gesture and speech across, 218–219
– defined, 160
– gestural vs. linguistic components of, 29
– gesture as predictor of, 100–105
– prelinguistic basis to, 52
Language acquisition, bilingual. *See* Bilingual language acquisition
Language and Communication Across Modalities Laboratory (Institute of Cognitive Sciences and Technologies of the Italian National Research Council), 113
Language proficiency, and bilingual language acquisition, 301–303
Languaging, 49, 61, 366
Langue, 7
Lao speakers, 26, 37

Laurent, A., 302
Lazaraton, A., 348
Leach, K. A., 99, 100
LeBarton, E. S., 9, 99
Léonard, J.-L., 212
Leroy, M., 58
Levelt, W. J. M., 249
Levinson, S. C., 55
Lexical explanation, 349
Lexical information, gestures of, 348–349
Lexical retrieval, impact of second language learners' gestures on, 338–339
Lexical retrieval hypothesis, 338
Limb apraxia, 279
Linell, P., 61
Linguistic pointing, nonlinguistic, 52–53
Lip-pointing, 27, 52
Listener gaze, 23
Liszkowski, U., 52, 53, 56, 58
Load-bearing points, 37
Load-sharing points, 37
Location-focus points, 37
Locatives, as analogues to pointing, 28–30
Long-term memory, 297
Lucca, K., 104
Lyons, J., 150

MacArthur–Bates Communicative Development Inventory (MB-CDI), 95, 121–123, 189
Maguire, M. J., 195
Mandarin–English bilinguals, 304, 306
Mandarin speakers, 189
Manner, 322
Manner fog hypothesis, 323, 325
Manner modulation hypothesis, 323
Marcos, H., 139
Markman, E. M., 309
Massini-Cagliari, G., 164
Masur, E. F., 102, 103, 138–140
Matthews, D., 99
Mazur-Palandre, A., 210, 230
McNamara, P., 282
McNeill, D., 4, 5, 79, 195, 206, 211, 215, 219, 228, 229–231, 248–249, 323, 325, 340
Meaning(s)
– extracting, from pointing, 51–52
– foundation of, 113
– gestures of negation for building complex, 170–176

Meaning correspondence, 119
Meaning making, in toddlers, 169–176
Mean length of utterance (MLU), 63, 168
Meltzoff, A. N., 94–95
Memory, 258–259, 273–275, 278, 297
Mental imagery, 271–272
Merleau-Ponty, M., 3
Mesh, K., 33–35
Mesoamerica, 27
Metaphoric gestures, 244, 269
Metaphors, understanding, 281
Methodologies, 7–9
Metonymic pointing, 24, 31, 32
Milan Congress, 367
Mimes, 337
Mixed-method (term), 164
Mocking, 25
Modalities, gesturing of, 223
Modalities of expression, early. *See* Early modalities of expression
Monolinguals, gesture production in, 299–301
Monologic discourse development, 205–235
– abstract concepts in, 219–227
– across language and culture, 218–219
– and adaptation of gestures to genre, 208–210
– and changes in narrative abilities, 213–215
– and emergence of reasoning, 224–227
– and functional repertoire of gestures, 207–208, 232
– introduction of referents in, 220–221
– and learning to comment, 215–217
– and marking of narrative complexity, 210–212
– narrative performance, levels of, 235
– narrative performance example, 233–234
Monologic pointing, 69–70
Montanus, 3
Morales, M., 97
Morgenstern, A., 162
Motamedi, Y., 8
Motherese, 126–127
Motion events, 339
Motor control, and pointing, 60
Motor cortex, 256
Motor simulation, 256
Mouth shrugs, 171
Movement, gestures drawing attention to, 194
Müller, C., 4–5, 227
Mumford, K. H., 191–192
Mundy, P., 97

Murillo, E., 140, 141
Murrinhpatha speakers, 27

Nagpal, J., 306–307
Nakatsukasa, K., 348
Nambiar, M. K., 338
Naming, 118
Narrative abilities, monologic discourse development and changes in, 213–215
Narrative coherence, 270
Narrative complexity, gesture for marking of, 210–212
Narrative performance
– example of, 233–234
– levels of, 235
Narratives, 79, 101, 206, 210–219, 228–230, 275, 278
Naturalistic methodologies, 7–8
Natural language, 128
Natural partitions hypothesis, 188, 194
Negation
– in adults, 160–162
– in toddlers, 158–159, 169–176
Neu, J., 338
Neurodegenerative disorders, 277–282
– Alzheimer's Disease, 278–279
– Parkinson's Disease, 281–282
– primary progressive aphasia, 279–281
Newborns, 247
Nheenghatú speakers, 27
Nicoladis, E., 300, 302, 306–307
Nominal gestures, 118
Noncommunicative points, 26
Nonlinguistic pointing, linguistic, 52–53
Nonrepresentational gestures, 271, 302
Nose-pointing, 27
Noun learning, 186–189

Object categorization, 117
Object recognition, 117
Olson, J., 102, 103
O'Neill, D., 58
Onomatopoeia, 8–9
Ontogenetic ritualization, 116–117
Open hand gestures, 27, 32, 34
– prone, 161, 220, 227
– supine, 162, 227
Opposable-thumb grasping, 115
Oral proficiency ratings, impact of second language learners' gestures on, 337–338

Ostension, deferred, 24
Özçalışkan, Ş., 126, 128, 187
Özer, D., 272, 278
Özyürek, A., 352

Palmar grasps, 115–116
Palm-up gestures, 162
Pantomimes, 337
Paper-folding tasks, 275
Parents
– early communication system of gestures + words and modeling by, 145–148
– early pointing gestures and input of, 63–66
Parietal cortex, 270
Paris Corpus, 49, 62–64, 163–164
Parkinson's Disease (PD), 281–282
Parole, 7
Parra, I., 338
Parrell, B., 248
Parrill, F., 228
Pavelin, B., 348
p but q clauses, 170–174, 179
PD (Parkinson's Disease), 281–282
Peabody Picture Vocabulary Test, 94
Pedagogical gestures, 337, 356
Pellenq, C., 217, 220, 224–226
Perception of gestures, 253–259
– cognitive processes in, 256–259
– and coordinated information, 254
– and integration of semantic information, 253–254
– visual/auditory/motor processes in, 254–256
Performative gestures, 207, 232
Performatives, 114
Petitto, L. A., 52
Phonemic fluency, 270, 276
Phonological and phonetic information gestures, 349
Piaget, J., 49
Pika, P., 299, 304
Pinheiro, M. B., 212
Playful imperative pointing, 70–73
Pointing, 10, 21–39, 139. *See also* Deictic gestures; Early pointing gestures
– baptismal, 25
– in Chatino gesture and sign, 33–35
– communicative vs. noncommunicative, 26
– coproduction of, with speech, 25–26
– in crosslinguistic comparison, 32
– declarative, 59, 95
– defined, 21
– direct, 24
– to establish and maintain reference, 30–31
– extracting meaning from, 51–52
– facial, 27
– grounding of, in shared attention, 50–51
– with index finger, 21, 50, 54, 116, 139
– informative, 58
– interactive, 66–69
– linguistic vs. nonlinguistic, 52–53
– metonymic, 24
– monologic, 69–70
– and perception of ambiguous speech signals, 253
– playful imperative, 70–73
– primary functions of, 23
– pronouns/demonstratives/locatives as analogues to, 28–30
– protodeclarative, 57–58, 73–75
– protoimperative, 57–58
– purpose of, 115
– secondary functions of, 23–25
– in sign languages, 30–32, 36–38
– social functions of, 25
– variation in, across contexts, 26
– variation in, across cultures, 27–28
Pointing signs, 28–32
Poking, 117
"Polysign" gesture, 228
Pouw, W. T. J. L., 274
Povinelli, D., 58
PPA (primary progressive aphasia), 279–281
Pragmatic (recurrent) gestures, 5, 6
Predicate gestures, 118
Prelinguistic basis (prelinguistic stage), 52, 58, 59, 76, 80, 117, 176–177, 229
Premotor cortex, 256
Primary progressive aphasia (PPA), 279–281
Primary uses of pointing, 23
Primates, pointing in, 55, 58–59
Primordial sharing situations, 49
Problem solving, 250, 256, 273–274, 281
Pronouns, 28–30, 149
Prosodic integration, 36
Prosody, 36, 52, 58, 79, 158, 164, 205, 212, 213, 231, 233, 235, 248, 257, 259
Protoassertive pointing, 57

Protodeclarative pointing, 57–58, 73–75
Protoimperative pointing, 57–58
Prototypical uses of pointing, 23
Protowords, 139, 148
Public reusability, 141, 147, 174
Public substrate, 176
Public visibility, 173

Quine, W. V. O., 51
Quintilian, 3

Reaching, 47, 55, 115, 138–140, 145, 148, 151
Reasoning, gestures and emergence of, 224–227
Recognizing others, 25
Recurrent gestures. *See* Pragmatic (recurrent) gestures
Reduction, 36
Redundancy, 50–51, 229, 255
Referential gestures of the abstract, 208, 232
Referential gestures of the concrete, 207–208, 232
Referential locus (R-locus), 30–31
Referents, 24, 220–221
Relational matrices, 144
Repetitions, 270
Reported gestures, 69
Representational gestures, 5, 118, 271, 297, 301–302, 307
Responding to joint attention (RJA), 97
Ritualized requests, 114
Romance languages, 305
Romanes, G. J., 54
Rowe, M. L., 94, 98–100, 104

Salo, V. C., 100
Salomo, D., 53
San Juan Quiahije, Mexico, 33
San Juan Quiahije Sign Language (SJQCSL), 33–35
Sansavini, A., 122–124
Sapir, E., 55
SAT (Scholastic Aptitude Test), 276
Satellite-framed languages, 304–305, 321–322, 339, 347
Scaffolding, 12–14, 49, 55, 61, 75, 77, 80–81, 113, 117, 146, 230, 335, 347, 348, 353
Schick, B., 52
Scholastic Aptitude Test (SAT), 276

Scolding, 25
SD (semantic dementia), 280–281
Second language acquisition (SLA), 318, 335, 337
Second language (L2) learners, 318, 323, 338, 339, 342
Second language learning and teaching, 335–357
– class management, gestures for, 351–356
– co-speech gestures, 336, 353–356
– and enhancement of learning via gestures, 347
– future teachers, gestures of, 353–356
– informing about language, gestures for, 348–349
– lexical retrieval, impact of learners' gestures on, 338–339
– oral proficiency ratings, impact of learners' gestures on, 337–338
– pedagogical gestures, 356
– performance assessment, gestures for, 350–351
– and task effects on learners' gestures, 345–347
– thinking in second language, learners' gestures as indicator of, 339–345
Second-language users, bimodal convergence in intermediate, 323–325
Sekali, M., 177
Self, pointing to the, 23
Semantic coordination, 244–245
Semantic dementia (SD), 280–281
Semantic fluency, 270, 276
Semantic information, perception of gestures and integration of, 253–254
Semantic roles, 9
Semiosis, 368
Sentence comprehension, 281
SES (socioeconomic status), 95
Shared attention, grounding of pointing in, 50–51
Shephard–Metzler Mental Rotations Test, 275
Shoulder lifts, 161, 162, 168, 170, 174, 176
Shoulder shrugs, 223, 232, 301
Showing, 93, 102, 115, 139–140, 145, 146, 148, 150
Showing off, 114–116, 122
Shrugs, 6, 159, 170–173, 176, 223, 232, 301
Sightseeing, pointing in, 23

Signers, 6, 11, 21, 24, 28–39, 53–55, 243–244, 327–328, 365, 368. *See also* Sign language(s)
Sign language(s), 5, 7, 30–32, 36–38, 365. *See also specific sign languages, e.g.:* American Sign Language (ASL)
Sime, D., 347
Singleton, J. L., 5
SJQCSL (San Juan Quiahije Sign Language), 33–35
SLA. *See* Second language acquisition
Slobin, D. I., 61, 339–342
Smith, L. B., 105
Smithson, L., 300
Snow, C. E., 125
Société de Linguistique de Paris, 367
Socioeconomic status (SES), 95, 98
Southgate, V., 103
Spatial agreement (spatial modulation), 30–31
Spatial skills
– of bilinguals, 298, 299
– gestures and, 275–276
Speaker gaze, 26
Speech, semantic/temporal coordination of gestures and, 246–253
– cognitive processes linking hand and mouth, 248–251
– methodological issues in study of, 251–253
– physiological processes linking hand and mouth, 247–248
Speech act theory, 57
Speech and discourse parsing gestures, 208, 232
Speech fluency, 276–277
Speech impairments, and aging, 270–271
Speech-linked gestures, 336
Spoken language production, bimodal convergence in multicompetent, 318–321
Spoon, using a, 116
Stam, G., 338, 339–347
Staties, L. J., 187
Stern, D., 63
Stern, W., 54
Storytelling, 25, 187, 210–211, 219, 232, 302, 306–309
Stress (spoken), 248
Substrate, 368
Sully, J., 54
Supplementation, 229
Support, 368

Supportive emotional colored attunements, 63
Symbolic (term), 22
Symbolic play schemes, 117
Synchrony, 63, 140–141, 176, 336
Syntactic development, 60, 96, 102–103, 105, 144, 157
Syntactic processing, 257, 270, 277, 280, 281

Tabensky, A., 345
Talmy, T., 321, 339
Tananhaus, M. K., 250, 256
Tannen, D., 306
Tardif, T., 189
Targets
– adult speakers referring to, 244
– pointing to, 23–24, 26, 27
Tavis Smiley Corpus, 36
Tellier, M., 347–348, 356
Temporal coordination, 245–247, 255
Theory of mind, 210–211
Thinking-for-speaking hypothesis, 339–342
Thumbs-down gesture, 336
Thumbs-up gesture, 93, 298–299
Time, indicating, 27
"Time out" sign, 303
Tip-of-the-tongue (TOT) situations, 272
Toddlers
– co-speech gestures in. *See* Co-speech gestures in toddlers
– emergence of gesture + word combinations in, 139–140, 145–148
– gesture repertoires of, 95
– iconic gestures in, 146
– and input from caregivers, 101–102
– interaction among modalities in, 113–129
– verb learning in. *See* Verb learning
Tomasello, M., 55–56, 62
Tower of Hanoi task, 250–251, 256, 274
Transcranial magnetic stimulation, 256
Transformative operations, 160–161
Transposition, gesturing under, 25

Ultrasound images, 54
UNESCO, 223

Verbal skills, gestures and, 276–277
Verb-framed languages, 305, 321, 323, 339
Verb learning, 185–197
– concepts underlying verbs, 194
– difficulty of, for children, 187–190
– and flexibility of context, 194–195

– gesture and facilitation of, 190–195
– and movement, 194
– and relationship between gesture and spoken language development, 185–187
Verbs, generating, 281
Vertical constructions, 75
Vertical palm (VP) gestures, 161
Visible utterances, 138
Visual–auditory integration, 255
Visual pattern tasks, 273–274
Visual–spatial skills, 275–276
Vocabulary development
– and gesture comprehension, 96–98
– and gesture production, 94–95
Voice, 212, 233, 235, 356
Volterra, V., 123
VP (vertical palm) gestures, 161
Vygotsky, L., 47, 49, 56, 61, 70

Wakefield, E. M., 190–193, 195
Waletzky, J., 211–212
Wallonia, 326
Waving, 10, 94, 118, 119, 138, 144, 148
Werner, H., 49, 54, 56
West, K. L., 128
Whorf, B., 55
Wilbourn, M. P., 104

Wilcox, S., 5
Wittgenstein, L., 4, 51, 53
WM. *See* Working memory
Woodward, A. L., 97
Word-finding difficulty, 280
Word–object associations, 124
Words and Gestures (WG) form (MacArthur–Bates Communicative Development Inventory), 121–122
Working memory (WM), 258, 270, 273–275, 277, 297, 300
Wu, Z., 102, 149
Wundt, W., 4, 7, 47, 54, 56

Yerian, K., 356
Yolngu Sign Language, 31
Yow, W. Q., 309
Yu, C., 105
Yucatec Maya speakers, 32
Yupno people, 24, 27

Zaire, 55
Zinacantec speakers, 63, 81
Zlatev, J., 10
Zukow-Goldring, P., 124
Zulu people, 218–219, 230
Zulu speakers, 218–219, 307

About the Editors

Aliyah Morgenstern, PhD, majored in English studies and linguistics at Ecole Normale Supérieure Fontenay-St Cloud in France. During and after her PhD at Sorbonne Nouvelle University, she taught at Brown, Harvard, Paris Descartes, Sorbonne Nouvelle and Ecole Normale Supérieure in Lyon. She is currently president of the Research Ethics committee and a full professor at Sorbonne Nouvelle University, where she teaches linguistics, multimodal interaction, and language acquisition. Her research is focused on language development using ethnographic methods and socio-pragmatic, functionalist perspectives. She combines analyses of gesture, phonology, morpho-syntax, pragmatics, and discourse to capture the blossoming of children's plurisemiotic practices in situated interactions.

Dr. Morgenstern has supervised over a dozen research projects and shared the multimodal data on open-access platforms in collaboration with Christophe Parisse. Her latest participations in internationally-funded projects were centered on sign language and gesture.

She has been the president of the French Association in Cognitive Linguistics, and she is currently the vice president of the International Society for Gesture Studies and on the board of the International Association for the Study of Child Language.

Susan Goldin-Meadow, PhD, is the Beardsley Ruml Distinguished Service Professor in the Department of Psychology and Committee on Human Development at the University of Chicago. While at Smith College, she spent her junior year at the Piagetian Institute in Geneva, which set the course of her academic career. She completed her PhD at the University of Pennsylvania under the direction of Rochel Gelman and Lila Gleitman. Her research focuses on the homemade gestures profoundly deaf children create when not exposed to sign language, and what they tell us about the fundamental properties of mind that shape language; and on the gestures hearing speakers around the globe spontaneously produce when they talk, and what they tell us about how we talk and think. Dr. Goldin-Meadow has been president of the Association for Psychological Sciences, the Cognitive Development Society, the International Society for Gesture Studies, and Chair of the Cognitive Science Society. She is a member of the American Academy of Arts and Sciences, and the National Academy of Sciences.

www.ingramcontent.com/pod-product-compliance
Lightning Source LLC
Chambersburg PA
CBHW080406230426
43662CB00016B/2333